Studying Singapore Before 1800

Studying Singapore Before 1800

Edited by

Kwa Chong Guan
&
Peter Borschberg

With the assistance of
Benjamin J.Q. Khoo & Xu Shengwei

NUS PRESS
SINGAPORE

Published by:

NUS Press
National University of Singapore
AS3-01-02, 3 Arts Link
Singapore 117569

Fax: (65) 6774-0652
E-mail: nusbooks@nus.edu.sg
Website: http://nuspress.nus.edu.sg

ISBN 978-981-4722-74-2 (paper)

National Library Board, Singapore Cataloguing in Publication Data

Names: Kwa, Chong Guan, editor. | Borschberg, Peter, editor.
Title: Studying Singapore before 1800 / edited by Kwa Chong Guan & Peter Borschberg; with the assistance of Benjamin J.Q. Khoo & Xu Shengwei.
Description: Singapore: NUS Press, [2018] | Includes index.
Identifiers: OCN 1020709665 | 978-981-4722-74-2 (paperback)
Subjects: LCSH: Singapore--History. | Singapore--Politics and government--History. | Singapore--Economic conditions--History.
Classification: DDC 959.57--dc23

Cover image: Hand coloured printed illustration of a Malay couple taken from the first edition of Jan Huyghen van Linschoten's *Itinerario and Reysgechrift* (Amsterdam, 1595–96). The Hague: Koninklijke Bibliotheek, Special Collections, 1702 B 4.

Typeset by: Ogma Solutions Pvt Ltd
Printed by: Mainland Press Pte Ltd

Contents

List of Abbreviations

A.N.	Author's Note
BEFEO	Bulletin de l'Ecole Française d'Extrême-Orient
BKI	Bijdragen tot de Taal-, Land- en Volkenkunde van Nederlandsch-Indië
BV	Isaac Commelin, Begin ende Voortgang Vande Vereenigde Neerlandsche Geoctroyeerde Oost-Indische Compagnie, 2 vols. (Amsterdam: Janssonius, 1645–46)
CD	Jan Ernst Heeres and Frederik Willem Stapel, eds., "Corpus Diplomaticum Neërlando-Indicum. Verzameling van politieke contracten en verdere verdragen door de Nederlanders in het Oosten gesloten, van privilegiebrieven, aan hen verleend, enz.", vol. 1 (1596–1650), *BKI* 57 (1907): 1–586
DRB	H.T. Colenbrander, ed., *Dagh-Register gehouden int Casteel Batavia vant passerende daer ter plaets als over geheel Nederlandts-India*, 31 vols. (The Hague: Martinus Nijhoff, 1896–1931)
EIC M.R.	*East India Company (EIC) Marine Records*
EIC Rec. A	East India Company, *Penang, Singapore and Malacca consultations, Sep 1806–Jun 1830*. Here (and for the subsequent series) the numbers first refer to the volume and subsequently to the folio or page number
EIC Rec. L	*Raffles Administration, 1814–1826*
EIC Rec. P	*Commissioner Young's Land Records 1837–1839*
EIC Rec. R	*Governor's Letters to Bengal, 1837–1867*
EIC Rec. S	*Governor's Letters from Bengal 1830–1866*
EIC Rec. U	*Governor's Letters to Resident Councillors, 1831–1867*
EIC Rec. V	*Series V of the Straits Settlements Records, Governor: Miscellaneous Letters Out, 1824–1867*
EIC Rec. W	*Governor: Miscellaneous Letters In, 1830–1866*
EIC Rec. Z	*Singapore: Letters from Governor 1827–1864*

E.N.	Editorial Note
Fol.	Folio. There follows a reference to the recto (front) or verso (back)
IOPO	M. Gotthard Artus, trans. and ed. and also J.I. de Bry and J.T. de Bry, *Indiae Orientalis Pars Octava Navigationes Quinque …* (Frankfurt/M.: n.p., 1607)
JAOS	Journal of the American Oriental Society
JASB	Journal of the Asiatic Society of Bengal
JCBRAS	Journal of the China Branch of the Royal Asiatic Society
JIA	Journal of the Indian Archipelago and Eastern Asia
JICH	Journal of Imperial and Commonwealth History
JMBRAS	Journal of the Malaysian Branch of the Royal Asiatic Society
JRAS	Journal of the Royal Asiatic Society of Great Britain and Ireland
JSBRAS	Journal of the Straits Branch of the Royal Asiatic Society
JSEAH	Journal of South East Asian History
JSEAS	Journal of Southeast Asian Studies
JSS	Journal of the South Seas Society
JSSB	Journal of the Siam Society, Bangkok
KA	Koloniaal Archief, The Hague. These materials are presently found in the Nationaal Archief van Nederland (National Archives of the Netherlands)
KITLV	Koninklijk Instituut voor Taal-, Land- en Volkenkunde; Royal Netherlands Institute for Southeast Asian and Caribbean Studies
P&O	The Peninsular & Oriental Steam Navigation Company
Rs	Rupees
SFP	Singapore Free Press
TBG	Tijdschrift van het Bataviaasch Genootschap
TINI	Tijdschrift voor Indische Taal-, Land- en Volkenkunde van Nederlandsch Indië
TKNAG	Tijdschrift van het Koninklijk Nederlandsch Aardrijkskundig Genootschap
VBG	Verhandelingen van het Bataviaasch Genootschap van Kunsten en Wetenschappen
VKI	Verhandelingen van het Koninklijk Instituut voor Taal-, Land- en Volkenkunde

List of Illustrations

Acknowledgements

This publication forms part of the Singapore History Anthology Project that is based in the Department of History at the National University of Singapore (NUS). It has been made possible through a number of generous grants obtained from the National Archives of Singapore (National Heritage Board, NHB), the Ministry of Education Singapore (under the grant number R-110-000-052-112), as well as the Lee Foundation (Singapore). A very special word of thanks is extended to the philanthropist and entrepreneur Dr Lee Seng Tee of the Lee Foundation who so generously sponsored the production of this book; Mr. Pitt Kuan Wah, the former head of the National Archives of Singapore (NAS) who provided funds for research and translation of texts, as well as Prof. Michael North, Chair of Modern European History at the University of Greifswald whose research team at "Baltic Borderlands" (DFG-IRTG 1540) has supported this publication in numerous ways. Singled out for special mention are also Paul Kratoska and Dato Henry Barlow of the Malaysian Branch of the Royal Asiatic Society; Maitrii Aung-Thwin, editor of the *Journal of Southeast Asian Studies*; and Mr Tim Yap Fuan of the Central Library at NUS. At the University of Greifswald the editors additionally thank Alexander Drost, Hielke van Nieuwenhuize, Cynthia Osiecki, Giovana Rossi, Jörn Sander and Lasse Seebeck.

Apart from the authors, the editors of this volume further acknowledge the original publication or copyright holders as follows:

Roland Braddell, Hsü Yün-Ts'iao, Richard O. Winstedt, Ian A. Macgregor and Leonard Andaya: The Malaysian Branch of the Royal Asiatic Society.
Pieter Gerritsz Rouffaer: The Royal Netherlands Institute for Southeast Asian and Carribean Studies (KITLV) and Koninklijke Brill.
Victor Obdeijn: The Royal Netherlands Geographical Society.
Purnadi Purbatjaraka, Brian Colless, Richard O. Winstedt: *Journal of Southeast Asian Studies*, Department of History, National University of Singapore.
Muhammad Yusoff Hashim: Dewan Bahasa dan Pustaka, Kuala Lumpur, Malaysia.
Paul Wheatley: Julian Wheatley and Marshall Cavendish, Singapore.
Carl-Alexander Gibson-Hill, David E. Sopher, Peter Borschberg, Kwa Chong Guan, and Timothy P. Barnard: National Heritage Board, Singapore.
Kwa Chong Guan: The Association of Muslim Professionals (AMP), Singapore.

Depository institutions and special collections departments singled out for special mention for their assistance or illustrations are: Special Collections Department,

Central Library, National University of Singapore; Amsterdam University Library; Rijksmuseum Amsterdam; National Library of Australia, Canberra; Koninklijke Bibliotheek, The Hague; Asia-Europe Institute, University of Malaya, Kuala Lumpur; Leiden University Library, Leiden; Asian Civilizations Museum, Singapore; National Archives of Singapore (NAS); National Library of Singapore (NLS); and NUS Museums, Singapore. Redrawn maps were prepared by Mrs Lee Li Kheng.

Editorial Note

This collection offers 19 contributions that, with the exception of Kwa Chong Guan's Introduction, have all been previously published. In collating and preparing the selected materials for publication, a number of rules were observed that are explained as follows.

The originals represented different types of publications and offer a mix of journal articles and chapters in books. As a result, they also followed different annotation and referencing styles which have been standardized for this collection. In order to make the text more easily legible, a number of interlinear comments have been placed in the footnotes and marked with A.N. This is notably the case in the article by Rouffaer. All endnotes have been converted to footnotes, and all interlinear references have also been moved into footnotes, rendering a consolidated bibliography at the end of each publication unnecessary.

In order to establish stylistic cohesion among the different chapters, a decision was made to abide by certain rules of the NUS Press house style without compromising the integrity of the original texts. This impacted chiefly the differences of British and American spelling and punctuation rules, or also the use of certain place names. References to centuries are all numerical (e.g. seventeenth century became 17th century, unless this referred to the title of a book or article), and references to *Anno Domini*, or AD, have been changed to CE, except where such a reference was used in the original title of a publication or in a direct quotation.

Colonial names and spellings have been retained as far as possible with certain exceptions. For example, Dutch colonial spellings such as "Djambi" or "Djohor" have been anglicized as Jambi or Johor; Atjeh becomes Aceh and Tjirebon has been adapted throughout to Cirebon, etc. The city name "Malacca" became "Melaka".

For the romanization of Malay, Dutch colonial orthography has been adapted to modern usage, such as for example "Radja Bongsoe" becomes "Raja Bongsu". The usage of the silent "e", spelled as "ĕ" in the Dutch colonial era, has been retained in the translations of the article by Rouffaer. Reduplications in Malay to denote a plural or an amplification that are indicated by number 2 placed after a given word have been fully spelled out and hyphenated. Hence the "Hikayat Raja2 Pasai" becomes "Hikayat Raja-raja Pasai", or the "Undang^2 Melaka" reads "Undang-undang Melaka".

A special word about the Rouffaer article is warranted. Rouffaer's use of diacritical characters, including those used in Malay and "italics" have been retained as in the original. This includes specifically the use of italics within quotation marks and providing translations from Malay. Only those passages have been translated from Malay where Rouffaer himself had provided one. Also, full bibliographic references have been provided when a source is cited for the first time. In one instance, a lengthy footnote with comments on folklore concerning Bukit Sebuntang and Bukit Lama has been omitted, since it is not immediately relevant to Singapore and its surrounding region.

For the romanization of Chinese, the spelling of the original has been retained. The different authors did not use a standardized system, and sometimes they employed multiple transliteration systems in the same article. Sometimes the authors have rendered place names from Chinese dialects. The original Chinese characters have been retained when and where originally used by the authors.

Internal cross-references that indicate a page number have been retained, and are marked "see above" or "see below" without indicating a new page number. This was most significantly the case with the long article by Gibson-Hill.

Journal titles now follow a standardized set of abbreviations which can be retrieved together with other abbreviations in a list found in the front matter of this volume.

Source references added at the end of a chapter have been reproduced in full together with the place of publication and name of the publisher when they are mentioned in a chapter for the first time. In some instances the original "op. cit." or "loc. cit." have been changed to conform to the NUS Press house style.

The editors have done their utmost to properly reference a source that has been cited, but it was inevitable that errors in the printed originals would be detected. These have been corrected or updated as far as possible. Some authors provided only minimal information on a publication involving for example the name of a journal and a year without any reference to an author, title of the article, or pagination. These have been updated for the reader's benefit. Publications that were in press or announced as forthcoming in the original publications have been updated with full details. Some items tagged as forthcoming, however, were never published, such as notably in the Gibson-Hill article. These have been identified in an editorial note marked as E.N. (Editorial Note). Less familiar measurements (fathoms, cables, league, knots, etc.) from the premetric era have an approximate metric equivalent placed next to it.

Square brackets are deployed either as brackets within brackets, or alternatively to mark an editorial note or comment. Longer editorial comments have been additionally marked within square brackets and marked with "E.N.".

Relevant maps have been redrawn and new digital images of essential illustrations secured for reproduction in this volume. The captions have only been retained or translated for those maps and illustrations that have been reproduced in the present collection. This volume also contains new illustrations that are not found in the original publications. A full list of the image captions that have been taken over or newly added are found in the front matter entitled *List of Illustrations*.

Finally a word about indexing. Editors tread a fine line between indexing what is absolutely necessary, and what might be potentially useful or of interest to readers and researchers who read and work closely with the publication. Words and names that appear very frequently across the texts have not been indexed. Since this collection does not feature a consolidated bibliography, all authors cited across the different chapters have been captured in the index. Readers should also bear certain collective terms in mind that are featured in the index. These include notably "hikayats" and "ship names". For example, if one is looking for a reference to a specific work, this would be found under "hikayat" and then under the sub-entry for the title. A specific ship is captured as a sub-entry under "ship name".

0.1 Staff photo of the University of Singapore History Department, 1966. Front row, from left: Sharom Ahmat, Jenny Chong, Mary Turnbull, Ken Tregonning, Eunice Thio, Irene Ee, Wong Lin Ken; Back row, from left: Yeoh Kim Wah, Edwin Lee, R. Suntharalingam, Chiang Hai Ding, Yong Ching Fatt, Png Poh Seng, Mat (Mohd. Ibrahim bin Baba). Singapore: History Department, National University of Singapore (NUS).

Kwa Chong Guan

Introduction

Wong Lin Ken's Puzzle

In an introduction to an exhibition catalogue of historical photographs of Singapore, former Raffles Professor of History Wong Lin Ken (1931–83) acknowledged the stories in the *Malay Annals* that relate how the island derived its fabled name, and inferred from them the following:

> What we know of the history of Singapore before 1819 indicates that its development could not be separated from the territorial ambitions of Srivijaya, Majaphit, Thailand and the Melaka and Johor sultanates. It has changed its overlord several times, according to the fortunes of the early empires in Southeast Asia. But no historian has yet adequately explained why Singapore failed to be a major trading centre before the 19th century.[1]

This introduction to *Studying Singapore Before 1800* provides a belated response to Wong's expectation of a major trading centre on Singapore Island before 1819 and the puzzle over why there was apparently none.

Wong Lin Ken was among the first group of graduates from the new History Department of the University of Malaya established in 1949. His postgraduate studies in economic history led him to study Singapore's emergence as a centre of trade after 1819.[2] He concluded that it happened as a consequence of Britain's strategic interest in and trade with China, and realized as a corollary that there was no trade or settlement on Singapore before that event. This puzzled Wong. He asked: "How do we account for Singapore's emergence as a strategic centre of trade linking the sea routes of the South China Sea with the Bay of Bengal and wider Indian Ocean beginning only in the 19th century, but not before?" Wong eventually solved the

[1] Wong, L.K., "A View of Our Past", in *Singapore in Pictures, 1819–1945*, ed. Lee Yik and C.C. Chang (Singapore: Sin Chew Jit Poh and Ministry of Culture, 1981), p. 15.

[2] Wong's MA thesis was published as "The Trade of Singapore, 1819–69", *JMBRAS* 33, 4 (1960): 11–204, and subsequent reprints.

puzzle he identified: Singapore, he argued, emerged as a trading centre only in response to the larger context of 18th-century Anglo-French rivalry and the possible spillover effects of that rivalry on the freedom of navigation on British traders sailing through the Straits of Melaka and Singapore to China.[3]

The Paradox of Singapore History

Wong Lin Ken's predecessor as Raffles Professor of History, K.G. Tregonning (1923–2015), also defined Singapore's historical significance within the framework of British commercial and strategic interest in the Malay Peninsula during the 18th century. Stamford Raffles' establishment of a settlement on Singapore Island was in order to protect British trade with China at the southern end of the Straits of Melaka, which Penang was not well situated to do.[4] Tregonning, however, went further to suggest the irrelevance of whatever answer we may deduce from Wong's puzzle because, as he famously declared in an essay commemorating the 150th anniversary of Stamford Raffles' arrival at Singapore:[5]

> Modern Singapore began in 1819. Nothing that occurred on the island prior to this has particular relevance to an understanding of the contemporary scene; it is of antiquarian interest only.

The fact that nothing occurred on this island prior to Raffles' arrival is not at issue here. Tregonning and Wong were aware of the studies compiled here, and the results of the search for historical developments on and around this island before 1800. Their former departmental colleague Ian Macgregor would have impressed on them the findings of his work on Portuguese interest and activities around Singapore and up the Johor River during the 16th century. They both would have studied Richard Winstedt's reference to Singapore as part of the narrative of Johor history and within the wider history of Malaya. They were also aware that Paul Wheatley, who joined the university's Geography Department in 1952, had embarked on extensive studies

---

[3] Wong, L.K., "The Strategic Significance of Singapore in Modern History", in *A History of Singapore*, ed. Ernest C.T. Chew and Edwin Lee (Singapore: Oxford University Press, 1991), pp. 17–35. Wong searched for more military and strategic explanations for Singapore's historical development after serving in government from 1968 to 1972, which included a stint as Minister of Home Affairs.

[4] K.G. Tregonning, *The British in Malay: The First Forty Years, 1786–1826* (Tucson: University of Arizona Press, 1965).

[5] K.G. Tregonning, "The Historical Background", in *Modern Singapore*, ed. Ooi Jin Bee and Chiang Hai Ding (Singapore: Singapore University Press, 1969), p. 14. "Antiquarian interest" as used by Tregonning appears to refer to how "relics" of the past were collected, studied and appreciated in Europe between the 15th and 19th centuries, and how the antiquarian scholarship was criticized in 19th-century historiography for its naïve approach to the past as performed by amateurs and dilettantes who randomly collected "relics" without offering any reference or relevance to the present. Elsewhere (as discussed in this introduction), Tregonning also dismissed the "Malayan studies" published in *JMBRAS* as literature "of antiquarian interest only". See A. Momigliano, "Ancient History and the Antiquarian", *Journal of the Warburg & Courtauld Institute* 13 (1950): 285–315, for a critique of antiquarianism.

of the historical geography of the Malay Peninsula. Instead, the issue is this: Why did Tregonning and Wong choose to ignore these studies and make the arrival of Raffles the incontestable foundational event in Singapore's past?

In arguing that Singapore's history began with Raffles, Tregonning was iterating an emergent perspective that since became the conventional and dominant view of Singapore's past. Constance Mary Turnbull (1927–2008), who joined the History Department in 1955 after a short stint in the Malayan Civil Service, provided the most sustained documentation of this reconstruction of Singapore's past starting with Raffles in her benchmark text, first published in 1975. In the third edition of *A History of Modern Singapore 1818–2005*, she continues to reiterate that Singapore's history is about the rise and development of a city-state, from its beginnings as the East India Company factory that Raffles established, through its transformation into a crown colony, to its take-off as a new nation-state after 1965. It is a history of *modern* Singapore, in which an earlier past has no place, because it is irrelevant and, in any case, virtually non-existent. Other textbooks and popular accounts of Singapore's past similarly situate Singapore's past within the framework of British colonialism and empire, of decolonization, and of the subsequent struggle for independence and other achievements of the new city-state.[6] In all these and other popular texts, Singapore's past before the arrival of Raffles is invariably and cursorily reviewed, usually to simply explain how it received its name.

Three categories of historiographical issues arise from starting Singapore's history in 1819.

The first is that it accords Raffles the prescience to recognise the strategic location of the depopulated island on which he landed at the end of January 1819, as he claimed in his official report to John Adams, Political Secretary to the Governor-General:

> A British station commanding the Southern entrance of the Straits of Malacca, and combining extraordinary local advantage with a peculiarly admirable Geographical position, has been established at Singapore, the ancient Capital of the Kings of Johor.

This elevation of Raffles to a "Great Man" of history has become an entrenched feature of not only the colonial historiography but also the post-colonial nationalist

---

[6] See Karl Hack's perceptive comment: "Turnbull followed the approach of … Tregonning with her 1972 book, *A History of Modern Malaya and Singapore*. There is some similarity here between the role of the *Sejarah Melayu* (Malay Annals) and that of these new 'Singapore' histories. The *Sejarah Melayu* aimed to provide a suitable genealogy and origin for the Melaka-Johor-Riau sultanate rulers during the 17th century when they had long lost Melaka and were threatened by rising Dutch power in the Straits. The new histories of the 1970s also aimed to give Singapore a past or 'genealogy' that would be meaningful and useful for the present." See Hack, "Framing Singapore's History", in *Studying Singapore's Past: C.M. Turnbull and the History of Modern Singapore*, ed. N. Tarling (Singapore: NUS Press, 2012), p. 18. See also Kevin Blackburn, "Mary Turnbull's History Textbook for the Singapore Nation", in *Studying Singapore's Past*, pp. 65–86.

narrative of Singapore.[7] It perpetuates a rather Anglo-centric perspective of Singapore's history—which, ironically, Tregonning stridently called on others to reject.[8]

Second, this emphasis on Raffles blurs the focus on Tengku Husain and Temenggong 'Abd'ur-Rahman and their reasons for positively responding to Raffles' approaches. It implies that they and all previous generations of sultans were unaware or at least unappreciative of the strategic significance of Singapore. It begs the counterfactual: What if Temenggong 'Abd'ur-Rahman and Tengku Husain had rejected Raffles' approaches? Would Raffles have continued sailing to the Johor River estuary, toward which he was headed, in search of a suitable site for the "British Station" that he had the authority to establish?

Third, it raises the question: How was a strategically significant island, which thrived after 1819, desolate and unpopulated, as both Raffles and John Crawfurd reported:

> With the exception of a single village of poor and predatory Malay fishermen, and that only formed in 1811, was covered with a primeval forest down to the 6th day of February 1819 ... [and that] ... for a period of about five centuries and a half, there is no record of Singapore having been occupied, and it was only the occasional resort of pirates.[9]

Crawfurd could precisely calculate that Singapore had been unoccupied for the five-and-a-half centuries before its takeover by the Honourable Company, because he was aware of an earlier settlement on the island. He saw its "antiquities" on a visit in 1822 and knew about their dating as well as Portuguese writings on these "antiquities".[10]

Richard Winstedt, the foremost Malayan Civil Service authority on Malay history and literature, appears to have recognized this paradox of Singapore. "How was it", Winstedt asks in his book, *A History of Malaya*, "that an island which Raffles found to be a mangrove-swamp inhabited by a few fishermen attracted attacks from the Cholas, Majapahit and Siam? As a colony, its fate was bound up with

---

[7] Evidence in the speeches delivered by Singapore's long-serving Minister for Foreign Affairs, S. Rajaratnam, collated in *S. Rajaratnam on Singapore: From Ideas to Reality*, ed. Kwa Chong Guan (Singapore: World Scientific and Institute of Defence and Strategic Studies, 2006), pp. 227–66.

[8] K.G. Tregonning, "A New Approach to Malayan History", *Straits Times*, 21 and 24 Nov. 1958. Tregonning was inspired by the debate in the 1950s about shifting the writing of Asian history from its dominant European perspective to that of an Asian point of view, as argued by the Dutch socioeconomic historian J.C. van Leur in the 1930s. See Blackburn, "Mary Turnbull's History", pp. 68–70, esp. n. 6, on the impact of Tregonning's call for writing Asia-centric history in school textbooks.

[9] Raffles' report transcribed by John Bastin in his *The Founding of Singapore 1819: Based on the Private Letters of Sir Stamford Raffles to the Governor-General and Commander-in-Chief in India, the Marquess of Hastings, preserved in the Bute Collection at Mount Stuart, Isle of Bute, Scotland* (Singapore: National Library, 2012), p. 45.

[10] J. Crawfurd, *A Descriptive Dictionary of the Indian Islands & Adjacent Countries* (1856, repr. Kuala Lumpur: Oxford University Press, 1971), pp. 395, 402. As Resident of Singapore from 1823 to 1826, Crawfurd wrote a history of events that he either observed or participated in; as such, what he reports must assumedly be reliable.

that of the empires of Srivijaya, Majapahit and Siam, each of which had owned it in turn."[11] He reiterated in 1964 (in an essay reprinted in this volume) that the Malay *datus* of Srivijaya, the first major emporium at the southern end of the Straits of Melaka, up the Musi River, where Palembang is today, must have been aware of Singapore's significance from the 7th century CE, which "was a time of great expansion for Srivijaya.... It is highly improbable that, possessing Bangka and being strong enough to attack Java, Palembang would not exercise control over Temasek or Singapura and the southern entrance to what was to become the Melaka Straits.... It would appear that Singapore was colonized by a ruler of Palembang, probably about the 7th century CE."

This paradox of Singaporean history, in which nothing happened on a strategic island until Raffles' arrival, has inspired three approaches in response. The first searches through classical texts and early-modern archival records for references to settlements on Singapore. The second pursues a much closer reading of these texts and records, attempting both a deeper along-the-grain reading in juxtaposition against a wider against-the-grain interrogation of the texts. The third contextualizes the integration of Singapore's pre-1800 and post-1800 pasts within the long cycles of history. The studies brought together in this anthology illustrate these three approaches to the study of Singapore before 1800.

Searching for Classical Texts

The lawyer and jurist by vocation, Roland St John Braddell (1880–1966) pioneered the search for references to early settlement on Singapore in classical texts. In 1935, he started writing a long and ambitious series of papers under the title "An Introduction to the Study of Ancient Times in the Malay Peninsula and the Straits of Malacca" for the *Journal of the Malayan Branch of the Royal Asiatic Society*.[12] For this series of papers, Braddell attempted to reconstruct an earlier history of Malaya in terms of a historical geography based on toponyms of emporia and polities described in the classical Graeco-Roman, Chinese, Arabic and Indian texts related to Southeast Asia. Braddell followed the French and Dutch scholars in tracing the shifts of these emporia identified in the classical texts from the Mekong after the 7th century CE to the South Sumatra port polity of Srivijaya, then to Temasek/Singapura and finally Melaka. Unfortunately, World War II disrupted Braddell's research, which he resumed after 1947 with a series entitled "Notes on Ancient Times in Malaya".[13]

Braddell's research was largely enabled by French and Dutch scholars working in the early decades of the 20th century on the pre-colonial history of their colonies. They included George Coedès, who in 1918 colligated fragmentary and elliptical Malay and Tamil epigraphy as well as Chinese and Arabic texts in order to

[11] Winstedt, *A History of Malaya*, revised and enlarged (Singapore: Marican & Sons, 1962), p. 42.

[12] Braddell's work has been compiled and reprinted by the MBRAS as *The Study of Ancient Times in the Malay Peninsula and the Straits of Malacca*, Reprint no. 7 (Kuala Lumpur: MBRAS, 1980).

[13] "Notes on Ancient Times in Malaya", *JMBRAS* 20, 1 (1947): 161–86; 20, 2 (1947): 1–19; 22, 1 (1949): 1–24; 23, 1 (1950): 1–36; 23, 3 (1950): 1–35; 24, 1 (1951): 1–27.

reconstruct the forgotten trading emporium of Srivijaya. Earlier, the sinologist Paul Pelliot reconstructed from Chinese texts the forgotten emporium of Funan in the Mekong delta. He was also the first to connect the Chinese reports of Tan-ma-hsi with Javanese references to Temasek and to link them to Singapore.[14] The toponyms related to Funan and Srivijaya were the starting points of Braddell's investigations. In line with these European scholars prioritising the Graeco-Roman texts, Braddell also attempted to read much into Ptolemy's reference in *Geographia* to a "Sabara" emporium at the southern tip of the Khryse Khersonese, the "Golden Peninsula", as a possible reference to an early settlement on Singapore. Braddell's 1969 discussion of the toponym "Lung-ya-men" as a reference to the Keppel Harbour passage as distinct from Ling-ya-men in the Straits of Lingga is reprinted in this anthology as an example of his contribution to the study of pre-1800 Singapore.[15]

Hsü Yün-ts'iao (Xu Yunqiao, 1905–81), whom Braddell refers to in his paper, was a leading public intellectual in the Chinese literary community in Malaya and Singapore beginning in the 1930s, when he migrated from his home in Suzhou. As a co-founder of the South Seas Society (Nanyang xuehui), Hsü edited its journal for some 18 years, making it Southeast Asia's leading Chinese-language scholarly journal.[16] His research into Chinese texts on Southeast Asia was part of a wider programme of documenting the long history of interaction between China and the Nanyang and the development of a distinct "Nanyang" Chinese identity.[17] "Singapore

---

[14] Pelliot, "Deux itinéraires de Chine en Inde à la fin du VIIIe siècle", *BEFEO* 4 (1904): 345n4.

[15] Braddell's discursive style of trying to tease meanings out of obscure texts that others had dismissed apparently did not go well with the Society's president, Richard Winstedt, who commented: "Mr. Braddell has made great play with a passage from pp. 34–5 of my *History of Malaya*, where I tried in too condensed a paragraph to deal with the telescoped myths of the *Malay Annals*. For years I practiced compression to save our Society printing costs, an example I venture to commend to all contributors" (*JMBRAS* 15, 3 [1937]: 142–4). Winstedt then elliptically critiqued several of Braddell's attempts to connect place names in different texts as speculative.

[16] See Leander Seah Tze Ling's MA thesis on the South Seas Society and Hsü's role as a public intellectual in the formation of a local Chinese identity ("Historicizing Hybridity and Globalization: The South Seas Society in Singapore, 1940–2000", MA thesis, National University of Singapore, 2006). See also Lew Bon Hui (Liao Wenhui), 许云樵评传 Xu yunqiao pingzhuan [A critical biography of Hsü Yün-ts'iao] (Singapore: Global Publishing, 2017); and Hsü 马来亚古代史研究 Malaya gudaishi yanjiu [Research on ancient Malayan history] (Singapore: Qingnian shuju, 1961) for Hsü's summary of his work.

[17] Others who joined Hsü in this search for early Chinese interactions with the Malay peninsula and the development of a new identity in an adopted homeland included Han Wai Toon, who established an expertise in Chinese ceramics, and the publisher and educator Tan Yeok Seong. (On Han Wai Toon, see Sharon W.Y. Wong, "Negotiating Identities, Affiliations and Interests: The Many Lives of Han Wai Toon, an Overseas Chinese", in *Reframing Singapore: Memory – Identity – Trans-regionalism*, ed. Derek Heng and Syed Muhd Khairudin Aljunied [Amsterdam: Amsterdam University Press, 2009], pp. 155–74.) Tan's library was donated to the National Library, which also includes a list of Tan's publications (see *Catalogue of the Ya Yin Kwan Collection in the Lee Kong Chian Reference Library*, comp. Ang Seow Leng and J. Wee [Singapore: National Library Board, 2006]). Hsü Yün-ts'iao's library and papers have also been purchased and donated to the National Library.

in the Remote Past" represents Hsü's summary of his 30-year search for evidence of early settlement on Singapore Island in Chinese texts and chronicles.

Some 20 years after Braddell started publishing his studies, Paul Wheatley arrived at the newly formed University of Malaya to assume an appointment in the Geography Department. He rose to the challenge of researching the historical geography of Malaya initiated by Braddell and Hsü, and as part of that challenge, he began to learn classical Chinese. The seminal influence of Braddell's pioneering work on Wheatley is apparent in the series of papers Wheatley produced, culminating in his benchmark text, *The Golden Khersonese, Studies in the Historical Geography of the Malay Peninsula before AD 1500* published in 1961.[18] *The Golden Khersonese* has become a standard reference for its colligation of not only the cryptic Latin and Greek references to the peninsula in their original languages but also the Chinese textual references. For the Arabic references to Malaya, Wheatley sought the help of his department colleague, Gerard R. Tibbetts, who then was researching early Arab trade in Southeast Asia, to collate references in Arab texts to the Malay Peninsula.[19] From their research of classical texts, Wheatley, Braddell and Hsü argued that Malaya's earlier history starts with the isthmus port of P'an-p'an in the 5th century and ends with the fall of Melaka to the Portuguese in 1511. Wheatley's summary of this history in "Century of Singhapura", reproduced in this compilation, outlines this emergence of Singapore as Melaka's 13th-century precursor.

The results of this search through classical texts for toponyms that can be linked with Singapore on the basis of phonemic similarity,[20] as attempted by Hsü and Braddell, is probably best summarized by Brian E. Colless' reconstruction, entitled "The Ancient History of Singapore" and reprinted in this volume, which links Ptolemy's Sabara with a place called Ban-zu in Wang Ta-yüan's 14th-century travelogue, which refers to the spring or *panchor* (as the Malays knew it) on Fort Canning. Colless' arguments drew much from a 1919 study by independent scholar

---

[18] P. Wheatley, *The Golden Khersonese, Studies in the Historical Geography of the Malay Peninsula before AD 1500* (Kuala Lumpur: University of Malaya Press, 1961). Wheatley's first article in *JMBRAS* was an appreciative "Belated Comments on Sir Roland Braddell's Study of Ancient Times in the Malay Peninsula", *JMBRAS* 28, 1 (1955): 78–98.

[19] G.R. Tibbett's *A Study of the Arabic Texts Containing Material on South-East Asia* (Leiden: E.J. Brill for Royal Asiatic Society Oriental Translation Fund, 1979) is a revision of an apparently much longer study that then Raffles Museum Director, C.A. Gibson-Hill, accepted for publication by the museum in 1956 but did not carry forward. See Tibbetts' work, "Early Muslim Traders in South-East Asia", *JMBRAS* 30, 1 (1957): 1–47. Tibbetts went on author *Arab Navigation in the Indian Ocean before the Coming of the Portuguese* (London: Royal Asiatic Society, Oriental Translation Fund, 1971), and later an article on Arab cartography for J.B. Harley and D. Woodward's multi-volume *History of Cartography* (Chicago: University of Chicago Press, 1992), bk. 2, vol. 2, p. 199, in particular on the limited role of charts in Islamic navigation in the Indian Ocean (see ibid., pp. 256–62).

[20] However, Wheatley realized the problems of making such phonemic comparisons of toponyms in his "Desultory Remarks on the Ancient History of the Malay Peninsula", in *Malayan and Indonesian Studies; Essays Presented to Sir Richard Winstedt on His Eighty-Fifth Birthday*, ed. J. Bastin and R. Roolvink (Oxford: Clarendon Press, 1964), pp. 34, 38–9. In this essay, he attempted to reconstruct the ancient Chinese pronunciations of the Chinese toponyms for the Malay Peninsula.

Gerritsz Pieter Rouffaer (1860–1928). Rouffaer, who became the deputy secretary of the Koninklijk Instituut voor Taal-, Land- en Volkenkunde (KITLV) in 1898, organized and expanded its library to become the best collection on the East Indies in the Netherlands.[21] Rouffaer spent a year travelling in the Dutch East Indies, and published a long discursive study of Melaka's origins in 1919, which included extensive digressions into early Singapore and Johor history. The paper has become an often-cited classic, which Richard Winstedt thought sufficiently significant to summarize for readers of the *Journal of the Straits Branch of the Royal Asiatic Society*. His summary is reprinted in this anthology. Rouffaer's comments on Batu Sawar, which the Dutch records indicate was one of the more significant of the peripatetic capitals of the Johor sultans, is also translated and reproduced in this compilation.

There are from the 13th century a series of more detailed Chinese reports on their growing maritime trade. Wang Gungwu, in his pioneering 1955 study of the Nanhai trade, was among the first to study these references to Chinese trade not so much for what they tell us about the historical geography of Southeast Asia but rather for how that trade shaped the historical development of the region.[22] A retired Malayan Civil Service officer turned historian, Oliver Wolters reconstructed from Chinese texts how a growing Chinese market enabled the development of a new series of ports in the Straits of Melaka to service this Chinese trade during the T'ang era, from which Srivijaya rose to pre-eminence.[23] Roderich Ptak has been looking at these cycles and circuits of Chinese trade in the Southeast Asia.[24] More

[21] The KITLV commissioned Frank Okker to write a biography of its honorary member, entitled *Rouffaer, de laatste Indische ontdekkingsreiziger* (Amsterdam: Boom, 2015).

[22] Wang Gungwu, "The Nanhai Trade; A Study of the Early History of Chinese Trade in the South China Sea", *JMBRAS* 31, 2 (1958): 1–135, reprinted in *Southeast Asia-China Interactions: Reprint of Articles from the Journal of the Malaysian Branch, Royal Asiatic Society*, ed. Geoff Wade (Singapore: NUS Press, 2007), pp. 51–167. See also Paul Wheatley, "Geographical Notes on Some Commodities Involved in Sung Maritime Trade", *JMBRAS* 32, 2 (1959): 3, 5–41, 43–139, reprinted in *Southeast Asia-China Interactions*, pp. 183–298, on what else he gleaned from his search of Chinese texts on the historical geography of the peninsula. This inventory has become a benchmark reference on the subject.

[23] O.W. Wolters, *Early Indonesian Commerce; A Study of the Origins of Srivijaya* (Ithaca, NY: Cornell University Press, 1967). See also his "Restudying Some Chinese Writings on Sriwijaya", *Indonesia* 42 (1986): 1–41, for a summary of his continued preoccupation with close readings of Chinese texts for not only the historical geography of Srivijaya but also how the cycles of Chinese trade and diplomacy shaped the historical development of Srivijaya. Wolters, like C.M. Turnbull, was a Malayan Civil Service officer who after early retirement turned to an academic career; see Craig J. Reynolds, "The Professional Lives of O.W. Wolters", in *Early Southeast Asia: Selected Essays: O.W. Wolters*, ed. Craig Reynolds (Ithaca, NY: Cornell University Southeast Asia Program Publications, 2008), pp. 1–38.

[24] See, for example, some of Ptak's essays republished in his collection, *China and the Asian Seas: Trade, Travel and Visions of the Other (1400–1750)*, Variorum Collected Studies (Aldershot: Ashgate Publishing, 1998), and *China's Seaborne Trade with South and Southeast Asia*, Variorum Collected Studies (Aldershot: Ashgate Publishing, 1999). His acclaimed monograph on the "Silk Road of the Sea" provides a sweeping overview of Asian trade over one millenium. R. Ptak, *Die maritime Seidenstraße: Küstenräume, Seefahrt und Handel in vorkolonialer Zeit* (Munich: C.H. Beck, 2007).

specifically, Derek Heng has been looking at Sino-Malay trade from the 10th to the 14th century as the underpinning of Temasek's rise in the 13th century as narrated in the *Malay Annals*.[25]

Reading the *Sejarah Melayu* (Malay Annals)

Stamford Raffles claimed that, but for his "Malay studies", he would "hardly have known that such a place [Singapore] existed". His Malay studies would have included reading John Leyden's 1810 translation of the *Malay Annals*, which Raffles published in 1821.[26] The *Malay Annals* continues to be a major source for an understanding and framing of Singapore history on two counts. The first seeks an understanding of the etymology of the island's name and history embedded in the annal's first six chapters. The second strives to use the source to reconstruct the destiny of Singapore during the centuries of the Melaka and Johor sultanate.

Interpreting the first six chapters of the *Malay Annals* about Sri Tri Buana's genealogy and dramatic arrival in Singapore continues to be problematic and controversial.

Richard Winstedt concluded that the account in the *Malay Annals* about the founder of Temasek is a "hotchpotch of Chola and Palembang folklore [out of which] little can be made".[27] Winstedt's literal reading of the Annals and other Malay literary texts as reliable sources of information raises fundamental issues about the content and intent of not only this text but also all other Malay literary texts. Winstedt's questioning the veracity of events described in the *Malay Annals* has vexed more than one generation of historians. The issue appears to balance Winstedt's against-the-grain interrogative reading of the text—turning to the objective language of the Portuguese reports, or the Chinese records as Oliver Wolters[28] had

[25] See Derek Heng, "Temasik as an International and Regional Trading Port in the Thirteenth and Fourteenth Centuries: A Reconstruction Based on Recent Archaeological Data", *JMBRAS* 72, 1 (1999): 113–24, reprinted in *Southeast Asia-China Interactions*, pp. 296–308; "Economic Relations between the Malay Region and the Hinterlands of Quanzhou and Guangzhou", in *Early Singapore 1300s–1819: Evidence in Maps, Text and Artefacts*, ed. John N. Miksic and Cheryl-Ann M. G. Low (Singapore: Singapore History Museum, 2004), pp. 73–83; and "Situating Temasik within the Larger Regional Context: Maritime Asia and Malay State Formation in the Pre-Modern Era", in *Singapore in Global History*, ed. Heng and Syed Muhd Khairudin Aljunied (Amsterdam: Amsterdam University Press, 2011), pp. 27–49.

[26] *John Leyden's Malay Annals*, with introductory essay by Virginia M. Hooker and M.B. Hooker, repr. no. 20 (Kuala Lumpur: MBRAS, 2001).

[27] Winstedt, *A History of Malaya*, [f.n. 11] p. 41. Muhammad Yusoff Hashim was among the historians preoccupied with the historicity of events described in the *Malay Annals*; see, for example, his book, *Persejarahan Melayu Nusantara*; *Kajian mengenai sumber, penghayatan, masalah dan tafsiran naskhah-naskhah terpilih Sejarah Melayu* (Kuala Lumpur: Teks Publishing, 1988).

[28] Wolters, in his *The Fall of Srivijaya in Malay History*, repr. (Kuala Lumpur: Oxford University Press, 1970), joins Winstedt in rejecting the historicity of the first six chapters of the *Malay Annals*, arguing that Sri Tri Buana and his successors were creations of a 16th-century Melaka court genealogist who sought to link his sultan to Alexander the Great and to verify his legitimate place in line as the divinely anointed successor to the Srivijayan chieftains.

attempted—with the along-the-grain hermeneutic understanding of the text. Umar Junus was among the first to shift the focus of reading the *Malay Annals* from issues of its historicity as a historical text to issues of how it should be "read as a literary text".[29] From this perspective, the issue is to make sense of the reality of the world that the author of the *Malay Annals* was seeking to convey and, as Kwa Chong Guan has attempted, to distinguish the literary tropes underpinning the historical imagination of the world of the *Malay Annals*.[30]

The *Malay Annals* also has relevance to the search for understanding Singapore's destiny in the centuries of the Melaka and Johor sultanates. In their chapters included here, Timothy P. Barnard and Leonard Y. Andaya both make the same point about the relevance of this text first composed in the 15th century to understanding Johor in the 17th and 18th centuries. Would a close reading of the *Malay Annals* confirm that the territory of Singapore was abandoned and unoccupied during the five centuries of the Melaka and Johor sultanates as John Crawfurd assumed? Or was it in fact integral to the development of Melaka and Johor?

The essays written by Muhammad Yusoff Hashim and Leonard Y. Andaya, although not referring directly to Singapore, show how a close reading of the *Malay Annals* provides insights into Singapore's place and role in the structures of political power in Melaka and Johor. Hashim's study of the court title of the Seri Bija Diraja draws attention to the significance of the office-bearer mentioned in Chapter 15 of the *Malay Annals*, who was based in Singapore and incurred the displeasure of his sultan, for which he was executed. Hashim reconstructs the situation in which the commander-in-chief of Melaka's military forces, whose members belonged to the orang laut, held this title of Seri Bija Diraja. Hashim admits that the title probably derived from the orang laut communities of Bintan and Singapore, which suggests that Singapore was a part of his "fiefdom".

The early 19th-century residents and observers of Singapore's orang laut, including John Crawfurd, had a very disparaging opinion of these communities, whose people still resided on their boats in the estuary of the Kallang River and at the mouth of the Singapore River. Could these nomadic communities have been warriors and emissaries of the Johor and earlier Melakan sultans?

The compilation includes David Sopher's summary of early modern Portuguese accounts of the orang laut. Sopher's ethno-historical background to underscore the significance of these communities in Melaka and Johor that the *Malay Annals* assumes. The contribution of these orang laut warriors to the defence and resilience

---

[29] Umar Junus, *Sejarah Melayu: Menemukan diri kembali* (Petaling Jaya: Penerbit Fajar Bakti, 1884); and more recently, G.L. Koster, *Roaming through Seductive Gardens: Readings in Malay Narrative*, Verhandelingen 167 (Leiden: KITLV Press, 1997). Cheah Boon Kheng has followed Umar Junus in perceiving the interaction of historicity, fiction and imagination in the *Malay Annals* to form a moral discourse for the education of the sultans in his article, "The Rise and Fall of the Great Melakan Empire: Moral Judgment in Tun Bambang's *Sejarah Melayu*", *JMBRAS* 71, 2 (1998): 103–21.

[30] Kwa, "Singapura as a Central Place in Malay History and Identity", in *Singapore from Temasek to the 21st Century: Reinventing the Global City*, ed. Karl Hack et al. (Singapore: NUS Press, 2010).

0.2 Melaka from the Sea, watercolour from the Charles Dyce Collection. Singapore: National University of Singapore (NUS) Museums. S1970-0052-024.

of the Johor sultans enabled them to swiftly rebound after repeated attacks by the Achenese and Portuguese on their capitals, which Andaya documents in his chapter. Led by the Seri Bija Wangsa, they were a key component in the structure of power in 17th-century Johor. However, Chuleeporn Virunha has attempted to show, in a study of the writing of autonomous histories about local pasts, that the orang laut were an extreme form of local autonomy on the periphery of the Melaka and Johor sultanates.[31] The nomadic nature of their communities and nomadic lifestyle in the mangroves and waterways feeding into the Singapore and Melaka Straits made them ungovernable, which provided them with opportunities to form multiple relationships with competing centres of authority. However, they also ran the risk of being marginalized and reduced to non-entities if they failed to establish a status under one centre of authority.

Besides the Seri Bija Diraja (later, Seri Bija Wangsa), as one of the Great Lords of Melaka, there was also a *shahbandar*, the "Lord of the Haven", who was in charge of administering the trade of Melaka. *Shahbandar*, as Purnadi in his contribution to this volume has pointed out, is a Persian institution introduced by Persian traders, or adopted by Melaka Straits emporia from the 3rd century CE and from there spread across the archipelago. By early modern times the *shahbandar* was the local ruler's representative not only in administering trade, but also in representing the ruler in his diplomatic and political relations with others. The office of *shahbandar* has become relevant to an understanding of Singapore before 1800 because we are today accumulating records and cartographic references to such an office on Singapore in the 17th century. For example, the Luso-Malayan *descobridor*, cartographer and explorer Manuel Godinho de Erédia marked a *xabandaria* on Singapore in his 1604 map of the island.[32] In another example, on 5 May 1606, Admiral Cornelis Matelieff de Jonge met the Shahbandar Seri Raja Negara in the Straits of Melaka, who had the authority to negotiate with the admiral on behalf of his sultan. Purnadi Purbatjaraka's 1961 essay, "Shahbandars in the Archipelago", included in this compilation, marks a first step toward understanding this office in the study of Singapore before 1800. His collation of Dutch references to the roles and responsibilities of a *shahbandar*, especially as a point of contact at ports and harbours between the ruler sequestered in his palace and traders and representatives of other rulers, provide an insight into the identity of this Seri Raja Negara whom Cornelis Matelieff de Jonge met.

Early Modern Records

From 16th-century Portuguese reports on Melaka, we derive not only an assessment of the military and political influence of the orang laut communities that differs from the marginalized tribal groups Crawfurd saw but also an alternative history about the

[31] Chuleeporn Virunha, "Power Relations between the Orang Laut and the Malay Kingdoms of Melaka and Johor during the Fifteenth to Seventeenth Centuries", in *Recalling Local Pasts; Autonomous History in Southeast Asia*, ed. Sunait Chutintaranond and Chris Baker (Chiang Mai: Silkworm Books, 2002), pp. 143–66.

[32] Cheah B.K. and J.V. Mills, ed. and trans., *Eredia's Description of Malaca, Meridional India and Cathay*, repr. no. 14 (Kuala Lumpur: MBRAS, 1997), p. 225.

beginnings of Melaka that differs from the history told in the *Malay Annals*. Most historians from Winstedt to Wolters have preferred the more mundane identification of the founder of Melaka as a renegade prince from Palembang who was forced to flee after an abortive coup against his east Javanese Majapahit overlord and who arrived at Temasek seeking refuge before taking flight again to Muar, where he fortuitously managed to establish a new settlement.[33]

Ian Macgregor began to re-examine Portuguese records and reports as part of his reconstruction of 16th-century Johor history when he joined the new History Department of the University of Malaya in 1950. His 1954 article, "Johore Lama in the Sixteenth Century", fixed the chronology of Johor history and established a possible timeline for the establishment of a shahbandar's office on Singapore. Macgregor's essay reprinted here, "A Portuguese Sea Fight off Singapore", illustrates what can be gleaned from the Portuguese sources for pre-1800 Singapore that were at his disposal.[34]

After Macgregor's departure, no further search and study of early modern Portuguese and Dutch records for a reconstruction of Singaporean history before 1800 was undertaken until the mid-1990s, when Peter Borschberg was diverted from his studies of Hugo Grotius to investigate the beginnings of the jurist's defence of free trade in his defence of Dutch freebooting in their seizure of a Portuguese carrack off Changi. Borschberg's research into the seizure of the *Santa Catarina* broadened into studies of 17th-century Luso-Dutch rivalry in the Singapore and Melaka Straits and the seascapes on which that rivalry played out. Admiral Cornelis Matelieff de Jonge emerges as a key personality in fundamentally shaping the early policies of the Dutch East Indies Company for the "East Indies", especially towards Johor and Singapore, as compiled by Borschberg's 2015 edition of his journal, memorials and letters.

Historians of Singapore largely focus on the historical development of the island; the waterways and seas surrounding the island, beyond the three-mile port limit and further ten-mile territorial boundaries, held no interest. However, a study of early-modern nautical charts and their accompanying rutters for providing sailing directions around the waters of Singapore provide a rather different perspective of the island's early history, as the polymath Dr Carl Alexander Gibson-Hill (1911–63),[35] the last British expatriate director of the old Raffles Museum and President of the Malayan Branch of the Royal Asiatic Society and also an editor of its journal, has shown.

---

[33] O.W. Wolters attempts in *The Fall of Srivijaya in Malay History* to correlate the Ming dynasty's records with the narrative of the *Malay Annals* on alternative reconstruction of the geneology of Melaka's founder.

[34] However, Macgregor died unexpectedly in 1956 after moving to a new appointment in Ghana. His papers were brought back to Singapore and deposited in the University of Singapore Library, with a listing in K.G. Tregonning, *Malaysian Historical Sources* (Singapore: Department of History, University of Singapore, 1962), pp. 78–90.

[35] See the tributes to and memoir of Gibson-Hill, as well as his encyclopedic interests in Malaysiana from archaeology to the zoology in *JMBRAS* 38, 2 (1965): 1–16, 17–21. Gibson-Hill's correspondence and papers are deposited in the Asian Civilisations Museum, while his library was acquired and donated to the National Library, on which see Bonny Tan, comp., *An Orientalist's Treasure Trove of Malaya and Beyond; Catalogue of the Gibson-Hill Collection at the National Library Singapore* (Singapore: National Library, 2008).

In a perceptive but under-appreciated paper first published in 1954 and expanded two years later, Gibson-Hill argued from a close examination of the Portuguese and Dutch rutters and nautical charts that indicate passage past Singapore—either via Philips Channel and Main Straits, the Keppel Harbour waterway, or the Tebrau or Johor Straits—dates only from the beginning to the middle of the 14th century but no earlier. Gibson-Hill also demonstrated that the mention of a passage through the Keppel Harbour Straits in the Chinese and European rutters, navigational charts and travelogues was only until the close of the 17th century. After these rutter references, no further mention of the Keppel Straits was made; its "very existence was forgotten", and it had to be rediscovered as a "new channel" in 1819. The significance of Gibson-Hill's findings to our understanding of Singapore's early history was lost until 1989, when Kwa Chong Guan reviewed it for a reconstruction of the local history of Tanjong Pagar.[36] Gibson-Hill's insights later became incorporated into Borschberg's studies of the remapping of the Straits of Singapore.[37]

Were the strange and foreign seascapes depicted in the early 16th-century maps and nautical charts a consequence of cartographic inadequacies and failures? Or had deeper geomorphological forces created a rather different seascape? The geologist Victor Obdeijn argued that the final post-Pleistocene submergence of the Sunda plain continued well into historical times. Obdeijn, followed by the geologist R.W. Bemmelen, speculated that Marco Polo did not mention Temasek or Singapura when he sailed through the region in 1292 because no navigable passage past Singapore existed. The Malayan Peninsula at that time formed a promontory that stretched to Bangka and Belitung. The islands, coral reefs and sandbars that define the seascape today were created over the past half-millenium by sea-level changes combined with a strong tidal scour and monsoon-driven currents.[38] Obdeijn's reconstruction of "The Old Naval Trade Route through the Strait of Melaka in Connection with the Geomorphology of the Selat Islands", translated for this compilation, was part of a series of studies on the geomorphology of South Sumatra in historical times. Indonesian historians and geologists have struggled with the implications of Obdeijn's reconstructions for their understanding of Srivijaya's historical development.[39]

---

[36] Kwa, "Sailing Past Singapore", in *Early Singapore*, pp. 95–105, is a revision of the 1989 essay.

[37] P. Borschberg, "Remapping the Straits of Singapore? New Insights from Old Sources", in *Iberians in the Singapore-Melaka Area and Adjacent Regions (16th to 18th Centuries)* (Wiesbaden: Harrassowitz, 2004), p. 95, and "Singapore and Melaka Straits", pp. 17–59.

[38] J.H.F. Umbgrove, *Structural History of the East Indies* (Cambridge: Cambridge University Press, 1949), p. 5; R.W. van Bemmelen, *De geologische geschiedenis van Indonesia* (The Hague: Stockum, 1952), p. 113.

[39] See the articles by the archaeologist Soekmono, "Garis pantai Sriwijaya", *Amerta: Warna warta kepurbakalaan* 3 (1955): 31–3; the geologist, S. Sartono, "Pusat-pusat keragaan Sriwijaya berdasarkan interpretasi paleogeografi", in *Pra Seminar penelitian Sriwijaya, Jakarta, 7–8 Des. 1978*, comp. Pusat Penelitisn Purbakala dan Peninggalan Nasional (Jakarta: Proyek Penelitian dan Penggalian Purbakala, Dept. P & K, 1979), pp. 43–73; Soekmono, "Geomorphology and the Location of Sri Vijaya", *Madjalah ilmu-ilmu sastra Indonesia* 1 (1963): 79–92; O.W. Wolters, "A Note on Sungsang Village at the Estuary of the Musi River in Southeastern Sumatra: A Reconsideration of the Historical Geography of the Palembang Region", *Indonesia* 27 (1979):

Historians and archaeologists studying pre-1800 Singapore may similarly need to reconsider Obdeijn's arguments.

Connecting the Study of Singapore before 1800 with the Study of Singapore after 1800

This introduction to some of the salient studies of pre-1800 Singapore brought together in this anthology suggests that Wong Lin Ken must have been aware of possible answers in these studies to his question asking why "no historian has yet adequately explained why Singapore failed to be a major trading centre before the 19th century". Wong, Tregonning and their colleagues had to be aware of what Paul Wheatley, inhabiting the Geography Department in the block next to the History Department offices on the Bukit Timah campus of the old University of Malaya and University of Singapore, was unearthing from classical texts information about settlement on Singapore during the 13th century, or Hsü Yün-ts'iao's arguments for Chinese textual references to possible earlier settlements on Singapore. Tregonning, Wong and their colleagues would also have been aware of Gibson-Hill's work at the old Raffles Museum and in the *Journal of the Malayan Branch of the Royal Asiatic Society*. But all these studies were ignored or dismissed. The point is that these answers were clearly not adequate from Wong's perspective.

For Wong, none of these answers of possible early settlement on Singapore constituted an "adequate" explanation of why a major trading centre comparable to what developed after 1819 did not happen before that date. In his unpublished MA thesis, Ho Chi Tim notes that Wong brought a very contemporary historical approach to his management of the *Journal of Southeast Asian History* and its transformation into the *Journal of Southeast Asian Studies* in 1970. Perhaps as a consequence of his participation in politics and stint in government service, Wong believed that history should have a practical influence on society. Utilizing this pragmatic function of history in the uncertain years following separation from Malaysia, Wong therefore challenged his colleagues to prove the relevance of Singapore's pre-1800 history to its post-1965 present.[40]

Tregonning dismissed Gibson-Hill and the *Journal of the Malayan Branch of the Royal Asiatic Society*, in the same terms he had used 20 years earlier to dismiss any historical development in the area of Singapore before 1800: "Malayan studies was of antiquarian interest only, the preserve largely of expatriates such as Charles (*sic*) Gibson-Hill, the eccentric, loveable genius who ran the Raffles Museum and edited the *Journal of the Malayan Branch of the Royal Asiatic Society* or Tom Harrison, editor of the *Sarawak Museum Journal*

33–50, esp. 42–6; and P.-Y. Manguin, "The Sumatran Coastline in the Straits of Bangka; New Evidence for Its Permanence in Historical Times", *SPAFA Digest* (Journal of the SEAMEO Project in Archaeology & Fine Arts) 3, 11 (1982): 24–8.

[40] Ho Chi Tim, "A Situated History of the *Journal of Southeast Asian History/Studies* (1960–1979)", MA thesis, Faculty of History, National University of Singapore, 2008, p. 41.

in Kuching."[41] Tregonning and Wong were right that this perspective of antiquarians was unable to connect their historical interest to present concerns. Braddell, Wheatley, Hsü and his South Seas Society colleagues, and Gibson-Hill did not, or could not, forge any connection between the possible early settlement on Singapore that they were studying and the origin and development of the colonial state that Tregonning, Turnbull and Wong were studying in the archived records of the East India Company and the Colonial Office in order to make sense of the phenomenon of decolonization they were witnessing around them.

For Tregonning and his colleagues, including Brian Harrison, C.D. Cowan and C.N. Parkinson, their new head of the History Department, it was these records of the East India Company, archived as the Straits Settlements Records in the old Raffles Museum and Library,[42] which provided the basic materials for the reconstruction of their immediate past. L.A. Mills was, in 1924, the first to draw on these archived records of the Honourable Company for his doctoral thesis, "British Malaya, 1824–67", published in the *Journal of the Malayan Branch of the Royal Asiatic Society* for 1925, which became the benchmark study of the political and administrative history of Singapore as a part of the Straits Settlements. C.D. Cowan, who preceded Tregonning as a lecturer at Raffles College, predecessor to the University of Malaya, selected 158 files from the Straits Settlements Records "to provide students [enrolling for the new course on the history of Malaya] with an original documentary basis for their studies".[43]

---

[41] K.G. Tregonning, reminiscing on his experience in *Home Port Singapore: An Australian Historian's Experience 1953–1967* (Nathan, Queensland: Centre for the Study of Australia-Asia Relations, Division of Asian and International Studies Griffith University, 1989), p. 11. This reflection is absent in the later edition of Tregonning's *Merdeka and Much More: The Reminiscences of a Raffles Professor 1953–1967* (Singapore: NUS Press, 2010), which focuses on history as the recent and contemporary events witnessed by the historian. Tregonning was clear in his rejection of *JMBRAS* and its focus on Malaysiana and his "need for a journal which would have a different emphasis and which would cover all Southeast Asia", to which end he established the *Journal of Southeast Asian History* in 1960, as he recalled in *Home Port Singapore*, pp. 31–3. See Ho's "Situated History" for a detail reconstruction of the launch, development and transformation of the *Journal of Southeast Asian History*. Ho's accounting shows that the journal and its successor published on topics that focused largely on 19th- and 20th-century subjects and issues. In its nine years, the *Journal of Southeast Asian History* published only three articles on subjects that occured before the 16th century—only 3.5 per cent of the total 172 articles published. By comparison, the *Journal of Southeast Asian Studies* published only three articles on pre-16th century topics, making up 1.9 per cent of the journal's content for its issues from 1970 to 1979.

[42] National Archives of Singapore, *Guide to the Sources of History in Singapore*, International Council on Archives Guide to the Sources of Asian History, vol. 10.1: Singapore (Singapore: National Archives of Singapore-UNESCO, c. 1991), vol.1 for an inventory of these East India Company records. In his study reprinted here, Gibson-Hill also refers to these records for information on later sailing past Singapore.

[43] Five hundred copies of this compilation were published as a "Special Edition" of *JMBRAS* (see 28, 2 [1950]), as it was "represented that these documents might be of use or interest to many outside the University of Malaya", according to Cowan in his "Editor's Note" to the publication.

That pioneering cohort of history students at the University of Malaya, who had to make sense of the Straits Settlements Records Cowan compiled for their study, were also directed to Mills' 1925 study as "the best general survey of the early history of Penang and Singapore". The legacy of Mills'[44] influence on Tregonning[45] and Turnbull[46] is evident in their research on the origins and the development of Singapore as a colonial state. Mill's pioneering work, elaborated by Tregonning and Turnbull, defined the paradigm for the study of the history of Singapore (and also Malaya), as a history about the establishment and development of a colonial state whose decolonization Tregonning and Turnbull observed, and whose continuing relevance in a post-colonial Singapore Turnbull urged.

However, as we recognize today, the Straits Settlements Records, which Tregonning and his colleagues taught students to mine for objective, verifiable "facts" for reconstructing Singapore's past as a colonial state, are about what the officials of the Honourable Company chose or were compelled to record or archive for their administration of the settlement. The Straits Settlements Records, therefore, constitute the institutional memories of East India Company officials about an unwanted settlement that one of their servants, Stamford Raffles, established against the wishes of the Honourable Company. The institutional memories that shape the succeeding Colonial Office records focus concern on governing a port city and its plural society as part of an expanding British empire. The consequence of this "archivalization" of institutional memories valued by the East India Company and Colonial Office is that it fundamentally shaped the writing of Singapore's past by Tregonning and Wong, and subsequently their students, as an appendage to the histories of the East India Company and British Empire,[47] rather than as the 19th-century successor to a longer series of earlier port settlements in the long cycles of the maritime history of the Melaka Straits archived in the Portuguese and Dutch records.

---

[44] In 1960, Turnbull and her colleagues Tregonning and D.K. Bassett edited for reprinting Mills' 35-year-old study of British Malaya as "the standard work in this field", entitled "British Malaya, 1824–67", and published in *JMBRAS* 33, 3 (1960): 1–424. Turnbull contributed a 97-page bibliography of writings in English on British Malaya, covering 1786 to 1867; D.K. Bassett, then at the University of Malaya, added a new introductory chapter on European influence in the Malay Peninsula between 1511 and 1787; and Tregonning amended Mills' ch. 2 on Penang in the light of his own work.

[45] Tregonning, in his 1958 PhD thesis submitted to the University of Singapore and published as *The British in Malaya: The First Forty Years 1786–1824*, Association for Asian Studies Mongraphs and Papers 18 (Tucson: University of Arizona Press, 1965). Here, he argued that Singapore was better located than Penang to service trade with China.

[46] Turnbull's 1962 University of London PhD thesis, later published as *Straits Settlements, 1826–67: Indian Presidency to Crown Colony* (London: University of London Athlone Press, 1972), firmly located Singapore within the Indian world of the East India Company.

[47] Kwa Chong Guan and Ho Chi Tim, "Archives in the Making of Post-Colonial Singapore", in *Colonial Legacy in South East Asia; The Dutch Archives*, Jaarboek 11, ed. Charles Jeurgens et al. (The Hague: Stichting Archiefpublicaties, 2012), pp. 125–50; also Kwa Chong Guan and Ho Chi Tim, "Archival Records in the Writing of Singapore History: A Perspective from the Archives", in *The Makers and Keepers of Singapore History*, ed. Loh Kah Seng and Liew Kai Khiun (Singapore: Ethos Books-Singapore Heritage Society, 2010), pp. 48–64.

The Portuguese records, which Ian Macgregor was beginning to examine before his premature death,[48] and the massive archives of the VOC, was *terra incognita* to the staff of the History Department at the University of Malaya, even though Graham Irwin, when he was with the department in 1953, had managed to arrange for some 33,000 pages of VOC records to be microfilmed for the university library.[49] It was only in the 1990s, when Peter Borschberg expanded his research on Hugo Grotius' work for the VOC in order to examine Luso-Dutch rivalry in the waters around Singapore, that we had an alternative framing of the beginnings of Singapore's past within the world of the VOC caught between war and diplomacy.[50] This is contrasted with the Mills-Tregonning-Turnbull paradigm of locating the beginnings of Singapore within the Indian world of the East India Company.

The data from 30 years of archaeological excavations in the environs of Fort Canning[51] have provided incontrovertible evidence to further stretch the beginnings of Singapore to the 14th century.[52] The artefacts recovered from a continuing series of archaeological excavations undertaken since 1984 provided a new starting point from which to re-examine the myth in the *Malay Annals* in which Sri Tri Buana/ Parmeswara saw a lion when he landed on the white sandy shore of Singapore— which Miksic and his colleagues found at the bottom of their trenches. These artefacts, which provide archaeological evidence of the first settlement on the island, enabled the old Singapore History Museum to mount an exhibition in 1998 commemorating Singapore's 700th anniversary. The museum also published a volume edited by

---

48 See Macgregor's survey, "Some Aspects of Historical Writing of the Sixteenth and Seventeenth Centuries on Southeast Asia", in *Historians of South-East Asia: Historical Writing on the Peoples of Asia*, ed. D.G.E. Hall (London: Oxford University Press, 1961), pp. 172–99.

49 For Irwin's summary of the VOC records he arranged to be microfilmed, see Irwin, "University of Singapore Library Dutch Archives Microfilm Collection", in *Malaysian Historical Sources*, ed. K.G. Tregonning (Singapore: Department of History, 1962), pp. 128–9. For a guide to these archives, see also M.A.P. Meilink-Roelofsz, *De archieven van de Verenigde oostindische Companie: The Archives of the Dutch East India Company (1602–1795)*, Algemeen Rijksarchief, eerste afd. (The Hague: Uitgeverij Konjinginnegracht, 1992).

50 For such a framing of VOC history, see G. Knaap and G. Teitler, eds., *De Verenigde oost-Indische Compagnie tussen oorlog en diplomatie*, Verhandelingen 197 (Leiden: KITLV Uitgeverij, 2002).

51 Ironically, neither the lecturers at the University or the curators of the old Raffles Museum appear to have thought of excavating Bukit Larangan, or the Forbidden Hill, directly behind the museum. Instead, Gibson-Hill led excavations of Johor Lama and Tregonning led an expedition to Kuala B'rang to look for the first signs of Islam on the peninsula. Perhaps they assessed that the construction of the artillery fort on the hill in 1859 and the digging of the reservoir in 1926 had destroyed the "antiquities" that Stamford Raffles and John Crawfurd saw on the hill. The old National Museum was therefore taking a very long shot in inviting John Miksic to conduct an archaeological excavation on Bukit Larangan or Fort Canning, in 1984, the results of which are reported in Miksic, *Archaeological Research on the "Forbidden Hill"*.

52 Thirty years of archaeological excavations have unearthed several tons of artefacts, the analysis of which lags behind the sorting and classification of the artefacts recovered. See Lim Tse Siang, "14th-Century Singapore: The Temasek Paradigm", MA thesis, Department of History, National University of Singapore, 2012, for insight into such archaeological issues such as the social complexity of society in 14th-century Temasek raised by analyzing finds from a single site.

Miksic and Low on early Singapore in 2004.[53] In her review of this volume, Turnbull conceded, "it will be impossible in the future to follow one 20th-century writer in ignoring pre-colonial Singapore as 'of antiquarian interest only', and the book's thought-provoking conclusions will challenge historians to look at Singapore afresh in an attempt to reunite the 21st century with its distant past".[54]

In the 2009 revision of her now classic *History of Singapore* (the title of which is now qualified as *History of Modern Singapore 1819–2005*), Turnbull however did not rise to the challenge of looking at Singapore afresh to try to reunite the history of modern Singapore with its distant past. Instead, she pointed out on page 4 of her revised book:

> The findings of careful archaeological work carried out in the late 20th century at Fort Canning and near the Singapore River, together with a study of pre-colonial records, charts and maps, supplement but basically support the previously known story, namely that Temasek appeared and flourished for a few decades as one of a number of moderately prosperous ports in the region but came to a sudden, violent and mysterious end at the close of the 14th century.... The thorough investigations of the late 20th century confirm that, after the fall of Temasek, nothing of significance took place on the island until Raffles' party landed in 1819.

It is a point that Miksic concurs with when he concludes: "archaeology and history both show that by 1650, Singapore had reverted to the marginal position which it had occupied before A.D. 1300".[55] Commenting on the contribution of archaeology to our understanding of Roman history, the classicist M.I. Finley observed in 1971 that archaeology has confirmed the beginnings of Rome as a primitive village and the chronology of Roman history as outlined in the texts.[56] Thirty years of archaeological excavations of the area demarcated by Crawfurd as the confines of the old settlement of Singapura appears to lead to similar confirmations about the contribution of archaeology to the reconstruction of Singapore before Raffles. Finley's "paradoxical conclusion that the contribution of archaeology to history becomes greater as the volume and reliability of non-archaeological evidence

---

[53] Miksic and Low, eds., *Early Singapore 1300s–1819.*

[54] Review in *JMBRAS* 78, 1 (2005): 122–4.

[55] Miksic, *Singapore and the Silk Road of the Sea*, p. 410. In a 2017 essay on "Singapore's Maritime Heritage" for the Republic of Singapore Navy, Miksic argued that Singapore was a centre of maritime activity, which Srivijaya from 680 to 1025 and Malayu from 1030 to 1300 sought to influence; see Miksic, "Singapore's Maritime Heritage", in *A Maritime Force for a Maritime Nation: Celebrating 50 Years of the Navy* (Singapore: Straits Times Press, 2017), pp. 19–21. Miksic points to the 14th century during the Temasek era and the 15th century when the island served as the Melaka and Johor sultanate's "main naval base", with a fleet of "40 three-masted cruisers", as times when Singapura rose to international prominence. However, "Singapura experienced a disaster sometime between 1605 and 1610. No archaeological remains from the period 1600–1800 have been found". As a consequence, these two centuries remain "the Lost Centuries".

[56] M.I. Finley, "Archaeology and History", *Daedalus* 100 (1971): 168–86.

increases (until the latter reaches the volume and nature of modern, even early modern, documentation)" may well apply to post-14th century Singapura.

In her review of *Early Singapore*, Turnbull also dismissed Kwa's attempts, reprinted in this anthology, to reconstruct the worldview of Husain, leading to his decision to accept Raffles recognition of him as a sultan, and so bringing about a convergence of the British and Malay past to create a new world. She argued: "while Singapore may not have been Raffles' first choice, he alone was responsible for persuading the British authorities to seek a base in the south of the Melaka Straits. Tengku Husain was an uninspiring claimant to the Srivijaya-Temasek-Melaka-Johor legacy, faltering as it was in 1819 towards an ignominious demise, with the throne in dispute and battered by Bugis, Dutch and British manoeuvring."[57] Turnbull may well be right about Tengku Husain and the larger historiographic issue of causally connecting the "ignominious demise" of the Srivijaya-Temasek-Melaka-Johor legacy to the 1699 regicide of Sultan Mahmud.

However, larger historical forces drive the actions of men and the events they enact. As Peter A. Coclanis, Raffles Visiting Professor, has argued (among others), there also exist cycles of historical forces complementing, or driving, the linear sequence of historical events.[58] These range from 50- to 60-year business cycles driven by technological innovation proposed by the business historians Joseph Schumpeter and Nikolai Kondratiev; to century-long cycles of geo-economic and geo-political change in Asia as tracked by the economic historian Andre Gunder Frank. Within these cycles of trade and commerce, Anthony Reid has defined 1450 to 1680 as an "Age of Commerce" in Southeast Asia, when the conjuncture of new economic forces and political change brought about revolutionary changes in Southeast Asia. Victor Lieberman has extended his initial work on precolonial Burma to a wide-ranging comparative analysis of "strange parallels" between Southeast Asia and Eurasia's history in a linear-cum-cyclic construction of Southeast Asia's history in a global context.

In his chapter, "From Temasek to Singapore: Locating a Global City-State in the Cycles of Melaka Straits History", Kwa Chong Guan argues for a linear-cum-cyclical construction of Singapore's history as a port that emerged and declined in response to cycles of regionalization of maritime trade in the Straits of Melaka. This framing of Singapore's past within hierarchies of trading ports and cities, and how they were networked and connected for the circulation of trade, assumes some underlying pattern of continuity within the longue durée.[59] Derek Heng has attempted to identify the key political, economic and social variables determining this framing of Singapore's past within the context of such a longue durée structure.[60]

---

[57] *JMBRAS* 78, 1 (2005): 124.

[58] P. Coclanis, *Time's Arrow, Time's Cycle* (Singapore: Institute of Southeast Asian Studies, 2006).

[59] Commenting on this attempt by Kwa, Heng, and Tan Tai Yong on their framing of Singapore within the longue durée in their teaching of Singapore history and in their 2009 text, Karl Hack notes: "this continuity consists more in place—the opportunities and dilemmas thrown up by [Singapore] sitting at the meeting of the monsoons on the Melaka Straits—than of institutions of even a 'nation'"; Hack, "Framing Singapore's History", p. 20.

[60] Derek Heng, "Casting Singapore's History in the Longue Durée", in *Singapore from Temasek to the 21st Century*, ed. Hack et al., pp. 55–75.

The challenge of studying Singapore both before 1800 and after 1800 depends upon whether, as Karl Hack has argued, we use alternative framings of Singapore within a 700- or a 200-year time frame.[61] Studying Singapore within a 200-year time frame leads to the historical trajectory of Singapore's beginnings as a 19th-century colonial state that was transformed by 20th-century decolonization into a post-colonial nation-state but which after 1965 had to disconnect itself from the Malay world after it tried but failed to merge with it.[62] For the founding fathers of the new nation-state, the historical analogies for Singapore's future as a city-state were, understandably, not the port cities and city-states of the Straits of Melaka, but rather 5th-century BCE Athens and 13th- to 16th-century CE Venice.[63]

The national narrative which emerges from this historical trajectory is, as the cultural theorist C.J. W.-L. Wee points out, "as linear in its historical emplotment as one centred on the story of a precolonial past destroyed by the imperialists". Wee goes on to identify two interrelated and dominant narratives that make for a distinctive national narrative. "The first has to do with a Whiggish telos of economic development, progress, modernity, and modernization since 1819." The second theme "has to do with the communist-, leftist- and communalist-inflected 1950s, from which the Lee Kuan Yew-led faction in the PAP emerged the victor".[64]

In contrast, a 700-year time frame focuses on the sea and the cycles and circuits of maritime trade in the South China Sea and the Straits of Melaka as the driving forces of Singapore's *raison-d'être*. It is about the conjunctures of cycles, circuits and networks of trade and commerce, driven by the geopolitical imperatives and constraints of the seascapes with their variable monsoons and changeable climates, that enabled the rapid rise of settlement on Singapore on three occasions—and on two occasions, their equally rapid demise.[65]

Studying Singapore before 1800 and after 1800 is more than about different ways of thinking about Singapore, and having to decide which is the "correct" way to think about Singapore's past. It is about the tensions inherent in locating Singapore

---

[61] Hack, in his edited volume *Singapore from Temasek to the 21st Century*, calls for "abandoning the idea of uninterrupted chronology"; instead, he prefers to see "Singapore as a location [that] has hosted diverse and partly discontinuous experiments on how to achieve centrality in the Straits; how to become a, or preferably, *the* pre-eminent entrepot for central Southeast Asia and the Melaka Straits."

[62] But not necessarily its "Malayan" legacy, as Hack has argued; Singapore's "Malayan" period was not just confined to a brief and traumatic merger with Malaysia, but was rooted in a deeper identity prior to 1960; Hack, "The Malayan Trajectory in Singapore History", pp. 243–91.

[63] Brigadier-General George Yeo, in his 1988 valedictory speech on resigning from the Singapore Armed Forces to enter politics, held up Venice as an example for Singapore to follow; see "Defending Singapore", in *George Yeo on Bonsai, Banyan and the Tao*, ed. Asad-ul Iqbal Laif and Lee Huay Leng (Singapore: World Scientific, 2015), p. 15.

[64] Wee, "Our Island Story; Economic Development and the National Narrative in Singapore", in *New Terrains in Southeast Asian History*, ed. Abu Talib and Tan Liok Ee, Ohio University Research in International Studies, Southeast Asia Series No. 107 (Athens: Ohio University Press, 2003), p. 141. Wee has reworked this essay into a wide-ranging critique, entitled *The Asian Modern: Culture, Capitalist Development, Singapore* (Singapore: NUS Press, 2007).

[65] Summarized in P. Borschberg, "Singapore in the Cycles of the Longue Durée", *JMBRAS* 90, 1 (2017): 29–60.

in the intersections of these two ways of thinking about Singapore's past in a global-historical context versus an autonomous history of local pasts. Embedded in this binary of studying Singapore before 1800 and after 1800 is the subjectivity of nationhood within the cycles of global capitalism and cosmopolitism.[66] Can Singapore's re-engineering of itself in the 1990s to become a global city continue to be bound up by the narrative of a nation-state/city-state's "disciplinary modernisation"[67] from a 19th-century colonial state? Attempting to locate Singapore within the intersections of these two framings of Singapore's past highlights fundamental tensions of a bounded and exclusive nation-state struggling to adapt to the demands of a global city as a de-territorialized, transient and open space within an increasingly complex and globalizing world of mega-size global cities.[68]

Oliver Wolters has extrapolated that the globalizing world of today, structured around a hierarchy of competing global cities whose ranks Singapore aspires to join, may, in a longue durée perspective, look like the political landscape of Southeast Asia a millennium ago, when kings envisaged themselves at the centre of a "circle of kings" or *mandala*, radiating their power and influence over other kings they claimed or manoeuvred as part of their circle of subservient vassals or allies.[69] Wolters saw "processual parallels" between competing global cities in the region today to create a neo-*mandala* order paralleling earlier eras of *mandala* time. The 200th anniversary of Stamford Raffles' arrival at Singapore would be an appropriate time to reflect on Raffles' place in connecting these two framings of Singapore history, and hopefully provide Singapore with an alternative framing and resulting understanding of its place as an aspiring global city in an emergent and volatile, uncertain and unpredictable global order.

Conclusion

The underlying logic of Wong Lin Ken's puzzle—why no historian had explained the absence of a major trading centre on Singapore prior to its rapid and unexpected rise in the 19th century—preoccupies many of the studies in this anthology. The tacit assumption is that Singapore, strategically situated between the trade routes of the South China Sea and the Indian Ocean, must have been settled from an early date. Wong followed Richard Winstedt in assuming that there should have been a settlement on Singapore as a consequence of efforts by a series of powers from

---

[66] See Reid's argument for the salience of the cosmopolis over the nation in the historical development of Singapore in the longue durée; "Singapore between Cosmopolis and Nation", in Hack, ed., *Singapore from Temasek to the 21st Century*, pp. 37–54.

[67] See Wee, *The Asian Modern*, pp. 143–60, for an analysis of the challenges to the "disciplinary modernization" which defined Singapore's development from the 1960s to the 1990s.

[68] See Simon Curtis, *Global Cities and Global Order* (Oxford: Oxford University Press, 2016), on the implications of the re-emergence of cities from the shadow of their nation-states to dominance in global politics.

[69] O.W. Wolters, *History, Culture, and Region in Southeast Asian Perspectives*, rev. ed. (Ithaca: Cornell University Southeast Asia Program Publications; Singapore: Institute of Southeast Asian Studies, 1999), p. 219.

Srivijaya to the Cholas and then Majapahit Java and the Melaka and Johor sultans to assert their influence over Singapore.

The authors of the studies in this anthology appear to accept this logic in their systematic combing of classical texts for possible references to an early settlement on Singapore. More than one generation of scholars, led by Richard Winstedt, have closely read the *Malay Annals*, trying to separate fable from facts with regard to Singapore's place in Malay historiography. Another generation of scholars dug deep into the Portuguese records and Dutch archives to reconstruct how Luso-Dutch rivalry shaped the historical landscape around Singapore.

But none of these studies impressed Wong, his predecessor K.G. Tregonning, or their colleague C.M. Turnbull. If history is about narratives, or stories, as in the case of Lee Kuan Yew's version in The Singapore Story, then every story should have a clear beginning, which can be documented and which legitimizes all subsequent developments. For Wong, Tregonning, Turnbull and Lee Kuan Yew, the beginning of their narrative is Raffles' arrival on a depopulated island in 1819. All before 1819 would be about the mythical origin of Singapore from lions sighted on the island or about inconclusive and ambiguous references in classical texts to possible early settlements.

This narrative of Singapore's beginnings as a colonial state has served Singapore well in its construction of a national history: surviving against all odds as a vulnerable city-state in a volatile and uncertain world. Turnbull successfully extended the legacy of the colonial state to explain the success of Singapore as a city-state. The challenge will be how much further this narrative can be extended to narrate Singapore's transformation into a global city. The studies contained in this anthology may provide that view back into a deep past to look further into Singapore's future as an aspiring global city.

Further Reading

Ahmat Adam. *Antara sejarah dan mitos; Sejarah Melayu & Hang Tuah dalam historiografi Malaysia*. Petaling Jaya, Selangor: Strategic Information and Research Development Centre, 2016.

Andaya, Leonard Y. *The Kingdom of Johor 1641–1728: Economic and Political Developments*. Kuala Lumpur: Oxford University Press, 1975.

Braddell, Roland. *The Study of Ancient Times in the Malay Peninsula and the Straits of Malacca*. Reprint no. 7. Kuala Lumpur: MBRAS, 1980.

Borschberg, Peter. *The Singapore and Melaka Straits; Violence, Security and Diplomacy in the 17th Century*. Singapore: NUS Press, 2010.

________, ed. *Iberians in the Singapore-Melaka Area (16th to 18th Century)*. Wiesbaden: Harrassowitz Verlag, 2001.

________, ed. *Journal, Memorials and Letters of Cornelis Matelieff de Jong: Security, Diplomacy and Commerce in 17th-Century Southeast Asia*. Singapore: NUS Press, 2015.

________, ed. *Jacques de Coutre's Singapore and Johor 1594–c.1625*. Singapore: NUS Press, 2015.

________, ed. *Admiral Matelieff's Singapore and Johor 1606–1616*. Singapore: NUS Press, 2016.

Borschberg, Peter, ed., and R. Roy, trans. *The Memoirs and Memorials of Jacques de Coutre: Security, Trade and Society in 16th- and 17th-century Southeast Asia*. Singapore: NUS Press, 2014.

Brown, C.C. ed and trans. "Malay Annals: A Translation of Raffles MS 18, in the Library of the R.A.S. London". *JMBRAS* 25, 2–3 (1952): 1–276. [Also *MBRAS* Reprint No. 28 (2009).]

Cheah, Boon Kheng, comp., and Abdul Rahman Haji Ismail, trans. *Sejarah Melayu: The Malay Annals: MS Raffles No. 18, New Romanised Edition*. Reprint no. 17. Kuala Lumpur: MBRAS, 1998.

Cleary, M. and K.C. Goh. *Environment and Development in the Straits of Malacca*. London: Routledge, 2000.

Coclanis, Peter A. *Time's Arrow, Time's Cycle: Globalization in Southeast Asia over la Longue Durée*. Raffles Lecture Series. Singapore: Institute of Southeast Asian Studies for the Department of History, National University of Singapore, 2006.

Crawfurd, John. *A Descriptive Dictionary of the Indian Islands & Adjacent Countries*. Reprint 1856. Kuala Lumpur: Oxford University Press, 1971.

Gibson-Hill, C.A. "The Orang Laut of the Singapore River and the Sampan Panjang". *JMBRAS* 25, 2 (1952): 161–74.

________. "Singapore: Notes on the History of the Old Strait, 1580–1850". *JMBRAS* 27, 1 (1954): 163–214.

________. "Johore Lama and Other Ancient Sites on the Johor River". *JMBRAS* 28, 2 (1955): 129–97.

Hack, Karl, Jean-Louis Margolin and Karine Delaye, eds. *Singapore from Temasek to the 21st Century: Reinventing the Global City*. Singapore: NUS Press, 2010.

Han, Wai Toon. "Study of Johore Lama". *JSS* 5, 2, pt. 10 (1948): 17–40.

Heng, Derek T.S. *Sino-Malay Trade and Diplomacy from the Tenth through the Fourteenth Century*. Nalanda-Sriwijaya Series 7. Reprint 2009. Singapore: Institute of Southeast Asian Studies, 2012.

________. "Temasik as an International and Regional Trading Port in the Thirteenth and Fourteenth Centuries: A Reconstruction Based on Recent Archaeological Data". *JMBRAS* 72, 1 (1999): 113–24.

________. "Situating Temasik within the Larger Regional Context: Maritime Asia and Malay State Formation in the Pre-Modern Era". In *Singapore in Global History*, ed. Derek Heng and Syed Muhd. Khairudin Aljunied. Amsterdam: Amsterdam University Press International Convention of Asian Scholars, 2011.

________. "Casting Singapore's History in the Longue Durée". In *Singapore from Temasek to the 21st Century*, ed. Hack et al., pp. 55–75.

Lapian, A.B. "Le rôle des Orang Laut dans l'histoire de Riau" [The Role of the Orang Laut in the History of Riau]. *Archipel* 18 (1979): 215–22.

Lewis, Dianne. *Jan Compagnie in the Straits of Malaca 1641–1795*. Athens, OH: Ohio University Center for International Studies, 1995.

Lewis, Dianne, "British Policy in the Straits of Malacca to 1819 and the Collapse of the Traditional Malay State Structure". In *Empires, Imperialism and Southeast Asia: Essays in Honour of Nicholas Tarling*, ed. Brook Barrington. Clayton, Victoria: Monash Asia Institute, Monash University, 1997, pp. 17–33.

Lin Woling 林我鈴. 龍牙门新考: 中國古代南海兩主要行道要衝的歷史地理研究/林我鈴著 Longyamen xin kao: Zhongguo gudai Nanhai liang zhuyao hangdao yaochong de lishi dili yanjiu [Long-ya-men re-identified: a historical-geography study of the two important junctions in the ancient Nanhai sea routes]. 新加坡: 南洋學會 [Xinjiapo (Singapore): Nanyang Xuehui], 1999.

Macgregor, I.A., C.A. Gibson-Hill, and G. de Sieveking. "Papers on Johore Lama and the Portuguese in Malaya (1511–1641)". *JMBRAS* 28, 2 (1955): 129–97.

Miksic, John N. *Archaeological Research on the "Forbidden Hill" of Singapore: Excavations at Fort Canning, 1984*. Singapore: National Museum of Singapore, 1985.

________. *Singapore and the Silk Road of the Sea, 1300–1800*. Singapore: NUS Press, 2013.

Miksic, John N. and Cheryl-Ann Low Mei Gek, eds. *Early Singapore 1300s–1819: Evidence in Maps, Text and Artefacts*. Singapore: Singapore History Museum, 2004.

Mills, J.V. "Arab and Chinese Navigators in Malaysian Waters in about A.D. 1500". *JMBRAS* 47, 2 (1974): 1–82.

Netscher, E. *De Nederlanders in Djohor en Siak 1602 tot 1865, historische beschrijving*. Verhandelingen 35. Batavia: Bataviaasch Genootschap, 1870: 1–309.

Ng, Chin-keong. "Commodity and Market: Structure of the Long-Distance Trade in the East Asian Seas and beyond Prior to the Early Nineteenth Century". In *Boundaries and Beyond: China's Maritime Southeast in Late Imperial Times*. Singapore: NUS Press, 2017, pp. 3–53.

Tarling, Nicholas. *Piracy and Politics in the Malay World: A Study of British Imperialism in Nineteenth-Century South-East Asia*. Nendeln: Kraus Reprint, 1978.

________, ed. *Studying Singapore's Past: C.M. Turnbull and the History of Modern Singapore*. Singapore: NUS Press, 2012.

Trocki, Carl. *Prince of Pirates: The Temenggongs and the Development of Johor and Singapore 1784–1885*. Singapore: Singapore University Press, 1979.

Turnbull, Constance M. *A History of Modern Singapore, 1819–2005*. Singapore: NUS Press, 2009.

Vos, Reinout. *Gentle Janus, Merchant Prince: The VOC and the Tightrope of Diplomacy in the Malay World, 1740–1800*. Verhandelingen 157. Leiden: KITLV Press, 1993.

Wade, Geoff, ed. and introd. *Southeast Asia: China Interactions: Reprints of Articles from the Journal of the Malaysian Branch, Royal Asiatic Society*. Reprint No. 25. Kuala Lumpur: MBRAS, 2007.

Wheatley, Paul. *The Golden Khersonese: Studies in the Historical Geography of the Malay Peninsula before A.D. 1500*. Kuala Lumpur: University of Malaya Press, 1961.

________. "Desultory Remarks on the Ancient History of the Malay Peninsula". In *Malayan and Indonesian Studies: Essays Presented to Sir Richard Winstedt on His Eighty-fifth Birthday*, ed. J. Bastin and R. Roolvink. Oxford: Clarendon Press, 1964, pp. 33–75.

Winstedt, Richard O. 1962. *A History of Malaya*, revised and enlarged. Singapore: Marican & Sons, 1962.

________. *A History of Johore (1365–1941)*. Reprint No. 6. Kuala Lumpur: MBRAS, 1979.

Winstedt, R.O., ed. "The Malay Annals or Sejarah Melayu: The Earliest Recension from MS. No. 18 of the Raffles Collection, in the Library of the Royal Asiatic Society, London". *JMBRAS* 16, 3 (1938): 1–226.

Wolters, O.W. *The Fall of Srivijaya in Malay History*. London: Lund Humphries, 1970.

1

Roland Braddell

Lung-ya-men and Tan-ma-hsi*

In a paper on Johor Lama, which appeared in a recent number of the *Journal of the South Seas Society*, Mr Han Wai Toon[1] has put forward several novel theories and has reopened the identification of the ancient Chinese toponyms Lung-ya-men and Tan-ma-hsi. His paper is fortified by a postcript written by Mr H.D. Collings, of Raffles Museum,[2] and is criticized by Mr Hsü Yün-ts'iao.[3]

Mr Han considers that "the so-called Lung-ya-men in Sung and Yuan Dynasties seemed to have been the general name for Kuala Johor in the east Strait of Johor. It could not have been either Lingga Island or Keppel Harbour". Mr Hsü, however, considers that it was Keppel Harbour.

Tan-ma-hsi was identified with Singapore Island in 1904 by the late Professor Pelliot.[4] This identification has been accepted generally ever since and is accepted by Professor Coedès in his latest work.[5] Mr Han, however, argues that it was the land adjacent to Kuala Johor and that Tan-ma-hsi-men (Tan-ma-hsi Gate), which is mentioned in the *Tung-hsi yang-k'ao*, represented the passage between "the Tanjong Tua and Tanjong Bulus of the west part of Johor Strait". Mr Hsü accepts the orthodox opinion that Tan-ma-hsi represents Singapore and considers that Lung-ya-men and Tan-ma-hsi-men were different names for Keppel Harbour.

---

* First published in *JMBRAS* 23, 1 (1950): 37–51, and reprinted in the Singapore 150th Anniversary Commemorative Issue of *JMBRAS* 42, 1 (1969): 10–24.

[1] Han W.T., "A Study on Johore Lama", *JSS* 5, 2 (1948): 17–35.

[2] H.D. Collings, "Postscript to a study on Johore Lama", *JSS* 5, 2 (1948): 35.

[3] Hsü Yün-ts'iao, "Notes on Malay Peninsula in Ancient Voyages", *JSS* 5, 2 (1948): 1–16.

[4] Paul Pelliot, "Deux itinéraires de Chine en Inde à la fin du VIIIème siècle", *BEFEO* 4 (1904): 345n4.

[5] Collings, "Postscript".

Mr Collings writes:

> For a number of years I have found it hard to believe in the old tale of the town of "Singapura" on this island. My reason is that, with three exceptions, no archaeological remains have been found here. This is all the more odd since there can be few places in the Far East which have been so messed about as Singapore Island. Foundations have been dug, hills have been cut away and swamps have been filled in, but the only finds ever reported were the Singapore stone, the fort on Canning Hill and the small hoard of Hindu jewellery from the same place. There have been no signs of the many odds and ends, the shards, the bits of metal, the graves and so on, which are always found on old sites. Only one conclusion can be drawn from this: there never was a settlement of any size or age upon this island.

He ends by saying: "In every way the Johor River is an ideal living place and Mr Han Wai Toon's argument based on old Chinese sources, should convince one that the so-called greatness of old 'Singapura' and the very existence of Temasek, are probably but the fancies of Malay folk tales and the religious and political yearnings of the then ruling royal house."

It is proposed in this paper to review the questions opened by Mr Han and Mr Collings; and we shall begin with the latter.

It seems to us impossible to deny the existence of Temasek. The Javanese form, Tumasik, occurs in *Pararaton*[6] and *Nagarakretagama*.[7] The *Sejarah Melayu* tells us that a settlement was made on the island of Temasek, which Dr Blagden says is pronounced by Malays as "Temasak",[8] and that the name of Singapura (or Singhapura) was given to this settlement. This custom of giving honorific names to places was obtained from the Hindus and persists among Malays to the present time. Singapura was a Hindu-Malay rajadom. Dr Linehan's latest dating gives Singapura an existence from 1299 to 1391,[9] and places its sack, so graphically recoded in the *Sejarah Melayu*, as having occurred in 1376. *Nagarakretagama* is dated as 1365, the *Sejarah Melayu* is now dated by Sir Richard Winstedt as a 15th-century history,[10] and *Pararaton* is stated by Professor Coedès to date at the end of the 15th century.[11] The last only is accepted as containing real history; but all three are perfectly good and convincing evidence that there was such a place as Temasek and, accordingly, all scholars so far have accepted its reality and its identification with the island of Singapore.

The existence of the settlement called Singapura is proved by those who saw its remains after the British first came to Singapore, when there was much more archaeological evidence of it than is enumerated by Mr Collings. We can, however, agree that its importance was exaggerated in the *Sejarah Melayu* and by Barros. The earliest European seamen who came to Malayan waters in the 16th century

---

[6] C.O. Blagden, "Notes on Malay History", *JSBRAS* 53 (1909): 143–9.

[7] Ibid., pp. 147, 149–50.

[8] Ibid., p. 144.

[9] W. Linehan, "The Kings of 14th Century Singapore", *JMBRAS* 20, 2 (1947): 117–27.

[10] Richard Winstedt, *The Malays: A Cultural History* (Singapore: Kelly & Walsh, 1947), p. 130.

[11] G. Coedès, *Les états hindouisés d'Indochine et d'Indonésie* (Paris: De Boccard, 1948), p. 314.

found the name Singapura attached to the island, which fact alone proves that name. Writing to Marsden on the 31 January 1819, Stamford Raffles said, "Here I am at Singapore, true to my word, and in the enjoyment of all the pleasure which a footing on such classic ground must inspire. The lines of the old city, and its defences, are still to be traced, and within its ramparts the British Union waves unmolested."[12] At that time the hill, now called Fort Canning, was a Malay *tabu* called Bukit Larangan (Forbidden Hill) and it must, beyond doubt, have been the one where the *Sejarah Melayu* records Sri Tri Buana as having been buried. We agree with Dr Linehan that "the neglected tomb there is probably the memorial of this founder of ancient Singapore";[13] though, in point of fact, it is not neglected and, naturally, the indentification is incapable of proof.

Stamford Raffles and Major Farquhar landed on Singapore Island on the morning of 29 January 1819, four-and-a-quarter centuries after the ancient settlement had been abandoned. In March of that year, Farquhar ascended Bukit Larangan and shortly thereafter the hill was cleared and a road made up it.[14] On 21 January 1823, Raffles wrote to Marsden: "We have lately built a small bungalow on Singapore Hill, where, though the height is inconsiderable, we find a great difference of climate. Nothing can be more interesting and beautiful than the view from this spot. I am happy to say the change has had a very beneficial effect on my, health, which has been better during the last fortnight than I have known it for two years before. The tombs of the Malay Kings are, however, close at hand; and I have settled that if it is my fate to die here, I shall take my place amongst these: this will, at any rate, be better than leaving my bones at Bencoolen."[15] The house was enlarged later but from the time of its construction, Bukit Larangan was known as Government Hill until Fort Canning was completed in 1861.

Another eyewitness, John Crawfurd, later to become Resident of Singapore, described the ancient Malay settlement in two entries in his journal on 3 and 4 February 1822.[16] As his book is a rare one and as well-known things are apt to be overlooked, the whole passage is reprinted in the appendix at the end of this chapter. So far as I have been able to ascertain, this is the only description of the ancient Malay settlement, and it is that of a dilettante, leaving much unsaid that a modern archaeologist would have recorded. It shows very clearly that, at all events on the hill, there were remains, or shards, bits of metal in the shape of dateable Chinese coins, and graves. But nothing has been preserved. Only the one Malay grave already mentioned remains now, and I have been unable to find out what happened to the rest, if there were any. Mr Buckley in 1902 wrote in connection with Farquhar's ascent of the hill in 1819: "The tombs of the old Rajahs were there, and it was

---

[12] Lady Raffles, *Memoir of the Life and Public Services of Sir Thomas Stamford Raffles, F.R.S., by His Widow* (London: John Murray, 1830), p. 376.

[13] W. Linehan, "Kings of 14th Century Singapore", p. 118n8.

[14] C.B. Buckley, *An Anecdotal History of Old Times in Singapore* (Singapore: Fraser & Neave, 1902), vol. 1, p. 53.

[15] Raffles, *Memoir*, p. 535.

[16] J. Crawfurd, *Journal of an Embassy to the Courts of Siam and Cochin-China* (London: H. Colburn & R. Bentley, 1830), vol. 1, pp. 68–73.

considered sacred, as it is to the present day. Malays were frequently seen until late years crowding up the hill and decorating old graves there."[17] I first went over Canning Hill in 1905, and I can recollect only the one which is still there. The plain truth is that until very recent times nobody bothered about archaeology. When the site of the old Malay settlement was cleared, when roads were made and buildings constructed within its confines, all kinds of debris might have come to light and, if so, would certainly have been regarded as rubbish. People who could blow up an ancient inscribed rock and not bother to protect its remains, would hardly have been likely to pay any attention to such bits of old pottery or of metal as the *changkol* might expose. The plain truth is that in Malaya an argument based on the absence of archaeological data does not stand upon a strong foundation.

But enough has been said to prove the existence of ancient Singapura and its identity with Temasek. That it was not a very big place would go, one imagines, without saying. What place in Malaya could have been in those times? Such importance as it attained came not from size but situation on the sea-route between China and India. An examination of the early part of Mr Buckley's *Anecdotal History*, combined with Mr Crawfurd's description, will show that the settlement was reasonably strong for defence purposes. In effect, it comprised the hill and the plain in front of it running down to the seashore. It was protected by the big wall and moat, which ran from the sea round the hill to the marshes, flanking it on the north, and to the west was protected by the salt creek (now the Singapore River) and the marshes on its right bank, which the British filled in to construct Battery Road, Circular Road, Raffles Place, etc. Let it also be remembered in connection with the size of the Malay settlement that the ground which the British first took for their factory extended only from Tanjong Malang on the west (that is, Telok Ayer) to Tanjong Katong on the east "and on the land side, as far as the range of cannon shot, all round from the factory".[18]

In his privately printed *Notes on the Historical Geography of the Malay Peninsula*,[19] Dato F.W. Douglas has an interesting note on the ancient name "Malaiur", in which he draws attention to Ramusio's version of Marco Polo. He says:

> Winstedt in his *History of Malaya* 1935 writes, "attempts to connect Marco Polo's Malaiur with Singapore have not hitherto been accepted". He quotes the Ramusio version of Marco Polo but omits the important sentence, "Chiamassie la citta de Malaiure case l'isola de Malaiur". No one seems to have noticed that Chiamassie is certainly a transcription of the Malay Tumasik, the old name for Singapore Island in the *Malay Annals*. Marco Polo's description would therefore read, "Not far from Bintang Island there are two other islands—proceed between these two islands for 60 miles [96.6km]. The water is only about four paces deep and big ships when they pass through must haul up their rudders because they draw nearly four paces of water. After these 60 miles one sails to the southeast for some 30 miles [48.3km]. Then one reaches a kingdom Tumasik the city of Malayur and thus the island of Malayur. They have a King and language of their own. The city

[17] Buckley, *Anecdotal History of Old Times in Singapore*, vol. 1, p. 53.

[18] Ibid., p. 58.

[19] F.W. Douglas, *Notes on the historical geography of Malaya and sidelights on the Malay annals* (published privately, 1949), pp. 22–3.

1.1 A clear view of the harbour of Singapore with dock and of the straits before development. Attributed to Lambert & Co, c.1870–c.1910. Rijksmuseum, Amsterdam. RP-F-F01104-Y.

is very large and noble". Yule rightly says this is a description of the voyage from Bintang, then through the Johor Straits (Selat Tebrau), but he does not attempt to define the position of Chiamassie or translate the Ramusio version referring to it.

We can agree that Chiamassie may well be a transcription of "Tumasik", but unfortunately Chiamassie is omitted from Benedetto's edition of the Marco Polo manuscript and also from the fuller edition by Moule. Benedetto (translated by Ricci),[20] after the passage dealing with Pentan (Bintan), has this:

> Let us leave this place, and proceed between these two islands for some 60 miles [96.56km]. The water is only about four paces deep, and big ships, when they pass through, must haul up their rudders, because they draw nearly four paces of water. After these 60 miles, one sails on to the southeast for some 30 miles, then one reaches an island that forms a kingdom; both it and its capital are called Malaiur. They have a king and a language of their own. The city is very large and noble. There is a great deal of trade in spices and other wares. For there is great abundance in that island of such products. There is nothing else worth mentioning. And so we will leave this place and proceed. We will tell you of Java the lesser, as you shall hear.

Marco Polo then describes Java the Lesser, which undoubtedly was Sumatra. The reader should also see Moule's edition from which the following passage may be noted: "And when one has gone *sailing* these sixty miles *and goes* again about *another* thirty miles forward toward the sirocco then soon afterwards one finds an island which is a kingdom, and the *chief* city is called Malaiur and the island is *named* Pentan."

Almost all the authorities take Malaiur to be Malayu (Jambi) in Sumatra, but on the data how can that be? Marco Polo distinctly separates Java the Lesser (Sumatra) from Pentan (Bintan) and says that the city of Malaiur was on an island of the same name, but not on Java the Lesser. Clearly Singapore would be a much better identification but for two facts: (1) according to present dating Singapore was not founded in 1292 when Polo passed by, and (2) a "large and noble city" would not seem to fit it. But Polo indubitably passed Singapore, because either he went through the Straits of Singapore or he went through the Selat Tebrau. If his *Malaiur* were Singapore, then the dating in the *Sejarah Melayu* would receive corroboration; if it were not, then where was it?

One thinks that more consideration is necessary. The late Professor Blagden discussed the question in Penzer's edition of Frampton's *Marco Polo*.[21] He thought that the place must have been Malayu in Sumatra: but, if that was so, why was it not mentioned in connection with Java the Lesser, and why did the language used

---

[20] Marco Polo, Aldo Ricci, and L.F. Benedetto, *The Travels of Marco Polo, translated into English from the text of L.F. Benedetto by Aldo Ricci; with an introduction and index by Siv E. Denison Ross* (London: G. Routledge & Sons, 1931), p. 281.

[21] John Frampton, ed., *The Most Noble and Famous Travels of Marco Polo, Together with the travels of Nicolò De' Conti*. Edited from the Elizabethan Translation of Frampton John, with Introduction, Notes, and Appendixes, by N.M. Penzer (London: Argonaut Press, 1929), pp. lviii–lix.

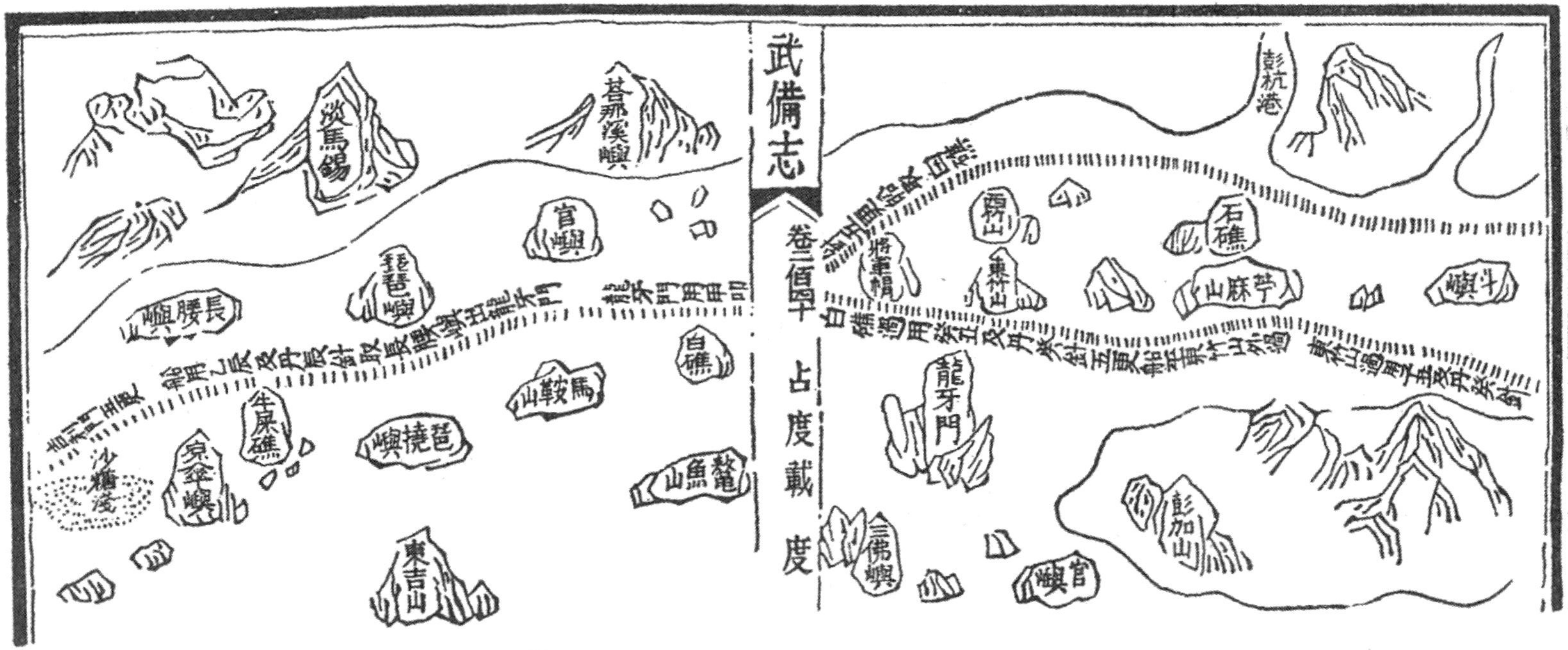

1.2 Mao Kun [茅坤] map from the *Wu Bei Zhi* [武备志], 1628. The map is thought to be based on the expeditions of Zheng He. The section depicted shows Singapore and part of the east coast of the Malay Peninsula. Temasek is located in the top left. Other places identified include Pulau Brani, Blakang Mati, Pedra Branca, Pulau Tinggi, Pulau Aur, Pahang River Estuary, and Pulau Tioman. Singapore: National Archives.

so clearly separate it from Java the Lesser? Marco Polo clearly did not actually visit Malaiur: and one can only say that, while it cannot be located with any certainty, the case for Singapore is less weak than that for Malayu (Jambi) in Sumatra.

The shallowness of the water could well be explained by the disappearance of stretches of sandbanks; and we know that along the southern coasts of Singapore there has been in the past 40 years a tremendous disappearance of sandbanks and coast. But the real difficulty is the date 1292, if Dr Linehan's dating is correct and 1299 was the year when Singhapura was founded.

Passing now to the two Chinese toponyms, we begin with their etymology. "Tan-ma-hsi" spells the pronunciation of the name's characters in the Pekingese dialect, as given in Giles' *Chinese-English Dictionary in the Pekingese Dialect.* Mr J.V. Mills, himself a sinologist, points out that the normal medium of transliteration in the *Wu pei chih* charts was the Amoy dialect and, using the spelling given in Douglas' *Chinese-English Dictionary of the Vernacular or Spoken Language of Amoy*, he gives "Tam-ma-sak" as the Amoy Hokkien pronunciation.[22] This latter is obviously the exact equivalent of the Malay "Temasek" (pronounced "Temasak") and the inference is irresistible that the indigenous name was carried back to China by Fukienese sailors. Mr Hsü, however, says that the name "should be pronounced as Tam-be-siak in Hokkien dialect and it could not be read as Tamasik".[23] Yet he agrees: "the Tan-ma-hsi of the Yuan Dynasty really derives itself from the term Temasek of the Javanese".[24] For ourselves, we prefer Mr J.V. Mills and think it safe to say that the Chinese name is a transcription of the Malay.

Lung-ya-men means "Dragon's Teeth Gate" or strait, and must clearly be a Chinese sailor's name. Mr Warren D. Barnes, who was Chinese Protector in Singapore at the time, wrote in 1911 that "the words Lêng-gê-mûy (Amoy dialect) translated by Groeneveldt the 'Straits of Lingga' mean dragon-teeth gate, strait or passage, and in the Amoy dialect 'dragon-teeth' is the name given to the two upright pegs in the bows of a ship through which the cable runs".[25] It would, therefore, be the kind of name that Amoy sailors would give to any strait which passed close between two hills, or to prominences that resembled cable pegs and so might well be applied to more than one strait.

Besides Groeneveldt, Rockhill and others write about the "Strait of Lingga" or the "Straits of Lingga" but, in point of fact, there is really no such thing, and it is not easy to know exactly what these writers mean, unless they mean a passage between Lingga and Singkep Islands. In any event, there is no such passage as could be called "Dragon's Teeth Gate". However, since the expression has been used so much, we retain it, though with this very necessary caution.

We pass now to the facts and, as Tam-ma-hsi is mentioned together with Lung-ya-men in most of the passages, we can consider them together.

---

[22] J.V. Mills, "Malaya in the Wu-pei-chih Charts", *JMBRAS* 15, 3 (1937): 47, 22; Mills, "Corrigenda", *JMBRAS* 16, 1 (1938): 154.

[23] Hsü, "Notes on Malay Peninsula", p. 12.

[24] Ibid., p. 16.

[25] Warren D. Barnes, "Singapore Old Straits and New Harbour", *JSBRAS* 60 (1911): 25.

In Chau Ju-Kua's *Chu fan chi* (1225), we get two references to a place called Ling-ya-men, or Leng-ya-men. The first passage says that a junk sailing to San-fo-ch'i (Palembang) from Ch'üan-chou in Fukien could reach Ling-ya-men in a little more than a month with the monsoon and that a third of the passing merchants put in there before proceeding to San-fo-ch'i.[26] The other refers to a foreign trade in mats at Ling-ya-men.[27] We agree with Hirth and Rockhill that Ling-ya-men must be referred to Lingga, since Singapura was not founded at that time. Mr Han and Mr Hsü, however, take this strait to be the same as the Lung-ya-men that appears a century later, and the question cannot be said to be settled beyond doubt. There is a long note by Rockhill on the subject in 1915 and the reader is referred to that.[28]

The master passage concerning Lung-ya-men occurs in the *Tao-i chih-lüeh*, dated 1349 and written by Wang Ta-yüan, "who visited for purposes of trade a considerable number of foreign localities during the Chih-cheng period of the Yuan (1341–67) and who recorded what he had seen in this work".[29] His evidence, therefore, is of primary importance. The notice on Lung-ya-men is translated in full by Rockhill.[30] It says that this strait of the Tan-ma-hsi barbarians (*fan*) is bordered by two hills that look like dragons' teeth, with a waterway between them. The people were addicted to piracy and neither fine products nor rare objects came from there, all they had of that sort being the product of their pillaging of the Ch'üan-chou traders; and later on, the natural products are given as coarse lakawood and tin, though doubtless these were not natural but imported. This passage shows that there was a trade but that in the middle of the 14th century Tan-ma-hsi could not have been a great entrepot. We are told of the defensive precautions against pillaging the Chinese junks had to take on their passage home, and that on their outward passage they were unmolested. There is a curious reference to the chief having found a jewelled cap while digging in the ground, and we are told that on the new year's day the chief, attired in his finest robes, wore this cap while receiving the congratulations of his people. Since Tan-ma-hsi must certainly have been Singapore, this last passage should be remembered in connection with the story in the *Sejarah Melayu* concerning the loss of the crown. Each shows that there was some local legend of importance in connection with the crown of Singapore, though the two do not agree as to the legend.

In another passage in the same work we get a notice on Hsien (Siam), in which it is said, "in recent years they came with seventy junks and raided Tan-ma-hsi and attacked the city moat".[31] Tan-ma-hsi closed its gates and resisted for a month when, an imperial envoy passing through, the Siamese withdrew. Mr Crawfurd tells of the

---

[26] Friedrich Hirth and W.W. Rockhill, trans. and annot., *Chau Ju-Kua: His Work on the Chinese and Arab Trade in the Twelfth and Thirteenth Centuries, entitled* Chu-fan-chï (St Petersburg: Printing Office of the Imperial Academy of Sciences, 1911), p. 60.

[27] Ibid., p. 220.

[28] W.W. Rockhill, "Notes on the Relations and Trade of China with the Eastern Archipelago and the Coast of the Indian Ocean during the Fourteenth Century", *T'oung Pao* 16, 1 (1915): 129–31.

[29] Ibid., p. 12.

[30] Ibid., pp. 129–32.

[31] Ibid., p. 100.

city moat of Singapura but not of any gates. The latter might possibly have been in an inner-palisaded stronghold; but that is speculation.

The *Tao-i chih-lüeh*[32] also tells us that Pan-tsu was the hill back of Lung-ya-men and that it was like a coil cut off, rising to a hollow-topped summit enclosed in a series of slopes, as a consequence of which the people lived all round it. This place had a ruler and produced cranes' nests of superior quality, middling quality lakawood, and cotton. Rockhill, doubtingly, suggests that the name represented Panchor, which he says in a Malay name occurring in several places, as indeed most Malay place names do. Since Lung-ya-men can only have been Singapore Main Strait or Keppel Harbour, as will be seen later, Pan-tsu, on the evidence above, must have been in the state of Johor and possibly Gunung Pulai.

Lastly, the *Tao-i chih-lüeh*, in its notice on San-fo-ch'i, says that one arrives in this country after a voyage of five days and nights from Lung-ya-men. Rockhill (who identifies Lung-ya-men with Singapore Strait) says in a footnote that this passage is a quotation from the *Chu fan chi*.[33] If that is the fact, then Wang Ta-yüan must have considered that his Lung-ya-men and Chau Ju-Kua's Ling-ya-men were one and the same, which would justify Mr Han and Mr Hsü in saying the same thing.

The *Wu pei chih* charts are considered to have embodied the navigational knowledge acquired from the various voyages of Cheng Ho, but Mr J.V. Mills thinks that the charts themselves cannot safely be dated prior to 1433.[34] Sailing directions are given from the Kerimun Islands through Lung-ya-men to Pedra Branca, and Tan-ma-hsi is marked in the map on the mainland of the peninsula. We are inclined to agree with Mr Hsü that this latter fact "shows that sailors in those days looked upon Selat Tebrau as an inland sea".[35] At all events, sailing past Singapore, there is no particular reason to realize that it is an island, the western and eastern entrances of the Selat Tebrau (Johor Strait) looking like river mouths; and there is no reason to think that the Chinese in Cheng Ho's time made Johor a place of call or entered the Selat Tebrau at all. Melaka at that time was the trading place *par excellence*, and the Malay rajas had not moved into Johor. In our view Mr Han's attempts to prove that the Chinese were trading to Pulau Tekong at this time are unsuccessful.

The *Hsing ch'a sheng lan*—dated 1436 and written by Fei Hsin, who was in Cheng Ho's suite during several voyages—has a notice on Lung-ya-men; but much of Fei Hsin's work was not original and this notice looks as though it had been copied from Wang Ta-yüan. It says that Lung-ya-men was to the northwest of San-fo-ch'i, an extraordinary statement, and repeats the facts in the *Tao-i chih-lüeh* as to the ships passing through a waterway between two hills that looked like "dragons" teeth. This same work, in its notice on Tung-hsi-chu, or Pulau Aur, says: "These islands in the sea face Lung-ya-men."[36] That again is strange, unless what is meant is that the group is passed on the way to Lung-ya-men. Pulau Aur, of course, has always been a much-used sailors' mark.

---

32 Ibid., p. 133.

33 Ibid., p. 134.

34 Mills, "Malaya in the Wu-pei-chih Charts", p. 50.

35 Hsü, "Notes on Malay Peninsula", p. 12.

36 Rockhill, "Notes", *T'oung Pao* 16, 1 (1915): 124.

Rockhill refers to sailing directions from Palembang (*Ch'iu-chiang*) to Melaka in the *Hsi-yang chao-kung tien*.[37] I have no note of the date of this work, but Rockhill points out that in the directions Melaka is called Wu-hsü (the Five Islets) and that name was only used by the Chinese prior to 1409, which may throw some light on the date of the directions. This passage in the Chinese work ends: "It is also said that one (can) arrive (at Melaka from Ch'iu-chiang) by the Strait of the Island of Lung-ya, the shape of which passage is like the horns of a dragon." In this passage, as Rockhill says, "the strait of the island Lung-ya can only be the Strait of Lingga". If that is so, then the passage confuses the "Strait of Lingga" with Lung-ya-men, since the former does not have the shape of the horns of a dragon.

1.3 Twin peaks of Lingga in the Riau Archipelago at dawn. © Huang Jianli, private collection.

The pilots' directory in the *Tung-hsi yang-k'ao* by Chang Hsi (1618), has a passage dealing with Lung-ya-men, which has been translated by Mr Hsü.[38] It begins by quoting from the *Hsing ch'a sheng lan* as to Lung-ya-men and then says: "At present the ships still dare not sail in the night on account of the pirates as well as the Liang-shan Rocks in its south. Measuring the water, it is 30 *t'o* (fathoms) in the middle, 20 *t'o* in its south. Passing the Gate of Tan-ma-hsi, a ship sails to 262.5° and 292.5° by three watches towards Chi-li-men Hill." This last is Kerimun, and the course therefore is east to west, that in the *Wu pei chih* charts being west to east. Mr Hsü takes Tan-ma-hsi-men and Lung-ya-men to be the same place in this passage,[39] and we agree.

---

[37] Ibid., pp. 130–1.

[38] Hsü, "Notes on Malay Peninsula", p. 10.

[39] Ibid., p. 12.

This concludes our review of the evidence, and we turn to the problem of identification. As we have said, we would separate Ling-ya-men from Lung-ya-men, and take the former to be the "Strait of Lingga" and the other a passage in Singapore waters, the choice lying between the Singapore Main Strait, which the Portuguese called Governor's Strait, and Keppel Harbour. The possibility of confusion between the two Chinese names seems obvious and may possibly explain the passages in the *Tao-i chih-lüeh* and the *Hsi-yang chao-kung tien*, where Lung-ya-men would seem to indicate the "Strait of Lingga" and so would be Ling-ya-men in reality.

The name "Dragon's Teeth Gate" seems to afford the best clue and was the one that led Mr Barnes to identify it with Keppel Harbour. The western entrance to that harbour presents a very different appearance from what it used to do in olden times. Linschoten (1598), in his full and very clear description of it, says: "The entrance of the straits is about a stone's throw across between two high mountains and runs a cannon-shot length to the East. The least depth in the straits is four and a half fathoms. At the entrance at the foot of the Northern mountain is a rock which looks like a pillar. It is commonly known as 'Varella del China'."[40] This last is the Batu Berlayar, which we call Lot's Wife, a very considerable part of which was blasted away in 1848 to widen the entrance.[41] The tops of the hills at the entrance were also higher before the British came to Singapore, and buildings were erected on them. Another passage, quoted by Mr Barnes and dating 1599, speaks of "so narrow a channel that from the ship you could jump ashore or touch the branches of the trees on either side".[42] This writer's vessel stuck on a shoal. Linschoten says, immediately after the description of the entrance that we have quoted above: "A little further on in the straits and on the south side is a bay in the middle of which is another rock below water and a shoal which reaches from this rock to the middle of the channel."[43] This quite likely is the Liang-shan Rocks mentioned in the *Tung-hsi yang-k'ao*, since each was on the south side of the channel.

I have come across what must, I think, be a description in 1804 of the western entrance to Keppel Habour and which accords well with those given in the 16th century. It occurs in *The Oriental Voyager* (1807), by J. Johnson, who was a surgeon in the Royal Navy. The passage is dated 16 September 1804 and reads: "The straits of Singapore are formed by a duster of innumerable little islands, lying off the most southern part of the Malay peninsula. They are covered with woods, have a great variety in their shapes, and are indented on all sides with pleasant little bays and sandy coves, where the finest turtle is found in great plenty. The passage between these islands is in some places so narrow, that we might have almost thrown a biscuit on shore; yet the water was deep, clear and smooth as glass."[44] It seems to me that this last sentence shows that Johnson's ship, HMS *Caroline*, passed through the

---

[40] Barnes, "Singapore Old Straits and New Harbour", p. 27.

[41] Buckley, *Anecdotal History of Old Times in Singapore*, vol. 2, p. 489.

[42] Barnes, "Singapore Old Straits and New Harbour", p. 29.

[43] Ibid., pp. 27–8.

[44] James Johnson, *The Oriental Voyager: Or, Descriptive Sketches and Cursory Remarks, on a Voyage to India and China, in His Majesty's Ship Caroline, Performed in the Years 1803-4-5-6* (London: James Asperne, 1807), p. 143.

present Keppel Harbour, though that, of course, is not completely certain. Another pointer to this strait is that he goes on to say: "The natives came off in their canoes laden with turtle, some of which weighed three or four hundred pounds, and these they sold for a dollar or a dollar and a half each." For very many years there was a well-known settlement of orang laut on Blakang Mati Island, which forms the south side of the entrance to Keppel Harbour, and Barros gives Cellates from *selat* (strait) as the name of the orang laut. But I do not know how old was the Blakang Mati settlement. Finlayson in his *Mission to Siam and Cochin China*, writing in 1821, says: "In the numerous bays, inlets and creeks that surround Singapore an inconceivable number of families of orang laut lived in boats. So it may well be that the Blakang Mati settlement produced Johnson's turtles."

It does not seem to us that Chinese sailors would have likened the entrances of the "Strait of Lingga" or the Singapore Main Strait to the cable pegs on their junks. On the other hand, it would have been most apt for the western entrance of Keppel Harbour. Mr Crawfurd sailed into that latter strait and recorded the fact in his journal on 27 January 1822.[45] He says that the Malay name for the strait was "Selat Panikam", as he writes it, a name which seems now to be lost entirely. Penikam means "a pointed weapon" and thus is as descriptive a name for Keppel Harbour as "Dragon's Teeth Gate" would be.

But Mr J.V. Mills, with assistance from Mr C.C. Best, who had done much sailing in Singapore waters, has studied the actual sailing directions in the *Wu pei chih* charts and is convinced that the Lung-ya-men mentioned there must have been the Singapore Main Strait.[46] Mr Hsü writes: "Even in Cheng Ho's Chart it also mentions 'One sails from Dragon's Tooth Gate to 82.5° by five watches to reach Pedra Branca'. Therefore it must be placed in the Strait of Singapore, and the most suitable place is Keppel Harbour which is called *Estreito Velho* (the Old Strait) in Manuel Godinho de Erédia's Map in the 17th century."[47] It will be noted that Mr Mills gives the course as *chia mao*, 75°, 90°, while Mr Hsü gives it as as 82.5°, presumably taking the midway between the two courses. The reader should see what Mr J.V. Mills says about Chinese compass directions.[48] Mr Mills and Mr Hsü are not in accord as to which passage was used.

Assuming that the *Wu pei chih* course did run through the Singapore Main Strait, there is the possible explanation that the Chinese changed their way of sailing and abandoned the Keppel Harbour passage for the one through the Main Strait but retained the old name. The Portuguese also changed their passage and mention the one through the Main Strait as Governor's Strait in 1615.[49] Eredia's map (1604), referred to by Mr Hsü, has been reproduced by Mr J.V. Mills in his paper.[50] The

---

[45] Crawfurd, *Journal of an Embassy*, pp. 66–7.

[46] Mills, "Malaya in the Wu-pei-chih Charts", pp. 23–4, 27–8.

[47] Hsü, "Notes on Malay Peninsula", p. 12.

[48] Mills, "Malaya", pp. 8–9.

[49] Ibid., p. 41; Barnes, "Singapore Old Straits and New Harbour", p. 30.

[50] J.V. Mills, "Eredia's Description of Malacca, Meridional India and Cathay", *JMBRAS* 8, 1 (1930): 1–288. Folio 45R, pl. 3.

plate faces page 225 and shows quite clearly that at that time the Keppel Harbour passage was known as "Estreito Velho" and the Main Strait as "Estreito Novo".

There is, however, one objection to thinking that the Chinese at the material times used the Main Strait; and it is stated by Mr C.C. Best as follows: "The tidal swirls, almost amounting to whirlpools, are worrying to a fully powered steamer and the depths sufficiently great, taking into accounts the strength of the tides, to make anchoring almost an impossibility for a small vessel. It is used today by all types of craft, but the men in charge of them are either skilled navigators or else have had long experience of Singapore waters. To newcomers, in clumsy ships equipped with primitive winches, cables and anchors it might well seem a place to be avoided, if an alternative and better known route was available".[51] The Portuguese had been in Malayan waters nearly a hundred years before they used the Main Strait in preference to the Keppel Harbour passage and, except for the working out by Mr J.V. Mills of the sailing directions in the *Wu pei chih* charts, the difficulties of the Main Strait would lead one to think that Chinese junks might not have used it in the 14th century, or even in the time of Cheng Ho.

Summarizing, it is submitted:

(1) Tan-ma-hsi is a transcription of Temasek and, beyond doubt, is Singapore;
(2) Ling-ya-men is the Strait of Lingga and probably is a transcription of that name;
(3) Lung-ya-men is a sailor's name taken from the cable pegs of a junk and used for a passage round Singapore Island;
(4) Lung-ya-men could not have been the Strait of Lingga, but must have been either the Keppel Harbour passage or the Singapore Main Strait;
(5) Lung-ya-men may have been confused with Ling-ya-men in some passages in the Chinese records;
(6) Lung-ya-men is a very apt name for the Keppel Harbour passage but not for the Singapore Main Strait;
(7) it is possible that Lung-ya-men was first used for the Keppel Harbour passage and then transferred to the Singapore Main Strait;
(8) but the balance of evidence, coupled with the difficulties of the passage through the Singapore Main Strait, may perhaps incline one to the opinion that Lung-ya-men was the Keppel Harbour passage.

The characters for the main places mentioned are as follows:

Tan-ma-hsi
Ling-ya-men
Lung-ya-men

Appendix

February 3. I walked this morning round the walls and limits of the ancient town of Singapore, for such in reality had been the site of our modern settlement. It was bounded to the east by the sea, to the north by a wall, and to the west by a salt creek

[51] Mills, "Malaya in the Wu-pei-chih Charts", p. 41.

or inlet of the sea. The inclosed space is a plain, ending in a hill of considerable extent, and 150 feet [45.7m] in height. The whole is a kind of triangle, of which the base is the seaside, about a mile in length. The wall, which is about 16 feet [4.9m] in breadth at its base, and at present about eight or nine in height, runs very near a mile from the seacoast to the base of the hill, until it meets a salt marsh. As long as it continues in the plain, it is skirted by a little rivulet running at the foot of it, and forming a kind of moat; and where it attains the elevated side of the hill, there are apparent the remains of a dry ditch. On the western side, which extends from the termination of the wall to the sea, the distance, like that of the northern side, is very near a mile. This last has the natural and strong defence of a salt marsh, overflown at high-water, land of a deep and broad creek. In the wall there are no traces of embrasures or loopholes; and neither on the seaside, nor on that skirted by the creek and marsh, is there any appearance whatever of artificial defences. We may conclude from these circumstances, that the works of Singapore were not intended against firearms, or an attack by sea; or that if the latter, the inhabitants considered themselves strong in their naval force, and therefore thought any other defences in that quarter superfluous.

February 4. On the stony point which forms the western side of the entrance of the creek, on which the modern town of Singapore is building, there was discovered, two years ago, a tolerably hard block of sandstone, with an inscription upon it. This I examined early this morning. The stone, in shape, is a rude mass, and formed of the one-half of a great nodule broken into two nearly equal parts by artificial means; for the two portions now face each other, separated at the base by a distance of not more than two feet and a half, and reclining opposite to each other at an angle of about 40 degrees. It is upon the inner surface of the stone that the inscription is engraved. The workmanship is far ruder than any thing of the kind that I have seen in Java or India; and the writing, perhaps from time, in some degree, but more from the natural decomposition of the rock, so much obliterated as to be quite illegible as a composition. Here and there, however, a few letters seem distinct enough. The character is rather round than square. It is probably the Pali, or religious character used by the followers of Buddha, and of which abundant examples are to be found in Java and Sumatra; while no monuments exist in these countries in their respective vernacular alphabets. The only remains of antiquity at Singapore, besides this stone, and the wall and moat before mentioned, are contained on the hill before alluded to. After being cleared by us of the extensive forest which covered it, it is now clothed with a fine grassy sward, and forms the principal beauty of the new settlement. The greater part of the west and northern side of the mountain is covered with the remains of the foundations of buildings, some composed of baked brick of good quality. Among these ruins, the most distinguished are those seated on a square terrace, of about 40 feet [12.2m] to a side, near the summit of the hill. On the edge of this terrace, we find 14 large blocks of sandstone; which, from the hole in each, had probably been the pedestals of as many wooden posts which supported the building. This shows us, at once, that the upper part of the structure was of perishable materials; an observation which, no doubt, applies to the rest of the buildings as well as to this. Within the square terrace is a circular inclosure, formed of rough sandstones, in the centre of which is a well, or hollow, which very possibly contained an image; for I look upon the building to have been a place of worship, and, from its appearance, in all likelihood, a temple of Buddha. I venture farther to conjecture, that the other relics of antiquity on the hill, are the remains of monasteries of the priests of this religion. Another terrace, on the north declivity of the hill, nearly of the same size, is said to have been the burying place of Iskandar Shah, King of Singapore. This is the prince whom tradition describes as having been driven from his throne by the Javanese, in the year 1252 of the Christian era, and who died at Malacca, not converted to the Mohammedan religion, in 1274; so that the story is probably apocryphal. Over the supposed tomb of Iskandar, a rude structure has been raised, since the formation of the new settlement, to which Mohammedans, Hindus, and Chinese, equally resort to do homage. It is remarkable, that many of the fruit trees cultivated by the ancient inhabitants of Singapore are still existing, on the eastern side of the hill, after a supposed lapse of near 600 years. Here we find the durian, the rambutan, the duku, the shaddock, and other fruit trees of great size; and all so degenerated, except the two first, that the fruit is scarcely to be recognized.

Among the ruins are found various descriptions of pottery, some of which is Chinese, and some native. Fragments of this are in great abundance. In the same situation have been found Chinese brass coins of the 10th and 11th centuries. The earliest is of the emperor Ching-chung, of the dynasty of Sung-chao, who died in the year 967.[52] Another is of the reign of Jin-chung, of the same dynasty, who died in 1067; and a third, of that of Shin-chung, his successor, who died in 1085. The discovery of these coins affords some confirmation of the relations which fix the establishment of the Malays at Singapore, in the 12th century. It should be remarked, in reference to this subject, that the coins of China were in circulation among all the nations of the Indian islands before they adopted the Mohammedan religion, or had any intercourse with Europeans. They are dug up in numbers in Java, and are still the only money used by the unconverted natives of Bali.

[52] [E.N.: The year should be 1022.]

2

Hsü Yün-ts'iao

Singapore in the Remote Past*

In 1969, Singapore celebrated the sesquicentennial of her founding by Sir Thomas Stamford Raffles in 1819, so most of the people in the world thought that Singapore has only a short history of 150 years. Local scholars all know that the name Singapore is derived from Sanskrit word "Singapura" or "Simhapura", literary meaning the "Lion City", which first appeared together with its previous name Temasek in *Sejarah Melayu*, the most famous example of Malay literature, written in 1535 and revised in 1612,[1] and that the term *Temasek* first appeared as *Tumasik* in *Nagarakretagama*, written in 1365, as well as in *Pararaton*, another Javanese record of the 15th century. Apart from these sources, no earlier account of Singapore can be found in Southeast Asia. Yet we have got a number of Chinese sources that provide evidence of the existence of old Singapore going back from the 13th century as far as the 3rd century.

The term *Temasek* or *Tumasik* has its corresponding name in old Chinese accounts. Writing in 1330, Wang Ta-yüan (汪大淵) made mention of the war between Tumasik and Siam in his book *Tao-i chih-lüeh* (島夷志略) under the heading of "Siam", as below:

> In recent years they (the Siamese) came with about seventy junks, and raided Tan-Ma-Hsi (單馬錫) and attacked the city moat. The town resisted for a month, this place (Tan-Ma-Hsi) having closed its gates and defending itself, and dared not stage any fight. It happened just then that a Java envoy was passing by (Tan-Ma-Hsi) for China, the men of Siam drew off and took shelter, after having looted Hsi-Li (昔里, probably a corruption of the Malay word "selat", strait).

---

* First published in *JMBRAS* 45, 1 (1972): 1–9.

[1] See Hsü Yün-ts'iao, "The Historical Evaluation of *Sejarah Melayu*", an appendix to his *Chinese Translation of the Sejarah Melayu* [馬來紀年] (Singapore: Singapore Youth Bookstore [新加坡青年書局], 1966).

If we notice the words "came" and "this place", we may understand that Wang Ta-yüan must have stayed here when he recorded the events. He recorded Tumasik as "Tan-ma-hsi" in Mandarin, if in the Hokkien dialect it should be pronounced as "Tan-ma-siak". This term also appeared in Cheng Ho's chart (鄭和航海圖 *Cheng-ho hang-hai t'u*) given in Mao Yüan-yi's (茅元儀) *Wu pei chih* (武備志), volume 240, as in the same pronunciation but in different characters as 淡馬錫 (*Tan-ma-hsi*) which in Hokkien pronunciation is *Tam-ma-siak* and more nearly corresponds to Tumasik.

In his *Malay-English Dictionary*, R.J. Wilkinson suggests that the term *Temasek* probably derives its etymology from *tasek* (sea or lake) by inserting the infix *-em-* in it, but this explanation is doubtful. The present writer suggests that it is a Greek loan word as a corruption of *Damascus*, in the same way that the place-name *Patani* is derived from the term *Bathany* in the Bible.

The war between Siam and Singapore, then known as Tumasik, has also been recorded in *Yüan shih* (元史, History of the Mongol dynasty), but Singapore was then called Ma-li-yü-r (麻里予兒) by the imperial court of China, which could correspond to Marco Polo's "Malaiur". Under the heading "Siam", it runs:

> In the first year of the reign of Yuan Tchen (元貞, 1295 A.D.) … on account of the wars between Siam and Ma-Li-Yü-R in the past, the Emperor gave an order that no Siamese could kill the people of Ma-Li-Yü-R as they had all submitted to China already.

Again, in *Tao-i chih-lüeh*, we find another interesting account under the caption "Lung-ya-men" (龍牙門), literally "Dragon's Teeth Gate", which also refers to Singapore. It reads:

> The gate (*men*) derives its name from two hills of the Tan-ma-hsi aborigines, facing each other as the teeth of a dragon. There is a channel passing through the gate. The soil is unfertile and yields only a little rice. The climate is warm, and in the fourth and fifth months there are heavy rains. The people are accustomed to pillage. At one time in the past, the chief dug the earth and found a crown made of jade. In the beginning of the year, people looked for the new moon to determine the new year's day, when the chief would wear the crown and put on dress to receive greetings. This custom is still transmitted down to the present generation. Both men and women, even those Chinese dwelling there, have their hair tied in a knot and wear a short jacket with a sarong of blue stuff. The country produces rough lakawood and tin blocks. The merchandise for trading consists of pure gold, blue satin, pattern cloth, porcelains from Ch'u-chou (*ch'u-tz'u-chou* 處磁器), iron pots, etc. As there is neither good timber in the mountain nor fine goods for tribute, they could only trade with Ch'üan-chou (泉州) with booty and plunder. When the vessels sail to the west sea, natives are quite at ease, but on their return voyage the crew have to put up arrow shelters and curtains, and sharpen their weapons to guard against pirates, especially when they arrive at Chi-li-men (吉利門, the Kerimon Islands). Two or three hundred boats of the pirates would come on silently and fight for several days. It would be fortunate if the travellers could meet a fair wind; otherwise the crew would be butchered and the merchandise would be looted.

2.1 The Old Straits Singapore, Teluk Blangan. Watercolour from the Charles Dyce Collection. Singapore: National University of Singapore (NUS) Museums. S1970-0052-059.

From the passage quoted above, we learnt that Tumasik was then a pirate-infested area, yet there were Chinese immigrants domiciled at the place and dressed as the natives. It was even so when Stamford Raffles started his colonization.

With regard to Dragon's Teeth Gate (Lung-ya-men), there is a note on it given in *Tung-hsi yang-kao* (東西洋考) by Chang Hsieh (張燮) written in 1617, which reads:

> At present the ships still dare not sail at night on account of the pirates as well as the Liang Shan Rocks (涼山礁, or Pulau Labon) in its south. Measuring the water, it is thirty *t'o* (托, fathoms) in the middle, twenty *t'o* in the north, and eight or nine *t'o* in the south. Passing the Gate of Tan-ma-hsi, ships sail by the directions of *keng-wu* (庚午, i.e. 262.5 degrees, due west by south) and *hsin-wu*, (辛午, 292.5 degrees, west southwest) for three watches (更, or thirty miles) towards Chi-li-men Hill.

This "Lung-ya-men" has been identified with Keppel Harbour and accepted by all authorities. It was also called the "Gate of Tumasik" by Chang Hsieh. Sir Roland Braddell made a valuable study, and told us:

> At the western entrance to Keppel Harbour, there used long ago to be two pointed rocks, one on the end of the island of Blakang Mati, and one where the present white stone marking the harbour limit stands, called Lot's Wife; but these rocks from their nearness to each other proved an obstruction to navigation, so they were blown up about 85 years ago, after Captain (the late Admiral of the Fleet, Sir) Harry Keppel had rediscovered the strait, which is now called Keppel Harbour after him, though it was at first and for a long time termed New Harbour. These two rocks reminded the Chinese of the two upright pegs in the bows of their junks through which the cable runs, and as these pegs are called the "Dragon's Teeth", they gave the name "Dragon's Teeth Gate" to the entrance to the strait. Old descriptions all refer to the narrowness of the entrance, one written in 1599, saying: "from the ship you could jump ashore or touch the branches of the trees on either side".

The term Lung-ya-men is in Mandarin and it should be pronounced as "Leng-ge-mun" in Hokkien dialect. Chau Ju-kua (趙汝适) recorded it as Ling-ya-men (凌牙門) in his *Chu fan chi* (諸蕃志), published in 1225. His reference runs as follows:

> San-fo-ch'i (三佛齊, also Srivijaya, now Palembang) lies between Chen-la (真臘, i.e. Cambodia) and She-p'o (闍婆, i.e. Java) dominating fifteen countries. It is also lies in the south of Ch'üan-Chou. People sail in the winter with the monsoon for a little more than one month to reach the Ling-ya-men, where they sell one third of their goods before entering this country (of San-fo-ch'i).

In a contemporary work *Tao-yi tsa-chih* (島夷雜志) by Chen Yüan-ching (陳元靚), under the caption "San-fo-ch'i", it states:

> Sailing from Canton (Guangzhou) due south by riding on the north wind in the winter for half a month, one reaches Ling-ya-men and in another five days enters San-fo-ch'i.

In the Yuan or Mongol dynasty, the term Lung-ya-men was seen as the name of a country; as in *Yüan Shih*, volume 27, under the caption of *Ying-tsung pen-chi* (英宗本紀), it states:

> In the ninth month of seventh year of the reign of Yen-you (延祐 1320), (the emperor) sent Ma-chah-man (馬札蠻) and others as envoys to Chan-ch'eng (占城, i.e. Champa); Chen-la (占臘, i.e. Cambodia) and Lung-ya-men, asking for tamed elephants.

From the passages quoted above, we learnt that Singapore was then called Lung-ya-men and had already established contact with the Chinese Empire during the Yuan dynasty (1280–1367) and had trade with Ch'üan-chou and Canton in the Sung dynasty (960–1279).

The historical position of Singapore was rather vague in T'ang-dynasty (618–959) Chinese chronicles. But we know that the sea communications in the T'ang dynasty had already been fully developed. In the *Geographical Records of the Hsin T'ang shu* (新唐書地理志), we find an appendix of Chia Tan's *Routes from China to Foreign Countries* (賈耽: 四夷路程), which runs as follows:

> Arriving at Chün-t'u-lung Hill (軍突弄山, that is, Pulo Condore), one sails for another five days to reach a strait called chih (質) by the natives. It is one hundred *li* (里) in breadth, with the state of Lo-yüeh (羅越) on the north shore and Fo-shih (佛逝, Srivijaya) on the south.

As one would take five days to sail from Pulo Condor to the Strait, it is most likely to be the Strait of Singapore. As for the word *chih* called by the natives, it is generally accepted by scholars to be the simplifiation and corruption of the Malay word *selat* (strait), derived from the Arabic *selahit*. Regarding the Lo-yüeh state to the north, it was suggested orally to me by the late Mr Han Wai Toon (韓槐準) ten years ago that the word *chih* corresponded to the Malay term *laut* (sea): This is quite a probable suggestion, because the T'ang tone pronounced 羅 (*lo*) as *la* and 越 (*yüeh*) as *jiwat* (now it is still pronounced as *uat* in Hokkien dialect). The suggestion is also supported by the fact that the proto-Malays now staying there are still known as orang laut (sea gypsy). This laut state might consist of Singapore Island and the southernmost part of the Malay Peninsula.

Prior to the T'ang dynasty, as the strait was infested with pirates, Chinese and Indian merchants used to transport their goods across the Isthmus of Kra, they were therefore quite ignorant of the conditions in the southern part of Malay Peninsula. However, it does not mean that Singapore was unknown.

In *Liang shu* (梁書) compiled in 629 CE by Yao Sze-lian (姚思廉, Ssu-lien), under the heading "Fu-nan" (扶南傳), it runs as follows:

> More than 3,000 *li* to the south of Fu-nan (today's Banam), there is the state of Tun-sun (頓遜), which situated on a isthmus (海崎 *hai-chi*) with a territory extending 1,000 *li*. The city lies 10 *li* away from the sea. There are five kings all of whom acknowledge the suzerainty of the state of Fu-nan. The eastern frontier of Tun-sun extends as far as to Chiao-chou (交州, Vietnam) and on the west it connects with India as far as with An Sih (安息, An-hsi, Parthia or Persia). All the foreign states come to trade here, the reason of this being that Tun-sun extends more than 1,000 *li* into the "Swell Sea", which is so vast that no ship has ever been able to cross it directly. To its market, people come from east and west, and thousands visit it daily. All kinds of valuable goods are found here. There is the wine tree resembling Parthian pomogranates, whose flowers' juice may be collected and kept in a jar, and will turn into wine in a few days.

The above passage is of great importance in the field of Malayan historical geography. Tun-sun was identified with Tenasserim, Lower Burma by G. Schlegel in *T'oung Pao* (1899), but I wish to point out that the term is also applied to the whole Malay Peninsula, as the above passage states that Tun-sun is on the Isthmus and extending more than 1,000 *li* into the "Swell Sea" (漲海, *chang hai*), which has been identified with Cankhay in early Arabic literature, that is, the present-day South China Sea, by the present writer.[2] Though the Chinese words "海崎" (*hai-chi*) originally meant "cliffy coast", in *Liang shu* it is either "isthmus" or "peninsula", and this interpretation also occurred in even earlier records, as we will discuss later.

The eminent position of Singapore as a focus of communications, although rediscovered by Sir Thomas Stamford Raffles only a little more than 150 years ago, yet was well known as far back as 1,700 years ago, as we have seen in Chinese texts. An illustrious chapter has been written in the history of the intercourse between China and Southeast Asian countries by the famous expeditions of "The Eunuch San-Pao to the Western Seas" (三保太監下西洋), which are well known to everyone in Southeast Asia. Nevertheless, there was another great event as eminent as the seven voyages undertaken by Admiral Cheng Ho (鄭和) in the early part of 15th century to South Seas, which took place more than a thousand years before the latter, but which has long been forgotten. It happened in about 231 CE, when General Lü Tai (呂岱) of the Wu kingdom (吳國) was the governor-general of Canton and Vietnam. In that year he sent Blazon Officer Chu Ying (宣化從事朱應) and Adjutant K'ang T'ai (中郎康泰) on a mission to the South Seas as Blazon Envoys. They set out from Chiao-chou (交州, Vietnam) and visited about a hundred countries in the South Seas. On their return about 15 years later, each wrote a book that contained the earliest and most valuable records about the Southeast Asian countries. Chu Ying's work was entitled *Fu-nan i-wu chih* (扶南異物志, Descriptions of the prodigies in Banam), also known as *Fu-nan i nan-chi* (扶南以南記, A record on the countries south of Banam), but it has long since been lost. K'ang T'ai's book was entitled *Wu-shih wai-kuo chuan* (吳時外國傳, The accounts of foreign countries during Wu period) also known as *Fu-nan t'u-su* (扶南土俗, The native customs of Banam), which also has been long lost, only some parts in fragmentary form are available from the old works of the T'ang and Sung.

More than 20 years ago, the present writer devoted himself to re-edit the K'ang T'ai's book with all the fragmentary passages collected from all those old works, such as *Shui ching chu* (水經注) by Li Tao-yüan (酈道元) of the Northern Wei dynasty (北魏 386–534); *Pei-t'ang shu-ch'ao* (北堂書鈔) by Yü Shih-nan (虞世南) of the Sui dynasty (隋朝 581–618); *Yi-wen lei-chü* (藝文類聚) by Ou-yang Hsün (歐陽詢) and others; *Ch'u-hsüeh chi* (初學記) by Hsü Cian (Ch'ien, 徐堅) and others; *Shih-chi cheng-i* (史記正義) by Chang Shou-cheh (Shou-chieh, 張守節); *Shih-chi suo-yin* (史記索隱) by Shih-ma Tchen (Ssu-Ma Ch'ien, 司馬貞), *T'ung tien* (通典) by Tu You (杜佑); and *Wen-hsüen chu* (文選注) by Li Shan (李善)—all published during the T'ang dynasty—and *Liu thieh* (Liu t'ieh, 六帖) by Pai Chü-i (白居易) and K'ung Ch'uan (孔傳); *T'ai-p'ing yü-lan* (太平御覽) and *T'ai-p'ing kuang-chi*

[2] Hsü Yün-ts'iao, "Notes on Malay Peninsula in Ancient Voyages", *JSS Society* 5, 2 (1948): 26–37.

(太平廣記) by Li Fang (李昉) and others; *Shih lei-fu* (事類賦) by Wu Shu (吳淑); *T'ung-chih* (通志) by Cheng Ch'iao (鄭樵); and *Wen-hsien t'ung-k'ao* (文獻通考) by Ma Tuan-lin (馬端臨)—all published in Sung dynasty.[3]

Among the numerous fragmentary passages, the present writer discovered two or three that might refer to ancient Singapore, so he studied them carefully for a long time and referred to the vast ocean of all the sources that he could obtain and read. At last he reached the conclusion that they are, briefly put, the earliest records of the remote days of Singapore. Only two passages have survived. Passage A is cited in *T'ung tien*, volume 187, by Tu You (735–812) as well as in *T'ai-p'ing yü-lan*, volume 791, by Li Fang (925–96). The latter reads:

> In the east of Kou-li (拘利), there are the people of P'u-lo chung (蒲羅中), each with a tail five or six inches long. They are accustomed to cannibalism. This place, together with the other P'u-lo (蒲羅) in the southwest, are the place-names called by the tailed tribes (Wei-p'u 尾濮).

Passage B has appeared only in *T'ai-p'ing yü-lan*, volume 787. It reads:

> Going from Kou-li due east *to approach the extremity of the peninsula* (Chih-chi-t'ou 極崎頭), there are inhabitants living by the sea, each with a tail five or six inches long. It is called P'u-lo chung state (蒲羅中國). They are accustomed to cannibalism.

First of all, the present writer has to explain the terms given in the above texts in order to clarify their identity.

Kou-li.—The present writer is of the opinion that Kou-li should be corresponding to Coli on the east coast of Aurea Chersonesus as mentioned in Ptolemy's *Geography* in the 2nd century. Aurea Chersonesus is none other than the Malay Peninsula. Kole or Coli has been identified with Chukai and Trengganu by Sir Roland Braddell.[4] Kou-li has appeared in various corruptions, such as Chiu-chih (九稚) in *Liang Shu*, volume 54, compiled by Yao Sze Lian (Ssu-lien 姚思廉) in 629; Chiu-li (九離) in *T'ung tien*, volume 188, compiled in 801; and Chü-chih (句稚) in Wan Tchen's *Nan-chou i-wu chih* (萬震：南州異物志) quoted in *T'ai-p'ing yü-lan*, volume 790, compiled in 983. In the present writer's opinion, "Chiu-li" is a different transliteration of "Coli", because the ancient pronunciation of "九" (*chiu*) is "kau", which is very near to "kou"; while the characters "稚" (*chih*) and "句" (*chü*) are the misprints of "離" (*li*) and "拘" (*kou*) respectively. Kou-li had a port called *Kou-li k'ou* (拘利口) recorded by K'ang T'ai; its citation in *Shui ching chu* reads:

> Starting from Kou-li k'ou (or the port of Kou-li) into the big bay, due northwest for one year or more to reach the entrance of an Indian river called Ganges.

There is a similar statement given in the *Account of Central India* (中天竺傳) in *Liang shu*, volume 54, which runs:

---

[3] The recompilation of K'ang T'ai's *Wu-shih wai-kuo chuan* [康泰吴时外国传辑注, 新加坡: 东南亚研究所, 1971] with annotations by this author, was published in Singapore in 1971.

[4] Sir Roland Braddell, "An Introduction to the Study of Ancient Times in the Malay Peninsula and the Straits of Malacca", *JMBRAS* 14, 3 (1936): 10–71.

> Starting from Funan *to go to* the port of Kou-li, thence the envoy sails in the big bay northwestward, passing by several states along the bay, for more than one year to reach the estuary of the Indian river, then sails up the river for 7,000 *li* to arrive at the country.

The phrase "to go to" in the above passage is the correct interpretation of the Chinese character "投" (*t'ou*) in the original text. However, the great authority Professor Sylvain Lévi unfortunately misinterpreted the word as a part of the term. "T'ou-kou-li" (投拘利), which he identified with Takola on the west coast of Aurea Chersonesus in Ptolemy's *Geography*, and Takkola in Maha Niddesa in the old Sanskrit literature.[5] Although the term "T'ou-kou-li" has never existed and is a fabrication, many scholars, among whom are Professor Paul Pelliot of France and Professor Fujita Tomohachi of Japan, allowed the mistake to pass. Due to an excessive respect for seniors among scholars, or because of complacency, some obvious mistakes and wrong records have gone uncorrected, sometimes for decades.

Kou-li or Coli has been identified with Chukai, Trengganu, yet that port is not on the east coast of the Malay Peninsula. The present writer has identified it with Muar, on the west coast of Johor for the following reasons:

(1) Since the northeast monsoon is so strong in the winter, all ports along the east coast used to be closed and no ship could sail out. So the sea communication is diverted to inland navigation. The people sailed up the Pahang River and turned south into the Sungai Serting over the Panarican (or Penarekan) portage to enter the Muar River, or vice versa.[6]

(2) As shown in Ptolemy's map, there is a river called Khrysoanas on the west coast of Aurea Chersonesus and the Attabas on the east coast, and they are connected in the middle by another river. Sir Roland Braddell had also identified them with the Muar and the Pahang respectively.[7]

(3) With reference to Bodhibhadra's (菩提拔陀) itinerary recorded by Yang Hsüan-chih (楊衒之) of the Later Wei dynasty (後魏 386–584) in his *Lo-yang chia-lan chi* (洛陽伽藍記), it reads:

> He started from Ko-ying state (歌營國) due north for one month to reach Chü-chih (句稚) and for another twelve days northward to reach Sun-tien (孫典 a reversed corrup-tion of Tun-sun 頓遜, in other words, Tenasserim); thence northward for thirty days to arrive in Funan (Cambodia).

Kuo Ying is also recorded by K'ang T'ai as Chia-ying (加營), because the ancient pronunciations of "歌" (*ko*) and "加" (*chia*) are the same as *ka*, and the present writer has identified it with Kalinga, a Hindunised state in Sumatra.[8] Chü-chih as we already know is the corruption of Kou-li. If the

---

[5] Sylvain Lévi, "Ptolémée, le Niddesa et la Brihatkathā", *Etudes Asiatiques* 2 (1925): 1–55.

[6] See Paul Wheatley, "Panarikan", *JSS* 10, 1 (1954): 1–16.

[7] Sir Roland Braddell, "An Introduction to the Study of Ancient Times in the Malay Peninsula and the Straits of Malacca", *JMBRAS* 14, 3 (1936): 10–71.

[8] Hsü Yün-ts'iao, *Nan-yang shih* [南洋史 or "History of the South Seas"] (新加坡：世界书局，1961), pp. 98–100.

2.2 Two Chinese junks, in the vicinity of the island Lamao (Lamma?) en route to Canton, August 1607. In the top right a cartouche with the view of the sea. Part of the illustrations in the report of the trip by Cornelis Matelieff de Jonge for the VOC to the East Indies and China, 1605–08, no. 10. Anonymous, 1644–46. Rijksmuseum, Amsterdam. RP-P-OB-75.455.

Chü Chih was situated between Sumatra and Tenasserim, it should mean that the port of Kou-li was located at Muar.

(4) K'ang T'ai mentioned that one started from Kou-li k'ou and sailed northwestward in the big bay to reach the estuary of the Ganges, so the place should be situated on the west coast, as Muar is, and it could keep touch with its capital on the east coast by inland navigation.

As to Takola, the present writer has identified it with Ko-ku-lo (哥谷) of the *Hsin Tang shu* (新唐書), volume 222B. The name is derived from the Sanskrit name Takkola, a place somewhere on the west coast of the Malay Peninsula, as recorded in the *Maha Nidesa* and the *Milindapañha* (2nd or 3rd century CE). In Sanskrit, "takkola" means nutmeg, which is also called *kakkula*. Nutmeg was also known to the Arabs and the Chinese. White nutmeg is called *chia-kou-le* (迦拘勒) in the *Pen-ts'ao shih-yi* (本草拾遺, The supplement to the book of herbals, ca. 725 CE). But in the *Yu-yang tsa-tsu* (酉陽雜俎) (ca. 863 CE), the nutmeg of Chia-ku-lo (迦古) is said to have been called *to-ku* (多骨). In Arabic geographical records, the terms Qaquallah, Jajullah, Gagulla or Kakula designate both the nutmeg and a place name on the west coast of Malaya. In Sanskrit initial *t* consonant occasionally become *k*, and thus Ptolemy's Takola would correspond to the *Hsin T'ang shu*'s Ko-ku-lo.[9]

P'u-lo chung.—The earliest name of Singapore in remote days, and should correspond to Pulau Ujong in Malay, the island on the extremity of the peninsula. It reminds us of Johor's old name, Ujong Tanah, the extremity of land. Therefore, *P'u-lo* is the transliteration of the Malay word *pulau* and *chung* corresponds to *ujong*.

The transliteration of the Malay term *ujong* in Chinese old books appears as 戎 *rong* or *jong* in Mandarin. For instance, Wang Ta-yüan referred to old Johor as "戎國 Jong state" in his *Tao-i chih-lüeh*.

As for the remarks that the natives each possessed a tail five or six inches long, and that they were accustomed to cannibalism, no further thought should be given to them, as they have no bearing on the actual facts. However, there are still natives with tails as Bontoks dwelling in Samti Village, Mount Province, Philippines, and in Sumatra some cannibals have found their existence in the wilds unaffected by modern civilization. Moreover, there is a fossil of burnt human bones left by the Malayan cannibals of the Mesolithic Age displayed in the Singapore National Museum.

These traces of the historical material of Singapore, rare as they are, can be dated back to more than 1,700 years ago. Its historical position, therefore, should not be as insignificant as some people used to consider. The discovery of Pulau Ujong, the oldest name for Singapore, has given the present writer a little consolation for his 40 years of historical research on Southeast Asia.

[9] Hsü Yün-ts'iao, "Notes on Studies of Ancient Malaya", *Eastern Horizon* 2, 6 (1962): 18–22.

3

Brian E. Colless

The Ancient History of Singapore*

It seems fitting that, on the occasion of the commemoration of the founding of modern Singapore 150 years ago, we should look further back than the year 1819 and see whether another examination of ancient documents can bring to light new data on the early history of Singapore. Accordingly it is here submitted that a previously unrecognised reference to Singapore, under another name of course, is to be found in a well-known Indian document written nearly 950 years ago. Such a discovery gives immediate rise to further speculation regarding the possibility that this island was also known to Chinese and Arab geographers and merchants as an important trading centre and possibly known as such as early as the 2nd century of the Christian era.

It is interesting to note that at the time of Singapore's centenary celebrations in 1919 Gerritsz Pieter Rouffaer commenced work on a gigantic study, in which he sought, among many other things, to push the known history of Singapore well back into the first millennium of our era, by establishing the equation "Mahasin = Hasin = Toemasik = Singhapoera".[1] Rouffaer has thereby bequeathed us a collection of important texts and materials together with some interesting suggestions about the early history of Singapore and Johor; but unfortunately he made a number of errors in the identification of certain toponyms, such as Langkasuka, which he would not have made if only he had been able to consult Paul Wheatley's magnificient handbook of Malayan historical geography, *The Golden Khersonese*, not published until exactly 40 years later, in 1961, but now freely available to us to assist in correcting older

* First published in *JSEAS* 10 (1969): 1–11.

[1] G.P. Rouffaer, "Was Malaka emporium voor 1400 A.D. genaamd Malajoer? En waar lag Woerawari, Mā-hasin, Langka, Batoesawar?", *BKI* 77 (1921): 1–174, 359–569. [E.N.: Selections from this article have been translated and included in this collection.]

discredited opinions.[2] At the same time there are some important points concerning Singapore that have been missed by Rouffaer and Wheatley also, which will be presented here for consideration. We shall consider these under three main headings, according to the historical period to which they belong, namely Majapahit (14th century), Srivijaya (before 1300), and Funan (before 550).

(1) The Majapahit Period

As is well known, Singapore was formerly called Tumasik or Temasek, a name included in the list of Majapahit dependencies in the 14th century. From the same period we have a Chinese description of the island and its trade, in the *Tao-i chih-lüeh*, compiled in 1349 by Wang Ta-yüan, who had personally visited the trading kingdoms of the South Seas. The texts relative to Malaya and Singapore have already been presented and analysed by Wheatley. On the one hand we are told of "Dragon-Teeth Strait" (Lung-ya-men), identified as the Keppel Harbour passage between the south coast of Singapore Island and Pulau Blakang Mati. Here lived and roved the notorious "Tan-ma-hsi (Temasek) barbarians" the orang laut of the region.[3] The most striking feature of this description is the statement that "the natives and the Chinese dwell side by side", which seems to be *the first record of a Chinese community in Malaya.*

On the other hand we have an important description of Pan-tsu, which was wrongly taken by Rouffaer to be Bintan.[4] This was an unfortunate choice, since his case for the antiquity of Singapore was thereby weakened considerably. As it is a vital link in the chain of reasoning to be constructed here, Wang Ta-yüan's account of Pan-tsu is reproduced here in Wheatley's translation:

> This locality is the hill behind Lung-ya-men. It resembles a truncated coil. It rises to a hollow summit (surrounded by) interconnected terraces, so that the people's dwellings encircle it. The soil is poor and grain scarce. The climate is irregular, for there is heavy rain in summer, when it is rather cool. By custom and disposition (the people) are honest. They wear their hair short, with turbans of gold-brocaded satin, and red oiled-cloths (covering) their bodies. They boil sea-water to obtain salt and ferment rice to make spirits called *ming-chia*. They are under a chieftain. Indigenous products include very fine hornbill casques, lakawood of moderate quality, and cotton. The goods used in trading are green cottons, lengths of iron, cotton prints of local manufacture, *ch'ih chin* (half-tael coins), porcelain ware, iron pots, and such like.[5]

As Wheatley observes, the hill behind Lung-ya-men or Keppel Harbour can only be the eminence that dominates Singapore City, namely Fort Canning Hill. The building operations of recent times have changed the face of this landmark, but we are fortunate in having John Crawfurd's description of the ruins of ancient Singapore,

---

[2] P. Wheatley, *The Golden Khersonese: Studies in the Historical Geography of the Malay Peninsula before A.D. 1500* (Kuala Lumpur: University of Malaya Press, 1961).

[3] Ibid., pp. 81–6, 303–5.

[4] Rouffaer, "Was Malakka emporium", p. 156n44.

[5] Wheatley, *The Golden Khersonese*, p. 83.

now readily accessible in Wheatley's indispensable manual. Crawfurd speaks of the remains of an extensive wall and a moat and then goes on to describe the features of the hill:

> After being cleared by us of the extensive forest which covered it, it is now clothed with a fine grassy sward, and forms the principal beauty of the new settlement. The greater part of the west and northern side of the mountain is covered with the remains of foundations of buildings, some composed of baked brick of good quality. Among these ruins, the most distinguished are those seated on a square terrace of about forty feet to a side, near the summit of the hill.... Another terrace, on the north declivity of the hill, nearly of the same size, is said to have been the burying-place of Iskander Shah, King of Singapore.[6]

Crawfurd made this examination of the site early in 1822. He also mentions a stone monument inscribed with Majapahit characters but in an unidentified language.[7] Chinese coins, the oldest from about the middle of the 10th century, are also mentioned by Crawfurd, but unfortunately these are unreliable for dating purposes.

Nevertheless, it will now be submitted that this hill was in fact occupied at that time and that Singapore was part of the Srivijayan commercial empire. To this end the evidence of the Tanjore inscription will be invoked, together with Arab and Chinese documents.

(2) The Srivijayan Period

(a) The Tanjore Inscription

This Tamil *prasasti*, which is inscribed on the south wall of the Rajarajesvara temple in Tanjore and which records the Cola raids on the empire of Srivijaya early in the 11th century (ca. 1025), has often been studied. Wheatley has an analysis of this document in which nine of the places are positively identified, leaving four still in doubt.[8] The established identifications are: Srivijaya = Palembang; Pannai = Pane, on the east coast of Sumatra opposite Klang; Malaiyur = Jambi; Ilangasoka = Langkasuka, shown by Wheatley to have been in the Patani region on the east coast of the Malay Peninsula; Talaittakolam = Ptolemy's Takola and, we may add, the Chinese Ko-ku-lo and the Arab Qaqullah, located at present-day Takuapa, more particularly on Kakhao Island; Madamalingam = Tambralinga, almost certainly located at Ligor; Ilamuri-desam = Marco Polo's Lambri in the north of Sumatra; Nakkavaram = the Nicobar Islands; Kadaram = Kedah.

The unidentified places are Mappappalam, Mayirudingam, Mevilimbangan, and Valaippanduru. The first of these, (Map)pappala(m), corresponds in my view to the P'an-p'an of the Chinese histories and to the *Fawfal* of Ibn Sa'id, located at Kra, for Ibn Sa'id places it north of Qaqullah (Takuapa) and the River Taragha (Trang).

---

[6] Ibid., pp. 120–2.

[7] Rouffaer, "Was Malakka emporium", pp. 35–67, 370–2, 404–6.

[8] Wheatley, *The Golden Khersonese*, pp. 199–203.

The full argument is presented elsewhere.[9] It would also appear that Mayirudingam represents Trang or else some kingdom along the transpeninsular route of the Trang River, for it certainly corresponds to Chau Ju-kua's Jih-lo-t'ing, located in the general area of Grahi and Ligor. This Chinese form led Rouffaer,[10] as also Gerolamo Emilio Gerini before him, to identify this place with Jelutong, the region around the River Jelutong, east of Singapore in Johor. This is highly unlikely and it is not even mentioned by Wheatley, but it was the best Rouffaer could do to get Singapore into the Tanjore inscription.

It is important to remember that according to the legends of the *Sejarah Melayu* Raja Shulan of Negapatam was said to have attacked Gangga Nagara, situated "at Dinding on the other side of the Perak River" (possibly corresponding to Ptolemy's Konkonagara); then he moved on to Ganggayu, a fort up the Johor River, thought to be on the Lenggiu, a tributary of that river; finally he occupied Temasek. It has often been asserted that this is a memory of Rajendra's Cola raids; if so we might expect to find mention of these places in the Tanjore inscription. The unidentified "Mevilimbangam" might be Gangga Nagara in Perak. I notice that there is a Belimbing on the Pergau, a tributary of the Kelantan River in Kelantan not far from the border of Perak; there is also a Bilimbim inland from Melaka on Eredia's map of the Melaka district (1613). Rouffaer suggested Mevilimbangam as Dinding (or perhaps Bruas or Klang, he added), but Valaippanduru he identified with Pandurang or Phanrang in Champa. Ironically, Rouffaer thereby sent into exile the very reference to Singapore that he was seeking. It has always been a puzzle why Panduru was prefixed with Valai, and it has been suggested that it represented the Cham *palei*, meaning "village" (perhaps influenced by Tamil *valai*, meaning "fortress") to go with the identification Phanrang.

If we accept the hypothesis that the Tamil form Panduru (giving it a more exact transliteration for purposes of comparison) corresponds to Wang Ta-yüan's Pan-tsu, with its rampart and ditch running down to the sea, the description "fortress", instead of an honorific Maha- or Sri, becomes intelligible. The Tamil and Chinese forms are perhaps representations of Malay "Panchur" (Pantjoer). In this regard we may note anyway that Rouffaer gives notes on a place of that name in D.F.A. Hervey's description of his trip up the Johor River in 1879. On one occasion Hervey wrote concerning Panchur (sited on Rouffaer's map just past Johor Lama): "Panchur itself is said to owe its name to an ivory conduit made by a former Raja to bring water to a pond in which he and his household might disport themselves." On another occasion he wrote: "At Panchur, where I also touched on my way down the river, the high bank … is *the site of an old fort*, traces of where the guns were placed

[9] For a discussion of this and many other new interpretations taken for granted throughout this study, see B.E. Colless, "Persian Merchants and Missionaries in Medieval Malaya", *JMBRAS* 42, 2 (1969): 10–47; "The Early Western Ports of the Malay Peninsula", *Journal of Tropical Geography* 29 (1969): 1–9. It should be noted that D.G.E. Hall, *History of South-East Asia* (London: Macmillan, 1961) includes, apparently erroneously, "Tumasik the old name for Singapore Island" in his list of places in the Tanjore inscription that can be identified (p. 59).

[10] Rouffaer, "Was Malakka emporium", pp. 76ff.

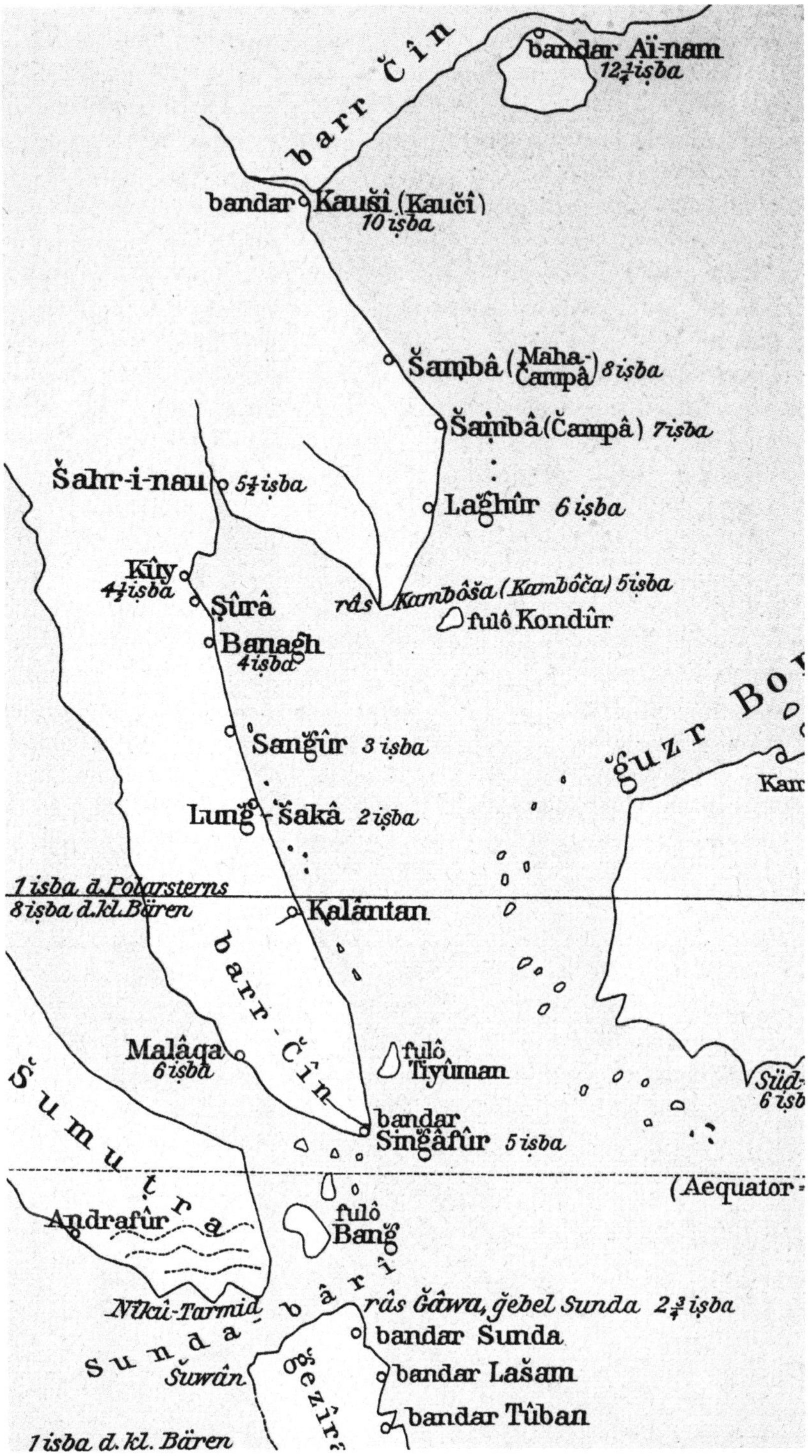

3.1 Section of a reconstructed map of the Singapore and Melaka Straits region based on the text by Sīdī ʻAli Čelebī, 1558. M. Bittner and W. Tomaschek, ed., int. and tr., *Die Topographischen Capitel des Indischen Seespiegels Moḥiṭ*, Vienna, 1897.

are still visible, but part of the site is now used as a burial ground."[11] This is rather striking: perhaps this Panchur was Panduru and perhaps also Pan-tsu. But there is another Panchur mentioned by Rouffaer,[12] namely Pantjoer Larangan, likewise a bathing place for the sultan's wives: this Panchur was on the Singapore hill once known as Bukit Larangan, as well as Bukit Bandera, Government Hill, Fort Canning Hill, and Singapore Hill.[13]

One difficulty with the equation Panduru = Panchur = Pan-tsu is the Chinese transcription, for whereas an initial or medial *r* is regularly represented by *l*, a final *r* is usually signified by *-n*. Possibly we might compare, however, the name *Sawar*, to be mentioned below, which is also written "Sawa" (but the *Ming History* has "Pan-tsu-eul").

The arguments presented are not conclusive, but we shall continue with the working hypothesis that Singapore was a centre of trade in the 11th century and turn to the Arab accounts of the Malay Peninsula and archipelago to see whether Singapore is hiding there under one of the many unidentified place names.

(b) The Arab Geographers

Wheatley gives information from Arabic sources on six places thought to be on or near the peninsula. These are (1) Kalah, for which Wheatley suggests Mergui, but which is seen quite clearly to be Klang in the Melaka Strait when compared with the Chinese evidence relating to Ko-lo, also called Ku-lei, etc.; (2) Qaqullah, for which Wheatley can offer no definite suggestion, but which is to be equated with Takkola and identified with Takuapa and Kakhao Island off the mouth of the Takuapa River, as stated above; (3) Panhang (wrongly written Fanjab and the like by Arab scribes), which is obviously Pahang; (4) Tiyumah, which is clearly Pulau Tioman near Pahang; (5) Sanfin, which is unidentified, but which may be the place known to the Chinese as Chan-pin, located between Coromandel and Ku-lo (Klang) and therefore not Singapore; the only possibility left is Mayt, also called Mayd or Mand by some writers.[14]

Mayt was close to Jaba—that is, Sumatra—and one day's sailing to the south of Tioman Island, according to Ibn Khurdadhbih, writing in about 850 CE. This certainly fits Singapore's position. For Buzurg (date unknown) Mayt lay between Champa and Srivijaya, and it produced gold, cotton and honey. The later books of Idrisi (12th century) and Ibn Sa'id (13th century) are very instructive. Each writer has two separate accounts in his works, doubtless because each has borrowed from various sources without realising that Mayt, Mayd, and Mand were only variants of the same place name.

Idrisi identified Mayt as a dependency of the king of Jaba (Srivijaya), situated one day from Pulau Tioman, and producing coconuts, bananas, sugar cane and rice.

---

[11] Ibid., pp. 424–5.
[12] Ibid., pp. 378–81.
[13] Ibid., p. 373.
[14] Wheatley, *The Golden Khersonese*, pp. 216–32.

Ibn Sa'id said that Mayd is north of the island Muja, from which it is separated by a channel some half a degree in width. The inhabitants take honey and wax to China. Here, the Indian Ocean ends, and the Encircling Ocean begins. Travellers sometimes reach thus far, but then turn away in order to reach al-Jawa (Sumatra). (This may be interpreted as saying that the Arabs' normal sailing route lay along the Malayan side of the Melaka Strait as far as Singapore, then crossed over to the Sumatran shore on their way to Srivijaya.) At the place where the two seas meet is the River Khumdan, which usually means Chang'an in China but in this context might mean Kuantan. Elsewhere he speaks of the Island of Mand and also Bintan,[15] which is obviously the large island of that name at the eastern end of the Straits of Singapore, one of the complex of three large islands—namely Singapore, Batam (south of Singapore), and Bintan (east of Batam). Now, combining Ibn Sa'id's two accounts we have Bintan and Muja, with Mayt north of Muja. It is thus highly likely that Mayt is Singapore, that Muja is Batam, and that Bintan is of course Bintan. In Idrisi's other account there is a similar group of three islands, namely Muja, Suma and Mayd, of which Suma is the largest and is situated two days from Muja (Batam) and four days from Mayd (Singapore).[16] Suma must therefore be an alternative name for Bintan.

Idrisi's statement concerning Mayd is important, in that it seems to explain how the Chinese community of Singapore came to be settled there:

> It contains a great number of towns, is vaster and more fertile than Muja (Batam), and its inhabitants are more like the Chinese than are the other peoples of the countries neighbouring on China. ... It is there that Chinese ships coming from the islands of China meet and stop; this is the island they head for and this is the point from which they set out to go elsewhere.

Perhaps we have here an indication that by the 11th century the situation described by Wang Ta-yüan in the 14th century, in which "the natives and the Chinese dwell side by side", was already established. It should be noted also that the first Arab reference to Mayt comes from the middle of the 9th century.

Wheatley points out that Mayt should be compared with a place mentioned by Fei Hsin (15th century), namely Ma-i-tung, which also produced cotton and sugarcane. This point will have to be followed up, but on the matter of cotton, because attempts to introduce it to the peninsula and the Riau-Lingga have failed in modern times, and it is today only cultivated in Java and South Sumatra, Wheatley is dubious about this detail. Yet it is surprising to note that the only reference to cotton in Ferrand's index to his historical geography[17] is to the Buzurg description of Mayt. It is also striking to note that the indigenous products of Pan-tsu were supposed to include cotton (a commodity also mentioned in connection with Hsia-lai-wu, which, situated "below Ku-lei" or Klang, is necessarily either Selangor or Sungei Ujong). All these coincidences seem to compel us to the conclusion that Mayt is Singapore.

---

[15] Gabriel Ferrand, *Relations de voyages et textes géographiques Arabes, Persans et Turcs relatifs à l'Extrême-Orient au VIIIe au XVIIIe siècles*, 2 vols. (Paris: Leroux, 1913–14), pp. 343–4.

[16] Ibid., pp. 189–91.

[17] Ibid.

There remains the account of Ibn Yunus, quoting Khwarizmi on Maydh, also called Kul, watered by a river and containing three villages. Some texts refer to Krk or Knk instead of Kul. These may be attempts to reproduce Kalang, the name of a river and a town in Singapore according to Rouffaer's map, while *Kul* may indicate Cape Gul in the southwest corner of the island. Then again, there may be a connection with the Galuh discussed by Rouffaer.[18] But what of the name Mayt? This paragraph is already thick with stabs in the dark, but the suggestion is offered that it represents all the Arabs and Persians could remember of the name Pulau Blakang Mati, but I have no idea how long that name has been attached to this island.

(c) The Chinese Records

Before attempting to identify Singapore in the earlier Chinese historical and geographical literature, we should first establish what the Chinese knew about the southern point of the Peninsula during the Srivijayan era. One source of information is Chia Tan's sailing itinerary of about 800 CE, preserved in the T'ang history. Here is the relevant portion of the route, from Pulo Condor off the coast of Vietnam:

> After five days' journey one reaches a strait, which the foreigners call *chih* (*selat?*) and which is 100 *li* from south to north. On its northern shore is the kingdom of Lo-yüeh; on its southern shore is the kingdom of Fo-shih (Srivijaya). Some four or five days' journey over the sea eastward from Fo-shih is the kingdom of Ho-ling (Java), the largest island in the south. Then emerging from the strait, in three days one reaches the kingdom of Ko-ko-seng-chih (somewhere on the east coast of Sumatra. Siak?).[19]

The strait mentioned is the Singapore Strait, so we would expect Lo-yüeh, on its northern shore, to be located in Johor, probably on the Johor River. Wheatley states that beads indicating early settlements have been found at Kota Tinggi and Johor Lama,[20] but he does not mention Moens' very credible identification of Lo-yüeh with Seluyut, the name given to a stream and to Bukit Seluyut on the Johor River between Kota Tinggi and Johor Lama. The T'ang history also records that Lo-yüeh was 5,000 *li* (emend to 50 *li*) inland, and that traders passing back and forth were accustomed to meeting there. This statement resembles the Arab statement that Mayt was the meeting place for Chinese ships.

But can we find a reference to Singapore itself from this period? Rouffaer suggested it was Mo-ho-hsin island, found in I-tsing's list of "islands"[21] or major kingdoms (*chou*) in the South Seas in the late 7th century:[22]

---

[18] Rouffaer, "Was Malakka emporium", pp. 96–7, 114–6.

[19] Wheatley, *The Golden Khersonese*, pp. 56–7. See also O.W. Wolters, *Early Indonesian Commerce: A Study of the Origins of Srivijaya* (Ithaca, NY: Cornell University Press, 1967), pp. 187–8.

[20] Ibid., pp. 59, 157.

[21] Rouffaer, "Was Malakka emporium", pp. 67–75.

[22] Wheatley, *The Golden Khersonese*, p. 54; Wolters, *Early Indonesian Commerce*, pp. 199ff.

> An enumeration from the west. There is P'o-lu-shih (Barus), Mo-lo-yu (Malayu, Jambi), which is now Shih-li-fo-shih (Srivijaya), Mo-ho-hsin, Ho-ling (Java), Tan-tan, P'en-p'en, P'oli, Chüeh-lun, Fo-shih-pu-lo (Vijayapura in western Borneo, aka Kalimantan), O-shan, and Mo-chia-man. There are also some small chou, which cannot all be recorded.

In Wolters' opinion all these places are situated in the Indonesian archipelago, and in this interpretation Mo-ho-hsin cannot be Singapore. But if I-tsing names "Barus" (which has been shown by Wolters to be distinct from the Barus on the west coast of Sumatra) on the northeast coast of Sumatra, why should he not also include some of the kingdoms in the lower regions of the Malay Peninsula? Thus, Tan-tan has to be squeezed into a somewhat overcrowded Java in Wolters' scheme, but it has been taken by Wheatley and others to have been situated on one of the kualas on the lower east coast of the Peninsula. My suggestion is to see in Tan-tan a transliteration of Kuantan. Wolters himself notes a case where the name Tan-tan designated a place on the Malay Peninsula: "in the 1785 addition to the *Wen-hsien t'ung-k'ao* the section on Johor states that Trengganu, Tan-tan and Pahang, all on the southern Malay Peninsula, were dependencies of Johor".[23] To my mind this is a clear reference to Kuantan, and even though the transliteration is faulty, it is quite intelligible.

Tan-tan is preceded by Mo-ho-hsin and Ho-ling and followed by P'en-p'en. This last name could conceivably be the same as P'an-p'an (Pappala, i.e. Kra), but this is really too far north for this list, and if we accepted it we would have to find a reason for the omission of Langkasuka and other east Malayan kingdoms. Rather, the suggestion of Pembuan on Borneo's southern coast for both P'en-p'en and Pu-p'en (mentioned elsewhere by I-tsing as being north of Ho-ling) is much more acceptable. Finally P'oli is also placed by Wolters on Java; but it is a perfect transliteration of Bali, and Wolters' reason for neglecting this is not clear, but he has no reference to Bali in his index. In any case the remaining toponyms in the list refer to Borneo and the rest of the archipelago, probably including the Philippines. Thus my interpretation sees I-tsing moving across the map from west to east naming the various South Sea countries of importance, not confining himself to the southernmost parts of the Java Sea, as in Wolters' interpretation, but moving from south to north and back again as he moves from west to east, thereby including the Malay Peninsula's southern portion.

On this interpretation of I-tsing's list, there is no serious impediment in the way of the suggestion that Mo-ho-hsin was Singapore, or else a kingdom on the Johor River. This neatly fills the apparent gap in I-tsing's writings, where apparently nothing corresponding to Lo-yüeh in the extreme south of the Peninsula is found.

But what is the meaning of the name Mo-ho-hsin? Rouffaer connected it with Hasin, found in the famous Airlangga inscription of the early 11th century, which he interprets as meaning "Salt-city" or "Sea-city".[24] One cannot help asking, however, whether it might not represent Mahacina, "Greater China". The Arabs and Persians considered that India stretched from the borders of Persia to Kalah (Klang) and,

---

[23] Ibid., p. 203.

[24] Rouffaer, "Was Malakka emporium", pp. 67–75.

loosely speaking, after Kalah came China. Thus Yaqut places Klang "at the beginning of India, on the edge of China". The name Masin seems to be the Arabic and Syriac form of Mahacina, but as far as I can see at the moment its appearance in these languages is rather late and when it is used it is not certain that it includes any country below Indochina. The 16th-century navigator al-Mahri has in his manual a "section on the sea routes of China" (*al-sin wa-ma'l-sin*), which commences at Singapura.[25] (At that time the lower Malay Peninsula was included in the term "the Siamese mainland".)

It would be foolhardy to go further and suggest that Singapore was called "Greater China" because a Chinese colony was established there as early as the 7th century. Nevertheless we shall see whether the equation Mo-ho-hsin = Mahacina can stand up to the critical scrutiny of other scholars. In any case we need to keep in mind the important point concerning Singapore in the Srivijayan period: it was an important meeting place for the Chinese (as also Seluyut on the Johor River), and Arab observers thought that the people of this island (Mayt) resembled the Chinese more than any other peoples along the route to China.

(3) The Funan Period

In his chapter on rumour and report about the Malay Peninsula in the 3rd century of the Christian calendar, Wheatley looks at the names of kingdoms that probably belonged on the Peninsula. From the *T'ai-p'ing yü-lan* we can extract the following names of kingdoms situated across the bay from Funan in Indochina to as much as 3,000 *li* southwards: Tien-sun (on the northern part of the isthmus), Pi-sung, Tu-k'un, Pan-tou (or Pien-tou), Chü-li, with Ko-ying situated one month's journey south of this last named place.[26]

The full argument for the synthesis of this material will be presented elsewhere in the context of a wider study on the significance of the Malay Peninsula in the Funan and Srivijaya periods. It is here submitted, however, that the picture of the Golden Khersonese presented in Ptolemy's *Geographia* is quite coherent and compatible with the early Chinese evidence from the 3rd century CE. This statement contradicts recent assertions that deny a 2nd-century date to Ptolemy's Southeast Asian data. The fact is that Ptolemy's place names find more coincidences with the Chinese forms from the 3rd century than from any other period. Here is a brief outline of the synthesis of the Chinese and Ptolemaic accounts:

(1) Besunga, in lower Burma, corresponds to Pi-sung.
(2) Beroba, a port on the isthmus, corresponds in position, though not in name, to Tien-sun.
(3) Takola is Chinese Tu-k'un (presumably a transcription of the term *takur* mentioned by Wheatley), later called Kakula by the Arabs and the Chinese, and is situated at modern Takuapa.[27]

---

[25] Wheatley, *The Golden Khersonese*, pp. 234, 237.
[26] Ibid., pp. 14–25.
[27] Ibid., p. 271.

3.2 Reconstructed map of Ptolemy's *Tabula Asiae XI* (Bengal and Southeast Asia). Giacomo Gastaldi, *Geografia di Claudio Ptolemeo Alexandrino*, Venice, Pedrazaro, 1548. © Peter Borschberg, private collection.

(4) Kalonka, placed on the same latitude as the Khrysoanas River along which gold was doubtless transported from the inland to the coast on the Melaka Strait, is to be compared with Ko-ying, which was known as a source of gold and, in my view, is to be identified with Klang.[28]

(5) Kolé was the main city on the east coast and corresponds to Chü-li, which was situated near a large headland jutting out into the sea, and for this and other reasons is to be located at Ligor.

(6) Sabara is the important place for our present purpose. (The other towns may be dismissed from this discussion with a tentative identification each: Konkonagara is the Gangga Nagara of the *Malay Annals* [or *Sejarah Melayu*], Palanda is a Greek attempt to pronounce Pahang, while Tharra might be Trengganu.) Sabara was an emporium on the southern tip of the Golden Khersonese, and Wheatley allows the possibility that it was Singapore.[29]

It would certainly seem that we should connect Sabara (or Sabana) with either Singapore or one of the sites up the Johor River. In this latter region, we have already placed Lo-yüeh on the Seluyut River, a tributary of the Johor River, between Kota Tinggi and Johor Lama, and we have noted that there is a place called Panchur in the same area. It is now time to notice that Rouffaer places Batu Sawar (or Batu Sawa) and Kota Sabrang on his map between Kota Tinggi and Seluyut. He discusses these names from the *Sejarah Melayu* at great length,[30] but he does not identify Ptolemy's Sabara with either. Rather, he leans towards the name "Sabang", the name of the strait ("Sabam" to the Portuguese) between Sumatra's eastern shore and Pulau Kundur, while not excluding the possibility that Sabara is Singapore.[31]

The significant point is that in the time of Ptolemy in the 2nd century there was an important trading centre in the extreme south of the Malay Peninsula. And the only name left on the Chinese list to couple with Sabara is Pan-tou. One can hardly overlook the fact that this looks remarkably like the Panduru and Pan-tsu of a much later age. Was the fort on the hill on Singapore Island in the 2nd century already the centre of a kingdom trading with India and Persia in one direction and with Indochina in the other?

Whatever the precise answer to that question, the picture built up by Wheatley of the early historical geography of the peninsula is in need of radical alteration. Wheatley found it impossible to fit Ptolemy's picture into his own frame, because, it needs to be pointed out, his synthesis was constructed on a faulty basis, namely the hypothesis that there was no important trading centre on the lower Malayan coast until Melaka was founded.[32] In this opinion, he has been followed by Wolters, and so the picture of early Malay history presented by these two scholars is somewhat distorted. It needs to be realised that since at least the 2nd century CE there has been a Malayan emporium inside the Melaka Strait as well as at either end: Klang

---

[28] Wolters, *Early Indonesian Commerce*, p. 60.

[29] Wheatley, *The Golden Khersonese*, pp. 151–2.

[30] Ibid., pp. 436–95.

[31] Ibid., p. 98.

[32] Ibid., pp. 159, 232, 303.

was flourishing as a trading kingdom and guarding the narrowest stretch of the strait more than a thousand years before Melaka took up this role, while Takola at the northern entrance and Singapore-Johor in the south beckoned to ships using the straits and solicited their trade.[33]

---

[33] See note 8 above.

4

Paul Wheatley

The Century of Singhapura*

In the 13th century a new star appeared in the firmament of Southeast Asia, namely the Tais.[1] As early as the 7th century CE this people had founded the kingdom of Nan Chao in western Yün-nan, since when they had been slowly filtering southwards. Enclaves of Tai *padi* farmers had settled among the Burmese, the Mons and the Khmers, and Tai mercenaries had served in the Cambodian armies. In 1096 one group had founded the independent state of P'a-yao at the confluence of the Me'p'ing and Me-wang rivers. Early in the 12th century other groups formed a number of principalities in the Chao Phraya valley. In 1238 a Tai confederacy ousted the Khmer garrison at Sukhothai, the capital of the northwestern province of the Cambodian

---

* First published as a book chapter in Paul Wheatley's *Impressions of the Malay Peninsula* (Singapore: Eastern Universities Press, 1964), pp. 101–18.

[1] This chapter as originally published contains three footnotes (*), 26 endnotes and preambles to the endnotes; all are combined here as footnotes. Wheatley's preamble to the endnotes reads: "There is no comprehensive synthesis of events on the Malay Peninsula during the 14th century, and I have compiled the interpretation here presented from the piecemeal works of Dutch, French, English and Chinese scholars. The primary sources are Malay annals and Javanese records, supplemented by Chinese and Tai more or less incidental allusions. The best account of the dynastic history of ancient Singhapura is Walter Linehan, "The Kings of 14th Century Singapore", *JMBRAS* 20, 2 (1947): 117–27. On this topic see also G.P. Rouffaer, "Oud-Singhapoera, en de Djohor-rivier", *BKI* 77 (1921). The rise of the Tai nation is summarized succinctly in English by Prof. D.G.E. Hall in ch. 7, "The Tais and the Kingdom of Ayutia", in his *A History of South-East Asia* (London: Macmillan Education, 1955), and in French by Professor George Coedès in chs. 12 and 13 of his *Les états hindouisés d'Indochine et d'Indonésie* (Paris: E. de Boccard, 1948). Earlier accounts, such as those in W.A.R. Wood's *History of Siam* (London: Fisher Unwin, 1926) and W.A. Graham's *Siam*, 2 vols. (London: Alexander Moring, 1924), are inaccurate on many points. The classic history of Java during this period is incorporated in N.J. Krom's *Hindoe-Javaansche Geschiedenis* (The Hague: Martinus Nijhoff, 1931), but more recent work by C.C. Berg and J.G. de Casparis has revised some of Krom's conclusions."

4.1 King Ramkamhaeng Monument in Old Sukhothai. The Siamese ruler who extended the realm of his kingdom into the Malay Peninsula during the 13th century. © Benjamin J.Q. Khoo, private collection.

empire, and founded the first Tai kingdom down on the plains of middle Chao Phraya. The Tais took advantage of the waning power of Cambodia consequent to the megalomaniacal excesses of Jayavarman VII (1181–ca. 1218) to extend their power yet farther afield. Qubilai Qan's conquest of Nan-chao in 1253 induced many able Tai leaders to change their fortune to the southward. Again and again Tais raided into Cambodian territory. Then in 1270 Rama K'amheng (Rama the Brave) came to the throne of Chao Phraya, and pushed the boundaries of his kingdom into the isthmian tract of the Malay Peninsula. An epexegesis to a famous inscription raised by Rama at Chao Phraya in 1292 detailed the boundaries of his realm. "Southwards he has subdued the country up to ... Ratburi, P'echaburi, Năk'ōn Sri Th'ammărat, and beyond to the sea which marks the frontier".[2] It is impossible to be certain of the precise boundaries here intended, but it is clear that Rama claimed control over most of the isthmus.

It is during the 14th century that we first find incontrovertible evidence of settlement in the extreme south of the Malay Peninsula (other, of course, than a few Mesolithic and Neolithic axes). At some time just before 1300 CE, there came into existence a settlement on Singapore Island, the ancient Singhapura, tales of which were, some five hundred years later, to inspire Sir Stamford Raffles to one of the world's great acts of creative statecraft. The traditional account of the founding of this famous settlement is contained in the *Sejarah Melayu*, the annals of the royal court of Melaka. According to this story a Sumatran prince, Sri Tri Buana, of the line of Raja Iskandar dzu'l-Qarnain,[3] was cruising in the Riau Archipelago when he had occasion to go hunting on Tanjong Bemian. From the summit of a hill whither his quarry had led him, Sri Tri Buana looked across the water to a crescent of sandy beach "so white that it looked like a sheet of cloth". He turned to his minister, Indra Bopal, and inquired the name of the pleasant island. Indra Bopal replied that it was the land called Temasek, whereupon Sri Tri Buana repaired thither. When the prince and his entourage reached the shore:

> The ship was brought close in and Sri Tri Buana went ashore with all the ship's company, and they amused themselves with collecting shellfish. The king then went inland for sport on the open ground at Kuala Temasek [the *padang* of present-day Singapore] and they beheld a strange animal. It seemed to move with great speed; it had a red body and a black head; its breast was white; it was strong and active in build, and in size was rather bigger than a he-goat. When it saw the party, it moved away and then disappeared. And Sri Tri Buana inquired of all those who were with him, "What beast is that?" But no one knew. Then said Demang Lebar Daun, "Your Highness, I have heard it said that in ancient times it was a lion that had that appearance. I think that what we saw must have been a lion".

Sri Tri Buana then established a city at Temasek, giving it the name of Singhapura—which, of course, signifies "Lion City". "And", the *Sejarah Melayu* concludes,

---

[2] G. Coedès, *Inscriptions de Sukhodaya* (Bangkok: Bangkok Times Press, 1924), pp. 37–48.

[3] The *epitheton ornans* [Dhū al-Qar-nayn] (bicornus) derives ultimately from the fable of King Midas' asses' ears (*vide* Ovid, *Metamorphoses*, bk. II, 11, pp. 146–93) and *JAOS* 81 (1961): 426. It is cause for suspicion that the genealogy of the Tribuanic dynasty includes the names of three apsarases from Indra's heaven.

"Singhapura became a great city, to which foreigners resorted in great numbers, so that the fame of the city and its greatness spread throughout the world."[4]

So much for tradition. The fact that lions are not found in Southeast Asia itself sufficiently evidences the mythological nature of this account. In the 19th century popular etymology favoured a more mundane derivation of the name from *singgah* and *pura*, meaning "the city where one breaks one's journey". But, despite its specious plausibility when applied to a city located as Singapore is, this was not a satisfactory derivation. Professor C.C. Berg of Leiden has proposed that a community of monks of the esoteric Bhairava-Buddhist sect from the Javanese kingdom of Majapahit settled on the island of Temasek late in the 13th century. Possibly their monastery was located on what is now Fort Canning Hill. In accordance with the demoniac and orgiastic sessions which characterized their religion, these monks adopted the sobriquet of "lions", and several cities within the Majapahit dominion, such as Singharājya in Bali and Singhasāri in Java, were designated "lions"—in this special sense. Professor Berg believed that Singhapura was another such settlement.[5]

Malay tradition preserves an interesting story of Sri Tri Buana's voyage from Tanjong Bemian to Kuala Temasek. The *Sejarah Melayu* reads as follows: "And when they were come out into the open sea, a storm arose and the ship began to fill with water. Bail as they might they could not clear her, and the boatswain gave order to lighten the ship. But though much was thrown overboard they still could not bale the ship dry. She was by now close to Telok Belanga, and the boatswain said to Sri Tri Buana, 'It seems to me, Your Highness, that it is because of the crown of kingship that the ship is foundering. All else has been thrown overboard, and if we do not likewise with this crown we shall be helpless with the ship.' And Sri Tri Buana replied, 'Overboard with it then!' And the crown was thrown overboard. Thereupon the storm abated, and the ship regained her buoyancy and was rowed to land."[6] As it has been preserved, this story fails to make sense. Clearly the weight of the crown would have had no ill effect on the stability of a dugout canoe, let alone on the *lanchang*, with its gilded figurehead, in which Sri Tri Buana was sailing. We must assume that the malign influence of the crown was inherent in its supernatural propertics, but what event real or imagined lay behind this story we cannot know. However, it is interesting to discover an apparent echo of this tale in another garbled description of Temasek, this time by a Chinese author writing in 1349.[7] In his version the story is somewhat different, but again focuses on a species of headgear. "In ancient times, when digging the ground, a chief came upon a jewelled headdress. The beginning of the year is calculated from the [first] rising of the moon, when the

---

[4] This and the following passages from the *Sejarah Melayu* are taken from C.C. Brown's translation in "Sejarah Melayu or Malay Annals", *JMBRAS* 25, 2–3 (1952): 1–276, hereafter *Sejarah Melayu*. An alternative thesis alluded to by Sir Richard Winstedt (in D.G.E. Hall, *Historians of South East Asia* [Oxford and London: Oxford University Press, 1961], p. 25) attributes the bestowal of the honorific "Singhapura" on the island of Temasek to Vira Rājendra, alias Nila Uttama, the Buddhist third son of Rājendra Cōla I, in 1068.

[5] C.C. Berg, Lecture to the University of Malaya Historical Society, Singapore, 29 Nov. 1956.

[6] Brown, *Sejarah Melayu*, p. 30.

[7] *Tao-i chih-lüeh* [Chih-fu-chai ts'ung-shu ed.], pp. 16a–b.

chief [formerly] put on this headdress and wore his [ceremonial] dress to receive the congratulations [of the people]. Nowadays this custom still continues." It is clear that a crown or other headdress played an important role in the mythology of Temasek or Old Singapore, but neither the Malay version nor that of the Chinese enables us to evaluate its precise significance. However, this theme of a lost crown is found in other Malaysian contexts. A variant version of the *Sejarah Melayu*, for example, relates that three sons of Alexander the Great—the legendary progenitor of the Śri Vijayan Sailendran dynasty—disputed over the succession. Eventually they were persuaded to surrender the crown of kingship to an angel, who thereupon let it fall into the Indian Ocean. Substantially the same myth occurs in the folklore of Johor, but here it was Alexander's eldest son who let the crown fall into the Strait of Singhapura. Finally, a Sumatran version comes very close to paralleling the account in the *Sejarah Melayu*. According to this, divers located the crown in the bed of the ocean, but were unable to recapture it from the coils of a serpent. It would seem that somewhere far back in the history of the Śailendra dynasty the lack of a crown had to be explained away, possibly by a usurper legitimizing his reign, and the Tribuanic kings, claiming descent in the line of Alexander Dzu'l-Qarnain through the supernatural births on Si-Guntang Mahameru, had evolved the legend as part of their dynastic mythology. Certainly in later Malay history the crown was considered essential for a valid coronation, so much so that in the 18th century Sultan Sulaiman of Riau-Johor declined to be installed until the Bugis had recovered his regalia, and Sultan 'Abdu'r-Rahman had to be installed for a second time in 1822 when the Dutch obtained his crown from Tengku Putri Hamidah.

Of the history of Singhapura, we know practically nothing for certain, though the *Sejarah Melayu* preserves the names and styles of some members of the dynasty founded by Sri Tri Buana. This name, incidentally, may not be without significance for it was borne, in the form "Tribhuvana", by a queen of 14th-century Majapahit and by two kings of Melayu in 1286 and 1378 respectively. According to the *Sejarah Melayu*, Sri Tri Buana reigned for 48 years and was buried on the hill of Singhapura.[8] He was succeeded by his son, who assumed the style of the Paduka Sri Pikrama Wira, and is memorable chiefly for his repulse of the Javanese forces of Hayam Wuruk. After reigning for 18 years he also died and was followed by his son, the Raja Muda, with the style of Sri Rana Wikerma. It was he who raised Badang, "the slave of a Sayong man" and performer of prodigious feats of strength, to the rank of a war chief. Badang repaid his master well for, in a trial of strength with the champion of Kalinga, he won for his royal patron the cargoes of seven ships sent specially by the Raja of Kalinga from the Coromandel coast as stakes for the contest. At the same time, he hurled a huge rock from Fort Canning Hill into the estuary of the Singapore River. Until the middle of the 19th century this boulder could be seen on the promontory that formed the southern side of the river estuary. Apparently, natural forces had split it into two pieces, which had fallen apart so that they faced each other at an angle. One of the surfaces thus exposed bore an inscription in 14th-century Majapahit Kawi, but it was so badly weathered that it could not be deciphered by the techniques available at the time. It is a great

[8] The mythology of the Singapore dynasty is related in *Sejarah Melayu* on pp. 31ff.

4.2 Photo of the old Raffles Museum and Library in Singapore, 1890–1910. Leiden: Royal Netherlands Institute for Southeast Asian and Caribbean Studies (KITLV).

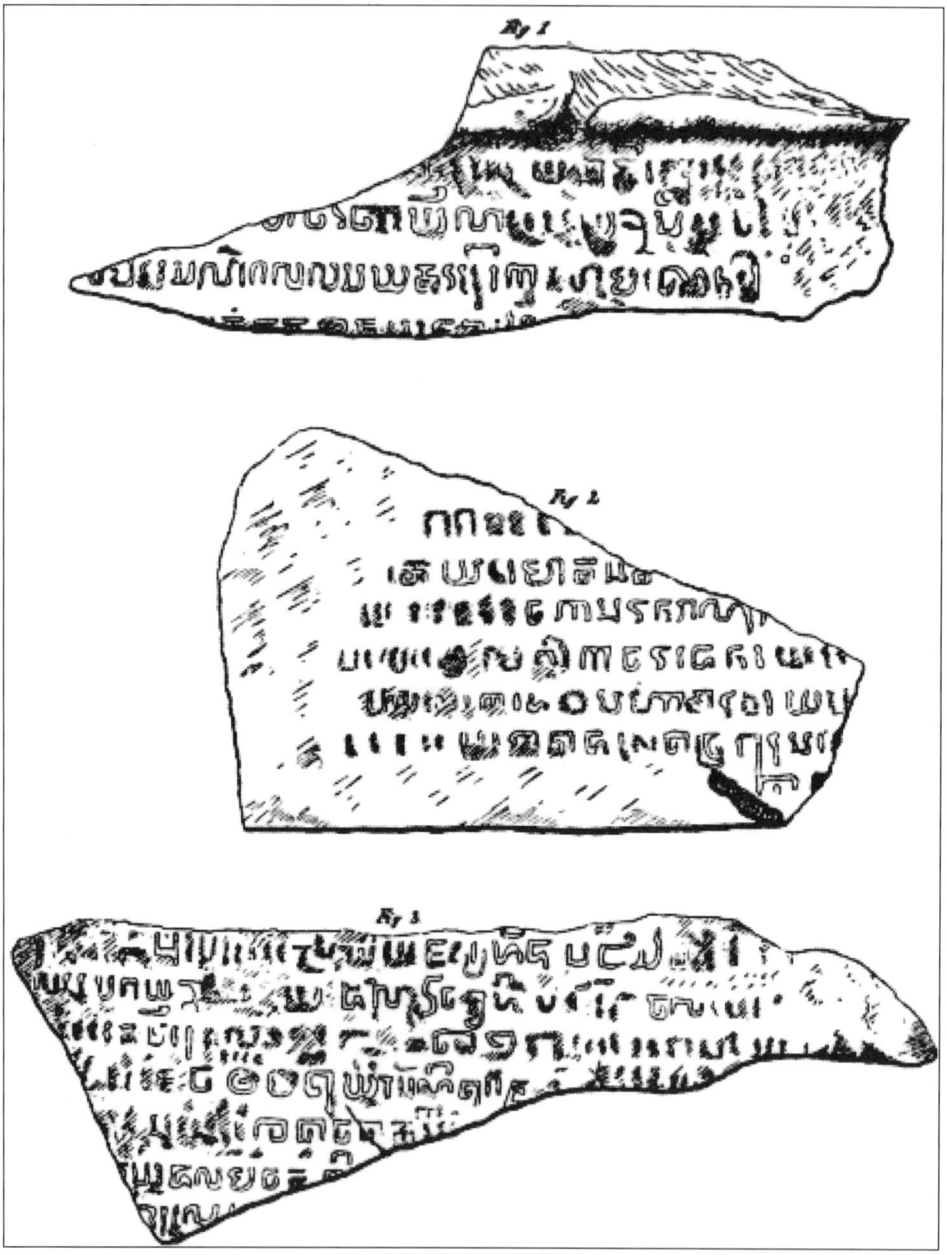

4.3 Sketch of three fragments of the Singapore stone. J.W. Laidlay, "Three fragments of the Singapore stone", *JASB* 17, 2 (1848).

misfortune for historians that the stone was destroyed by explosives in 1843 during the clearing of the ground preparatory to the building of a government bungalow. Had it been possible to re-examine the inscription in light of modern scholarship, there is every likelihood that, though it would probably not have substantiated the tale of Badang, it would almost certainly have provided valuable information about ancient Singhapura. Today there appear to be only fragments of the inscription preserved on a few small pieces of the original stone that Colonel James Low rescued immediately after the explosion. One is now in the Raffles Museum in Singapore, the rest in the Museum of the Asiatic Society of Bengal.[9]

The *Sejarah Melayu* relates that after a reign of 13 years Sri Rana Wikerma was succeeded by his son Damar Rajah, who then took the title Paduka Sri Maharaja. He reigned for 12 years and 6 months. Malay tradition asserts that he was succeeded by his son, with the style Sri Sultan Iskandar Shah, but there is reason to believe that this last ruler of Singhapura, elsewhere known as the Sri Parameswara, was in fact a Javanese or Sumatran renegade, who murdered Sri Rana Wikerma before usurping his throne. In any case, he himself was deposed after a brief reign and fled with his household, first to Seletar and then to Muar. According to Malay lore and one European source[10] the instrument of his defeat was the Javanese, but according to other early European writers[11] it was either the Tais themselves, or one of their peninsular vassals, who ousted the usurper.

No single date in the history of Singhapura can be fixed with certainty, but it is fairly clear that it was a flourishing settlement during much of the 14th century. Dr Linehan has sought to establish a chronology by correlating the evidence of the *Sejarah Melayu* with a remark in the *History of the Ming Dynasty* (*Ming shih*), but in my opinion it is by no means certain that the Chinese phrases on which he has based his argument refer to Singapore at all. Readers who are interested in evaluating Dr Linehan's arguments for themselves will find them set out in volume 20 of the *Journal of the Malayan Branch of the Royal Asiatic Society*, published in 1947. Yet despite the uncertainty as to events during the 14th century, the internal geography of Singhapura is better known than that of any other contemporary peninsular settlement. The nucleus seems to have been sited on terraces on the slope of Fort Canning Hill.[12] Today these terraces have been obliterated by builders and landscapers, so that it is impossible to say whether they were natural wave-cut platforms or were carved by the hand of man, but at least one writer remarked on their distinctive

---

[9] Illustrations of fragments of the Singapore monolith were first published by J.W. Laidlay in *JASB* 17, 2 (1848): pl. 3. Subsequently this article was reprinted in *Miscellaneous Papers relating to Indo-China*, ed. R. Rost (London: Trubner & Co., 1886), vol. 1, pp. 227–32. Recently both Mr S. Durai Raja Singam and Dr C.A. Gibson-Hill have reproduced Laidlay's plate, the former in *India and Malaya through the Ages*, 3rd ed. (Singapore: S. Lazar & Sons, 1954), p. 49, the latter in "Singapore Old Strait and New Harbour, 1300–1870", *Memoirs of the Raffles Museum*, no. 3 (Singapore: Government Printing Office, 1956), p. 23. [E.N.: The text of this publication has been reproduced in this collection.]

[10] Brown, *Sejarah Melayu* and Diogo do Couto.

[11] Bras d'Albuquerque, João de Barros, Tomé Pires, and Godinho d'Eredia.

[12] The topography of ancient Singapore is described in chs. 8 and 20 of *The Golden Khersonese* (Kuala Lumpur: University of Malaya Press, 1961).

appearance in the 14th century. This was Wang Ta-yüan, who in 1349 compiled a Chinese geographical handbook entitled *Description of the Island Foreigners* (*Tao-i chih-lüeh*).[13] He described Fort Canning Hill as resembling—presumably from the seaward—a truncated coil rising to a hollow summit and surrounded by interconnected terraces. Four centuries later John Crawfurd, second resident of the resuscitated Singapore, commented on the ruins on the hill, the most distinguished being those "seated on a square terrace ... near the summit". Subsequently he referred to "another terrace, on the north declivity of the hill".[14] The ruins mentioned by Crawfurd comprised brick and stone foundations of undetermined date, which were most probably remains of shrines contemporaneous with the ancient settlement. Among the ruins Crawfurd also noticed sherds of pottery, which he unfortunately neglected to particularize, and Chinese coins, which in any case would almost certainly have been valueless for dating purposes. The only remains which have come to light since Crawfurd's time are some gold ornaments of Majapahit workmanship discovered during the construction of a reservoir on the summit of Fort Canning Hill in 1928.[15] In later years, when old Singhapura had become but a memory, the shrines on the hilltop were thought to be the tombs of the Tribuanic dynasty, and as such were avoided by Malays, who called the hill Bukit Larangan (the Forbidden Hill). Munshi Abdullah, writing in 1849, recalled that when Colonel Farquhar, first Resident of modern Singapore, wished to explore the hill, he was accompanied by Melakan men, for no Singapore Malay would venture with him.[16]

The extent of the ancient settlement can be estimated with some degree of accuracy. As long ago as 1819 Sir Stamford Raffles discerned the "lines of the old city and its defences".[17] Presumably he was referring to the rampart and ditch which formerly ran inland from the sea to the base of Fort Canning Hill along the

---

[13] *Tao-i chih-lüeh*. This is a description of 99 countries, ports and noteworthy localities ranging from the Moluccas to Arabia and the African coast. Wang Ta-yüan, the author, had traded in a considerable number of foreign localities in and subsequent to 1330.

[14] The remains of ancient Singhapura as they existed in 1819 were described by John Crawfurd in his *Journal of an Embassy from the Governor-General of India to the Courts of Siam and Cochin-China* (London: Henry Colburn, 1828), pp. 44–7.

[15] The jewellery found on Fort Canning Hill has been described in detail and illustrated by Sir Richard Winstedt, "Gold Ornaments Dug up at Fort Canning, Singapore", *JMBRAS* 6, 4 (1928): 1–4. Originally the hoard included a pair of large, flexible five-strand, gold bracelets weighing 50 *mayam* each. One was in perfect condition, the tongue of its clasp sliding into its socket with ease; the other had its fastening partially crushed and two of its strands broken. Each bracelet bore a plaque with an incised *kala*-head. In addition there was a signet ring with a bird in flight incised on the bezel, three pairs of earrings set with small diamonds, a jewelled clasp and an elliptical ornament set with a ruby *en cabochon*. The gems were all of inferior quality, but the gold was of 24 carat fineness. In this description the past tense has been used because, during the Japanese occupation of Singapore, all except three of the earrings and the broken bracelet disappeared from the Raffles Museum. The present whereabouts of the rest of the hoard is unknown.

[16] *Hikayat Abdullah*, trans. A.H. Hill, *JMBRAS* 28, 3 (1955): 130–1.

[17] Raffles' remarks on the ruins of early Singapore are contained in letters that he wrote to William Marsden on 31 Jan. 1819 and 21 Jan. 1823.

line of the Beras Basah River. On the east the settlement apparently reached to the sea, though no archaeological remains have ever been discovered on the plain of Singapore; on the south it was bounded by the Singapore River and the swamps that formerly occupied the present central business district. With its shrines rising from the terraces of Fort Canning Hill and its rampart, which as late as 1822 was 16 feet [4.9m] wide and 8 feet [2.44m] high, Singhapura must have presented an impressive appearance to voyagers passing through the strait.

At this time Keppel Harbour afforded the only practicable passage for vessels rounding the peninsula. To Chinese mariners it was known as Dragon-Teeth Strait. "Dragon Teeth", originally the name applied by Amoy sailors to the two vertical pegs at the bow of a junk through which was carried the anchor cable, was a term easily transferred to twin peaks or headlands or other similar coastal features. In this instance the "dragon teeth" were prominent rocks that had weathered out from strongly jointed granite at the western entrance to Keppel Harbour. One still stands as the last Singapore landmark seen by travellers leaving the island by ship. For those who have not travelled by this means, we may quote John Thornton who, in his *Oriental Navigation* of 1703, described it as a "Bluff-Rock and smooth aloft with Trees, and Grass". The other rock, known to Malays and Europeans as Batu Belayar and Lot's Wife respectively, was demolished in 1848 during the widening of the strait, but was characterized by Thornton as "a scragged Rock, shewing like a ruinated Wall".[18]

Wang Ta-yüan leaves us in no doubt that the main dangers of the strait came not from the hazards of navigation, but from the communities of orang laut who lurked in the channels. These sea gypsies forbore to attack Chinese merchantmen outward bound, but lay in wait for the day when they should be returning through the strait, heavy laden with cargoes of spices, aromatics, drugs, apotropaia and cloths. As they were forced to rely on their sweeps to negotiate the narrow channel, the junks were especially vulnerable to piratical assault at that time. As soon as they cleared the Karimon Islands their crews donned their armour and erected padded screens as a protection against the arrows of the orang laut pirates, for they knew, so Wang Ta-yüan continued, that "of a certainty some two or three hundred *perahu* would put out to attack them.... Sometimes the junks were fortunate enough to escape with a favouring wind", but on other occasions the crews were butchered and their merchandise pirated by the orang laut. This, of course, was not an unusual fate for a South Seas trader. All round the shores of the peninsula and among the islands to the southward, both Malays and coastal aborigines turned to piracy whenever it offered a better livelihood than fishing or petty trading. As late as 1900 old men living on the Kallang River claimed they could recall piratical voyages of former days, which had taken them as far afield as Thailand and Cochinchina.[19]

The relationship of the sea gypsies of Dragon-Teeth Strait to the settlement of Singhapura is not at all clear. Living outside the enceinte of the town, they probably

---

[18] There is in the Raffles Museum a watercolour of this rock by an unknown artist. The painting has been reproduced by Dato Sir Roland Braddell in "Lung-ya-men and Tan-ma-hsi", *JMBRAS* 23, 1 (1950): pl. 5; and by Dr C.A. Gibson-Hill, "Singapore Old Strait and New Harbour", pl. 1.

[19] W.W. Skeat and H.N. Ridley, "The Orang Laut of Singapore", *JSBRAS* 33 (1900): 248.

had little commerce with the religious and trading communities on the hill, and the rampart may have served to protect the city as much from these turbulent neighbours as from foreign raiders. The boom that, the *Sejarah Melayu* relates, closed the estuary of the Singapore River, probably also performed a similar service for the inhabitants. Though this boom is mentioned on two occasions in the *Sejarah Melayu*, there are several traditions to account for its origin. *Raffles Manuscript* number 18 preserves two versions. According to the first, the construction of the boom was one of the labours of the mighty Badang, whose chief exploit was described above. According to the second version, the boom was laid by one Benderang, a champion of the Raja of Perlak. Yet a third account in the Shellabear recension describes the feat as a joint effort of both Badang and Benderang. When ancient contemporary authorities were so at variance, how can the sceptical historian hope to divine the truth?

One last point is worth mention before we leave the orang laut. In his *Island Foreigners*, Wang Ta-yüan remarked in a tantalizingly obscure manner that "Natives and Chinese dwell side by side" in Dragon-Teeth Strait. Who these Chinese were we do not know. Whether Wang assumed that the presence of Chinese among the orang laut was so well known as not to merit explanation, or whether he was simply careless in his composition can only be guessed. Perhaps the Chinese in question were traders, for Wang later added that the orang laut themselves produced no fine or rare goods for trade. All such commodities, he said, were obtained from commerce with Ch'üan-chou merchants. In any case, whatever the explanation, this is the earliest extant mention of Chinese residing in any part of the peninsula.

We have seen that Tai southward expansion went some way towards filling the power vacuum left by the decline of Śrī Vijaya. Another threat to the peninsular states came from Java, an old enemy of the Śailendra dynasty. In 1293 Prince Vijaya, son-in-law of the great Kṛtanagara of Singhasari who had dreamed of organizing a pan-Malayan union to withstand the encroachments of Qubilai Qan in the South Seas, founded the Kingdom of Majapahit with its capital in the Brantas valley. For the first half-century or so of its history, its rulers were occupied with domestic revolts, but in 1331 a natural leader by the name of Gajah Mada became Mapatih (Chief Minister) of Majapahit. For over 30 years he was the real ruler of the kingdom, and inaugurated a programme of military expansion in direct contrast to the diplomatic policies of his predecessors. In 1350 the famous Hayam Wuruk became Bhaṭāra of Majapahit. Of him the Buddhist poet Prapañca wrote: "Truly King Hayam Wuruk is a great potentate. He is without cares and worries. He indulges in all pleasures. All beautiful maidens in Janggala and Kediri are selected for him, as many as possible." This same poet, in 1365, composed *Nāgarakṛtāgama*,[20] an encomium in honour of Hayam Wuruk, in which he claimed to enumerate the territories comprising the empire of Majapahit. According to Prapañca this included all Sumatra, the Malay Peninsula as far north as Patani, Borneo (Kalimantan), Bali, Makassar, the Banda Islands and the Moluccas. In other words, Prapanca would have us believe that Hayam Wuruk's

[20] The *Nāgarakṛatāgama* was first translated into Dutch by H. Kern and annotated by N.J. Krom (The Hague: Martinus Nijhoff, 1919). Professor C.C. Berg's re-interpretation of the implications of this text are set out in "De sadengoorlog en de mythe van Groot-Majapahit", *Indonesië* 5 (1951): 385–422.

domains were as extensive as present-day Indonesia, together with the southern half of the Malay Peninsula. Alas, the inexorable progress of historical research has stripped away the imposing facade of grandeur and shown that Majapahit at its greatest extent probably comprised little more than East Java, Madura and Bali. The other names in the impressive catalogue merely reflect the received geographical knowledge of medieval Java, and were incorporated only to glorify the Kingdom of Majapahit in a paean of resounding praise. Southeast Asian rulers have not normally been too critical of such eulogies.

In the *Nāgarakṛtāgama* the whole of the southern half of the Malay Peninsula is known as Pahang. The list of place names within Pahang—presumably those which in Javanese eyes were of some importance—opens with Hujung Tanah (land's end), the contemporary name for Johor, and then proceeds coastwise from the northeast to the northwest: Langkasuka, with a history already of over a thousand years; Sai, an old name for Telubin; Kelantan; Trengganu; Nashor, an unidentified name; Paka; the *muara* (estuary) of the Dungun River; Temasek (Old Singapore); Sungei Ujong; Klang; Kedah; Jerai; and another unidentified toponym, Kanjapiniran. Several of the names in this list also occur in Wang Ta-yüan's geographical handbook. Langkasuka (p. 13 a–b), for example, was thickly populated, "the inhabitants settled all around like ants, even though the soil was of low fertility". Kelantan soil was even worse: "sterile" is the word he used (p. 6b). But the people were great lovers of ceremony. Both men and women wore black cotton *sarong*, except on festival days when they donned garments of red cotton. The Chinese were no more favourably impressed with the soils of Trengganu, which they classed as middling to poor, though they admitted that "even the poorest folk had sufficient food" (p. 7a). The men of Trengganu, it was recorded, were a superstitious crowd, who worshipped Kālī, the consort of Śiva in her fierce and bloody aspect, with Tantric rites that included human sacrifice. Similar rites were performed in Pahang, of which a rather later writer says: "They cut slips of aromatic wood with which to bring about peoples' deaths, sacrifice with human blood, and pray for good fortune to avert calamity".[21]

Among other peninsular states described by Wang Ta-yüan was Tāmbraliṅga (pp. 5a–b), which at least as early as 1230 had declared its independence of the Śri Vijayan empire. We have seen that in that year its king, Dharmaraja Candrābhanu, had erected a stele at Ca'iya, the inscription on which showed that he not only considered himself an autonomous ruler but was also annexing neighbouring states on his own initiative. During the next 40 years the fortunes of Tāmbraliṅga prospered. Concurrently Dharmaraja Candrābhanu seems to have rejected Mahayana Buddhism in favour of the Theravada discipline, an action that procured him the favour of the rulers of the expanding state of Chao Phraya in the north, also a pillar of the Theravada school. So confident of his power was the ruler of Tāmbraliṅga that in 1247 he dared to interfere in the affairs of Ceylon. Singhalese and South Indian records[22] lead us to believe that a colony of Malays had been established somewhere

---

[21] Fei-Hsin, *Hsing-ch'a sheng-lan* [Triumphant visions of the starry raft (that is, the ship carrying the imperial ambassador)], Ts'ung-shu chi-ch'eng ed., ch. 2, pp. 2a–b.

[22] For Paṇḍyan inscriptions of 1263 and 1264, see *BKI* (1927): 470–1 and *Cūḷavamśa*, vol. 83, p. 40.

in Ceylon for some years prior to this, and it would seem likely that Candrābhanu's intervention was in some way connected with the affairs of this settlement. Possibly the settlers were, in fact, men from Tāmbraliṅga. The Singhalese chronicle known as the Cūḷavaṃśa states, probably correctly, that Candrābhanu's mission was of a peaceful nature but that subsequently friction developed between him and the Singhalese. The "wicked Javaka soldiers invaded every landing place and, with their poisoned arrows like terrible snakes … laid waste, raging in their fury, [to] all Laṅkā [the island of Ceylon]". The outcome of the conflict seems to have been indeterminate, and Candrābhanu returned to Tāmbraliṅga, leaving "his son in command of the Malay colony". A decade or so later Sundara Pānhdya invaded Ceylon from South India and eventually imposed his suzerainty over most of the island, including the Malay territory. In an attempt to free his son from the Pāṇḍyan shackles, Candrābhanu, "the Lord of Men" as he is called in Singhalese chronicles, in 1270 again invaded Ceylon, this time supplementing his Malay army with South Indian levies. Alas for Malay imperialism, "the Lord of Men was sent flying defenceless by a Pāṇḍyan general".[23] So severe were the losses suffered by Candrābhanu that they probably undermined his power to resist Tai southward penetration, and by the dawn of the 14th century his kingdom had been incorporated in the realm of Rama K'amheng. Nevertheless, during the first half of the new century Tāmbraliṅga flourished under Tai suzerainty. Wang Ta-yüan remarked that the *padi* fields of the country produced more grain than the inhabitants could consume, but added, "Newly harvested grain was put aside for future use, for the people were economical in their manner of life."[24]

The outstanding feature of the 14th century on the Malay Peninsula was the increasing definition of states in the southern tracts. As far as we can tell, economic life was still more developed on the isthmus, but Kelantan, Trengganu and Pahang were each allotted a section in Wang Ta-yüan's *Island Foreigners*, and several other names in the southern reaches were incorporated in Prapañca's panegyric. The nature of the trade conducted by these states had changed little since the 12th and 13th centuries, but the range of commodities had widened, tin, tortoiseshell and "cranes' crests" (in reality hornbill casques) having been added to the schedule. Coarse-quality lakawood was a staple export from nearly all the states; Tāmbraliṅga was a source of tin of outstanding quality, and Kelantan prided itself on the excellence of its gharu. As these petty kingdoms came to participate more actively in the commerce of Southeast Asia, so they developed specialized markets for Chinese trade goods. Tāmbraliṅga, Langkasuka and Trengganu, for example, preferred blue-and-white porcelain, but Kelantan took plain blue. The peninsular textile market was apparently even more individualistic. Whereas pongees were popular in Pahang and Trengganu, Vietnamese cottons were the best line in Kelantan, and prints in Langasuka.

It is virtually impossible that the isthmian states were ever subject to Majapahit dominion, but there is some reason to believe that the settlement at Temasek in the extreme south was nominally within the Majapahit sphere of influence. For example,

---

23 The imbroglio involving the rulers of Tāmbraliṅga and Ceylon has been most ably evaluated by Prof. K.A. Nilakanta Sastri, in "Srīvijaya, Candrabhānu and Vīra-Pāṇḍya", *TBG* 77 (1937): 251–68.

24 Based on Wang Ta-yüan's account.

during the reign of Sri Pikrama Wira (possibly ca. 1347–62), Hayam Wuruk, Bhaṭāra of Majapahit, sent envoys to Singhapura to demand allegiance. The *Sejarah Melayu* relates the story of the embassy in some detail. Apparently the envoys brought with them as the customary present "a wood-shaving seven fathoms long, which had been cut without a break in it: it was as thin as paper and rolled up in the form of a girl's ear-stud". Sri Pikrama Wira interpreted this as impugning the manliness and valour of the Singapore warriors, but the Javanese envoys repudiated this implication, saying, "No, your Highness, that was not the intention of the Bhatara. What he signifies is simply, 'Is there at your Highness's feet a man who can use an adze like that?'" Nevertheless, the real significance of the gift was not lost on the wily men of Singapore. A carpenter named Sang Bentan was called and, in the presence of the Javanese envoys, commanded to shave a boy's head with his adze. "Though the boy cried and kept moving his head this way and that, the carpenter went on with his work, and in the twinkling of an eye the hair was gone as though it had been taken off with a razor." Sri Pikrama Wira then gave the adze with which the feat had been performed to the envoys to take back to Majapahit as the customary present. This time there was no doubt as to the significance of the gift. The Bhaṭāra of Majapahit knew that the Raja of Singapore implied that if the Javanese invaded his realm their heads would be shaved as was the boy's. To this impudent challenge Hayam Wuruk could make only one reply. He ordered his war-chiefs to prepare a fleet of a hundred ships of the line, "together with small craft beyond number", and sailed for Singapore. "And the Javanese troops landed and fought the men of Singapore; and a great battle ensued. Loud rang weapon on weapon; terrifying was the roar of the warriors shouting; the din was unimaginable.[25] On either side many were killed and the ground flowed with blood." But the men of Singapore stood firm, and as the sun sank the Javanese retreated to their ships. The author of the *Sejarah Melayu* concludes: "So long is the story of the battle between Singhapura and Java that were I to tell it in detail, listeners would have more than their fill. That is why I shorten it, for diffuseness makes no appeal to the intelligent."

It was not to be expected that the mighty Hayam Wuruk, whose court poet had set him over all the peoples of Malaysia, would countenance the existence of an intransigent kingdom situated in such a strategic position for the collection of tolls and the control of trade. Accordingly, in the latter half of the 14th century a new and larger Javanese fleet appeared off Singapore. For some days the forces of Hayam Wuruk besieged the city without notable success. What the outcome would have been can only be guessed, had not treachery played a hand. An officer of the treasury, who felt he had been wronged by the Raja of Singapore, opened the gate of the city at dawn, "whereupon the Javanese entered and fought with the men of Singhapura inside the fort. So many were killed on either side that blood flowed like a river in spate and flooded the fort of Singhapura on the sea shore". According to Malay tradition it was this blood which stained bright red the ferrallitic soils on the plain of Singapore, which not even equatorial rainfall has since been able to cleanse. The same tradition attributes the almost complete absence on Singapore Island of

[25] See also note 6 in Paul Wheatley, *Impressions of the Malay Peninsula* (Singapore: Eastern Universities Press, 1964), ch. 7.

padi, the staple crop of the Malaysian world, to the cosmic disturbance effected by this battle rather than to a lack of low-lying, level land. But although the Javanese sacked Singapore, they apparently made no attempt at permanent occupation, and sailed back to Majapahit with their loot.

Meanwhile the Tais, having established their authority over the isthmus, were claiming suzerainty over the rest of the peninsula. As early as 1295 the emperor of China had placed his veto on this policy. A mission to the Tai court at Chao Phraya had conveyed the stern injunction, "Do thou no evil to the Malays", but apparently with no tangible result. Certainly a Tai fleet of over 70 vessels attacked Singapore in the 1340s. The town resisted for a month, and the outcome was still in doubt when a Chinese imperial envoy sailed through the strait. Fearing to incur the wrath of the Dragon Throne, the Tai forces scattered into creeks amid the mangrove, and, after raiding coastal villages, sailed back to their homeland. The story as told by Wang Ta-yüan smacks of banditry and piracy rather than organized conquest. Peninsular Malays have ever been prone to label any man or thing from the northward as "Siam", and it is probable that these so-called Tai raiders were actually Malay or orang laut pirates from one of the Tai-controlled states on the isthmus, rather than the official fleet of Chao Phraya, a state that was ruled from 1317 to 1347 by T'amrnaraja Lü-t'ai, a monarch more interested in works of Buddhist merit than in the vain panoply of war. Nevertheless, we must not forget that three Portuguese historians claim that the last ruler of Singapore, himself a usurper, was forced to flee the country by a peninsular vassal of the Tai power, though there is disagreement between them as to whether the instrument of vengeance was Pahang or Patani.[26]

There are some indications that, after its final sack by Javanese or Tais and the flight of its ruler, Singhapura was not wholly abandoned. According to the younger Albuquerque, for example, the laksamana of Melaka went to live there after the fall of that city in 1511,[27] and at a slightly later date the ruler of Singhapura was strong enough to be able to defend the settlement against an attack by Melaka.[28] Both Eredia's maps[29] and Valentijn's text[30] also refer to a settlement on the island, presumably the same one mentioned in Portuguese records as late as 1613. But these later references depict a decayed settlement. They leave the impression that the prosperity that had invested the city-state during the 14th century had departed. In any case, the 15th century belonged to a new city that had grown up on the western seaboard of the peninsula. This city became the focus of an empire which overshadowed and eventually subsumed the city-states of the peninsula as a strangling *pipal* envelops its host.

---

[26] Based on Wang Ta-yüan's account.

[27] *Comentários*.

[28] Shellabear edition of *Sějarah Mělayu* (Singapore: Methodist Publishing House, 1910), p. 250.

[29] J.V. Mills, "Description of Malaca and Meridional India and Cathay", *JMBRAS* 8, 1 (1930): plate 6.

[30] D.F.A. Hervey, trans., "Valentyn's Account of Malacca", *JSBRAS* 15 (1885): 134.

5

Pieter Gerritsz Rouffaer

Was Melaka an Emporium Named *Malayur* before 1400 CE? And Where was Wurawari, Ma-Hasin, Langka and Batu Sawar?*

5.1 Portrait photograph of Pieter Gerritsz Rouffaer in Amsterdam. Leiden: Royal Netherlands Institute for Southeast Asian and Caribbean Studies (KITLV).

* In 1921, Rouffaer published this piece as a long article in two parts. They appeared under the same title in *BKI* 77, 1 (1921): 1–171, and 77, 3–4 (1921): 359–604. The text reproduced here in English translation represents a partial translation from part II of the article, covering pp. 436–81 in the Dutch original. Internal references made by Rouffaer to different parts of his article have been indicated as "part 1" and "part 2". Some interlinear comments have been moved into newly-created footnotes and marked with "A.N.".

Penatih

Although it was unfortunately garbled to "Petatek" on the English Admiralty Map no. 795 (1913) as well as on the Straits Branch Map (1911), Viator's "Bukit Panate" and Hervey's more accurate "Pĕnâtih" leave no room for doubt as to what the correct name was.

A place name such as this, here at the Johor River, is most noteworthy; for it is a place "joined to a patih". Of course, we are immediately reminded of Gresik on East Java, where a prominent widow—still well-known nowadays as Nyahi Gede Pinatih[1] played an important historical role in the time of Java's religious transition (ca. 1475–1525). Kampong Kebungson, where her old-fashioned grave is still located, is now just north of the centre of *kota* Gresik, and was essentially a Malay kampong,[2] whereas south of that centre lay the old Arab quarter—Jaratan or Pajaratan (Yoartan), with the grave of the Islamic apostle Malik Ibrahim (d. 8 May 1419).

Here at the Johor River, the curious name "Penatih"[3] immediately gives rise to the question: Could this have been the "residence of a Patih" in the older Johorean period? That is, the residence of a Patih of the Sultans during the 18th and 19th centuries, when they themselves had moved their residence first to Riau and then in 1788 to Lingga (Daik)? Was there a vice-viceroy living here who reported to the temenggong at Johor Lama or Singapore? Only local research can shed light on this strange place name.

---

[1] A.N.: Grand Dame, First Lady of the Patih or in this case, the Dowager-Patih. This is according to, for example, J.L.A. Brandes, *Pararaton (Ken Arok) of het boek der koningen van Tumapel en van Majapahit* (Batavia: Albrecht and Rusche, 1896), p. 71n5, and H.N. van der Tuuk *Kawi-balineesch-nederlandsch woordenboek* [Kawi-Balinese-Dutch dictionary] (Batavia: Landsdrukkerij, 1912), vol. 4, p. 177a.

[2] Compare the survey of this person's significance in P.J. Veth's *Java, geographisch, ethnologisch, historisch*, 2nd ed. (Haarlem: De Erven F. Bohn, 1896), vol. 1, pp. 235–6 and the reference there to Brumund's description of her grave in "Verhandelingen Bataviaasch Genootschap der Kunsten en Wetenschappen" [Proceedings of the Batavia Society of Arts and Sciences] 33 (1868): 186. On 11 Aug. 1909, I visited this grave in Kampung Kebungson[!], in other words, in a Malay "younger brother's kampung" (compare Jav. *bungsu* as Mal. *bongsoe*, in J.F.C. Gericke, T. Roorda and A.C. Vreede, *Javaansch-Nederlandsch handwoordenboek* [Leiden and Amsterdam: J. Muller and E.J. Brill, 1901], vol. 1, p. 771a); only the little entrance gate, also mentioned by Brumund, still holds an interest. It was visited neither by J. Knebel in his 1907 *Oudheidkundig Rapport* [Antiquarian report] (pp. 248–9), nor by Van Hoëvell in 1847. Jasper in *Eigen Haard* (1910) has a brief note that ends: "around the shed's raised floor pieces of stone have been arranged on which one can still see fragments of inscriptions" (pp. 639–40). [E.N.: An attempt to identify the sources by Knebel and Jasper was unsuccessful.]

[3] A.N.: Be it for a hamlet at the foot; or perhaps at the top, of a low hill with the same name; and a small river bearing the same name.

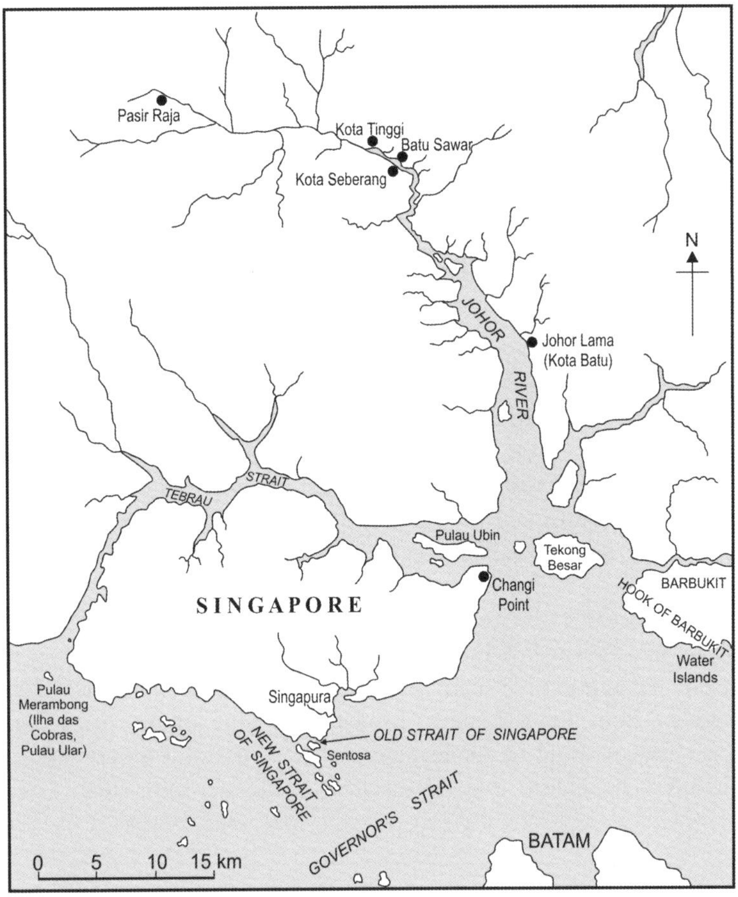

5.2 Map of Singapore and Johor River region with the historic upstream towns. Drawn by Mrs Lee Li Kheng.

Batu Sawa(r)

Out of deference to Hervey, who speaks of "Batu Sawa", I have placed the *r* between brackets. The correct form, however, is certain:

- Batu Sawar;[4]
- Batusauar on the map dating from ca. 1604 (before 1613, in any case);[5]
- Batusauwer repeatedly in Cornelius Matelieff's wonderful narrative from September 1606;[6]

[4] W.G. Shellabear, *Sejarah Melayu; or, The Malay Annals* (Singapore: American Mission Press, 1898), p. 2, l. 11; see also appendix, story 38, p. 189r.

[5] M.G. de Eredia, *Malaca, l'Inde Méridionale, et le Cathay: Manuscrit original autographe de Godinho de Eredia appartenant à la Bibliothèque Royale de Bruxelles*, ed. M.L. Janssen (Bruxelles: Librairie Européenne C. Muquardt, 1882), fol. 45 recto, and esp. fol. 60 verso.

[6] I. Commelin, *Begin ende Voortgang Vande Vereenigde Neerlandsche Geoctroyeerde Oost-Indische Compagnie*, 2 vols. (Amsterdam: Joannes Janssonius, 1645–46, hereafter *BV*), vol. 2, 13, pp. 29b–31a.

- Batusabar repeatedly (sometimes Batusauwer) in Willem Verhoeff's no less wonderful log from January 1609,[7] often interchanged with a synonymous Iohor, in the sense of Johor proper as it was known then (for he calls Johor Lama "Old Johor");
- Batu Sawar, in the blustering letter written in Malay characters, from the Acehnese Sultan Iskandar Muda (r. 1607–36) to King James I of England (r. 1603–25)—first published by Shellabear in 1898,[8] then discussed by, among others, Gerini[9] and Ferrand,[10] a letter dating from 1024 AH/1615 (*not* 1612) CE.[11]

Besides, when later in his travelogue Hervey mentions a second "Batu Sâwâ"—with two long *a*'s here—some distance upstream from Seluang, he also gives the English translation to the Malay word *sāwar*: "fishing-weir rock". For *sāwa* in Malay means "bog, marsh" and *ular*, "python", whereas *sāwar* means "barrier of branches" for catching fish or game.[12] To use a Dutch word commonly used on the Eastern Scheldt (*Oosterschelde*) in fishing and lobster trapping, Malay *sawar* is like our *weer*, or *visch-weer* [fishing weir]; equivalent to Malay *jĕrmal*, well known throughout the Strait of Melaka.

Thanks to Hervey's text, it is now possible to reliably indicate on a map where this historical Batu Sawar lay. For no one seems to know that anymore, or to have asked himself that question in earnest; it is brushed aside with the statement that it was upstream from Johor Lama.[13] Eredia's mapping of the place, dating from ca. 1604 (see above) could be misleading as far as his folio 45 recto is concerned; although it has been placed a good distance upstream from Pulau Layang (Pulo

---

[7] Ibid., vol. 2, 15, pp. 41b–45a.

[8] W.G. Shellabear, "An Account of Some of the Oldest Malay MSS. Now Extant", *JSBRAS* 31 (1898): 123–30.

[9] G.E. Gerini, *Researches on Ptolemy's Geography of Eastern Asia, Further India and the Indo-Malay Archipelago* (London: Royal Geographical Society, 1909), pp. 705–6.

[10] G. Ferrand, *Relations de Voyages et textes géographiques arabes, persans et turcs relatifs à l'Extrême-Orient du VIIIe au XVIIIe siècles* (Paris: Ernest Leroux, 1914), vol. 2, pp. 670–1.

[11] Shellabear's error (*Sejarah Melayu* [1898], p. 111: "1024 AH or 1612 CE") was copied by Gerini and Ferrand. But 1024 AH lasted from 31 January 1615 through 19 January 1616. The blustering letter dates from the period after the second and definitive destruction of Batu Sawar by Aceh in the beginning of September 1615 (see below) because it twice mentions "the subject places of B.S. [Batu Sawar]" as belonging to Aceh. See also G.P. Rouffaer, "Was Malaka emporium vóór 1400 A.D.?", part 1, *BKI* 77, 1 (1921): 127.

[12] H.C. Klinkert, *Maleisch-Nederduitsch Woordenboek* [Malay-Dutch Dictionary], 3rd ed. (Leiden: E.J. Brill, 1916), p. 539b.

[13] Even the accurate E. Netscher, in the introduction to his *De Nederlanders in Djohor en Siak, 1602 tot 1865* [The Dutch in Johor and Siak, 1602–1865] (Batavia: Bruining & Wijt, 1870), says only: "Batu-Sawar, further up the river", namely the "capital Seluyut, on the Johor River" (p. 5). An effort at mapping, albeit mistaken, was made by W. Marsden on his "Map of the Island of Sumatra", attached to the third edition of his *History of Sumatra* (London: Longman, Hurst, Rees, Orme, and Brown, 1811); there, one sees "Johor or Batu Sabar" on the east bank and "Kota Sabrang" opposite to it on the west bank. So here Johor Lama was mistakenly identified with Batu Sawar.

Layan) there, the latter is depicted as lying straight west from Kota Batu (*cottabato*, which is Johor Lama), and as an insignificant little island at the west bank of the great fjord, which continues beyond *batusauar*—this is completely wrong. Much better is his sketch on a smaller scale, in folio 60 verso; there we see *cottabatu* at the north side of the fjord (an exaggeration), but marked *batusauar* at the left bank of a far narrower upper river—this is reasonably realistic. From Matelieff's beautiful description of 18 September 1606, which will follow below, we know that the "city of *Batusauwer*" lay in the freshwater area of the Sungai Johor, even if the sea's ebb and flow by the rise of the river water were still clearly present in the city. So Batu Sawar must have been some distance upstream from Pulau Linau, as it appeared above from Viator.

Hervey's text goes:

> A mile further on, that is, past "Pûlau Patâni" mentioned above, is Tanah Sĕroh (Sunken Soil), the scene of a terrible catastrophe said to have taken place long ago, a sudden subsidence of the soil, which buried the whole kampong with its inhabitants. This calamity is attributed to a tremendous fall of rain.... Not far above this at a bend of the river on the same side Batu Sâwa comes into view, with red and white soil shewing [sic] on the bank where the river has eaten into rising ground.[14] Just beyond is Tanjong Putus (Severed Point), indicating no doubt the spot which the river, as it often does during the rainy season, has cut right across the neck of a bend and made for itself another channel. A short way beyond on the left may be descried, with some trouble, a tiny creek which bears the name of *Dânau Sĕrâ* (Midge Lake);[15] it widens out a little way from the main stream into a lake, which from its name may supposed to rejoice in swarms of a little stinging creature more minute than the redoutable *agas* (sand-fly).
>
> Thus from here we go upstream from Pĕnatih (which was to the *left*—that is, on the right bank), and then to the *right*: Pulau Patani, Tanah Sĕroh, Batu Sawa(r), and Tanjung Putus; and further on, but to the *left* now: *Danau Sĕra*. This alone, together with that "bend of the river", would suffice to justify the way I have located Batu Sawar on our sketch map, since the position of Pĕnatih ("Petatek", as it were) has been established. Batu Sawar, the "fish-weir rock", must have lain at the sharp bend—even *in* that bend—which the S. Johor makes between Kota Tinggi and Pĕnatih, coming from the west and bending toward the south.

That this location is correct is further proven by Viator. As he sails on from "Bukit China" and "Bukit Pahang" (or "Bukit Chîna" and, more or less, "Pûlau Patâni" in Hervey) to Kota Tinggi (Kota Tingeh) he makes no mention of Batu Sawar, but mentions "Tanjong Pootoos" on the return trip, including the tale of Badang's fishing and wrestling with an evil spirit in this place, as it was immortalized at the beginning of story six of the *Sejarah Melayu* in 1612 (the Badang "Hantu" episode). Viator, with his "fellow travellers",[16] had thus viewed "the place ... called *Kota tingeh*"[17] with the Malay royal graves present there (see below) and were headed downstream back to Singapore in a rowboat. He writes:

---

[14] That this is "the eastern bank" will soon be made apparent by Viator.

[15] Malay *sĕra* as midge. This meaning is not in Klinkert, who only has the synonymous *rĕngit*.

[16] Rouffaer, part 1, p. 264.

[17] Ibid., p. 268.

> About two miles lower down, we came to a sharp angle of the river [!] where the eastern bank is about 20 feet high and worn by the force of the stream; hence it is called *Tanjong Pootoos*. On the convex side (or on the opposite shore, the SW side) there was a ripple as if the water was passing over sunken rocks; this, in the native tradition, is the remains of the weir made by Si Badang celebrated in the Malay Annals for his feats of strength.[18]

Viator—who simply cannot be anyone else than Crawfurd—then adds a detail that amuses modern readers:

> It was this same Si Badang, who, having been chosen champion to the Rajah of Singapore, in a trial of strength with a Kling champion, took up a large rock which his antagonist could not lift and pitched it into the sea at the entrance of the Singapore river, where it still remains a stumbling block to the orang Kling [namely when they navigate into the *kuwala*]; but the members of the Singapore Yacht Club have put a beacon upon it for the public benefit, finding that none of their number was strong enough to pitch it back again.[19]

Does not this testimony from August 1826 indirectly support what the ex-Singaporean W.H.(M.) Read remembered in 1884, when he said of this stone with the Old-Javanese inscription: "It used to be decorated with flags and offerings when at the entrance of the Singapore River"?[20]

Now that we have collected these 19th-century data regarding the location of Batu Sawar, first of all, that which the *Sejarah Melayu* narrates so nonchalantly in its closing chapter 38 (Appendix of the *Sejarah Melayu*)—apparently even forging the true history—becomes clear. After all, it claims that up to 1621 (1021 AH) no less than five *kota* were founded by the successive sultans, namely:

1. Johor (Lama), with a canal between the S. Johor (upstream) and the S. Kerting (downstream), founded by Sultan Alauddin Ri'ayat Shah II.[21]
2. Seluyud, at or near the Kuala Seluyud, founded by his son Sultan Mudhafar Shah II and also inhabited by his successor (indecisive, young, and soon simply "deceased").[22]
3. Tanah Putih, renamed Batu Sawar. Founded by Raja Umar of Pahang, who (as a factual usurper and brother-in-law of Mudhafar Shah) worked his way to the throne as Sultan (Ali Jala) Abdu'l Jalil (Ri'ayat) Shah I. Said to have served only as a residence *sa-kira-kira duwa tahun*![23]

---

[18] A.N.: "The story goes; Si Bandang, etc.". Viator continues with a long story based on Leyden's 1821 translation of the *Sejarah Melayu* (London: Longman, Hurst, Rees, Orme, and Brown), pp. 53–6.

[19] Ibid.

[20] See the full quotation from Read in Buckley in Rouffaer, part 1, p. 54n1.

[21] Shellabear, ed., *Sejarah Melayu* (1898), p. 176, l. 18–9.

[22] Ibid., p. 184, ll. 10–1 and 6 from the bottom. This ephemeral sultan bears the name of S. Abdu'l Jalil Shah here, being Raja Umar's son by a daughter of S. Alauddin Ri'ayat Shah (and a full sister of S. Mudhafar Shah). He was appointed sultan by his dying uncle Mudhafar, but soon died a natural death at the age of nine himself, having refused on his deathbed to appoint his very own uncle (Raja Umar) as successor! See also Rouffaer, part 1.

[23] Ibid., p. 189, ll. 1 and 3–4.

4. Makam Tauḥid [Impregnable Residence], situated *di hulu S. Damar, di dalam S. Batu Sawar itu*. Founded by Sultan Abdu'l Jalil as well.[24]
5. Pasar Raja [Our Raja], situated *di hulu kuwala S. Riun*. Founded by the former's son, the rash (preferably drunk, that is) new Sultan Alauddin Ri'ayat Shah III, formerly called Raja Mansur; the "youngest brother", Raja Abdullah,[25] who was more suitable, had turned down the throne when the bendahara (patih, chief minister) offered it to him. This Raja Abdullah was *beristana di sabrang, Pangkalan Raya*; which is why the people also called him Raja Sabrang.[26]

The big forgery lies exactly in the duration of Batu Sawar as a *kota* [city]. Instead of "roughly two years", Batu Sawar was certainly the centre of the state of Johor for *over 25 years*: from after the destruction of Johor/Johor Lama by the Portuguese on 15 August 1587,[27] until 6 June 1613, when Aceh in turn destroyed the second centre of state.[28] Although for a short time after that catastrophe, Batu Sawar regained its position as the centre of the state, from ca. October 1613 to September 1615 (*two years, just!*) under the new sultan Abdullah Ma'ayat Shah who was sent there from Aceh.[29] This sultan was no other person than Raja Abdullah (Raja Sabrang) who was just mentioned, who had been taken prisoner by Aceh on 6 June 1613, dragged off, but pardoned shortly after; aka Raja Bongsu (Young Prince), aka Raja Ilir, more correctly *Raja di Ilir* (Downstream Prince), who will shortly be discussed in more detail.

But then, Batu Sawar's days were really over. For the new king[30] was not submissive enough toward the Acehnese. In August 1615, Sultan Iskandar Muda (r. 1607–36) dispatched another fleet from Aceh, allegedly against Melaka but actually against Johor, and razed Batu Sawar to the ground. On (?) September was Batu Sawar indeed so totally destroyed, that Sultan Abdullah Ma'ayat Shah—also called Sultan Hammat Shah, it seems—fled to Bintan, later to flee to Lingga (Daik),

---

[24] Ibid., ll. 7–8 and 10.

[25] Perhaps this "youngest brother or half-brother" (Raja Bongsu of the Portuguese and also Dutch reports, see below) should be taken with a pinch of salt. The *Sejarah Melayu* claims that he was a secret child of S. Mudhafar Shah by an older *istri* of Raja Umar (from Pahang), who was later repudiated by the latter and silently remarried with Mudhafar; and, therefore, a son of the *legitimate* S. Mudhafar, *not* of the usurper Abdu'l Jalil.

[26] Ibid., p. 190, ll. 7–8 and 3–4; also, the end of the entire text but for one paragraph which can be called the colophon of the appendix; see below.

[27] See also above. The "1588" in Eredia, *Malaca l'Inde Méridionale et le Cathay*, fol. 44 verso (dating from 1613) is incorrect. See the extensive survey of this destruction, based on Diogo do Couto's *Década*, vol. 10 (dating from 1595, 1788 ed. [see note 34 below]), part 2; and J.H. van Linschoten's *Itinerario* (Amsterdam: Cornelis Claesz., 1596), cap. 92, fol. 122b, in P.A. Tiele, "De Europeërs in den Maleischen Archipel", part 5, *BKI* 29, 2 (1881): 173–7.

[28] This is discussed in Rouffaer, part 1, on the occasion of the unreliable date in the introduction to that same *Sejarah Melayu*.

[29] This is likewise mentioned in the Introduction.

[30] A.N.: Who as Raja Sabrang (the former Sultan Alauddin Ri'ayat Shah III, r. ca. 1597–6 to June 1613), had been his elder brother, was a prisoner in Aceh, and soon died there as a factotum.

constantly hunted by the men of Aceh, and ended his life as a pretender on Greater Tambelan (one of the Pulau Tujuh) in the middle of 1623 (*not* later!). Only in 1641 did a resurrection there follow, which came to a disgraceful end in 1673.[31]

Thus the bendahara, Tun Muhamad, with his childhood name (*timangan*) Sri Lanang or Tun Sri Lanang,[32] the author-compiler of the *Sejarah Melayu*, Paduka Raja according to his official title (*gĕlaran*), committed two shameless forgeries, with his fantastic *dal* 1021 AH in the introduction as well as his "two years at an estimate" at the end of chapter 38 regarding the duration of the *nĕgĕri* of Batu Sawar. This is all the more shameless since he dates that introduction *from* "Bātu Sāwar dār as-salām" (B.S., land of peace). And in chapter 38 he also narrates that he himself, Tun Sri Lanang, was raised to the office of bendahara—five days after the death of his father, Bendahara Paduka Raja—by Sultan Ali Jala Abdu'l Jalil (Ri'ayat) Shah, mentioned above, who, according to Portuguese reports, which call him Raja Ale (pronounced "Razya Ali"), had usurped the throne of Johor in 1580 or 1581 (before mid-1582 in any case);[33] and he took office before Batu Sawar was founded, that is, before the destruction of Johor Lama in August 1587.[34] We can conclude that he was appointed bendahara around 1585 and that he moved with his king to the newly founded Batu Sawar around 1588, and that according to his own testimony in the introduction he still lived there in 1021 AH (4 March 1612 through 20 February 1613), holding his full office and wielding his full power.

The mere fact is that until now no one knew any longer (I am not afraid to state) where exactly this Batu Sawar, cradle of the *Sejarah Melayu*, had been. This caused people to overlook it, mistranslate it, or put it aside as too elusive.[35] But now it is time for clear light to be shed upon it by serious local research. There need not be any doubt that the *kota* of that name used to be where I have mapped it. And

---

[31] See below.

[32] In Dulaurier's introduction in *Collection des principales chroniques malayes (deuxième fascicule, la suite des annales malayes)* (Paris: Imprimerie nationale, 1856), ed., p. 4, l. 16, he is called "Tun Muhamad namanya, Seri Lanang timangannya, Paduka Raja gelarannya, Bendahara, anak" (W.G. Shellabear, *Sejarah Melayu; or, the Malay Annals*, 2nd ed. [Singapore: M.P.H., 1910], introduction, p. 2), also correcting the punctuation in the 1898 edition: "Tun Muhamad namanya, Tun Seri Lanang timang-timangannya, Paduka Raja gelarannya, Bendahara, anak", etc. For the rest of the text see below.

[33] J. de Barros and D. do Couto, *Décadas da Asia. Dos feitos que os Portuguezes fizeram no conquista, e descubrimento das terras e mares do Oriente* (Lisbon: Na Regia Officina Typographia, 1788), vol. 10, part 1, p. 272: *Rafale* (typographical error for *Rajale*); Eredia in his 1613 *Declaraçam de Malaca* (Janssen ed., 1882), fol. 44 verso: *Raya Ale* and *Raja Ale*. For the date and the correct spelling *Rajale* in Do Couto (this spelling on pp. 421, 468), see Tiele, "De Europeërs", part 5, pp. 169–70.

[34] Shellabear, ed., *Sejarah Melayu* (1898), pp. 188–9.

[35] Leyden translates: "*Malāka* [or arabified *Malākat* in other texts; compare with the end of story 1] nĕgĕrinya. Bātu Sāwar dār as-salām". With "the signet of whose country is of the Sawal gem" (p. 2)! L.M. Devic, *Legendes et traditions historiques de l'archipel Indie* (Paris: Leroux, 1878) and A. Marre, *Sadjârah malâyou* (Vaucressons: n.p., 1900) took the easy and indeed safest way out and neglected to translate the complicated introduction altogether! See the translation of this sentence beginning with "Batu Sawar" below.

"Tanah Putih" (which must have been its former name, as appears in the *Sejarah Melayu*: "Hata Sulṭan Ali Jala Abdu'l-Jalil Shah pun pindah dari Seluyud, membuwat negeri di Tanah Putih, maka di-namaï Batu Sawar"),[36] is already clarified by Hervey's description of his "Batu Sâwa": "with red and white soil shewing on the bank where the river has eaten into rising ground". Closer local research will certainly confirm this and will also reveal where the S. Batu Sawar, and the S. Damar that in turn flows into it, lie exactly. On the latter,[37] Sultan Abdu'l Jali Shah appears to have had his private *kota*, his *dalam*, and his Makam Tauḥid (lit. "Grave in God's unity"), in which he could imagine himself at one with Allah and therefore invulnerable.

No wonder that foreigners coming to Batu Sawar (namely some Portuguese and after February 1603, mostly Dutchmen with Jacob van Heemskerck's factor,[38] in particular Admiral Matelieff in September 1606 and Admiral Verhoeff [or Verhoeven] in January 1609) paid no attention to the decayed secondary residence Seluyut from 1567–87,[39] nor mention this Makam Tauḥid, which in any case must have been very close to Batu Sawar, but knew only of Batusauwer or Batusabar. These two admirals' travelogues, included in part 2 of Isaac Commelin's *Begin ende Voortgangh* (edited in 1645 or 1646), especially that of Matelieff, provide invaluable details regarding the location and nature of this centre of Johor's power, which was deserted first in 1615 and definitively after 1673 and where the *Sejarah Melayu* must have been started and finished by the aforementioned bendahara between 1612 and 1614. Matelieff's log not only portrayed the two sultans at whose instigation he wrote his history—Alauddin Ri'ayat Shah and Abdullah Ma'ayat Shah, aka Raja Sabrang, both glorified in the introduction and at the end of the appendix, especially the latter—but also the bendahara himself!

The first fact was cleverly brought back to memory by Wilkinson in 1908 in his *Papers On Malay Subjects: History*, based on the Dutch data in E. Netscher's standard work[40] but without mentioning Netscher as his source, as was his wont. The latter fact has so far escaped everybody's attention; yet in order to get a feel for the *spirit* with which the *Sejarah Melayu* was in part composed from older Malay (probably even Melakan) hikayat, in part continued for the new Johor era until about 1612 by the bendahara, this is extremely important.

Here are those three portraits, painted by Abraham van den Broeck, secretary to Admiral Cornelis Matelieff de Jonge, at the Melaka roadstead on the 17 and 27 May 1606:[41]

---

[36] Shellabear, ed., *Sejarah Melayu* (1898), as cited.

[37] See above.

[38] Jacob Buys (or Buysen), who was merchant at Batu Sawar from Feb. 1603 to the end of 1605; see Netscher, *De Nederlanders in Djohor en Siak*, pp. 7–9; and esp. P.A. Tiele, "De Europeërs in den Maleischen Archipel", part 6, *BKI* 30, 2 (1882): 197 (where "Ruys" is a typographical error), 217, 239–40.

[39] See above.

[40] See also Netscher, *De Nederlanders*, p. 35.

[41] It appears from Admiral Matelieff's log, p. 85, and in Dec. 1609 from that of Admiral Verhoeff (*BV* 2, 15: 40b) that Abraham van den Broeck, factor at Johor from October 1607 to February 1609, was Matelieff's "secretary".

Sultan Alauddin Ri'ayat Shah, aka Yang-di-pertuan:

> In order to understand his situation, one should know that the old king of Johor (namely, Sultan [Ali Jala] Abdul Jalil [Ri'ayat] Shah, r. ca. 1580–ca. 1597), who was a good warrior and was often at war with the Portuguese, left four sons. The eldest now rules and is called *Ian de Patuan* by the *Malays*, but that seems to be his title rather than his name.[42] King Ian de Patuan equally (like his half-brother, the *Raja Siak*) is a person of little activity, used to sleeping until it is almost noon; then he eats and washes and proceeds to get drunk, so that he is impossible to deal with after noon, for one has to drink with him and do drunkards' things. He does not trouble himself with anything, leaving everything to the noblemen (that is, in the first place the bendahara or patih) and *Raya Zabrang*. He does not want to hear about any difficulties, and if one urges him to do something, mustering men or things like that, he simply is silent; and if one asks him two or three times, it is all the same. To sum up, there is nothing he is less capable of than being a king; he does not think of his kingdom or his subjects as long as he has wine and women.[43]

Raja Sabrang (aka Raja Abdullah, Raja Bongsu, Raja di Ilir), appointed Sultan Abdullah Ma'ayat Shah by Aceh in Batu Sawar ca. October 1613:

> By his second wife [who also bore the *Raja Siak*], the [old] king of *Iohor* had *Raya Bonsu* who is now called *Raya Zabrang*, meaning "king of the other side", because he lives on the other side of the river from the city of *Battusabar*, where he has a fortress as well [namely the *Kota Sabrang*, see below], and part of his subjects; but he is a vassal of *Ian de Patuan*. He is about thirty-five years old [therefore born ca. 1571], almost white, not very tall, but wise, forgiving, not choleric, and very prudent; an enemy of the Portuguese [and, as becomes apparent further on in the text,[44] even more so of Aceh, albeit in secret], industrious in his business, which he would also conduct energetically if he had the power. In short, worthy of being king of *Iohor* and *Melaka*. He would also recognise the help one would spend on him, and inasfar as could be judged, he is completely loyal to us. He always respects his brother *Ian de Patuan*, who loves him much as well,

---

[42] The sentences skipped here in the main text describe a second son, a certain Raja Siak: "By another woman he had *Raia Siacai*, which means *king of Siaca*; Siaca is a fief of the crown of *Iohor*. He married the king of *Patane*'s daughter and is a man of little activity and not blessed with any kingly virtues, but a naïve fool; he always stays in *Siaca* and rarely goes to *Iohor*." According to the *Sejarah Melayu*, end of story 38, he was called Hasan as a boy.

[43] *BV*, vol. 2, no. 13, p. 11.

[44] For after various meetings regarding a combined attack against the city of Melaka, "He [*Raja Bonsu* or *Zabrang*] then took the admiral and the interpreter apart and whispered into their ears that he asked that an expedition to Aceh be made with him, to drive out its king. But the admiral said…." (ibid., p. 13a). This is also on 17 May 1606.

> but of course *Ian de Patuan* secretly harbours quite a bit of jealousy....[45] All the brothers drink wine, except *Raja Zabrang*, who has never tasted wine or spirits; and as the lord is, such are the noblemen of all these kings.[46]

But now the so-far unnoticed portrait of the bendahara, that is, the author of the *Sejarah Melayu*, Tun Muhamad aka Sri Lanang ("little guy-fellow"?):

> The bendahara even had the audacity [after Matelieff had tried in vain to conquer the *kota* Melaka since 18 May, weakly supported by the allied Johor fleet] to say to the admiral [on 27 May], in the king's presence while he was in his council [i.e. in a *majelis*; think of the Introduction of the *Sejarah Melayu* which speaks of a *majelis* of the high courtiers held in Batu Sawar six years later, probably on Mawlid Day (Muhammad's Birthday) of the year *Jimawal* (*not* Dal) 1021 AH (Sunday, 13 May 1612) and in which the *idea* of the *Sejarah Melayu* was first brought up by a "most high orang besar", namely, Raja Sabrang], that our people [the Dutch] had conquered Ternate [here read *Tidore*] and *Amboyna* [Ambon] without the inhabitants' help [on 19 May and 23 February 1605 respectively], and therefore they ought to do so in this case [Melaka] as well; for he [the bendahara] had not come to fight, but to watch the fight. To which the admiral replied: "I have come here as a servant to the king *Ian de Patuan*, whose war this was. And if you do not wish to be his servant, nor do him any service, you may say so; and if king *Ian de Patuan* commands me to, I will make such people leave here". When the king heard this, he was annoyed with the bendahara, and many noblemen were quite pleased that the admiral spoke to him like that, since [!!] he was an arrogant fool and a rude beast, who seemed to be more on the Portuguese than on the Dutch side. His position was that of the king's vice-regent.[47]

Isn't it delicious, this snapshot of 27 May 1606, this time on the Melakan shore in the northern Kampung Kling (Upih), which had been conquered on 18 May? And how palpable is Van den Broeck's (who stayed behind at Batu Sawar as Matelieff's factor in October next and remained in function there until February 1609) partiality in favour of the pro-Dutch Raja Sabrang[48] and against the anti-Dutch bendahara! The bendahara took his revenge in his *Sejarah Melayu*: he does not mention a single Dutchman in Johor or anywhere else. They do not exist for him in his history, although he had continuous political and commercial dealings with them for 10 to

---

[45] Here follows the portrait of the fourth son, a certain Raja Laut: "From his third wife, the old king of *Iohor* has a son named *Raja Laud*, that is 'king of the sea'—a man incapable of anything but smoking *tobacco*, drinking *arak* and eating *bettele* with it, indeed worthy of being bound hands and feet and sunk into the sea; a big drunkard, killer and fornicator, and everything to do with those three things he knows inside out" (ibid., p. 11b). This person is *not* mentioned in the *Sejarah Melayu*.

[46] Ibid., pp. 11b–2a.

[47] Ibid., p. 18b.

[48] Raja Bongsu's (Eredia calls him "Raja Benco" or Bonço) goodwill toward the Dutch is explicitly acknowledged by Eredia in his *Declaraçam de Malaca*, dated Goa, 24 Nov. 1613; see Janssen's 1882 ed. (albeit *very careless and unsatisfactory*), fol. 44b at the bottom; translation p. 53. Eredia, temporarily staying at Goa, had no knowledge at the time of what had happened in Johor on 6 June 1613.

12 years! And Wilkinson was mainly right when after a survey of this Dutch narrative from Matelieff's voyage he cleverly noted in 1908:

> But we must not condemn these men too hastily. The bendahara or prime minister of these princes was the author of the Annals, our great source of information on Malay history. The royal drunkard, Alaedin Riayat Shah, was the man who ordered the Annals to be written.[49] The "great hand at driving hard bargains"[50]—Raja Abdullah—is the patron of the history: "Sultan Abdullah Maayat Shah, the glory of his land and of his time, the chief of the assembly of true believers, the ornament of the abodes of the Faithful—may God enhance his generosity and his dignities, and perpetuate his just government over all his estates" [another free rendering of a few sentences from the end of the Introduction of the S.M.]. These men must have been something more than mere drunkards; and the historian has reason to be grateful to them.[51]

Now, however, we can make statements with a much sharper outline regarding the three protagonists from the introduction and conclusion of the *Sejarah Melayu* (in its complete form) than what Wilkinson wrote down here, in part rightly, in part rather superficially. This is more so because the passage on the bendahara was not noticed by Netscher and therefore remained unknown to Wilkinson. Here are my conclusions:

1. Two persons, *not* three, are behind the birth of the *Sejarah Melayu* at Batu Sawar in 1612–14: Bendahara Tun Muhamad as its author, Raja Sabrang as the instigator of its conception and beginning (certainly) and further execution (probably). Neither was a drunkard: nor the raja (later sultan), as Matelieff's secretary expressly acknowledges, nor in all likelihood the patih, whose portrait Van den Broeck renders in a highly one-sided and hostile way.
2. The drunkard-Sultan Alaudin Ri'ayat Shah III (ca. 1596/97 to June 1613) plays a purely symbolic part in the introduction. Of course, he is extolled in byzantine fashion, because *up to* that fateful date as Yang-di-pertuan, he had officially been the high king; but *after* "he had departed [to meet his Maker] at Aceh" he was the "Marhum yang mangkat di Aceh", who had ended his life there as a prisoner and ousted sultan, probably murdered or else because he drank himself to death. Merely symbolically, he is mentioned

---

[49] A.N.: *Wrong*—see below.

[50] A.N.: A free interpretation of the Dutch translated above as "industrious in his business, which he would also conduct energetically if he had the power".

[51] R.J. Wilkinson, *Papers on Malay Subjects: History*, parts I–II (Kuala Lumpur: F.M.S. Government Press, 1908), p. 46. Reprint of part I in the same year (only omitting the chapter "Early British Trade With Eastern Asia") in the slightly abridged and in the luxury edition of the *Twentieth-Century Impressions of British Malaya* (London: Lloyd's Greater Britain Publishing Company, 1908); see ibid., pp. 90, 93. Wilkinson practically understands Dutch, as he told me himself when I had the privilege to make his acquaintance at Taiping (Perak) on 26–28 May 1909. Shellabear understands it well.

In the 2nd revised edition of Wilkinson's aforementioned work—this time under the title *A History of the Peninsular Malays, with Chapters on Perak and Selangor*, 2nd rev. ed. (Singapore: Kelly & Walsh, 1920)—this was reprinted word for word, apart from the last paragraph, which goes: "These men were not mere drunkards; and the historian, at least, has reason to be grateful to them."

twice in it: first as Sultan Alaudin Ri'ayat Shah (A.R.S.), *during* whose reign the idea of the *Sejarah Melayu* was brought up; and immediately after that as the "baginda", who "just" (*sedang*) "resided at Pasai" (*bernegeri di Pasai*) when the "high order" (*titah*) reached the bendahara from "*Yang-di-pertuan-di-hilir*, Sultan Abdullah Ma'ayat Shah" to begin writing his hikayat. Since by far the most scholars of Malay had not acquainted themselves with this history and some like Netscher, Wilkinson and Dr Hussein lacked any notion of the location of Batu Sawar and Pasar Raja,[52] these words remained mysterious and were airily ignored. But in less diplomatic words, this last statement says: *after* Sultan A.R.S. had been captured and taken from Batu Sawar to Pasai in Aceh on 6 June 1613, and *after* the younger half-brother Raja Abdullah (Bongsu or Sabrang or *di ilir*), who had equally been taken away as a prisoner, had been brought back by an Aceh fleet in September or October 1613 and installed at Batu Sawar as the new *Yang-di-pertuan*—who apparently remained in personal residence at his old Kota Sabrang (aka *di ilir*)[53]—*then* that high order reached the bendahara to really start "making" (*perbuwatkan*) that hikayat. The *true* portrait which the bendahara (Tun Sri

[52] See Rouffaer, part 2, pp. 504–5 at j.

[53] In his important study—"Critisch overzicht van de in Maleische werken vervatte gegevens over de geschiedenis van het Soeltanaat van Atjeh" [Critical survey of the data concerning the history of the Aceh Sultanate found in Malay works], *BKI* 65 (1911): 179.—Dr Hussein Jayadiningrat on occasion defended the position that it was *not* Raja Sabrang who was sent back to Johor by Aceh as the new sultan shortly after the destruction of Batu Sawar on 6 June 1613, but that it *was* the old drunkard sultan who was reinstated to the throne. Wrongly so. It was in fact Raja Sabrang (as the Dutch mostly called him) or Raja Bongsu (as the Portuguese used to say) who ascended to the Johor throne as the *new Yang-di-pertuan* in the autumn of 1613, as Aceh's middleman and Sultan Iskandar Muda's brother-in-law. It was *because* he was a creature of Aceh that he was sometimes "summoned" there, which caused the apparent contradiction in what Tiele wrote in "De Europeërs", part 8, *BKI* 35, 3 (1886): 303, 305, 307 (see Hussein's note 3). To confirm Tiele's view, we may point out the following information from a Portuguese source, published after Tiele's essay had been printed:

(1) R.A. de Bulhão Pato, ed., *Documentos remettidos da Índia ou Livros das Monções*, vol. 3 (Lisbon: Typographia da Academia Real das Sciencias, 1885), p. 380, where "Raja Bonso" is the ruler of Johor who had made the *same* agreement with the Dutch as the one on which Adriaen van der Dussen reported from "Batosawar" in his role of envoy to that ruler, 25 Aug.–28 Sept. 1614 (see his "Cort Verhael" [Brief report] dated Bantam, 10 Nov. 1614 in P.A. Tiele and J.E. Heeres, ed., *Bouwstoffen voor de Geschiedenis der Nederlanders in den Maleischen Archipel*, 3 vols. [The Hague: Martinus Nijhoff, 1886], vol. 1, pp. 70–9).

(2) R.A. de Bulhão Pato, ed., *Documentos remettidos da India ou Livros das Monções*, vol. 4, pp. 314–5, where mention is made of Aceh's attack with a large fleet, first against "the king of Johor" and unsuccessful (because the said king had left for Bintan, as we know from Abraham van den Broeck and Steven van der Haghen among others; see Tiele, p. 308), then against "the kingdom of Pahang, where a son of the king of Johor reigned", which corresponds to what Steven van der Haghen reported around 1 Dec. 1615, in his letter to the Directors dated Jacatra, 10 March 1616 (Tiele, *Bouwstoffen*, vol. 1, pp. 118–9).

Lanang or Tun Muhamad or Paduka Raja) dares to give of this former sultan at the end of story 38 is not flattering: transferring his kraton very rashly to the higher position of Pasar Raja, despite the prudent advice of "his younger brother, Prince Raja Abdullah, and Bendahara Paduka Raja" (*adinda Baginda Raja Abdullah dengan bendahara Paduka Raja*),[54] in other words, of Raja Sabrang *and himself*, Tun Muhamad!

Perfect reading for anyone who likes human comedy and the diplomatic phrases that go with it.

3. The true *auctor intellectualis* [instigator] of the *Sejarah Melayu*, in fact, was Raja Sabrang, before 6 June 1613. After his metamorphosis to sultan in September or October 1613, it was *he* as well who *ordered* the bendahara—now *his* bendahara—to write that hikayat. As the messenger of that order the new sultan used a certain Tun Mambang, a prominent person from Patani. There need not be any doubt: Those veiled words of praise were meant for no one else but Raja Sabrang in the first part of the introduction, "sa-orang orang besar, terlebih muliyanya dan terlebih martabatnya daripada yang lain",[55] as the person who first brought up the idea of such a historiography during a crown council (*majelis*). And when that most distinguished person (second only to Yang-di-pertuan) begins to speak to that end—"My insignificant self heard that someone from Goa brought a Malay hikayat" and then encourages the making of a better one[56]—this again is no one but Raja Sabrang, to whom, after all, any "foreign" matters were addressed first, and who had personally—*not* the Yang-di-pertuan—sent a high-ranking Johorese envoy, Megat Mansur, with a retinue including an Encik Kamar as its most important member, to Prince Maurice in the spring of 1603 on Jacob van Heemskerck's ship.[57]

Incidentally, one need only read Matelieff's story of his negotiations with Raja Sabrang in *1606* (*BV*, vol. 2, 13, pp. 12–5 and 31–4) first, and then Van der Dussen's Brief Report from *1614* just mentioned, to recognise the very same Malay prince: an apparently mysterious, very calculating, not to say cunning intellectual who as a Malay prince had more power in his brains than in his hands. He lacked courage.

Now see also H.T. Colenbrander, ed., *Jan Pieterszoon Coen: Bescheiden Omtrent Zijn Bedrijf in Indië* (The Hague: Martinus Nijhoff, 1919), vol. 1, pp. 27, 35, 135, 180, 204, 349, 414, 739.

[54] Shellabear, ed., *Sejarah Melayu* (1898), p. 190, ll. 8–9.

[55] Ibid., p. 1.

[56] Ibid., pp. 1–2, or Shellabear, ed., *Sejarah Melayu* (1910), p. 2, ll. 20–2. The original quote here is: "Hamba dengar ada hikayat Melayu di bawa oleh orang dari Goa; barang kita perbaïki kiranya dengan istiadataya, supaya". Wilkinson *mistakenly* thought (see above) that these were the "royal drunkard's" words.

[57] Few facts are known about this Johorese embassy. Megat Mansur (see Verhoeff's log in *BV*, vol. 2, 15, p. 204b) died on board Van Heemskerck's ship (the *Witte Leeuw* [White Lion], which left Bantam for Holland in October 1603 and arrived there in July 1604, with the rich Portuguese carrack taken at Ujung Tanah on 25 Feb. 1603) before he ever saw Holland. Encik Kamar, and probably the entire Johorese retinue, boarded Matelieff's fleet, which sailed from Texel on 12 May 1605 and arrived at Melaka on 30 April 1606. That same evening, Matelieff sent two Dutchmen and "Ambassador *Camar* to the king of *Johor* in a yacht, to announce his arrival, and to say that His Majesty should join him immediately with all his troops" (Matelieff's

However, we can fortunately determine with overwhelming probability the *terminus a quo* on which such a "Malay (historical) hikayat" could have been brought to Batu Sawar by "someone from Goa"—again, this should be understood in less diplomatic language as "a Portuguese official from Melaka"!

Namely: 1 October 1610, when "the Ambassador from Melaka, who was a born Portuguese named Joan Lopez de Morere Tonbongon" arrived at "Jhoor" (the capital of Johor or Batu Sawar) in order to make the peace between Johor and Melaka, which was subsequently ratified in Melaka at the end of that October by two Johorese envoys who had travelled there with this João Lopes d'Amoreira, temenggong of Melaka.[58]

A beautiful addition to this is the date mentioned in the introduction as the day of the crown council (majelis), in which the said "most high lord" brought up the idea of such an improved (historical) hikayat: the Mawlid holiday (12 Rabi'ulawal 1021 AH which is Sunday, 13 May 1612) (the forgery of Chamis for the weekday and Dal for the cycle year [Malay Arabic *daur*; here the *daur ketjil* or Jav. *windu*] has been calculated away). And lastly, one will note in the very wording of the introduction that the train of thought in which this *sa-orang orang besar* utters his *wish* on this Mawlid Day (Malay *kiranya* which means "o that … !" or "o, may … !") is exactly the same as that in which he phrases his *high order* (*titah*) once he has become "*mahamuliya*"—namely, *Yang-di-pertuan* (*Besar*) as "great king".[59]

4. Thus, the honour of taking the initiative and the honour of giving the royal commission both belong to the definitely quiet intellectual Raja Sabrang

---

log, in *BV*, vol. 2, 13, p. 7a). On 13 May this cutter, once more with "Yntse Camar" on board, was back before Melaka carrying a letter from Raja Sabrang (ibid., pp. 10b–1a), while on 17 May Matelieff himself says to Raja Sabrang: "although he (Raya Zabrang) had sent his envoys [!!] to Holland with presents for His Excellency (Prince Maurice), nonetheless it was *Ian de Patuan* (Sultan Alaudin Ri'ayat Shah) who was ruling king; therefore he asked *Raya Zabrang*" (ibid., p. 15b). See also the note in Netscher, *De Nederlanders in Djohor en Siak*, p. 8n2, and compare with p. 35. This is all we know about it!

[58] We know his true name from Bulhão Pato, ed., *Documentos remettidos da India*, vol. 4, p. 315, in a letter from the governor general dated Goa, 9 Feb. 1619 (translated): "João Lopes d'Amoreira, citizen of Melaka and temenggong of the foreigners—a great friend of the king of Johor's father", that is, a great friend of the deceased Sultan Abdu'l Jalil Shah (d. ca. 1597); see also p. 313. This sheds full light on the aforementioned Dutch statement by Jacques Obelaer, senior merchant of the Dutch lodge at Batu Sawar, dated "Jhoor", 25 Nov. 1610 (J.K.J. de Jonge, *Opkomst van het Nederlandsch gezag in Oost-Indië* (The Hague: Martinus Nijhoff, 1865), vol. 3, p. 305; Tiele gives a faulty excerpt of this in "De Europeërs", part 7, *BKI* 32, 1 [1884]: 111). Moreover, his correct name is still found nowadays on a gravestone in Melaka (transferred to the Old Dutch Church aka Christ's Church), inscribed: "S[epultura] d[e] I[oão; the *I* has a little *o* over it] Lopes Damoreira e d[e] seus herdeiros", therefore his own and his heirs' grave; see the picture, with a reasonably good explanation, in R.N. Bland, *Historical Tombstones of Malacca, Mostly of Portuguese* [or rather "Dutch"] *Origin* (London: Elliot Stock, 1905), pp. 14–5.

[59] In both transliterated editions by Shellabear, ed., *Sejarah Melayu* (1898), p. 2, l. 13 from the bottom; (1910), p. 3, l. 14 from the bottom), one has *neglected* to place closing quotation marks at the end of the "bunyi titah yang Mahamuliya itu". The quotation ends after "daripadanya".

> (Sultan Abdullah Ma'ayat Shah); but the *author-compiler* of the *Sejarah Melayu* remains Bendahara Tun Muhamad. Without a doubt he was a haughty Malay, so much so that his fellow orang kayas felt tacit pleasure when Matelieff squarely told him off in the presence of princes and noblemen on 27 May 1606. Nor should it be doubted that he was pro-Portuguese and anti-Dutch; but it is just as certain that he was the contrary of a "rude beast", as Van den Broeck simply wrote.
>
> Now can we perhaps also lift a tip of the veil behind which he partially wrote his "Malay genealogy" and partially borrowed its substance from the writings of others?

He must have been born around 1565 at the latest; for, as we learnt earlier from his own information.[60] In about 1585 he succeeded his father (Bendahara Paduka Raja I) as bendahara with the same official title (Bendahara Paduka Raja II). Since Matelieff in 1606 describes Raja Sabrang as "a man of about 35 years old", the bendahara was about 40 years old then and a little over 45 on the Mawlid Holiday when Raja Sabrang's idea "fell so heavy on the poor man's body" (*jadi beratlah atas anggota fakir*). The next year, on that fatal 6 June 1613, with a probability of 99 per cent he was amongst the numerous orang kayas dragged off into captivity by the men of Aceh at Batu Sawar—together with Sultan Raja Sabrang, and no less than 22 Dutchmen! But with the same degree of probability, he belonged to the Johorese who were pardoned and who returned in or about September next in the retinue of the new sultan, with the sultan's new spouse—a sister of Sultan Iskandar Muda, the formidable Aceh prince—and his escort of "protectors" from Aceh commanded by Lela Wangsa. He must have lived at Batu Sawar once more then, which he, as the new sultan's right hand, had to rebuild from its ashes; while Sultan Abdullah Ma'ayat Shah[61] kept

---

[60] See above.

[61] Or as Netscher calls him, apparently based on ruler chronicles continued at Riau and Lingga, "Sulthan Hammat Shah" in Netscher, *De Nederlanders in Djohor en Siak*, pp. 31–2. This name in Netscher was copied by Tiele in "De Europeërs", part 8, *BKI* 35, 3 (1886): 305 and further. It appears to have been taken from what Netscher in his elaborate work of 1870 calls "the great Malay chronicle" or "the great Malay chronicle [*Sejarah Melayu*]". On those pages he gives a translated survey of 1699–1721 from it, that is, from a version of the *Sejarah Melayu* that was continued later (on Riau, Lingga or elsewhere in this Malay island group). For this vague description, we find a perfect match in the great "Shajarah Raja Raja Malayu", described by Dr Van Ronkel as manuscript no. 354 in his *Catalogus der Maleische HSS in het Museum Bataviaasch Genootschap van Kunsten en Wetenschappen* [Catalogue of the Malay manuscripts in the Museum of the Batavia Society of Arts and Sciences], vol. 57 (Batavia: Albrecht & Co., and The Hague: Martinus Nijhoff, 1909), pp. 274–5: it was written in *1272 AH or 1855/6 CE* by the Malay scribe of Assistant Resident H. von de Wall, the well-known scholar of Malay who then was assistant resident at Sukadana (in southwest Borneo). In this Tengku Said's *Sejarah*, 341 pages long, the entire older *Sejarah Melayu*, modified here and there, is given first on pp. 1–197, 38 stories long (so including the *Sejarah Melayu*'s appendix. It is followed by the "younger" Malay history, ca. 1610(?)–1842 (Governor-General Merkus's time). Of course, in this case Tengku Said also was both author and compiler from Malay from the 17th- to 18th-century manuscripts he had at his disposal. A single comparison of this manusript in Batavia by

his residence in his old Kota Sabrang, at the other side, but "downstream" from his predecessor's last kraton, Pasar Raja. This also sheds light on how it is narrated in the introduction that the Patani prince—the royal families of Johor and Patani were closely linked indeed, as were those of Johor and Pahang—a certain Tun Mambang,[62] came to "lay upon" (*menjunjungkan*) him, Tun Muhamad, the "command" (or "high order", *titah*) from the *Yang-di-pertuan di hilir* to start composing his hikayat. The experience of exile in Aceh apparently gave the intellectual sultan a desire to own such a "Malay" history to the glory of Minangkabau-Palembang-Singhapura-Melaka-Johor, *against* the arrogant and forceful upstarts, the people of Aceh, had been since almost a century (from ca. 1525). And to whom could he turn for this purpose better than his bendahara?

Indeed the latter in his introduction proudly states that he is:

- son of the orang kaya Paduka Raja (namely, Bendahara P.R.I just mentioned);
- son of Bendahara Sri Maharaja II;

---

a scholar of Malay can establish for us whether indeed Netscher in 1870 meant *this* Shajarah R.R.M. from 1855 with his "great Malay chronicle"; or that Netscher still stuck to the "three manuscripts" of the "Malay historiographical work Sulalatus Salatin" mentioned by him (then former resident of Riau-Lingga and secretary of the Batavia Society) in *TBG* 2 (1854): 144n1, and of which "one, property of the present Sultan of Lingga, is quite old and has apparently been updated over time", so that, on pp. 145–6, he was able to compile from it "a name list of the sultans, starting from Sri Tri Buana", which in fact continues until after 1841! For in this list of 1854—which incidentally shows continuous big *mistakes* in names and dates *up to* ca. 1811, where the list begins to become reliable—it is exactly the aforementioned Sultan Abdullah Maäyat (aka Hammat) Shah who is *missing*; who indeed reigned from the autumn of 1613 to the spring of 1623 (d. on Greater Tambelan), our "Raja Sabrang". But in his great work of 1870, on pp. 30–1, Netscher only knows a "Sulthan Hammat Shah", whose reign he dates 1615–23, completely neglecting the information printed in Dulaurier's edition of the *Sejarah Melayu* (1856), where the introduction mentions (p. 4 at the bottom) the "marhum yang mangkat di Atjeh, Sulthan Ala'ud-din Ri'ayat Shah", making Netscher's note 4 on p. 31 a certain mistake (copied in good faith by Tiele, "De Europeërs", part 8 [1886], p. 305n5). The question therefore is: in which Malay source could Netscher have drawn between 1854 and 1870 for his Sultan "Hammat" Shah? From von de Wall's manuscript no. 354, in Batavia? And during on-site research, it can also become clear whether the man who wrote it, Tengku Said, was its author-compiler or its copyist-plagiarist.

[62] According to the text, Raja Dewa Sayyid (aka Sĕri Narawangsa) was (again according to the text) a son of Sĕri Akar, the king of Patani. He probably even was a full nephew of Raja Sabrang, the new sultan. According to the information of January 1609 in the appendices to Verhoeff's log *BV* 2, 15: 204–7a (dated "October 1625" by a very silly mistake in a margin on p. 204a there; corrected already by Netscher, *De Nederlanders in Djohor en Siak*, p. 17n3—see also his note on p. 22). Sultan Abdu'l Jalil Shah had six sons instead of the four mentioned by Matelieff's log (1606). The eldest of the six was married to the king of Patani's daughter; one of his younger brothers was having an affair with this woman, for which the elder brother killed him, and later his wife as well; then, in revenge the father-in-law killed the son-in-law. I suspect that Sĕri Akar was the name of this eldest son of Sultan Abdu'l Jalil Shah, next to whom the *Sejarah Melayu* mentions a Hussein (Raja of Kelantan) and a Mahmud (Raja of Kampar), as well as other sons (story 38; Shellabear, ed., *Sejarah Melayu* [1898], p. 189). That the family tragedy occurred in Patani is clear from the old Dutch text, p. 205b; but the brothers' names are not given there.

- son of Bendahara Tun Narawangsa;
- son of Bendahara Sri Maharaja I; son of Sri Nara Diraja Tun Ali; and
- son of "Prince Mani Purendan" (Baginda M.P.), who was "of Malay blood, from the mountain Si-Guntang Mahameru [the Merapi in Minangkabau],[63] living in Melaka".[64]

So here is the family tree along which Tun Muhamad in "Batu Sawar, land of peace", the bendahara from a line of bendaharas, in the year Dal 1023 AH or 1614 CE counts back to his forebear of six branches ago, the "prince" with the beautifully Dekhan name (Mani Purendan),[65] but in fact a Minangkabau man living in Melaka. That in turn means: he counts back to a forefather who at least 6 times 20, at most 6 times 40, but in all probability the average of 6 times 30 years earlier gave rise to his (Tun Muhamad's) life in the seventh degree. Since the bendahara was born around 1565, as we have just seen, this Minangkabau ancestor must have been born around 1325 at the earliest, around 1385 most probably, and around 1445 at the latest. As according to the true sense of Tun Muhamad's genealogical list, this Minangkabau man was a Melakan immigrant, and since Melaka started to flourish as a trade centre in about 1400, the possibility that Mani Purendan was born around 1325 can be eliminated immediately. Again taking 20 or 30 years respectively as the age at which M. P. settled in Melaka, around 1415 (which is the most probable) and 1465 (which was the last possible year) was when this Minangkabau Malay became a Melakan Malay and started to engender the later line of bendaharas of which Tun Muhamad speaks with pride in his introduction, and regarding which story 12 of the *Sejarah Melayu* reveals further legends.[66]

If we stick to that most probable time of Mani Purendan's arrival in Melaka as a man in the prime of his life in about 1415, then he *arrived* there (as we know from the Chinese and Portuguese historical documents) during the reign of the Islamising Raja Ahmad (ca. 1414–24) and undoubtedly also lived there under the first so-called Sultan Muhamad Shah (ca. 1424–ca. 1450), the "sultan" to whom story 11 of the *Sejarah Melayu* ascribes the first regulation of the Melaka court, describing it elaborately in its *istīādat* or etiquette. Now, at the end of that story there is a very conspicuous stop: so conspicuous that Devic in 1878 rightly decided to end the "*première partie*" [first part] of his translation there.[67] Translated as literally as possible, the paragraph goes as follows:

---

[63] For the correctness of this identification, see below.

[64] Shellabear, ed., *Sejarah Melayu* (1898) or (1910), p. 2. The text goes: "Tun Muhamad [see above] … bendahara, anak O.P.R., chuchu B.S.M., chichit B.T.N., piyut B.S.M., anak S.N.T.A., anak Baginda Mani Purendan, kaddasa, Allâhu sirrahum, Malayu bangsanya, dari bukit Siguntang Mahameru, Melaka [var. Malakat] nĕgĕrinya." We can see here that the Malay words for "son, grandson, great-grandson, great-great-grandson" counts no further than "anak, chuchu, chichi/chichit, piyut".

[65] Dr van Ronkel noted: "Mani Purendan could be the Tamil *manippurandān*, 'keeper of the jewels', Malay *bendahara*". Thus, in this proper name there would be hidden yet another glory to the Melakan-Johorese line from which Tun Muhamad was born.

[66] See below.

[67] A.N.: It was never continued.

> This is the court etiquette of the Malay kings of yore. What I [*sanda*, "your servant"] have heard I have retold; if there be a mistake in it, may it be corrected by whomsoever has paid attention to its story, [but] please let me not be ridiculed.[68]

This is immediately followed by: "The narrator's words (*kata rawi*) [are as follows]: When this Sultan Muhamad Shah, etc.".

One *feels* the makeshift later addition here. And after one large paragraph of that unmistakeable addition—in which the curious statement (among others) is made that the port of Malāka was called Malākat by the *orang Arab* because of its many merchants, "*artinya perhimpunan segala dagang*"; an "explanation" which makes *no* sense at all and is therefore very much posterior as well![69]—story 11 *closes*, and story 12 *begins*, with a legend-filled ode to Baginda Mani Purendan, the bendahara's grandfather to the fifth degree.

In any case, this "Prince" M.P. is called a prince's son from Kling country, from "the city of Pahali",[70] who after some vicissitudes of fortune at Pasei comes to Melaka during the reign of "Sultan" Muhamad Shah, is received with great honour, marries the daughter of the Panghulu bendahari (Sri Nara Diraja) and begets a certain "Tun Ali" by her. With this we have already reached Bendahara Tun Muhamad's grandfather to the fourth degree, whom in 1612–14 he calls "Sri Nara Diraja Tun Ali". But story 12 gets even better, for Mani Purendan from that same high marriage also had a daughter, Tun Wati, who marries none less than "Sultan" M.S.; the offspring from this union is a certain Raja Kasim. But this maternal grandson of "Prince" M.P. does not succeed the sultan (as he had hoped), but is passed over in favour of a younger half-brother named Raja Ibrahim, "Sultan" M.S.'s son by a Rokan princess. The father sultan dies; Raja Ibrahim succeeds him as "Sultan" Abu Shaid, but is soon murdered—the later byzantine representation of this murder can be found in said story 12—by Raja Kasim, who takes the throne as Sultan Mudhafar Shah—the *first* real sultan of Melaka, as we know from Chinese reports (*Su-lu-tân*

---

[68] Shellabear, ed., *Sejarah Melayu* (1898), p. 49; (1910), p. 68. The text goes: "Inilah istiādat Raja-Raja Mĕlayu dĕhulu kala. Barang pĕnĕgaran sanda [= sĕhaya-nda] itulah sanda chĕritĕrakan, dan jikalau ada salahnya hĕndak-lah di-pĕrbaïki oleh barang-siapa yang ingat akan chĕritĕranya, jangan kiranya sanda di-gonjakkan." This last verb is rare, as is clear from the inconsistent transliterations in Shellabear: "ganjakkan" in 1898, "gonjokkan" in 1910. In Dulaurier's edition in Arab letters it starts with a *k* ([1856], p. 155, l. 2); the correct form however is *gonjak*, as Wilkinson has in his *Malay-English Dictionary* (Singapore: Kelly & Walsh, 1903), p. 578a, while H.C. Klinkert, *Nieuw Maleisch-Nederlandsch Woordenboek*, has *gonja-gonjak*, to ridicule, also Jav. (pp. 876–7).

[69] This fake learning (or rather: wilful misinterpretation), however, predates Bendahara Tun Muhamad's bringing it up again in 1614 by at least 60 years; for it is found as early as 1557 in Bras d'Albuquerque's *Comentarios de Afonso d'Albuqerque*, text of the 2nd ed. of 1576 ed. and introd. by J. Veríssimo Serrão, 3rd ed., 4 vols. (Lisboa: Na Regia Officina Typografica, 1774), vol. 3, p. 88, as alternative explanation to "*Malāka*" as Portuguese "*encontrar*". Compare with Ferrand, *Relations de voyages*, vol. 1, p. 418n2, who for his part points to Arabic "*mulākā*" as "to meet"—Arabic *malākat* as possession.

[70] A.N.: A *mangled* adaptation perhaps of the language name, *Pāli*?

Wu-ta-fu-na-sha), whose reign started about 1450 (before 1456 in any case),[71] the Soltão Modafaixa of the historian Albuquerque in 1557.[72]

Now we have solid historical ground under our feet! But now also we have collected precious information that enables us to recalculate all of Bendahara Tun Muhamad's diplomatic historical account from Batu Sawar in 1614, when he proudly goes back to his forebear Mani Purendan with the title of "baginda". In his introduction, Tun Muhamad calls him a Malay from Minangkabau; in his story 12, he calls him a Klingalese from "Pahali" ("Pāli country"?). The real truth, no doubt, lies somewhere in between: M.P. probably was a so-called *jawi pekan*, in this case: a half-breed from combined Minangkabau and Klingalese origins.

By a simple calculation based on six generations of 30 years each on average before birth, we saw that M.P. most probably lived in Melaka under Raja Ahmad and Maharaja Muhamad Shah (who probably did not have a higher title), sometime between 1414 and 1450 CE; and in story 12 Tun Muhamad himself says that this M.P. arrived in Melaka during Sultan Muhamad Shah's reign. This proves that our calculation was correct. We further noted, again according to the man's own story, that Sultan Mudhafar Shah, son of this Muhamad Shah and maternal grandson of M.P., was a *usurper* who deposed and killed his half-brother of higher birth. How does Tun Muhamad, seventh-degree descendant of M.P., in 1614 commemorate in his introduction the glorious origins of the Johorese Sultan Alaudin Ri'ayat Shah III from 1612, who in the meantime (after 6 June 1613) had died in Aceh? In the following diplomatic and formal way, in which perceptive readers can also see now the intention to glorify the said ancestor Mani Purendan—in other words, to glorify the author himself—Tun Muhamad (for convenience's sake I have added all dates as well as the correct *numbering* of the sultans in an ascending series):

> [In] Batu Sawar, land of peace, thus [was] His word [in other words, that of the *sa-orang orang besar*, Raja Sabrang as we saw above in the time of the Hijrah [then the date is given in the usual elaborate way, which after correction equals Mawlid Day, 1021 AH which is Sunday 13 May 1612], in the time circle of the reign of Him of Blessed Memory who passed away in Aceh, Sultan *Alaudin Ri'ayat Shah* [III, ca. 1597–6 June 1613], Shadow of God on earth, son of Sultan Ali Jala Abdu'l Jalil [Ri'ayat] Shah [ca. 1580–ca. 1597; *usurper*], brother [meaning "brother-in-law" here] of Sultan Mudhafar Shah [II, ca. 1564–ca. 1580], son of Sultan Alaudin Ri'ayat Shah [II, ca. 1530–ca. 1564, first sultan of Johor], son of Sultan Mahmud Shah [ca. 1488–ca. 1528; last sultan of Malaka, expelled by d'Albuquerque on 16 August 1511], son of Sultan Alaudin [Ri'ayat] Shah [I, end of 1477–ca. 1488], son of Sultan Mansur Shah [the Great, ca. 1458–d. October 1477], son of Sultan Mudhafar Shah [I, the *usurper*, see above, and Mani Purendan's grandson; ca. 1450–ca. 1458], son of "Sultan" Muhamad Shah

[71] Groeneveldt, *Notes on the Malay Archipelago and Malacca* (Batavia: W. Bruining, 1876), p. 131; or *Notes*, 2nd ed. (London: Trubner, 1887), p. 251. Compare with Rouffaer, part 1, p. 23 and especially below.

[72] Albuquerque, *Commentarios*, vols. 3, 17.

> of Blessed Memory [Mani Purendan's son-in-law ca. 1424–ca. 1445 or–ca. 1450, depending on the more or less ephemeral character of "Sultan Abu Shaid", ca. 1445–ca. 1450]—may Allah make his reign and rule enduring.[73]

So we see: first Tun Muhamad glorified himself directly as a descendant of Baginda Mani Purendan in the male line; then he covertly glorifies himself behind the nine sultans of Johor and Melaka he names, through that same Mani Purendan, who had been son-in-law to the first self-proclaimed sultan of Melaka and thus become the first real sultan's grandfather, who by the grace of Allah had perpetuated the usurped throne by his most royal offspring. Blue blood (or in good Malay, white blood, *darah putih*) thus coursed through Tun Muhamad's veins from left and from right; and the sultans of Johor under whom he served as bendahara really ought to acknowledge him as a distant cousin.

That was what he wanted to make clear, in his way, in his introduction, in between all the *sembahs* and *salāms* to the recently deceased and the living sultan. Beneath all the obligatory humility, he was in fact utterly "arrogant", as Van den Broeck wrote in Matelieff's log in 1606.

With him we are also in the atmosphere of the authentic Eastern and especially authentic Malay court history, where regicide is a normal means of ascending the throne.

While he ends the list of his six ancestors[74] with the mystical eulogy "*kaddasa Allāhu sirrahum*" (may God hallow their secret),[75] for the critical reader of Tun Muhamad's own stories concerning the three oldest (in story 12 and story 27 in

---

[73] Shellabear, ed., *Sejarah Melayu* (1898), p. 2; or, somewhat corrected (1910), pp. 2–3. The text *immediately* following after the one printed above goes: "[Di] Batu Sawar, dār as-salām, dĕmikiyan katanya tatkala Hijratu … saribu duwa puluh satu tahun, kapada tahun Dal [read Jimawal], pada duwa bĕlas hari bulan Rabi'ul-awal, kapada hari Khamis [read Ahad], … pada zaman kĕrajaän Marhum yang mangkat di Aceh, Sultan Alaudin Ri'ayat Shah, lil Allah fi'l-alam, anak Sultan Ali Jala [this should be the reading; Shellabear's *al-ajal* is nonsensical, as Van Ronkel tells me] Abdu'l Jalil Shah, akh [Arab. *akh* = "brother"], but the sense here is "brother-in-law" (see story 38 in Shellabear, ed., *Sejarah Melayu* [1898], pp. 176, 182, 186–8); but also that brother-in-law's *murderer*, as we know from Couto, although he calls the murderer "the brother of his [Mudhafar's] mother" as uncle, Sultan Mudhafar Shah, ibnu as-Sultan Alaudin Ri'ayat Shah, ibnu as-Sultan Mahmud Shah, chuchu Sultan Alaudin Shah, chichit Sultan Mansur Shah, piyut Sultan Mudhafar Shah, anak Sultan Muhamad Shah al-marhum, khaladu Allah mulkahu wa sultanahu". The *Di* with which the passage should begin is missing in all editions.

[74] See above.

[75] Regarding this phrase, Dr Snouck Hurgronje wrote to me: This eulogy is used in Muhammadan literature after mysticism had won its place in Islam. Where such eulogies are well understood and distinguished, its purpose is to signal that the man using it regards—either really or politely—the man to whose name he adds it as illuminated by a higher mystic light. The *sirr* is not a secret in the sense of something that must be hidden, but the mystery, the most hidden being of that person, and thus *sirrahum* here indicates those ancestors who are thought to have had a very special relationship to Allah. Sometimes one says, "qaddasa 'llâhu rûhahu" (may Allah sanctify his spirit), entirely in the same sense. As to whether the Malay author really thought that those bendahara ancestors were such mystical luminaries or merely supposed *this* out of deference, or did not realise the specific value of this phrase as opposed to, for example, "rahîmahum Allâh" etc., I have to leave it unanswered.

connection with 33) these three great men turn out to be far from saintly, but were in fact born conspirators as soon as they saw an advantage to treason. Regarding his great-great-grandfather, Tun Mutahir, who had played a disastrous part in the years of Melaka's fall (1509–11) as the city's Bendahara Sri Maharaja, Tun Muhamad simply could not forge history so completely that this intriguer would appear a faithful servant of his king; his violent death had been too dramatic for that and was too deeply engraved on the minds of all Johorese Malays.[76] But, in turn, Tun Mutahir's father, Bendahara Sri Nara Diraja (Tun Ali), and *his* great father Mani Purendan, both glorified in story 12—were they without blame? Quite the contrary: both had been protagonists in the murder of the ephemeral ruler of Melaka "Sultan (?) Abu Shaid", and as a consequence, a grandson of Mani Purendan had been able to usurp the throne. Grandfather and uncle had thus become the patrons of Melaka's first sultan, Mudhafar Shah.[77]

---

[76] Shellabear, ed., *Sejarah Melayu* (1898), pp. 56–7 and 62, see story 13. This bendahara Sri Maharaja, son of Sri Nara Diraja Tun Ali and therefore grandson of "Baginda" Mani Purendan, was born from his already senile father's marriage to a young princess, Tun Kudu, after the old man had very successfully taken "chula" (*chula badak*, rhinoceros horn – used as an aphrodisiac). Shellabear, ed., *Sejarah Melayu* (1898), p. 84, l. 13, end of story 16. As a boy he was called Tun Mutahir, and his future greatness was predicted from the flame that sometimes shot up from his young head, "its shine going straight to heaven". In women, as we know from Java, the equivalent shine of greatness comes from their "secret place" (*rahasya*); see esp. *Pararaton*, ed. Brandes, pp. 46–7 and 54–5, or 2nd ed. 1920, pp. 58 and 66–7). He first became temenggong (chief *fiscaal*) of Melaka, with the title of Sri Maharaja (ibid., p. 85), then in a highly comical way—by means of the "Unterrocks-Politik" which Bismarck finds so annoying—becomes bendahara under Sultan Mahmud Shah (in Melaka ca. 1488–1511) (ibid., p. 122, beginning of story 27), then in accordance with all the predictions (compare with ibid., pp. 110, 112, story 26) becomes an impressive orang besar (ibid., p. 122), but finally in story 33—that is, *between* story 32, with the first arrival of Portuguese ships at Melaka (under "Gangsālu Parairā" = Gonçalo Pereira; but this should be Diego Lopes de Sequeira in Sept. 1509) and story 34, with the arrival of the conqueror Albuquerque on 1 July 1511—turns into a rebel and meets his death by an order of Sultan Mahmud (ibid., pp. 148–53). Of course the representation of facts concerning Sri Maharaja in story 33 is still very one-sided. The fact that the *Sejarah Melayu* makes such a gross mistake by naming Gonçalo Pereira as the first Portuguese admiral who came to Melaka in 1509—while in fact G.P., as newly appointed *capitão* [captain] of Ternate, made a quick stop at Melaka as late as May 1530, coming from Portugal via Goa, sailed on to the Moluccas over Brunei, arrived at Ternate on about 1 November, and was killed there by the Sangajis on 27 May 1531 (compare with Tiele in "De Europeërs", part 2, *BKI* 27, 1 [1879]: 11–6)—is proof that (1) this murder had made a huge impression; and (2) that story 32 errs in good faith.

[77] For in that story 7, a "Sri Nara Diraja" is the great patron of Raja Kasim (see above) in the latter's effort to dethrone his half-brother Raja Ibrahim (Sultan Abu Shaid) and ascend the throne himself. Compare with Shellabear, ed., *Sejarah Melayu* (1898), pp. 50–2, and (1910), vol. 1, pp. 70–3. But *which* Sri Nara Diraja was that? Raja Kasim's maternal great-grandfather, the old chief treasurer (*panghulu bendahari*) of that name from story 11, *or* his uncle Tun Ali, whose full name is given in the introduction as "Sri Nara Diraja Tun Ali"? In itself, the probability of the story is in favour of the relatively young uncle, not the ancient great-grandfather. But before that, there is a little sentence in the story which provides conclusive evidence, if one corrects the forgery in the name. It tells the story of how, when Raja Ibrahim had been made sultan,

It is most noteworthy that even from the wording of the *Ming Annals* (book 325), we can infer the dynastic drama that played out in Melaka between 1445 and 1456.

In 1424, Hsi-li Ma-ha-la (Sri Maharadja [Muhamad Shah?]) ascended the throne in an honest way as son of Mu-kan Sa-u-ti-r-sha (Megat (?) [Sekandar (?) Shah]).[78] This Hsi-li Ma-ha-la had a long reign, up to 1445 at least, for in that year, envoys went to China "who asked that the king Hsi-li Pa-mi-si-war Tiu-pa-sha [Çri Parameçwara Abu Shaid (?); and then also the "Sultan Abu Shaid" of the *Sejarah Melayu*] might obtain a commission for ruling the country", while "the [old] king" was still alive, that is, envoys with the request that the former be allowed to act as Raja Muda. But then suddenly, without any transition: "In the year 1456, *Su-lu-tân Wu-ta-fu-na-sha* sent as tribute horses and products of his country, and asked to be invested as king", while in 1458 he was succeeded by his own son as follows: "In the year 1459 this king's son [!], *Su-tan Wang-su-sha* [Sultan Mansur Shah, the Great; his name was mangled to *Wang-su* by the Chinese, like the *M* in his father

---

Raja Kasim was exiled due to the efforts of R.I.'s grandfather, the prince of Rokan, and out of desperation became a fisherman. The high noblemen were displeased at this and gathered at the house of the bendahara (Sri Amar di Raja at the time, earlier in story 11, *perdana manteri*), but the bendahara shrugged and said: "What can we do about it?" The noblemen silently return to their homes. Then there follows (I give the correct translation by Marre, corrected with regard to the forgery): "Cependant Sri Nara Di-Radja pensa dans son coeur à cette affaire; bien souvent il avait invité Radja Kâsim à venir manger avec lui dans sa maison, *car la mère de Radja Kâsim était sa soeur*" (see Marre, *Sadjârah malâyou*, p. 75). Thus, we are clearly dealing with Raja Kasim's uncle: Sri Nara Diraja (Tun Ali), who is already rebelling in his heart and will later be the promoter of the coup d'état, accompanied by the murder of "Sultan" Abu Shaid, and subsequently is given the office of bendahara as a reward. Now *all* the Malay texts (Singapore *editio princeps*, ca. 1840, p. 112; Dulaurier [1856], p. 163; [following Abdullah's original text], [1884], pp. 128–9; Shellabear [1896], pp. 102–3; Shellabear [1898], p. 51) do have the concluding causal clause, "karena bonda Raja Kasim itu saudara padanya"; but all these five editions also have "Maka Sri *Bija*-di-raja" at the beginning of the sentence, appearing out of the blue without any connection whatsoever to the preceding or the following text of chapter 7: apparently a forgery of the original and correct "Maka Sri *Nara* Diraja". So Shellabear restored this reading in his second transliterated edition of 1910 (vol. 1, p. 71, l. 15 from the bottom). It is funny that in the copy of the Singapore edition by Abdullah that came into the possession of the Koninklijk Instituut in 1915, a studying Dutch former owner (from idiosyncrasies in the handwriting, I suspect it was Dr Niemann) wrote with pencil in Arab letters in the margin of this passage: "Nāra?" The degree to which this passage was tampered with at an early stage is clear from the mangled representation in Leyden's translation: "Sri Vija [or Bija] di Raja, however, reflected in his own mind what was to be done; he had been constantly in the habit of inviting Raja Kasim to his house to eat and drink, *because his brother had been bandahara to Raja Kasim*" (p. 113)! Or is this a translation error?

[78] See Rouffaer, part 1, p. 20. In 1414 he had succeeded his father, the first ruler of Melaka, Pai-li-su-ra (Pĕrmaisura or Raja Iskandar Shah), and who after all can be identified with the Raja Ahmad (Raja Besar Muda) mentioned in the beginning of story 11.

Mudhafar's name to *Wu-ta-fu-na*], sent envoys to bring tribute, on which the Emperor ordered some officers to go and invest him as king".[79]

One simply feels the *argumentum ex silentio*: Sultan Mudhafar Shah was not a son of the preceding ruler of Melaka, but a usurper who between 1445 and 1446 managed to become an absolute monarch and founded his own dynasty.

What sources did Tun Muhamad use in 1612–14; or what sources did he possibly have at his disposal? There are only three hikayats he mentions by name:

(1) *Hikayat Iskandar*, at the beginning of story 1;
(2) *Hikayat Sayyidina Hamzah*, at the end of story 1 and again at the beginning of story 34 as *Hikayat Amir Hamzah* and *Hikayat Hamzah*;
(3) *Hikayat Muhammad Hanafiyah*, in the same passage of story 34.

This only proves that these three Malay hikayats, inspired very strongly by Persian originals, already existed *before* 1614. In 1896, Dr Van Ronkel found a piece of the last one among the Malay manuscript at Cambridge, from the estate of the Leiden orientalist Thomas Erpenius (d. 13 November 1624); the "history of hamsa in malay" and "ditto on Alexander the Great" were numbers 7 and 8 in the estate of the Councillor of the Indies, Isaac de Saint-Martin in Batavia (d. 14 April 1696), as well as three copies of "the chronicle of the Malay kings" (no. 11–12), as we know since 1900 thanks to Dr De Haan.[80]

Moreover, Wilkinson in the introduction to his *Malay–English Dictionary* (1903) pointed out that the Rajput author[81] of the *Bustan as-Salatin* (the "Pleasure Garden of the Kings") who, in Aceh in *Shawal* 1047 AH (March 1638 CE), commenced his work by an order of Sultan Iskandar Thani (January 1637–d. 15 February 1641; that is, the successor of Johor's designer, Sultan Iskandar Muda, in 1613 and definitively in 1615), "mentions having written a history of Alexander, so that the *Hikayat Iskandar dzû'l-karnain* had not been long in existence in 1611 [read 1612, and actually 1614]".[82] We should probably add:

---

[79] See Groeneveldt's *Notes*, 1st ed. (1876), pp. 129–32, or 2nd ed. (1887), pp. 249–51. I owe the transliteration of some Chinese characters to Mr B. Hoetink.

[80] Compare respectively to P.S. van Ronkel, "Account of Six Malay Manuscripts of the Cambridge University Library", *BKI* 6, 2 (1896): 1–2, 5, 9, and esp. 54–6, and F. de Haan, "Uit oude notarispapieren, I" [From Old Notarial Papers, I], *TBG* 42 (1900): 299.

[81] The author's place of birth "Ranir" (see next note) is in fact the village Raner in the land of Bikanir (or "Bikaner"), straight north from its capital of the same name, in Rajputana. So he was a highly malaified Rajput Arab, *not* a Gujarat Arab as it is still thought.

[82] Wilkinson, *Malay-English Dictionary*, pp. 6–7. By mistake Wilkinson wrote on p. 6: "The Bustânu's-salâtin is dated A.D. 1636". The correct date is given above. On the date of the main work and the later addition, see Dr Husein Jayadiningrat, "Critische overzicht van de geschiedenis van het Soeltanaat van Aceh" [Critical overview of the history of the Sultanate of Aceh], *BKI* 65 (1911): 136–7, correcting the date given earlier by H.N. van der Tuuk, "Kort Verslag der Maleische Handschriften Toebehorende aan de Royal Asiatic Society te Londen" [Short report concerning Malay manuscripts belonging to the Royal Asiatic Society in London], *BKI* 3, 1 (1866): 424: "in the year 1040 according to the Muhamadan calendar". For it became clear to Dr Husein that in the interlinear Malay translation the number "*tudjokh*" had been forgotten.

(4) the Malay version (likewise inspired by a Persian original) of the *Taju as-Salaṭin* (Crown of the kings), which after all bears the chronogramme 1012 AH (1603–04 CE) (the word *ghaib* is 1000 + 10 + 2) and mentions an author whose nickname can be read as al-Jauharī (the Jeweller) or as al-Johorī (the Johorese). This is in all likelihood a Malay at Johor or Batu Sawar, in the middle of the reign of Sultan Alaudin Ri'ayat Shah (ca. 1597–6 June 1613) and his factotum Raja Sabrang, while following a Persian original from ca. 1160 (by *Bokhārī al-Jauharī*; between 1152 and 1176 CE) was consciously playing with this Jauhar/Johor.[83] Do we not believe that the very *title* alone of this Aceh *Bustān as-Salaṭin* from about 1638 was a literary *countermove* to the Johorese *Taju as-Salaṭin* from ca. 1603 and the Johorese *Sulalat as-Salaṭin* from about 1614 combined?

The author, Nurad-dīn ibn Alī ar-Rānīrī had—once more—arrived at Aceh on Sunday, 31 May 1637. In the list of his numerous Arabic-Malay writings, partly from before 1637 (for these are pamphlets, in part against Sultan Iskandar Muda's [d. 27 Dec. 1636] protégé Shamsudīn as-Samatranī [the man from Pasei], who died on 24 Feb. 1630), given by H.N. van der Tuuk, "Kort Verslag", *BKI* 3, 1 (1866): 462–4, there is however *no Hikayat Iskandar*. Wilkinson's statement quoted above cannot be verified—as usual, he does not say where his data are to be found—and may be false. On the other hand, Wilkinson is a specialty in the *Bustān* [*sic*] (see footnotes just below). *Today* regarding ar-Rānīrī, we can refer to Dr H. Kraemer's dissertation, *Een Javaansche primbon uit de 16e eeuw* [A Javanese *primbon* from the 16th century] (Leiden: Trap, 1921), pp. 32–3, where in note 8 it is stated, based on Dr Van Ronkel's, *Catalogus der Maleische handschriften*, p. 514, that he "returned to Rānīr" in 1054 AH (Mar. 1644–Feb. 1645 CE), thus concluding his career as a Malay author.

[83] On the original Persian author (in all likelihood at least, for the Persian original has not been found yet) see Dr Van Ronkel's paper, "De Kroon der Koningen", *TBG* 41 (1899): 55–69, esp. 62–3 and 67. However this paper in my opinion pays too little attention to the possibility that the Malay translator in 1012 AH may in fact have been a Johorese who had kept "*Bokhārī*" as his nom de plume and was deliberately ambiguous with "*al-Jauharī*". The extent to which the Malay translator was also a Malay *adaptor* can be verified by anyone in the translation by Marre from 1878 (*Makôta Râja-Râja ou la Couronne des Rois*), since he had the useful idea to add not only various notes but also registers; in this case, see the passages under the lemma "Malais" and the indicated passages in chs. 1, 5 (3 passages) and 21; those on p. 100 in ch. 5 and on p. 322 in ch. 21 are the most significant. The *chronogramme* is in the *Malay introduction* to the Book of 24 Chapters. See A. Marre, ed. and trans., *Makôta Râja-Râja ou la Couronne des Rois* (Paris: Maisonneuve, 1878), p. 13, and P.P. Roorda van Eysinga's text edition with Dutch translation, *De Kroon der Koningen* (Batavia: Landsdrukkerij, 1827), p. 7. The other passages referred to above are in Roorda van Eysinga's, *Kroon der Koningen*, on pp. 26, 53, 55, 61 and 201. The highly particular nature of this introduction, in which the Malay adaptor/author mentions no less than seven sources by name—one of which, the *Akhlāq-i-Muhsinī*, was determined as completed before 1495 CE by Dr Van Ronkel – and the highly particular nature of the systematic division of the actual book into 24 chapters in my opinion not only indicate that this introduction was *entirely* written by the Johorese adaptor/author, but even that this Malay "*Bokhārī al-Jauharī*" and Bendahara Tun Muhamad of the *Sejarah Melayu* (which also has an introduction and a systematic division into stories) *possibly* knew each other personally. The year 1012 AH lasted from 11 June 1603 through 29 May 1604. For Johor or Jauhar, see Rouffaer, part 1, pp. 123 and 133–4, with notes.

To my historical sense, the battle for hegemony over the Malay lands between the upstart Aceh and the old Melaka-Johor was between about 1550 and 1613. We also see here the reason why these three prominent Malay texts have similar titles. Incidentally, the later Aceh work can be called a kind of theological-historical Malay encyclopedia in seven books, the "Pleasure Garden" of scholarly Aceh,[84] albeit written by a man who was born in *Rajputan*, and by order of a prince who was not from Aceh either, but from *Pahang*.

The four aforementioned Malay hikayats, all certainly existing before 1614, only prove that a literary-historical work like the *Sejarah Melayu* did not fall from the sky like a meteor. But which "Hikayat Melayu" could have been meant in the introduction, "brought by someone from Goa"; or as Leyden translates in 1821, "a Malay story, which had been lately brought by a nobleman from the land of Gua"?[85] This must have been a work of *history*, as opposed to the four theological-mythological and theological-moralising texts mentioned above; a historical work that had Melaka's earlier history for its main subject.

For otherwise it made no sense for Raja Sabrang (*sa-orang orang besar*) at the ceremonial meeting (*majelis*) on Mawlid Day 1612 to say that this Malay hikayat brought from Goa (which should of course be understood as *Melaka*) should be "corrected in its statutes that they may be known to our children and grandchildren and observed by them all, and they may have use thereof".[86] Or as Leyden translated: "that it would be proper for some person to correct it [namely that "Malay story"] according to the statutes of the Malays, that it might be useful to posterity".[87] After all, one cannot "correct" something that is not already present, albeit in a bad or unsatisfactory form. It must therefore have been an *historical* hikayat in the spirit of the later *Sejarah Melayu*.

---

[84] Wilkinson has published two little volumes of this text in seven books—see the summary contents in Van der Tuuk, "Kort Verslag", p. 425—in Singapore in 1899 and 1900, unfortunately in Arabic script only. They include all of book 1 (27 chapters) and all 13 chapters of book 2, but the last one is incomplete (according to a personal communication from Dr Van Ronkel). Publication was discontinued *deliberately*, because—as the chief printer of the Methodist Mission Press told me in May 1909 upon enquiry *in situ*—the rest became so "indecent"!

[85] John Leyden, trans., *Malay Annals: Translated from the Malay language with an introduction by Thomas Stamford Raffles* (London: Printed for Longman, Hurst, Rees, Orme, and Brown, 1821), p. 1.

[86] Shellabear, ed., *Sejarah Melayu* (1898), pp. 1–2; or (1910), vol. 1, p. 2. In its full context as an utterance from Raja Sabrang at this *majĕlis* the text goes (compare above): "Dan pada suwatu masa bahwa [indeed] fakir [Tun Muhamad] duduk pada suwatu Majĕlis dengan orang besar-besar bĕrsĕnda-gurau [to amuse oneself, to play a jeu d'esprit]. Pada antara itu ada sa-orang orang besar [Raja Sabrang], tĕrlĕbih muliyanya dan tĕrlĕbih martabatnya daripada yang lain; maka bĕrkata iya kapada fakir [so Raja Sabrang now adresses the bendahara directly]: 'Hamba dĕngar ada hikayat Melayu di-bawa oleh orang dari Goa; barang kita [one or the other of us] pĕrbaïki kiranya [o! as an optative] dĕngan istiādatnya, supaya di-kĕtahuï oleh sĕgala anak-chuchu kita yang kĕmudian daripada kita, dan boleh di-ingatkannya oleh sĕgala marekaïtu syahadan adalah bĕroleh faïdah iya daripadanya'. Satĕlah fakir mĕnĕngar dĕmikiyan, jadi bĕratlah atas anggota fakir al-ladzi murakkabcala jahila [according to a personal communication from Dr Van Ronkel: Arabic 'the one founded on ignorance' or ignorant me, poor me] Tun Muhamad namanya, Tun Sĕri Lanang timang-timangannya, Paduka Raja gelărannya, bĕndahara, anak" (see also above).

[87] Leyden, trans., *Malay Annals* (1821), p. 1.

Only one Malay hikayat appears to fit this description: the *Hikayat Koris*, of which a manuscript can be found in the University Library of Cambridge. This was donated by Wilkinson in 1902 or earlier, from which he has taken a very large amount of lexicographical material for his *Malay-English Dictionary* (1903), and in which he gives us a most noteworthy piece of information in the introduction:

> The *Hikâyat Koris*, which is exceptional in that it contains many local references, clearly belongs to the period of Portuguese rule in Melaka [16 August 1511–14 January 1641; then taken over by the Dutch]. It was probably written in the Peninsula as it contains descriptions of the Sĕmang and Pangan aborigines.[88] The *Hikâyat Indĕra Mĕngindĕra* approaches the *Hikâyat Koris* so closely in point of style as to suggest the same authorship or at least the same school of authorship".[89]

Unfortunately no more can be said of this. Until a time when the Cambridge manuscript may be studied by a wider circle[90]—in an edition transliterated into Latin script, please, so that not only scholars of Malay, but also historians may use it!—I shall advance the following proposition in connection with what was already concluded from Dutch and Portuguese information from between 1600 and 1615 above.

João Lopes d'Amoreira, born Portuguese, temenggong of the foreigners at Melaka, former friend of the deceased Sultan Abdu'l Jalil Shah (d. ca. 1597), undoubtedly friend of the pro-Portuguese Bendahara Tun Muhamad as well, when he arrived at Batu Sawar to make peace between Melaka and Johor on 1 October

---

[88] A.N.: Mainly frizzy-haired inhabitants of the *rimba* and it shows a friendly spirit to Europeans, a rare thing in those days. The Dutch are not mentioned [nor in the *Sejarah Melayu*], incidentally; compare above.

[89] Wilkinson, p. 7. A.N.: One might think that the two manuscripts from the von de Wall collection in Batavia, described as *Hikayat Kuraish* 1–2 by Dr Van Ronkel in his catalogue of 1909 (Verhandelingen der Bataviaasch Genootschap, dl. 57), pp. 139–43 (in the second manuscript, the main character is even called Kuris or Koris) are similar to Wilkinson's *Hikayat Koris* from the Straits. However one needs only go over Dr Van Ronkel's summary and compare it to Wilkinson's summary quoted above (however brief) to see that they have nothing in common. According to a personal communication from Dr Van Ronkel there is a manuscript of the *Hikayat Indĕra Mĕngindĕra* (in a corrupt version) among the Klinkert (d. 20 Nov. 1913) collection with the title *Hikayat Dewa Indĕra Mĕngindĕra alias Hik. Bĕlah Tunggul*. Compare with the list of his manuscripts Klinkert himself gives in 1866 in *Vergadering der Directie van het Bataviaasch Genootschap van Kunsten en Wetenschappen, op Dienstag, den 31sten Julij 1866, Notulen van de Algemeene en Directie-vergaderingen van het Bataviaasch Genootschap van Kunsten en Wetenschappen*, vol. 4, p. 201n80. It appears from Wilkinson's list of abbreviations (p. 715) that a lithographic edition of the *Hikayat Indĕra Mĕngindĕra* appeared in Penang (so before 1903)".

Thus Wilkinson's manuscript of the *Hikayat Koris*, now kept at Cambridge University, appears to be *unique*; just as, incidentally, the manuscript of the *Hikayat Raja-Raja Pasai* has remained unique so far, as well as the *Hikayat Charang Kolina*, both kept in the Raffles collection at the Royal Asiatic Society in London, nos. 67 and 14.

[90] A.N.: Question—wasn't the definitely curious passage in "On the wild tribes of the Malay Peninsula" from T.J. Newbold, *Political and Statistical Account of the British Settlement in the Straits*, vol. 2 (1839), pp. 394–5, which reads "a copy of an old Malay manuscript which was sent to me by one of the Salangore chiefs" translated from a manuscript which in turn could be a descendant of the *Hikayat Koris* dating from ca. 1700?

1610, brought the *Hikayat Koris*. This hikayat was resurrected in its "improved" form as *Sejarah Melayu* after Raja Sabrang's encouraging words on Sunday, 13 May 1612 and his "high order" as sultan to his bendahara in the autumn of 1613.

But Tun Muhamad must have had *at least* one other source: the tribal and family tradition Si-Guntang[91]—Palembang—Singhapura—Melaka; a kind of ancient family hikayat. I am convinced that its outlines can even be traced in the *Sejarah Melayu*: story 2 through story 11 (the latter without its appended final paragraph). The strange sentence with which story 11 then ends, discussed at length above, and the immediate abrupt transition to story 12 with its exaltation of the author's forebear Mani Purendan and his son Sri Nara Diraja (Tun Ali), the revolutionary and patron of the first real sultan of Melaka, Mudhafar Shah (ca. 1450–ca. 1458), indicates that story 2–11 could very well be an adapted hikayat, or let us say: *cherichera*, which was *written* in the olden days by that honoured Baginda Mani Purendan; but that story 12 and all that follows it by definition is of a later age, when that ancestor and his son had become legendary-historical figures. To make the abrupt transition between that ancient part and the modern sequel less halting, the author Tun Muhamad in my opinion added the final paragraph discussed above to story 12, starting with *Kata rawi* (The narrator's words [are as follows]); in which Melaka's political power is overstated as reaching, under the first "Sultan" Muhamad Shah (ca. 1424–ca. 1450) already, from "Beruwas Ujung Karang" in the west to Trengganu in the east—that is, from Tanjung Karang[92] at the northern mouth of the Larut River (4° 47' n.l.)

---

[91] In interpreting this Si-Guntang (Mahameru or the Měrapi volcano) in Minangkabau I completely agree with Westenenk's earlier solution (see Rouffaer, part 1, pp. 29–30 with note and p. 90, note; also above) and reject the recent solution—with which, in my opinion, someone fooled him in Palembang—which he defends in passing in the first issue (received in this country on 30 April 1921) of the new magazine *Djâwâ* (*Orgaan van het Java-Instituut*), published at Weltevreden, pp. 7–8. This latter view is the *local Palembang* one, in opposition to the Minangkabau tradition; of which the oldest traces can be found at the beginning of story 2 of the *Sejarah Melayu*. While the oldest description of that local Palembang tradition was given by W.L. de Sturler, *Proeve eener beschrijving van het gebied van Palembang* (Groningen: J. Oomrens, 1843), pp. 28, 189–90, and subsequently by A.L. van Hasselt in "*Midden-Sumatra*", *I. Reisverhaal* [Travelogue] (Leiden: E.J. Brill, 1882), part 2, pp. 42–5; and now, with complete faith in the truth of these local claims, by Westenenk, supported by his highly surprising find of two inscriptions in Pallawa script (genre of the Kota Kapur and Karang Brahi [sic] inscriptions) at Putih Kuku and … (name as yet unknown), 5 kilometres WNW and … resp. from Bukit Sěbuntang (for that *is* the correct name; the name "Sěguntang" for this hill, 26 metres high, straight W from Kota Palembang, is a *forgery* by the local Malays; the only true name even seems to be Bukit Lama, see below). The oldest mention, in which the Palembang "Bukit Sebuntang" and a mutilated "Pagar-rudung" from Minangkabau are mingled already, in the Lampong tongue to be precise, comes from J.A. du Bois, supervisor in the Lampongs (1819–33), in his description "De Lampongsche distrikten op het eiland Sumatra", *Tijdschrift voor Nederlandsch-Indië* 14, part 1 (1852): 245–75 and 309–33. In the final chapter, "Legenden en fabelen". [E.N.: There follows a three-page note by Rouffaer in which he provides details of folklore concerning Bukit Sebuntang and Bukit Lama. It was not thought necessary to translate this for the present collection.]

[92] Garbled to "Tanjung Krong" on the English nautical charts; "Tanjung Krang" on the Straits Branch Map (1911); "*hoek Krang*" [Hook of Krang], in *Zeemansgids voor den Oost-Indischen Archipel* [Sailor's Guide to the East Indian Archipelago], vol. 1 (Utrecht: Departement van Marine,

on the west coast to Trengganu (ca. 5° 20' n.l.) on the east coast. A damned lie! Not to mention the nonsensical etymology brought up in that concluding paragraph concerning *Malāka* (Arabic *Malākat* or *malā-kah*) = trade centre ("*perhimpunan segala dagang*").

Story 1, however, certainly cannot be counted as part of that oldest historical core; for specifically Johorese-Tumasik legends have been worked into its final part, while in the beginning of this first story we see a reflection of the Alexander/Iskandar legend that may point to a secondary influence from Aceh, since after all Tun Muhamad as bendahara had also been taken from Batu Sawar to Aceh as a prisoner on 6 June 1613. To sum up: story 1 flowed entirely from Tun Muhamad's own pen.

As to the question about whether he may have used other older *cherichera*, apart from what I would call "the oldest core", stories 2–11: although with more hesitation, I would nonetheless give a positive answer here as well. I have the impression that stories 12–16—starting with the praise of Mani Purendan and ending with Hang Kasturi's death at the hands of Hang Tuah ordered by Sultan Mansur Shah (ca. 1458–d. October 1477), constitute a younger, second cycle of histories, written down at the time in *Melaka itself*, before the city's fall in 1511. If one leaves out the following *two* stories, 17–18, as lacking in both Leyden (so before 1811) and several Malay manuscripts[93] and therefore probably inserted later, I think that the remaining stories 19–34 of the *textus receptus* Abdullah-Dulaurier were largely written down by Johor Malays during the existence of the new capital, Johor, ca. 1530–64, in its first flourishing period under Sultan Alaudin Ri'ayat Shah II; before Sultan Alaudin al-Kahhar's (ca. 1539–28 September 1571) Aceh fleet came and attacked the city ca. 1564 and led the Johor sultan away in captivity and put a new sultan on the throne as Aceh's first middleman (Mudhafar Shah II, ca. 1564–ca. 1580), no doubt caused the foundation of the secondary residence Seluyud.[94]

This "third cycle" of stories in the *Sejarah Melayu*, as I would call this group, begins with that curious story 19 on the naval power of Ujung Tanah (Langka or Galuh!) in the days of yore[95] and ends with the fall of Melaka in 1511 and the flight to Bintan of Sultan Mahmud Shah (I, ca. 1488–d. ca. 1528), expelled by the Portuguese. Then finally, as "most recent history", there follows the delightful appendix, constituting stories 35–38, for the knowledge of which in a broader circle we have Shellabear to thank, since 1896 and especially since the transliterated edition of 1898—the appendix which in my firm opinion is once more entirely the work of Tun Muhamad, just like story 1 and the introduction; work, therefore, dating from 1614 in *Batu Sawar*.

Afd. Hydrographie, 1916). N.B. Dennys, *A Descriptive Dictionary of British Malaya* (London: London and China Telegraph Office, 1894) is correct: "Tanjong Karang". It lies at the entrance of the present-day port town Port Weld. The preceding Bĕruwas—the mouth of S. Bruas, in the ancient landscape Bruas = Dinding (just about; see Rouffaer, part 1, p. 42 with note 2, and p. 83), lies a bit farther to the south, at 4° 27' northern latitude—serves to distinguish it from other capes of that name, among others in Selangor, on the west point of Singapore Island, etc.

93 See Rouffaer, part 1, p. 121.

94 See above.

95 See Rouffaer, part 1, pp. 116ff.

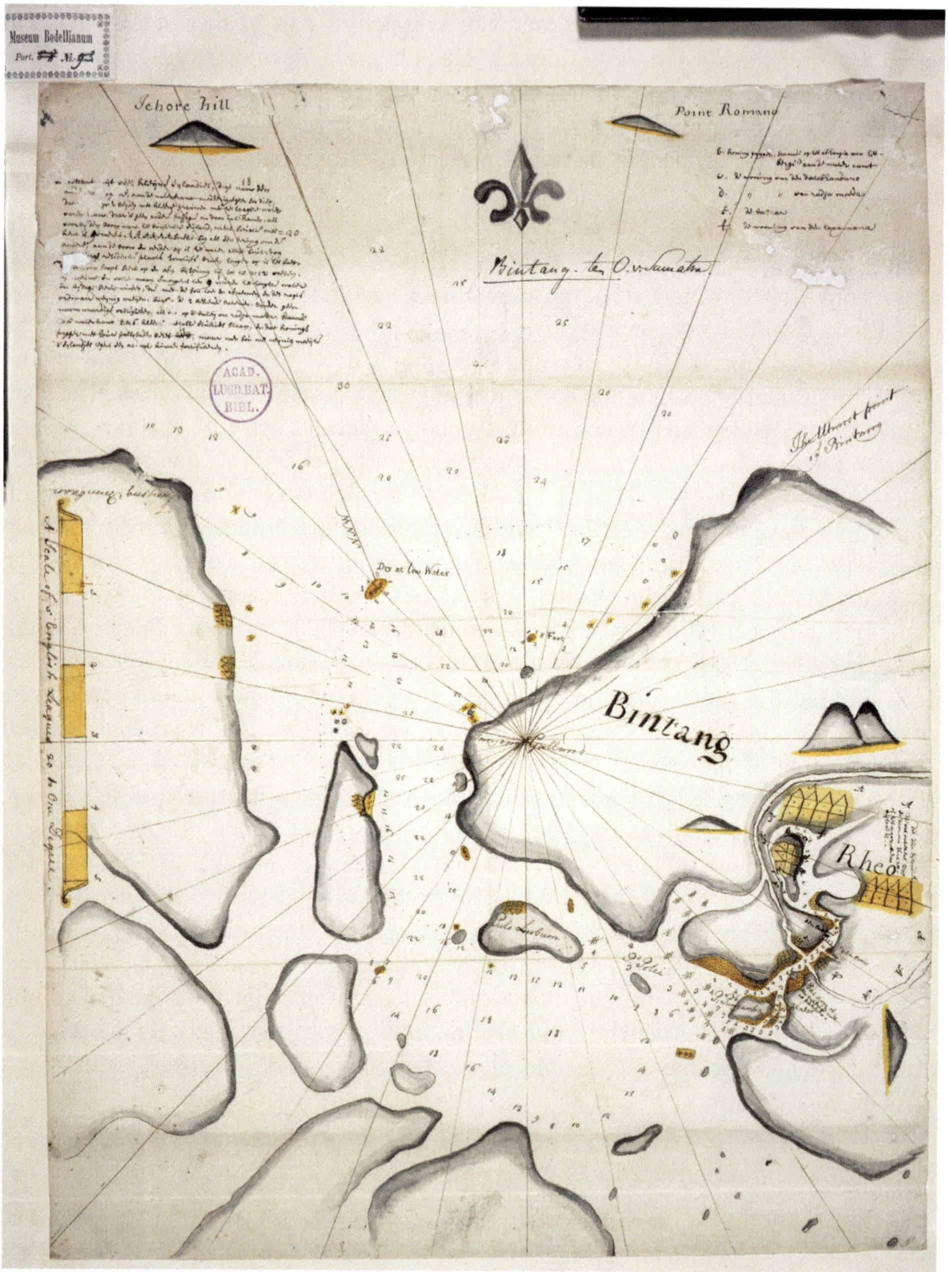

5.3 Map of the Riau Straits and Bintan, probably 18th century. Leiden: Collectie Bodel Nijenhuis, 006-15-003, Leiden University Library.

But I should not like being misunderstood concerning the nature of what I think I can distinguish here as the oldest core, younger cycle and third cycle of the *Sejarah Melayu*. I am fully convinced that Tun Muhamad is the author of the entire book; but, like all writers of older history and like all writers of historical novels until today, he has used earlier sources as much as possible, in keeping with the system (which is healthy in itself) of "je prends mon bien, où je le trouve"—taking, adapting and remodelling the contents of those sources and whole pieces from them to suit the author's own interest and purpose.

I have merely tried to show, not just in general terms but by clear, albeit entirely provisional indication of a small number of dividing lines in this native historical text, that just as the *Sejarah Melayu* did not appear out of the blue in 1614 as to its *literary* aspect, so this history book of the Malays equally was not without older historical examples when it was produced.

The introduction's own words about the "Hikayat Melayu" from "Goa" which had to be "improved" would suffice on their own to refute such an exclusivist view; but they go back no further than Sunday, 13 May 1612. The argument however goes back much further which has been preserved for us in the Portuguese sources that antedate it by 50 to 60 years: Barros' second *Década* from 1553 and d'Albuquerque's *Commentarios* from 1557. In those years, they were able to publish a foundational history of Singapore-Melaka and a history of the city of Melaka up to 1511 which in essence are parallel to stories 2–34 of the *Sejarah Melayu* (in a much shortened summary). Both Portuguese historians worked in Lisbon, so one should take into account a fair number of years for their information to become available from Melaka. As a consequence we may propose that ca. 1540 the essence of that Malay history *must* have been *present* among civilized Melakans in the form of notes, a *cherichera* or a *shair*—so that they were able to provide gifted half-bred Portuguese or curious commanders of the fortress (*capitães*), with an oral or written summary of it, which was subsequently used in the motherland by the keeper of the state archives, Barros and by the conqueror's son (Albuquerque). Indeed, when some 40 years later, Couto, keeper of the records at Goa, working so much closer to Melaka, says in his 4th *Década* (completed in 1597 and printed at Lisbon in 1602) that he wishes to partially correct what Barros, Albuquerque and Damião de Goes[96] wrote regarding Melaka, and in that context mentions proper names like Mrs "Milãotania" from Singapore (Mr Sang "Nila Utama" in stories 2–3 of the *S.M.*, place names like "Sencuder" (Sekudai) near "Ujantana" (Ujung Tanah) (to which the Malays driven from the city of Singapore by the Javanese retreated before they went and founded Melaka;[97] then we recognise authentic Malay information, in part misunderstood, in part used well and still of importance *today*, foreshadowing the *Sejarah Melayu* that was to come into existence ca. 20 years later. Not to mention the half-breed Manoel Godinho de Erédia, born in Melaka in 1563, who briefly in his *Informação da Aurea*

---

[96] Couto's mentioning Damião de Goes in this context—compare with Ferrand, *Relations de voyages*, vol. 1, p. 444n3—is a mistake. Goes in his *Chronica do rei D. Emmanuel III* (Lisbon: Em casa de Francisco Correa, 1568–7) gave a superficial sketch of Melaka in chapter 1, without mentioning any earlier rulers' names.

[97] Compare with Rouffaer, part 1, p. 32n1 and pp. 149–50 with notes.

Chersoneso (1599)[98] and over a whole chapter in his *Declaraçam de Malaca* (1603)[99] speaks of the enchanted Putri of the Gunung Ledang (aka Mount Ophir) in Melaka's inland[100]—of which the end of story 27 of the *Sejarah Melayu* likewise tells such a curious story, as the residence of a kind of Sibyl virgin.

But no less important than that appendix itself is the *colophon* of story 38, whose riddles have not been solved yet. At the end of this story, which has brought us to one of the last years of the "reign" of the drunkard-Sultan Alaudin Ri'ayat Shah III (ca. 1597–6 June 1613), it says (mainly in Dr Van Ronkel's translation of 1901):

> This is what was found by me, insignificant servant; as read in the hikayat of the illustrious father (God the Most High have mercy upon him), the datuk who passed away at Tanjung Batu. At the time when Johor was attacked and conquered by Jambi, I, insignificant one, was favoured by that illustrious father [*ayahenda itu*] with reading the Malay hikayat, how the glorious prince of the Bukit Si-Guntang descended to Palembang, proceeded from Palembang to Bintan, from Bintan to Singapura, which was conquered by the Javanese from Majapahit, then [went] to Melaka, which was conquered by the Portuguese, returned to Bintan once more, [and] from Bintan [proceeded] to Johor.
>
> This is what was read by me, insignificant one [literally: by the *datuk*'s slave]. And Allah knows best.[101]

---

[98] Eredia, "Informação da Aurea Chersoneso", in *Ordenações da Índia do Senhor Rei D. Manoel, etc.* ed. A.L. Caminha (Lisbon: Na Impressão Regia, 1807), p. 81.

[99] Eredia, *Declaraçam*, ed. Janssen (1882), ch. 15.

[100] On this chapter 15 (*not* 9) compare with the short summary in Ferrand, *Relations de voyages*, vol. 1, pp. 452–3. "Gunung Ledang" however is not "la vaste montagne", as Favre (1875) translated, but "Twilight Mountain, Hazy Mountain"; it does not have the incredible height of "4.186 mètres", nor is it "à l'ouest de Malaka", as Ferrand adds in a note, but it is 4,137 feet or 1,261 metres high and lies East-North-East from the city of Melaka. Eredia's "Informação" dates either from 1599 or from the spring of 1600 at the latest, since it is dedicated to Governor-General Dom Francisco da Gama (during his first term in this office, 25 May 1597–25 Dec. 1600), and on the other hand mentions (pp. 114–5) 1597 as the year of the safe return voyage of "Cornilio de Ortiman's" (Cornelis de Houtman's) fleet, which arrived at Texel on 14 Aug. 1598. For the author's biography see E.T. Hamy, "Le Descobridor Godinho de Eredia" in *Bulletin Société de Géographie*, ser. T.15 (1878): 511 [most of it copied in Ruelens' preface to the Janssen ed. of 1882, pp. 9–10; partly in Ferrand, *Relations des voyages*, vol. 1, p. 447n] and now particularly Sousa Viterbo in his valuable study, "Trabalhos nauticos dos Portuguezes nos seculos XVI e XVII", in *Memorias da Academia Real das Sciencias de Lisboa*, part 1 (Lisbon: Na Officina da Academia Real das Sciencias, 1898), pp. 153–9. It tells us that he died in Goa in March 1623, almost 60 years of age and that he is usually taken for a dreamer.

[101] Shellabear, *Sejarah Melayu* (1898), p. 190; compared with Shellabear (1910) vol. 2, pp. 264–5, a few words changed. The text reads: "Pada zaman itu hingga inilah yang dapat oleh pachal yang dlaif di-bacha di dalam ḥikayat ayahenda itu, rahúm Allah Ta'āla, iyaitu Datuk yang hilang di Tanjung Batu. Kapada masa Johor alah di-sĕrang Jambi, pachal Datuk di-kurniaï ayahenda itu mĕmbacha hikayat Mĕlayu oleh Baginda tĕrjali dari Bukit Si-Guntang turun ka-Palembang, dari Palembang lalu ka-Bintan, dari Bintan lalu ka-Singapura, maka alah Singapura oleh Jawa Majapahit, lalu ka-Malaka, alah Malaka oleh Fĕringgi, bĕrbalek pula ka-Bintan, dari Bintan lalulah ka-Johor. Had itulah yang tĕrbacha oleh pachal Datuk. Wa Allahu a'lam". The sole change I have made in this transliteration consists in starting a new sentence with "Kapada"; likewise in the translation. For Dr Van Ronkel's translation see "Toevoegsel op de Sadjarah Malajoe", *TBG* 44 (1901): 371. I prefer translating *ayahenda* with "illustrious father" to "princely father".

It remains uncertain if *datuk* should be translated as "grandfather" or "head of the family" here, or should be taken as an ancient title of high honour—not unlike our "Lord". The location of Tanjung Batu in the text is uncertain as well, since more than one cape of that name is known until today. One thinks first of the place name at the beach in central Pahang, 3° 12' n.l., where a *Kuala Tanjung Batu* runs into the sea, close to a kampung Tiring (lama); a closer investigation of the "great Malay chronicle" at Batavia[102] will make that clear in due course of time.[103] Concerning the *time* however when this colophon was written we need not be in doubt even for a moment: *after May 1673*.

For it was early in May 1673 that the Jambians surprised and destroyed Makām Tauḥīd, then capital of Johor (on a small river near Batu Sawar, see p. 441 above) and forced the Johorese sultan, Abdul Jalil Shah II (r. 1623–d. 22 Nov. 1677), son of the drunkard-sultan and therefore nephew of Raja Sabrang (Sultan Abdullah Ma'ayat Shah) in the *Sejarah Melayu*, to seek refuge in Pahang.[104] It was then, in that year 1673 which was once again so fateful for Johor, that the unnamed writer of the

---

[102] Manuscript no. 354. See above.

[103] Of course one can also think immediately of the Tanjung Batu which is mentioned at the end of story 19 of the *Sejarah Melayu* as lying in the Selat Ungaran, namely, in the southern part of the Strait of Melaka, between the "islands of Ongarangh" (as they are called in *Dagh-Register 1640–1641* [*DRB*, 1887], p. 226) or the islands at Sumatra's east shore, South-East of Bĕngkalis and West of Karimun on the one hand, and the southernmost part of Malaya's west shore on the other hand (the regions therefore of Muar, Batu Pahat, Bĕnut and Kukub). But *where* exactly in these Selat Ungaran of yore—a name that is now completely forgotten, but mentioned again at the beginning of story 35 of the *Sejarah Melayu*—this Tanjung Batu meant in story 19 lay and lies I have not been able to ascertain. I suspect it is the cape at Batu, Batu Pahat in full, at the southern mouth of the river of the same name (compare Rouffaer, part 2, p. 407). The "Tanjung Gading" in the Selat Ungaran mentioned in story 35 is the cape, protruding very little, of that name between the mouths of the Muar and Kĕsang rivers.

[104] On this disaster see Netscher, *De Nederlanders in Djohor en Siak*, p. 34, and on the Sultan of Johor at that time, ibid., pp. 32–4. His residence, "Makam Tolhied", is mentioned on p. 33. In 1641 (François Valentijn, *Oud en Nieuw Oost-Indiën, Vervattende een Naauwkeurige en Uitvoerige Verhandelinge van Nederlands Mogentheyd in de Gewesten, etc.*, 5 parts in 8 vols. [Dordrecht and Amsterdam: Johannes van Braam and Gerard Onder de Linden, 1724–26], 5, 1 [1726], fol. 345a) spells this "from Maccam Thoeheet (or from Johor)"; see also in the *Dagh-Registers* for 1640–41 (*DRB*, 1887) and 1641–42 (*DRB*, 1900) passim, the register references to "Makam-toehel" [!] and "Maccam Toeheet" [Makham Tāuḥid].

Netscher however only mentions the *year*: "in 1673". It appears from the *Dagh-Register* for 1673 (*DRB*, 1901), pp. 128 and 146, that the correct date of the destruction must be *ca. 10 May* of that year. For it was done by Pangeran Dipati of Jambi, who had left for Johor from Palembang under the guise of a peaceful mission on 3 May, while already on 15 May news reached Palembang of the treacherous surprise attack, "and that furthermore the king of Johor had fled to Pahan" (over land on an elephant, to be precise). In this context it is noteworthy that the so-called *Hikayat nĕgĕri Johor*—see Dr H.H. Juynboll's *Catalogus van de Maleische en Sundanesche HSS der Leidsche Universiteits Bibliotheek* (Leiden: E.J. Brill, 1899) [Catalogue of Malay MSS, Leiden], pp. 236–7, *starts* with this catastrophe at the end of 1083 AH (more correctly the beginning of 1084 AH, since it started on 18 April) and then continues up to the end of the 18th century. The same goes for the two manuscripts at Batavia; see Dr Van Ronkel's *Catalogue* (1909), pp. 275–6.

colophon had obtained from his *ayahenda* (in general "illustrious" and hence also "princely" father), that is, "the datuk who passed away at Tanjung Batu" the favour of … reading the "Hikayat Melayu", that is the *Sejarah Melayu*, which was "what was found" by him, that is, up to and including the end of story 38.[105]

This then is the extraordinary meaning of this colophon: dating from a year between 1673 and, say, ca. 1700, it tells us that the text of the entire *Sejarah Melayu*, written by Bendahara Tun Muhamad at Batu Sawar in Dal 1023 AH or 1614 CE (as we learned earlier), ends only with story 38. The *textus receptus* of 34 stories as given by Abdullah and Dulaurier and in fact Leyden as well, indeed as even Reverend P. van der Vorm must have known it before 1708 and as Reverend Father Valentijn became acquainted with it between 1708 and 1726,[106] and as Reverend

---

[105] For this *correct* count I expressly refer to the warning at the end in Rouffaer, part 1, p. 123. The true *numbering* is found in Malay Manuscript no. 1703 at Leiden, described in Juynboll's *Catalogus* (1899), p. 231; the same division—albeit without numbering—is found in the Leiden Manuscript, 1716 (Dulaurier's "MS A"!), 1736 and 3210, as well as the Batavia Manuscripts 343 and 345 (see Van Ronkel's *Catalogue* [1909], pp. 268–70).

[106] On pp. 8–9 of his anonymous preface of 1708—see above; the preface and the *Verhandeling des Taals* [Treatise on the language] following it are signed "Batavia, in the year of our Lord 1708" and "Fare thee well"—Van der Vorm gives a list of the Malay works known to him:

1. *Makota sĕgala Raja* or *Taju as-Salatina*;
2. *Indraputra* (indara patara);
3. *History of Alexander the Great*;
4. *Kalilah dan Daminah*;
5. *Sulalet as-Salatina* or *Pĕnurunan sĕgala Raja*;
6. *Hikayat Hamzah*;
7. *Hikayat Muhamad Hanafiyah*; to be added (having been mentioned by him on p. 5);
8. *Shamsuddin's Mir'at al-mu'min*; and
9. *Hikayat Isma Yatim*.

No. 5 he describes as follows: "Finally it must be said that the *aficionado* should take a serious look at the book called *Sula'letu's-salathyna* or *pennuruwnan segalla ra'ja-ra'ja*, not only for its language but also for its content, which shows us the origins of the *Malay kings* and the vicissitudes of the *Malay kingdom* and *country*, up to [!] the arrival of the Portuguese" (p. 9). Valentijn, who provided the second printed list of Malay manuscripts in his *Ambonsche zaaken van den Godsdienst*" [Ambonese Matters of Religion] (1726), ch. 2 part 3, p. 1, fols. 26–7 (*not* fol. 16, as Werndly erroneously refers in the preface to his *Maleische Spraakkunst* [Malay Grammar] of 1736 [Amsterdam: R. and G. Wetstein], p. 67), mentions among the "24 Malay texts in an Arabic letter which the author possesses" (plus two which he had been unable to acquire) as no. 10, quarto: "*Sulalet Essalatina*, or *the Origins of the Kings of the Malay Coast, and of Malacca*; however I do not have this in Arabic, but in Dutch script". Now [Valentijn] in his part 5, 1 (1726), fols. 316–7, he digresses on this work in his *Description of Malacca*, and strangely calls it *Kitab Hantuwa or Hangtuha* as well as (see also below) acknowledges: "before I possessed this last book, I was much enlightened by a preface by my former fellow-minister Petrus van der Vorm, published in the reprinted *Dictionarium* of [D. Heurnius and] F. Gueynier [Batavia: Andries Lambert Loderus, 1708], and in part used it here", and *ends* his chapter 2 (which is taken entirely from the *Sejarah Melayu* of 32 to 34 stories; partly in accordance with Van der Vorm's brief summary on his pp. 4–5 and apparently partly based on his own more elaborate summary) with the *arrival* of the

G.H. Werndly knew it before 1736, is *not* the full text, but the text with 38 stories, as edited by Shellabear, *is*. Toward the end of that last story there appears the same Tun Sri Lanang who became bendahara around 1585, and of whom we now have a picture, seen through hostile Dutch eyes, made by Matelieff's secretary on 27 May 1606; and who in his introduction of 1614, with a fitting mixture of subject humility and orang kaya pride, presented us with his genealogy and the genesis of his book.

Thus the colophon is a *tammat* of the highest value—who it was exactly who wrote it, and apart from the other stories, still scattered about, that *may* belong to the text.[107]

Portuguese under "Sultan Mahhmud Shah" (fol. 320b), after which he starts summarising the Portuguese sources. And finally G.H. Werndly, who in the preface to his *Maleische spraakkunst* [Malay grammar] (Amsterdam: R. & G. Wetstein, 1736), p. 68, states that "in the library room of the Malays' books" he was able to use:

a. "the printed catalogue of the books from the estate of Rev. *Petrus van der Vorm*, as they were sold publicly at Batavia", that is, an auction catalogue printed soon after 17 May 1731 (the date of Van der Vorm's death);
b. Valentijn's list from 1726 mentioned above;
c. "a list of books and papers from the estate of Sir *Isaac de St Martin*" dated 4 May 1696, found by Dr De Haan in the National Archives at Batavia in 1899 (compare above);
d. a list Werndly himself made "of the Arabic, Malay and Javanese books from the estate of Rev. *Hermannus Kolde de Horn*", deceased in Batavia on 31 May 1719; and finally
e. "my own book treasure" (Werndly, p. 68).

Werndly, in his famous "Room of Malay Books" at the end of his book, mentions as no. 51 of the 69 + 8 (nearly three times the number Valentijn gave) Malay manuscripts he lists and briefly describes: "*Sulâtetu*[sic]-'*lsalâthîn*, or in Malay *Penurûnan segala raja* [The line or descent of the kings]. This book is most commendable, not only for its language but also for its subject matter, to wit, the descent of the Malay kings from Alexander the Great, and the vicissitudes of the Malay kingdom and country up to [!] the arrival of the Portuguese" (pp. 352–3). So we have here beginning and end of the textus receptus, stories 1–32 or 34. Werndly likewise mentions the "SS." (*Sulâletu-'lsalâthîn*) among the sources of his quotations (Werndly, p. 68), and on p. 186 one indeed finds the quotation, "Maka berperanglah 'awrang Malâka dengan 'awrang Pâhang", although the manuscript page no. has *not been filled in* ("p. ..."). This is a pity, for Werndly's information could serve to identify an old manuscript of the *Sejarah Melayu*; the quotation comes from story 13, in Shellabear (1898), p. 59, ll. 23–4, with a variant reading: "Maka orang M. pun bĕrpĕranglah d.o.P.". But *where* is this manuscript of Valentijn's hiding, "in Dutch script" and therefore older than 1726? It is strange that Valentijn's old and important list of 27 manuscripts (26 + 1; all of them, with the exception of three, also mentioned in Werndly's "Room of Books": nos. 5, 9–10, 14, 18–9, 21, 25–6, 28–9, 32, 34–5, 39–43, 45, 51, 59 and 63) has received so little attention from Malayists thus far. *What*, for example, does Valentijn's number 18 in part 3, 1: "Het Voorbeeld van de vertroosting van 't herte, behelzende verscheide "oude Geschiedenissen der Maleyers [The Example of the Solace for the Heart, Comprising Various Old Histories of the Malays] (fol. 26b)" mean?

[107] I am referring first of all to H.N. van der Tuuk's remark about Manuscript no. 18 of the Raffles collection at the Royal Asiatic Society in London: "This manuscript however contains chapters that are not found in other copies and have not been translated by Leyden. The

5.4 Photomechanical reproduction of a self-portrait by Manuel Godinho de Erédia, c.1613. M.G. de Erédia, *Malaca l'Inde Méridionale e le Cathay: Manuscrit original autographe de Godinho de Eredia appartenant à la Bibliothèque Royale de Bruxelles*, tr. M.L. Janssen (Bruxelles: Librairie Européenne C. Muquardt, 1882). © Peter Borschberg, private collection.

Was it a digression to detail the *histoire intime* (intimate history) of the *Sejarah Melayu* when we came here only for the recently recovered location of Batu Sawar?

I am deeply convinced that it was not. After all, this work is the only text that one may call an old history book of the Malays, no matter how unsatisfactory it is in our modern view. Everything that came after it in the 17th and 18th centuries—the bulky *Hikayat Hang Tuah* first, the *Bustān as-Salatīn* which we already mentioned and which has hardly been disclosed so far, the 18th-century *Hikayat Raja-Raja Pasai*—is either much closer to a novel or of much less general interest.[108] And older Malay sources are unknown thus far, apart from the *Hikayat Koris*, whose riddles yet remain unsolved. Is it not true that now, for the first time, the knowledge of the author and genesis of the *Sejarah Melayu* has alighted on proper firm ground from the old cloud of careless babble?[109]

---

penultimate chapter for instance deals with *Sang Naja*'s conspiracy against the Portuguese at Mălaka" (Van der Tuuk, "Kort Verslag", p. 426). Are these perhaps "apocryphal stories"? At present, in 1921, *still nothing further* is known!

[108] Apart from Dulaurier's edition of the *Hikayat Raja-Raja Pasai* in Arabic script based on the unique manuscript in the Raffles collection (1849), there is a useful French translation with notes by A. Marre, *Sadjârah malâyou*. The *Hikayat Hang Tuah* was, again, edited in transliteration by W.G. Shellabear—practical as ever, being a born American—as no. 3 of the Malay Literature Series (Singapore, 1908–9), in four parts.

The claim that the *Hikayat Hang Tuah* was written "shortly after 1600" by Dr R. Brandstetter, in his translation "*Die Geschichte von Hang Tuah*" [The Story of Hang Tuah] (Luzern: Geschwister Doleschal, 1894), p. 3, is quite incorrect. It would be about right to say that it was written around *1700*. For it must have been written after 1641 (the year of the Dutch seizure of Melaka, the event with which the *Hikayat* ends) and before 1726, when Valentijn in his part 5, 1, fol. 316, in his *Description of Malaka* mentioned the work for the very first time, as follows: "and Kitab Hantuwa or Hangtuha, that is, the book of Hang Tuah, otherwise commonly known to the scholars of that language by the name of *Sulalet essalathina*, that is: the line or family tree of the kings (namely, the Malakan ones)". This confusion of the *Hikayat Hang Tuah* and the *Sejarah Melayu* is even worse in Werndly (1736), no. 43, in his "Room of Malay Books": there, Hang Tuah is even called the "author" of both works! On the other hand, Hang Tuah does not yet occur in the estate of Isaac de Saint-Martin in 1696 (compare above), nor in the preface by Rev. P. van der Vorm dating from 1708 (see above).

[109] What should one think of a man like Wilkinson, being able to write in 1907: "The Sejarah Melayu was written at Aceh [!] in 1612 CE" (*Papers on Malay subjects. Malay Literature*, pt. 1, p. 15)? The article "Sajarah Malayu" in the *Encyclopaedie van Nederlandsch-Indië* [Encyclopaedia of the Dutch Indies], 2nd ed. (Leiden: E.J. Brill, 1919), part 3, deserves mention in this context as well. Wilkinson incidentally also dared to write: "From internal evidence we can infer that the 'Romance of Hang Tuah' was written about the middle of the 16th century" (p. 16); which is not an error for "17th". Later, in 1911, Wilkinson changed his opinion regarding the time of the *Sejarah Melayu*'s composition. He then claimed in "Notes on the Negri Sembilan" (in *Papers on Malay Subjects: Malay History*, ed. R.J. Wilkinson [Kuala Lumpur: F.M.S. Government Press, 1911], p. 11), mainly on the grounds of a sentence at the end of story 26 ("*Maka Raja Sulung ... sĕkarang ini*" [Shellabear, ed. *Sejarah Melayu* (1898), p. 120, ll. 12–9 from the bottom]): "The 'Annals' cannot have been written in their present form prior to 1635 CE"; and in a note: "The last chapter [that is, the appendix of four stories] was added very much later than 1636". (See, however, the rebuttal in Rouffaer, part 2, *appendix* 2, p. 596, note, for this concerns a few later interpolations.)

6

Richard O. Winstedt

The Early History of Singapore, Johore and Melaka: An Outline of a Paper by Gerrit Pieter Rouffaer*

6.1 Sir Richard O. Winstedt, a prominent colonial administrator who had a hand in preserving several works of Malay literature. Kuala Lumpur: Malaysian Branch of the Royal Asiatic Society.

In the 1921 edition of *Bijdragen tot de Taal- Land- en Volkenkunde van Nederlandsch-Indie* (vol. 77), G.P. Rouffaer, who first identified *tanah* Melayu as the basin of the Jambi, has published a startling paper on the geography of the Malayan Peninsula. It is probable that his surmises as to the situation of Langkasuka and several other theories will not be accepted, but his paper should be in the hands of every serious student of peninsular history.

* First published in *JSBRAS* 86 (1922): 257–60.

Rouffaer brushes aside G. Ferrand's recent theory (*Journal Asiatique*, 1918) that Melaka existed, as the unreliable Gaspar Correia wrote, for 700 years before the coming of the Portuguese, under the name Malayu, Marco Polo's Malayur. Malayur is only a Tamil form of Malayu, the original home of the Malays in Jambi. Would Fra Odorigo van Pordenone (Friar Odoric) and Ibn Battuta have been silent over the existence of such an early Melaka? Would the *Nāgarakṛtāgama* (1365 CE), recording the conquests of Hayam Wuruk, the famous ruler of Majapahit, have then referred to the peninsula simply as Pahang?

On the other hand it is hardly likely that in 1403 Melaka "belonged to Siam", as the *Ming Annals* say; from 1405 to 1413 was a Hindu state under Permaisura and becoming Muslim under Gujarati influence in 1414 suddenly won trade and empire. The *Pararaton* mentions two Malay princesses captured at the fall of Jambi and one Tuhan Wuruju (Bongsu), a *dewa-putĕra* (that is, son of a Ksatriya *dewa*) of Pamelekahan or "Melaka lands", a captive in Majapahit in 1328. Again Gerini tells how Siamese laws enacted in 1360 cite as tributary to Siam "Ujong Tanah, *Malaka*, Malayu, Worawari" (*Researches* [1909], pp. 531–2). Probably Barros (1553) and the *Sejarah Melayu* are right in saying that Melaka existed as early as the middle of the 13th century and became a commercial centre about 1400 owing to immigration of Malays from Singapore or Tumasik, the "sea country".

Barros (1553), the most reliable of Portuguese chroniclers, relates how one Sangesinga (? Sangyang Singha) ruler of Singapore was murdered by his guest Permaisura, who was a fugitive *from East Java* owing to disturbances on the death of Pararisa (O.J. Bhra Wicesa, who ascended the throne of Majapahit in 1389 and ruled some 40 years). The king of Siam attacked the usurper who fled to Pago on the Muar. His whilom followers, the Cellates (Orang Laut) opened Bertam near Melaka.

D'Albuquerque (1557) relates how, when Melaka was founded, a Bhatara ruled Tumapel in Java and the Permaisura fled to Singapore, murdered its chief and ruled it for five years, until the ruler of Patani, brother of the murdered chief, drove him to Muar, whence he went to Bintão (Bertam) and founded Melaka. The reference to Tumapel is valuable.

The *Sejarah Melayu* (chapters 5 and 10) give the Malay tradition of Singapore's relationship with Java. The end of chapter 10 refers to its destruction by Hayam Wuruk *after* 1338 when according to the *Pararaton* Gajah Mada took his famous oath not to eat *palapa* until ten countries including Palembang, Pahang and Tumasik had been subjected to Majapahit and *before* 1365 when the *Nāgarakṛtāgama* tells how all the islands and states in the east and west of the Malay Archipelago had been subdued. The lettering on the fragment of the Singapore monolith, now in Raffles' Museum, is said by Dr Krom to resemble Majapahit characters and to antedate somewhat 1360. Dr Krom is studying a cast of the fragment.

How old is Singapore? I-tsing mentions in 690 a state "Mo-ho-hsin" at the south of the peninsula = Mahasin "the great salt state", which Rouffaer identifies with a Malay land "Hassin" recorded in a Majapahit inscription of 1034 to have been conquered by Airlangga, a prince in East Java (b. 991; r. 1019–42). Probably it is Ibn Khordadybeh's "Schalahit" (Selat). According to Rouffaer it was Tasik = Temasik (of the 14th century) = old Samudra = Singapura (of the 15th century), while on the mainland was Wura-wari (old Javanese, henceforth O.J. = "clear water") from the 10th to 11th centuries = Ganggayu, i.e. Gangga ayu (O.J. = "fresh water"), before

1450 but still known at the time of the *Sejarah Melayu* (1612) = Johor of the 16th century. An inscription of 1006 in Sanskrit and old Javanese, in the Calcutta Museum, tells how Wurawari had brought disaster to Java, and the Siamese laws of 1360 count it among places subject to Siam. In the Tanjore inscription of Rajendracola I (1030), Kadaram = Kedah, Srivijayam = Palembang and Malayur = Jambi; and Rouffaer suggests Mayirudingam = Great Yirudingam = Chau Ju-kua's Great Ji-lo-t'ing = Mahasin = Singapore; Ilangacogam = Langkasuka = Ganggayu = Wurawari; and Ma-Ppappalam = ? Pahang or Penang, and Mevilimbangam "the walled" may be the Dingings or Klang. Langkasuka = Chau Ju-kua's Ling-ya-ssi-kia (1225) = the Nāgarakṛtāgama's Langkasuka (1365) = I-tsing's Lang-ka-su (692) = Langgasu or Langga of the Chinese annals of the Liang dynasty (502–56) = ? the Lanka of the *Ramayana*. The Calcutta inscription speaks of Luaram (= *lwah* O.J. "river, water" and ram Skt. = *rama* "sweet, charming") as its capital.

An inscription of 924 CE of prince Sri Wijayaloka of East Java speaks of Ujong Galoh = Ujong Putri = Jong Galoh or the Hujung Galoh of Airlangga's inscription. *Galoh* "jewel" = *jauhar* (Arabic) = Johor, and the name fits the honorific Ratna-parayana of the old Javanese *Ramayana* and the "Golden Chersonese" of Ptolemy, whose Sabana will correspond with the 16th century Straits of Sabang and be the Karimuns, Hasin or Galoh. Was it from the Biduanda Kallang of Kallang River that the mysterious Kalangs, prisoners of war mentioned in old Javanese romance, came? Among the Solo regalia (*upachara*) are a Snake (*Ardawalike*) and a Roc (*Garuda*); among the Jokja regalia only the Snake. These must be symbols of the victory of Airlangga's as Vishnu's Garuda over the "snake" princes of Wurawari, Hasin and Langka; as of the other regalia in which an Elephant symbolizes Patih Gajah Mada, a Cock Hayam Wuruk and a Buffalo-Calf Java's victory over Menangke(r)bau; and so on. To this day a Garuda is the symbol of Hindu Bali (first conquered by Java in Airlangga's time), while the Muslim mosques and art of Java took a snake as the symbol of Islam's victory over Hinduism.

Apparently about 1135 Daha brought Galoh nearly to ruin. A Panji tale (*BKI* 2, 7 [1863]) speaks of a Klana Tunjong-Seta, prince of the island Kenchana, (= "gold" and ? the "Golden Chersonese"), who desiring to win a Daha-princess, Dewi Angreni, (or Raden Galoh), attacked Java and failed, slain by Pangeran Klana Jayang Sari, *alias* Raden Panji Kuda Wanengpati, a prince of Jenggala in the service of the ruler of Kediri. The people of Kenchana and three princes were carried captive to Java. Perhaps the *Sejarah Melayu* (chapters 14 and 19) show that Middle Java and Ujong Tanah once came to grips and that Melaka, or really Galoh, had to do with Daha in the Panji period.

Though the early Portuguese knew nothing of Galoh, Ganggayu or Langka, the *Sejarah Melayu* (chapter 1) connects Ganggayu with Johor and interprets the word to mean "a treasure-house of jewels", which fits both *galoh* and *jauhar*.

Between 1275, when Kertanagara of Tumapel sent his ill-fated expedition against Palembang and Marco Polo's visit in 1292, apparently Kertanagara had destroyed Mahasin, that is, old Singapore (*Sejarah Melayu*, chapter 5). But Marco Polo mentions "Pentam" or Bintan, whither perhaps one band of fugitives had fled, and the *Sejarah Melayu* records how the founders of the new town Tumasik came from Bintan. The Javanese name, Tumasik, may have been given by men of Tumapel, who, after Majapahit triumphed over their country in 1293 owing to the absence of

Tumapel's forces in Palembang, stayed in Sumatra and the Malay islands. Probably Kertanagara's attack on Hasin drove sea Malays (*wong asin*) not only to Bintan but also to Muar and "Melaka lands", opposite of which were the "Five Islands" that in early Chinese charts take the place of Melaka. Majapahit's attack about 1360 must have sent a yet further band in the same direction. From 1328 to the death of Hayam Wuruk, the great Majapahit conqueror, in 1389, the Melaka Straits would be under Javanese influence and only later under the Siamese suzerainty of which Chinese annals and Siamese laws speak.

Such in briefest outline is Rouffaer's paper, which fills 174 pages and is to be continued further.[1]

Though it has no direct bearing on this paper, it is interesting to note that Raffles' Museum has not only a neolithic celt from Singapore but also several from Kota Tinggi in Johor, all made from local stone.

[1] [E.N.: Rouffaer's article was published in two parts. Winstedt refers here to the first section published in *BKI* 77, 1 (1921): 1–174. The second half was published later that year in *BKI* 77, 3–4 (1921): 359–604.]

7

Richard O. Winstedt

A Note on the Founding of Singapore*

In both versions of the *Malay Annals* the founder of Singapore is a prince of Indian descent who had been given the throne of Palembang by a chief with the corrupt name of Demang Lebar Daun, and both versions make this chief a descendant of a Raja Shulan. Shulan is generally taken to be a corruption of Chola, but if Demang Lebar Daun were a Chola, it would mean that the Indian dynasty which ruled Palembang (or Śri Vijaya) was installed after 1025, the date of the first Chola raid on that country. In fact Palembang bore the Indian name of Śri Vijaya and had rulers with Sanskrit titles as early as the time of the Buddhist monk I-tsing, who stayed there for six months in 671 CE to study Sanskrit. Demang Lebar Daun, whatever his correct name, must have been an aboriginal chief who welcomed Indian rule and Indian trade.

According to the *Malay Annals* the Indian prince who had been installed as ruler of Palembang sailed away first to Bintan and thence to Tumasik, where he settled, giving it the new name of Singapura and bringing with him from Palembang the title of Sri Tri Buana, "The glory of three worlds". No ruler of Palembang and probably no king ever settled at Singapore: only a governor or representative of its respective suzerains. But though the title "glory of three worlds" was a title of Chola kings and a queen regent (1329–30) of Majapahit, Ming chronicles record that it was also assumed by rulers of Śri Vijaya, and it may well have been ascribed anachronistically to the Palembang king in whose reign Singapura was founded. The oldest version of the *Malay Annals* gives that king the name of Sang Utama and says that his eldest brother became ruler of Minangkabau and was styled Sang Sapurba, though Minangkabau does not come into history until the 14th century, when it succeeded Śri Vijaya's successor Jambi (or Melayu). The later version of the *Annals* makes Sang Sapurba the title of the founder of Singapore.

* First published in *JSEAH* 5, 2 (1964): 15–6.

Such a jumble of legend and history mixed up with the story of Alexander the Great as ancestor of Malay royalty is hardly promising. Yet the central core that Singapore was under Palembang rule has been corroborated by the discovery by Professor Coedès nearly half a century ago of a far-flung Malay Buddhist empire Śri Vijaya that, comprising Palembang and Kedah, exercised such authority over the Malay peninsula and the adjacent sea-passage to China that its colonies were raided successively by the Cholas, Majapahit and Siam.

Four inscriptions in old Malay, two in Palembang, one in Jambi and one on the island of Bangka, are evidence that the 7th century CE was a time of great expansion for Śri Vijaya, and the Bangka inscription mentions an expedition against Java in 686. It is highly improbable that, possessing Bangka and being strong enough to attack Java, Palembang would not exercise authority over Tumasik or Singapura and the southern entrance to what were to become the Melaka Straits. Confirmation of the early founding of Singapore is to be found in the fact that the father of Balaputra, the first Śailendra ruler of Śri Vijaya, reigned in Java from 812 to 832, and that neither the Śailendra title of Sri Maharaja nor the name Śailendra is attached in the *Malay Annals* to the founder of Singapore, as might be expected if he were a Śailendra. The title Sri Maharaja is, however, given in those annals to both the father and son of the Palembang prince Parameswara, afterwards Iskandar Shah, the last lord of Singapore and founder of Melaka (1344–1424).

It would appear certain that Singapore was colonized by a ruler of Palembang, probably about the 7th century.

But the folklore of the *Malay Annals* has so confused research, that Dr Linehan, for example, adding up the reigns of five so-called kings of Singapore, concluded that Singapore was founded in 1299, when Śri Vijaya was in decay and its successor Jambi had been conquered by the Javanese Kritanagara and deprived of control of the Melaka Straits.[1]

[1] Walter Linehan, "The Kings of 14th Century Singapore", *JMBRAS* 20, 2 (1947): 117–27.

8

Timothy P. Barnard

Confrontation on a River: Singapore as an Eighteenth-century Battleground in Malay Historiography*

Introduction

> When they arrived in the Straits, the Riau ships anchored at the mouth of the Singapore River. [Upon seeing the boats] ... the people from Siak went downstream. The Riau ships fired at them, but the people from Siak showed little concern. As the Siak ships neared fighting broke out; there were even cannon shots. They were at war.[1]

In 1767 representatives of two Malay states fought a battle on the Singapore River. Accounts of this confrontation appear in various traditional local texts, as well as the Dutch East India Company archives, but it has yet to gain the attention of any recently produced histories of Singapore.[2] This absence is understandable since it was but a minor clash in a larger conflict. In the fighting that ensued, Raja Ismail

* First published as a chapter in *Early Singapore: Evidence in Maps, Texts and Artefacts*, ed. J.N. Miksic and C.A.M.G. Low (Singapore: National Museum, 2004), pp. 118–23.

[1] Tengku Said, *Hikayat Siak*, intro. and ed. Muhammad Yusoff Hashim (Kuala Lumpur: Dewan Bahasa dan Pustaka, 1992), pp. 157–8.

[2] Ibid., pp. 157–63; Raja Ali Haji ibn Ahmad, *Tuhfat al-Nafis* [The precious gift], trans. and annot. Virginia Matheson and Barbara Watson Andaya (Kuala Lumpur: Oxford University Press, 1982), pp. 128–33; "Hikayat Negeri Johor", in *The History of Johore* (1365–1895), by Richard Winstedt (Kuala Lumpur: MBRAS, 1979), pp. 267–8; The Hague, National Archives of the Netherlands, Ms. VOC 3245 (2nd Part), Incoming Letters from Outer Areas: Letter from Sri Sultan Abdul Jalil bin Marhum Sultan Muhammad, to Governor and Council at Malacca (received 4 Nov.

of Siak lost to a Bugis force from Johor-Riau led by Daeng Kemboja. The official reason for the battle in 1767 was a complicated Siak attempt to assist the Malay nobility of Johor-Riau. Although Johor-Riau was momentarily triumphant, the war continued since it involved contentious issues between the two states, particularly their legitimacy as Malay states, which was often determined by their status within the historiography of the region. This status was based on the maintenance of texts that glorified the rulers and emphasized links to previous idealized states. These traditional Malay texts were not simply tales of a distant past; they functioned, more importantly, as guides to how a state and its rulers could achieve status, power and authority. With regard to this historiography, Singapore played a significant and considerably vital role.

The tensions between Siak and Johor-Riau, and their corresponding histories, had developed earlier in the 18th century. At the beginning of the century the Johor sultanate was facing considerable adversity. Its dependencies were dissatisfied with the increasingly dominant role that Johor was playing in their societies, and many of them rebelled against attempts to supervise and funnel trade through Johor ports. While some of the resentment can be traced to economic turmoil in the area, many of the residents of the Melaka Straits traced the origins of their troubles to the events surrounding the misrule of the Johor sultan in the late 17th century. In both Malay texts and Western accounts, this sultan, known as Mahmud, committed numerous sadistic acts toward the Johor populace and eventually was murdered by his ruling council when they could not accept such behaviour any longer.[3] This murder, which occurred in 1699, severed the links that legitimized Johor's position in the Malay world, which was based on Sultan Mahmud being a direct descendant of the sovereign line of rulers that stretched back not only to the idealized state of Melaka but also to its earlier model, Srivijaya.[4]

In 1718 a man calling himself Raja Kecik appeared in the east Sumatran port of Bengkalis and began to gather followers among the ethnic groups that traded in the port. Raja Kecik was able to defeat the warriors protecting Johor with these followers. After a series of conflicts with Bugis mercenaries brought in to protect the Johor rulers, Raja Kecik retreated to Sumatra and developed his own Malay sultanate along the Siak River. But the enmity that developed between Raja Kecik's Siak and the newly reformed Johor-Riau sultanate remained. Siak acted as a counter to

1767). For an excellent history that understandably does not contain the battle, see Malcolm Murfett et al., *Between Two Oceans: A Military History of Singapore from First Settlement to Final British Withdrawal* (Singapore: Oxford University Press, 1999).

[3] There are numerous accounts of how Sultan Mahmud mistreated the residents of Johor, For example see Said, *Hikayat Siak*, pp. 107–8; Alexander Hamilton, *Alexander Hamilton: A Scottish Sea Captain in Southeast Asia, 1689–1723*, ed. Michael Smithies (Chiang Mai: Silkworm Books, 1997), pp. 74–6.

[4] The implications of the murder of Sultan Mahmud are most clearly handled in Leonard Y. Andaya, *Kingdom of Johor, 1641–1724* (Kuala Lumpur: Oxford University Press, 1975), ch. 7. The tracing of sovereignty back to Melaka and ultimately Srivijaya is found in the early chapters of the *Sejarah Melayu*. O.W. Wolters reconstructed much of this in *The Fall of Srivijaya in Malay History* (London: Cornell University Press, 1970).

Johor-Riau in its attempts to dominate trade, politics, and even Malay historiography in the region.

Militarily, battles were fought between the two states through constant raids on shipping, and even extended on occasion to open warfare, throughout the 18th century. The 1767 battle along the Singapore River was simply one among these numerous clashes. The conflicts, however, were fundamentally based on local concepts of power, since a state could only prosper if it fulfilled the ideals which were laid down in traditional Malay texts. For both Siak and Johor-Riau the key Malay text was the *Sulalat Us-Salatin* (Genealogy of the Sultans); it was a work of traditional Malay literature describing the basic governmental structure of Malay Melaka, interspersed with tales of its great leaders. This text is better known as the *Sejarah Melayu* (Malay Annals).[5]

The Role of Traditional Malay Histories

The *Sejarah Melayu* was relevant to both states due to connections they had with Melaka. The fleeing Melaka leadership had formed the Johor polity in the 16th century and commissioned the recording of the *Sejarah Melayu*. In this context, the political-historical narrative came to be a guide for Johor and other Malay states in matters related to status, power and identity. The death of Sultan Mahmud in 1699, however, had severed the connections that Johor had possessed to the idealized Melaka portrayed in the *Sejarah Melayu*. Into this vacuum stepped the leaders of Siak, who also used historiography to fight their battle by maintaining their own legitimizing court text, the *Hikayat Siak*.

The *Hikayat Siak* can be conveniently divided into two sections.[6] The first half is basically a copy of the *Sejarah Melayu*. In this first section of the text, links between Melaka and Siak are based on the subjugation of Siak to the will of Melaka. East Sumatran leaders who operated independently are incorporated through marriage into the Melaka royal family and are granted royal titles. When this does not achieve the desired effect, Siak is attacked and controlled through force. Once the Melaka rulers transferred their state to Johor, however, the text falls silent. The story continues with the death of Sultan Mahmud, and the tale is given an interesting twist. In the *Hikayat Siak*, Mahmud is portrayed as the father of Raja Kecik.[7] Thus, proponents of this text could use this claim as evidence that Siak was the legitimate heir to the glorious heritage of Melaka, since the sacred line of rulers that stretched back to Melaka through Johor could be traced to, and seen as continued in, Siak.

---

[5] For a discussion of the pre-eminent place that the *Sejarah Melayu* has achieved in the study of Malay literature and history, see H.M.J. Maier, *In the Center of Authority: The Malay Hikayat Merong Mahawangsa* (Ithaca: Cornell Southeast Asia Program, 1988), pp. 29–30, 42.

[6] The Cod. Or. 7304 version of the *Hikayat Siak* is 647 folio pages, the first 400 being a version of the *Sejarah Melayu*. Even the modern transliteration and publication of the *Hikayat Siak* does not publish the first 401 folio pages of the text. R.O. Roolvink, "The Variant Versions of the Malay Annals", *BKI* 123 (1967): 309.

[7] The implications of this claim are discussed in Timothy P. Barnard, *Raja Kecik dan Mitos Pengabsahaannya* (Pekanbaru: Pusat Pengajian Melayu, 1994).

As a traditional Malay narrative, the *Hikayat Siak* has not received the attention it deserves, perhaps because it is seen as derivative of the *Sejarah Melayu*, and the outrageous nature of the claims over the connections between Sultan Mahmud and Raja Kecik. The significance of these historiographical battles, however, can be seen in a rival text, the *Tuhfat al-Nafis*, a history of Johor-Riau that is focused on the denigration of Siak as a Malay state and successor to the illustrious legacy of Melaka and its royal line. The author of the *Tuhfat al-Nafis*, Raja Ali Haji, summarized the attitude of the leaders of Johor-Riau toward Siak's legitimizing text when he described it as a "history, which from beginning to end has no years, nor dates, let alone months or days—I could not find one ... whoever wrote it did not carefully examine material to verify it. That is my opinion".[8] Historiographical claims to the idealized state of Melaka were not to be taken lightly. With this in mind, the fact that the *Hikayat Siak* is derivative of the *Sejarah Melayu* is a testament to the power of these historical narratives. They were not simply tomes of dusty tales filled with facts and dates, which were to be taken off a shelf to remind people of their place in society. They were to be emulated, experienced and recreated.

Singapore in Traditional Malay Narrative

Singapore played an important role in these traditional texts. In the Malay text that legitimized Johor and Siak, the *Sejarah Melayu*, Singapore is the place where a prominent Malay prince develops a state prior to moving to Melaka. The tales of this ruler, known variously as Sri Tri Buana, Sang Nila Utama or Parameswara, are well known throughout the Malay world, even to those who have never read the text. This trend continues even today. Residents and visitors of Singapore can learn of his exploits through a series of cartoons displayed on Fort Canning Hill, which the famous Malay satirist Lat has drawn, while the *keramat* grave of Sultan Iskandar Shah nearby may also commemorate the same person.[9]

According to the *Sejarah Melayu*, Sri Tri Buana fled Palembang, one of the centres of the Srivijaya Empire, and following a consecration ceremony gained the trust of the orang laut who populated the southern end of the Melaka Straits. With their help, Sri Tri Buana settled in Temasek, which he soon called *Singapura*, the "Lion City", after having glimpsed a strange beast, which he mistook for a lion. For five generations Singapura was prosperous, but it ran into difficulties when the last two rulers unjustly punished their subjects. These punishments contravened the social contract between rulers and subjects in Malay states. Disasters such as the famous swordfish attack thus beset Singapura. One of its wronged subjects invited the Javanese to attack the city, which resulted in the ruler's flight to the Malay Peninsula, where he founded the city of Melaka.

Recent archaeological work has uncovered proof of a 14th-century community in Singapore.[10] While the analysis of the evidence has boosted our understanding

---

[8] Raja Ali Haji, *Tuhfat al-Nafis*, p. 96.

[9] Wolters, *Fall of Srivijaya*.

[10] John N. Miksic, *Archaeological Research on the "Forbidden Hill" of Singapore: Excavations at Fort Canning, 1984* (Singapore: National Museum, 1985).

of the pre-19th century history of the region, which is also supported by Chinese accounts, it does not provide a narrative of the prosperous trading settlement as is described in the *Sejarah Melayu*. Despite the function that such tales provide, they have been little appreciated in historical texts to be found in Singapore today. One prominent study of Singapore history, echoing the earlier words of Raja Ali Haji, describes the Malay texts as "often incomplete, vague or contradictory, imprecise in dating and … presented in such as way as to make it difficult to separate historical event from legend".[11] Such an attitude places an emphasis on very antiquated notions of historiography and does not satisfactorily deal with the power and ambiguities of memory. This is further emphasized in their portrayals of Singapore's history between the 14th and 19th centuries, in which the lack of a permanent settlement or archaeological remains during the period is emphasized. This resulted in many histories referring to Singapore as simply empty or a lair for pirates "pillaging helpless craft and slaughtering their crews".[12]

However, the early tales of Singapore in these traditional Malay narratives were known throughout the region, and even influenced Raffles' choice of the island as a British trading base. These tales were not "simply incongruous" or "fantasy without foundation", as John Crawfurd referred to them.[13] They had a power that extended beyond their role as histories. During times of upheaval, such as the 18th century, the traditional texts were often a method of not only spreading the basic tenets of a society but also reinforcing claims of sovereignty and identity. They functioned both as moral guides for the populace at large and also as "teaching manuals" throughout the Malay world.[14]

Pre-Melaka Singapore was a transition point in Malay history that played an iconic role in the collective memory of the Malays, as exemplified in the *Sejarah Melayu*; thus these tales from Singapore were present to teach a lesson to listeners to a particular text. Sri Tri Buana fled Palembang, or Srivijaya, and made his home in Singapura, from where his descendants made their later move to Melaka. This was a period of commercial and social upheaval as the traditional trade route with China had been disrupted. Sri Tri Buana had fled an oppressive Javanese overlord and attempted to create an ideal state, while his own descendants had encountered difficulties due to their own problematic policies. The same was true some 300 years later. Siak had arisen during a similar period of commercial and social upheaval. Trading practices were changing given the presence of Dutch, English and other European traders who frequented the region in search of new products. This was further complicated by the arrival of various groups, ranging from Minangkabaus to Bugis, in search of their own fortunes. The sadistic rule of Sultan Mahmud resulted in the destruction of the Johor sultanate, just as the unwise actions of Singapura's

[11] Arthur Lim Joo-Jock, "Geographical Setting", in *A History of Singapore*, ed. E.C.T. Chew and E. Lee (Singapore: Oxford University Press, 1991), p. 3.

[12] C.M. Turnbull, *A History of Modern Singapore: 1819–1975* (Singapore: Oxford University Press, 1977), p. 5.

[13] John Crawfurd, *History of the Indian Archipelago* (London: Cass, 1967), vol. 2, pp. 293–4.

[14] A.C. Milner, *Kerajaan: Malay Political Culture on the Eve of Colonial Rule* (Tucson: University of Arizona Press, 1981), p. 89.

ruler had done prior to the founding of Melaka. As Wolters stated in his study of the transfer of sovereignty to Singapore and then Melaka, "we are in the presence of a situation more suitably described as the end of an unsuccessful period in Malay history ... an improvement in Malay fortunes was accompanied by disasters".[15]

The *Hikayat Siak* portrays the founding of Siak as the long-awaited improvement in Malay fortunes after the disastrous rule of Johor earlier in the 18th century. Within this context, and to establish its legitimacy as a Malay state, the rulers of Siak portrayed its history as a continuation of the *Sejarah Melayu*. The disasters that accompanied the fall of Singapore and the rise of its successor, as portrayed earlier in the text, are recreated within the pages of the *Hikayat Siak*; but they now are related to the rise of Raja Kecik and the founding of Siak. Not only had Johor fallen due to the unjust practices of Sultan Mahmud, but Raja Kecik, much like Sri Tri Buana, had travelled over great distances and suffered the injustices of oppressive officials. Once he had gained the trust of the orang laut, also like the founder of Singapura, Raja Kecik was able to develop his own Malay state, one that would be as glorious as Melaka.

The similarities between early Siak and Singapura would not have been lost on the Malay audience of the *Hikayat Siak*. That an important battle in 1767 took place in Singapore would have also resonated in the tales of swordfish attacks and Javanese attempts to assert control over Malay polities. Raja Ismail, after all, had come to Singapore to assist Malay nobility whose power was being usurped by Bugis mercenaries. As a defender of Malay sovereignty Raja Ismail was not simply willing to help them; rather, he saw it as his duty. The location was symbolic, a powerful reminder of the role Singapore played in local understandings of Malay history, identity and memory. The fact that he was defeated in the battle was of little significance. He was a successor to the glorious line of Siak, Johor, Melaka and Srivijaya, and that line had run through Singapura.

Conclusion

The confrontation between a Siak prince and the Bugis of Johor-Riau on the Singapore River in 1767 is simply a footnote in the history of Singapore. Its absence in the histories of Singapore should not be a surprise. It was part of a larger battle between Siak and Johor-Riau over their Malay identities and pasts, and such confrontations occurred throughout the Malay world during the 18th century. However, Singapore played a role in that past. It was not simply a pirate's lair. While raiding did take place from Singapore, a common practice in the region, it played a more prominent role in the collective memory of the Malay heritage. Singapura was part of a larger Malay heritage. To judge pre-British Singapore by the absence of stone buildings, dwellings, or even substantial trading communities simply misses the point. It was part of a larger Malay legacy, one in which history played an active role. As the *Hikayat Siak* portrayed the battle between the two competitors over the Malay legacy, "they were at war". It was a war fought both with cannon shots as well as the pen, as traditional Malay literature reminded the audience of the text of their role within

---

[15] Wolters, *Fall of Srivijaya*, p. 7.

history. Singapore played a significant role in that history as a location of epic battles, brave warriors, and a harbour in which those fleeing their enemies could take refuge. It was firmly located in the collective Malay memory and operated as a powerful teaching tool, which emphasized the importance of heritage to those living in the region. This was a legacy more important than the remains of any building or settlement.

9

Muhammad Yusoff Hashim

The Seri Bija Diraja in the Tradition of the Great Lords of Melaka in the Fifteenth and Sixteenth Centuries*

Seri Bija Diraja was one of the most important titles of nobility in Melaka during the period of the Malay sultanate. In connection with this traditional high office of state, Tun Seri Lanang, quoting other compilers in the *Sejarah Melayu*, says:

> and the minor captains stood in the place of honour in the audience hall, bearing their swords ... and the chief herald on the ruler's right is descended from captains who provided the Laksamana and the Seri Bija Diraja.[1]

When Melaka was under Sultan Muhammad Shah (Seri Maharaja, 1414–44), the third ruler and the second to embrace Islam,[2] the Seri Bija Diraja was accorded third place in rank and precedence in the audience chamber at court after the four great lords of Melaka, and sat on the royal verandah immediately after the royal princes. He also stood in the place of honour in the audience hall along with the minor captains. His duties were reported to have been the same as those of the Laksamana, as is explained in the *Sejarah Melayu*:

---

* First published as a chapter section in Muhammad Yusoff Hashim, *The Malay Sultanate of Malacca: A Study of Various Aspects of Malacca in the 15th and 16th Centuries in Malaysian History* (Kuala Lumpur: Dewan Bahasa dan Pustaka / Ministry of Education, 1992), pp. 98–103.

[1] See W.G. Shellabear, ed., *Sejarah Melayu: The Malay Annals* (Singapore: Malaya Publishing House, 1961), p. 72.

[2] Wang Gungwu, "The First Three Ruler of Malacca", *JMBRAS* 41, 1 (1968): 18.

> All the royal regalia, including the cuspidor and cruse (*kendi*), fans and the like were arranged alternately, with the exception of the betel-caddies and the swords, were borne by bearers on the left and right, and the sword of State was borne by the Laksamana or by the Seri Bija Diraja.[3]

While it is clear that Seri Bija Diraja is in fact a title, the office was held by those who carried the title Hulubalang Besar (Captain-in-Chief), the fourth most important post after those of the Bendahara, Penghulu Bendahari and Temenggong. This was before the reign of Sultan Mansur Shah (1456–77) and before the creation of the post of Laksamana. Looking at the designation of the post itself, and taking note of the military functions it embraced, the Seri Bjia Diraja was obviously the head of all the captains or military commanders of Melaka, and was held responsible for all matters pertaining to the military affairs of the Melakan sultanate.

The Seri Bija Diraja and the Laksamana

As far as we are aware, the Four Great Lords in the hierarchy of nobility in Melaka, and in other traditional Malay states which arose after Melaka and continued with the traditions of the Melaka nobility, historians and sociologists have always shown a disposition to place the four lords according to the following: the Bendahara, the Penghulu Bendahari, the Temenggong and the Laksamana,[4] and not in this order: the Bendahara, Penghulu Bendahari, the Temenggong and the Shahbandar as proposed by other researchers on this subject.[5] In consequence, the role and political position of the Seri Bija Diraja was frequently overlooked.

The question arose, if the Seri Bija Diraja was the holder of the post of Hulubalang Besar and the head of all the captains in Melaka, a post supposedly held by the Laksamana, what was his true status and position within the system of the "Four Great Lords"?

---

[3] Shellabear, *Sejarah Melayu*, p. 72.

[4] See the relevant article by R.O. Winstedt, "A History of Malaya", *JMBRAS* 13, 2 (1935): 1–270; R.J. Wilkinson, "The Malacca Sultanate", *JSBRAS* 13, 2 (1935): 22–67; J.M. Gullick, *Indigenous Political Systems of Western Malaya* (London: The Athlone Press, 1958), and so forth.

[5] In fact, this proposal is based on the evidence in the *Undang-undang Melaka*, which states: "And to serve the rulers, there was appointed in the first place the Bendahara, second the Temenggong, third the Penghulu Bendahari, and fourth the shahbandar; and so the affairs of the rulers and the people were taken care of." This passage in the *Undang-undang Melaka* requires a reexamination. To begin with, the original draft of the *Undang-undang* was "done" during the reign of Sultan Muzaffar Shah, before the creation of the office of Laksamana. The Portuguese chronicler Tomé Pires claimed that Melaka had at least four shahbandars. If this is correct, how could they all be placed together in the fourth position? Foreigners such as Raja Mendeliar were appointed shahbandar of Melaka; however, it is inconceivable that a foreigner could have been made one of the four great lords of Melaka. For further reference, see Liaw Yock Fang, ed., *Undang-undang Melaka* [The Laws of Melaka] (The Hague: Martinus Nijhoff, 1976), p. 620; and also Armando Cortesão, ed. and trans., *The Suma Oriental of Tomé Pires: An Account of the East from the Red Sea to Japan. Written in Malacca and India in 1512–1515* (London: Hakluyt Society, 1944), pp. 284–6.

9.1 Photomechanical reproduction of a sketch depicting a Malay *Lancha* or *Lanchara.* M.G. de Erédia, *Malaca l'Inde Méridionale e le Cathay: Manuscrit original autographe de Godinho de Eredia appartenant à la Bibliothèque Royale de Bruxelles*, tr. M.L. Janssen (Bruxelles: Librairie Européenne C. Muquardt, 1882). © Peter Borschberg, private collection.

Until more studies are carried out, we are only able to suggest that before the creation of the post of Laksamana within the tradition of the Melaka nobility, the office of the Seri Bija Diraja ranked fourth in the hierarchy of the nobility: namely, the Bendahara, the Penghulu Bendahari, the Temenggong, and the Seri Bija Diraja. This hypothesis was advanced based on a number of observations. Firstly, when Sultan Mansur Shah went to Java, the *Sejarah Melayu* reported that the administration of Melaka was left in the hands of the Bendahara Paduka Raja, Tun Perak, and that he was assisted by several other noblemen including the Penghulu Bendahari Tun Ali and the Seri Bija Diraja.[6] In several wars between Melaka and other powers like Siam, Pahang, Siak and Tungkal, the Bendahara Paduka Raja or the Seri Nara Diraja were put in charge of the Melakan forces, and were usually supported by the Seri Bija Diraja.[7]

The *Ceritera Asal Raja-raja Melayu Punya Keturunan*, believed to be the earliest and oldest version of the *Sejarah Melayu* extant and regarded as the closest to the original in its historical contents,[8] reported that the most influential political figures in Melaka were the Seri Nara Diraja Tun Ali and the Seri Bija Diraja, namely, before the rise of Bendahara Tun Perak and Laksamana Hang Tuah.

But once the post of Laksamana, first held by Hang Tuah during the reign of Sultan Mansur Shah, was instituted, the position and status of the Seri Bija Raja steadily declined, although his political and social functions remained unchanged. As far as the status and position of the the Melaka nobility was concerned, the Laksamana was placed on a par with that of the Seri Bija Diraja, as reported in the *Sejarah Melayu*:

> After that, Hang Tuah was given the title of "Laksamana", and he was taken in procession around the city, in the manner reserved for princes, and was placed on a par with the Seri Bija Diraja, according to ancient custom.[9]

As a result, two problems arose in relation to the system of nobility in Melaka. Firstly, if the functions and status of the Seri Bija Diraja were equal to those of the Laksamana, where would their position be in the hierarchical system of the Melaka nobility? It would be impossible for them both to share the fourth place. Secondly, as a result of this difficulty, a shahbandar was made one of the Great Lords instead of either of them.

---

[6] Shellabear, *Sejarah Melayu*, p. 116.

[7] Ibid., passim.

[8] R. Roolvink, "Variant Version of the Malay Annals". This article was added to the book by C.C. Brown (ed. and trans.) entitled *The Malay Annals or Sejarah Melayu* (Kuala Lumpur: Oxford University Press, 1970), pp. 15–35. The original text is kept in the University of Leiden Library, Holland. The microfilm copy is kept in the University of Malaya Library, Kuala Lumpur. In Leiden, it is known by its reference Cod. Or. 3199 (3), Part 4.

[9] Shellabear, *Sejarah Melayu*, p. 137.

The Deputy Laksamana

If we study the genealogy of the first Laksamana of Melaka and also that of the Seri Bija Diraja, there is no doubt that both of them were of pure Malay descent. Although we lack historical evidence on this, we are clear on their social and political functions. It seems highly likely that the Seri Bija Diraja was descended from the orang laut Malays from Bentan and Singapore.[10] The orang laut were in actual fact the backbone of Melaka's military and naval striking power.[11] It is probable that because of the Seri Bija Diraja's familiarity with the role of the orang laut, and being a descendant of this Malay group, he should be put in charge of the Melakan forces, particularly on the naval side. It was equally appropriate that Singapore should become the "fief" of the Seri Bija Diraja, since politically and traditionally, Singapore had always been his area.[12] Since both the Laksamana and the Seri Bija Diraja were of Malay stock and played the same political and military roles, there was no personal friction between them or occurrence of conflicts over their official appointments. When Hang Tuah was officially made the Laksamana of Melaka, the Seri Bija Diraja was probably appointed as his deputy. When the ruler of Melaka sent the Bendahara to make war on foreign countries such as Pasai, Rokan and Inderagiri, the Laksamana and *the* Seri Bija Diraja were appointed to accompany the Bendahara, one on his left and the other on his right. In the writing tradition of the *Sejarah Melayu*, Tun Seri Lanang provides similar information on this. The title Seri Bija Diraja is often mentioned with the office of Laksamana, as if to show that the functions of the Laksamana and the Seri Bija Diraja were of equal importance and the hierarchy is as follows:

Bendahara
Penghulu Bendahari
Temenggong
Laksamana
or
Seri Bija Diraja

This situation is certainly an interesting phenomenon in the development of the society and the official establishment in Melaka. This phenomenon is in contrast to the historical relationship between two other great lords of Melaka, namely the

---

[10] For further explanation on this point, see Alfred Rubin, *The International Personality of the Malay Peninsula* (Kuala Lumpur: University of Malaya Press, 1974), pp. 3–28. See also C.A. Gibson-Hill, "The Orang Laut of the Singapore River and Sampan Panjang", *JMBRAS* 25, 1 (1952): 161–74.

[11] See Sherard Osborn, *My Journal in Malayan Waters, or the Blockade of Kedah*, 2nd ed. (London: Routledge, Warne and Routledge, 1861), pp. 255–60; O.W. Wolters, *The Fall of Sri Vijaya in Malay History* (Ithaca: Cornell University Press, 1970); Shellabear, *Sejarah Melayu*, passim.

[12] Bentan was given to the Bendahara as his fief. See Shellabear, *Sejarah Melayu*, p. 202; Yusoff Iskandar and Abdul Rahman Kaeh, *Sejarah Melayu: Satu Perbincangan Kritis daripada Pelbagai bidang* (Kuala Lumpur: Heinemann, 1978), pp. 172–3.

Bendahara Paduka Raja Tun Perak and the Penghulu Bendahari (Seri Nara Diraja) Tun Ali. Tun Ali was of Malay-Tamil descent. The appointment of Tun Perak as Bendahara engendered intense personal rivalry between him and Tun Ali. The people of Melaka became divided into two opposing factions.[13] The first faction belonged to the supporters of Tun Perak, while the other faction comprised those who supported Tun Ali.

This social phenomenon brings to mind the historical development of the relationship between the social groups in the Melaka society on a still broader scale. The Bendahara Seri Wak Raja II, the Bendahara of Melaka of pure Malay descent, disapproved Sultan Muzaffar's scheme to absorb the Seri Nara Diraja Tun Ali who was of Tamil descent into the Melaka nobility. He demonstrated his disapproval by committing suicide by poison.[14] This conflict between the Malay and Tamil-Malay factions continued right until 1511. This rivalry became the "thorn in the flesh" which ultimately constituted one of the underlying causes for Melaka's downfall.[15]

Similarly, the Seri Bija Diraja who was also of Malay descent, supported the Seri Wak Raja II, who had committed suicide. The Seri Bija Diraja Tun Kerutup revealed his attitude and position when he refused to recognize Sultan Mahmud as ruler of Melaka. The sultan was of Tamil descent on his mother's side. Seri Bija Diraja Tun Kerutup's strong pro-Malay sentiments became obvious when he declared that he owed a greater allegiance to Raja Menawar Shah in Kampar, who was the son of Sultan Alauddin Riayat Shah by the daughter of a Malay nobleman in Melaka. He apparently preferred to die than give his allegiance to Sultan Mahmud, and in the end he was indeed put to death on the orders of the sultan.

The Geneology of the Seri Bija Diraja

There are no reliable local sources available on the genealogy of the family of the Seri Bija Diraja. The *Sejarah Melayu* records that the office of the Seri Bija Diraja was included in the traditions of the great lords of Melaka since the reign of Sultan Muhammad Shah. By 1511, Melaka had at least three leading Malay figures who held the office. The first person to do so was Tun Hamzah,[16] who was called Datuk Bongkok. He was reckoned to have enjoyed the same status as the Seri Nara Diraja (the Penghulu Bendahari) in position and function before the creation of

---

[13] See Muhammad Yusoff Hashim, "Masyarakat Melaka Zaman Kesultanan dan Sifat Kosmopolitannya", in *Melaka: The Transformation of a Malay Capital, c. 1400–1980*, ed. Kernial Singh Sandhu and Paul Wheatley, 2 vols. (Kuala Lumpur: Oxford University Press, 1983), vol. 1, pp. 113–27.

[14] Shellabear, *Sejarah Melayu*, p. 89; see also P. Wheatley, *Impressions of the Malay Peninsula in Ancient Times* (Singapore: Eastern Universities Press, 1964), p. 149. However, the compiler of the 1612 version of the *Sejarah Melayu*, who is said to be of Malay-Tamil descent, appears to have tried to conceal what really happened by stating that the Bendahara killed himself because of the humiliation he suffered at the palace of the Melakan ruler.

[15] See Muhammad Yusoff Hashim, "Masyarakat Melaka, 1400–1511, dengan Tumpuan Khas tentang Orang-orang Asing", unpublished working paper presented at the Congress of Malaysian History, University Kebangsaan Malaysia, Bangi, March 1978.

[16] See P.E. de Josselin de Jong, "Who's Who in the Malay Annals", *JMBRAS* 24, 2 (1961): 1–89.

the Laksamana post and before the appointment of Tun Perak as the Bendahara of Melaka. He died during the reign of Sultan Alauddin Riayat Shah.[17]

Tun Hamzah was succeeded by his son, Tun Kerutup. He was reported to have been put to death on the orders of Sultan Mahmud because of his strong pro-Malay sentiments.

Tun Kerutup's place was taken by his nephew, Sang Setia Tatayan,[18] a grandson of the late Tun Hamzah and son of the Tun Bija Diraja.[19] He died in battle whilst defending Pagoh from a Portuguese attack in 1511. In short, just as was the case with the title and office of Laksamana, so the title Seri Bija Diraja or the office of Hulubalang Besar was the hereditary monopoly of one family.

The Change in Title

The social and political role of the Seri Bija Diraja as head of the captains of Melaka, and his position as deputy to the Laksamana in the aristocratic system of Malay administration, was probably adopted by the officials of the Johor sultanate. However, some changes occurred. In Johor the title Seri Bija Diraja was changed to Seri Bija Wangsa.

Genealogical Tree

Tun Hamzah* (Datuk Bongkok)

- Tun Kerutup* (executed)
- Tun Bija Diraja
  - Sang Setia Tetayan* (Bentayan)
- Tun Umar
- Tun Chandera Panjang

Note: * Holders of the title of Seri Bija Diraja.

The Seri Bija Wangsa in charge of the orang laut forces who constituted a large proportion of the naval striking power of Johor.[20] In 1699 and 1719 it was the Seri Bija Wangsa who attempted to manipulate politics in Johor during the disturbances surrounding the attempts to keep out Bugis influence. According to the *Hikayat Siak* and a contemporary report of the Dutch *Dagh Register*, he was the personal bodyguard of Sultan Mahmud II and played a leading role in defending the sultan

[17] Shellabear, *Sejarah Melayu*, p. 178.

[18] In the 1536 version of the *Sejarah Melayu*, this figure is given the name of *Sang Setia Bentayan*. See C.C. Brown, ed. and trans., *Sejarah Melayu "Malay Annals"* (Kuala Lumpur: MBRAS Reprint, 1970), pp. 186–7.

[19] Shellabear, *Sejarah Melayu*, p. 178; Haji Buyong Adil, *Sejarah Melaka dalam Zaman Kerajaan Melaka*, Siri sejarah nusantara, Siri pelajaran menengah DBP no. 93 (Kuala Lumpur: Dewan Bahasa dan Pustaka, 1973), p. 158; R.J. Wilkinson, *A History of the Peninsular Malays*, 3rd ed. (Singapore: Kelly & Walsh, 1923), p. 196.

[20] See L.Y. Andaya, *The Kingdom of Johore, 1641–1728: Economic and Political Developments* (Kuala Lumpur: Oxford University Press, 1975), pp. 58–77; see also his article, "The Structure of Power in Seventeenth Century Johor". [E.N.: reproduced in this collection.]

from the attempts made by the Bendahara Tun Abdul Jalil and the Laksamana Megat Seri Rama in 1699 to betray and overthrow him.[21]

The *Hikayat Siak* relates that in the midst of all this political intrigue, the Seri Bija Wangsa appeared to be invulnerable and could not be wounded by ordinary weapons. He died only after his own *keris* had been spat upon and was plunged into his abdomen, upon which white blood gushed forth, before he was finally vanquished.[22] The evolution of Johor history, a legacy of Melaka, thereupon changed course and assumed a different pattern. However, despite this change, the role of the Seri Bija Diraja (Seri Bija Wangsa in Johor) had not lost its significance.

---

[21] *Hikayat Siak*, Cod. Or. 1304, pp. 404–8. In citing the prowess of the *Seri Bija Wangsa*, the *Hikayat* stated: "There was no captain to compare with him in all Johor" (p. 405).
[22] Ibid., pp. 406–7. The *Hikayat* adds, quoting the *Seri Bija Wangsa*: "Apart from my own *keris*, there is no steel in Johor which can pierce my flesh."

10

Leonard Y. Andaya

The Structure of Power in Seventeenth-century Johor*

Any discussion of the traditional Johor polity would be difficult without understanding Johor's historical ties with the kingdom of Melaka. When Sultan Mahmud Syah, the last ruler of Melaka, died in Kampar on the east coast of Sumatra sometime between November 1527 and July 1528, he was succeeded by his son by a non-royal wife who became Sultan Alauddin Riayat Syah. In the early 1530s Sultan Alauddin moved his residence to the Johor River and became the first ruler of the Melaka dynasty to establish a permanent settlement in Johor.[1] The "foundation" of the kingdom of Johor did not mark a significant event in the area but was merely a continuing episode in the history of the Malays of Melaka. In describing the structure of power in "traditional" Johor, therefore, one must take into account many features that had their origins in the Melaka kingdom.

Reference to the *Sejarah Melayu*, a work which was begun in Melaka sometime in the 15th century but which contains later interpolations including the early history of Johor, is essential for an understanding of the attitudes, ideals and basic power structure of the court in Melaka and in Johor. Using a text from an earlier period to describe a later situation in a kingdom's history may not always be wise, yet in this case there may be some justification for it. In none of the extant Malay texts known to this author, except for perhaps a recently published work by Ernst

* First published as a chapter in *Pre-Colonial State Systems in Southeast Asia: The Malay Peninsula, Sumatra, Bali-Lombok, South Celebes*, ed. A. Reid and L. Castles (Kuala Lumpur: MBRAS, 1975), pp. 1–11.

[1] I.A. Macgregor, "Johore Lama in the Sixteenth Century", *JMBRAS* 28, 2 (1955): 74–5, 81.

10.1 Map of insular Southeast Asia centred on the historic kingdom of Johor. Drawn by Mrs Lee Li Kheng.

Ulrich Kratz,[2] is there any extensive treatment of events in 17th-century Johor. The Shellabear recension of the *Sejarah Melayu* continues into the late 17th century, but the treatment is sketchy with none of the colour and enlightening episodes that characterise the sections dealing with the Melaka kingdom.[3] In an unpublished version of the *Sejarah Melayu*, which has been appropriately given the title of *The Siak Chronicles* by a Dutch scholar of classical Malay literature,[4] there is nothing but a list of rulers for the 17th-century history of Johor. The various Malay histories of Johor such as the *Tuhfat al-Nafis*, *Silsilah Melayu dan Bugis*, *Hikayat Negri Johor*, *Aturan Setia Bugis dengan Melayu*, etc., make certain references to events in this period with little or no elaboration.[5] The scarcity of Malay material and the decidedly Buginese slant in these "Malay" histories from Johor make these texts an unsatisfactory source for studying the Malays in Johor in the 17th century. The *Sejarah Melayu*, on the other hand, while not dealing with events in Johor during this period, focusses on subjects pertinent to Malay courts whether in Melaka, Perak, or Johor.[6]

There is another reason for regarding the *Sejarah Melayu* as an important text for the study of the Kingdom of Johor in the 17th century. After examining numerous references to Johor during this period from the records of the Dutch East India Company (VOC) in the General State Archives in The Hague,[7] it was interesting to discover that the power structure and the attitudes of the court Malays in Johor were basically similar to those portrayed in the *Sejarah Melayu*. Many events in Johor that

---

[2] Ernst Ulrich Kratz, *Peringatan Sejarah Negeri Jobor: Eine malaiische Quelle zur Geschichte Johors im 18 Jahrhundert* (Wiesbaden: Harrassowitz, 1973). The text used by Kratz is listed in the Leiden University Library in The Netherlands as Klinkert 24B. While Kratz transcribed the whole of this text, he also used another copy of this text, von de Wall 196 from the Museum Pusat in Jakarta, to show variations in the two manuscripts. Although the treatment of the 17th century in this text is as limited as in the other Malay works, it contains certain detailed descriptions of a particular episode in Johor history in the late 17th century, the overthrow and the death of Paduka Raja Tun Abdul Jamil, which are found in no other Malay text.

[3] W.G. Shellabear, *Sejarah Melayu*, romanized from an 1896 Jawi text (Kuala Lumpur: Oxford University Press, 1967).

[4] This manuscript is listed in the University of Leiden Library as Cod. Or. 7304 and Cod. Or. 6342, and in the Museum Pusat in Jakarta as von de Wall 191. Dr R.O. Roolvink describes this work as "a Malay history which is an edited and in several places abbreviated text of the *Sejarah Melayu*, followed by an 18th century history of the Straits of Melaka told from the Siak point of view". See R.O. Roolvink, "The Variant Versions of the Malay Annals", *BKI* 123 (1967): 309. This text will be quoted henceforth as the *Siak Chronicles*.

[5] Perhaps one of the reasons that events in 17th-century Johor are not given prominence is that these texts all originate from the Buginese families of the Malay world. Events which occurred prior to the period of Buginese ascendancy in Johor, which dates from about the beginning of the second decade of the 18th century, would have been of only peripheral interest to these chroniclers.

[6] In this paper the Raffles 18 manuscript of the *Sejarah Melayu* will be used. This manuscript is considered to be the oldest recension extant and has been transcribed into Rumi and edited by R.O. Winstedt in *JMBRAS* 16, 3 (1938): 1–226, and also translated into English by C.C. Brown in "Sejarah Melayu or Malay Annals", *JMBRAS* 25, 2–3 (1952): 1–276.

[7] [E.N.: Presently the Nationaal Archief, the National Archives of the Netherlands.]

seemed incomprehensible at first became clearer when studied in conjunction with Malay attitudes and ideals propounded in the *Sejarah Melayu*. This text, therefore, proved to be a much more relevant document for the study of Johor up to the end of the 17th century than any of the Johor histories.

Although the new centre of the old kingdom of Melaka was now located on the Johor River, it continued to be a maritime state highly dependent upon the rivers and the sea which were its principal means of communication and livelihood. By 1641 this Johor kingdom had lost some of the areas that had originally been dependencies of Melaka. Nevertheless, it was still an extensive kingdom consisting of Johor, Selangor, areas on the Kelang, Linggi, Siak, Kampar, Muar and Batu Pahat Rivers, and the islands of Ungaran, Karimum, the Riau-Lingga Archipelagos and Singapore.[8] During the course of the 17th century it reasserted its authority on the east coast of Sumatra as far north as Deli and in Pahang and Trengganu in east coast Malay Peninsula. In terms of distance Johor could very well be termed a "far-flung" kingdom; but with the sea and the rivers providing easy access to even the most remote dependency, Johor was a much closer-knit kingdom than the distance would indicate.

The outlying areas were important only insofar as they contributed to the glory of the court and the enhancement of the ruler in the centre. The ruler was an essential ingredient in the perpetuation of the kingdom. Without his presence to justify all activity and to reward, the labours of the people with titles and robes of honour, the kingdom would be indistinguishable from many other riverine or estuary settlements in the Malay world. He enhanced the status of the particular Malay community in which he lived, and his glory and splendour were shared by it. When the last ruler of Melaka was fleeing from Bentan, he was assured by his minister that ten countries could be found for him.[9] Land and people were always available but not rulers with an illustrious and impeccable lineage. Despite the repeated destruction of the capitals of Johor by the Portuguese and the Acehnese in the 16th and early 17th centuries, only in 1564 and in 1613 was the ruler of Johor actually taken prisoner. But on both of these occasions another ruler from the same royal family was set on the throne by the conquerors. In all of the other cases the ruler eluded his pursuers and re-established his residence as before, thus assuring the perpetuation of the kingdom.[10] It did not matter that the land was ravaged and the people scattered. As long as the ruler and the dynasty survived, there was no danger of the dissolution of the kingdom and a reversion to an earlier situation of the small, individual *kampung* under a minor chieftain, like those located at any number of places on the rivers, estuaries, or coasts of the Malay world.

Through the efforts of the whole kingdom, wealth through trade, piracy and wars flowed to the ruler's coffers. It was this practice which elicited the following remark

---

[8] *Dagh-Register gehouden in't Casteel Batavia van't passerende daer ter plaetse als over geheel Nederlandts-Indië, 1624–1682* (The Hague: Martinus Nijhoff and Batavia: Landsdrukkerij, 1887), 3 Apr. 1641, p. 226.

[9] Brown, "Sejarah Melayu", p. 189.

[10] P.A. Tiele, "De Europeërs in den Maleischen Archipel", part 5, *BKI* 29 (1887): 169–70; and part 8, *BKI* 35 (1886): 303.

from the last sultan of Melaka when asked by the bendahara why all the wealth of the kingdom had been given in dowry which left nothing but "the bedragoned sword of kingship" for his successor, the Sultan Muda: "If the Sultan Muda has but the sword of kingship, he will have gold as well". To this remark the author of the *Sejarah Melayu* added in explanation: "That is to say, where there is sovereignty, there is gold".[11] In return the faithful subjects shared not merely in the material wealth but also in the glory and prestige of a ruler descended from an ancient and illustrious line.

The ruler's exalted and indispensable role in the society is reinforced by the attitude expressed in the *Sejarah Melayu* that a ruler is responsible solely to Almighty God. No matter how unjust and cruel a ruler may be, the loyal Malay subject is admonished to be loyal since only the hand of God would be able to render appropriate justice to the ruler.[12] This is the ideal expounded in court literature, which, if not followed totally in practice, conditioned the relationship between ruler and subjects.

Since the wellbeing of the ruler was of such great importance to the Johor kingdom, the choice for the site of his residence, hence the principal settlement was determined more by considerations of security than of accessibility to the international trade flowing through the Straits of Melaka. Many of the rulers of Johor had their residences on the banks of the Johor River whose winding course and numerous branches afforded an excellent avenue of escape into the interior.[13] With the Orang Laut (sea people) patrols at the mouth of the Johor River to report the approach of an enemy fleet, and with thick, impenetrable jungle at his back, the ruler was well safeguarded at any one of a number of sites on the Johor River. During the 17th and early 18th centuries, the ruler usually moved his residence to the Johor River whenever there was any threat of attack.

On the other hand, selecting a site in Riau on the island of Bentan seemed to indicate a determination to meet any danger openly. When the last ruler of Melaka was urged to flee Bentan to escape from the Portuguese, he replied:

> When I came here, Sri Nara Diraja, I knew full well that Bentan was an island; and it was because I was determined that there should be no retreating that I took up my abode here! If I had thought of retreating, I should have done better to stay on the mainland.[14]

These words could very well have been uttered by the rulers of Johor in the 17th and first decade of the 18th centuries when they shifted their residences from the Johor

[11] Brown, "Sejarah Melayu", p. 187.
[12] Ibid., pp. 26–7.
[13] When Admiral Verhoeven offered to build a fort for Sultan Alauddin in Johor in 1609 as a defensive measure, Sultan Alauddin refused, saying that if the Portuguese came with a large fleet he and his subjects could always flee upriver. Isaac Commelin, *Begin ende Voortgang van de Vereenigde Nederlandtsche Geoctroyeerde Oost-Indische Compagnie*, vol. 2 (Amsterdam: [Janssonius], 1646), p. 43.
[14] Brown, "Sejarah Melayu", p. 189.

10.2 Sketch of a Malay man and woman. John Crawfurd, *Journal of an embassy from the Governor-General of India to the Courts of Siam and Cochin-China*. Singapore: Henry Colburn and Richard Bentley, 1828. NUS Libraries, Special Collections.

River to Riau.[15] The principal attraction of Riau as a place for the ruler's residence was the proximity of the various Orang Laut tribes that formed the backbone of Johor's navy. The considerable naval skills of the Orang Laut proved even more effective in their home waters in and around the Riau-Lingga Archipelagos. Since the seas in these archipelagos abound with sand shoals, reefs and tiny atolls, a numerically weaker naval force with a knowledge of the area could wreak havoc on a much larger fleet unfamiliar with the dangers in these waters. Riau was thus ideal as a forward base to meet any foreign invasion.

While the presence of the ruler was indispensable in guaranteeing the survival of and providing a purpose for the kingdom, he alone could not assure the proper functioning of the government:

> for no ruler, however great his wisdom and understanding, shall prosper or succeed in doing justice unless he consults with those in authority under him. For rulers are like fire and their ministers are like firewood, and fire needs wood to produce a flame....[16]

For the proper governing of the community, the ruler depended upon his ministers who served as the purifying filter that protected the sacred kingship from the vulgarities of mundane affairs of state. The areas on the Malay Peninsula outside the immediate vicinity of the principal settlement on the Johor River were governed by individuals appointed by and accountable to a chief minister at the court. An episode in the *Sejarah Melayu* illustrates what was expected of these ministers by the ruler. When one of the ministers was accused of poor management of his fief, he replied:

> As for the business of us who administer territory, what concern is that of yours? For territory is territory even if it is only the size of a coconut shell! What we think should be done we do, for the Ruler is not concerned with the difficulties we administrators encounter; he only takes account of the good results we achieve.[17]

---

[15] When Raja Seberang of Johor was sent back by Sultan Iskandar Muda of Aceh (1607–36) to rule his ravaged kingdom, he did not return to the former site on the Johor River but went instead to Bentan, where he began immediately intriguing with the Dutch and the Portuguese to force the Acehnese to leave his kingdom. He recognized that his strength lay among the Orang Laut in these islands. Tiele, "De Europeërs in den Maleischen Archipel", part 8, p. 308. To avenge Jambi's destruction of Johor Lama in 1673, the laksamana assembled the population and moved them to Bentan to make preparations for an invasion of Jambi. KA 1184, OB 1674, Missive from Governor Bort of Melaka to Batavia, 27 September 1673, fol. 763. (The KA number refers to the files of the Colonial Archives of the General State Archives in The Hague. The OB number is the year in which a certain document was received in Amsterdam. These files of the Colonial Archives are documents of the Dutch East India Company, including letters and reports of rulers and natives of the various areas.) In 1709 the capital was again transferred to Riau in a self-confident move to meet any threat from the Siamese. Soon thereafter the Raja Muda Tun Mahmud set sail with a fleet to meet the supposed invasion force in Trengganu. KA 1668, OB 1709, Second Melaka Register, Missive from Governor Rooselaer to Batavia, 26 December 1709, fols. 192–4.

[16] Brown, "Sejarah Melayu", p. 124.

[17] Ibid., p. 66.

The ruler was unconcerned with the manner in which these ministers managed their fiefs as long as there was peace in the kingdom and wealth continued to flow to the ruler's coffers. In case of rebellion or other disturbances in an outlying area, the chief minister himself was despatched to the scene to supervise the normalization of affairs. In such cases it was common for the official in whose area of jurisdiction a disturbance had occurred to be removed and another favourite of the chief minister put in his place.[18] When a chief minister fell out of favour with the ruler, the area would again be placed at the disposal of the ruler to be assigned to another chief minister or to be disposed of in whatever way he saw fit. Yet from an examination of the Dutch sources for the 17th century, it appears that more often than not, even a chief minister out of favour with the ruler retained certain traditional areas as apanages.

On the east coast of Sumatra there were various systems of governance that reflected the true degree of control exercised from the centre in the 17th century.[19] Indragiri was governed through its own ruler who was, however, handpicked by Johor. This arrangement did not prove entirely satisfactory and led to some difficulties when expeditions had to be sent to Indragiri to prop up an unpopular figure against someone more favoured by the local population. Kampar, Siak and Rokan were governed by *shahbandars* who were responsible to a chief minister of Johor. Since most of the interior Minangkabau products of gold and pepper came down these rivers, they were much sought-after fiefs and were usually administered by the most powerful minister of Johor. Batu Bahara and Deli acknowledged the overlordship of Johor but retained their own heads. They exercised an independence of policy and were less responsive to the wishes of the centre than most of the other territories. Once a year a Johor mission headed by a chief minister was sent to the outlying dependencies to collect tribute and receive the homage from the heads of governments.[20]

The ministers acted on behalf of the ruler and were the guardians of those matters that constituted a threat to their sovereign lord, hence a threat to the kingdom. Despite the apparent independence and authority exercised by some of the chief ministers, the rivalry between the bendahara and the laksamana families in the 17th century vividly illustrated the fact that their position and power depended ultimately not on their own innate shrewdness and ability, nor on their wealth, but on the sanction of the ruler. Although traditionally the bendahara was acknowledged as the

---

[18] For example, in 1683 a Minangkabau adventurer, Raja Hitam, came from Kalimantan and led a revolt among the Minangkabau settlements on the Siak River against Johor rule. After the revolt was suppressed, the Paduka Raja Tun Abdul Jamil came personally to Siak and replaced the *shahbandar* whom he had appointed to govern the area. KA 1274, OB 1684, Missive from Governor Qualbergen of Melaka to Batavia, 1 May 1683, fols. 821 verso–822 recto.

[19] The generalizations about the manner in which Johor administered its east coast Sumatra dependencies are based on various reports in the 17th-century VOC records from Melaka, Palembang and Jambi.

[20] In the Dutch reports the laksamana was once mentioned as the leader of the mission, and at another time, the Sri Bija Wangsa, who is considered to be a "deputy" laksamana, headed the mission. There is too little evidence to be able to say definitely that they were the only officials expected to lead such missions. KA 1315, OB 1687, Missive from Governor Comans of Melaka to Batavia, 12 September 1686, fol. 1857; KA Melaka to Batavia, passim.

principal minister in the kingdom, the prestige of the laksamana rose in the 16th and early 17th centuries because of his role as the supreme authority of the naval forces that were frequently called upon to defend the kingdom from Acehnese and Portuguese invasions. By the beginning of the 17th century the laksamana family had already eclipsed the bendahara family in importance. The bendahara was forced to play a less prominent role within the administrative structure of the kingdom than was traditionally proper.

After 1641 the influence of the laksamana family under the Paduka Raja Tun Abdul Jamil steadily grew until every important office was held by this family to the detriment of all other Orang Kaya, and especially of the bendahara family. This blatant usurpation of power forced the bendahara to gamble desperately on a plot to seize the young ruler from the control of the laksamana and thus remove the source of sanction on the laksamana's activities. Once the bendahara succeeded in gaining control of the young ruler, he had the royal drums and reedpipes (*nobat* and *nafiri*) played to indicate that the ruler was with him. This sign was sufficient to make the Orang Laut desert the laksamana's ships and return to the side of their ruler. With this one stroke the bendahara reduced a once seemingly invincible minister into a dishonoured refugee seeking safety from his erstwhile supporters.[21] When the Bendahara Tun Habib Abdul Majid again took his rightful place within the kingdom, he preserved his position by maintaining the proper relationships within the society and conducting affairs with an awareness that he was but a regent for the young ruler. In 1691 he refused to commit himself and the kingdom to any written agreements with the Dutch until the ruler had reached his majority and could understand the full implications of such documents. In a letter to the Dutch governor-general in Batavia, the bendahara wrote:

> According to *adat* I have no right in the disposition of the kingdom, so how much less have I the right to give it to others. If I were to do so, I would be cheating my own king.[22]

When his son and successor ignored this basic precept and acquiesced in the assassination of the ruler in 1699,[23] he unleashed a series of events that changed the course of Malay history in the 18th century.

In addition to the ruler and his chief ministers, the Council of Nobles (Orang Kaya) was a third important component in the power structure of the Kingdom of Johor. The chief minister in theory consulted the council when acting on the

---

[21] KA 1341, OB 1689, Letter from the Bendahara of Johor to Melaka, received 2 July 1688, fols. 1580–3; Kratz, p. 44.

[22] KA 1388, OB 1692, Letter from the Bendahara of Johor to Melaka, received 13 April 1691, fols. 357.

[23] The *Siak Chronicles* indicate that the bendahara family was directly implicated in the plot to murder Sultan Mahmud Syah (*Siak Chronicles*, pp. 405–6). According to an Indian Muslim trader who arrived in Melaka from Johor shortly after the event, the assassination had occurred with the complicity of most of the nobles in the kingdom. KA 1515, OB 1700, Missive from Governor van Hoorne, 17 October 1699, fols. 126–7. If this report were accurate, it is likely that the bendahara knew of the plot and most probably agreed to it.

wishes of the ruler or in attending to other matters of government. Neither the Dutch nor the Malay records describe the composition or the function of the council, but certain features can be gleaned from these two sources. These principal Orang Kaya formed individual centres of power within the kingdom. In times of war they would assemble their men and lead them as a group in battle. Whenever the Orang Kaya were called to perform certain services for the ruler in court, they brought their people and organized them to carry out the ruler's wishes. In return the Orang Kaya provided their people with an intermediary with the ruler and protection from excessive demands from both the ruler and from other Orang Kaya.

The Orang Kaya were also essential figures in the international trade conducted in the ports of Johor under the system of patronage. In this system business transactions were left entirely in the hands of the traders, but the latter could not buy or sell anything without money provided by their patrons. For this vital service the patrons retained a substantial commission, sometimes amounting to 25 per cent of the total money required by the traders. In addition to the large sums that went into the pockets of the Orang Kaya in this purely monetary transaction, a sizable share of the traders' profits had to be shared with their patrons.[24] The benefits to the traders, however, were well worth the cost of this patronage. The patrons guaranteed the traders protection against hounding creditors, and if they were sufficiently powerful, even against crimes. Since the Dutch at Melaka provided free passes to all Johor Orang Kaya to trade in areas restricted to other kingdoms because of their role in the conquest of Portuguese Melaka in 1641, these traders were able to fly the flag of their patrons and carry on a lucrative trade protected by the Dutch. Many of the Orang Kaya also participated indirectly in the trade by selling and buying goods through their clients.

Through this profitable system of trade, the Orang Kaya obtained the revenues necessary to acquire followers and slaves to serve them. The Orang Kaya were thus understandably sensitive to the ability of the chief minister to attract trade to Johor's ports and to protect their trading ships. These Orang Kaya proved to be a force capable of righting any imbalance in the exercise of power resulting from either a usurpation of proper roles or the inordinate devotion toward the acquisition of wealth by any chief minister or any other Orang Kaya. When they were ignored or abused, they lent their assistance to a rival contender in order to improve their position within the kingdom. When they were courted, they responded favourably and contributed toward a successful working relationship with the ruler and the chief minister.

The fourth principal component in the power structure of Johor was the Orang Laut. Because of their intense loyalty to the rulers of the Melaka dynasty, they were an effective counterforce to the strength of the Orang Kaya. Although "Orang Laut" is a convenient term, it obscures the reality of numerous tribes and status groups subsumed under this rubric for seafaring peoples in the Malay world. These Orang Laut inhabit the islands and estuaries in the Riau-Lingga Archipelagos, the Pulau Tujuh islands, the Batam Archipelago, and the coasts and offshore islands of eastern Sumatra and southern Malay Peninsula. The more powerful and prestigious Orang

---

[24] KA 1327, OB 1688, Missive from Governor Slicher of Melaka to Batavia, 29 August 1687, fols. 853 verso–61 recto.

Laut groups were associated with the larger islands or those islands which were favourably situated on major sea trading lanes, such as the Orang Suku Bentan, Orang Suku Mepar, Orang Suku Bulang, Orang Suku Galang and the Orang Laut on the island of Singapore.[25]

The duties of the Orang Laut were to gather sea products for the China trade, perform certain special services for the ruler at weddings, funerals, or on a hunt, serve as transport for envoys and royal missives, man the ships and serve as a fighting force on the ruler's fleet, and patrol the waters of the kingdom.[26] Except in times of actual warfare when their services were needed for the fleet, the Orang Laut were usually on patrol providing protection for Johor's traders or to those wanting to trade in Johor while harassing all other shipping. It would have been against Johor's own interests to maintain these Orang Laut idle near the capital city; consequently, the capital was at times vulnerable to surprise attack, as occurred in the 16th century and in the destruction of Johor Lama in 1673. Yet because the Orang Laut were not confined to the capital, it was possible for the ruler whose capital was destroyed by the enemy to assemble these forces within a short time to launch a counterattack or re-establish a new capital elsewhere in his large kingdom. On one occasion after Bentan had been conquered by the Portuguese in 1526 and the population scattered, one of the principal Orang Kaya, the Paduka Tuan, told his son Tun Pekerma:

> "Go and collect all the people living on the coast [the Orang Laut], and we will then go and fetch the Ruler". Tun Pekerma went accordingly and called the coast tribesmen who thereupon assembled.[27]

Only a few months after the Dutch reported "the complete destruction" of Johor Lama in 1673 and the large booty and numerous prisoners taken, a Johor fleet appeared at the mouth of the Jambi River and threatened "victorious" Jambi.[28] The surprising resilience shown by the kingdom of Johor, despite the repeated destruction of its capital cities in the 16th and 17th centuries, may be attributed to the mobility of the Orang Laut groups and their total devotion to the person of the ruler.

Another factor contributing to the influence of the Orang Laut in the kingdom prior to the 19th century was their large numbers in relation to the Malays. The Dutch calculated in 1714 that out of 6,500 soldiers that the ruler of Johor could assemble from all of his territories, approximately 700 would come from the islands off the coast of Pahang, 2,000 from Riau, 500 from Lingga and 400 from Bengkalis and the Siak River.[29] These were areas of principally Orang Laut populations; thus, even

---

[25] J.G. Schot, "De Battam Archipel", *De Indische Gids* 4, 2 (1882): 164–5; J.R. Logan, "The Ethnology of the Johore Archipelago", *JIA* 1 (1847): 336.

[26] Schot, "Het stroomgebied der Kateman, bijdrage tot de kennis van Oost-Sumatra", *TBG* 29 (1884): 575–6; Schot, "De Battam Archipel", 5, 1 (1883): 473.

[27] Brown, "Sejarah Melayu", p. 191.

[28] KA 1185, OB 1674, Missive from Governor Bort of Melaka to Batavia, 21 December 1673, fol. 636.

[29] KA 1746, OB 1715, Missive from Governor Moerman of Melaka to Batavia, 12 August 1714, fols. 146–9.

discounting the figures at the capital city of Riau, which had a substantial Malay population, the Orang Laut still constituted, at a conservative estimate, about one-fourth of the military manpower of the kingdom. A VOC official visiting Riau in July 1714, observed that according to his estimation there were no more than 2,000 men on the island: "the rest live in the surrounding islands called Singapore, Pulau Papan, Pulau Bawang, and the Brouwer Straits, etc".[30] Since the size of a population was an important index of power in the Malay world, the Orang Laut played a decisive role in the politics of Johor. Of added significance was the fact that the sacredness of the ruler of the Melaka-Johor dynasty was more totally accepted within the ranks of the Orang Laut than in any other group in Johor. Their complete trust and loyalty to the Melaka-Johor ruler is difficult to explain because it was not merely wealth that bound them to the ruler. Despite chests of rials and gold that the Paduka Raja Tun Abdul Jamil possessed, he was not able to buy the loyalty of the Orang Laut against a child ruler in 1688.[31]

In face of the evidence from 17th and 18th century VOC records, which contain letters and verbal reports from Malays themselves and from later Malay histories dealing with this period, one is inclined to seek a reasonable explanation for the Orang Laut's loyalty to the Melaka-Johor family from a suggestion made by O.W. Wolters. After analysing the sources dealing with late 14th-century Srivijaya history, he suggests that the future founder of the Melaka dynasty had undergone in Srivijaya an *abhiseka* ceremony, in which "a consecration rite was performed accompanied by the prince's assumption of a new name identifying him with a god".[32] Judging from the sequel to these events in which the Orang Laut from Bentan and from the coastal areas of Palembang played a conspicuous part,[33] one can perhaps suggest that a possible source of the devotion of the Orang Laut to this prince was their belief in the special powers acquired by their lord in this special ceremony. The possession of *sakti*, "the supernatural power associated with the gods",[34] placed the ruler in a sacred realm far above the common people and thus worthy of their veneration.

The *sakti* of the prince from Palembang would have been perpetuated among his descendants, the rulers of Melaka, but would have been described by a term that was more in accordance with the new Muslim belief in that kingdom. In the

---

[30] KA 1746, OB 1715, report of van Aldorp on the layout of Riau, 24 July 1714, fols. 210–1.

[31] KA 1341, OB 1689, Letter from the Bendahara of Johor to Melaka, received 2 July 1688, fols. 1580–83.

[32] O.W. Wolters, *The Fall of Srivijaya in Malay History* (Ithaca, NY: Cornell University Press, 1970), p. 124.

[33] According to the *Sejarah Melayu*, the Queen of Bentan sent men, elephants and horses "without number" to help the prince from Palembang to settle in Singapore (Brown, "Sejarah Melayu", p. 31). Tomé Pires, an early 16th-century Portuguese observer who collected stories and other material in an attempt to reconstruct Melaka's history, states that the Orang Laut discovered the sites of Bertam and Melaka for their lord when he was expelled from Singapore. They told him, "We too belong to thy ancient lordship of Palembang; we have always gone with thee", Armando Cortesão, ed., *The Suma Oriental of Tomé Pires*, 2 vols. (London: Hakluyt Society, 1944), vol. 2, pp. 233–5.

[34] R.J. Wilkinson, *A Malay-English Dictionary* (romanized), 2 vols. (London: Macmillan, 1959), vol. 2, p. 1004.

Muslim Malay court this divine quality of kingship and the powers associated with this position were incorporated in the Arabic-derived term, *daulat*. This concept of *daulat* was such an awesome one that along with this belief grew a particularly abhorrent sin described as *derhaka*, treason to the ruler, to the *negeri* (community). *Derhaka* was regarded with such repugnance that transgressors received unusual punishments from a force surrounding kingship (*timpa daulat*). In one of the Malay chronicles the assassin is lamed by a wound inflicted on his foot by the dying ruler. "By the decree of the Almighty", grass begins growing in the assassin's wound, and for four years the wound remains unhealed until he dies.[35] In the *Sejarah Melayu* there is a story of a treasury officer (Bendahari) of Melaka who betrays his ruler to the Batara of Majapahit in revenge for the shameful murder of his daughter. For this act of *derhaka* he is punished by "the will of Almighty God" and his house and wife turned into stone.[36] As long as the rulers of the Melaka-Johor kingdoms could claim descent from the prince from Palembang, whether referring to the mythologized Sri Tri Buana (Sang Utama in the Shellabear recension) from court literature, or to some remote historical figure whose memory remained among the Orang Laut and the Malays, they could continue to enjoy the privileges and powers of kingship. To the Orang Laut this link with the original prince in Palembang endowed with the special powers through a certain ceremony may have been the vital element in their devotion to the Melaka ruling house that approximated the relationship of a lord and his personal retainers.

These, then, were the principal elements of Johor's power structure in the 17th century. Only with the murder of Sultan Mahmud Syah in 1699 was this traditional structure undermined. This overt act of regicide meant not only the death of a ruler, but the demise of a set of values which had been maintained with regard to the sacredness of the ruler, the depth and extent of loyalty which should be accorded him, and the special nature of his position within the society. If the ruler's position were no longer guaranteed by the sacred force of kingship, the ruler himself could not be regarded as the "sacred lodestone" around which the community evolved and gained its meaning and purpose. Instead, the ruler was now forced to rely upon apparent and visible manifestations of power and on close, personal ties with powerful individuals within the kingdom. The new bendahara dynasty that came to power in 1699 after Sultan Mahmud's death seems to have been unaware of these monumental changes in the traditional concept of power. It continued to conduct itself as in the past until forced to submit to the realities of the power structure in the kingdom during the Minangkabau invasion of 1718.

The Orang Laut were clearly stunned by the assassination and threatened to take vengeance on Johor. They refused to give their allegiance to the new bendahara dynasty and openly announced their willingness to serve the ruler of Palembang "because there were no descendants of the old royal blood of the Yang Dipertuan left; thus there could no longer be any King of Johor".[37] This statement may have been an implicit recognition by the Orang Laut that without a legitimate ruler from the

---

35 *Siak Chronicles*, p. 409.

36 Brown, "Sejarah Melayu", p. 51.

37 KA 1515, OB 1700, Missive from Governor Van Hoorn to Batavia, 30 November 1699, fols. 12–13.

Melaka line on the throne of Johor, the logical successor should come from the ruling house of Palembang. The collective memory of the Orang Laut may have retained some belief in the link between Melaka and Palembang, as portrayed in the *Sejarah Melayu* and in Pires' account of early Melaka, for as recently as 1967/68 one of the Orang Laut groups in Johor told a French anthropologist that "the first ruler of the Malays was one of ours".[38] Of interest also is the fact that after the regicide, only two Malay states sought ways of wreaking vengeance on the bendahara dynasty. They were Perak and Palembang; the two states which had the greatest claims to being the successors of the Melaka dynastic line.[39] All of these separate threads make fascinating material for the reconsideration and reconstruction of early Malay history.

A year after the assassination some of the Orang Laut groups decided to pay homage once again to the Malay ruler in Johor. However, their allegiance to the former dynasty did not wane. When a Minangkabau adventurer named Raja Kecil claimed in 1718 to be the son of the last male heir of the Melaka dynasty in Johor, he quickly gained the support of almost the entire Orang Laut population of Johor.[40] Some of the Orang Laut groups never wavered in their belief that Raja Kecil was the legitimate heir and thus their only lord. They remained faithful to him and continued to serve him even after his expulsion from Johor and his establishing of a new kingdom in Siak. When Dutch observers paid a visit to the ruler of Siak in the late 19th century, they noted the presence of the Orang Suku Bentan and the Orang Suku Bulang among the ruler's personal retainers. According to the traditions at the court, they were the descendants of the principal Orang Laut groups that had followed Raja Kecil from Johor to Siak in the early 18th century.[41]

The Malay reaction to the regicide was much more guarded than that of the Orang Laut because the bendahara family and many of the Orang Kaya had been implicated in the deed. There was no open opposition against the plotters, yet the abhorrence felt was much stronger than appeared on the surface. Despite continuing Dutch reports on the favourable trade and prosperity enjoyed at the principal settlement of Johor, revolts were rampant in the outlying areas of the kingdom. For all the admirable efforts of the bendahara dynasty under some very able ministers to attract international trade and continue the accustomed flow of wealth into the kingdom, the memory that the new dynasty had committed such a heinous act

---

[38] Chr. Pelras, "Notes sur quelques populations aquatiques de l'Archipel nusantarien", *Archipel* 3 (1972): 144. See also page 118 and footnote 32 in this paper for a discussion of the relationship between Palembang and Melaka as mentioned in the *Sejarah Melayu* and by Tomé Pires.

[39] The case for Palembang has already been discussed in the paper itself. As for Perak, its first ruler was Sultan Muzaffar Syah, the eldest son of Sultan Mahmud Syah, the last ruler of Melaka, by a royal wife. Although he was designated the heir–apparent (Raja Muda) by his father, the crown went to his half-brother by a non-royal mother (*gundek*) who became Sultan Alauddin Riayat Syah, the first ruler of Johor. Muzaffar was then invited by the people of Perak to become their ruler. Brown, "Sejarah Melayu", p. 193.

[40] KA 1803, OB 1719, Report of the refugee Bendahara of Johor to Melaka, 26 May 1718, fols. 25–32; T.D. Hughes, "A Portuguese Account of Johor", *JMBRAS* 13, 2 (1935): 129–31.

[41] A.A. Hijmans van Anrooij, "Nota omtrent het rijk van Siak", *TBG* 30 (1885): 330.

served to undermine the loyalty of the Malay subjects. When the bendahara dynasty confidently moved its capital to Riau in 1709 to meet a Siamese force said to be coming down the Peninsula to invade Johor, some 400 Johor subjects, or about one quarter of the entire population at the capital, fled to Trengganu hoping to link up with the Siamese to destroy the new Johor dynasty.[42] Yet the new rulers of Johor never really comprehended the extent of the disaffection within the kingdom until 1718, when mass desertions occurred among the Orang Laut and the Malay subjects to the side of Raja Kecil.

When the bendahara dynasty regained the throne of Johor with the help of the Buginese in 1722, it no longer deluded itself with the pretence of being upheld by the same pillars of support of the former Melaka dynasty. The new ruler of Johor, Sultan Sulaiman Syah, was now propped up by the Buginese rather than by his own Malay subjects or Orang Laut retainers. Although he and his descendants attempted to inculcate in their subjects the same devotion to the bendahara family as the former Melaka-Johor dynasty had enjoyed, these efforts were partially nullified by the presence of an alternative focus of loyalty in the form of the position of the Buginese Raja Muda. Since the latter received the allegiance of all the Buginese groups on Riau and the outlying areas of Johor, he was a figure of great influence in the kingdom. The Buginese were an effective power bloc in Johor and were unwilling to become merely tools of Sultan Sulaiman. Instead, they sought compensation in terms of security, acceptance and prestige for themselves and their descendants within their adopted homeland. They assumed the important trading, patrolling and military role in Johor once exercised by the Orang Laut, and they became essential to the ruler in maintaining his position from both internal and external enemies.

The Orang Kaya were no longer in great favour with Sultan Sulaiman because of their betrayal of his father in 1718 and because of their minor role in the recovery of the kingdom from the Minangkabaus. Their positions in the court were now usurped by the Buginese princes and war leaders. For the greater part of the 18th century the Buginese posts of Raja Muda and Raja Tua became of greater importance in the principal decisionmaking within the kingdom than the chief Malay ministers and the Council of the Orang Kaya.

But of all the traditional sources of power within the Kingdom of Johor, the group that suffered most was the Orang Laut. The death of the last male line of the Melaka dynasty in 1699 destroyed any lasting ties that they had maintained with that ruling family. While they had been attracted to this family because of the creation of a unique *daulat* in a distant past, the *daulat* in turn had acquired a certain cogency and credibility because of the power the Orang Laut brought to the throne. The shock of the regicide of 1699, which resulted in confusion within the ranks of the Orang Laut and culminated in the betrayal of the new dynasty in 1718 in favour of the supposed son of the last Melaka dynastic line, was a significant turning point in the history of the Orang Laut within the Malay world. Refusing to offer their total devotion to a new ruling family, but also unwilling to transfer their loyalty wholly to Raja Kecil in Siak, the Orang Laut vacillated between Riau-Johor and Siak, thereby

[42] KA 1687, OB 1711, Report of Backer and Encik Aman on their mission to Johor, 20 October 1710, fols. 540–4.

weakening their impact in the affairs of these kingdoms. Those who remained in the service of the new Sultan Sulaiman were soon subject to demeaning behaviour by the ruler's new champions, the Buginese. Their principal task of serving as the ruler's navy and fighting men was now admirably filled by the experienced seamen and warriors of southwest Sulawesi. The Orang Laut underwent such a significant metamorphosis in the 18th century that by the 19th century foreign observers were wont to characterize the Orang Laut groups they occasionally encountered as a shy, nomadic sea-people of little consequence.

These were significant changes that altered the very nature of power and kingship in Johor. Whereas in 1691 the Malay bendahara serving as regent to a child ruler could justifiably say that according to *adat* he had no right in the disposition of the kingdom,[43] such an attitude would have been both unconvincing and risible had it come from Daeng Kemboja, the Buginese Raja Muda who served as regent to another child ruler of Johor in 1761. Until the end of the 17th century the concept of authority in the Kingdom of Johor was governed by a long tradition of belief in the sacredness of the ruler. His presence and well-being were considered essential in providing a purpose and a focus for all activity in the kingdom. When this basic assumption was rejected by the Malays themselves, it undermined the entire system of roles and beliefs which had been the strength of the kingdom from the founding of Melaka in the early 15th century until the death of the last male ruler of the Melaka dynasty in Johor in 1699.

[43] See the statement of Bendahara Tun Habib Abdul Majid quoted above.

11

David E. Sopher

Boat People in the Western Archipelago during the Portuguese Period*

The history of Melaka's rise to eminence as the emporium of the Indies in the century preceding its capture by the Portuguese was well preserved in local traditions and annals in the early 16th century. In the story of the founding of Melaka, of which several Portuguese versions exist, the boat people called *Celates* play an important role. The Celates appear in the same light as the Lutaos described by Combés: they have the nomadic, boat-dwelling habit, are simple collectors and fishermen, but are most renowned and feared for their piratical activities. Like the Lutaos, some of them acquire considerable power, undergoing complete cultural and social transformation. Contemporary descriptions of them by Portuguese in Melaka during the 16th century are scarce, but are adequate to show that the primitive character of the nomadic boat people is retained by a large segment of the Celate population, despite the high rank of some of their sedentary relatives.

The sudden rise of Melaka as the chief transhipment point for goods from East Asia to India occurred, according to the events described in the Portuguese accounts, at the very end of the 14th century. Majapahit, the Javanese power, which for a brief period had maintained nominal control over the coasts of Malaya, eastern Sumatra, western Borneo and the islands of the South China Sea, began to decline rapidly after 1389, when the prosperous reign of Hayam Wuruk ended. From the north, a considerable rival, Thailand, sought to fill the growing vacuum, and established its representative as governor of the port of Singapore, which was then a mart of some importance, sharing the rather local trade in the Strait of Melaka with Pasai on the opposite shore of Sumatra.

On this scene there appeared shortly after the death of Hayam Wuruk a Javanese nobleman known by the title of Parameswara, who, together with some

---

* First published as a chapter in David E. Sopher, *The Sea Nomads: a Study of the Maritime Boat People of Southeast Asia* (Singapore: National Museum, 1965), pp. 314–33.

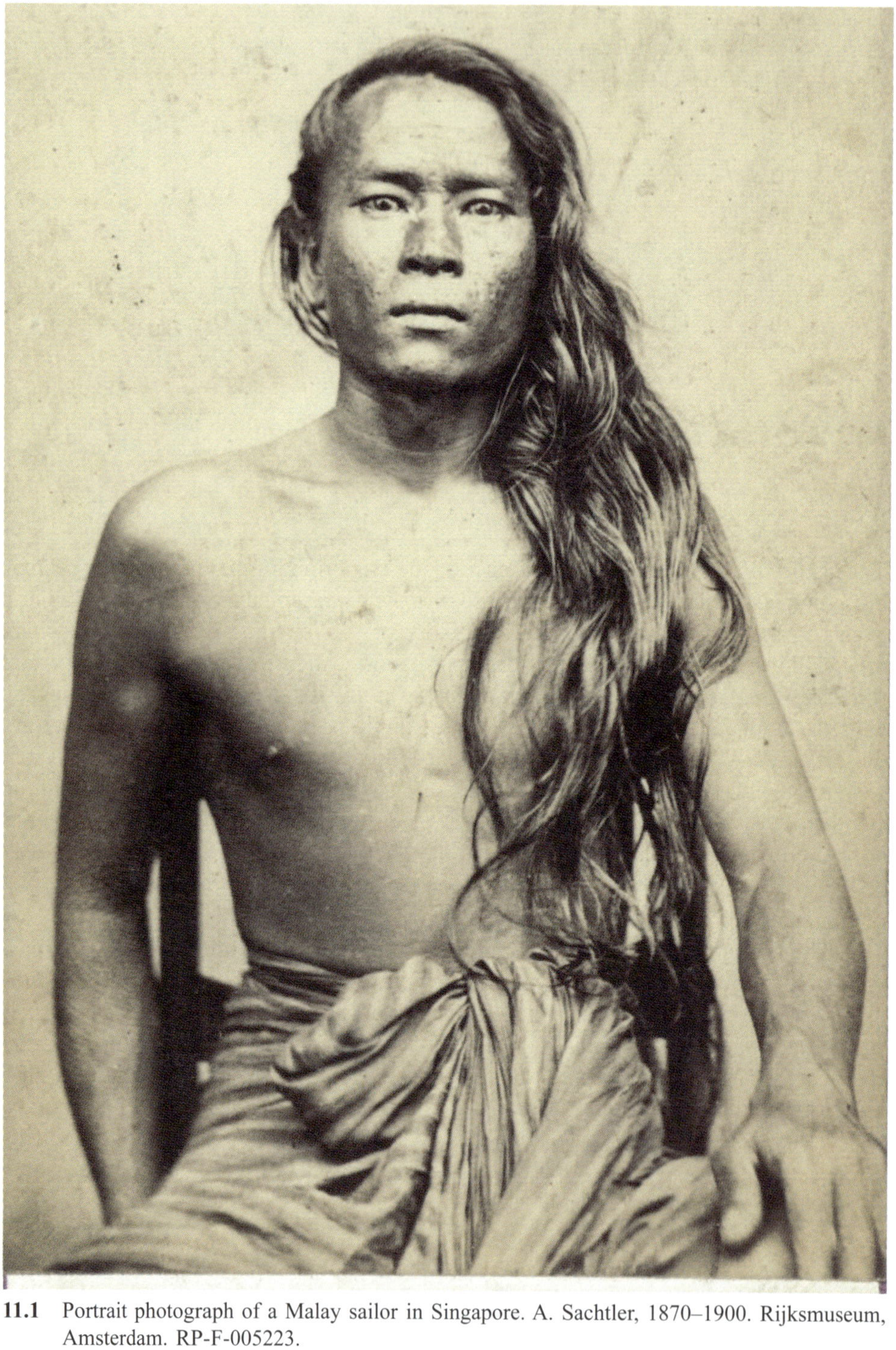

11.1 Portrait photograph of a Malay sailor in Singapore. A. Sachtler, 1870–1900. Rijksmuseum, Amsterdam. RP-F-005223.

of his followers, had fled his country after an unsuccessful coup. In Singapore he was more fortunate, but his violent access to power there threatened to bring Thai retaliation, and he fled once again, this time up the coast, eventually settling at Melaka. This place is not mentioned in the chronicles of Majapahit, and the local tradition retold by the Portuguese was that it was founded as a result of this particular episode, but its name appears about a half century earlier in a Thai document, so that a small coastal port and fishing village must have existed on the site for some time before 1400, as the Portuguese historian Barros supposed. Undeterred by his earlier misfortunes, the Parameswara at Melaka set about organizing his friends and dependents among the boat people into an effective naval force which could cut off trade from Singapore and other ports and direct it to Melaka.

By masterly statesmanship the Parameswara proceeded to secure his position and to build the foundation of Melaka's wealth. Under the early Ming rulers of China there was active and official interest in the South Seas, and an embassy to these parts under the renowned Cheng Ho found eager co-operation from a potential ally, the Parameswara, who saw here an opportunity to balance the friendship of China against the enmity of Thailand and the disgruntled annoyance of decadent Java. He himself visited the Chinese court at Beijing, and was duly honoured with tokens of regard and official recognition; perhaps on this account a face-saving agreement was reached with Thailand, which was to receive an annual tribute from Melaka. Apparently, too, the Parameswara quickly reached an understanding with the Muslim Indian merchants who handled much of the international commerce of the Indies, and who must have gone through difficult times under Hindu Majapahit. At least, his son, the second ruler of Melaka, had a Muslim name and title: Muhammad Iskander Shah. Under him the Muslim merchant community grew large and prosperous, while maritime control of the Strait now made it possible to bring the all-important spices of the Moluccas via eastern Java to Melaka for transshipment to India.[1]

This historical digression provides the context of the early Portuguese references to the Celates, which will now be considered.

The best known and reputedly most reliable historian of the earliest years of Portuguese power in the Indies is João de Barros, who as an official in Melaka a generation after its capture by Albuquerque in 1511 was able to use existing Portuguese records and local Malay sources. The following is a summary of his account of the founding of Melaka from the second "Decade" of *Da Ásia*, originally published in 1553:

> When the Parameswara ("Paramisóra") fled Singapore he took with him "a people called *Celates* ('Cellates'), persons who live on the sea, whose occupation is robbing and fishing, with the [ruler's] favour", with whose aid the Parameswara

[1] See especially R.O. Winstedt, *The Straits Settlements and the Federated and Unfederated Malay States* (London: Constable & Co., 1923), pp. 130ff; Bernard H.M. Vlekke, *Nusantara: A History of the East Indian Archipelago* (Cambridge: Harvard University Press, 1943), pp. 68–71; F.W. Stapel, *Geschiedenis van Nederlandsch Indië*, 4 vols. (Amsterdam: N.V. Uitgevermaatschappij Joost van den Vondel, 1938), vol. 1, pp. 320–3. These modern writers rely on the Chinese records and the Portuguese accounts that here are considered in connection with the information they provide concerning the Celates.

had made himself master of Singapore for a period of five years. The Parameswara settled at Muar (Bandar Maharani), south of the site of Melaka, but fearing the Celates and not wishing them to live in his settlement, suggested with simulated reasons that they settle further up the coast.

> "The Celates, although their habitation is more on the sea than on the land, for there their children are born and there they are brought up without making any establishment on shore, however, because they were hated by the people of Singapore and all the islands in its territory, did not dare to return to those parts", but settled near the mouth of the river of Melaka. There they found some people of the land, "half-savages in their manner of living, whose language was the proper Malay, which was used by all that people, and with which also the Celates were familiar". In the beginning these two groups avoided one another because of the difference in their manner of living, but because of the women, who were becoming scarce among the Celates, they joined to form one settlement, each group retaining the occupation to which it was accustomed, the Celates living on the products of the sea and the Malays on the fruits of the earth.
>
> The Celates found the area above Melaka spacious and well supplied with fruit trees, particularly durians, and sent word of this to the Parameswara at Muar, who subsequently moved his settlement to the new site at Melaka. Although the memory of his father's quarrel with the Thai at Singapore had lapsed when the Parameswara's son came to rule, the latter, Iskander Shah (in Javanese, "Sekender Shah"; hence the Portuguese "Xaquem Darxá") confirmed his settlement at Melaka in order that his people might profit from the sea, which was the principal means whereby he hoped to come to great estate.
>
> And although the Celates folk were a low, vile people, and the natives half savages, Paramisóra and his son Xaquem Darxá found them loyal friends in their deeds, or rather, in the evils which they committed with their blessing. Chiefly, in order to make use of many of them in the settlements, particularly Melaka, they gave them nobility, marrying them with the most noble of the Javans whom they had brought from Java; and from those Celates and wild Malays come all the Mandarins who are now the Fidalgos of Melaka, by grant of these former kings, as being the first settlers of Melaka, the which title of king [i.e., Sultan] began with Xaquem Darxá. For after the death of the king of Siam, whom his father feared, aided by the fleets of war boats with which the Celates were very familiar, he began to compel the ships which formerly navigated in the Strait between Melaka and Sumatra that they should no longer go to Singapore and also the ships from the East which used to come there to exchange merchandise with those from the West, according to old custom; as a result of this Singapore began to become empty of merchants who came to live in Melaka.[2]

The *Commentarios do Grande Affonso d'Albuquerque*, written by the son of the conquistador and containing in the main selections from his father's papers, relates substantially the same story but does not give more information about the Celates. Barros scarcely mentions the contemporary Celates in his account of the Portuguese conquest and rule of Melaka. Other Portuguese writers, however, in particular the

---

[2] João de Barros, *Da Asia. Dos Feitos que os Portuguezes fizeram no descubrimento e conquista dos mares e tarras do Oriente*, déc. II, pt. II (Lisbon: Na Regia Officina Typografica, 1777), pp. 6–9; a partial English translation is to be found in John Crawfurd, *A Descriptive Dictionary of the Indian Islands and Adjacent Countries* (London: Bradbury & Evans, 1856), p. 242.

discerning Tomé Pires, supply additional information, which is in part contemporary description and in part popular conception concerning earlier conditions at Melaka.

Godinho d'Eredia, for instance, in his *Declaraçam de Malaca e India Meridional com o Cathay*, written in 1613, has these notes on the Celates ("Saletes"):

> Before the foundation of the town [Melaka], the place was inhabited by a fisher-folk, the Saletes, who gathered in the shade of the myrobalan trees.[3] These fishermen employed pointed darts called "soligues",[4] with which they transfixed the fish swimming at the bottom of the sea: they used no other devices for catching fish. They were a wild, cannibal race, who inhabited the coast of Ujontana[5] in the southern sea.[6]

Eredia's "Map of the Malacca Territory"[7] has the name *Regiam de Saletes* inscribed near the mouth of the *Rio Panagim*, which has been identified as the Sungei Linggi, a small river flowing through a mangrove swamp to the sea about 25 miles [40.2km] northwest of Melaka.

A quarter of a century later, on the eve of Portuguese Melaka's capitulation to the Dutch, Barretto de Resende briefly noted the chief characteristics of the contemporary Celates, in a passage which appears to be based on more direct observation than the other accounts.

In the Strait of Singapore, he says, where the water, though deep, is so clear that fishes can be seen swimming about in it, fish is bought by the merchants on board the ships

> from the Saletes, or inhabitants of the Straits, who live in very swift baloons with their families. They catch fish by spearing them in the water and then sell them. These Saletes are a wicked people and especially so to the Portuguese. They are evil-hearted and treacherous and the best spies the Dutch possess. Wherever, of the many places in this vicinity, our ships may be, they immediately inform the Dutch and lead them there; so that most of our losses are due to them. This is because the Dutch give a great share of all thus seized, and thus it is very necessary that our fleets of *jaleas* [armed galleys] and ships that go to these straits to wait for the said fleets should make war as much as possible on these Saletes and drive them from these parts.[8]

The piratical nature of the Celates is always stressed by Portuguese writers, but Resende's remarks indicate that other political and economic factors were involved. Unhappy personal experiences with pirates were bitterly remembered by the victims, who condemned the entire boat population out of hand. For instance, the usually temperate Fernão Mendes Pinto refers to a narrow escape he had on the way to

---

[3] *Myrobalan trees*. Mal.: *kayu laka*, giving, in the folk etymology, the name of the town.

[4] "*Soligues*". Mal.: *saligi*, a wooden or bamboo lance, the point being simply the sharpened end of the shaft.

[5] *Ujontana*, Singapore Island.

[6] J.V. Mills, ed. and trans., "Eredia's Description of Malaca, Meridional India and Cathay", *JMBRAS* 8 (1930): 16.

[7] Ibid., pl. 1, p. 207.

[8] George W. Maxwell, "Barretto de Resende's Account of Malacca", *JMBRAS* 60 (1911): 10.

Macao in 1555. He was in a lifeboat, their ship having run aground, and their craft was twice approached by apparently hostile craft, once by two longboats, and the second time by a fleet of 50 or 60 boats, but the Portuguese barely eluded their pursuers on both occasions. The crew of these boats, says Pinto, were "Saletes", "who are robbers who live in those islands, who fight with blowpipes using poison ['*pelejao com zaravatanas de peconha*'], and are the most treacherous people in the whole world".[9]

The use of blowpipes and poisoned darts by the Celates is a remarkable feature about which some additional information is provided by other writers. Barros tells how in the hard-fought battle for Melaka in 1511, some of the Portuguese were wounded, several fatally, by poisoned darts. "The Malays say that the invention of this poison was made by the inhabitants of Sumatra and is compounded with the bone of a fish which in this kingdom we call *bagre*, and the Malays charged with this manufacture were the Cellates folk who live on the sea".[10] The fish is the *ikan pari*, the Malay name for the stingrays and eagle rays (see below) of these seas; the caudal spine of the ray was sometimes used in Malaya as a spearhead, but more often among the forest tribes was ground up with other ingredients, some magical, of which the *ipoh* derived from *Antiaris toxicaria* was usually the effective poisonous agent.[11] The Celates were probably charged with obtaining the spines of the rays, which would be dangerous work requiring the cooperation of several boats.

These incidental details concerning the Celates would remain hanging in air were it not for the framework of support provided by the factual statements of Tomé Pires, an unparalleled source, only recently published, on the economic geography of coastal Southeast Asia at the beginning of the 16th century. The *Suma Oriental* is an amazing work, characterized by remarkable perception and an accurately detailed comprehensiveness; written in 1512–15, it contains the earliest succinct geographical statement concerning the Malaysian boat people.

In his account of the early history of Melaka, Pires mentions the Celates, "who are corsairs in small, light craft, men who go out pillaging in their boats, and fish, and are sometimes on land and sometimes on sea, of whom there are a large number now in our time. (They carry blowpipes with small arrows of black hellebore which, as they touch blood, kill, as they often did to our Portuguese in the enterprise and destruction of the famous city of Melaka, which is very famous among the nations.)"

Then Pires refers to the boat people by a name that does not occur in other Portuguese writing. These people are, in the orthography of the manuscript, *celates bajuus*, men who lived near Singapore and also near Palembang, and of whom some 30 accompanied Paramisura on his "flight from Singapore" (he had altogether about a thousand followers with him). "When Paramisura had been in Palembang, they served as fishermen; after they came to Singapore, they lived in Karimun, an island near the channel; and at the time when Paramisura came to Muar, these

---

[9] Maurice Collis, *The Grand Peregrination, Being the Life and Adventure of Fernão Mendes Pinto* (London: Faber & Faber, 1949), p. 268.

[10] Barros, *Da Ásia*, II. 2, p. 65.

[11] I.H. Burkill, *A Dictionary of the Economic Products of the Malay Peninsula* (London: Crown Agents for the Colonies, 1935), vol. 1, pp. 179, 181.

thirty came to live in the place which is now called Melaka. After they had apprised the Parameswara of the site's advantages, the Celates, now only 18 in number, petitioned him for a reward and he made them mandarins, they and their sons forever. They always accompanied the king, serving him with great faith and whole-hearted friendship, and the honour of the newly created Mandarins lasted continually right down to the coming of the Portuguese to Melaka, when their fifth grandson was the *Laksamana* and the *Bendahara*....[12] Paramisura had a son, born in Singapore, who was married to the principal daughter of the Mandarin lords who had formerly been Celates ... Xaquem Darxá endeavoured to populate Melaka as much as possible. People began to come from the Aru side and from other places, men such as Celates robbers and also fishermen, in such numbers that three years after his coming Melaka was a place of 2,000 inhabitants and Siam was sending rice there."[13]

In the latter part of the 14th century, Melaka acquired "many islands belong to the Celates. Through his captains, he [the sultan] took the islands of Lingga which are on this side of Bangka, almost opposite to Palembang."[14] This expansion was of course accompanied by the zealous spreading of Islam.

In addition to these historical references to the Celates, Pires gives their distribution as precisely as he had been able to determine it. He gives a short description of each section of the coasts of the Malay Peninsula and eastern Sumatra and the intervening islands, referring to the Celates in the following cases:

(a) *Dependencies of Melaka*. "Beyond the Rio Fremoso [Sungei Batu Pahat, that is, south of the modern Bandar Penggaram] is the Singapura channel. It has a few Celate villages; it is nothing much. From here onwards the said kingdom does not extend any farther on land. This channel is a thing of little importance—I mean the people who live there."[15]

(b) *East coast of Sumatra*. The kingdom of Aru [north of Rokan estuary]: "Aru has a town in the land of Arqat [between the Deli and Rokan mouths] where

---

[12] *Bendahara*. "The most important person near the old Melaka, Johor and Perak thrones was an officer who was at once prime minister and commander-in-chief. He bore the Indian title of Bendahara.... Of local as opposed to foreign Indian origin, [it] was his duty of providing the ruler with a palace and with a daughter of his own house for consort.... He had jurisdiction over nobles and officials. And he was the leading figure at all court ceremonies and receptions.... It is possible that the Bendahara represents a submerged indigenous chief, the equivalent of a proto-Malay Batin" (R.O. Winstedt, *The Malays: A Cultural History* [New York: The Philosophical Library, 1950], pp. 73–4). *Laksamana*. This official was a Mentri of the second rank; the Mentris had general judicial functions as well as special administrative functions. The *Laksamana* was the Admiral, whose title, of Hindu provenance, had originated in Melaka. "The Perak Laksamana held sway 'up-river as far as the tide can reach, down river to the line where the surf breaks on the bar and the grey mullet come to the surface'. He had charge of the coast and it was his duty to guard against foreign foes and assist those in trouble at sea" (ibid., pp. 75–6).

[13] Armando Cortesão, ed. and trans., *The Suma Oriental of Tomé Pires. An Account of the East, from the Red Sea to Japan, written in Malacca and India in 1512–1515* (London: Hakluyt Society, 1944), vol. 2, pp. 233–8.

[14] Ibid., p. 250.

[15] Ibid., p. 262.

11.2 Map of the Riau Archipelago, Singapore and the Lingga Archipelago, 1848. National Archives of the Netherlands. 4.AANW-1447.

11.3 Photograph of an *orembaii* (a type of Bugis freight ship) which is followed by a *kole-kole*, taken in the Bay of Amahai in southern Seram. Leiden: Royal Netherlands Institute for Southeast Asian and Caribbean Studies (KITLV).

a slave market of men and women is held on certain months … and they also deal in other merchandise there, and that is the way it happens with the Celates, as will be told when we speak of the Celates robbers.… The kingdom of Arqat: the people on the sea-coast are Celates robbers and those inland live on their crops."[16] Rokan: the ruling mandarin was a vassal of the late king of Melaka and had to help him during his war with the Portuguese with rowers and men-at-arms, who had to serve gratis, just for their food. "Many of these people are Celates, which is the Malay for sea robbers." Purim [vicinity of Bengkalis]: Also, a vassal to the king of Melaka and helps with rowing men in great numbers. "And most of the people in this place are Celates, robbers, and they are brought up on the sea and are great rowers".[17] "Purim is almost entirely a country of Celates.… The robbers come to make a fair of the things they steal."[18]

(c) *Riau-Lingga Islands*. Lingga Archipelago: "thickly populated … must have four or five thousand men.… The king is like a king of the Celates. He is feared and powerful.… Off Jambi, the islands of Berhala [between Singkep and Bangka] are uninhabited. Some Celates sometimes take shelter there; they have plenty of water."[19] Lingga has a king called Raja Linga, "who is greatly beloved by the Celates. The Celates are thieving corsairs who go to sea in small *perahus* robbing where they can. They are obedient to Melaka. They make Bintan ('Bimtam') their headquarters. These men serve as rowers when they are required by the king of Melaka, without payment just for their food, and the governor of Bintan brings them when they have to serve for certain months of the year."[20]

Yet more remarkable than this itemized account of the Celates is the description given by Pires of the people called Bajuus. These people resemble the Bajaus (Bajus) in one or two characteristics, but in general appear to be much more akin to the Bugis (Wajus). Although the Malay annals of the 15th century refer to the Bugis and Makassarese as sea rovers, Pires is the only one of the chief Portuguese historians to refer to them at length.[21] Bugis and Makassarese history only begins with the early years of the 17th century, when conversion of the rulers to Islam was accompanied by great territorial and commercial expansion. Pires' account is particularly interesting because it deals with a period several decades earlier than this.

Pires refers to Celebes as "the islands of Macassar", which reflects the general ignorance, even among Malays, of the coastal geography of that oddly shaped island. His account, which is not very well organized, is quoted in full.

"The islands are numerous. It is a large country. One side goes up to Buton and Madura and the other extends far up north. They are all heathens. They say

[16] Ibid., vol. 1, p. 148.
[17] Ibid., vol. 1, p. 149.
[18] Ibid., vol. 2, p. 262.
[19] Ibid., vol. 1, pp. 156–7.
[20] Ibid., vol. 2, p. 264.
[21] Crawfurd, *A Descriptive Dictionary*, p. 74.

that these islands have more than fifty kings. These islands trade with Melaka, Java, Borneo, Siam and with all the places between Pahang and Siam. They are men more like the Siamese than other races. Their language is peculiar to them, different from the others. They are all heathens, robust, great warriors. These men in these islands are greater thieves than any in the world, and they are powerful and have many praos [*perahu* or *prahu*]. They sail about plundering, from their country to Pegu and from their country to the Moluccas and Banda and among all the islands around Java; and they take women to sea. They have fairs where they dispose of the merchandise they steal and sell the slaves they capture. They run all round the island of Sumatra. They are mainly corsairs. The Javanese call them Bajuus and the Malays call them this and Celates. They take their spoils to Jumaia[22] which is near Pahang, where they sell and have a fair continually. Those who do not carry on this kind of robbery come in their large well-built *pangajavas*[23] with merchandise ... [there follows a brief description of the merchandise] ... These islands have many inhabitants ... they all wear krises. They are well-built men. They go about the world and everyone fears them, because no doubt all the robbers must obey these with good reason. They carry a great deal of poisoned weapons and shoot with them. They have no power against the junks which can all defend themselves, but every other ship in the country they have in their hands."[24]

It is possible to see, in this hazy *aperçu* of a land and people scarcely mentioned at all in the contemporary literature, references to two kinds of people: the thieving pirates who yet take their women to sea, and the swaggering, keris-wearing, honoured sea captains, traders and warriors, who are the conventional type of the Bugis of Wajo in later years.

Most of the description, however, undoubtedly refers to the pre-Muslim Bugis. Inconsistencies between the general characteristics of the people described as Bajuus and those of the Bugis in later centuries are: the thieving character ascribed to them, the taking of women and presumably whole families aboard, and the equating of them by name with the Celates. The Bugis had the reputation of colourful adventurers, playing an active part in local wars on the Malayan and Sumatran coasts in the 17th and 18th centuries, and although their commercial activities included the

---

[22] *Jumaia*. Jemaja, in the western Anambas islands. Hamilton, writing in the 1720s, remarked that the inhabitants of the Anambas and Natuna islands "are called *Bougies*, a fierce desperate People ... the Religion is Mahometan" (Alexander Hamilton, *A New Account of the East Indies*, ed. W. Foster [London: Argonaut Press, 1930], vol. 2, p. 80). Earlier in the 14th century, the larger islands were territories of Majapahit. In the early 19th century, islands nearer the Malayan coast like Pulau Aur and Pulau Tinggi had the same functions as Jemaja had in the 16th century: a harbour for pirates, a place for disposing of stolen and smuggled goods and a market for slaves (J.T. Thomson, "Pulo Aor", *JIA* 4 [1850]: 194).

[23] *Pangajavas*. *Perahu penjajap*. (D.G. Stibbe, ed., The *Encyclopaedië van Nederlandsch-Indië*, 2nd ed. [The Hague: Martinus Nijhoff, 1919–39], supplement vol. for S, p. 118) on the basis of earlier information wrongly identifies it as follows: "*Perkayuhan* or *Pankayuhan* (Mal.). 'A boat which is paddled' (*kayuh*: 'paddle'). By the term pangajaoa derived from it, the Portuguese formerly apparently referred to a certain kind of rowing boat."

[24] Pires, *Suma Oriental*, vol. 1, p. 226.

11.4 A Melayu Captain. Johan Nieuhof, *Voyages and Travels, into Brazil, and the East-Indies: Containing, an exact description of the Dutch Brazil, and divers parts of the East-Indies*. London: Printed for Awnsham and John Churchill at the Black Swan in Pater Noster Row, 1703. NUS Libraries, Special Collections.

merchandising of slaves, a legitimate activity until the advent of European control, they were to be trusted as men of the strictest honesty.

> The Bugis ... in honesty, energy of character and general conduct, are far superior [to the Malays]. They are deservedly praised for their upright conduct in commercial transactions; greater reliance being placed on their bare word, by those who are acquainted with the native character, than on the most sacred oaths taken by the natives of Bengal and Coromandel.... It is supposed by strangers that the Bugis are addicted to piracy. That individuals of the Bugis nation are to be found, who, as the Chinese say, "indulge in disorderly thoughts and actions, and go about madly scheming irregular profits", I do not pretend to dispute, but during my sojourn in Eastern India I never heard of a single instance of a piratical attack by a Bugis trader; and, on the contrary, several circumstances have come to my knowledge which would go to prove that their inclinations tend the contrary way.[25]
>
> The Bugis ... are by far men of the most honour of any of the Malay cast and dignified in their manner superior to other Malays. The Macassars and Bugis people who come annually to trade at Sumatra, are looked upon by the inhabitants as their superiors in manners, the Malays affect to copy their style of dress, and frequent allusions to their feats and achievements are made in their songs. Their reputation for courage, which certainly surpasses that of all others in the eastern seas, acquires them this flattering distinction; they also derive part of the respect showed to them from the richness of the cargoes they import and the spirit with which they spend the produce—Marsden.[26]

Pires describes the legitimate trading activities of the people called *Bajuus*, and some of his condemnation of them as pirates probably arises from a tendency, characteristic of those times, to label in this way any manifestation of vigorous commercial competition. The fact that the Bajuus took their women to sea is the opposite of modern conditions, as Collins points out, for an important distinction between the Bajaus and the Bugis is that the latter do not take their families with them, even on extended trips such as those to the coast of Australia, during which they are absent from home for 6 to 18 months. The statement by Pires may actually represent a confused reference to the Bajaus.

A more specific source of confusion is the explanation of the name *Bajuus* given by Pires. Bajuus as a Javanese name, and as a Malay alternative to Celates, immediately suggests *bajau* with its common meaning of "pirate" and "sea-rover" as it occurs in the western part of the archipelago; such a meaning must be involved in Pires' use of the combination *celates bajuus* in referring to the associates of the Parameswara.[27] But the description of the Bajuus obviously refers to the Bugis, who are alternatively called Wajos from their most common place of origin in southwestern Celebes.

[25] George Windsor Earl, *The Eastern Seas, or Voyages and Adventures in the Indian Archipelago, in 1832–33–34* (London: Wm. Hallen & Co., 1837), pp. 390–1.

[26] Thomas Forrest, *A Voyage from Culcutta to the Mergui Archipelago, Lying on the East Side of the Bay of Bengal* (London: J. Robson, 1792), p. 85.

[27] See above. Cortesão translates this as "Bugis *Celates*", but does not explain.

The following relationships are therefore suggested. Baju/Waju, originally a toponym of southern Celebes, referred to the far-ranging Bugis who in pre-Muslim times appear to have had some traits of the Orang Laut or Orang Sarna character, traits which later disappeared. In the western part of the archipelago, the name acquired a more general, but pejorative sense, perhaps suggested by a chance resemblance to a Javanese word for "pirates". In the Celebes area, however, the specific geographic meaning of the name was retained for the majority of the maritime Bugis; in addition, it must be supposed, there were in that area boat people, ancestors of the later Bajaus of the Celebes coasts, perhaps related to and symbiotically dependent on their more advanced maritime neighbours in the familiar ecological pattern of the Riau-Lingga Islands and the North Borneo coasts of the 19th century. These people might also be known as "the Wajo people" or "the Wajo sea people" the slightly different forms (Wâjó and Bâjo) in which the two ethnic names were perpetuated being due to dialect differences. In support of this it may be noted that the name Orang Johor has, in addition to its regular meaning of "Johore people" or "Johor man", the general significance of "pirate" on the Java coast, while a people of Orang Laut habit called Orang Johor were found on Pulau Laut in the first half of the 19th century.[28]

In another place, Tomé Pires again mentions Celates and Bajuus together. In the Sumatran coast of Aru, he says, the mandarins and the people (who are not identified as Celates) go robbing at sea and share the booty with their chief. Aru and Melaka were traditional enemies (that is, economic rivals), "whence comes the saying 'Aru against Melaka, Achin against Pedir, Pedir against Kedah and Siam, Pahang against Siam on the other side, Palembang against Lingga, Celates against Bajuus, etc.', and all these nations fight one against the other and they are very rarely friends".[29] The examples show that the pairs all comprise similar and neighbouring, but distinct, political geographic entities. The Celates and Bajuus, therefore, were both predominantly seafaring people with strong piratical tendencies, but with suggestions of the same basic economy as that of the sea nomads of the 19th century; there was, however a geographic distinction between them which was probably this: the Celates were the indigenes of the Strait, while the Bajuus had an eastern origin. Such a conclusion, clearly indicated by the evidence, must imply the existence at one time of a close relationship between the Celebes sea nomads and the maritime Bugis.

An additional note on the distribution of the Celates concerns the occurrence, in the *Suma Oriental* and in early Portuguese maps of the Strait of the name "Islands of the Celates". In the account of Antonio Galvão's voyage to the Moluccas only a few months after the taking of Melaka, the route is given: "through the strait of Sabam [Sabam is identified as Pulau Kundur, so this would be Durian Strait] along the island of Sumatra and in sight of many others—leaving them on the left hand and towards the east—which are called *Salites*, past the islands of Palimbao [Bangka, and possibly Singkep]".[30]

---

[28] See D.E. Sopher, *The Sea Nomads: a Study of the Maritime Boat People of Southeast Asia* (Singapore: National Museum, 1977), p. 152.

[29] Pires, *Suma Oriental*, vol. 1, p. 147.

[30] Ibid., vol.1, p. lxxx.

11.5 Photograph of a Malay carpenter surrounded by children in the Straits Settlements. Leiden: Royal Netherlands Institute for Southeast Asian and Caribbean Studies (KITLV).

In the year following, Albuquerque sent the king a map of the Indies, said to have been copied by the pilot Francisco Rodrigues from a Javanese map, with the notation: "Your highness can take this map as a very accurate and ascertained thing. The archipelago of the islands called Celates, which lie between Java and Melaka, is missing."[31]

In these two instances, the islands called Celates appear to be the Riau and Lingga archipelagos or some part of them. In three separate references, however, Pires speaks of them as being located in the northwestern part of this area, being either the islands of the western part of the Batam archipelago, or an adjacent group, the small islands between Karimun and Kundur. Thus, in a list of the islands forming a channel from Kampar to Palembang, he has: "In front of Siak, the islands of Pulau Pisang [the alluvial islands Rangsang, Merbau, etc.]; in front of Kampar the islands of Karimun and the Celates and Kundur. These produce a few foodstuffs and are inhabited."[32] Elsewhere, he refers to the same group as "the islands of the Celates which are called Çelaguym gim";[33] this may be identified with Sugi Strait (Selat Sugi).

The foregoing information on the Celates during the 16th century will now be critically reviewed. There has been some disagreement about the derivation of the name itself, although it is not clear why this is so. Tomé Pires is wrong in saying explicitly that Celates is Malay for "sea robbers"; in his time, however, the name may have acquired a generic connotation of that sort.

The etymology of the name was given by Resende as "inhabitants of the straits", which in Malay would be *Orang Selat*. Crawfurd accepts this derivation, equating the Celates with the Orang Laut[34] and Ferrand defines the name as "a Portuguese neologism" from the Malay *selat*.[35] The form "Celates" or "Saletes" is a Portuguese term that disappeared from use in the middle of the 17th century, although it is retained in modified form in Dutch and English writings.

Contradicting these opinions, Dalgado in his *Glosário Luso–Asiático* (1919) says that the Malay language does not admit of such derivations as Celates from *selat*, which is beside the point, for the Portuguese language certainly does. Wilkinson, who is sometimes unreliable,[36] is not satisfied with the commonly accepted derivations and looks for the origin of Celates in a corrupted form of a hypothetical Besisi-Laut, or "Sea Besisi"! Winstedt apparently follows his colleague, for he says that Celates is "usually though perhaps wrongly interpreted, 'People of the Straits'".[37]

---

[31] Ibid., vol. 1, p. lxxix.

[32] Ibid., vol. 1, p. 156.

[33] Ibid., vol. 1, p. 136.

[34] Crawfurd, *A Descriptive Dictionary*, p. 49.

[35] Mills, *Eredia's Description*, p. 89.

[36] Compare, for example, his sketch of a Melakan sea gypsy before the arrival of the Javanese fugitives (Wilkinson, "The Malacca Sultanate", *JMBRAS* 13 [1935]: 27). The sea gypsy's food resources included "gourds, onions, leeks, Malay mustard, water-melon, sago-flour, maize and occasionally rice".

[37] R.O. Winstedt, "A History of Malaya", *JMBRAS* 13 (1935): 4.

11.6 Makassar Soldiers who blow Poisoned Darts out of Trunks. Johan Nieuhof, *Voyages and Travels, into Brazil, and the East-Indies: Containing, an exact description of the Dutch Brazil, and divers parts of the East-Indies.* London: Printed for Awnsham and John Churchill at the Black Swan in Pater Noster Row, 1703. NUS Libraries, Special Collections.

These are scarcely valid objections to an explanation that is simple and very probable. *Selat* not only means "strait", but in particular, either in this form or in the adjectival form *selatan*, refers specifically to the Strait of Singapore and the many narrow water passages of the Batam archipelago, so that the derived meaning of *selatan* in Malay is "southern" (such as Tanjung Selatan, the southernmost point of Borneo). The Malays on the Inderagiri coast of Sumatra customarily refer to Singapore as Selat,[38] and *Tanah Selat*, "the Land of the Straits", is the Malay term for a European geographical one, namely, "Riouw-Lingga archipelago".[39]

There is also a more localized use of *selat* in the case of the islands so called by the Portuguese. Finally, there is among the 19th century Orang Laut Pesukuan one clan known as the Suku Selat, frequenting the western islands of the Batam archipelago,[40] which are probably those meant by Pires as "islands of the Celates".

Celates, then, is simply the Portuguese plural form derived from "Orang Selat", just as Malaios is derived from "Orang Malayu" or Jaos from "Orang Jawa". The Malay original would mean "the people of the Singapore and Batam Straits", which, as the comments of Pires, Barros, Eredia and Resende show, would apply very well to the Celates.

One aspect of this nomenclature is curious: the disappearance of Orang Selat from modern usage and the lack of reference in early European accounts to the generally used modern "Orang Laut". It would appear that the Portuguese gave the former wider use than was the case among the Malay-speaking population, while in time the Malay term developed in the opposite direction, becoming restricted in application to one small group of the sea people. There are indications that "Orang Laut" had currency in the 16th century; for instance, the Italian traveller Ludovico di Varthema, who visited Melaka before the Portuguese conquest, noted that when the sultan of Melaka attempted to interfere with his people, they would threaten to abandon the land, because they were *men of the sea*.[41]

The richness of detail in the *Suma Oriental*, combined with the corroborative information in other Portuguese writings of the 16th century, gives positive value to the absence of references to the Celates on the better-known coasts of the Peninsula, Sumatra and Java. The Celates were to be found in the Riau-Lingga archipelago and on Singapore Island, in scattered places on the west coast of Johor and Melaka, and on the east coast of Sumatra between the mouths of the Rokan and Kampar Rivers.

---

[38] J.J. de Hollander, *Handleiding bij de Beoefening der Land- en Volkenkunde van Nederlandsch Oost-Indië*, 4th ed. (Breda: Koninklijke Militaire Academie, 1895), vol. 1, p. 727.

[39] Crawfurd, *A Descriptive Dictionary*, p. 367.

[40] T.J. Newbold, *Political and Statistical Account of the British Settlements in the Straits of Malacca* (London: John Murray, 1839), vol. 2, p. 413; J.R. Logan, "The Ethnology of the Johore Archipelago", *JIA* 1 (1847): 336; J.G. Schot, "De Battam Archipel", *De Indische Gids* 4, 2 (1882): 165.

[41] Winstedt, *The Malays*, p. 15. Also: "Et quando el re se vol mettere fra loro, essi dicono che desabitarano la terra perché sonno omini de mare" [And when the king wants to interfere with them, they reply that they deserted the land because they are men of the sea] (*Itinerario de Ludovico de Varthema Bolognese*, ed. Paolo Giudici [Milan: Edizioni Alpes, 1926], p. 271). This indirect reference is the only one Varthema makes to boat people or their descendants; it is, incidentally, the earliest European reference of this kind.

Their distribution along the Strait of Melaka is not duplicated by the occurrence of actual boat-dwelling Orang Laut in the 19th century, but there were in the later period, on both sides of the Strait, indications that an Orang Laut element had at one time lived in the vicinity and mingled with other elements in the population.

The Portuguese accounts show that the Celates did not frequent the Achin, Batak, and Lampongs coasts on the eastern side of Sumatra, the Pahang-Thailand east coast of the Malay Peninsula, or the coast of Java. Evidence regarding the coasts of Borneo, Celebes and the Philippines cannot be regarded as reliable enough for any conclusions of this kind to be drawn.

A coast which was well travelled, with several ports at which Portuguese ships would stop, was the west coast of the peninsula from Mergui to Trang, all of which was then under Thai rule. There is no mention in the Portuguese literature of boat people at any of the mainland points, while the islands such as those of the Mergui archipelago remained untouched and unexplored, except by accident, so that here, too, the evidence is almost entirely negative regarding the presence of sea nomads.

No positive conclusion can be drawn from this, however. Tenasserim at the time was a prosperous agricultural province of Thailand, more densely populated than at present, with its commercial center at the delta town of Tenasserim, upriver from Mergui which later superseded it, and despite the rise of Melaka, playing an important role as a transshipment point in the trade in luxury articles between India and eastern Asia. The inner islands in the narrow straits leading to Mergui and the Tenasserim River mouth were mantled with groves of fruit trees. Shy, nomadic boat people like the Mawken would remain concealed in the islands farther west or south, or in the creeks in the mangrove swamp fringing the mainland coast. They would be inconspicuous, off the trade routes, and would form an insignificant fraction of the total population.

Fernão Mendes Pinto recounts an incident that suggests some of the simple boat people may have been in the Mergui archipelago in the 16th century. (Malay and Bugis trading ships were found at Tenasserim, presumably carrying local trade between the ports of the west coast of the Malay Peninsula.) In 1542, Pinto sailed from Melaka for Martaban. Before they reached Mergui, while they were threading their way through the small islands to the south, a boat put out from a small island ("Pulo Hinhor", "Coconut Island"). "Six swarthy men, poorly dressed", came aboard, evidently delighted to find that there were Portuguese on the ship. The leader presented Pinto with "a letter wrapped in a filthy rag",[42] which was a recommendation from a Portuguese saying the bearer was a newly converted Christian who had given the Portuguese valuable intelligence in a sea fight. He was chief of the little island, but this had lately been usurped by a Muslim. Pinto wanted to help him, and the Muslim Malay *nakhoda* of his ship amiably consented to do so. "He gave him a little rice and some linen to cover him withal, for he was so ragged, that one might

[42] J.I. de Brito Rebello, *Peregrinação de Fernão Mendes Pinto* (Lisbon: Livraria Ferreira, 1908–10), vol. 3, p. 32.

feel his naked skin everywhere about him".[43] The enemy was in a straw cabin, with not more than 30 fishermen, weak and unarmed, with no weapons but spears and one arquebus.

These being defeated, the rescuing party went on to a settlement, "where there were not above twenty poor low cabins, covered with straw; in it were found some threescore and four women, with a many of little children, who no sooner perceived us but all of them with tears fell a crying out *Christian, Christian, Jesus, Jesus*". However, the *nakhoda* could not keep his men from sacking the cabins "though in them all was not found the value of five ducats. ... For the people of this island are so poor, that scarce one of them is worth a groat; they feed on nothing but a little fish, which they take with angling, and eat it broiled on the coals without salt; yet are they so vain and presumptuous that no one amongst them but terms himself a king of some vile piece of ground, wherein is little more than one poor cabin. And neither the men nor the women have wherewithal to cover their nakedness."[44]

The nomadic boat-dwelling habit is not mentioned in the case of these non-Muslim fishermen, but the circumstantial account of them, contrasted with the Mon-Thai pattern of high culture prevailing on the mainland, suggests a resemblance to the Mawken and Orang Laut Kappir of the 19th century.

Apart from this nebulous situation in the Mergui archipelago, however, within the small but geopolitically significant part of the Indies in which the Celates were found, they were known to the Portuguese as nomadic fishermen, living with their families in boats, in the vicinity of small wooded islands or among the channels of mangrove tidal forests. Some of them would form more permanent settlements on land. Fishing was done almost exclusively with the wooden fish spear. The small, light family boats of the Celates were built up dugouts, reinforced with a bulwark of palm stems, having square mat sails and rigging of rattan.

An element of material culture associated with the Celates that is not characteristic of the 19th-century sea nomads is the use of the blowpipe with poisoned darts. Neither the blowpipe nor the use of poison is mentioned in any account of the modern sea nomads. In addition, the contemporary accounts of piracy in the Strait of Melaka and Singapore and areas adjacent, such as the account carried in each issue of the *Journal of the Indian Archipelago*,[45] do not mention the blowpipe in the pirate arsenal, which was meager enough, being made up largely of *saligis* of *nibong* wood in addition to a few guns and a small cannon of native manufacture.

The Orang Laut Kappir had no weapons, other than the fish spear and harpoon, and had never heard of blowpipes, according to Annandale.[46] However, on Pulau

---

[43] Henry Cogan, *The Voyages and Adventures of Ferdinand Mendez Pinto, the Portuguese*, 3rd ed. (London: J. Macock, 1692), p. 191. The story is told in detail in Maurice Collis, *The Grand Peregrination: Being the Life and Adventures of Fernão Mendes Pinto* (London: Faber and Faber, 1949), pp. 169ff.

[44] Cogan, *The Voyages*, p. 191.

[45] Compare "Piracy and slave trade, etc.", *JIA* 3–5 (1849–51).

[46] Nelson Annandale and Herbert C. Robinson, *Fasciculi Malayenses: Anthropological and Zoological Results of an Expedition to Perak and the Siamese Malay States, 1901–1902* (London: Longmans, Green & Co., 1903), p. 62.

Peringai near Trang, Evans acquired from a settlement of "Sea Gypsies" there several short toy bamboo blowpipes for shooting pellets. Such toy blowpipes are found in other parts of the archipelago within the general area of blowpipe distribution, as at Melaka, on Java and Sarawak and among the Bugis,[47] and are usually taken to be survivals of the blowpipe as a hunting and occasional fighting weapon.

Although all the Toraja tribes used the blowpipe as a hunting weapon, it is not found among the Bugis; Kennedy, however, says that they had heard of its use in former times. Pires provides valuable confirmation of this, but no doubt he exaggerates its importance as an offensive weapon. Blowpipes and the associated use of *ipoh* poison are "native in the western part of the Malay archipelago, being found all over Sumatra, and on Java, Bali, Borneo and Celebes". It is used chiefly as a hunting weapon for small game, but among many Dayak tribes and a few Toraja the blowpipe serves as a fighting weapon and is used in the hunting of larger game. In Java and Sumatra, including Minangkabau, it is only used as a hunting weapon.[48]

The blowpipe is used by all the forest people of the Malay Peninsula, as well as the Sabimba and Muka Kuning of the interior of Batam Island. It is, however, "quite certain that the Semang only learnt the use of the blowpipe from the Sakai.... It appears on the whole most reasonable to suppose that the blowpipe was introduced into the Malay Peninsula by the Sakai, that it has since been perfected by the same race, and that the modem blowpipe of the Malayan tribes in the Peninsula (as well as that of the archipelago) was either an inferior imitation of the Sakai weapon, or else that the wooden blowpipe was an altogether independent invention, which appear at the best most improbable."[49]

This would appear to be especially valid for the sea folk, among whom it is almost never found in any form in later centuries, while it would only have extremely limited use in a way of life specializing in strand collecting and fishing. Two factors must be considered in connection with the Celates of Melaka and the Singapore channel of the 16th century. First, at Melaka there was strong cultural mixing between the boat folk and the forest peoples (the half-wild Malays) who used the blowpipe, and who must have been drafted into the forces defending Melaka against the Portuguese siege. Barros, it should be noted, does not say that the Celates used the blowpipe, but only that they supplied one of the ingredients—and by no means the most important one—of the poison, namely, the *ipoh* produced from *Antiaris toxicaria*, the manufacture of which was no doubt known exclusively to the forest peoples. The Celates at Melaka may have learnt the use of this weapon and have used it in a limited way in warfare and piratical raids, perhaps principally for its psychological effect. Secondly, the novelty of this deadly weapon and the initial terror inspired by it among the Portuguese would lead to considerable exaggeration of its importance as a fighting weapon among the Celates, and even perhaps an

---

[47] For example Reymond Kennedy, *Field Notes on Indonesia: South Celebes 1949–50* (New Haven: Human Relations Area Files, 1953), p. 77; Walter W. Skeat and Charles O. Blagden, *Pagan Races of the Malay Peninsula* (London: Macmillan & Co., 1906), vol. 1, p. 259.

[48] Stibbe, *Encyclopaedië*, vol. 4, p. 683.

[49] Skeat and Blagden, *Pagan Races*, vol. 1, pp. 255–6.

erroneous extension to the sea people of its use among the non-Muslim forest people, accounting for the statements of Pinto and Pires.[50]

A "wild, treacherous, evil-hearted, piratical people, hated by the sedentary population of the coast"—such is the Portuguese description of the Celates, but it is paralleled by the comments on the Rayats or Orang Laut of this area by Dutch writers in the early part of the 19th century. Yet, as closer investigation was to show, it was often these groups who were most consistently the victims of pirates. This aspect of the Celate mode of life—their loose organization in small, defenceless groups of families living in boats—hardly appears in the Portuguese accounts, although its existence is suggested in Pinto's circumstantial anecdote of the people of "Coconut Island".

However, it does clearly appear from the Portuguese accounts that the organization of groups of these people into a significant factor in the economic and political struggles of this area was provided by leaders foreign to the group. The Parameswara at Singapore and Melaka, his son Muhammad Iskander Shah and the succeeding sultan of Melaka were the organizing force behind these skirmishes in a struggle for economic supremacy. When the Portuguese conquered Melaka and the sultanate was later transferred to Johor, the Celate vassals of Johor could be used to carry on a guerrilla warfare at sea against Portuguese shipping. On the Sumatra side, too, rival princelings must have financed the Celate population of their coasts in piratical activities in the Strait of Melaka, as the booty was shared openly, according to Pires.

The political aspect of the Celate harassment of the Portuguese is indicated by Resende's reference to their active support of the rising Dutch competitors of the Portuguese at the beginning of the 17th century. The nomadic habits of the Celates made them particularly useful as spies, as one or another European power was to find in the case of other groups of sea nomads, and Resende's belated call to arms was prompted by considerations of political and military strategy rather than by moral indignation.

The dependent relationship of the Orang Laut *sukus* under a foreign ruling class is duplicated in the relationship of the Celates to the sultan of Melaka and his deputy at Bintan. As vassals the Celates performed a service as rowers in the warboats of the ruler. Yet their loyalty was not always to be counted on; the Parameswara distrusted his uncivilized associates, and in later times, those who had settled on land at Melaka were inclined to be factious and restless, threatening to return to the life at sea.

Some of the Celates were rapidly assimilated by intermarriage with the ruling high culture group after the founding of Melaka. Although they retained the tradition of Celate descent, the members of the laksamana and bendahara families were Muslim Malays of high standing when the Portuguese took Melaka. However, their kinship ties with the Celates made it easier for them to command the services of the boat people, which their charge of the maritime affairs of state would make necessary on occasion.

This must also have been the way in which individual Lutaos acquired power and noble connections in the Sulu archipelago, as is suggested by Combés' account

[50] See above.

of them. Perhaps something similar is involved in the hints of Bajau participation in the creation of the ruling class of Gowa and Wajo. The similarity between the Celates and the Bajaus (Bugis with one or two elements of the Bajau way of life), which is implied by Pires, must mean that many of the piratical Celates had been considerably acculturated by their contacts with Melaka. This is in accordance with the situation in the Riau-Lingga archipelago in the 19th century: the population there appeared to be stratified culturally, the different layers dating back to different periods of active acculturation. Thus, the Celates on the islands, conquered by Melaka and pressed into its service, would, at least in part, become sedentary, acquiring new economic techniques, although their chief interests would remain maritime, very much like the Orang Sarna and the acculturated Lutaos. They would still after many decades, however, retain their connections with the nomadic boat people through their interrelationship within the *suku* structure.

In this way, for instance, the temenggong of Singapore[51] in 1819 was very distantly related to the boat-dwelling families he had in his charge. The temenggong was a member of the bendahara family of old Melaka, and was also related to the ruling family at Riau, so that the trace of descent from the Celates of Melaka ran through all the noble families of the Riau-Lingga Islands; in addition, intermarriage with women from the boat-people, daughters of important headmen, no doubt added strength to these remote ties. This tradition of Celate ancestry may have been important in the socio-political organization of the boat people under the rulers at Riau and Lingga, but no mention is made of it. The temenggong of Singapore was a Muslim Malay of high social status, one of the chief officers of the sultan of Johor; he had all the appearance of a foreign governor among the still pagan and primitive boat-dwelling Orang Laut.

The relations of the Celates with the "wild Malays", apparently coast-dwelling Jakun, indicate rather close mingling in a few places, although the initial contact between the two groups in the vicinity of Melaka was a hesitant one. This fortuitous mixing at places on the west coast of Malaya suggests an explanation for references to Orang Laut on that coast in the 19th century.

In Part II[52] it was shown that the classification of the Besisi as "Orang Laut" by Skeat and Blagden was improper, as it could not be justified by a comparison of their economy and culture with the sea nomad *genre de vie* and the culture traits associated with it. Yet allusions to the sea people and some traces of their culture were present, so that the Besisi preferred to speak of themselves as "Orang Laut".[53] It is likely that these traces survive from cultural mingling of the kind described by Barros, which may have taken place long before the 19th century. In this connection, Vaughan-Stevens, who is never fully reliable, relates a long and involved traditional history of the Blandas, mixed tribes of the interior of Selangor adjacent to the area occupied by the Besisi. In this story there is, at an early period of Blandas history, friendly intercourse with the Orang Laut, who appear to be vaguely related to the Blandas; following this there are references to the places and events which appear

---

[51] See Sopher, *The Sea Nomads*, p. 105.

[52] Ibid., pp. 67–8.

[53] Skeat and Blagden, *Pagan Races*, vol. 1, p. 22.

in the history of Melaka's founding, so that the connection with the Orang Laut may refer to an old tradition, perhaps learned from some other group, of a mixed population of Celates and forest people several centuries past.

From all this it is seen that the Celates of the Portuguese literature were the same people as the 19th-century Orang Laut, and that several features which characterize the relationship between the Orang Laut and Malays of the Riau-Lingga area appear to have existed in the 15th and 16th centuries.

12

Kwa Chong Guan

From Temasek to Singapore: Locating a Global City-State in the Cycles of Melaka Straits History*

The Problem of Singapore before Raffles

Outlining the historical background of Singapore for a University of Singapore volume commemorating the 150th anniversary of the founding of Singapore in 1969, then-Raffles Professor of History K.G. Tregonning argued, "modern Singapore began in 1819. Nothing that occurred on the island prior to this date has particular relevance to an understanding of the contemporary scene; it is of antiquarian interest only".[1] "Antiquarian" as used by Tregonning in this statement appears to be an attempt to distinguish history, usually of the recent political past which can be rigorously studied through an analysis of documents, from an older past which is known only through the collection of its relics and antiques, physical artefacts which might be considered too fragmentary to be worthy of systematic study.[2]

* Abridged from the original version published in *Early Singapore, 1300–1819: Evidence from Maps, Texts and Artefacts*, ed. John N. Miksic and Cheryl-Ann Low Mei Gek (Singapore: Singapore History Museum, 2004), pp. 124–46.

[1] K.G. Tregonning, "The Historical Background", in *Modern Singapore*, ed. Ooi Jin Bee and Chiang Hai Ding (Singapore: Singapore University Press, 1969), p. 14.

[2] *Antiquarianism* as a European historiographical category refers to how the past was studied and appreciated between the 15th and the 18th centuries. This antiquarian interest in the "relics" of the past for its own sake came under increasing criticism in 19th-century histography as a naive approach to the past by amateurs and dilettantes randomly collecting bits and pieces of

The "Antiquities" of Singapore

Some of the "antiquities" of Singapore to which Professor Tregonning may be referring were seen by Sir Stamford Raffles when he landed at the mouth of the Singapore River in January 1819. These included an earthen rampart running along the banks of what is now the Stamford Canal from where the canal enters the sea to near the old National Museum, at the base of Fort Canning, then known as the Forbidden Hill or Bukit Larangan to the Malays, as ghosts of old rulers were believed to haunt it. The "tombs of the old Malay kings" on Fort Canning were another series of "antiquities" also noted by Raffles during his last visit to Singapore in October 1822 when he built himself a bungalow on the hill. Raffles at the time gloomily accepted that he could well be buried among these tombs should he die in Singapore of the severe headaches which afflicted him.[3]

In February 1822 Dr John Crawfurd, who was to become Singapore's second resident, also saw these "antiquities" when he visited Singapore en route to the courts of Siam and Cochinchina as an envoy of the East India Company. Crawfurd spent two days walking around Singapore and climbed the Forbidden Hill. There he recorded sighting a number of old brick platforms, which he rightly concluded were the foundations of wooden buildings. Exploring further, he found blocks of sandstone around these platforms, which he correctly inferred were the bases of wooden pillars of buildings, Chinese coins and fragments of green porcelain or celadon. Crawfurd also noted the earthen rampart Raffles had seen three years earlier, and estimated it to span 4.8 metres broad and rise to a height of 2.7 metres.[4]

---

evidence of the past which have no relevance to the present. A. Momigliano's "Ancient History and the Antiquarian" (*Journal of the Warburg and Courtauld Institutes* 13 [1950]: 285–315) remains the best introduction to the concept of antiquarianism.

[3] Raffles' comments on the defences of Singapore are in his 31 Jan. 1819 letter to William Marsden, which is reproduced in Lady Sophia Raffles, *Memoir of the Life and Public Service of Sir Thomas Stamford Raffles*, reprint of 1830 ed. (Singapore: Oxford University Press, 1991), p. 376. His resignation to dying and being buried on Government Hill can be found in his letters to Marsden written on 21 Jan. 1823 and to the Duchess of Somerset on 23 Jan. 1823 (during his last visit to Singapore), both also reproduced by Lady Sophia Raffles in her *Memoir*, p. 535.

[4] John Crawfurd, *Journal of an Embassy from the Governor-General of India to the Courts of Siam and Cochin China*, reprint of 1828 ed. (Singapore: Oxford University Press, 1967), pp. 44–7. Crawfurd's account was critical to historical geographer Paul Wheatley in reconstructing the geography of early Singapore, and to archaeologists led by John Miksic in planning which areas to excavate. For a reconstruction of what Crawfurd may have seen at Fort Canning, see C.G. Kwa, "Narrative and Structural History of Fort Canning", in Fourth Intra-ASEAN Archaeological & Conservation Workshop, Report, Singapore, 1–21 Nov. 1987, pp. 204–8; and "What Was It Crawfurd Saw on Fort Canning?" *Heritage* 6 (1984): 1–4. For an attempt to reconstruct not only what was at Fort Canning but also on the banks of the Singapore River, on the basis of more recent archaeological data and extrapolations from what we know about the layout of other contemporaneous emporia, see Derek Heng, "Reconstructing Banzu, a Fourteenth-Century Port Settlement in Singapore", *JMBRAS* 75, 1 (2002): 69–90.

12.1 Inner harbour of the Singapore River with Fort Canning Hill (formerly Bukit Larangan) in the background. Anonymous, c.1890–c.1910. Rijksmuseum, Amsterdam. RP-F-00-5018-39.

12.2 Incense burner of stoneware in the form of a tripod, covered with a green glaze. On the outside marked by embossed floral scrolls and a decorative band with a zigzag pattern in relief. Celadon (Longquan), c.1400–c.1599. Rijksmuseum, Amsterdam. AK-MAK-1695.

Systematic archaeological excavation of Fort Canning was unfortunately undertaken only in 1984,[5] by which time the brick platforms Crawfurd saw and the Malay "tombs" Raffles wrote about had been demolished for the fortress built in 1859. Other artefacts were lost in the construction of the covered reservoir in 1926 and the underground command centre for the British Far East Command in the 1930s. It was therefore fortunate that a cache of gold ornaments,[6] which have become national treasures, was found intact in the area. Reporting this find of gold ornaments, Winstedt identified the style of the rings and the armlets engraved with a *kala* as Majapahit. But no coherent narrative could be made out from these chance finds. The developments on Fort Canning have irretrievably destroyed much of the archaeological evidence, and what we have been recovering since 1984 is therefore fragmentary and incomplete.[7]

One other major piece of evidence was an inscription standing at the south bank of what used to be the mouth of the Singapore River before reclamation projects extended the coastline. Crawfurd saw this inscription during his visit in 1822 and described it as carved into one face of a large 3-by-3 metre sandstone boulder that had been split into two. Unfortunately the rock with its inscription was destroyed in 1843 to enable development of the area around the mouth of the Singapore River, and only fragments of this inscription were saved and deposited in our National Museum and the Calcutta Museum.[8] These fragments have proven to be inadequate

---

[5] Dr John N. Miksic was invited by the old National Museum to undertake the excavation with funding provided by the Shell Corporation in Singapore. This museum initiative was coordinated by then-Senior Curator of Art, Ms Constance Sheares. The Museum's case for initiating excavations was made in the wider context of preserving Fort Canning as the earliest seat of government in Singapore. A public version of this case for preserving Fort Canning drafted with inputs from C.G. Kwa is in "Fort Canning: Earliest Seat of Government in Singapore", *Heritage* 5 (1983): 13–21. Miksic's findings from his excavation at Fort Canning in 1984 (see *Archaeological Research on the "Forbidden Hill" of Singapore: Excavations at Fort Canning, 1984* [Singapore: National Museum, 1985]) formed the basis for planning further and more extensive excavations by an Intra-ASEAN Archaeological Workshop in Nov. 1987. A report of the workshop was drafted and submitted to the ASEAN Secretariat but never published. This workshop was significant for its excavation of a pit north of Keramat Iskandar Shah, which proved unusually rich in artefacts and has since been redeveloped into a site museum.

[6] R.O. Winstedt, "Gold Ornaments Dug Up at Fort Canning, Singapore", *JMBRAS* 6, 4 (1928): 1–4, and reprinted in "Singapore 150th Anniversary Commemorative Issue", *JMBRAS* 42, 1 (1969): 49–52. Part of the cache, including one of the two bracelets found, were lost during the Japanese occupation of Singapore.

[7] The results of these excavations are reported in Alexandra A. Choo, *Report on the Excavation at Fort Canning Hill Singapore* (Singapore: National Museum, 1986); John N. Miksic, "Beyond the Grave: Excavations North of the Keramat Iskandar Shah, 1988", *Heritage* (1989) 10: 34–56. [E.N.: See J.N. Miksic, *Singapore and the Silk Road of the Sea 1300–1800* (Singapore: NUS Press, 2013), pp. 222–65 for a summary of what Miksic excavated on Fort Canning and other sites around Fort Canning.]

[8] Background to the stone is contained in G.P. Rouffaer, "Was Malaka emporium voor 1400 A.D. genaamd Malayoer? En waar lag Woerawari, Ma-hsin, Langka, Batoesawar?", *BKI* 77 (1921): 35–67. [E.N.: Portions of this long article have been published in this collection.] W. Bland, a naval surgeon on the HMS *Wolfe*, provided another contemporary description of the

for the epigraphists who have examined it. The estimates that were given by the epigraphists for the date of the inscription range from 14th-century Majapahit *kawi* script to earlier *kawi* (ca. 925–1250).[9]

Locating Singapore in the Cycle of Melaka Straits History: The Heritage of Srivijaya

A series of old Malay inscriptions recovered in the estuary of the Musi River, and especially around the vicinity of Palembang, announced the establishment of a new emporium in the 7th century CE by a group of Malay chieftains or *datus* to service the growing trade between West and South Asia to East Asia. These old Malay inscriptions indicate that the Malay *datus* upriver along the Musi successfully exerted their influence over other emporia in the Straits of Melaka and the isthmus. These emporia included Langkasuka, then the main port of call on the east coast of the Malay Peninsula, the Merbok River estuary in Kedah, and Barus on the north Sumatra coast. Near Palembang, on the Batang Hari, Melayu was another major port of call and significant contender against Srivijaya to be the *primus inter pares* emporium in the Straits. Through conquest and control of these rival ports, the Srivijaya *datus*, as they termed themselves in their epigraphy, established a *negara* built on trade that survived for the next several centuries.[10]

The geographical imperatives however provided only the necessary, but not the sufficient, conditions for the rise of the Srivijayan *datus* to preeminence. Srivijayan success and prosperity was founded on a new cycle in the trade of the South China Sea and the Indian Ocean. In the centuries preceding the 7th century, Indian, Arab, Persian and Jewish traders sailed across the Bay of Bengal, then crossed the Isthmus of Kra before sailing across the Gulf of Siam to stop at Oc-Eo in the Mekong Delta before proceeding to Canton (Guangzhou). These early traders linked a booming Roman market for eastern luxuries with an incipient Han Chinese market. Also, a new generation of Islamic traders from West Asia sprang up. These traders were seeking new routes to China and the sources of the aromatics and spices demanded in the markets of mediaeval Europe, which was coupled with a new Chinese market under the Tang dynasty for Buddhist artefacts, drugs, aromatics and other exotica from the South Seas. These markets therefore provided the Srivijayan *datus* with

---

inscription *in situ* in "Inscription on the Jetty at Singapore", *JASB* 6 (1837): 68–82. Bland's copy of the inscription is reproduced in S. Durai Raja Singam, *India and Malaya through the Ages* (n.p., 1954), p. 48.

[9] Probably the best guide to the dating of the inscription remains J.G. de Casparis, *Indonesian Palaeograph: A History of Writing in Indonesia from the Beginnings to c. AD 1500* (Leiden: Brill, 1975), p. 45.

[10] For a reconstruction of the nature of the Srivijayan city-state and its influence, see P.-Y. Manguin, "City-States and City-State Cultures in Pre-15th Century Southeast Asia", in *A Comparative Study of Thirty City-State Cultures: An Investigation Conducted by the Copenhagen Polis Centre*, ed. M.H. Hansen (Copenhagen: Det Konelige Danske Videnskabernes Selskab, 2000), pp. 409–16.

the opportunity to develop their home base up the Musi River into the preferred entrepot on the Maritime Silk Road.[11]

The Srivijayan *datus*' rise to eminence was therefore made possible by their monopolizing an incipient Tang market for a new range of rare merchandise and luxuries. Through a series of tribute missions to the Tang court begun in 724, they established themselves as the dominant supplier of these rare goods to the Chinese. With Chinese acquiescence, Srivijaya moved against other polities and emporia in the Straits that were challenging its right to monopolize the Chinese market. But the Srivijayan *datus* apparently failed to detect and adapt to fundamental changes in China's demographic, political and economic structures after the An Lushan Rebellion in 755. By the 11th century it had lost out to its old rival on the Batang Hari River, Melayu.[12]

It is to the credit of the Srivijayan *datus* that they were able to establish their home base some 50 kilometres up the Musi River, and therefore somewhat off the natural sailing routes, as the preferred emporium in the Straits of Melaka for several centuries. Over these centuries, the Srivijayan dominance of this assemblage of ports and harbours built on a network of alliances and allegiances waxed and waned in response to challenges from rival ports of call. But the mystique of the Srivijaya name persisted. The image of Srivijaya as the major and dominant trading *negara* in the Straits of Melaka recorded in the imperial Chinese histories, travelogues and topographies, the Arab rutters and other texts,[13] is a testament to the achievement of the Srivijayan *datus* and their political legacy. It is a legacy that both the Portuguese reports and the classical Malay text, the *Sejarah Melayu*, were carried to Temasek by a member of the Srivijayan ruling oligarchy,[14] which is testament to the importance of the text in maintaining the legitimacy of those in power.

---

[11] O.W. Wolters reconstructed the events leading to the establishment of Srivijaya in his classic, *Early Indonesian Commerce: A Study of the Origins of Srivijaya* (Ithaca: Cornell University Press, 1967), n. 20.

[12] The relationship between Srivijaya and Melayu on the Batang Hari River, probably at Muara Jambi, has preoccupied most historians and archaeologists of Srivijaya. See O.W. Wolters, "Restudying Some Chinese Writings on Srivijaya", *Indonesia* 42 (1986): 15–25; his earlier essay, "A Note on the Capital of Srivijaya during the Eleventh Century", in *Essays Offered to G.H. Luce*, ed. Ba Shin et al., 2 vols. (Ascona: Artibus Asiae, 1966), vol. 1, pp. 225–39; and J.G. de Casparis, "Srivijaya and Malayu", in *SPAFA Final Report*, Consultative Workshop on Archaeological and Environmental Studies on Srivijaya (I-W2b), Jakarta, Padang, Prapat and Medan, Indonesia, 16–30 September 1985 (Bangkok: SEAMEO Project in Archaeology and Fine Arts [SPAFA] Co-Ordinating Unit, 1985), pp. 245–56.

[13] Gabriel Ferrand collated most of these texts in 1922 for his "L'empire sumatranais de Çrivijaya", *JA*, sér. 11, vol. 20 (1922): 1–104, 161–262.

[14] Wolters' *Fall of Srivijaya in Malay History* (Oxford: Oxford University Press, 1970) collates the Portuguese accounts of Melaka with the Chinese records to reconstruct the sequence of events in the transmission of this Srivijayan legacy from Palembang to Melaka and the intent of the narrative underlying the *Sejarah Melayu*. Wolters rejects the historicity of these six chapters of the *Sejarah Melayu*, arguing that Sri Tri Buana and his successors were creations of a 16th-century genealogist of the Johor *istana* seeking to link his sultan to Alexander the Great, and furthermore to prove his lineage and right as the divinely appointed successor of Srivijaya.

From Srivijaya to Temasek: The Transmission of a Heritage

The archaeological evidence recovered since excavations were made in 1984 confirms that Temasek—where a member of the Srivijayan ruling oligarchy, Sri Tri Buana or Parameswara (depending on whether we are reading Fires or the *Sejarah Melayu*), unintentionally arrived after leaving Palembang—was a thriving settlement. Evidence found on Fort Canning and along the banks of the Singapore River provides definitive corroboration of scant textual references by Wang Ta-yüan and others to a 14th-century settlement on Singapore, whose remains Stamford Raffles and John Crawfurd saw.

According to the Portuguese reports, Parameswara (Sri Tri Buana) assassinated his Temasek host a mere eight days after his arrival in 1390 or 1391, evidently hoping to recreate the Srivijayan *negara* he had fled from. Six years into his reestablishment of a new trading *negara* on Temasek, Parameswara had to again flee, this time from a Thai expedition[15] dispatched to avenge their Temasek vassal, whom Parameswara had murdered. The *Sejarah Melayu* provides a rather different account of Sri Tri Buana's arrival and reign in Temasek, in which he renamed it Singapura in honour of the mythical *felis leo* he sighted ambling on the shores of the island. The *Sejarah Melayu* describes Sri Tri Buana as one of three brothers who descended from heaven onto the sacred hill of Bukit Seguntang in Palembang, where he was elected monarch of in honour of his prowess. However, he abdicated his throne in search of a new realm, which he found in Temasek. The text traces the line up to Iskandar Shah, who was fifth in the line of Singapura rulers descended from Sri Tri Buana, and who was forced to abandon Singapura after it was besieged by forces from Majapahit Java. He withdrew north of Singapura, to Muar and then to the Bertam River, where he established a new emporium he named Melaka, which his descendants ruled until they were driven out by the Portuguese, who were contesting the area, in 1511.

Parameswara or Sri Tri Buana evidently intended to create a new emporium at Singapura to service a new Chinese market that developed during the Yuan and Ming dynasties.[16] During the Yuan dynasty, an expanding Chinese market, created by the preceding Song dynasty, was closely linked to the West Asian and Indian markets controlled by the Mongol cousins of the Yuan emperors, and to the mediaeval European markets via both the overland and maritime Silk Roads. A *Pax Mongolica* thus facilitated the creation of an interlinked global trading system.[17] In preceding

---

[15] The expedition was probably launched by Suphanburi, which replaced the Dvaravati centres of Nakon Fathom and Utong as the major naval and military power in the central Menam basin from the 11th century; Charnvit Kasetsiri, *The Rise of Ayudhya: A History of Siam in the 14th and 15th Centuries* (Kuala Lumpur: Oxford University Press, 1976), pp. 22–4, 53, 84.

[16] The Ming was, perhaps more than earlier dynasties, a society dependent upon commerce to satisfy their conspicuous consumption of luxury goods and "superfluous things"; see Timothy Brook, *The Confusions of Pleasure: Commerce and Culture in Ming China* (Berkeley: University of California Press, 1998).

[17] Or "world system", according to Janet Lippman Abu-Lughod; see "The World System in the Thirteenth Century: Dead End or Precursor?", in *Islamic & European Expansion: The Forging of a Global Order*, ed. M. Adas (Philadelphia: Temple University Press, 1993), pp. 75–102. The perspective that the nation-states, economies and communities of the modern world interact (in

centuries, traders would embark from Siraf or Kanchipura and sail the entire journey across the Bay of Bengal to Srivijaya and on through the South China Sea to Quanzhou, incurring not only time, but also high risk. From the 12th century on traders saved time, reduced risk and cut costs by segmenting the Maritime Silk Road into three sectors: an Indian Ocean sector linking ports from Aden and Hormuz to Cambay and Calicut, a Bay of Bengal sector linking Cambay and other South Asian ports to Melakan strait ports like Singapura, and a South China Sea sector linking the Chinese ports with Southeast Asia emporia. Traders now specialized in trading across only one sector, rather than the entire Maritime Silk Road.[18]

The segmentation of this Maritime Silk Road was made possible by the trust and confidence traders had in each other within a system of trade founded on Islamic concepts and principles. Arab traders who had been travelling and trading on the Maritime Silk Road since the 7th century had, by the 13th century, made their institutional framework for the raising of capital and formation of partnerships to obtain credit for the payment, transport and storage of merchandise for trade, adjudicating disputes where they arose and providing channels of information about demand in different markets and where supplies to meet this demand were to be found, as well as the preferred mode of conducting trade. Conversion to Islam among the trading communities of the Silk Road, especially after the 13th century, helped consolidate Islamic rules and trade practices in an increasingly integrated Indo-Islamic world. This *al-bahr al-hindi* or monsoons drew the northern half of the Indian subcontinent and the "land below the winds" tighter together to the Islamic core region in West Asia.[19]

Temasek-Singapura was one of a new generation of emporia that emerged to service the trade that transpired in the Indo-Islamic world during the 14th century. It played a critical role in transforming and transmitting the Srivijayan heritage. Srivijaya, on the other hand, operated within a Buddhist trading world. Buddhist missionaries were the pioneers of the routes across the deserts of central Asia and the Indian Ocean–South China Sea route that traders followed and developed. Buddhist monasteries may have been centres of refuge for traders and shippers in foreign territories, acting as repositories of information and literacy.[20] Like Islam later,

---

trade, politics, war, information and kinship) to form a system that interlinks them and in turn impacts their domestic structures has become a paradigm for the social sciences that is most associated with Immanuel Wallerstein. The argument is that premodern communities and empires were similarly linked in a series of earlier world systems.

[18] Chaudhuri, especially chs. 2 and 5 on the distinction between emporia and pre-emporia trade.

[19] André Wink documents this Indo-Islamic world in *Al-Hind, The Making of the Indo-Islamic World: Early Medieval India and the Expansion of Islam, 7th to 11th Centuries*, vol. 1: *The Slave Kings and the Islamic Conquests, 11th to 13th Centuries* (Leiden: Brill, 1990, 1997). Wink has presented an overview of his arguments in "Al-Hind, India and Indonesia in the Islamic World Economy, c. 799–1800", in *India and Indonesia during the Ancien Régime*, ed. Taufik Abdullah and A. Lapian (Leiden: Brill, 1988), pp. 33–76.

[20] The link between Buddhism and trade is explored in James Heitzman, "Early Buddhism, Trade and Empire", in *Studies in the Archaeology and Palaeoanthropology of South Asia*, ed. K.A.R. Kennedy and G.L. Posehl (Delhi: Oxford University Press, 1984), pp. 121–37; and more specifically, Himanshu P. Ray, *The Winds of Change: Buddhism and the Maritime Links*

Buddhism provided the basis for trust and confidence among traders in each other. Srivijaya in its heyday was a major centre for Buddhist studies, attracting some 3,000 missionaries and scholars, according to 7th-century Chinese pilgrim I-tsing. That Buddhist trading world came to an end in Temasek-Singapura. The archaeological evidence recovered suggests that Temasek-Singapura was a Buddhist settlement, and this can be confirmed by the Buddhist symbolism underlying the choice of the *felis leo*, a venerable Buddhist symbol, to launch a new emporium. However, the *Sejarah Melayu* seems to imply that the last king of Singapura, Iskandar Shah, and possibly his successors as well, were Muslims.

Melaka: "City for Merchandise"[21]

Parameswara successfully carried the *galang-galang*, the sacred anklets symbolising his sovereignty, with him to the Bertam valley, on the basis of which he claimed the political legacy of Srivijaya for the new trading *negara* he established. Like his Srivijayan ancestors in the 7th century, Parameswara had to contend with challenges and threats to his new *negara* from rival emporia in the Straits of Melaka, notably Samudera-Pasai and Aru in north Sumatra and especially the Thais, who appeared not to have forgotten or forgiven him for his assassination of their Temasek vassal. Parameswara successfully surmounted these challenges because he had the foresight to welcome an envoy from the Ming court of Emperor Yongle in 1403,[22] and opted to offer with alacrity tribute to the Ming court, which he visited several times. Ming patronage of Melaka evidently enabled Parameswara and his successors to fend off the Thai threat and challenges from Lamuri-Pasi and Aru in northern Sumatra.

However, Melaka depended not only on Ming political patronage but also on its market for its survival and prosperity. Ming China was an expanding market, especially for luxury consumer goods. Pepper, aromatics and jungle products from the South Seas, rare products in the Song dynasty, became items of everyday consumption. The seven voyages of the Eunuch Admiral Cheng Ho further stimulated

of Early South Asia (Delhi: Oxford University Press, 1994). This link was first articulated by Sylvain Lévi, "Les 'marchands de mer' et leur rôle dans le bouddhisme primitif", *Bulletin de l'Association française des Amis de l'Orient* 3 (1929): 19–30, reprinted in *Memorial Sylvain Lévi* (Paris: Paul Hartmann, 1937), pp. 133–44.

[21] This was how the 16th-century Portuguese apothecary Tomé Pires described the emporium in Pires, *The Suma Oriental of Tomé Pires: An Account of the East from the Red Sea to Japan, Written in Malacca and India in 1512–1515*, trans. and ed. A. Cortesão (London: Haklyut Society, 1944), pp. 284, 286. Pires' report was apparently so highly classified and its circulation so restricted that it was not until the 20th century that copies were found in the Paris and Lisbon archives.

[22] Wang Gungwu's collation of the Chinese records established that the Ming envoy Yin-qing visited Melaka in October 1403, providing a benchmark date for the establishment of Melaka. See "The Opening of Relations between China and Malacca, 1403–1405", in *Malayan and Indonesian Studies: Essays Presented to Sir Richard Winstedt*, ed. J.S. Bastin and R. Roolvink (London: Oxford University Press, 1964), pp. 86–104.

Chinese interest in the world of the South Seas and its products.[23] Tribute trade scaled new heights. Ayutthaya led the Southeast Asian kingdoms in sending some 50 tribute missions to the Ming court from 1371 to 1420. Chinese traders ventured forth in greater numbers, even after the Ming emperors banned private trade and terminated state trade in 1433. Trade with China continued via Ryukyu. Merchants in Fujian and Ryukyu linked up with Melaka, Ayutthaya and Pasai to supply an insatiable Chinese market until the 16th century.

Melaka, more than Srivijaya, also depended upon the West Asian and early modern European markets for its prosperity. Black pepper (*Piper nigrum*) was one of the main items of Melaka's trade, not only with China but also with the West. Originally a native of Kerala, the vine was introduced to Sumatra probably in the late 14th century in response to the growing demand for its seed, where it rapidly became a major cash crop. Cloves, nutmeg and mace were other major items of export to the West via Gujarati merchants. Melaka benefited from this growing prosperity in China, Europe and the Indo-Islamic world, creating an age of commerce in Southeast Asia[24] in which Islam was the defining feature.

Parameswara's successor took the major step of converting to Islam, thereby locating the new trading negara firmly within the moral universe of the Indo-Islamic world.[25] Melaka's official adoption of Islam probably was to maintain its comparative advantage vis-à-vis its competitors, especially Samudera-Pasai, which had earlier converted to Islam.[26] Conversion to Islam meant that the negotiation of trade, adjudication of conflicts and formation of diplomatic alliances could be made within an Islamic framework, and appeared to have helped make Melaka a more attractive port of call for Muslim traders.

Melaka, like Srivijaya before it, prospered because its facilities, port charges and taxes attracted traders, and not because it was able to control the shipping and trade passing through the Straits more successfully by coercing mariners and traders to call at its ports as the Portuguese and Dutch were to attempt later. Melaka, in

---

[23] T'ien Ju-Kang, "Cheng Ho's Voyages and the Distribution of Pepper in China", *JRAS* 2 (1981): 186–97. Economic growth and commercialization made for a rather materialistic society in Ming-dynasty China, concerned as it was with conspicuous consumption and the collection of objects for social status; on this, see Craig Clunas, *Superfluous Things: Material Culture and Social Status in Early Modern China* (Oxford: Polity/Blackwells, 1991).

[24] As defined in Anthony Reid, *Southeast Asia in the Age of Commerce: 1450–1680* (New Haven: Yale University Press, 1998–93); see esp. vol. 2.

[25] The Portuguese records and Malay texts differ on who were the successors of Parameswara and the reception of Islam, on which see Wang Gungwu, "The First Three Rulers of Malacca", *JMBRAS* 42, 1 (1968): 11–22; and C.H. Wake, "Melaka in the Fifteenth Century: Malay Historical Traditions and the Poltics of Islamization", in *Melaka: The Transformation of a Malay Capital, c. 1400–1800*, ed. Kernial Singh Sandhu and Paul Wheatley (Kuala Lumpur: Oxford University Press, 1983), ch. 5.

[26] Conversion to Islam in the western half of Island Southeast Asia was a central feature of the "age of commerce" Anthony Reid has defined. Reid reminds us that Theravada Buddhism was introducing a more "rational" universalist ethic into Mainland Southeast Asia west of the Mekong, while east of it, in Vietnam, the Nguyen were contemporaneously introducing a neo-Confucian orthodoxy while Christianity was making inroads into the eastern half of Island Southeast Asia.

12.3 View of Borobodur. Leiden: Royal Netherlands Institute for Southeast Asian and Carribbean Studies (KITLV).

contrast, was a free port at which traders could choose whether to call or not.[27] This was necessary, because Melaka did not have the resources and wherewithal to impose its will on shippers and traders and to control their movements.

As a settlement, Melaka was not the typical Malay settlement that emerged from the 10th century on the west and east coasts of the peninsula, most of which were based on wet rice cultivation and its related features.[28] Melaka, apparently like Srivijaya before and Johor-Riau after it, did not have any hinterland to support the cultivation of crops and depended upon imports of food and other necessities of life. The jungles of the hinterland were also the source of the resins and other products collected by the forest peoples, which were traded at Melaka.[29] Like Srivijaya, Melaka's relationship with its interior—especially Selangor, Dinding—was therefore complex and potentially difficult. For it was not only an economic relationship that linked Melaka to its interior, but perhaps more importantly, a political and symbolic link that defined Melaka and other Malay emporia.[30]

---

[27] A generation of historians from Van Leur to Meilink-Roelofsz argued for Srivijayan prosperity being based on its control of shipping transiting in the Straits of Melaka. However, this image of Srivijayan and Melakan success based on control and coercion of traders appears to be a projection of the medieval Low Countries' practice of "compulsory stapling" of trade, that is, the assertion of the right to "staple" or exclusively market certain categories of goods. This image of Asian trade as "controlled" and "stapled" appeared to be supported by Chinese travelogue descriptions of Srivijayan naval vessels compelling shippers to call at its harbour. But the Chinese reports are better read as descriptions of periods of anarchy, when the Srivijayan *datus* were weak and unable to hold the allegiances of the sea nomads or orang laut, who then roamed freely as "pirates". Srivijayan, Melakan and Johor prosperity is better interpreted as a symbiosis of the aura or charisma of the ruler, which attracts trade and wealth and in turn enhances the aura and charisma of the ruler, a relationship which A.C. Milner has argued is central to the concept and structure of the Malay polity (*Kerajaan: Malay Political Culture on the Eve of Colonial Rule* [Tucson: University of Arizona Press, 1982]). The structure of power in Melaka and its successor Johor was a tripartite structure of the sultan, who provided the aura and symbolic centre of the realm, the leading merchants or orang kaya and the naval element provided by the sea nomads. See Leonard Y. Andaya, "The Structure of Power in Seventeenth Century Johor", in *Pre-Colonial State Systems in Southeast Asia*, ed. A. Reid and L. Castle (Kuala Lumpur: MBRAS, 1975), pp. 5–9; K.S. Sandhu and P. Wheatley, "The Historical Context", *Melaka: The Transformation of a Malay Capital*, ed. Sandhu and Wheatley, 2 vols. (Kuala Lumpur: Oxford University Press, 1983), pp. 3–69; D. Lombard, "Le sultanat malais comme modèle socio-économique", in *Marchands et hommes d'affaires asiatiques dans l'Océan indien et la Mer de Chine, XIIIe–XXe siècles*, ed. D. Lombard and J. Aubin (Paris: École des Hautes Études en Sciences Sociales, 1988), pp. 117–34.

[28] Defined by Zaharah binte Hj. Mahmud, "The Period and the Nature of 'Traditional' Settlement in the Malay Peninsula", *JMBRAS* 43, 2 (1970): 81–113. Wheatley and Sandhu locate Melaka in the wider context of other early Southeast Asian urban centres in their chapter, "The Historical Context", in Sandhu and Wheatley, *Melaka*, pp. 3–69.

[29] F.L. Dunn, *Rain-Forest Collectors and Traders: A Study of Resource Utilization in Modern and Ancient Malaya* (Kuala Lumpur: MBRAS, 1975), ch. 7.

[30] O.W. Wolters has argued that Srivijaya was not only a coastal entity, but maybe better defined as a riverine entity stretching upriver into the highlands and defined by the prowess of the ruler to mobilize the inhabitants of the interior to collect the resins and other forest products that Srivijaya traded; see "Studying Srivijaya", *JMBRAS* 52, 2 (1979): 1–33. Bennet Bronson has

Given this constraint, Melaka could not maintain a large naval force to defend itself, much less force traders into its harbour. It was the spiritual prowess or daulat of the sultan, who was the link between the divine and earthly planes, and from whom spiritual salubrity flowed as a consequence of his actions at the apex of society, which defined Melaka and was the basis for the network of alliances it made and allegiances it forged. In particular, Melaka and its successors depended very much upon an allegiance that the Srivijayan *datus* had forged with the hardy sea nomads or orang laut whose habitat lay in the inhospitable mangrove swamps of the Straits, to defend the body of the white-blooded ruler and his trading *negara*. According to Pires, it was a group of Bajau sea nomads who accompanied Parameswara on his flight from Palembang to Temasek, brought him to Muar, and helped him establish Melaka. It was these orang laut who, according to the *Sejarah Melayu*, responded to the call of the Melaka sultans to defend the realm from threats and challenges and who carried the last sultan of Melaka away from his burning city.[31]

The network of alliances that Melaka built and developed, and allegiances it had claimed and asserted which formed the underpinnings of its success, was not captured by Alfonso d'Albuquerque.[32] He captured only the empty shell of a port. Instead, it was sustained by Sultan Mahmud Shah as he made flight through the jungles to the court of his cousin at Pahang and then continued to Bintan in the Riaus. The loss of the port of Melaka was not the end of the Melaka *negara*. Inasmuch as the focus of the *negara* was on the person of the sultan in whose body ran the white blood of Sri Tri Buana and his descendants, then the *negara* was wherever the sultan chose to locate himself. The Sri Nara Diraja's reply to Sultan Mahmud

---

attempted to generalize this relationship in his "Exchanges at the Upstream and Downstream Ends: Notes Toward a Functional Model of the Coastal State in Southeast Asia", in *Economic Exchange and Social Interaction in Southeast Asia*, ed. K.L. Hutterer (Ann Arbor: University of Michigan Center for South and Southeast Asian Studies, 1978), pp. 39–52.

[31] In his annotated translation of Pires, Cortesão erroneously transcribed Pires's "celates bajuus homees" in folio 165r of his text as "celates Bugis" on page 233 of his translation. There is at the western end of Singapore today a river and hillock that both have traditionally been known by the name Bajau. Pires provides us one of the more insightful reports of the critical role played by these sea nomads in the politics and security of Melaka, on pp. 233–6 of Cortesão's translation. In his book, *Sea Nomads*, David Sopher analyzes accounts of the orang laut by Pires and other Portuguese; see *Sea Nomads: A Study of the Maritime Boat People of Southeast Asia*, reprint (Singapore: National Museum, 1977), pp. 314–34. The link with Palembang appears to continue in the collective memory of the orang laut communities down to today and is recorded by C. Pelras, "Notes sur quelques populations aquatiques de l'Archipel nusantarien", *Archipel* 3 (1972): 144. The role of the orang laut as one of three pillars in the structure of power in Johor is analyzed by Leonard Y. Andaya, *The Kingdom of Johor 1641–1728* (Kuala Lumpur: Oxford University Press, 1975), pp. 37–54. It was an orang laut, Batin Sapi, who went to Bintan to fetch Tengku Long to Singapore to be recognized as sultan by Stamford Raffles.

[32] M.A.P. Meilink-Roelofsz, *Asian Trade and European Influence in the Indonesian Archipelago between 1500 and about 1630* (The Hague: Martinus Nijhoff, 1962), pp. 136ff, for an assessment of the impact of the Portuguese on Asian trade, which she concluded was "limited".

when he decided to stand and fight Alfonso d'Albuquerque to the end for the city of Melaka is significant:[33]

> The Sri Nara Diraja urged him [Sultan Mahmud] to leave Bentan now that the city had fallen. But he [the sultan] replied, "... it is the custom of the Rajas that when their country falls to the foe, they die". And the Sri Nara Diraja said, "Your Highness is mistaken. Every country has a raja and if Your Highness is granted length of days, we can find ten countries for you".

Kerajaan Johor

It was not to be Sultan Mahmud's fate to have the chance to re-establish the glory of Melaka elsewhere. That opportunity fell to his son and successor, 'Ala'ud-din, who left Pahang in 1530 to establish a new *negara* up the Johor River. In selecting the Johor River for his new *negara*, 'Ala'ud-din was not moving into a backwater region separated from the trading activity of the Melaka Straits. The archaeological evidence—primarily the range and volume of earthenware and blue-and-white Ming and Qing export ware sherds—points to the Johor River as a node in the trade of the Melaka Straits from perhaps the beginning of the 15th century.[34] From his new *negara*, 'Ala'ud-din and his successors ventured forth to alternately challenge the Portuguese and the Acehnese for control of the shipping and trade in the Melaka Straits.

Aceh in the 16th and 17th centuries, especially under Sultan Iskander Muda (1603–37), was a rising power that challenged Johor for the heritage of Srivijaya-Melaka as the dominant trading *negara* in the Straits. But the successful Acehnese attacks on Johor Lama in 1564 and Batu Sawar in 1613 did not undermine the comparative advantage of Johor for traders. Neither did the Portuguese attack in 1530 on Sayong Pinang on the upper reaches of the Johor River, where Sultan 'Ala'ud-din had first established himself, and the sacking of Johor Lama in 1587, succeed in pulling the Straits trade from the Johor River back to Melaka. The Johor sultans merely shifted themselves and their courts to a different location on the Johor River whenever the Portuguese or Acehnese attacked them, and from their new location successfully maintained the Johor River as the preferred port of call in the Straits. If Sultan 'Ala'ud-din and his successors were able to successfully establish a new trading *negara* up the Johor River, which took off and prospered in the face of strong competition and threats from Aceh and the Portuguese, then it was probably because they (and their competitors) continued to enjoy the benefits and

---

33 *Sejarah Melayu*, quoted from the translation by C.C. Brown in his article, "Sejarah Melayu or Malay Annals", p. 189. The symbolic significance of the person of the sultan/raja for the Malay political system was outlined by J.M. Gullick (*Indigenous Political Systems of Western Malaya* [London: Athlone Press, 1958]), and further developed by A.C. Milner in *Kerajaan Kerajaan* (1982).

34 C.A. Gibson-Hill, "Johore Lama and Other Ancient Sites on the Johore River", *JMBRAS* 28, 2 (1955): 177ff. On the archaeological data from the Johor river sites, see W.G. Solheim II and E. Green, "Johore Lama Excavations, 1960", *Federation Museums Journal*, special issue 10 (1965); and C. Jack-Hinton, "Further Investigations at Johor Lama: Preliminary Notes", *Federation Museums Journal*, n.s., 8 (1963): 24ff.

profits from the boom years of the age of commerce that had sustained Melaka from 1570 to 1630.

More critical to Johor's survival and prosperity was the entry of the VOC (*Vereenigde Oostindische Compagnie* [Dutch East India Company]) into the Straits of Melaka. Different from the *Estado da Índia*, which was a royal monopoly, the VOC (like its English competitor) was a joint-stock company that was professionally managed yet given sovereign powers by the Dutch government to enter into treaties and make alliances, recruit troops and take over foreign territory. These factors, coupled with substantial capital and aggressiveness, made the VOC a formidable power and helped make the Netherlands the primary global trading power in the "long 16th century".[35] The Johor sultans welcomed the Dutch as an ally in their long-standing conflict with the Acehnese and the Portuguese, and joined the Dutch in successfully besieging Melaka in 1640–41. Fortuitously, the Dutch had in 1612 captured Jayakarta, which they renamed Batavia and made their regional headquarters. Melaka, which they had captured at some cost, was left to languish. With the Acehnese reduced and the Portuguese eliminated, and with a supportive VOC Council in Batavia, Johor rose to become the pre-eminent power in the Riaus.[36]

The Dutch had entered Southeast Asia, like the Portuguese, as a trading power determined to establish a new trading state in the Straits and to control its traffic and trade to Europe. In this they were initially successful, for during much of the 16th century they acted as a trading state seeking to control not only the Straits of Melaka, but also to control the trade of eastern Indonesia from Batavia. However, Dutch involvement in the succession politics of the Javanese *kratons* from 1676 slowly diverted their attention from the Melaka Straits to Java and its rich natural resources. By the 18th century the Dutch were more governors of territories than merchant-princes. In the Straits of Melaka their presence and control of its trade was challenged by the British, who in 1786 had established a factory on Pulau Pinang (Penang) to service their vessels crossing the Bay of Bengal to China; meanwhile, their neutrality towards the Johor sultans was being tested by the Bugis who had already established a dominant presence in the *istana* of the Johor sultans. The Bugis had by 1780 built a thriving entrepot at Tanjong Pinang on Bintan Island, serving

---

[35] Jonathan I. Israel, *Dutch Primacy in World Trade, 1585–1740* (Oxford: Clarendon Press, 1989), traces the factors leading to Dutch primacy in world trade from the fall of Antwerp in 1585 through its zenith in the latter half of the 17th and decline in the course of the 18th centuries. Niels Steensgaard argues that it was the institutional innovations which the VOC as a joint-stock company could bring about that disrupted the emporia trade more effectively than the *Estado da Índia* did ("The Dutch East India Company as an Institutional Innovation", in *Dutch Capitalism and World Capitalism*, ed. M. Aymard [Cambridge: University of Cambridge Press, 1982], pp. 235–57).

[36] Reinout Vos, *Gentle Janus, Merchant Prince: The VOC and the Tightrope of Diplomacy in the Malay World, 1740–1800* (Leiden: KITLV, 1993), and Dianne Lewis, *Jan Compagnie in the Straits of Malacca 1641–1795* (Athens, OH: Ohio University Center for International Studies, 1995), studies the ultimately disruptive impact of the VOC on the Malay trading *negara*.

12.4 A Bugis or Boekjes. Johan Nieuhof, *Voyages and Travels, into Brazil, and the East-Indies: Containing, an exact description of the Dutch Brazil, and divers parts of the East-Indies*. London: Printed for Awnsham and John Churchill at the Black Swan in Pater Noster Row, 1703. NUS Libraries, Special Collections.

not only the Asian traders, but also the growing "country trade".[37] The Dutch thus felt sufficiently threatened by these developments to invade the Riaus in 1784 to drive the Bugis out and establish a presence there.

The "Malta of the East"[38]

In 1795 Britain found itself thrust into the role of caretaker government for Melaka as a consequence of Napoleon's takeover of Holland. European interests dictated that Britain support the Dutch crown by returning Melaka and Java which Britain had occupied. This decision did not go down well with some East India Company officials, notably Stamford Raffles, who predicted that a resurgent Dutch East Indies would be a threat to British mercantile interests. In particular, the return of Melaka, from where the Dutch were moving to re-establish their influence in the Riaus, was perceived by Raffles as a direct threat to East India Company's trade to China. It was to forestall Admiral Wolterbeek's proposed mission to the Riaus to reassert Dutch control that Raffles raced to establish an East India Company factory at the southern end of the Straits of Melaka.[39]

Raffles' service on Pinang and as Lieutenant-Governor of Java had convinced him of the immense commercial value of Java, the Spice Islands to its east, the Sumatran east coast where he was based as Lieutenant-Governor of Bencoolen, and the Malay Peninsula. It was a view not shared by most of his superiors in Bengal, who were more preoccupied with developing the Company's Indian possessions and thought of the Straits of Melaka as a passage where their ships had to transit en route to Guangdong. With some difficulty, Raffles managed to persuade the Governor-General, Lord Hastings, to allow him to establish a new port "beyond Melaka, such as may command the southern entrance of the Straits".[40]

Singapore had not been Raffles' first choice. The Riaus, which lay to its south, were his preferred destination. But he found the Dutch already there, and had to look at his second choice, the Karimun Islands. And when no suitable harbour could be found there, Raffles looked to the Johor River estuary where his studies of Malay history informed him the Johor sultans were based prior to their relocation to Bintan

---

[37] Dianne Lewis, "The Growth of the Country Trade to the Straits of Malacca", *JMBRAS* 43, 2 (1970): 115–7; and more recently Lee Kam Hing, "The Shipping Lists of Dutch Melaka: A Source for the Study of Coastal Trade and Shipping in the Malay Peninsula during the 17th and 18th Centuries", in *Karpal dan Harta Karam: Ships and Sunken Treasure*, ed. Mohd. Yusoff Hashim et al. (Kuala Lumpur: Persuatuan Muzium Malaysia, 1986), pp. 53–76; and Anthony Reid and Radin Fernando, "Shipping on Melaka and Singapore as an Index of Growth, 1760–1840", *South Asia* 19 (1996): 59–84.

[38] "What Malta is in the West, that may Singapore be in the East" was how Raffles described Singapore in a letter to Colonel Adenbrooke, quoted in C.E. Wurtzburg, *Raffles of the Eastern Isles* (London: Hodder & Stoughton, 1954), p. 461.

[39] On the factors underlying Raffles' search for a new EIC factory, see Nicholas Tarling, *Anglo-Dutch Rivalry in the Malay World, 1780–1824* (St Lucia: University of Queensland Press, 1962), pp. 84–94.

[40] On the influence of the China trade on the British in Malaya see K.G. Tregonning, *The British in Malaya: The First Forty Years, 1786–1826* (Tucson: University of Arizona Press, 1965).

Island. En route Raffles, as John Crawfurd recorded, "touched at Singapore to make enquiries, and then for the first time, the advantages and superiority of its locality presented themselves".[41]

The advantages of Singapore included not only good berthing facilities around the mouth of the Singapore River, but also the prospect of Malay assent to a British presence. Tengku Long, the elder son of Sultan Mahmud and heir presumptive, had been passed over in the succession when his father died in 1812. He was in Pahang celebrating his wedding when he was persuaded by the temenggong, whom Raffles had met, to welcome Raffles and the British as a counter-force to Dutch support for the Bugis and his brother Abdur Rahman, who had been installed as sultan on his father's death and in his absence. Tengku Long probably welcomed Raffles' recognition of him as sultan with the hope that British backing would enable him to establish a rival trading *negara* on Singapura to challenge his younger brother and his Bugis and Dutch backers on Bintan.[42]

But this was not to be so. Singapore under the East India Company took off in a way that surprised not only Raffles and his superiors in Bengal, but also Sultan Husain. The increasing number of country traders plying the Straits en route to China and the Spice Islands relocated themselves from Batavia and Tanjong Pinang to Singapore. Asian traders—the Fujian merchants from China and Melaka, the Bugis traders, the Indians and Arab merchants—also found the new port a less restrictive place to trade in than other Dutch and regional ports.[43] The success and potential of its new port probably persuaded the East India Company and Britain to stand firm and hold on to their new possession in a "paper war" with the Dutch over it, which was resolved after much negotiation in an 1824 treaty.

Raffles had succeeded where Antonio van Diemen and Alfonso d'Albuquerque had failed: to successfully capture the legacy of Srivijaya-Melaka from the Johor sultans. For Singapore, like Melaka and Srivijaya, rose to eminence as the new trading *negara* in the Straits of Melaka servicing the trade to China, a collection point for the spices and other products of the archipelago and a distribution centre for merchandise from India and the West. Sultan Husain evidently failed to anticipate the new economic, political and demographic forces driving the trading world of Asia in the 19th century. It was beyond Husain to comprehend the complex contradictory political economics of mercantilism and liberal free trade driving British actions

---

[41] John Crawfurd, *A Descriptive Dictionary of the Indian Islands & Adjacent Countries*, reprint of 1654 ed. (Kuala Lumpur: Oxford University Press, 1971), p. 403. The selection of Singapore was made after dinner on 27 Jan. on board Raffles' ship, the *Indiana*. On the morning of 28 Jan., Raffles sailed from Karimun for Singapore and "anchored off the intended port of Singapore, near a fine sandy beach".

[42] C.H. Wake, in "Raffles and the Rajas: The Founding of Singapore in Malayan and British Colonial History", *JMBRAS* 48, 1 (1975): 47–73, reconstructs the intentions and minds of Temenggong Abdur Rahman and Tengku Long in welcoming Raffles.

[43] On the place of trade in the rise of modern Singapore, see Wong Lin Ken, "The Trade of Singapore, 1819–69", *JMBRAS* 33, 4 (1960): 1–315.

in his world;[44] nor the dynamics of Chinese trade and migration under the Ch'ing [Qing] dynasty, which flooded his world with Chinese traders and planters.[45] Sultan Husain and the temenggong thus became irrelevant once the British and the Dutch decided to divide this world in 1824.

But the East India Company was a reluctant heir of this Srivijaya-Melaka-Johor legacy, which they inherited in 1824. They were ambivalent about it through their 40-odd years of responsibility for the area. In 1867 this legacy was then passed to the Colonial Office, under which Singapore became the administrative and political capital of British Malaya and main economic centre for the development of the Malay Peninsula from the third quarter of the 19th century. Singapore became a staple port that prospered on the export of tin, rubber, petroleum and other staples not only of British Malaya, but also the Dutch East Indies.[46] British Malaya thus became the hinterland for Singapore and the other two Straits Settlements in Penang and Melaka.

Separation from Malaysia and British plans for the formation of a Malayan Union at the end of World War II created a crisis that in large part defined the goal of the emerging post-colonial struggle for independence as some form of federation with Malaya. This imperative to reunite Singapore with Malaya, coupled with British proposals for decolonization through some form of dominion among their colonies in the region, underlay the formation of Malaysia in 1963.[47] Singapore's separation

---

[44] See Eli F. Heckscher's classic study, *Mercantilism* (London: Allen & Unwin, 1935). See also the critique by J. Viner, "Power versus Plenty as Objectives of Foreign Policy in the Seventeenth and Eighteenth Centuries (1948)", reprinted in his *Essays on the Intellectual History of Economics* (Princeton: Princeton University Press, 1991).

[45] On the build-up and dynamism of the Fukien trade which enabled it to take-off in the 18th century into Southeast Asia, see Ng Chin-Keong, *Trade and Society: The Amoy Network on the China Coast, 1683–1735* (Singapore: Singapore University Press, 1983); see also A. Reid, "Flows and Seepages in the Long-term Chinese Interaction with Southeast Asia", in *Sojourners and Settlers: Histories of Southeast Asia and the Chinese*, ed. A. Reid (St Leonard: Allen & Unwin, 1996), pp. 15–50.

[46] See W.G. Huff, *The Economic Growth of Singapore: Trade and Development in the Twentieth Century* (Cambridge: Cambridge University Press, 1994), for the argument that it was Singapore's role as a staple port that attracted immigrants and made possible the island's rapid urbanization and development.

[47] See M. Noordin Sopiee, *From Malayan Union to Singapore Separation: Political Unification in the Malaysia Region, 1945–65* (Kuala Lumpur: Penerbit University of Malaya, 1974), ch. 5, for documentation of the question of merger and a united Malaya leading to Malaysia. Singapore's struggle for independence should also be seen within the context of British strategies for decolonization; on which see A. Stockwell, "British Imperial Policy and Decolonisation in Malaya, 1942–52", *JICH* 13, 1 (1989): 68–87; and D.S. Ranjit Singh, "British Proposals for a Dominion of Southeast Asia, 1943–1957", *JMBRAS* 26, 2 (1998): 27–40; and A. Stockwell, "Malaysia: The Making of a Neo-Colony", *JICH* 26, 2 (1988): 138–56, reprinted in *Managing the Business of Empire: Essays in Honour of David Fieldhouse*, ed. P. Burroughs and A. Stockwell (London: Cass, 1999).

12.5 Portrait etching of Alfonso d'Albuquerque. Taken from Gasper Correia, *Lendas da Índia*, ed. R.J. de Lima Felner. Lisbon: Academia Real das Sciencies, 1858–66. © Peter Borschberg, private collection.

from Malaysia created an even more profound crisis that it continues to grapple with in the new millennium.[48]

In summary, this attempt to locate Temasek-Singapura in the cycles of Melaka Straits history differs from that attempted by Paul Wheatley[49] and more recently Michel Jacq-Hergoualc'h.[50] In their reconstruction, Temasek-Singapura is the last in a series of Mon city-states and emporia that were located primarily in the isthmus and Kedah after the dissolution of Funan. The theme of their reconstruction is how these city-states and emporia were networked with each other and into the dominant Srivijaya *mandala*. Where Wheatley and Jacq-Hergoualc'h looked at the northern end of the Straits of Melaka and the emporia on both the west and east coasts of the isthmus, this essay looks at the southern end of the Straits of Melaka. The underlying theme of the reconstruction attempted in this essay is the contest among a network of Malay city-states at the southern end of the Straits of Melaka for the legacy of Srivijaya following its dissolution. Temasek-Singapura had established a niche in this network in the 14th century by becoming the "epicentre of the Johor-Riau archipelago regional trade network".[51] Temasek-Singapura was, in the classical Malay historiography of the Straits, a critical point in the transmission and diffusion of Srivijaya's legacy.[52] Parameswara may have abandoned Singapura towards the end of the 14th century, but control of its waterways linking the Indian Ocean with the South China Sea and its orang laut communities remained crucial to the survival of the Melaka and Johor sultans. Likewise, the Portuguese, Spanish, Dutch and English found control of these waterways critical to their commercial and strategic interests in the region.[53] Their importance was not lost on the British, and it was to secure these waterways for the English East India Company that Sir Stamford Raffles sought out Singapore in 1819.

Conclusion: Linking Singapore Before and After Raffles

In stating that Singapore's history started with Sir Stamford Raffles because there was nothing of significance before that, Tregonning was stating what was and continues today to be the conventional and dominant view of Singapore's past. Mary Turnbull

---

[48] See the volume produced by the National Heritage Board, *Singapore: Journey into Nationhood* (Singapore: Landmark Books, 1998), for a dramatic retelling of this narrative of crisis. Lee Kuan Yew's memoir, *The Singapore Story*, is a more authoritative telling of this narrative of crisis.

[49] See also Wheatley, "Desultory Remarks on the Ancient History of the Malay Peninsula", in *Malayan and Indonesian Studies*, ed. Bastin and Roolvink (Oxford: Oxford University Press, 1963), pp. 33–75 (esp. note 39) for a succinct summary of his longer studies.

[50] Michel Jacq-Hergoualc'h, *The Malay Peninsula: Crossroads of the Maritime Silk Road* (100 BC–1300 AD) (Leiden: Brill, 2002), p. 491.

[51] Derek Heng's description, in Heng, "Temasik in the 13th and 14th Centuries", *JMBRAS* 72, 1 (1999): 113–24.

[52] See Wolters, *The Fall of Srivijayan Malay History* (London: Lund Humphries, 1970), p. 33 for an extended argument of this thesis.

[53] As Peter Borschberg has pointed out, the Portuguese, Spanish and Dutch felt compelled to plan for a fort in the Straits of Singapore; see "Portuguese, Spanish and Dutch Plans to Construct a Fort in the Straits of Singapore, c. 1584–1625", *Archipel* 65 (2003): 55–88.

also documents this view in what has become the standard textbook on Singapore's history. Singapore's history is about the rise and development of a city-state from its beginnings as a factory of the East India Company and its transformation as a crown colony to its take-off after independence. It is a history of modern Singapore in which an earlier past has no place because it is virtually non-existent.[54] Other textbook and popular accounts of Singapore's past similarly situate Singapore within the framework of British colonialism and empire, decolonization and the struggle for independence and the achievements thereafter.[55] Singapore's past before Raffles is invariably cursorily reviewed, usually to explain how it received its name.

Using 1819 as a starting-point for Singapore's history, however, creates three categories of historiographical problems. The first is that it accords to Thomas Stamford Raffles the prescience to recognize the strategic significance of Singapore.[56] This elevation of Raffles to a "great man" of history has become an entrenched feature of colonial historiography. It is well captured in Sir Frank Swettenham's

---

[54] C.M. Turnbull, *A History of Singapore 1819–1988*, 2nd ed. (Singapore: Oxford University Press, 1988). H.F. Pearson was among the first to draw attention to Singapore's earlier past in his *Singapore: A Popular History, 1819–1960*, first published in 1956 (Singapore: D. Moore for Eastern University Press, 1961). There were no other attempts at writing a history of Singapore until Turnbull attempted it in 1977. Reviewing research on the historiography of Singapore, undertaken largely within the Department of History at the University of Singapore, Edwin Lee felt he had to defend his inclusion of a section on "pre-modern history", "even though Singapore does not appear in it until the very tail end", because the people described in it—the Chinese, Malays, Indians and others—are the people of Singapore. Lee is uncertain whether any of the evidence that he discussed touches on Singapore, because he is uncertain whether Singapore existed in this early period. See Lee, "The Historiography of Singapore", in *Singapore Studies: Critical Surveys of the Humanities and Social Sciences*, ed. Basant K. Kapur (Singapore: NUS Press, 1986), pp. 1–4.

[55] There is, as C.J.W.-L. Wee points out, a dominant narrative of "a Whiggish telos of economic development, progress, modernity, and modernization since 1819" underlying this telling of Singapore's story. As Wee recognizes, there is another narrative of crisis from the threat of communism and the response to it; see Wee, "Our Island Story: Economic Development and the National Narrative in Singapore", in *New Terrains in Southeast Asian History*, ed. A.B. Ahmad and Tan Liok Ee (Athens, OH: University of Ohio Press; Singapore: Singapore University Press, 2003), pp. 141–67.

[56] Despite Raffles' claims to Singapore as "a child of [his] own", which he would not have known about but for his Malay studies (in his letter dated 10 June 1819 to Colonel Addenbrooke, reproduced in Lady Sophia Raffles' *Memoir*, p. 379), the records indicate that Singapore was not Raffles' first choice of a location for the East India Company factory he was seeking to establish. The islands to its south, the Riaus, were Raffles' first choice. But he found the Dutch had re-established their old presence there, and had to look at his second choice, the Karimun Islands. When no suitable harbour could be found on it after three days of surveying, Raffles turned to the Johor River estuary, where his study of Malay history informed him that the Johor sultans were based prior to their relocation to Bintan Island. En route to the Johor River—as Dr John Crawfurd, who lived through this era and may therefore have had a personal recollection of the events leading to the founding of Singapore, recorded—Raffles "touched at Singapore to make enquiries, and for the first time, the advantages and superiority of its locality presented themselves" (Crawfurd, *A Descriptive Dictionary of the Indian Islands & Adjacent Countries*, p. 403).

eulogy of Raffles—"to him we owe the possession of Singapore, the Gate of the Farther East, and a naval base of the highest importance, a great commercial centre, and the most prosperous of British crown colonies".[57] This reverent gaze cast upon Raffles leads to a focus on the other personalities, principally made up of the colonial officials and the leaders of the immigrant communities in Singapore who opted to work with them. This view of Singapore's history ends in the confrontation of two "great men", General Arthur E. Percival and Japanese commander Yamashita Tomiki, facing each other on the evening of 15 February 1942. Thereafter our gaze then shifts to a new procession of "great men" who will make Singapore's post-World War II history.

The second category of problems is that it may have exacerbated Singapore's post-1965 identity crisis.[58] Bereft of its origins as a 14th-century Malay city-state, Singapore after 1965 could only debate its future as a postcolonial city-state, seeking analogies for its future in the Athenian, Venetian and Swiss city-states.[59] In the new millennium Singapore has chosen to identify itself as a global city-state.[60] Singapore's decision to elevate itself from the regional stage to the global stage means, in the words of long-time astute Singapore observer Michael Leifer, that Singapore has to "suffer the region" and yet has to "drive it". Will linking Singapore before and after Raffles lead Singaporeans to a deeper understanding of their place in the region, a better appreciation of why they are "suffer[ing] the region" and a more nuanced approach towards understanding how they "drive it"?[61]

---

[57] Frank Swettenham, *British Malaya: An Account of the Origin and Progress of British Influence in Malaya*, rev. ed. (London: Allen & Unwin, 1955), pp. 72–3. Swettenham not only made history, but lived long enough to write it, although, as his obituarist Sir Richard Winstedt noted in L.G.W. Legg, ed., *Dictionary of National Biography, 1941–50*, 6th suppl. (Oxford: Oxford University Press), p. 856: "his education had not been such as to qualify him for research". He revised his book *British Malaya* twice, in 1929 and 1948, and the book went through seven reprints between 1906 and 1955. For better or worse, *British Malaya* has shaped our template for the history of Malaya. Certainly, his explanation of the prosperity of the Straits Settlement—because of "three factors: (1) the geographical positions of Singapore and Pinang … (2) the fact that all the ports of the colony are free; [and] (3) the development of the Malay hinterland"—would resonate with the "Singapore Story" being told today, as summarized in Singapore Heritage Board, *Singapore's Journey into Nationhood* (Singapore: Landmark Books for National Heritage Board, 1998).

[58] Elaborated further in C.G. Kwa, "Remembering Ourselves", in *Our Place in Time: Exploring Heritage and Memory in Singapore*, ed. Kwok Kian-Woon et al. (Singapore: Singapore Heritage Society, 1999), pp. 47–58; see also Albert Lau, "The National Past and the Writing of the History of Singapore", in *Imagining Singapore*, ed. Ban Kah Choon et al. (Singapore: Times Academic Press, 1992), pp. 46–68.

[59] Yong Mun Cheong, "Singapore: The City-State in History", in *Imagining Singapore*, pp. 9–45.

[60] M. Perry, L. Kong and B. Yeoh, *Singapore: A Developmental City State* (Chichester: John Wiley, 1997), pp. 15–22; Linda Low, "The Limits of a City-State: Or Are There Any?", in *Singapore in the New Millennium: Challenges Facing the City-State*, ed. D. da Cunha (Singapore: ISEAS–Yusof Ishak Institute, 2002), pp. 1–25; and C.G. Kwa, "Relating to the World: Images, Metaphors, and Analogies", in *Singapore in the New Millennium*, pp. 1–25, 108–32.

[61] Michael Leifer, *Singapore's Foreign Policy: Coping with Vulnerability* (London: Routledge, 2000), pp. 131–56.

The third category of problems is that it blurs the focus on Sultan Husain. It implies that entire generations of earlier Malay sultans and their courts were largely ignorant and unappreciative of the strategic significance of Singapore and were taken advantage of by Raffles and Crawfurd who either "persuaded" or "pressured" (depending upon one's moral perspective) Sultan Husain and the temenggong to sign away Singapore to the Honourable Company in August 1824. It is what Tregonning in his other writings has condemned as "Euro-centric" history: the viewing of Southeast Asian history through the eyes of the European actors rather than the Asian actors. For Tregonning (ironically), "Asia, not the European in Asia, must be our theme, and suddenly, if you think of that, it makes the Portuguese and the Dutch most insignificant ... they were a few heretical fish in a Muslim sea...."[62] An underlying goal of this essay, and indeed this whole programme of recovering Singapore's pre-1819 history, is to explore whether a greater awareness of this longer past could be the basis for a shift to a more "Asia-centric" view of Singapore's past.

Raffles' arrival in Singapore will continue to be an essential chain in linking pre- and post-1819 Singapore. The challenge will be to go beyond the intentions of Raffles and Tengku Husain in signing their treaty and the context of their intentions.[63] For Raffles this context will be the East India Company and how he perceived his role in it. For Husain the context will be the complex interplay in the *istana* of Bugis and Malay politics on Pulau Penyengat.[64] Going beyond the context of the East India Company and Malay *Istana* politics would mean exploring the wider world that the Company and Raffles were working within, and the future of the *alam*

---

[62] K.G. Tregonning, "A New Approach to Malayan History", *Straits Times*, 21 and 24 Nov. 1958; he reasserts this in *A History of Modern Malaya* (London: University of London Press, 1964), pp. 46–7. Tregonning's call for an Asia-centric history is ironic, because his published works were Eurocentric in content, theme and focus. Perhaps as a teacher, he was exhorting his students to go beyond what he was doing.

[63] The Russian Marxist philosopher Georgi Plekhanov's 1898 essay, "The Role of the Individual in History", remains one of the seminal discussions about the issue of whether "great men" or their social setting and institutions played a greater part in historical development, and whether "great men" are born or made by their times. Plekhanov's essay reflects in a way the challenge from Marxism and the emerging social sciences to the prevailing practice of biography as the fundamental building block of historiography. Plekhanov argued that Marxism was not antithetical to "great men" who could work within their social setting and yet shape it. Sidney Hook's *The Hero in History*, published in 1943, is still the only sustained critique of Plekhanov and the "great men" issue, which is a major methodological and philosophical problem in the social sciences. Emile Durkheim was an early and leading advocate of the argument for structures (including social structures, institutions and norms) pre-dating and therefore conditioning the actions of persons/agents. Max Weber led the case for human agency and rationality in creating and maintaining structures. Much social science theorizing has sought to reconcile this dualism by attempting to reduce agency to structure or vice-versa. Currently, the debate is not how to reduce one to the other, because that would be bad metaphysics and poor methodology, but how to link and connect structures and agency; on which see J. Bohman, *New Philosophy of Social Science: Problems of Indeterminacy* (Cambridge: MIT Press, 1991), pp. 146–85. This essay introduces this debate into the telling of the Singapore Story by introducing the cycles of maritime history in the Melaka Straits into the biographies of the "great men" of Singapore's past.

[64] A story successfully told by Wake, "Raffles and the Rajas", n. 58.

Melayu or Malay world that Tengku Husain and his brother Sultan Abdur Rahman were concerned about.

Within this context of the structures of the world that defined the Company and its servants, including Raffles, then Raffles' "child" (as he has described Singapore) was born into the modern world that Paul Johnson[65] argues was formed during the 15 critical years that followed the Napoleonic Wars. As Johnson narrates it, between 1815 and 1830 a new international order was constructed around the nation state, and the mercantilism of the preceding centuries gave way to free trade advocated by economic liberalism, during which time colonialism was changing the geopolitical landscape outside Europe. All these political, economic and social transformations, accompanied by seismic changes in culture and the arts, were unprecedented in their scale and impact on the future of the world. What we are observing at the start of the 19th century is, in the paradigm of the 21st century, the start of an era of globalization.[66] Modern Singapore was therefore born into this climate of 19th-century globalization that defined the modern world, and survived because its peoples were able to adapt and respond to the demands of this "modern globalization". In contrast, the East India Company failed to respond and adapt to the demands of modern globalization, and hence was dissolved in 1858.

Likewise the Malay world of Sultan Husain failed to understand these demands that they were caught in, and was effectively undermined. The idea of the *kerajaan* which was centred on the sultan as the rallying point of the Malay community, the exemplar of moral righteousness from which status and well-being flowed and to whom homage and tribute was due, was contrary to the ideology of both mercantilism and free trade. Both of these ideologies undermined the conspicuous consumption and display of wealth by the sultan as an indication of his role and introduced a challenge to his function as the dispenser of patronage and redistributor of wealth. Raffles' Malay language teacher Abdullah bin Kadir appeared to recognize this "destruction of the old world" he was living in and the "creation of a new world" in its place.[67]

Four centuries earlier, Parameswara had recognized the changes in his world and had moved to exploit in 1403 it by welcoming the Ming envoys that called on him, and subsequently offering Melaka as a base for the fleets of the Three-Jewel Eunuch

---

[65] Paul Johnson, *The Birth of the Modern: World Society 1815–1830* (London: G. Weidenfeld & Nicolson, 1991). See ch. 4 on Raffles and the founding of Singapore.

[66] The term *globalization* entered discourse in the 1980s to describe the closing decades of the 20th century. However, there is growing recognition that it is a recurrent trend of global history, on which see W.H. McNeill, "The Rise of the West After Twenty-Five Years", and V. Roudometof and R. Robertson, "Globalization, World System Theory and the Comparative Study of Civilizations", both essays in *Civilizations and World Systems*, ed. S.K. Sanderson (Walnut Creek: Altamira, 1995). A.G. Frank and B. Gills made the case for a multiplicity of world-systems from before 1500; see Frank and Gills, eds., *The World System: Five Hundred Years or Five Thousand?* (New York: Routledge, 1996). See especially the essays from a Cambridge University Faculty of History series of Millennium Lectures in *Globalization in World History*, ed. A.G. Hopkins (London: Pimlico, 2002), which argue for the "globalization of history".

[67] See A.C. Milner, *The Invention of Politics in Colonial Malaya*, 2nd ed. (Cambridge: Cambridge University Press, 2002) on the challenge to the Malay *ancien régime* in the writings of Abdullah bin Kadir.

Admiral Zheng He (Cheng Ho). Parameswara may not have recognized that the "city for merchandise", as the Portuguese apothecary Tomé Pires described Melaka, was built upon an earlier cycle of pre-modern or anarchic globalization[68] which was driven by the markets of Ming China and early modern Europe. Parameswara had earlier abandoned his Srivijayan homeland for Temasek probably due to the fact that he had been caught up in and had lost out in an earlier cycle of pre-modern globalization wrought by the Song transformation of the southern Chinese economy, which his Srivijayan forefathers had apparently failed to recognize, much less understand, to their final detriment.[69]

The maritime history of the Melaka Straits could be said to be driven by these cycles of globalization, which link Singapore before and after Raffles. The city-states along the littoral of the Melaka Straits rose and fell in relation to their ability to recognize these changes in the global networks they were linked to. The cycle of modern globalization on which Singapore rode to affluence in the 19th century and first half of the 20th century reached its nadir with the end of decolonization and the Cold War. The challenge for Singapore in the 20th century is thus to recognize the nature of the post-colonial or post-modern cycle of globalization it is caught in, and to decide how best to respond to it. Looking at the impact of earlier cycles of globalization on the maritime history of the Melaka Straits may provide Singaporeans with a better understanding of their city-state's vulnerabilities.

---

[68] C.A. Bayly on "'Archaic' and 'Modern' Globalization in their Eurasian and African Arena, c. 1750–1850", in Hopkins, ed., *Globalization*, pp. 47–73.

[69] So Kee-Long, "Dissolving Hegemony or Changing Trade Pattern? Images of Srivijaya in the Chinese sources of the Twelfth and Thirteenth Centuries", *JSEAS* 29, 2 (1998): 295–308.

13

Ian A. Macgregor

A Sea-Fight Near Singapore in the 1570s*

The object of this paper is to give an account of a naval battle that took place off the island of Singapore, probably on 1 January 1577. This battle was the first of three that were fought between the Acehnese and the Portuguese during the time that Mathias d'Albuquerque was Captain-Major of the Seas of Melaka. Despite this, the story of these battles, or of any one of them, has not appeared in any history of events in Malaya written since 1800. This omission is probably due to the fact that no account of the fight exists in the *Décadas* of Diogo do Couto. As Tiele noted,[1] the extant version of the *Décadas* makes no mention of happenings at Melaka between 1575 and 1580.[2] The *Ásia Portuguesa* of Manuel de Faria e Sousa is equally barren of information.

In the following account, three sources have been used: one of them is printed, but the other two are in manuscript form. The printed evidence is contained in *O Oriente conquistado á Jesú Christo pelos Padres da Companhia de Jesús*, written by Padre Francisco de Sousa, S.J., and published in Lisbon in 1710.[3] One of the manuscripts, preserved in the Public Library and District Archives at Évora, is a biography of Mathias d'Albuquerque.[4] This work does not name its author, although

* First published in *JMBRAS* 29, 3 (1956): 4–21.

[1] P.A. Tiele, "De Europeërs in den Maleischen Archipel", the citation made being from part 4 which appeared in *BKI* 29 (1881): 153–214, esp. p. 167.

[2] For the misfortunes of Couto's MS, see C.R. Boxer, *Three Historians of Portuguese Asia* (Macau: Instituto Português de Hong Kong, 1948). See also Diogo do Couto, *Décadas da Asia*, vols. 10–24 of *Da Ásia* by João de Barros and Diogo do Couto (Lisbon: Na Regio Officina Typografica, 1778–88).

[3] Francisco de Sousa, S.J., *O Oriente conquistado á Jesú Christo pelos Padres da Companhia de Jesús*, 2 vols. (Lisbon: Valentim da Costa Deslandes, 1710).

[4] *Vida de Mathias d'Albuquerque*, a work of 231 folios, codex CXV/1–13 in the Public Library and District Archives, Évora. Henceforth cited as *Vida*.

13.1 Portrait etching of the Indian Governor and Portuguese militaryman António Moniz Barreto. © Peter Borschberg, private collection.

Cunha Rivara thought that it had been composed during the lifetime of its subject.[5] The other manuscript, which is in the National Library at Lisbon, is the *História dos serviçǫs com martírio de Lúis Monteiro Coutinho*, written by Manuel Godinho de Erédia and dated 1615.[6] Until recently it was thought that this work had been lost without a trace.[7]

Events Prior to the Battle

Acehnese war fleets were very active in Malayan waters between 1564 and 1585. In 1564 it seems that the Acehnese attacked the capital of Johor, which then lay on the banks of the Johor River, possibly at Johor Lama. They are said either to have killed the sultan of Johor in the attack, or else to have carried him off as a prisoner to Aceh where he was later murdered. For a few years Johor may have been a vassal state of Aceh.[8]

In 1568 the Acehnese unsuccessfully besieged Melaka. At this time the state of Johor seems to have been on friendly terms with the Portuguese, but this amity did not last for long.[9] The Acehnese launched a further attack on Melaka in 1573; their example was copied by a Javanese force in 1574 before a further, rather feeble, Acehnese attempt occurred in 1575.[10] By the end of 1574 Johor also seems to have turned against the Portuguese. Referring to this period, a Portuguese writer asserted that the sultan of Johor and Bintan had given refuge to Javanese supply craft and had secretly helped the Acehnese against Melaka.[11]

Writing in Goa at a later date, Couto mentions friendly negotiations between Johor and Aceh at this time, but dubs them "tricks and stratagems". Nevertheless, it is true that, in the late 1570s, Acehnese vessels could sail in Malayan waters without risk of opposition from Johor. As a result, it was noted that the seas became infested with Acehnese. This was especially true of the approaches to the Singapore Straits: strong Acehnese fleets cruised there, impeding the passage of shipping and able, if need arose, to take refuge in the Johor River.[12]

---

[5] J.H. da Cunha Rivara, *Catálogo dos Manuscritos da Bibliotheca Pública Eborense* (Lisbon: Imprensa Nacional, 1850), p. 315.

[6] National Library of Portugal, Lisbon, Fundo Geral, ms. 414, *História dos serviços com martirio de Luís Monteiro Coutinho*, by Manoel Godinho de Erédia. Henceforth cited as Eredia.

[7] See translation Eredia's *Declaraçam de Malaca*, in J.V. Mills, "Eredia's Description of Melaka, Meridional India and Cathay", *JMBRAS* 8, 1 (1930): 257. See pp. 265–8 of this article for some account of Eredia's life.

[8] I.A. Macgregor, "Johore Lama in the Sixteenth Century", *JMBRAS* 28, 2 (1955): 86–7; C.A. Gibson-Hill, "Johore Lama and Other Ancient Sites on the Johore River", *JMBRAS* 28, 2 (1955): 144–6.

[9] Ibid., pp. 91 et seq., 146.

[10] For accounts of these three sieges see Couto, *Décadas*, vol. 19, pp. 121–31, 226–46; and s.n., "Descripçam dos cercos de Malacca, sendo Capitão Tristão Vaz da Veiga, e de huma vitória naval que teve da armada do Achem", codex CXVI/1–26, Évora Public Library and District Archives.

[11] "Descripçam dos cercos", fols. 22 and 23.

[12] See Macgregor, "Johore Lama in the Sixteenth Century", pp. 86–7. Gibson-Hill, "Johore Lama and Other Ancient Sites", pp. 144–6.

After the siege of Melaka in 1568, the news of Acehnese activities in Malayan waters caused perturbation in Portugal. The Portuguese now began to think of sending an expedition to conquer Aceh. It is possible that this idea was in mind when the government of Portuguese India was divided between three governors in 1571. It was also said that António Moniz Barreto, the governor appointed to take charge of affairs in the south, that is the Malay Archipelago and Macau, was named governor of the conquest of Sumatra. However, any scheme to realise this conquest in the early 1570s was frustrated by dissension between the governor of India and the governor of the south, a dissension largely due to the Portuguese lack of resources in the East.[13] Moniz Barreto never came to Melaka, the proposed headquarters of his government, and the plan for dividing Portuguese India into three governorships soon collapsed.

The home government did not forget the needs of Melaka. Indeed, awareness of trouble there must have been sharpened considerably when reports reached Portugal, in 1575 at the latest, of the attack made by the Acehnese in 1573. It is not surprising therefore that, early in 1576, the Portuguese government should have decided to send Mathias d'Albuquerque to the East as Captain-Major of the Seas of Melaka.[14] Albuquerque was a man of high social position, a collateral descendant of Alfonso d'Albuquerque, Governor of Portuguese India 1509–15, and he himself was to become Viceroy of Portuguese India in 1591.[15] Moreover, he already knew the East, as he had served there before, though not at Melaka.[16]

Albuquerque left Lisbon on 2 March 1576, with two vessels, the *Santa Catherina*, under his own command, and the *São Jorge*, under the captaincy of Bartolomeu Passanha. The two vessels were ordered to proceed directly to Melaka without halting at any place along the way.[17]

They did not make a good passage. The crews suffered badly from sickness during the voyage through the Atlantic, and Albuquerque was forced to put in at Mozambique—at least, so said the priest quoted by Francisco de Sousa. Near Mozambique the galleon *São Jorge* foundered, but it was claimed that all the crew and stores were saved.[18]

It is not absolutely certain how long Albuquerque stayed at Mozambique. Both the priest quoted by Sousa and Albuquerque's biographer agree that the Captain-Major reached Melaka a short time before the battle was fought.[19] The biographer states that the battle occurred on 1 January 1577; this is also consonant with the priest's evidence.[20] However, the battle mentioned by Eredia is dated 1 January 1578,

---

[13] Ibid., p. 94n190. Some time before, in 1558, Francisco Barreto, Governor of Portuguese India, had assembled a large fleet for an expedition against Aceh. Before he could set out he was replaced by Dom Constantino de Bragança, who abandoned the plan. See Couto, *Décadas*, vol. 16, pp. 396–7; vol. 17, pp. 12–6, 23–6.

[14] *Vida*, fol. 20.

[15] Macgregor, "Johore Lama in the Sixteenth Century", p. 87n156.

[16] Couto, *Décadas*, vol. 19, pp. 13, 22–4.

[17] De Sousa, *O Oriente conquistado*, vol. 2, p. 337; *Vida*, fols. 20–20 verso.

[18] Ibid.

[19] Ibid.; *Vida*, fol. 21 verso.

[20] *Vida*, fol. 22; de Sousa (*O Oriente conquistado*, vol. 2, p. 337) says that the day previous to the battle was the eve of the feast of the Circumcision, 1577.

13.2 Glazed tile painting of a Portuguese-style *caravela* (caravel) from the mid-16th century. © Peter Borschberg, private collection.

and he supports his assertion with a verbatim reproduction of a certificate issued by António Moniz Barreto.[21] The matter is further complicated by the fact that on three occasions in the same work Eredia gives dates that are inconsistent with other dates or circumstances that he mentions.[22] One of these inconsistencies concerns the certificate of António Moniz Barreto. It is dated from Lisbon, 9 March 1578. Since Eredia himself states that Luís Monteiro Coutinho, to whom the certificate was issued, did not reach India until 25 January 1578, its emanation from Lisbon is a physical impossibility, which, if the dates are right, can only be resolved by assuming that Lisbon should "read" Goa. Moreover, Eredia's account of the battle is at variance with the other evidence[23] and, except in the matter of the date of the battle, his variations are unsupported by the certificates that he reproduced in his work.[24] Indeed, it seems likely that he confused the battle of 1 January 1577 with a later combat which seems to have taken place off Changi Point and which may have occurred on 1 January 1578. Such an assumption, however, would mean that Eredia changed the date of the battle in Moniz Barreto's certificate, which clearly refers to the earlier engagement[25] and which, equally clearly, was a source for part of Eredia's story of the battles.[26] And even if no such change of date can be proved,

---

[21] Eredia, fol. 5.

[22] The three inconsistencies: (i) in fol. 3 Eredia says that Luís Monteiro Coutinho reached Melaka in June 1574: in fol. 4, when referring to the same occasion, he quotes orders to proceed to Melaka dated 13 Apr. 1576; (ii) in the introductory page headed "To the reader", he states that Coutinho's martyrdom occurred on 24 Mar. 1588; in fol. 11 verso, the date is given as 24 Mar. 1583; (iii) the example given in the text is drawn from fol. 4 verso and fol. 5. For reasons given below it appears that the place is wrong and not the date.

[23] Eredia, fol. 4 verso, is at variance with both the other accounts on three points: (i) in saying that the Portuguese first sighted the Acehnese as they were entering the Johor River, whereupon Albuquerque at once set sail and attacked them. *Vida*, fol. 21 verso, and de Sousa, p. 337, say that the Acehnese approached the Portuguese, coming in search of them; (ii) in saying that the Portuguese pursued the Acehnese to *Cotabatu* (Johor Lama). *Vida*, fol. 23, and de Sousa, p. 338, say that the Portuguese pursuit had to stop because the wind fell, and *Vida*, ibid., adds that the wind fell as the Portuguese were about to pass *Taniambur* (Tanjong Rhu? Tanjong Buai?); (iii) in saying that some Acehnese galleys, galliots and foists remained outside *Tanjong ruça* (Beting Kusah) sandbank, and that these craft were captured by the Portuguese in addition to the vessels of the Acehnese admiral and vice-admiral. *Vida*, fol. 23 mentions no prizes; de Sousa, p. 338, mentions three prizes, a figure which agrees with the certificate quoted by Eredia in fol. 5.

[24] Eredia, fol. 5 verso, Certificate of judges, aldermen and city of Melaka, dated at Melaka, 14 Dec. 1581, mentions that Luís Monteiro Coutinho went against the fortress of *Jor* (Johor Lama) twice, once with Dom Pedro de Menezes (this must have been between Coutinho's arrival in Melaka in June 1576 and Albuquerque's in December of the same year) and once with Mathias d'Albuquerque. But this certificate says nothing to indicate that the second visit occurred immediately after Albuquerque's first fight with the Acehnese.

[25] The text bears a marked resemblance to the letter quoted in Sousa and translated below.

[26] In his account of the battle in fol. 4 verso, Eredia used Moniz Barreto's certificate for (i) the numbers of the Acehnese vessels; (ii) the numbers of Portuguese vessels engaged, though besides the twelve given in the certificate he adds many foists and bantins; (iii) Luís Monteiro Coutinho's attack on a large Acehnese galley, though this was also mentioned in the certificate of the judges, aldermen and other officials of Melaka (Eredia, fol. 5 verso).

there are enough inconsistencies in Eredia's work to make it possible to have some doubt of his general trustworthiness.

Apart from the question of Eredia's reliability, certain factors point to a short stay in Mozambique and an arrival in Melaka in December 1576. These factors are the winds that governed the navigation of Portuguese vessels in the East in the 16th century. Sailing from Europe and going by way of the Mozambique Channel, Portuguese vessels normally reached western India in August or September, though an arrival in October was not unknown. Vessels sailing from Goa or Cochin to Melaka in the second half of the year normally set out in September to take advantage of the northerly wind then blowing off the western coast of India and also of the frequent westerly winds which blow in October and November from Lat. 8° or 10° N to the equator between Ceylon and the entrance to the Straits of Melaka. These westerly winds are especially strong about the Nicobar Islands. Vessels making this voyage usually reached Melaka in September or October. Assuming that Albuquerque left Mozambique in September 1576, it would have been possible for him to reach Melaka in December. He would have set out by way of the northern Mozambique Channel. Having passed the northern tip of Madagascar, he would have found East and ESE winds south of the equator until late October or early November, when the wind changes to NW. After crossing the equator, he could have picked up the tail end of the westerly winds blowing from Ceylon [Sri Lanka] towards the Nicobars. If he failed to reach the Nicobars before the NE monsoon began north of the equator in November, he would probably have had a difficult passage there—a presumption that would gain support from the statement of Albuquerque's biographer that his hero had a toilsome journey. For, as Horsburgh noted, "Ships from Madras or Ceylon, if bound for the Melaka Strait in the NE monsoon, will be liable to have a tedious passage."[27]

If this sequence of events can be accepted, it would have brought Albuquerque to Melaka in December 1576. Indeed, an arrival in December, which is vouched for by two authorities, one of them an eyewitness, cannot be explained except on the assumption that Albuquerque reached Melaka in the same year as he set out. Had he waited a long time in Mozambique, he would surely have tried to leave port in the middle of 1577 in time to make sure of catching the westerlies between Ceylon and the Melaka Strait.

Soon after reaching Melaka, Albuquerque set out for the Singapore Straits to meet the annual trading vessel from China and escort it to Melaka.[28] From here onwards, the accounts of the three sources are fairly similar. I have therefore furnished translations of the accounts of de Sousa's witness, the Jesuit Amador da Costa and the certificate of António Moniz Barreto which was reproduced by Eredia. Differences between the two are mentioned in the notes to da Costa's account, as is

---

[27] James Horsburgh, *India Directory*, 2nd ed. (London: Black, Parbury & Allen for the East India Company London, 1817), vol. 1, pp. 115–6; vol. 2, pp. 146–8. The quotation in the text is from vol. 2, p. 148. For some references to Portuguese *roteiros* which mention routes to Melaka, see Macgregor, "Johore Lama in the Sixteenth Century", p. 95n195.

[28] De Sousa, *O Oriente conquistado*, vol. 2, p. 337; *Vida*, fol. 21 verso.

13.3 Glazed tile painting of a Portuguese-style *fusta* (foist) from the mid-16th century. © Peter Borschberg, private collection.

additional or different information given by Albuquerque's biographer. The certificate of Moniz Barreto is collated with the one granted to Luís Monteiro Coutinho by the judges, aldermen and other officials of the city of Melaka, a document which is also reproduced by Eredia.

Amador da Costa's Account of the Battle and its Aftermath[29]

Our voyage to Mozambique was not so good as we had wished, because there was much sickness in all the ships, which was the reason of our putting into port[30] against the instructions which the Captain, Mathias d'Albuquerque, had from the king, ordering him to stop at no other place but Melaka. By this haste it seems that the heart of our Lord the King foresaw the great trouble in which Melaka would be, for it was so great, from lack of men[31] and from the great pressure of this Moor,[32] its neighbour, that with our arrival it seemed to them to be their resuscitation from death to life. Until the monsoon and the time for leaving for China arrived,[33] I was always with the fleet in the company of the Captain Mathias d'Albuquerque who, a few days after his arrival, prepared a fleet of 13 sail, that is, three high-sided vessels, three galleys and seven foists,[34] and went with it to await the China ship,[35] of which, together with a junk in its company, we had news in passing the Strait of Singapore. And, having joined it, the whole fleet was together and about to re-enter

---

[29] De Sousa, *O Oriente conquistado*, vol. 2, pp. 337–9.

[30] *Vida*, fol. 20, mentions the loss of Passanha's galleon near Mozambique, and says that Albuquerque went from there to Melaka.

[31] *Vida*, fol. 21, says that when Albuquerque reached Melaka he found a lack of almost all things needed to supply a fleet and soldiers, while the Portuguese captains who were there were anxious to return to India.

[32] The normal Portuguese term for Muslims in the 16th century. "This" Moor of the text was the sultan of Aceh.

[33] Ships normally left Melaka for China in the middle of the year. See C.R. Boxer, *Fidalgos in the Far East* (The Hague: Martinus Nijhoff, 1948), p. 15.

[34] *Vida*, fol. 21 verso, says that there were 12 vessels: one galleon, two galleasses, three galleys, three galliots and three brigantines. Moniz Barreto's certificate (below, p. 17), says 12 vessels: one galleon, two galleasses, three galleys and six foists. Eredia, fol. 4 verso, copies this, substituting the word *galliots* for *foists* and adding "many foists and bantins". *Vida*, fol. 21 verso, names the captains of the fleet: galleass *Santiago*, Albuquerque; another galleass (*Santa Catharina*?) António de Ataíde; galleon *Samorin*, Pedro Lopes de Sousa; galleys, Luís de Carvalho, Roque de Brito, Baltesar de Sequeira; galliots, Gaspar da Costa, Gaspar Diaz, Manuel Monteiro; brigantines, António Padrão, Gaspar de Paiva, Pedro Velho. High-sided vessels (galleon and galliot), see above.

[35] *Vida*, fol. 23 says that the Portuguese fleet met the "junk" from China, but does not state when the meeting occurred. Ibid., fol. 21, states that Albuquerque went to the Singapore Strait because he had news that the enemy fleet was there. It seems that the expected arrival of the vessel from China and the presence of the Acehnese fleet near the Singapore Strait were the things that made Albuquerque set out so hastily.

the Strait,[36] when, on the eve of the Circumcision, 1577,[37] we caught sight of the Acehnese fleet,[38] which consisted of 150 sail,[39] very well furnished with men and munitions of war[40] and, above all, a will to fight, for they were promising themselves victory. They came with 40 royal galleys with two rows of oars and other vessels of lesser size.[41] But, as the Captain-Major of the fleet had instructions from his king not to fight the Portuguese in the open sea, but only along the shore, he stationed the galleys in order, according to his instructions.

Although the proportion between the fleets was so unequal, both in the number of sails and in the artillery, for all their pieces were spheres and basilisks which, with much fury, fired a shot as large as a man's head while we had no more than two spheres,[42] still Mathias d'Albuquerque laboured all that night to reach them. Nor was his labour in vain because, on the morning of the day of Jesus,[43] we anchored near the enemy, though not so near as all desired. The Portuguese were excited to see themselves near and the Moors much more, thinking they had us in their hands.

---

36 *Vida*, fol. 21 verso, says Albuquerque took his fleet to a watering place which lay on the other (that is, eastward) side of the Singapore Strait. It could have been near the mouth of the Singapore River: see J.I. de Brito Rebello, ed., *Livro de marinharia* (Lisbon: Imprensa Lipanio da Silva, 1903), p. 203. But it could also have been one of the watering places near Pulau Remunia: see Horsburgh, *India Directory*, 2nd ed., vol. 2, p. 190. The latter is possibly the more likely place.

37 The eve of the feast of the Circumcision of 1577, or 31 Dec. 1576. The feast of the Circumcision is celebrated on 1 Jan., the first day of the year.

38 *Vida*, fol. 21 verso, says that, after reaching the watering place, Albuquerque sent Luís Carvalho with his galley and a brigantine to the river of *Jor* (Johor) to get some information about the enemy. Carvalho soon returned saying that the enemy fleet was coming to look for them.

39 Moniz Barreto's certificate agrees with this figure, but *Vida*, fol. 21 verso gives a total of 115 vessels.

40 *Vida*, fol. 22 states that the fleet was commanded by "Ciri maralela" (Sri Maharaja Lela) and contained 10,000 fighting men and much artillery. It adds that the fleet was accompanied by "Raiale" (Raja Ali), who was married to a daughter of the sultan of Aceh and to whom the sultan wished to restore Melaka. Eredia, fol. 4 verso, says that the soldiers on board were Turks, Arabs, Deccanis and Acehnese.

41 Moniz Barreto's certificate agrees with this number, but *Vida* fol. 21 verso says 36 royal galleys, 50 galliots, foists and launches, and 29 light craft.

42 The *sphere* was a gun smaller that the serpent. (Damião de Goes, *Chrónica do felicissimo Rei Dom Emanuel* [Lisbon: Escritorio, 1909–12], vol. 4, p. 52). The weight of shot fired by the various muzzle-loading cannon varied both with time and by country during the 16th century. In England, towards the end of this period, the *basilisk* had a calibre of about 5 inches, and with 9 lbs of powder was capable of firing a ball weighing 14 to 15 lbs (William Laird Clowes, *The Royal Navy, a History*, 1st ed. [London: Dampson, Low, Marston & Co., 1897], p. 410). The *serpent* or *culverin* was a long cannon of slightly larger bore, with a projectile of about 18 lbs. With increased standardization of cannon in the 17th century, the *basilisk* became, or was replaced by, the 12-pounder, and the *culverin* became the long 18-pounder. At the request of the Acehnese, the Turks are said to have sent 500 men, "many big bombards", supplies and many engineers and gunfounders to Aceh in the 1560s (Couto, *Décadas*, vol. 18, p. 131). For contacts of Aceh with Turkey see also Lisbon, Arquivo Nacional / Torre do Tombo, Coll. São Lourenço, no. 4, fol. 375.

43 Of the feast of the Circumcision of Christ, 1 Jan. 1577.

The game of bombard shots began from each side, lasting with considerable fury for six hours,[44] from the morning until after midday. It lasted so long because our fleet could not reach the enemy, who lay to the windward, until that Jesus, in whose name and trust the Portuguese were fighting, suddenly turned the wind on our side.[45] With this favour the Captain, Mathias d'Albuquerque, had the trumpets sounded and all sails unfurled and he at once put himself and his galley in the midst of all the enemy fleet and so pressed them that they began to become confused, each one seeking his own salvation. But the Captain, making no account of those remaining behind, but only of the enemy flagship, made chase, but when the bows (of his galley) were near the stern and he was in terms of grappling with it, our Lord God mortified us and calmed the wind,[46] and the enemy had time to gain safety,[47] to our considerable vexation. They left with us only three galleys of the whole fleet,[48] including the Vice-Admiral's vessel,[49] which had all the powder and the most noble men of the Acehnese who, being noblemen, ever refused to surrender and, with courageous heart, resisted to the death. The Captain of the galley, seeing that he could not escape, cut his hair, saying, *Amoucou*,[50] that is, let us all die. On this he was embraced by all his men and, forming themselves into one body they charged like lions; but their valour, although it profited them, gaining them temporal honour, could not save their lives. Thirteen of ours died in this conflict[51] and the enemy killed and captured reached 1,600.[52]

Returning towards Melaka, the Captain-Major sent a *bantin*[53] ahead to go and give the news of the good success. It arrived at midnight. Beating on the gates of the fortress and uttering great shouts, the men of the bantin gave the good news they carried. The Captain of the Fortress, Aires de Saldanha,[54] at once had all the artillery fired off in the space of a creed, for it was all ready charged. Behold then the city, which knew not what it was, put into confusion, attributing that noise to the fortress

---

[44] *Vida*, fol. 22 verso, says the Acehnese galleys approached, having the wind in their favour, and bombarded the Portuguese for three hours. The Portuguese suffered many casualties and their vessels were badly damaged, but their resistance was so great that the Acehnese finally withdrew and gave Albuquerque time to effect some repairs. On this matter of the approach of the Acehnese the *Vida* and da Costa are at variance with Eredia's own report (fol. 4 verso) (see above, n. 22), but not necessarily with Moniz Barreto's certificate.

[45] *Vida* fol. 23, agrees about the wind turning and the Portuguese then attacked the Acehnese.

[46] *Vida*, fol. 23, says that Albuquerque had completed the defeat of the enemy fleet if the wind had not failed him as he was about to pass Taniambur (Tanjong Rhu? Tanjong Buai? The latter is possibly more likely).

[47] *Vida*, fol. 23, says that the Acehnese retired towards *Jor* (Johor) where Albuquerque could not seek them out. Eredia's version see above n. 22, item (ii).

[48] *Vida* does not mention prizes; Moniz Barreto's certificate (see the next section below) says it was two galleys and a foist. For Eredia's version, see above, n. 22, item (iii).

[49] Eredia, fol. 4 verso, says that Luís Monteiro Coutinho captured this galley.

[50] In other words, *amok*.

[51] *Vida* does not enumerate the Portuguese casualties; for Moniz Barreto's certificate, see below.

[52] *Vida* gives no figures. For Moniz Barreto, see below.

[53] *Bantin*, swift, oared craft. See Eredia's *Description* in Mills, "Description", p. 159.

[54] Later Viceroy of Portuguese India, 1600–05.

being besieged. All came out, some with two-handed swords in their hands, others with lances, others with shields and swords, large and small, all running towards the fortress, thinking that it was entered by the enemy. The shouting of men rent the air, the bells sounded the alarm. But, on learning the news which had arrived, the sadness turns to joy, the vows made to thanks given to God. Some knelt down in the streets, raising their hands to heaven; others ran to the temples where, before the holy sacrament, they gave thanks in a loud voice for such a great favour. And from that hour till morning they never stopped running to the churches. The Bishop, Dom Jorge de Santa Luzia,[55] came out with the clergy in a solemn procession accompanied by many people and by the tears which all were shedding. Two days later the fleet arrived and your Reverence can imagine the joy with which it was received.

My office in all this time was to encourage the soldiers, cure the wounded and do the other things of our Institute.[56]

A few days later we went out again along the coast of this Moor and burned and ravaged many places and captured many men.[57]

Certificate of António Moniz Barreto

I, António Moniz Barreto, of the Council of our Lord the King, make known that while I was governing the states of India and the Southern Parts, Mathias d'Albuquerque, being commander in them, with 2 galleasses, 1 galleon, 3 galleys and 6 foists, (which, with other vessels, I from time to time sent to the succour of those parts), on 1 January 1578 met a great fleet of the king of Aceh, consisting of 150 sail, of which 40 were royal galleys and the rest foists and *lanchara*. After exchanging a great number of bombard shots he put them to flight and burned the vessel of the Vice-Admiral of the fleet, 300 Muslims dying in the fight; and he captured another galley and a foist in which many of the enemy also died. Ten to twelve Portuguese died and many were wounded. And because Luís Monteiro Coutinho[58] was present in the engagement, in a galleot in which I sent him to the help of Melaka, and grappled with the galley of the enemy and was badly wounded,[59] for they threw many powder pots and other weapons inside, harming him and the soldiers of his company; and also, considering that he has served in the Melaka waters in the same

---

[55] The first bishop of Melaka, who reached the city in 1561. He is generally considered to have renounced the bishopric in 1576. For some occurrences during his stay in Melaka see Frei João dos Santos, *Ethiópia Oriental* (*varia história de cousas notaveis do Oriente*) (Lisbon: Bibliotheca de Classicos Portugueses, 1891), vol. 2, pp. 145–50.

[56] The Institute of St Ignatius Loyola.

[57] *Vida*, fol. 23, says that Albuquerque went out again in search of the enemy fleet which was retiring towards Aceh. See section called "Later Events" below.

[58] For Luís Monteiro Coutinho, see Appendix.

[59] The certificate of the judges, aldermen and officials of Melaka, 14 Dec. 1581; Eredia, fol. 5 verso, states that Luís Monteiro Coutinho grappled with a very big galley of the Acehnese and defeated it, but was wounded so badly that he was near death. The same source states that many of his soldiers were also badly wounded in the fight.

vessel for more than three years[60] and with much expense of his own goods, all of which I have learned from Mathias d'Albuquerque, [António Moniz Barreto issues this certificate]. Lisbon [*sic*, Goa?], March 1578.

Later Events

According to his biographer, Albuquerque set out again soon after his return to Melaka. This time he went to try and intercept the enemy fleet, which was retiring towards Aceh. But the Acehnese vessels were hidden among the islands and Albuquerque failed to find them. He returned to Melaka at the end of the monsoon.[61] It was probably on this voyage that there occurred the burning and ravaging of places mentioned by da Costa.

Some time later Albuquerque sailed back to the Singapore Straits, While he was there he received news that four Acehnese galleys and one lanchara[62] were in the Kedah River. To deal with them he sent Dom Henrique Bendarra, with 2 galleys and 9 bantins. Dom Henrique was a member of the royal family of Tidore, in the Moluccas; he had become Christian and been made *bendahara* of Melaka by the Portuguese.[63] He now accomplished his task successfully, burning the lanchara and one of the enemy galleys and capturing the three others, which he brought back to Melaka, loaded with much pepper[64] and other merchandise. Among the booty were also 23 pieces of artillery, 3 of them bearing the Portuguese arms.[65]

Despite these defeats, the Acehnese, according to Albuquerque's biographer, were still not averse to fighting the Portuguese, who were much inferior to them in numbers of men and vessels.[66] Two more combats occurred, but each time Albuquerque is said to have routed the Acehnese.[67] One of these engagements was probably the one that Eredia confused with the battle of 1 January 1577. On this occasion the Portuguese were, possibly on 1 January 1578, anchored "nearer to Baru Buquet"—perhaps at the "indifferent watering place" mentioned by Horsburgh, lying between Johor Point and South Cape.[68] This watering place would have been

---

[60] An exaggeration. As the certificate of the officials of Melaka stated, Coutinho served in Malayan waters for a "little more or less" than two years, from June 1576 to January 1578 (Eredia, fol. 5 verso).

[61] *Vida*, fol. 23.

[62] See Eredia in Mills, "Description", p. 159.

[63] "Descripçam dos cercos", fol. 27 verso, describes Dom Henrique as an uncle of the king of Tidore and as "bendara", "which is governor of the people of the country". As bendahara he received a pension of 100,000 *reis* a year (Lisbon, Arquivo Nacional/ Torre do Tombo, Livraria, Orçamento do Estado da Índia do que rende da António de Abreu, no. 320, fol. 95 verso.) See also Couto, *Décadas*, vol. 16, pp. 332–3, where he is described as "Cachil Labuzaza", a cousin of the king of Ternate, and a great knight whom the king of Portugal made a knight of the Order of Christ. Couto said that he lived in Melaka with his family.

[64] Kedah produced some pepper in the 16th and early 17th centuries.

[65] For this campaign see *Vida*, fol. 24.

[66] *Vida*, fol. 24.

[67] Ibid.

[68] James Horsburgh, *India Directory*, vol. 2, p. 190.

a good place to wait for the vessels from China, in order to escort them past the mouth of the Johor River and through the Singapore Strait and thence to Melaka. While anchored there Albuquerque is said to have sighted the Acehnese fleet at dawn one morning; it was then sailing towards the mouth of the Johor River, presumably approaching it from the southwest. Albuquerque at once set sail and attacked the enemy. He engaged them when only part of their fleet had passed Changi Point. Some of the leading craft seem to have fled towards Calder's Harbour; others ran for the Johor river, pursued by the Portuguese, perhaps as far as Johor Lama. Still other Acehnese craft tried to escape from the Portuguese by edging close in shore, with the result that they went aground and were captured.[69] However, the story of this fight, which is the one shown in Eredia's illustration, is not mentioned in the *Vida* or in de Sousa's work and, except for the mention of Albuquerque going against Johor Lama, it does not occur in either of the certificates copied by Eredia. In writing of the two combats, Albuquerque's biographer merely said that he captured the galley of the king of *Cuncal* (Trincal? = Trengganu) which was coming to the help of the Acehnese, and also a vessel carrying the king of Lingga;[70] whether or not these successes were obtained in the same engagement as the one mentioned by Eredia it cannot yet be said.

Albuquerque's biographer claimed that, as a result of his hero's efforts, it was many years before the Acehnese again infested the seas ef Melaka as they had previously been accustomed to do.[71] This, however, is not the whole truth, for the accession of a new ruler in Aceh in 1579 was followed by events that weakened the power of Aceh and broke its alliance with Johor.[72]

Albuquerque wished to take advantage of this weakened position of Aceh to attempt its conquest and in 1580 he sailed to India to get support for this scheme. But the plan was not carried out. Mathias d'Albuquerque did, it is true, return to Melaka later in the same year, but he stayed for only a short time. In February 1581, he was in Colombo where he was instrumental in raising a siege that had lasted for nearly two years.[73]

Appendix

Luís Monteiro Coutinho

Monteiro Coutinho was born in the Lamego district of Portugal on 25 August 1527 [*sic*]. He apparently came to India in the time of Luís de Ataíde's first vice-royalty (1568–71). After serving in campaigns off the west coast of India, he was one of the two Portuguese sent to the Mogul court at Akbar's request in 1573. They were well

---

69 Eredia, fol. 4 verso.

70 *Vida*, fol. 24.

71 *Vida*, fol. 25.

72 See Macgregor, "Johore Lama in the Sixteenth Century", p. 88; Gibson-Hill, "Johore Lama and Other Ancient Sites", pp. 144–6.

73 *Vida*, fols. 35–7.

received by the emperor at Agra, and Coutinho is said by Eredia to have astonished the Muslims by beating them at fencing.

In 1576 the Governor, António Moniz Barreto, sent him to Melaka as captain of a galleot, with 40 men. His brother, Domingos, went in another galleot and the original idea seems to have been that both should go to the Moluccas. In fact, Luís Monteiro Coutinho remained at Melaka for about 18 months. During his stay in Malayan waters he is said to have gone up the Johor River as far as Johor Lama on two occasions, once with Dom Pedro de Menezes (c.1576) and once with Mathias d'Albuquerque (1578). In 1578 he seems to have returned to India. Two years later he was sent back to Melaka, on his way to become Captain of the Sea (naval commander) at Amboina. On his way to Amboina he was wrecked near Solor, where he spent four months, during which he raised the siege of the fortress of Solor and performed other useful tasks. On his return to Melaka he was made Captain of the Sea, in 1581, according to Eredia. In 1582 (Eredia's date of 1583 must be a mistake) a large Acehnese fleet appeared off Melaka while Coutinho was away in the area of the Singapore Strait. Disobeying orders, Coutinho returned and attacked the Acehnese fleet with one vessel. A fierce fight took place off Melaka, between Pulau Jawa and Pulau Upeh. Coutinho managed to inflict some damage on the Acehnese, but, through carelessness with a powder pot, his own vessel blew up. Coutinho and 12 other survivors were taken prisoner by the Acehnese and martyred at Aceh on 24 March 1583, Coutinho meeting his fate by being placed in front of a basilisk that was then fired at him.[74]

---

[74] See Eredia, passim; Couto, *Décadas*, vol. 20, pp. 280–1.

14

Carl Alexander Gibson-Hill

Singapore Old Strait and New Harbour, 1300–1870*

14.1 Photograph portrait of Carl Alexander Gibson-Hill. He had served as the director of the Raffles Museum in Singapore and also president of the Malayan Branch of the Royal Asiatic Society between 1956–61. Kuala Lumpur: Malaysian Branch of the Royal Asiatic Society.

* This monograph or long article was first published in the *Memoirs of the Raffles Museum*, no. 3 (Singapore: Government Printing Office, 1956), pp. 11–115. It substantially expands an article by Gibson-Hill published earlier as "Singapore: Note on the History of the Old Straits, 1580–1850", *JMBRAS* 27, 1 (1954): 165–214. Bibliographic details were collected by referencing *An Orientalist's Treasure Trove of Malaya and Beyond: Catalogue of the Gibson-Hill Collection at the National Library Singapore*, ed. Irene Lim and comp. Bonney Tan (Singapore: National Library Board, 2008).

> Keppel Harbour, between Singapore island on the north and Pulau Blakang Mati and Pulau Brani on the south, has a least width of 1½ cables [150 fathoms, 274.3m]. Situated as it is in the very centre of Eastern commerce, Keppel Harbour possesses extensive dock and wharf accommodation, the property of the Singapore Harbour Board. There is a large basin fitted with all modern appliances, and several dry docks. The whole of the above establishments are situated on the northern side of Keppel Harbour ... The western entrance is one cable wide between the 6-fathom [11m] lines off Kubu Batu Berlayar and Tanjong Rimau, and has a least depth of 39 feet [11.9m] in the fairway. The eastern entrance lies between Tanjong Pagar and Teregeh spit, where it is about 4½ cables [731.5m] wide. There are three channels in the eastern entrance: north channel, with a least depth of 28 feet [8.5m]; middle channel, 24 feet [7.3m]; and south channel, 18 feet [5.5m]. (*Malacca Strait Pilot*, 3rd ed. (1946), pp. 195–6)

The waterway now known as Keppel Harbour[1] has, in the past, been given a number of different names, some of which have tended to obscure rather than record its history. It is, however, now clear that it was the "Straight of Sincapura" that Linschoten describes in his *Reys-Gheschrift*,[2] and thus during the latter part of the 16th century an essential and well-marked section of the only route known to have been in use between the south end of the Melaka Strait and the South China Sea. As we shall note in more detail below, during the succeeding century it gradually passed out of common employment as a passageway for European vessels, though notice of it remained in sailing directions and on maps until early in the second half of the 18th century. Even then, when it was otherwise forgotten, native craft continued to

---

[1] For the use of the name Keppel Harbour, after Admiral the Honourable Sir Henry Keppel and his association with the waterway, see below.

[2] Jan Huyghen van Linschoten was born in Haarlem, in or about 1563. In 1583 he went with the Portuguese East India fleet to Goa, where he remained until Jan. 1589, when he sailed for Europe. He delayed for two years in the Azores on the way and did not reach the Netherlands until Sept. 1592. In 1594 and again in 1595 he participated in the Dutch voyages to the Arctic. He apparently began to write his account of the Indies soon after his return home in 1592, and a licence to publish the work was granted him on 8 Oct. 1594. The first section to appear (Book II of the original edition, but called Book III in the English translation of 1598, which is divided into four books, not two) interests us here: this is his summary of the routes followed by the Portuguese pilots, the title-page of which bears the date 1595. His *Itinerario* (Book I in both Dutch and English versions) appeared the following year (1596). The *Reys-Gheschrift vande Navigatien der Portugaloysers in Orienten* is a compilation of the routes to India, the Eastern Seas and the American coasts, translated from the manuscripts of Spanish and Portuguese pilots, and in part acquired by personal conversation with Portuguese pilots in Goa. In particular it contains full details of the courses beyond Melaka, in the Malay Archipelago and on the coast of China. Since it is not the record of a single, particular voyage, the routes described are not compromises between the pilot's preferences and the run of the wind and weather: they represent the considered opinions of experienced men over the 15 to 20 or more years before Linschoten left Goa. The English and German translations of both works appeared in 1598, two Latin versions in 1599, and a French translation in 1610. The English version of the *Reys-Gheschrift* has never been reprinted. A revised edition of Linschoten's *Itinerario* was published in 1885 in two volumes by the Hakluyt Society; see *The Voyage of John Huyghen van Linschoten to the East Indies*, ed. A.C. Burnell and P.A. Tiele, 1st ser., 2 vols. (London: Hakluyt Society, 1885).

14.2 Coloured etching of Jan Huyghen van Linschoten. Taken from the first edition of Jan Huyghen van Linschoten's *Itinerario* published in Amsterdam in 1596. The Hague, Koninklijke Bibliotheek, 1702B4.

travel by it. Subsequently, some five to seven months after the establishment of the present settlement of Singapore, it was re-discovered; but from this point onwards, under the title of New Harbour, it was looked on primarily as a possible refuge for shipping in time of war, and later as the obvious site for the docks which Singapore urgently needed.

This much of the history of Keppel Harbour is now clear. We also know that it was inhabited by a group or groups of orang laut[3] from at least the beginning of the 16th century. We find interesting references to these people in some of the 17th-century accounts of the waterway, and again in notes by Crawfurd and Finlayson, who visited New Harbour in 1822.[4] Initially, probably, all the orang laut lived with their families in small boats, but it appears that a few had houses raised on pillars over the shore line by the latter part of the 17th century.[5] This custom spread gradually, until by the middle of the 19th century we find no references to boat dwellers in Keppel Harbour, though by this time there were at least two well-established villages of these people on Pulau Brani, one in Telok Saga on the north coast, and the other at Kampong Kopit, on the south side of the island, facing the Selat Sengkir. The fate of the one or more communities that once lived ashore on the north side of the waterway is not clear; it is likely that they were absorbed into the Malay settlement in this area when, in 1823, Temenggong 'Abdu'r Rahman and his numerous followers moved from their site on the Singapore River to Telok Blanga, on orders from Sir Stamford Raffles.[6]

---

[3] *Orang Laut.* In the area of the Melaka Strait and the Riau-Lingga archipelagos they are generally taken to be aboriginal Malays (not proto-Malays, a term which should be avoided in this context). They were known to the Portuguese, and through them to later writers, as Cellates, a word with a fairly wide range of variant renderings, and in origin a neologism coined by the Portuguese from the Malay term *selat*, a strait. The term Cellates is applicable in the sense in which it was first used, for those groups inhabiting the waters of the southern part of the Melaka Strait and the Singapore Strait, but in general these people apparently themselves after the estuaries or coasts where they had taken up their abode. There does not appear to be any satisfactory term for the genre as a whole, though it is clear that the Cellates were but one group of a widespread series of cognate groups existing in varying numbers from the Sulu Sea (at least), through the waters of the Makassar Strait, off parts of South Borneo, and so through the archipelagos to the Melaka Strait, and thence north to the waters of the Mergui archipelago: in addition they occurred among the Natuna Islands, the Anambas and on Pulo Condor. In most cases these people lived by scavenging, fishing and mild piracy, and normally they were boat-dwellers, though they appear to have formed settlements ashore to an increasing extent, and their offshoot in North Borneo, the Bajau, are in parts entirely terrestrial. It is clear that the early traders of the archipelagos, coming from Celebes, South Borneo and adjacent islands, were also a branch of these people, and it is significant to find that Tomé Pires used the terms *bajus* and *bujuus* for the traders, suggesting a link between Bajau and Bugis, as they were called respectively in the 19th century.

[4] See also below.

[5] MS map by Wilde, ca. 1680; see below. Tomé Pires refers to "Celate villages", but it is clear that he meant floating villages (the expression used by most later writers), in other words, congregations of boats, as he defines the Cellates elsewhere as boat-dwellers.

[6] See also below.

The Strait of Singapura

Linschoten's account of Keppel Harbour, based on information that he collected from the Portuguese pilots at Goa in the 1580s, provides us with a definite fixed point in the history of the waterway.[7] Its significance and importance at this time are stated unequivocally, and his description leaves no doubt about the channel to which he is referring. In an earlier account of Keppel Harbour over the period 1580–1850,[8] we began with Linschoten's notice, as it was then necessary to correct a number of errors that existed in regard to the subsequent history of the waterway and the names given to it. Actually we can carry the account back as far as the early part of the 16th century. It is certain that the Strait of Singapura was known to the Portuguese from the beginning of their occupation of Melaka. According to Antonio Galvão:[9]

---

[7] In his description of the route from Melaka to Macau (*Reys-Gheschrift*, ch. 20). In the English edition of 1598 (printed in London by John Wolfe), this chapter appears on page 336 (incorrectly marked 318) through page 346. The account of the passage through Keppel Harbour and some of the surrounding portion of the narrative is reprinted with annotations in the 2 Nov. 1848 edition of the *SFP*, as part of an unsigned article (probably by J.R. Logan, who was the brother of the editor, Abraham Logan). See also Gibson-Hill, "Singapore: Notes on the History of the Old Strait, 1580–1850", *JMBRAS* 27, 1 (1954): 167–9, with annotations by the present writer. W.D. Barnes provides an English translation of the 1610 Paris edition covering the same section; see Barnes, "Singapore Old Straits and New Harbour", *JSBRAS* 60 (1911): 26–9. From this latter version it appears that the French version is shorter than the English one, but Barnes may have omitted some passages in preparing the translation. We hope to publish in a later volume in the present series, annotated texts of a selected number of sailing directions and accounts of voyages over waters in the neighbourhood of the Malay Peninsula, to illustrate the routes in current use from 1400–1850. [E.N.: This volume was never published.]

[8] Gibson-Hill, "Notes on the History of the Old Strait", pp. 163–214.

[9] See Samuel Purchas, *Purchas His Pilgrimes*, 4 vols. (London: William Stansby for Herrie Fetherstone, 1625), 2 Oct. 1681. In the reprint, *Hakluytus Posthumus or Purchas His Pilgrims*, 12 vols. (Glasgow: James MacLehose & Sons, 1903–05), see vol. 10 (1905): 27–8. Antonio Galvão's *Tratado* was published in Lisbon in 1563. The English translation printed by Purchas was prepared for Hakluyt and first published by the latter in 1601. It has also been reprinted, together with the Portuguese text of 1563, by the Hakluyt Society as *Discoveries of the World*, 1st ser., no. 30 (London: Hakluyt Society, 1862), p. 112, gives the passages quoted here), edited by Vice-Admiral Bethune, together with textual notes. Galvão cites as his sources Barros, *Década* 2, bk. 5, ch. 10; bk. 6, ch. 2; and bk. 6. ch. 5.

The incident given here is also mentioned in Brás d'Albuquerque's *Commentaries of the Great Afonso Dalboquerque, Second Viceroy of India*, ed. and trans. W. de Gray Birch, 4 vols. (London: Hakluyt Society, 1875–84), vol. 3 (1880), 1st ser., no. 62, pp. 113–4, but the latter account does not indicate the route followed from Melaka to the Gulf of Siam. It occurred shortly after d'Albuquerque's arrival at Melaka, before the capture of the city, which did not occur until August. The presence of the Portuguese fleet in the seas, however, constituted a partial blockade, whatever their intentions may have been at this stage. The masters of the Chinese vessels requested permission to return home as it was by then the normal season for their departure. They were sent off, with a few presents, but asked to take the proposed Portuguese envoy to Siam with them and leave him at Cuy on their way. This suggests that they were in the habit of coasting round the South China Sea, at least when eastward bound, at this period: if not, d'Albuquerque was asking them to go a long distance off their course.

> In the yeere 1511, in the moneth of Aprill, Alfonso de Albuquerque went from the Citie of Cochin unto Malacca. In which yeere and moneth the Chineans went from Malacca into their owne countrey, and Alfonso sent with them for Master[10] a Portugall called Duarte Fernandes, with letters also and order unto the King of the Mantias, which is now called Sian. Standing in the south they passed through the Streight of Cincapura, and sailed towards the North, went along the coast of Patane unto the Citie of Cuy, and from thence to Odia, which is the chiefe Citie of the Kingdome.

Dom Fernandez was one of the men who had been imprisoned by Sultan Mahmud. He was, it seems, "greatly honoured and welcomed" by the king of Siam, and on his return brought back with him ambassadors from the Siamese court to d'Albuquerque. When they came, "they passed overland towards the west unto the Citie of Tanazerim standing upon the sea on the other side [of the peninsula], where they imbarked themselves in two ships, and sailed along the coast unto the Citie of Malacca, leaving it all discovered". In addition to the ambassadors, Dom Fernandez also carried back with him several interesting stories of the marvels of Siam; how the king could "bring forth into the field thirtie thousand Elephants" when he went to war; how he much esteemed "a white Elephant and a red one also, that hath his eyes like unto flaming fire"; and how the men of the country delighted "to carrie round bels within the skin of their privie members", a relaxation which was forbidden to the king and the religious people.[11]

There is also a reference to use of the Keppel Harbour channel at this period in the *Commentaries of the Great Afonso Dalboquerque*. Here it is called the "gate of Singapura", an expression which recurs in the form the "Gate of Tan-ma-hsi" in a Chinese pilots' directory dated 1618.[12] In speaking of the *Guores* of the Liu

---

[10] *Sent with them for Master*. In the *Commentaries*, d'Albuquerque is reported as telling the Chinese that "he wished to send in their company a messenger with letters for the king" of Siam. "Messenger" is therefore much more likely than "Master". Certainly Dom Fernandez could not have gone as sailing master of the Chinese vessel, as he could not have had experience of the craft or the course. He is said to have become well acquainted with "the language" while in prison; but which language—Siamese or Malay—is not clear; probably it was the former, as a knowledge of Malay would not necessarily be of value to an envoy to the Siamese court.

[11] Ralph Fitch reported these whimsical oddities from Pegu, and according to Hakluyt took some back with him to London when he returned there in 1596, but we are not told if he found any sale for them. Tomé Pires, among other writers, noted the custom, though he was never in Burma, and in spite of the several references to it, it may have been only a travellers' tale. Pires says: "Our Malay women rejoice greatly when the Pegu men come to their country, and they are very fond of them. The reason for this must be their sweet harmony"; but it is by no means certain that the Pegu men trafficked much by sea, their carrying trade being at least very largely in Indian and Malay hands. Only 10,000 elephants were recorded by Niccolò di Conti, but apropos of this number Purchas dryly remarks, "and that of ten thousand elephants nourished by a King not knowne by fame, are hard to be beleeved: but longinquitie cannot easily be confuted" (Purchas, *Pilgrimes*, bk. III, ch. I, p. 139; or the ed. of 1905, vol. II, p. 399).

[12] See also below. The source is Hsü Yün-ts'iao, "Notes on the Malay Peninsula in Ancient Voyages", *JSSB* 5, 2 (1948): 10. The Tan-ma-hsi barbarians were the people of *Singapura*.

Kiu [Ryukyu] Islands, who then sent two or three junks a year to Melaka, the *Commentaries* says:[13]

> They set out for Malacca in the month of January, and begin their return journey in August and September. The usual course of their navigation is to beat up the channel between the Islands of Celate [the Riau Archipelago and adjacent islands][14] and the point of *Singapûra*, on the side of the mainland. At the time when Afonso Dalbuquerque set sail for India, after having captured Malacca, there arrived two of their ships at the gate of *Singapûra*, and they mere coming on to Malacca, but by the advice of the *Lassamane*, who was the king of Malacca's admiral of the sea, they remained where they were, and would not pass up, having learnt that Malacca had been taken by the Portuguese; but when the governors of the land were informed of their position, they sent a safeguard for them, and a flag of truce, and then they came on immediately.

---

[13] D'Albuquerque, *Commentaries*, vol. 3, pp. 89–90. Tomé Pires, *The Suma Oriental of Tomé Pires. An Account of the East from the Red Sea to Japan. Written in Malacca and India in 1512–1515*, ed. Armando Cortesão, Hakluyt Society, 2nd ser., nos. 89–90, 2 vols. (London: Hakluyt Society, 1944), pp. 128–30, says: "The *Lequeos* are called *Guores*—they are known by either of these names. *Lequios* is the chief one. The king is a heathen and all the people too. He is tributary vassal of the king of the Chinese [a point which the Japanese chose to ignore when they occupied the islands in 1879]. His island is large and has many people; they have small ships of their own type; they have three or four junks which they are continuously buying in China, and they have no more. ... One, two or three junks come to Malacca every year, and they take a great deal of Bengal clothing. Among the *Lequjos* Malacca wine is greatly esteemed. They load large quantities of one kind which is like brandy.... The *Lequjos* bring swords worth thirty *cruzados* each, and many of these." The last item provides a possible source for Malay weapons hitherto ignored. The *Commentaries* calls the men Gores, and says that they came from Lequea. This seems more likely to be correct. The trade died shortly after this, and we hear no more of these men; but there is no doubt that the Liu Kiu islanders are not a maritime people, nor does the description of the Guores given by Pires fit the modern islanders. It seems more likely that they were a pocket of Min-yüeh people surviving on the Liu Kiu coast, and since absorbed. There is no doubt that the islands referred to here were the Liu Kiu group, as Pires mentions them again in his notice of China. See also, Pires, *Suma Oriental*, p. lxxviii. C.R. Boxer supposes the Guores who visited Melaka to have been Japanese traders, as the latter were certainly in this area at the close of the 16th century, but the Guores do not seem to have behaved in the customary Japanese manner: Chassigneaux suggests a pocket of Koreans who had settled in the Liu Kiu group, but he is matching sounds, without considering other points about the people.

[14] Alfonso d'Albuquerque to Dom Manoel, 1 Apr. 1512, referring to a map by Francisco Rodrigues, writes of "The archipelago of the islands called *Celates*, which lie beween Java and Melaka" (for a note on this map, see Armando Cortesão, *Cartografia e cartógrafos portugueses do séculos XVI e XVI*, 2 vols. [Lisbon: Seara Nova, 1935], vol. 2, pp. 122–30). Pires, *Suma Oriental*, vol. 1, p. 136, refers to "islands of the *Celates* which are called *Celaguym gum* [not identified], Sabam [Kundur], Buaya, Lingga, Tiga, Pulau Berhala, Bangka and *Monomby* [northwestern Bangka]". Elsewhere Pires, *Suma Oriental*, vol. 2, p. 241, he speaks of people "from Singapore and the neighbouring islands of *Celates*", and other people "arriving to help establish Melaka". The Celates were the orang laut of the straits (Malay *selat*, a strait)—"thieving corsairs who go to sea in small *perahus*, [undecked boats] robbing where they can".

A rutter for a voyage from Melaka to the Canton River, noted briefly by Francisco Rodrigues, and probably taken down about 1513 from directions given by a Chinese pilot, also carries the route past Singapore.[15] Rodrigues writes the name as "Syngapura", and in time places it half way between the Karimun Islands and Pedra Branca. Again a rutter by João de Lisboa [John of Lisbon] of a voyage that he made from Melaka to Brunei in 1526, shows that his course clearly lay through the Selat Sembilan and Keppel Harbour (which he calls the "Estreito Cimquapura").[16]

We know from a brief note by Tomé Pires—"Beyond [the Batu Pahat River] is the *Sijmgapura* channel. It has a few *Celate* villages"—that the orang laut were present in the strait as early as 1512–15 and, the apothecary adds sadly, "of little importance" commercially.[17] Pires also says that it was Sultan Muzaffar Shah (d. ca. 1460) who added the Strait of Singapore and the island of Bintan (*o canall de simgapura com a Jlha de bimtam*) to the dependencies of Melaka—"and he went to war over the said channel with the king of Pahang, and of Trengganu and of Patani, and he always had the best of it, and therewithal he retained the land and jurisdiction";[18] at this period these three rulers were all vassals of Siam, and it looks, therefore, as if the settlement and waterway passed within the Siamese sphere of influence when Parameswara fled to Muar, after killing the last representative of the line of the kings of early Singapore.

In the time of Muzaffar Shah's grandson, Sultan 'Ala'u'd-din, Singapore Strait became the fief of the Seri Bija Diraja. On one occasion after Mahmud Shah had succeeded his father, in place of an elder brother, the Seri Bija Diraja arrived from Singapore to attend a festival in Melaka a day late. Mahmud chose to take the incident as an intentional affront, and after accusing him of disloyalty, gave orders that he should be killed. The fief passed to Seri Bija Diraja's nephew, Sang Setia

---

[15] In Pires, *Suma Oriental*, vol. 2, pp. 301–2. "From Malacca to *Pulo Param* it is five *jaos*, and from there to Pisang another five, and from Pulo Pisang to Karimun it is three *jaos*, and from Karimun to Singapore it is five, and from Singapore to Pedra Branca five, and from [Pedra Branca to] Pulo Tingi five *jaos* to the northeast, and by this route another five *jaos* to *Vioma* [Tioman], and from Pulo Tioman to Pulo Condore it is forty-five *jaos*." Amando Cortesão tries to give a distance for the *jaos*, but in this case it is clearly a measure of time—a watch—the distance varying with the difficulty of the course. Compare with the watches cited on the *Wu pei chih* charts. See also *JASB* 18, 1 (1849): 155, which states: "The junks of the Central Nation [China] are not to be compared with those of the Western Ocean [European Seas]. Those make use of sextants and quadrants to determine the sun's altitude, and measure the time, and so find out the ship's position. The Central People use the compass and the sandglass, and as the wind is strong or light, fair or foul, determine the number of *keng* [2.4 hours]. Each keng is equal to a sea-distance of about 60 *li*. If the wind is fresh and fair the amount may be doubled. When the current and wind are contrary, they reduce the reckoning. In this way they know their position [maybe]" (quoted from a Chinese geographical work, dated 1731).

[16] J.I. de Brito Rebello, ed., *Livro de marinharia: Tratado da agulha de marear de João de Lisboa, Roteiros, sondas e outros conhecimentos relativos a navegação* (Lisbon: Imprensa Silvio Lipano, 1903), pp. 268–9 (confirmed, I.A. Macgregor, 1954).

[17] Pires, *Suma Oriental*, vol. 2, p. 262.

[18] Ibid., p. 244.

Tetain or Bentayan.[19] From the manner of the anecdote it seems likely that the Seri Bija Diraja was in fact displeased at Mahmud's succession, and he may have been plotting with the sultan of Pahang, a state by this time within the Melaka fold. But the point of interest here is the suggestion that Singapura was of sufficient importance for the Seri Bija Diraja to reside there. It seems clear that at this period there must still have been a settlement somewhere in the vicinity of the Singapore Strait and, as we have suggested elsewhere,[20] it was probably on the site of the old Malay capital at the mouth of the Singapore River. The chroniclers are not unanimous in saying that the latter was destroyed at the end of the 14th century,[21] and it is probable that the usurper Parameswara fled prematurely to Muar, leaving Singapura undefended. Certainly, according to the *Commentaries*, the *laksamana* went to live at Singapura after the fall of Melaka to the Portuguese. Again the Shellabear recension of the *Malay Annals*[22] says that during the reign of the first Sultan 'Ala'u'd-din of Johor, the "penglima ra'ayat Raja Nagara, batin Singapura", put up a stout defence of his position against an attack from Melaka. Later, in one of his maps dated 1604, Eredia[23] shows a "Xabandaria" (*Shahbandaria*, port commander's office) situated near the mouth of the Singapore River; and Valentijn,[24] writing about Dutch contacts with Johor, says, "on the 5th of May [1606] two perahus of the king of Johor with the Shahbandar of Singapura, Sri Raja Negara, reached our fleet". Floris[25] writes as if there were a settlement of "Sinca Pura" in this neighbourhood early in 1613, and we know that later that year the Portuguese burned a Malay post at the mouth of the Singapore River.[26] It is likely that it was at this point, and not earlier, that the ancient settlement of Singapura went up on flames. The point is of some significance here. While the settlement lasted, Keppel Harbour was the gate, or strait, or Narrow Strait

---

[19] "Malay Annals, Raffles MS no. 18", ed. and trans. C.C. Brown in *JMBRAS* 25, 2–3 (1952): 125. See also Leyden's text, rev. T. Braddell, *JIA* 5 (1851): 738.

[20] Gibson-Hill, "Five Early Watercolour Sketches of Penang and Malacca", *JMBRAS* 31, 1 (1958): 163–71.

[21] D'Albuquerque (*Commentaries*), Barros and Couto say that the city was attacked and the wayward ruler driven out; the attackers are described as men sent by the king of Patani, of Siam and of Majapahit (respectively). Eredia says that he fled in fear of an attack from the king of Pahang, Pires that he fled in fear of an attack from Siam. The latter also mentions men from Singapore as among those who gathered a little later at Melaka, to take part in establishing the new settlement there, but he groups them with other peoples from the neighbouring area, so there is nothing to suggest that they were refugees. Patani and Pahang were at this time vassals of Siam. Accordingly, Couto and the *Malay Annals* alone tell the story of the successful attack by the *batara* of Majapahit. On this point, see Gibson-Hill, "The Malay Annals: The History Brought from Goa", *JMBRAS* 29, 1 (1956): 185–8. Couto probably had access to the MS of the *Malay Annals* in Goa, where he was working as keeper of the Goa archives from 1595/1604 to 1616.

[22] Reprint of 1910 romanized ed., ed. Shellabear (Singapore: Harmony Press, 1948), p. 250.

[23] See also below.

[24] D.F.A. Hervey, ed. and trans., "François Valentyn's Account of Malacca", *JSBRAS* 15 (1885): 134.

[25] *Peter Floris, His Voyage to the East Indies in the Globe, 1611–1615*, ed. W.H. Moreland, Hakluyt Society, 2nd ser., no. 74 (London: Hakluyt Society, 1934), pp. 102–3.

[26] I.A. Macgregor, *in epistola*, 1954. [E.N.: The reference made here by Gibson-Hill appears to refer to a private unpublished letter by I.A. Macgregor.]

14.3 A Map of the Dominions of Johor and of the Island of Sumatra with the Adjacent Islands. Alexander Hamilton, *New Account of the East Indies*. London: Printed for C. Hitch and A. Millar, 1744. © Peter Borschberg, private collection.

of Singapura: once the settlement had gone, the way was open for the terminology to grow laxer.

As we have seen, the first Portuguese to pass through the Strait of Singapore went as passenger on a Chinese junk returning home from Melaka. When the Portuguese came to sail vessels under their own command southwards from the city they must, as was customary, have borrowed local pilots. Had there been any other channels in use at this time, they would have heard of them from this source, just as they found the way to the Moluccas easily enough. The only other major strait in this region with which they were acquainted is the one they called the Strait of Sabam (present-day Selat Kundur).[27] It is entered by running down west of the Karimun Islands, and beyond it, still keeping close to the Sumatran coast, one reaches the Bangka Strait and so passes on to Sunda and western Java. It is not, in fact, the best route from the Melaka Strait to Java, but it is a coasting passage, and it has the advantage of providing access to the ports of southeast Sumatra on the same course. Between Lingga and Singkep in the north, and Bangka in the south, a broad, clear channel, the Berhala Strait, runs out eastwards, from which one can turn north towards the South China Sea and Pedra Branca, or bearing south, pass below the Karimata Islands to Tanjong Sambar, the south coast of Borneo (Kalimantan) and thence on to the Moluccas by way of southern Celebes (Sulawesi). The first Portuguese expedition to the Moluccas went by way of the Bangka Strait and the north coast of Java as many of the local merchants did, the latter taking this course so that they could trade along the line of the Lesser Sunda Islands en route. The Portuguese also knew of the passage by way of the Berhala Strait and the Karimata Islands: already in Tomé Pires' time they had learned that this was the course followed by the vessels from Tanjongpura and other points on the south coast of Borneo. But the Portuguese were not, apparently, aware of any practical channel through the mass of islands comprising the Riau Archipelago and adjacent groups. They do not even seem to have known of the Durian Strait, running down east of the island of Kundur, which is a much better passage than the Selat Kundur, and is now used in place of it.

There is no doubt that the sea routes the Portuguese followed, initially at least, were routes taken over from local pilots. With the exception of the Singapore channel,

---

[27] The Portuguese refer to the island of Kundur as Sabam. This may have been an alternative name, or the name of a part of the island, in the same way that a number of 16th-century maps (and among texts, at least Tomé Pires) refer to Bangka by names based on Bukit Menumbing (Monopin Hill, 455m), a conspicuous hill at the northwest corner of the island. We suspect also that Billiton [Belitung] may once have been known as Panten or Pantan in the same way, from a district on the island. An alternative possibility to consider in the case of Sabam is that the place in question really lay further south, and that by the Selat Sabam the 16th-century local pilots meant the strait leading to Sabam, in which case the latter could have been the defunct "Sabana emporium" of the *Geographike Huphegesis* attributed to Claudius Ptolemy. It is not usual for Malays to regard straits as "roads" (or jungle paths) and name them by the place to which they lead, but the normal European practice is to name them from the island, or islands, which they separate from the adjacent mainland. Hence the early Portuguese pilots meeting with a Selat Sabam would automatically take it that one of the more prominent islands on the seaward side of the strait must be known as Sabam.

they were clearly the passages that had been in use from the very beginning of regular sea traffic in this region, and they were few in number. At the start they must inevitably have been worked out by craft travelling coastwise, and it is thus that the old north-south link came to lie as close as practicable to the east coast of Sumatra, while the original east-west route crossed from Borneo to Sumatra along a chain of islands. Very few peoples have the peculiar idiosyncrasy of exploring for its own sake. By far the greater part of the human race treats it as a practical matter. So long as local politics permit the existing routes to function reasonably satisfactorily, they suffer no urge to risk their lives trying to discover what lies beyond the shoals and mangrove forests along the horizon. At any one time, the search for new routes can well wait until the need is pressing. After all, if there is a better world it is more likely to be under the counter in this one, rather than round the corner. The only people who stood to profit personally by investigating the complex waterways east of the Strait of Sabam, were the orang laut; and they must have penetrated the "Islands of Celate" much as rabbits burrow into a sandy bank, worrying out a vast warren of channels in which to shelter and breed. From their tunnelling would come no knowledge of through straits, except by the slenderest chance: their requirements were not to be met by passing through, but merely by passing in.

The question, then, of when Linschoten's course[28] past Singapore Island first came into regular use as a passageway must depend on the manner in which the trade routes were opened up in this region. We believe, in fact, that the date must almost certainly be very late, clearly well after the beginning of the 2nd millenium CE, and probably as late as the second half of the 13th century. Moreover, it seems likely that the founding of the city-port of Singapura was an indication of the growing use of this route. Clearly, of course, there were already orang laut here, though we have no documentary evidence of their presence. Singapura must have begun in much the same way as Melaka, roughly a century later, a leader with a few followers settling among a group of orang laut and gathering in other neighbouring units by the strength of his personality and the success of his undertakings.[29] It is interesting to note how easily the orang laut peoples have at different times accepted leaders from other communities. In the 18th and early 19th centuries nearly all the leaders of the Bajau (Samal) groups among the islands near or dependent on Sulu were Sulu *datu*.[30] During the same period in the Riau archipelago and neighbouring waterways, the leaders of the orang laut were generally men from one of the Malay courts, and

---

[28] See above.

[29] Compare Tomé Pires, *Suma Oriental*, vol. 2, pp. 232ff, a good account, much less widely known than it should be.

[30] The Sulu *datu* were the sons of sultans by concubines, or inferior wives, and their descendants in the male line. In a few cases *datu* appear to have been created by sultans (other than by procreation), but this was not usual. Amirul Mu'minim, one of the best remembered and respected of the sultans among the Sulus, was claimed as their ancestor by the majority of the 19th-century *datu*. On the position of the *datu* among the Samal see Otley Beyer (*Population of Philippine Islands in 1916* [Manila: Philippine Education Co., 1917], p. 67), who wrote, "their rulers are almost without exception Sulu chiefs".

it was, in fact, under the influence of the latter that some of them foresook their normal scavenging habits and became notorious as full-blooded pirates.[31]

The earliest finds on the Johor River take us back only as far as the beginning of the 15th century, or possibly to some time in the latter part of the 14th century.[32] So far as we know the first trading settlements there were roughly contemporary with the last phase of the Singapura of the *Malay Annals*. They might have been founded by refugees, if by any chance Singapura was destroyed shortly before 1400, but it is more likely that they emerged first as trading posts connected with the port during the latter part of its first period of prosperity. So far as Singapura is concerned, we have no reason to doubt the story that it flourished during the 14th century, possibly beginning a little earlier, and that it ceased to be important, for a time at least, round about 1400. The association between the bricks in some of the remains originally on Fort Canning Hill and those in one of the structures at Kota Tinggi, requires careful consideration,[33] and may well be of appreciable significance. But none of this takes us back with certainty before the beginning of the 14th century, nor have there as yet been any archaeological finds in this area which do so. A more precise analysis of the script on the surviving fragments of the Singapore stone[34] might

---

[31] Notoriously the men of Pulau Galang, who even achieved the posthumous honour of mention in a poem by Rudyard Kipling. In Singapore during the 1830s, and the early 40s, it was currently believed that a number of the Malays round the temenggong's court at Telok Blanga were leaders of groups of Bajau freebooters.

[32] See Gibson-Hill, "Johore Lama and Other Ancient Sites on the Johore River", *JMBRAS* 28, 2 (1955): 126–97, esp. 177–94.

[33] *Viator*, "Trip to the Johore River", *Singapore Chronicle*, Aug. 1826, repr. in J.H. Moor, Notices of the Indian Archipelago (Singapore: n.p., 1837), pp. 264–8, esp. 268. Viator is generally assumed to have been John Crawfurd, though there is a possible objection to this identification (see Gibson-Hill, *JMBRAS* 28, 2 [1955]: 128n7). For the association of the bricks, see ibid., pp. 181–3, including the references cited there.

[34] The Singapore stone; see *JMBRAS* 30, 1 (1957) [*sic*]. The stone was situated on the point at the south side of the mouth of the Singapore River. Contemporary accounts by Crawfurd (Jan. 1822) and Tyerman (Sept. 1825) agree in describing it as a large boulder that had been split into two pieces, apparently by natural forces. The two surfaces thus exposed faced each other at an angle, and one, measuring about eight feet by ten, had been smoothed artificially and covered with an inscription in letters approximately 1¼ inches [32mm] high. Unfortunately the surface had weathered badly, and the characters were indecipherable. A number of attempts were made to copy the inscription, of which the most successful was that undertaken by a naval surgeon from HMS *Wolfe* (see *JASB* 6, 2 [1837]: 680–6 and pl. 37). In 1843 the stone was blown up by Captain Stevenson, acting settlement engineer, to clear the ground for the erection of a bungalow, designed by Denis McSwiney to provide quarters for the officer in charge of Fort Fullerton (McSwiney had been clerk of the works under G.D. Coleman prior to July 1841, and the design was almost certainly inspired by the latter's work, an association that probably formed the basis of Munshi 'Abdu'llah's erroneous statement that the stone was destroyed by Coleman). Colonel James Low arrived on the scene immediately after the event and rescued a small number of pieces bearing part of the inscription, one of which is now in the Raffles Museum; the remainder are in the Museum of the Asiatic Society of Bengal in Calcutta, whither they were sent by Low and Colonel Butterworth in 1848–49. From these the late Professor Krom decided that the inscription was in Majapahit Kawi earlier than 1361; but if the Ptolemaic trans-peninsular canal (see below) is significant, the inscription could date as early as the 8th or

possibly put the origin of the settlement back a little further. A cast has recently been made of the piece now in the Raffles Museum, and it has been sent to Leiden for re-examination in the light of information collected from other sources over the last 20 years. Meanwhile, we have Professor Krom's verdict that it was incised in Majapahit Kawi of the form used prior to 1361. This leaves open the possibility that it was cut to commemorate the founding of the settlement, or even the time when the latter came under Majapahit's influence.

We have no information, then, from either the Johor River or the south coast of Singapore Island that can give us a certain date for these settlements earlier than the 14th century.[35] Nor have we any significant local legends or traditions indicating a belief in habitation of the area prior to the founding of Singapura. Indeed we might say that the only suggestion that there was an earlier knowledge of the passageway across from the Karimun Islands to Pedra Branca (and here we definitely say only "knowledge", not regular use), is the river system given to the Malay Peninsula in the *Geographike Huphegesis*.[36] The unknown compiler tells us nothing of the important archipelago lying immediately to the south of the peninsula, and the obvious conclusion is that it is included in the landmass. Such is by no means an uncommon error in the initial stages of the mapping of an area from the sea. The three largest islands in the Andaman group were recorded as one long

---

9th centuries. [E.N.: The forthcoming article indicated for *JMBRAS* (1957) was never published. From the Gibson-Hill papers now preserved in the Asian Civilizations Museum in Singapore, it transpires that Gibson-Hill did receive a paper by Richard Winstedt on the Singapore Stone, and the former discussed it with Linehan (1954–55) and De Josselin de Jong (1956).]

[35] Chinese coins of the 9th and 10th centuries (John Crawfurd, *Journal of an Embassy from the Governor-General of India to the Courts of Siam and Cochin-China*, 2nd ed., 2 vols. [London: Henry Colburn and Richard Bentley, 1830], vol. 1, p. 73), beads from Rome and the Roman Orient (references, Gibson-Hill, "Johor Lama and other Ancient Sites on the Johor River", *JMBRAS* 28, 2 [1955]: 183–5), beer bottle stoppers from Amsterdam, are all too mobile. Particularly beads, compare Tom Harrisson in R. Braddell, "A Note on Sambas and Borneo", *JMBRAS* 22, 4 (1949): 13. They were a common article of trade during at least the first half of the 2nd millenium CE throughout the Indian archipelago (until, apparently, their place was taken by cloths from eastern India), and seemingly formed the principal (or at least the most notable) article worn by the women. For *Hsing-ch'a sheng-lan*, dated 1436, by Fei Hsin, on beads in Pahang, see W.P. Groeneveldt, "Notes on the Malay Archipelago and Malacca", *Miscellaneous Papers relating to Indo-China and the Indian Archipelago*, 2nd ser. 1 (1887): 255: "Men and women have their hair in a knot, and are clad with a single piece of cloth. Girls of rich families wear four or five golden circles on their foreheads, and the daughters of the common people use strings of coloured glass beads instead". It is almost certain that the beads reached the Johor River area by trade from, or a migration of these people. And where there was not migration, in coastal areas there was piracy: and how many young girls when being abducted would have the sense to take off their beads lest they should confuse future archaeologists?

[36] The Greek text of this passage in the *Geographike Huphegesis*, with a translation and comment, is published by Wheatley, "Belated Comments on Sir Roland Braddell's Studies on Ancient Times in the Malay Peninsula", *JMBRAS* 28, 1 (1955): 84ff. It occurs in book 7, ch. 2 of the original work. For a discussion of the texts of the Ptolemaic geography, see Wheatley, "Belated Comments", *JMBRAS* 28, 1 (1955): 78–84. Also L. Bagrow, "The Origin of Ptolemy's Geographia", *Geografiska Annaler* 27, 3–4 (1945): 318–87.

island until after the beginning of the 19th century; a number of the earlier maps of the Malay Peninsula omit the Selat Tebrau (the Johor Strait); and there is much lumping of the islands south of the present Main Strait—though certainly this strait, which was by then an important seaway, is shown as open water. But if we refer the data in the *Geographike Huphegesis* to the 10th or 11th centuries CE,[37] it is by no means impossible that enough was known about the main channels in this region to ascribe them to the delta of "a river greater than Ganges", and not enough to define their true nature. Admittedly this hypothesis does not help us to identify the emporia (Sabana, Palanda and Tharra), but no one seems to have been particularly successful in placing them securely under existing interpretations of the text. And there is certainly a pleasing neatness in equating "the river that rises in the nameless mountains dominating the Golden Chersonese" with the Sungai Johor; the Palandas with the Riau Strait, between Pulau Bintan and Pulau Bulang; and the Krysoanas and the Attabas with the strait running from the Karimun Islands to Pedra Branca. It also saves us the trouble and worry of the Penarikan, and provides the most reasonable explanation for the attempt to fit a version of the Ptolemaic river system into the peninsula itself after direct Portuguese contact had been established with the area and firsthand information about it was becoming available in Europe.[38] Belief in the pattern, dating from before the employment of the waters south of Singapore as an important passageway, lived on strongly; but even the earliest Portuguese navigators found and sailed on a seaway in this region, and so the requirements of the Ptolemaic system had to be met from among the existing rivers further north. Finally, we must note that under this interpretation the latitude for the southern tip of the "peninsula" given in the *Geographike* is substantially correct as it stands.

On Lung-ya-men

There can, of course, have been little chance of the discovery of the channel past Singapore Island at a very early period. It seems reasonably certain that the first contacts between the archipelago and the area now designated as China were formed by the Yüeh traders from the independent kingdoms of Nan-yüeh and Min-yüeh. They must clearly have travelled south via the Philippines and the seaway between Borneo and Celebes, spreading thence eastwards, and west along the south coast of Borneo and across to southern Sumatra. There, on the Pasemah Plateau, they left

---

[37] For a note on the date of the *Geographike Huphegesis*, see Wheatley, "Belated Comments", *JMBRAS* 28, 1 (1955): 78–84, and references given therein. On this and other grounds we would have dated the text rather later, say the 12th to 13th centuries, but this point must be left to classical scholars; the latter, as summarized by Wheatley, give the 10th to 11th centuries as the date of the completion of Ptolemy's work in the form now known to us.

[38] Wheatley, "Belated Comments", *JMBRAS* 28, 1 (1955): 90–5. The whole of this paper, "Belated Comments on Sir Roland Braddell's Studies of Ancient Times in the Malay Peninsula" (pp. 78–98) is a most valuable and well measured contribution to the study of the history of the Malay Peninsula during the 1st millenium CE. For an account of the 16th-century maps showing the trans-peninsular canal, see Wheatley, "A curious feature on maps of Malaya", *Imago Mundi* 2 (1954): 67–72; Wheatley interprets it as a portrayal of the Penarikan route, a point with which we cannot concur, but the data presented are of considerable interest.

perhaps the most extensive tangible evidence of their influence.[39] The first Indians to reach this region must have landed on the west coast of Sumatra and passed into the hills of the Menangkabau and Battak countries, where those who were not summarily eaten introduced at least the broad outlines of the system of matrilineal inheritance found among the ruling castes of Malabar.[40] From the Menangkabau country they must have spread southwards to the Pasemah Plateau, arriving via the summit of Mount Dempo, almost as the *Malay Annals* tell us (when we allow for the exaggeration common to historical romances).[41] Earlier, emigrants from eastern India, sailing from Telingana and later Orissa, had niggled round by way of the northern shores of the Bay of Bengal to reach the Môn country in southern Burma. Others who came later from these regions and from the Coromandel Coast struck out across open water towards the northern part of the Malay Peninsula, and landed (as one would expect) below the Isthmus of Kra and south as far as Kedah. From this area some of them must have journeyed on down the Melaka Strait, keeping to the west side as Marco Polo did. In this way they would pass through the Strait of Sabam, and so reach the Tanah Malayalee, and the groups around Palembang.

Clearly the earliest Indianizing movements further eastwards must have come from the Pasemah-Palembang region, and passed thence by way of the islands to southern Borneo. There, the culture heroes penetrated far up the Kapuas River (the Lawe), and in eastern Borneo reached the middle Kutei, possibly travelling by way of the Barito or Negara, from the region that later became known as Tanjongpura. In South Borneo they founded the river states whose successors survived to the early 16th century as the minor Hindu kingdoms of Tanamasim (Old Sambas), Lawe (the Kapuas River) and Tanjongpura (Tanah Laut and the lower reaches of the Barito River),[42] to be replaced within the next hundred years by the Muslim states of Sambas,

---

[39] See R. von Heine-Geldern, "Prehistoric Research in the Netherlands Indies", in *Science and Scientists in the Netherlands Indies*, ed. P. Honig and F. Verdoorn (New York: Board for the Netherlands Indies, Surinam and Curaçao, 1945), pp. 129–66, esp. 147–53; see also Gibson-Hill, "On the Alleged Death of Sultan Ala'u'd-din of Johore at Acheh in 1613", *JMBRAS* 29, 1 (1956): 125–45. On Pasemah, see A.N.J.Th. van der Hoop, *Megalithic Remains in South Sumatra* (Zutphen: Thieme, 1932), and references in Heine-Geldern, "Prehistoric Research".

[40] See J.R. Logan, "A General Sketch of Sumatra", *JIA* 3 (1849): 343–65, esp. 363–4. See also T.J. Willer, "The Battas of Mandheling and Pertibi", *JIA* 3 (1849): 366–78.

[41] Brown, ed. and trans., *Sejarah Melayu*, pp. 24–8. Rather different versions are given in the Leyden text, revised by T. Braddell in *JIA* 5 (1851): 173–9; and in summary by T.S. Raffles, *History of Java*, 2nd ed., 2 vols. (London: John Murray, 1830), vol. 2, pp. 116–9. See also Gibson-Hill, "On the Alleged Death of Sultan Ala'u'd-din of Johore at Acheh in 1613", *JMBRAS* 29, 1 (1956): 125–45.

[42] For a discussion of these localities, see G.R. Tibbetts, "Early Muslim Traders in South-East Asia", *JMBRAS* 30, 1 (1957): 1–45. They are all late names, extant when the Portuguese first reached the archipelago, though references to Tanjongpura apparently go back to events contemporary with the founding of Singapore; but they can be localized, we have no earlier names from South Borneo that can be determined in this way, and it is clear that Indianization occurred early in that region; accordingly, the names are used here to represent the apparent localities of settlement. Lawe, appearing in Portuguese accounts and early maps as Laoe, Laue, Lave and Lava, seems to have puzzled most commentators, but the name was still used in Raffles' time for the Kapuas River in West Borneo. The original capital of Lawe, which appears

Landak, Sukadana and Banjermasin. From South Borneo, soon after their arrival, colonizing groups must have passed over to Java, probably in greatest numbers in the east, where the link with Tanjongpura appears to have been the strongest of these associations. There may well have been several such lemming-like waves of adventurers; and seemingly there was one as late as the 12th or 13th centuries. They must also have spread up the west coast of Borneo; certainly they got far enough round Tanjong Datu to establish Puchavaram[43] on the east side of Datu Bay. But further than this takes us beyond our immediate concern here. The significant point is that long before the end of the 4th century CE, Indianized groups must certainly have formed trading ports in southern Sumatra and West and South Borneo.

The landings among the Môns in the area south of the Gulf of Martaban were sufficient to produce a new hybrid group, the Talaings. Further south, where the hazards of the crossing were greater, the newcomers apparently arrived in much smaller numbers; and since the areas they reached were much larger, they came, metaphorically, only as unemployed princes. From Lower Burma the immigrants followed the earlier Môn movement over the passes to southwestern Siam. For a time, a confederacy there of (five) petty states, lying in the area between the Tenasserim coast and the Inner Gulf of Siam, flourished under the name Tun-sun.[44] From Tun-sun the contact spread east to the delta of the Mekong, where Funan, a state greater

---

to have been some distance inland, was destroyed by men from Brunei in 1521, after which its place was apparently taken by Landak, seemingly on the river of that name, and then by Sukadana, which was the important centre in this area during the 17th century. Tanjongpura was in the neighbourhood of the present Banjermasin: it was still the most important centre in South Borneo in Pires' time, but during the 16th century it was superseded by Banjermasin. Indian inscriptions dating from the 4th century have been reported from some distance up the Kapuas and Kutei rivers.

[43] Puchavaram was apparently situated somewhere in or inland from Datu Bay. From the photographs published by Tom Harrisson in "Gold and Indian Influences in West Borneo", *JMBRAS* 22, 4 (1949): 33–110, it might appear that Santubong was the port for Puchavaram, but since then we have heard little of Indian material from this region; and it is not clear how much, if any, investigation has been undertaken along the east side of the bay. Nonetheless, there can be little doubt that there was an Indianized settlement in the area at one time, possibly destroyed (as non-Muslim) by Brunei shortly before the Portuguese arrived. The name appears on a number of early maps, and then drops out before one can pin it down.

[44] *Tun-sun*. The Chinese notices on Tun-sun have been collected and edited by Wheatley, "The Malay Peninsula as known to the Chinese in the Third Century A.D.", *JMBRAS* 28, 1 (1955): 1–9. For an analysis of this and other data relating to the kingdom, and leading to the identification of the site occupied, see Gibson-Hill, "A Critical Examination of the Kingdom of Tun-Sun", *JMBRAS* 28, 1 (1955): 157–93. It must have occupied the most northerly section of the Malay Peninsula, from about 11° north latitude northwards to a little above the latitude of Tavoy, and thence eastwards as far as the west bank of the Menam. It was apparently founded in the 1st century CE, and declined in importance from the latter part of the 3rd century. It flourished again as a Buddhist kingdom under the name "Lanka-Açoka" (Langkasuka) at the beginning of the 6th century, but was later absorbed in the growing power of Dvaravati. Subsequently, the name "Langkasuka" was born by another kingdom on the east coast of the Malay Peninsula, further south, in the region of Singgora and Patani (see Wheatley, "Langkasuka", *T'oung Pao* 44, 4–5 [1957]: 387–412; and Gibson-Hill, cited above, appendix B).

than Tun-sun, rose to power; a state, moreover, that was nearer to China and large enough to attract attention.

The Yüeh voyages down through the islands to the Makassar Sea and beyond it to the northern shores of the Java Sea may not have ceased completely at this stage. It is possible that the Guores from Liu Kiu, whom d'Albuquerque, Tomé Pires, Duarte Barbosa and Barros mention as sending two or three junks a year to Melaka early in the 16th century, were the last of their line.[45] But their trafficking southwards was clearly no longer of much importance by the beginning of the 2nd century CE, and when in the 3rd century, the kingdom of Wu looked again for contact with the barbarians of the Southern Ocean, the envoys were sent round the coast of Annam and Champa to Funan.

Deep-water traders have a marked, and by no means unreasonable, preference for sailing from point to point. To the natural seamen, as rare as poets, "all shores of the earth are but as doors of an inn", and they seek

> Only a wider sea; room for the winds to blow,
> And a world to wander in.[46]

But the sea trader, the rag-and-bone man of the open waters, demands a port at his journey's end: he traffics for profit, and if there is a spark of fire left in the tepid spirit coursing his bloated flesh, he only adds wine and women to spend it on. When seaborne trade began between China and the west, and between India and the archipelago, the deep-water traffic inevitably appeared first between established centres. And the details of the route were determined as much by their quality as by the ease of the sea passages, which could never be free of an element of uncertainty and risk. Progress was slow, the boats were ill found, and space was limited for men and stores. An intermediate port was essential, on any count. Even more, it appears that initially the traffic was carried on by men from the region of the intermediate ports, the centres in West Borneo and southern Sumatra communicating with both India and China, until finally there was a through traffic. At first it was in the hands of the Kun-lun sailors; later, once the practice was established, it was broached by the Arabs passing eastwards from India and finally by the Chinese themselves.

The monsoons, the seasonal set of winds and currents in a changing cycle through the year, favour western Borneo as the area for the half-way ports, and thereafter the southern fringe of the Riau-Lingga group, where Sabana, Thana and Palanda must have lain (though seemingly under rather different names). From here, connections passed easily to the south Sumatran ports—where in Palembang a strong Buddhist centre grew up—but the latter were not so conveniently placed as stages on the main route. In a matter of deep-water traffic this point should have proved the deciding factor, but almost habitually man's urge to save his soul is second only to his desire to save his skin, and so Palembang rose to prominence, first as a religious centre and later for its wealth and local entrepôt trade. But whether the port were Palembang or an estuary in western Borneo, the course must have lain along the

---

[45] See also above.

[46] Laurence Binyon, *The Sirens: An Ode* (London: Macmillan & Co. Ltd., 1925).

east coast of Sumatra, with the east-west run through the Berhala or Dempo Straits. In neither case would there be any incentive to seek out the Singapore Strait, nor under these conditions there could have been little through traffic for it. It was not possible for a vessel to run profitably or safely from southern India to the China coast without a break, a rest for the boat while the strained lashings were tightened and leaking seams re-plugged, and a rest for the men while fresh supplies of water and food were taken on board:[47] all this, apart, of course, from the added profits to be derived from bartering en route.

The Singapore channel became of value when it was possible to cut out the jungle-girt ports of western Borneo and Palembang, affluent and powerful but tediously placed. It became of potential value as soon as trading ports were developed in north Sumatra and in the region of Junk Seylon (Jungceylon).[48] Then, an altered rhythm was possible, with the break in the voyage no longer at its southern angle but at the end of the run across the eastern Indian Ocean. In terms of time, this point was reached when the Arab hold on the China trade weakened and Chinese seamen entered increasingly into competition with them, seemingly from about the 9th century onwards. Logically, at any point after this, the China traffic could have passed through the Singapore Strait. But apparently the Chinese themselves were very interested in the products of the Palembang entrepôt trade,[49] and there is no

[47] It is clear that Kun-lun, Arab, Po-sse (Po-ssu), and Indian boats had a dugout base, with the freeboard increased by planks fitted and then lashed together by coir (coconut fibre), or in some cases *ijau*-fibre ropes. No metal was used in their construction, and trenails were seldom employed. They lacked a complete deck and were powered by one or two rectangular sails of pandanus matting or coarse cotton cloth. Except for the Chinese junks and the later junks of the East Indies, these conditions prevailed until after the arrival of the Portuguese in India. In parts, they prevailed until the 17th century at least. For accounts of voyages in vessels of this kind, at different periods, see, inter alia, *The Travels of Fa-hsien or Records of the Buddhist Kingdoms*, ed. and trans. H.A. Giles (Cambridge: Cambridge University Press, 1923), pp. 77–80; anon., ca. 919, from Buzurg, quoted by Hourani, *Arab Seafaring* (Princeton: Princeton University Press, 1951), pp. 118–20; *A Narrative of the Voyage of Abd-er-Razzak, Ambassador of Shah Rukh*, 1st ser., no. 22 (London: Hakluyt Society, 1858), pp. 45–9; Cæsar Frederike, ca. 1567, in *Purchas His Pilgrimes* (1625), IL.II.X, 1710–1.

[48] In spite of the eloquent pleading of Sir Roland Braddell, who summarizes the available data admirably ("Notes on Ancient Times in Malaya", *JMBRAS* 23, 1 [1950]: 21–6), we think that Kalah (Kilah) of the Arab accounts from the 10th century onwards is more likely to have been Jungceylon (Junk Seylon) than Kedah. Certainly some of the descriptions which he cites could not have applied to Kedah; and at the same time they are surprisingly similar to the early European notices of Jungceylon. Above all, when has there ever been a tin mine in Kedah? Kedah tin was tin brought overland from Patani.

[49] It was indeed some of the articles about the Palembang entrepôt trade which interested them as much as anything; birds' nests, "kingfisher" feathers, rhinoceros horn, "cranes crest" (hornbill casques), semi-precious stones, etc. See Groeneveldt, "Notes", pp. 185–201. Friedrich Hirth and W.W. Rockhill, trans. and annot., *Chau Ju-kua: His Work on the Chinese and Arab Trade in the Twelfth and Thirteenth Centuries, entitled Chu-fan-chï* (St Petersburg: Imperial Russian Academy of Sciences, 1911), passim; Rockhill, "Notes on the Relations and Trade of China with the Eastern Archipelago during the Fourteenth Century", *T'oung Pao* 15, 3 (1914): 419–47; ibid., 16 (1915): passim.

evidence suggesting that they used the shorter route prior to the era when Palembang began to lose its predominant position in the western half of the archipelago. The 13th century, in fact, appears to be the period when the change came.

In spite of the labour that has been expended analysing it, one cannot honestly say that Marco Polo's route has been established with reasonable certainty. He may have passed through the Singapore Strait, or he may not. There is most certainly no inevitability about his Pentam being Pulau Bintan; and the best grounds for equating it with Bintan would be to make a passage through the Singapore Strait possible.[50] This apart, Polo's Pentam could as well have been Friar Odoric's Panten, if we are to play with sounds;[51] in which case it was also Thalamasyn, and thus in western Borneo, and Lochac or Locac was up towards the northern end of the northwest coast—possibly even connected with Wan-lai and Ki-li-man, which "in ancient times" constituted the kingdom of Po'lo.[52] But on this topic, inevitably, we still come out by the same door as in we went. Fortunately one significant point is clear without argument: Marco Polo most certainly did not travel via Palembang, and his personal knowledge of Sumatra was confined to its northern end.

The good Friar Odoric,[53] 25 years later, went from Lambri, in northern Sumatra, to Thalamasyn (Tanamasim) in West Borneo, and thence to Champa, where the king kept many women and 14,000 tame elephants.[54] Ibn Battuta, following him

---

[50] Ramusio and the older Latin editions (such as Miller's), say that the fleet passed "between the kingdom of Locac and the island of Pentan", which would be the Singapore channel, if Locae (Lochac) = Malay Peninsula, and Pentan (Pentam) = Bintan. Part of the problem is that the Bintan of Raffles MS no. 18 of the *Malay Annals* might not originally have been Bintan. The version quoted by Raffles, *History of Java*, pp. 116–9, suggests a settlement on Lingga. Why was the present Pulau Bintan so important at this stage? Lingga, yes; but the importance of Bintan came after the establishment of Singapore.

[51] The travels of Friar Odoric of Pordenone; see H. Yule, *Cathay and the Way Thither*, 2nd ed., rev. by H. Cordier, 4 vols. (London: Hakluyt Society, 1913–16), vol. 2 (2nd ser., no. 33), pp. 155–63 (of the land called "Thalamasyn", and of the trees that give flour and other marvels). Yule suggests Banjermasin for Thalamasyn, but we know that Tanjongpura was in that neighbourhood. A number of maps show Tamenasim or Tamenaserim, or variants of that name in the region of Old Sambas.

[52] J.W. Laidlay, "Notice of a Chinese Geographical Work [Dated 1731]", *JASB* 18, 1 (1849): 137–64, esp. 150–1. Wan lai = Brunei, Ki-li-man = North Borneo. The same author notes Kinabalu as the "Great Hill of Si li".

[53] Friar Odoric's voyage from India to China; see Yule, *Cathay and the Way Thither*, vol. 2, pp. 146–76. He also mentions Samudra, Rejang and Java, but he does not say that he visited them (compare with the case of Tibet, on his return journey): he does, however, refer to being at Lambri, Thalamasyn and Champa, as well as giving rather better notices of these places. He also puts in a muddled passage about the Andamans, Nicobar Islands and Ceylon (Sri Lanka), after leaving Champa, but this may be due to a sheet having been displaced in the original manuscript.

[54] He also saw in that country a tortoise with a shell higger in compass than the dome of St Anthony's church in Padua (in Yule, *Cathay and the Way Thither*, vol. 2, pp. 165–6). Thomas Bowrey, writing of the viceroy of the king of Golconda, says "Hee keeps many Stately Elephants, and a huge number of Concubines, which are the 2 Chiefe pieces of State Esteemed on amonge the Inhahitants of Asia" (Thomas Bowrey, *The Countries around the Bay of Bengal*, ed. R.C.

eastwards, went to Samudra, then to an uncertain point probably somewhere near Aru or Kampar, and finally to the port of Kailukari, in Tawalisi,[55] The latter is clearly Champa again, though Ibn Battuta, believing himself at last beyond the reach of the pedantic, here adds an account of an imaginery warlike female ruler who knew no Arabic but the name of Allah. To add to the glamour of her city, a thick mist is said to have engulfed the vessel on the return journey before they reached Champa, so that the sailors knew not on what sea they travelled, and a *rukh*[56] as large as a volcano rose up before them. One point, however, stands out clearly; none of these three men give any indication that they sailed via Palembang; and by now we are beyond the stage when, refreshingly unequivocal after all that has gone before, we have the first Chinese record of a voyage through the Singapore Strait.

When we turn further to the Chinese accounts of the islands of the Southern Ocean, we find an undoubted reference to the Keppel Harbour strait under the designation Lung-ya-men in the *Tao-i chih-lüeh* of 1349. Its author, Wang Ta-yüan, "visited for the purposes of trade a considerable number of foreign localities during the Chih-ch'êng period of the Yuan (1341–67), and recorded what he had seen in this work".[57] Rockhill gives a translation of the complete passage on Lung-ya-men, the main points of which can be summarized as follows: the strait was bordered by

---

Temple, 2nd ser., no. 12 [London: Hakluyt Society, 1903]: 125). And Marco Polo, of Kail, in Tinnevelly, "This King has some 300 wives; for in those parts the man who has most wives is most thought of" (H. Yule, ed., *The Book of Ser Marco Polo Venetian*, 3rd ed., rev. by H. Cordier, 2 vols. [London: John Murray, 1926], vol. 2, p. 371).

[55] The travels of Ibn Battuta; see Yule, *Cathay and the Way Thither*. After leaving *Samudra*, Ibn Battuta sailed for 21 days along the coasts of the country, and then arrived at Mul-Jawa, a region inhabited by pagans, which had an extent of some two months' journey, and produced excellent aromatics, especially the aloes-wood of Kakula and Kamara, places which were both in Mul-Jawa. Yule suggests that Mul-Jawa should be the Malay Peninsula, but if Ibn Battuta travelled only along the coast from Samudra, it must be somewhere on the east side of Sumatra (or the whole of Sumatra). Kakula was a fine city with a wall of hewn stone wide enough to admit the passage of three elephants abreast—but nothing like that has come to light anywhere in this region. Tawalisi was 71 days from Kakula, 37 of which lay through the Calm Sea, where "The boats were brought into play to tow the ship, and the great sweeps of the junk were pulled likewise". Tawalisi was only 17 days from China. On the return journey they sailed for ten days with a fair wind, and were then near Tawalisi again, when the storm came up. Finally, two months out from China, they reached Samudra, this time without having put in at any intermediate port. For the identification of Tawalisi, see T. Yamamoto, "On Tawalisi described by Ibn Battuta", *Memoirs of the Toyo Bunko* 8 (1936): 93–133.

[56] On the *rukh*, see the adventures of Sinbad. The archipelago appears to have been the legitimate habitat of the rukh, before increasing knowledge of the Malayan region localised it in the neighbourhood of Madagascar. Yule (*Book of Ser Marco Polo*, vol. 2, pp. 415–6) suggests that the Garuda of the Hindus, the Simurgh of the old Persians, the 'Angka of the Arabs, the Bar Yuchre of the Rabbinical legends and the Gryps of the Greeks were all versions of the same original fable. And to reassure travellers in our day quotes the Arabic proverb from Bochart, "Good Faith, the Ghul and the Gryphon [*'Angka*] are three names of things that exist nowhere." In the present instance, the rukh was probably Pulau Tioman, or possibly Pulau Lingga.

[57] Rockhill, "Notes", *T'oung Pao* 16, 1 (1915): 129–32.

two hills of the Tan-ma-hsi barbarians, which looked like dragons' teeth,[58] with a waterway between them; the people were addicted to piracy, and themselves produced nothing of value; all that they had for barter being stuff that they had pillaged from the Ch'üan-chou (Fukien) traders returning home. Wang Ta-yüan also tells a story of the chief having found a jewelled cap, buried in the ground, which he wore on New Year's day, together with his ceremonial robes, when he received the homage of his people. The anecdote is interesting and worth considering in other contexts. We do not suggest that it is an attempt to relate the story of the loss of Sri Buana's crown at Telok Blanga (in Keppel Harbour) as it is told in the *Malay Annals*,[59] but it seems likely that there was a common belief underlying the two accounts that have not come down to us. So far as the pillaging is concerned, we may remark that it apparently occurred only on the homeward journey: the Chinese junks were not molested when outward bound. The three successive rulers of Melaka, the Malays, Portuguese and Dutch, all tried to collect dues from vessels passing up the strait, as though they owned the whole waterway, and not only their own harbour. With this, and the apparent paucity of trade goods, we must clearly bear in mind the probability that Singapura was not founded as a trading centre, but as a station to collect tolls from passing shipping—officially or unofficially.

As we have said, Wang Ta-yüan's notice of Keppel Harbour dates from the middle of the 14th century, roughly 55 years after Marco Polo's voyage to the west via Lochac, Pentam and northern Sumatra. A shorter but somewhat similar account appears in the *Hsing-ch'a sheng-lan* of Fei Hsin, dated 1436.[60] Fei Hsin accompanied

---

[58] The important point about the accounts of passages through Keppel Harbour is that they place the course between the hills like dragons' teeth, or between the dragons' teeth. It is suggested that the term referred to the pillar rocks formerly at the western entrance to the waterway, on the grounds that these were faintly reminiscent of the two vertical pegs at the bow of a junk through which the anchor cable runs, and to which the same name is given. Early references to Ling-ya-men (not Lung-ya-men) must be to the modern Berhala Strait, the passageway south of Lingga, or to Lingga itself (compare Hirth and Rockhill, *Chau Ju-kua*: *Chu-fan-chi* [1225], pp. 60, 220), but there was scope for confusion, because Lingga has two prominences at the south end which seen from some directions appear to stick up like the horns of a dragon, as in the case of the two rocky pinnacles on Tioman (the Chulia Naga): the south end of Lingga, and later Tioman, must have been important sailing marks in their time. Braddel says there is no such waterway as the Straits of Lingga: this name was employed for the Dempo Strait in the latter part of the 18th and early 19th centuries, at least.

The characters for Tan-ma-hsi, Ling-ya-men and Lung-ya-men are as follows:
Tan-ma-hsi 單馬錫 and 淡馬錫;
Ling-ya-men 凌牙門;
Lung-ya-men 龍牙門.

[59] Brown, ed. and trans., "Malay Annals", p. 30.

[60] In Groeneveldt, "Notes", p. 203. Here the passage is erroneously attributed, by Groeneveldt, to the island of Lingga, possibly because of its opening phrase; Lung-ya-men (the "Dragons' Teeth Strait") is situated to the northwest of San-bo-tsai (Palembang); but it continues, high mountains face each other as the teeth of a dragon, and between these the ships must pass, which is clearly correct for Lung-ya-men; the Keppel Harbour Strait. "Northwest of Palembang"

the Grand Eunuch Ho on several of his voyages (1405–33),[61] but much of his work was taken from the *Tao-i chih-lüeh* of Wang Ta-yüan. It is probable that his account of Keppel Harbour was derived in this way; but surely, if he did thus make use of the earlier work, it can safely be assumed that he regarded the passages which he plagiarised as a fair enough description of the locality? He uses the same name Lung-ya-men for the strait, and refers to the vessels passing through a waterway between two hills that looked like dragons' teeth, a point which certainly could not apply to any other channel in this neighbourhood. Fei Hsin adds:[62]

> The soil is barren and yields only little rice; the climate is warm, and in the fourth and fifth months there are heavy rains. Men and women have their hair in a knot, and wear a short jacket with a sarong of striped stuff. They chiefly live from piracy, and when they see native vessels they go out with many hundreds of small boats to attack them; when there is a favourable wind these ships may escape, but otherwise they are plundered and the crew killed. Therefore ships are very careful in this neighbourhood.

On six of the seven voyages, Cheng Ho's fleet passed from the South China Sea to Java or Palembang, from the necessity of visiting these places, and thereafter it must have reached the Melaka Strait by way of the Straits of Bangka and Kundur (the Estreito Sabam of Portuguese accounts). But he probably passed directly into the Melaka Strait (via the Singapore channel) outward bound on the sixth voyage (1421–22); in addition, his ships may well have used this route on the return run on any of the missions except the first, and certainly he must have sailed that way homeward bound from the seventh (last) voyage in 1433.[63] Moreover, in the much-discussed *Wu pei chih* charts,[64] we have definite and unequivocable sailing directions

---

is a little confusing, but when we remember that the passage would have been made through the Selat Kundur, the first leg would have been almost northwest, from the north end of the Bangka Strait.

[61] Seven voyages were undertaken between 1405 and 1433 under the direction of the Grand Eunuch Cheng Ho, but it appears that he did not go on all of them, and on one or two occasions the fleet appears to have split, part going to one place and part to another. See J.J.L. Duyvendak, "The True Dates of the Chinese Maritime Expeditions in the Early Fifteenth Century", *T'oung Pao* 34 (1939): 341–62; Duyvendak, "China's Discovery of Africa" (London: Arthur Propsthian, 1949); and J.V. Mills, "Notes on Early Chinese Voyages", *JRAS* 1–2 (1951): 3–25, esp. 14–23.

[62] Translated in Groeneveldt, "Notes", p. 203. See also above.

[63] J.V. Mills, "Notes on Early Chinese Voyages", *JRAS* 1–2 (1951): 21–3. The fleet left *Samudra* on 1 May and reached Melaka on 9 May after a good passage down the strait (Aceh to Melaka could take anything up to three weeks). We are not told when Cheng Ho left Melaka, but he reached the K'un-lun Sea (the southern part of the South China Sea) on 28 May and Ch'ih K'an (Cape St James, near Saigon) on 10 June—roughly 650 miles [1046km] in 12 days, or an average of just over 2 knots [3.7km/h] over the whole run.

[64] Published in the *Wu pei chih*, by Mao Yüan-yi, vol. 64, ch. 240; see notes on military [preparation and selection] from sea voyages. The preface of this work is dated 1621, but it was not offered to the throne until 1629, and so it cannot have been printed before the latter year, at the earliest. The author was a grandson of a certain Mao K'un, who lived from 1511 to 1601, and collaborated with Hu Tsung-hsien, an expert on coast defence. Seemingly, therefore, the

for a course through the Singapore channel, from the vicinity of the Karimun Islands to Pedra Branca; and, in spite of J.V. Mills'[65] courageous though misguided attempt to interpret this as a passage through the Singapore Main Strait, the route therein laid down most certainly ran through Keppel Harbour. The sailing directions given in the relevant sections of the *Wu pei chih* charts translate as follows:[66]

> From *chi-li-men* [the Karimun Islands] following a course of *yi ch'en* [105°, 120°] and then of exactly *ch'en* [120°] the ship after five watches makes *ch'ang-yao-hsu* [Long-waist Island] and passes out through *lung-ya-men* [Dragons' Teeth Strait]. In lung-ya-men following a course of *chia-mao* [75°, 90°] the ship after five watches makes *pai-chiao* [White Rock, that is, Pedra Branca].

The characters used for Lung-ya-men here are the same as for the two previous accounts (see above). We may also draw attention again to the rutter for a voyage from Melaka to Macau noted by Rodrigues, which Armando Cortesão says he probably obtained from a Chinese pilot; there the directions run "and from Karimun to *syngapura* it is five [*jaos*], and from *syngapura* to Pedra Branca five";[67] we have no reason to doubt that this passage was through the Keppel Harbour strait, as there is no evidence that the Portuguese, or anyone else at that time, were aware of any other route.

There are in addition certain technical objections to Mills's analysis of this section of the route, including his interpretation of the double compass bearings, his decision that variation could safely be ignored at all stages, and his acceptance of varying speeds for the two legs of the passage. Unfortunately, this matter cannot be dealt with briefly, as a more correct reading of the bearings given in the rutter leaves us with a course that cannot be fitted to either route: possibly a character has been left out; the addition of a further *chia* [that is, a course of 75°) at the beginning, immediately after leaving the vicinity of the Karimun Islands, together with an allowance for variation, gives us a simplified form of the route through Keppel Harbour laid down by Linschoten. We hope to be able to analyse the routes in this area given in the *Wu pei chih* charts more fully on another occasion—particularly as the tracings published by Mills in all cases omit the lower half of each sheet, and thus leave out the passage through the Selat Kundur (the Strait of Sabam) and others

---

charts formed part of the geographical material collected by Hu Tsung-hsien's circle, and must be held to date at least from the second or third quarter of the 16th century; see Duyvendak, "Ma Huan Re-examined", *Verhandelingen der Koninklijke Akademie van Wetenschappen te Amsterdam, Afd. Letterkunde* 32, 3 [1933]: 17–22; and W.Z. Mulder, "The *Wu Pei Chih* Chart", *T'oung Pao* 37 (1942): 1–14. The introductory note to the maps concludes with the statement that his (Cheng Ho's) maps record carefully and correctly the distances of the routes and the various countries, and that they have been inserted for the information of posterity and as a memorial of (his) military achievements. On the strength of this it is generally accepted that the *Wu pei chih* charts show the routes of Cheng Ho's various expeditions, and accordingly depict the courses followed in the first half of the 15th century. A copy of the *Wu pei chih* charts, re-cut and showing some small variations. was also included in the later *Wu pei shu* [Records of military affairs] and the *Hai-yün yao-lüeh* [An epitome of sea transport].

[65] J.V. Mills, "Malaya in the *Wu-pei-chih* Charts", *JMBRAS* 15, 3 (1937): 1–52.

[66] Ibid., p. 21.

[67] See above.

further south. Meanwhile, for this reason, and in view of the scarcity of the originals, we reproduce here the three sheets covering the passage past Singapore Island, joined together to form a continuous run: they have been copied photographically from an edition of the original work in the Library of the University of Malaya.[68]

Apart from the question of the points noted above, we must remember that the description given by Fei Hsin could only apply to a passage through Keppel Harbour; and to assert that he lifted it from the *Tao-i chih-lüeh* of Wang Ta-yüan can scarcely be said to meet this objection. There is no doubt that Fei Hsin accompanied Cheng Ho's later expeditions, including the last one. He must, therefore, have passed through the strait taken by Cheng Ho in this region, and he would scarcely have made use thereafter of an account that he knew to be grievously inaccurate, as Wang Ta-yüan's notes become when applied to the Main Strait. Much of Ralph Fitch's account of Pegu is clearly derived from the narrative published by Cæsar Frederike,[69] who visited Lower Burma some 20 years earlier. Here again we know that Fitch did reach the area (and even brought back with him some of the famous bells); we find moreover that all the sections wherein he summarised Frederike's work in his own journal cover matters which Fitch would have known or could well have believed, to be true. He paraphrases, as many occasional writers do, statements he would have been fully prepared to make himself. There seems no reason why the same point should not apply to Fei Hsin.

There are, of course, still other objections to the interpretation of the course given in the *Wu pei chih* charts as a passage through the Singapore Main Strait. They are themselves sufficient to raise serious doubts, even if the directions as printed did fit such a passage.[70] We must remember that the Main Strait was the preference of masters of deep-water European sailing vessels, particularly from the 18th century

[68] *Wu pei chih*, by Mao Yüan-yi, vol. 64, ch. 240, and fols. 15 recto–16 recto. See also above. [E.N.: These reproductions have been taken over from the original publication.]

[69] "In the yeere of our Lord God 1563, I Cæsar Frederike being in Venice, and very desirous to see the East parts of the World, tooke my journey to Alepo"; "Extracts of Master Cæsar Frederike his eighteene yeeres Indian Observations", in *Purchas His Pilgrimes* (1625), II.X.1702–22 (repr., 1905, vol. 10, pp. 88–143). "In the yeere of our Lorde 1583, I Ralph Fitch of London, Merchant, being desirous to see the Countries of the East Indie ... did ship my selfe in a Ship of London called the Tygre, wherein wee went for Tripolis in Syria: and from thence wee tooke the way for Alepo" ("The Voyage of Master Ralph Fitch, Merchant of London, to Ormus, and so to Goa in the East India ...", in Purchas, *Pilgrimes* (1625), II.X.1730–44 (and repr. [1905], vol. 10, pp. 165–204).

[70] We must not, of course, forget that the *Wu pei chih* charts were not printed for the first time until 1629, or later, and by then some of the European shipping reaching the Canton River, or the Philippines, was probably using the Main Strait. We do not suggest that Chinese vessels were then travelling by that route, but rutters could easily have been available in Canton based on courses along it. As the figures in the sailing directions on the chart stand, they are not, when properly interpreted, correct for any possible course. We have already suggested that with the addition of a *chia* (75°) on leaving the Karimun Islands, when proper allowance is made for variation, we get a rough approximation to the route through Keppel Harbour laid down by Linschoten. In making this point, we had in view an accidental omission of the character. But it is possible also that an attempt was made to doctor the figures in the MS to bring them into line with what was taken to be the current route.

14.4 William Dampier on a small open *perahu* on his way to Aceh illustrated by Caspar Luyken. William Dampier, *A New Voyage Round the World.* Den Haag: Abraham de Hondt, 1698, dl. I, p. 358. Rijksmuseum, Amsterdam. RP-P-1896-A-19368-1317.

onwards. Prior to that time—all through the 17th century—a considerable number of passages were clearly made via Keppel Harbour, even after the existence of the Main Strait was widely known. The strait offered great value to fullrigged vessels requiring plenty of sea room, which they were well able to use beating up against a contrary wind whenever there was occasion for it. The disadvantages were the greater depth, which made anchoring impossible for ill-equipped vessels with short cables (and inefficient windlasses, which was partly the reason for the short cables), and the numerous eddies and tide swells which such a vessel would normally have countered by anchoring or warping. Moreover, as Dampier's passage homeward bound on the *Swan* in 1688 shows, it was not a very easy strait to pick out, before the erection of Raffles Light. The old route through Keppel Harbour (in its original condition) was undoubtedly a much safer and surer route for Chinese junks provided with sweeps (as apparently the majority were until well into the 19th century).[71] On the other hand,

[71] See also the account by Ibn Battuta, who travelled to China by sea in the second quarter of the 14th century: "The boats were brought into play to tow the ship, and the great sweeps of the junk were pulled likewise" (Yule, *Cathay*, vol. 2, p. 473). "And aboard these ships, you must know, when there is no wind they use sweeps, and these sweeps are so big, that to pull them requires four mariners to each. Every great ship has certain large barks or tenders attached

of course, it would certainly have been very dangerous and troublesome for a large square-rigged vessel, and she would have had to be warped through the passage—a tedious procedure which was not popular with European crews, who learned to express their resentment at an earlier period than their counterparts on Chinese boats.

To these points we must add the fact that discovery of the Keppel Harbour strait must unquestionably have predated discovery of the Main Strait. The former is the route described by Wang Ta-yüan in the 14th century, and it was the only route used and known in the 16th century, prior to Sultan Ali Jalla's pleasant little jest in trying to block the Keppel Harbour passage.[72] Even then, the fact that he did make such an attempt is a good indication that he firmly believed that the junks from the Moluccas and China could not pass through any other route. If he or anyone around him had known how to follow a course through the Main Strait, he would have realized that he was wasting his time—and worse: he had a better chance of waylaying vessels in Keppel Harbour than in the open strait; if pilots could follow either passage, he did himself more harm than good by shutting the mice out of the only place where he could set an effective trap. Furthermore, it seems highly probable that the *Wu pei chih* charts were not an original work by Cheng Ho: they must almost certainly have been adapted from Arabic originals (or an Arabic original);[73] and if that is so, they represent the general maritime practice of the period. If Cheng Ho alone had found out the Main Strait, used it, and kept the information to himself, we could understand the subsequent sequence of events. But if his pilots followed the accepted course, the Main Strait must have been in common use during the early part of the 15th century. That is clearly impossible. As we have said, it never was, and never could have been, the preferred practice of the masters of the shallow-draft, beamy, full-bottomed craft of that period, and if it had been, knowledge of it could not have faded away completely by the beginning of the 16th century. Knowledge of the Keppel Harbour passageway never disappeared to this extent: it only came to pass that European ships' masters knew nothing of it, because it had long been out of use among them. But native craft were still using it, and the first edition of "Horsburgh's Directory" (1811) contains information from Robert Scott of Penang

---

to it … and they are likewise moved by oars; they assist the great ship by towing her, at such times as her sweeps are in use". Marco Polo, on the large ships of southern China (Yule, *The Book of Ser Marco Polo*, vol. 2, p. 250). According to J.R. Logan, commenting on the second passage in Marsden's translation, in the late 1840s the junks then visiting Singapore still carried sweeps for use in calm weather (J.R. Logan, "Antiquity of Chinese Trade with India and the Indian Archipelago", *JIA* 2 [1848]: 607). It is possible that the sketches by European travellers, which apparently show junks fitted with sweeps on the quarter for steering, represent erroneous interpretations of the sweeps used for helping the vessel forward, in calm weather or in port. We have no reason to think that the Chinese ever employed steering paddles on deep-water junks, and as we have already shown ("Further Notes on the Old Boat found at Pontian, Southern Pahang", *JMBRAS* 25, 1 [1952]: 111–33, esp. 126–8) a bas-relief showing a *wang-kang* on the Bayon at Angkor, dated ca. 1200, indicates clearly that the Chinese form of the central rudder as we know it today was already in use at this time.

72 See below.

73 P. Pelliot, "Les grandes voyages maritimes Chinois au début du XV siècle", *T'oung Pao* 30 (1933): 231–65; see esp. p. 268.

to the effect that he had been through it in a Bugis *perahu* and considered it too narrow for square-rigged vessels to sail through in safety, which was fair enough.

Finally, we may add that the important thing here about the passage given in the *Wu pei chih* charts is that they unquestionably cover a run from the Karimun Islands to Pedra Branca (Chi-li-men to White Rock). To a large extent so far as the present argument is concerned, the exact course is immaterial. We have made the points given above to keep the history of Keppel Harbour itself in full order. But the significant detail that we have to consider here is that use of the run past Singapore apparently began about the beginning of the 14th century, and that it was a fully accepted course from the 15th century onwards. Thus, we find that known use of the Keppel Harbour channel dates from about the time of the founding of the old settlement of Singapore. Which, in fact, almost certainly means, as we have suggested above, that Singapura was established when pilots began to make regular use of the waterway between Pedra Branca and the Karimun Islands.

In a review of the rulers of Singapura, Dr Linehan suggests that the settlement was established in the year 1299.[74] In effect, he obtains this date by working backwards from later ones that can be accepted with reasonable certainty, but his date for the foundation of Singapura rests on the unsupported testimony of the *Malay Annals*, and depends on Sri Tri Buana having reigned for 48 years. As he can scarcely have been less than 20 or 25 years old when he first reached Temasek (which he renamed Singapura), 48 years seems a little too long. If, at the same time the list is not complete, the interval could have been longer. For the present, it is probably safer to take the date of the establishment of the first ruler at Singapura as "about the year 1300".

According to Raffles MS no. 18 of the *Malay Annals*, the founder of the settlement was one of three brothers who appeared suddenly on the slopes of Mount Dempo under miraculous circumstances.[75] Two of the brothers were carried off to rule the peoples of Menangkabau and Tanjongpura (southeast, not southwest, Borneo),[76] while the third ruled for a time at Palembang, then went to Bintan, and finally reached the island of Temasek. Thus, if we strip the story of its impossible elements, we have a prince reaching the north shore of the Singapore Strait via Palembang and Bintan around 1300 and there founding a small city-state. Is this probable? And if so, from where did he get the *Singha* in Singapura?[77] According to the *Malay Annals* a strange beast ambled across the plain of Kuala Temasek[78] while the prince and his party were viewing the landscape speculatively. His chief minister recognized it,with

[74] W. Linehan, "Notes on the Text of the Malay Annals", *JMBRAS* 20, 2 (1947): 117–27.

[75] Brown, ed. and trans., *Malay Annals*, pp. 24–6.

[76] See Gibson-Hill, "The Malay Annals; the History Brought from Goa", *JMBRAS* 29, 1 (1956): 185–8.

[77] The spelling should, correctly, be *Singha-pura*, but we have employed *Singa-pura* here because it is much more general in use and lies nearer to the modern form *Singapore*.

[78] The plain of *Kuala Temasek* must have begun about where Empress Place is now situated, and stretched from there towards the present *padang*. The area on the south side of the river was uneven and marshy until 1823/24, when Crawfurd honoured Raffles' pledge that a small hillock should be dug up and the soil used to fill in neighbouring hollows.

diffidence, as a "lion", an animal that he said was formerly known in his country. It cannot, of course, have been an example of *Felis leo*, as accepted by zoologists; but if the original Indianizing element in these peoples was from Orissa or elsewhere in southern India, their descendents could still have been relaying traditional stories of lions, and at least one of the Orissa dynasties was very partial to peculiar "lion" forms in the decoration of the temples built under its aegis. Clearly from its description the animal seen on the plain of Temasek is more likely to have been a peculiar lion-form than a specimen of *Felis leo*.

The years around 1300 were a troubled period in the history of Palembang.[79] Early in the 13th century a revolution drove out the ruler of Kadiri in East Java, and a new regime was instituted with its centre at Singhasari, north of present-day Malong. It proved to be relatively short-lived, but it survived for long enough to break the already weakened power of Srivijaya, before it succumbed to the house that was to build the empire of Majapahit. The greatest of the Singhasari rulers was its last, the warrior king Kertanagara, who flourished from about 1268 to 1292. He conquered a large part of Java, and about 1286 established his sovreignty over the kingdom of Malayu north of Palembang. Javanese forces remained in Sumatra, and for the next 17 years threatened Palembang itself. Meanwhile Kertanagara had also forced Pahang and the kingdoms of southwest (or south) Borneo to acknowledge his suzerainty. Following his defeat by the founder of the Majapahit empire in 1292, Kertanagara's overseas possessions broke away, and they were not gathered up into the Majapahit fold for another 60 to 70 years.[80] Clearly a prince of Palembang could have founded Singapura about 1300, possibly inspired by the realization that Palembang was a weakened power liable to fall at any time. Alternatively, and this seems more likely, the settlement may have been established as an outpost of the Singhasari empire shortly before 1292, either as part of Kertanagara's encircling movement around Palembang, or to milk the traffic that was passing through the new channel in view of the troubled conditions further south. Or again, the founder of Singapura might have been a refugee prince of the house of Singhasari, either from Sumatra or western Borneo, who fled there when news reached him of Kertanagara's death. This is, of course, all pure speculation. But we introduce it because the association with the house of Singhasari alone gives significance to the selection of the name Singhapura. Moreover, if that association is valid, it further confirms the approximate date of the foundation of Singapura, and hence of the opening of the Keppel Harbour route.

[79] Much of the material in this paragraph is taken from Brian Harrison, *South-East Asia. A Short History* (London: Macmillan, 1954), pp. 46–9.

[80] That is, ca. 1360, during the reign of Hayam Wuruk (r. 1350–89), allegedly a grandson of Vijaya, the founder of the dynasty. By 1365, Majapahit could claim dominion over most of Sumatra, the Malay Peninsula north to Kedah, Patani and Langkasuka, the kingdoms of South and West Borneo, southern Celebes and the Moluccas. Much of this was due to Pateh Gajah Mada, who held office as chief minister from 1331 until his death in 1364. The account in the *Malay Annals* (Raffles MS no. 18) suggests that Hayam Wuruk came from Tanjongpura, and was not of the house of Majapahit; but it also makes him a contemporary of Sultan Mansur Shah of Melaka, so too much reliance should not be placed on it. At the same time, we cannot ignore the possibility that the house that built up the empire of Majapahit came originally from Tanjongpura.

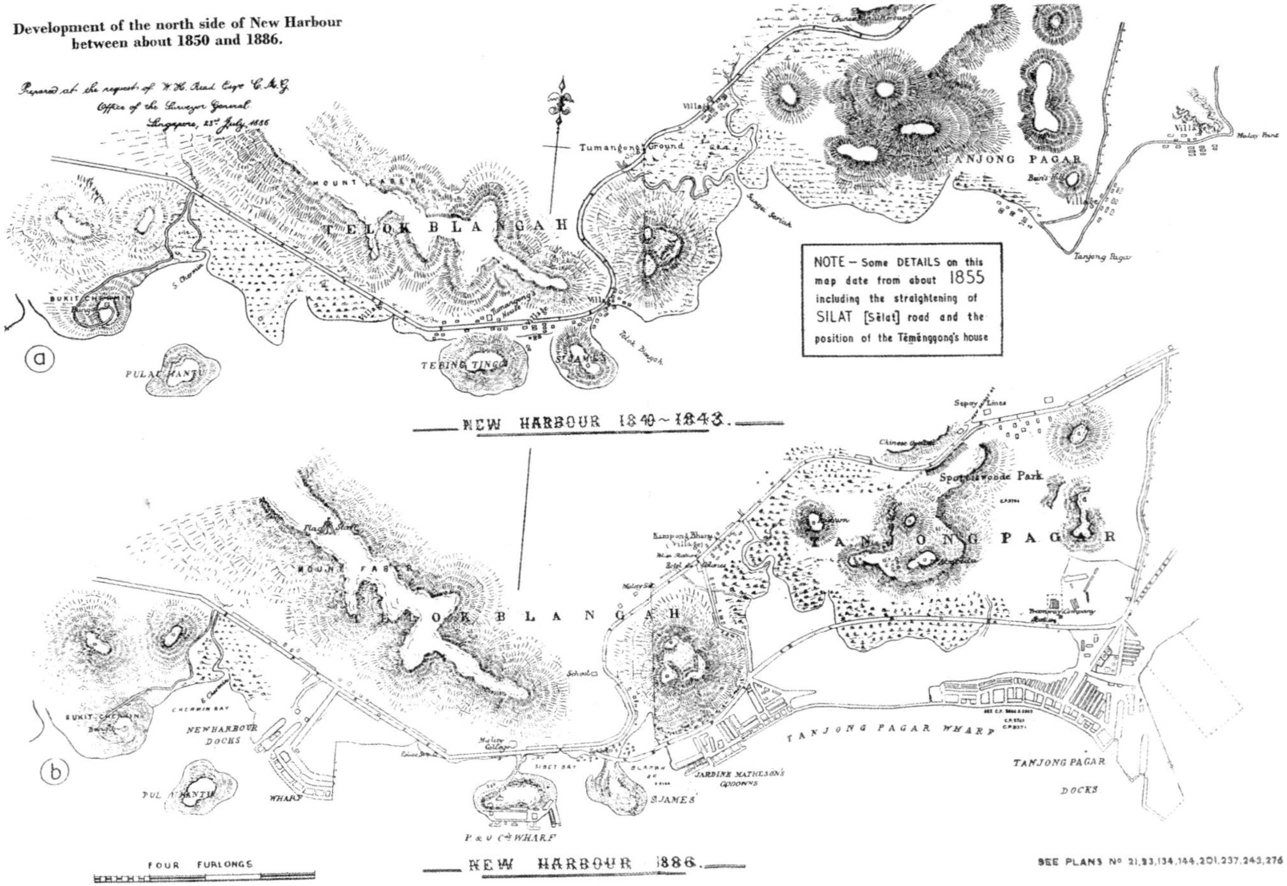

14.5 Development of New Harbour, 1840–86. C.A. Gibson-Hill, "Singapore Old Strait and New Harbour, 1300–1870", *Memoirs of the Raffles Museum*, no. 3. Singapore: Government Printing Office, 1956. © National Heritage Board, Singapore.

It also shows that the change took place during the period of increasing instability around Palembang, and when conditions were probably unsettled in the West Borneo kingdoms. Finally, it draws attention to the fact that in asserting their suzerainty over Singapura, the Majapahit rulers were merely gathering up one of the outlying pieces of the Singhasari empire, whose place they had effectively taken in Java itself.

At this point we can perhaps leave the early history of Keppel Harbour and turn to rather firmer ground, noting that the channel was certainly in use by the middle of the 14th century and probably in use 50 to 100 years earlier, but that we have no indication that it was employed as a full-scale passageway prior to this period.

The Channel of Santa Barbara

Although Linschoten never went further east than Goa, his *Reys-Gheschrift* had a high reputation in the earlier part of the 17th century. Peter Floris, when referring to his own passage westward-bound from the Selat Sembilan to Great Karimun on the *Globe* in November 1613, says that the course "is so well described in the 20th chapter of the *Deroutes* of John Hugens van Linschoten that it cannot bee mended for wee have founde all juste as hee hath described it, so that a man needeth no other judge or pilote butt him".[81] If we examine Linschoten's work, we find that he writes of only one course for a voyage from the south end of the Melaka Strait to the South China Sea. From the vicinity of Tanjong Piai[82] he runs eastward to the Selat Sembilan ("the first straits through which you must pass"), then southeast to the level of the Cyrene Shoal (which at this period and later was marked by a low, sandy island, since disappeared, near its eastern end)[83] and thence due east through

---

[81] Moreland, ed., *Peter Floris*, p. 101.

[82] This headland, the most southerly point of the mainland of Asia, was formerly known as Tanjong Bulus, and in most of the early maps it is marked with variations of the latter name: Linschoten calls it Tanjambuco, Floris, Tanjang Bouro, and Eredia, Tanjon Buro and Tanjon Buras. Bulus = *bolos*, the fish Sillago sp. Piai is a common salt-marsh fern, *Acrostichum aureum* (Linnaeus).

[83] It is clear that this small sandy island with a clump of trees (probably coconut palms) of Linschoten's account was at the eastern end of the Cyrene Shoal, and it undoubtedly afforded a most valuable mark to anyone sailing through the two straits. The sandy strand survived until the last century, but apparently by 1797 it boasted only one tree. Presumably, it was slowly breaking up during this period. It appears as an island as late as Franklin's map of 1822 (Pulau Boosing = Pulau Busing in the version amended by Crawfurd and Jackson). Busing, no meaning, may be from *busong*, a spit of sand, or (more likely) it may be a corruption of *pusing*, from *pusing luan*, to alter the course of a vessel. Captain Daniel Ross (1830) marks it as "Cyrene's Reef and Sand, Dry at 2/3 Ebb", and as far as I know this is the first association of any *Cyrene* with it on a map. The absence of the original mark was very noticeable when I went over Linschoten's course from Pulau Merambong eastwards in a launch in 1951, and one felt that the disappearance of the trees might have been one of the factors that led to the final disuse of this route. The name Pulau Busing is now given to a small island west of Pulau Bukum, and about 1½ miles [2.4km] south of the western end of Cyrene Shoal. It must, I think, have been transferred to this island when the original sailing mark ceased to be recognizable as an island. Pulau Boosing makes its first appearance in its present location on the map by Ross et al. of 1840. Earlier, the latter island (when named) is given variants of Pulau Ular, the toponym now born by the small islet between it and Pulau Bukum.

the passage now known as Keppel Harbour, and out into open water again east of Brani Reef. From this point there is a fairly clear run north-of-east to the east end of Singapore Island, thence across the mouth of the Kuala Johor, and on to the vicinity of Pedra Branca.

We have already reprinted Linschoten's account of the course through Keppel Harbour,[84] on a previous occasion, and nothing would be achieved by repeating it here. It is abundantly clear that his text could only refer to a passage through this straight; and, moreover, that he regarded it as the only safe, workable route between the southern end of the Melaka Strait and the South China Sea, other than by going round to the south of Singkep and Lingga. He also refers to the channel between Singapore Island and the mainland, but he shows that it was certainly not in regular use at this period. He describes the western end of the Johor Strait as a river, and notes that it runs through to the present Kuala Johor. He adds that one "Antonio Mello by chance did once enter [it from the west] with a ship of eight hundreth Bhares great … and came out again at the ryuer Iantana", but this was obviously a unique event, in contrast to the "many ships" that had gone the other way. Since Antonio Mello is considered to have been lucky to get out again safely, it is obvious that Linschoten is not suggesting that anyone should follow his example. Nor, one may add, does his ship appear to have been a large vessel: she can only have been about half the size of the *Globe*, roughly 270 to 300 tons net by present measurements.

In giving his directions for sailing in eastern waters, Linschoten paraphrased the accepted practise of the Portuguese pilots as relayed to him in India—though actually, while he was still at Goa, the Portuguese were forced (or believed themselves forced) to seek a new route south of Singapore Island. It is possible that information about the change of course did not reach him, although he certainly heard of the Portuguese sack of Johor Lama in August 1587 that followed it.[85] A more likely explanation is that he considered that the trouble was only temporary—as it was, relatively—and that Keppel Harbour would again be the normal passageway by the time his book was in common use. In the latter assumption he was wrong: once the pilots of European vessels were compelled to find a route other than through Keppel Harbour, they passed on to discover the Main Strait of Singapore. Thereafter, as we shall see, they continued to use the Keppel Harbour channel until some time towards the end of the 17th century, but the easier, southern route was slowly gaining ground. Ultimately, the latter carried all the vessels of European rig, and only the native craft remained faithful to the Old Strait.

A most helpful paper by I.A. Macgregor provides a very good survey of relations between the Malay court on the Johor River and the Portuguese of Melaka in the 16th century.[86] During the 1570s, a personal link kept Aceh and Johor on moderately

---

84 Gibson-Hill, "Notes on the History of the Old Strait", *JMBRAS* 27, 1 (1954): 167–9.

85 "[A]lso the Towne of Ior was by the Portingals wonne and by them rased to the ground, and for ever made wast, wherein they founde about 150. Brasse pieces smal and great" (Burnell and Tiele, ed., *Voyage of John Huyghen van Linschoten*, vol. 1, p. 110).

86 I.A. Macgregor, "Johore Lama in the Sixteenth Century", *JMBRAS* 28, 2 (1957): 48–125. [E.N.: This article is found in the present collection.] See also Gibson-Hill, "Johore Lama and other Ancient Sites on the Johore River", *JMBRAS* 28, 2 (1955): 126–97.

friendly terms, and though the Malays made no direct attacks on Melaka, they were certainly assisting the Acehnese.[87] Then in June 1579, Sultan Ali Ri'ayat Shah of Aceh died, and shortly afterwards he was succeeded by 'Ala'u'd-din Mansur Shah, a member of the royal house of Perak, and thus one born with no great love for the rulers of Johor. The latent antagonism between Johor and Aceh flared up again, and in 1582 the Acehnese besieged Johor Lama. The Malays asked the Captain of Melaka for assistance, and he sent a Portuguese squadron to the Johor River, where it drove off the Acehnese galleys. Sultan Ali Jalla of Johor followed his retreating enemies, and when near Melaka landed to express personally his gratitude for the help given him. He was, says Couto,[88] much satisfied with his reception, and later that year, or early in 1583, a Malay mission was sent to Goa to arrange for a treaty between the two governments, the chief clause of which (significantly enough) was that the sultan of Johor should not re-establish friendly relations with Aceh.[89] There never was a really satisfactory alliance of long duration between the two Malay powers, but it was the one eventuality above all others that the Portuguese had reason to fear during the 16th century. Had it ever occurred, they would inevitably have been driven from Melaka.

At this point, relations between the Portuguese and Johor had entered a friendly phase, and to the sanguine it must have seemed as if this condition would last for some time. Admittedly, there was a little awkwardness over a richly laiden Melakan boat that was wrecked through negligence at the mouth of the Johor River. But in the end, the Captain of Melaka received back her cannon and a part of her cargo.[90] Oil spread on the ruffled waters, and the bristling hairs on the neck of the sleeping dog sank to rest again. More serious trouble began later, innocently enough, with an order sent from Portugal in 1584, which forbade any Captain of Melaka to maintain an agent at the port of Johor. The prohibition was aimed only at protecting the Melaka customs, the revenue from which had dropped steeply. According to Couto, the amity between the Portuguese and the Malays had led to the junks from Java going to Johor instead of Melaka. In Johor the Portuguese factors were able to buy goods at Melaka prices, less the Melaka customs duty, which they were thus saved from paying. They were also exempt from paying duty to the sultan, which cost the

---

[87] Sultan Ali Jalla'Abdu'l Jalil of Johor married a daughter of Sultan Ali Ri'ayat Shah of Aceh, ca. 1571. Sultan Ali Ri'ayat Shah died on 8 June 1579, leaving no male heir, but his daughter had a son by Sultan Ali Jalla, a young lad called Raja Ashern, who was passed over in 1579. Then, after much dissension, the throne of Aceh was offered to a member of the Perak royal house, who ruled as Sultan 'Ala'u'd-din Mansur Shah until his assasination in 1586/87. Raja Ashern then succeeded, but he was in his turn assisted over the bridge within two years.

[88] See Macgregor, "Johore Lama", pp. 90–1.

[89] Ibid.

[90] See Macgregor, "Johore Lama", pp. 91–3. It must, of course, be born in mind that a vessel wrecked on the shore of most of the countries round the Bay of Bengal became, by local law, the property of the ruler. Even a vessel putting in from stress of weather was liable to confiscation. Sultan Ali Jalla probably thought he was being very generous in returning the guns and part of the cargo; the remainder of the cargo, he said, had been taken by the orang laut, an extremely plausible excuse if not for the common report that said all the cargo from the wreck reached the sultan's godowns in safety.

sultan nothing, as he collected the duty plus a present from Javanese traders. And the traders were content, because they had a shorter run, with less risk of falling into the hands of the Acehnese or getting caught in trouble between Johor and the Portuguese; and, furthermore, they paid no harbour dues at Johor. Everyone, in fact, liked the system except the scrutineers of revenue returns at Goa and Lisbon. So to set a few figures right, an arrangement which satisfied a number of people had to come to an end.

Early in 1585, João da Silva was sent from Goa to take up the Captaincy of Melaka, with instructions to enforce the new order. Sultan Ali Jalla sent a message of goodwill on his arrival, and invited da Silva to station a factor in Johor, as his predecessors had done, promising him even more profitable trading there. The new Captain, bound by the order that reached Melaka with him, refused Ali Jalla's offer. At the same time he sent out vessels to enforce the shipping regulations and compel the local craft to put in at Melaka. To the Malay leaders, it was clear that a new pharaoh who knew not Joseph had arisen; but at first the arrival of fresh naval reinforcements, which were used to strengthen the Portuguese patrol in the Straits, rendered it inexpedient for Ali Jalla to take any immediate action.

It seems likely that the Portuguese reinforcements had been sent primarily with a view to a possible attack on Aceh, a project which was much in the minds of men at Goa in 1584/85. The plan never developed along more material lines, and early in 1586 the extra ships returned to India. Their departure was the signal for action by the Johor Malays. For a time the Portuguese countered it by blockading Kuala Johor and forcibly diverting all local shipping to Melaka, but their depleted squadron could not remain at sea indefinitely. As soon as it withdrew, Ali Jalla's galleys came down the river and began to force the local craft to trade at Johor. At the same time, to increase the effectiveness of their patrol, they attempted to close the Singapore Strait by sinking several barges and old junks laden with stones across one of the ends of the Keppel Harbour passageway. This action was directed principally against the larger vessels sailing from China and the Moluccas to Melaka: Craft from Java could indeed have circumvented it by using the Strait of Sabam [Strait of Kundur]. It suggests that at this time the China and Moluccas junks, at least, did not venture on an East-West crossing south of Blakang Mati. Otherwise, blocking the strait would not have forced them to go to Johor, though in any case the strait cannot really have been closed completely. To a large extent the effectiveness of the Malay blockade must have depended on the patrol maintained by their galleys.

When news of Ali Jalla's action reached Melaka, Dom da Silva[91] immediately sent a squadron to the Johor River again. Apparently, the Portuguese sea captains did not care to risk forcing the passage of the blocked strait, and describing it as completely closed, they cast about for an alternative route. According to Couto:[92]

---

[91] [E.N.: The captain-major or "governor" of Melaka, João da Silva Pereira.]

[92] J. de Barros and D. do Couto, *Da Ásia. Dos feitos que os Portuguezes fizeram no conquista, e descubrimento das terras e mares do Oriente*, 24 vols. (Lisbon: Na Regia Officina Typographia, 1777–78), vol. 21, pp. 210–11. The passage was kindly translated for publication here by I.A. Macgregor. Winstedt, "A History of Johore", *JMBRAS* 10, 3 (1932): 23, following P.A. Tiele, assumes that the attempt was made to block the Selat Tebrau, a truly heroic undertaking, and

> And seeing that the strait was completely impeded by the junks which had been sunk there, he [Dom Manoel de Almada, the Portuguese Captain] ordered the *bantins* to investigate the islands and to see if they could find another channel through which might pass the vessels he was expecting from China and the Moluccas. These *bantins* reached the Varela channel [canal da Varela], as the commonly used strait which was impeded is called (and which is ordinarily called that of Singapore) and passing to the south of that island, they found another channel which had not been used. Entering it, they went on, slowly sounding and noting it and found 7, 8 and 9 fathoms [13 to 16m] there, it being no longer than a *camelete* shot and at its largest 100 fathoms [183m] wide, while at the entrance and in the middle it was no more than 14 fathoms wide. They decided that the vessels could very easily pass through it and gave it the name of the channel of Santa Barbara [O canal da Santa Barbara].

The reference to "that island" in the eighth line is clumsy and confusing, but "the island" would be all right. Presumably, it is this point that trapped Tiele (and Winstedt following him) into believing that the original passage lay through the Selat Tebrau (that is, between the island of Singapore and the mainland), though it is inconceivable that anyone in their senses could have set out to close the latter strait by sinking a few barges and junks in it. Equally certain is the fact that the "canal da Varela" can only be the passage past Batu Berlayar, the western entrance into Keppel Harbour. There is no possible stack on the strait north of Singapore Island, and we must remember that the old lady, Lot's Wife, was still standing at this period.[93] Linschoten wrote about the approach from the west, "in the entrie at the footes of the hill on the North side there lieth a stone Cliffe, which sheweth

---

quite unnecessary. [E.N.: The reference to Pieter Anton Tiele is to his series of articles entitled "De Europeërs in den Maleischen Archipel" (The Europeans in the Malay Archipelago), published in 8 parts. Gibson-Hill refers here to part 5, published in *BKI* 29, 2 (1881): 153–214. The passage concerned can be found ibid., p. 171.]

[93] She was blown up by convict labour, on instructions from J.T. Thomson in Aug. 1848 (see below). Prior to her demise she was, presumably, one of the dragons' teeth that gave the strait its Chinese name, Lung-ya-men (see above). *Varela* = Malay *berhala*, an image or an idol, or by projection a place where joss is burnt. Hence the Berhala China or Batu China elsewhere among the islands in a number of cases refer to points at which the Chinese pilots burnt joss before setting out on a voyage: that is, they were Batu Berlayar. The name Berhala in the sense of Rumah Berhala was also used for a pagoda, and this indeed appears to have been the sense in which the Portuguese employed Varela, but again Pagoda Rock was not a bad term for Lot's Wife.

Thomson (map of 1844) calls this headland Sinki Point, presumably a corruption of Singkeh, a coolie fresh from China; it cannot be a Malay word. Perhaps Singkeh was a joking appellation for the Varella da China dating from the late 1820s, or later, and that the present Sinki Strait takes its name from it. Before 1848 the stack must have been an excellent sailing mark for a vessel running east on the last section of that rather featureless course. The Sinki Strait, one may add, is a relatively new passageway. Older maps block up the area. The channel is shown by soundings (but with no name) on Ross's map of 1830 and again on Tassin's map of 1836, still without a name. Ross et al. (1840) call it New Channel. Sinki Strait appears first on Thomson's revised chart of 1846. Thereafter, it is printed by Hobbs (1852), who took much material from Thomson's chart, Thomson (1854), and so on.

like a pillar, this is commonly called of all nations that passe by it, the Varella of China". Again, the new channel—no longer than a *camelete* shot[94]—is too short for Keppel Harbour, which is about 2¼ miles [3.6 km] long, or roughly 4,000 yards.

From this point we can safely leave the bickering between the Malays and the Portuguese, and move on in search of further references, if any, to the new channel of Santa Barbara. Actually, we find that the toponym does not seem to have gained any immortality, but we do get later notices of the new channel. It is clearly the *estreito nouo* recorded on Eredia's maps, and the route followed by the *Globe* when westward bound in 1613. But these appear to be all the available references to it. If, therefore, the route was first used in 1586, it had a life of a little less than 30 years. Thereafter, as we shall see, vessels used either the old route, as apparently the *Globe* could have done in 1613, or a new channel still further south, and ultimately the Singapore Main Street.

Emanuel Godinho de Erédia completed his *Declaraçam de Malaca* at Goa in 1613.[95] Among his maps are six that include the neighbourhood of Singapore Island and the south end of the Malay Peninsula. All of them are spoilt by a rather troublesome mistake: the south point of the island (Tanjong Pagar) is much accentuated, and the whole island is twisted in an anti-clockwise direction, so that the southeast coast from Beting Kusah to Tanjong Pagar faces due east, and the coast from Keppel Harbour to Tanjung Gul (at the western entrance to the Johor Strait) appears to face due south. One may also add that where the scale allows him to show the narrow channel between Pulau Brani and Blakang Mati, he makes it run from north to south (cutting Pulau Blakang Mati in half), instead of from east to west. Nonetheless, these errors in no way confuse the fact that he clearly recognized two passageways, in parallel, running roughly east-west off the south coast of Singapore Island. One is undoubtedly the route described by Linschoten:

---

[94] *Camelete*, a small camel. The camel probably fired a shot in the region of 12 to 16 lbs. [about 5.4 to 7.3kg]. The camelete was clearly not a very large piece of ordinance; but it was probably a bit larger than the falcon, which in the 16th century fired a shot weighing 1½ to 3 lbs. [about 0.7 to 1.4kg], and had a range of 320 yards [292.6m] point-blank. A camelete shot as a measure of distance is, therefore, likely to have been in the region of 350 yards [320m], or possibly as much as 400 yards [365.8m], but clearly nowhere near 4,000 yards [3657.6m].

[95] Actually, it seems likely that all Eredia's maps of Singapore Island and its vicinity in point of information date from 1604, when he was in this neighbourhood accompanying an abortive Portuguese attack on the Johor capital of Batu Sawar. In 1605 he was said to be suffering from beriberi, and he returned to Goa; so far as is known he thereafter remained in India until his death. The *Declaraçam de Malaca e India Meridional com o Cathay*, completed in 1613, was first published by Léon Janssen (Brussels: Librairie Européenne C. Muquardt, 1881), with a French translation and commentary (Brussels, 1882). An annotated English translation was later published by J.V. Mills "Eredia's Description of Malaca, Meridional India and Cathay", *JMBRAS* 8, 1 (1930): 1–288. Janssen reproduced tracings of all the six maps noted here. Mills drew from folios 25 verso, 45 recto, and 61 recto, and reproduced them photographically, albeit reduced in size. The most important of the maps is folio 61 recto, dated 1604, which shows the two straits of Singapore, both old and new. The other five maps are undated, and are accordingly known by the year in which Eredia completed the *Declaraçam*. He did not reach Melaka from Goa until 1600 and, as we have noted, he returned to India about 1605.

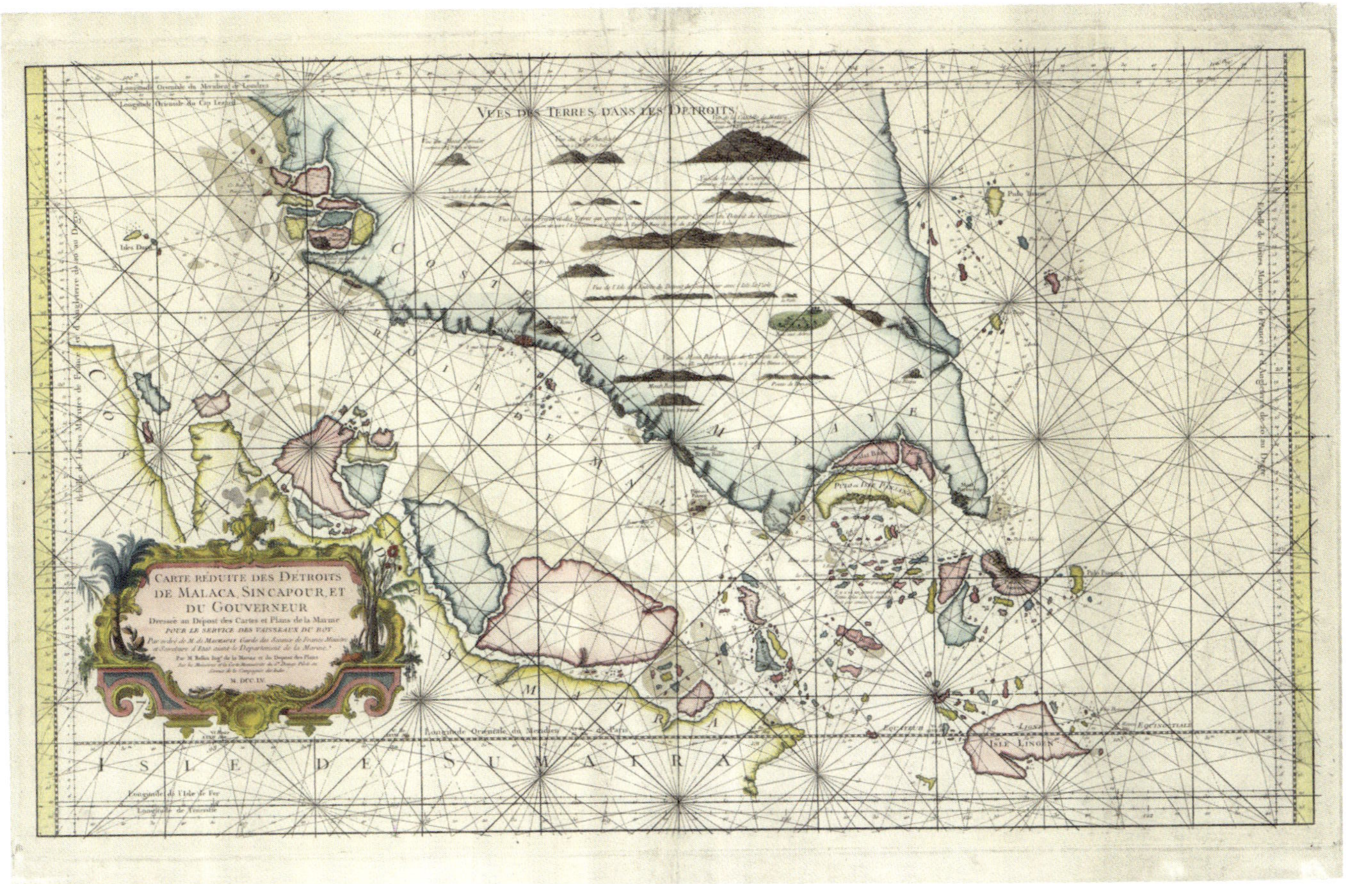

14.6 Carte Réduite des Détroits de Malaca, Sincapour, et du Gouverneur [Reduced Map of the Melaka, Singapore and Governor Straits]. Paris: Dépôt de la Marine, 1755. © Peter Borschberg, private collection.

and in one of his maps (folio 61 recto),[96] which bears the date 1604, Eredia marks this as *Estreito Velho* (Old Strait). His second passageway, which he labels *Estreito Nouo* (New Strait), lies further south. Westward it begins outside the western entrance to Keppel Harbour; from there, it runs along the south side of Pulau Blakang Mati and thereafter turns east, passing north of Pulau Sakijang Bendera (western St John's Island) to rejoin the other passage east of Pulau Brani. Pulau Tekukor lies in the gap between the south point of Pulau Blakang Mati and the western St John's Island. It is not clear on which side of Tekukor Eredia takes the channel, but there can be no doubt that he contemplates a passage close to Pulau Blakang Mati and north of the St John's Islands.

Eredia's *Estreito Nouo* was not, therefore, the present Main Strait. It is most important that this point be appreciated. With this in mind we can now turn to the westward passage past Singapore Island made by the *Globe* in November 1613, as recorded by Peter Floris. Nothing would be gained by giving his account of the full length of the run from Tanjong Datok to Tanjong Piai; we can profitably reduce it by starting with the *Globe* passing the mouth of the Kuala Johor (which Floris calls the "river of Johor") and finishing as he enters the eastern end of the Selat Sembilan:[97]

> Wee were buysie every daye in turning upp with the flood, til wee were `paste the river of Johor, and came aboute 2 leagues [11.1km] from Sinca Pura.
>
> Dyvers prawes came aboorde of us hard by the Straighte, being of the Salettes under the King of Johor, which for the mooste parte keepe in the prawes with their wyves and children, living chiefely by fishing[98]. Heere wee tooke a pilott to bring us thorough the Straighte of Sinca Pura for 7R8 [7 ryals of 8]; and hee counselling us to go thorough the newe straighte, wee followed his counsell; which wee entered aboute the noone tyde, after they had fyrste sette of with beacons the hidden rocks, which lye verye dangerous and are very perillous to passe, [the channel] not being paste one-eight of an Englishe mile [200m] broad. And the flood being done, which runneth heere very strong, wee were forced to come to an ancker juste by the rocke which lyeth in the middest of the Straighte, att larboord aboute 1½ faddem [2.74m] under water; and although wee did not touche it, yett were wee not 2 faddem from it, having in the middle shipp 5 faddem [9.1m] and in the fore parte 9 faddem [16.4m]. Butt in regard it was very fayre wether and calme, the danger was the lesse, the ebbe running so strong that wee coulde not

---

[96] Eredia marks his straits very clearly, and labels them as *estreito*; for examples, see fols. 45 recto, 60 verso and 61 recto. The Johor Strait is shown as a narrow channel separating the island from the mainland, and it is only labelled once, when it is called Selat Tubrau (= Malay, Selat Tebrau). The next appearance of a variant on Selat Tebrau is in Hamilton's text of 1727 (see below), where he refers to it as Salleta de Brew, possibly Bellin's map of 1775 (Selat Buro) and Mannevillette's maps of the 1770's (Det[roit] de Salete Baro). The term was in common use in the 19th century, but presumably the Malays must have been employing it before 1600.

[97] Moreland, ed., *Peter Floris*, pp. 102–3.

[98] I have omitted here a short passage, which relates news told to Floris by the Orang Laut about the dispute between Aceh and Johor and is not pertinent to the present discussion. It appears in Gibson-Hill, "On the Alleged Death of Sultan Ala'u'd-din of Johore at Acheh in 1613", *JMBRAS* 29, 1 (1956): 125–45.

> carrye oute a warping ancker. Heere wee rode till the ebbe was spente, being 12 of the clock att night, the ebbe having lasted heere 12 houres. Then wee sette thorough the Straighte, not being paste ½ Englishe myle [800m] in lengthe.
>
> In the morning, being passed the fyrste straighte, wee made N.W. for the second, passing by the olde Straite of Sincapura, which wee coulde see from ende to ende, being betweene 2 high ilands and very narrowe, so that the newe straighte is better for greate shipps to passe. Taking thus oure course towards the second straighte....

Moreland, in editing Floris's text for the Hakluyt Society, says that the *Globe* passed through Keppel Harbour,[99] which thus for him becomes the "newe straighte". This not unnaturally lands him in several difficulties, of which the most troublesome is the location of the old channel. He disposes of the latter by assuming it to have been the Selat Sengkir, between Pulau Brani and Pulau Blakang Mati. The suggestion is quite untenable, and it is, in fact, difficult to think of a more impossible solution to the problem; Linschoten had already said that the latter passage "is shallow all ouer, serving only for smal foists to passe through", and a modern chart and reference to the *Malacca Strait Pilot* easily confirm this point.[100] The Selat Sengkir would have been a most dangerous passage for any seagoing vessel, even at the size then current. Furthermore, there is no reason whatever why eastbound boats should have turned into it, as a regular practice, when they had a much easier way out of Keppel Harbour between Pulau Brani and Tanjong Pagar. Both Eredia and Couto indicate plainly enough that the new channel lay to the south of the old one, not to the north of it, as Moreland maintained. Moreover, Floris himself tells us that the *Globe* passed the western entrance to the Old Strait, "being passed the fyrste straighte" and making northwest for the Selat Sembilan. There can he no question of "an afterthought", as Moreland suggests, in so definite a statement: it is not a question of a sentence being misplaced, as certainly occurs in some manuscript accounts. If the Selat Sengkir had

---

[99] Moreland, ed., *Peter Floris*. The use of the word "iland" here is the only excuse that Moreland can have had for putting Floris's "newe straighte" in Keppel Harbour [E.N.: See ibid., p. 100], but it is not an important point, nor of any value as evidence. Several later cartographers chopped bits off Singapore Island and made them into separate islands, including Horsburgh (1806) who cut the west end off the island and called it *Tooly* just as in other cases islands were added to the adjacent land mass as headlands. It is often very difficult to detect from the sea whether or not a headland rising to a hillock at its end is or is not an island, and Floris must have been about a mile [about 1.6km] off-shore when he passed the western entrance to Keppel Harbour.

[100] *Malacca Strait Pilot, Comprising Malacca Strait and its Northern Approaches, Singapore and the West Coast of Sumatra*, 3rd ed. (London: Hydrographic Department, Admiralty, 1946), p. 200: "Sĕlat Sengkir, the channel between the northern side of Pulau Blakang Mati and Pulau Brani, has a least depth of 15 feet (about 4.6m) in the fairway, and is navigable for small vessels, but owing to the gusts of wind caused by the adjacent high land, it can scarcely be considered safe for sailing vessels". Actually, the fairway is dog-legged, with a shoal in mid-channel, and some charts show a maximum depth of only 13 feet [about 4m] over the bar. It is, however, clearly not a fit channel for a deep-sea sailing vessel far from home, as one can see easily by traversing it. One could get a small vessel through it, but no master with any sense or seamanship would have voluntarily hazarded his ship in it when he could have run along Keppel Harbour or gone outside Pulau Blakang Mati.

been part of the Old Strait, the *Globe* would have passed the entrance to it while still in what Floris calls "the fyrste straighte", and sailing west, not northwest.

A careful reading of Peter Floris' narrative shows that the *Globe* must, in fact, have followed Eredia's New Strait, Couto's channel of Santa Barbara. She ran westward off the Singapore coast until she lay southeast of Tanjong Malang, where her commander had picked up a local pilot. On the advice of the latter, they then bore south off the shoal east of Pulau Brani, east of the Buran Darat reef, and then passed through the channel between Pulau Tekukor and Blakang Mati, instead of entering the eastern end of Keppel Harbour. The first, short strait that Floris describes was the passage north of Pulau Tekukor, where the chart shows a shoal in mid-channel. Thereafter, the *Globe* sailed northwest, as Floris says quite correctly, making for the Selat Sembilan. In doing so, she would have coasted along the southwest flank of Blakang Mati, and then, still on the same bearing, have passed the western entrance to the Old Strait, where she rejoined Linschoten's course off Pasir Panjang.

We have seen, in Couto's narrative, the reason why the boats stopped using Keppel Harbour in the 1580s. It is clear from Floris's account that the old passage was open again by this time, as one would expect. The fastenings on the sunken boats must have rotted fairly quickly, and once that happened they would break up with the action of the current setting through the channel. Nonetheless, apparently some boats were still using the New Strait, presumably because the difficult section was much shorter, and the pilot had less far to go to get back home; but it cannot have been at all satisfactory during the southwest monsoon. And as we have said, 1613 is the last year in which we get a definite reference to it. Thereafter, all the passages recorded in this immediate vicinity are through the Old Strait again, that is, through Keppel Harbour.

Before we examine some of these records we may well note a further voyage in these seas quoted by Yule in *Hobson-Jobson*. It refers to the return westward of the Spanish governor of the Philippines, in 1616:

> The Governor sailed from Manila in March of this year [1616] with ten galleons and two galleys. ... On arriving at the straits of Sincapur. ... and passing by a new strait which since has taken the name of *Estreito do Governador*, there his galleon grounded on the reef at the point of the strait and was a little grazed by the top of it.

This, we may remark, was the incident that gave its earliest name to the Main Strait: from this period on, with many variants in spelling, the latter frequently appears as Governor's Strait. Nonetheless, this does not prove that His Excellency's fleet was following the full length of the channel. If it were, his galleon must have grounded off Pulau Satumu (Raffles Light),[101] which was very careless of her pilot, as he had

---

[101] *Satumu* is from the Malay *tumu*, the large mangrove tree *Bruguiera conjugata Merr.*, and a fair translation would be "One-tree Island", but the latter name was sometimes used for another island. The building of a lighthouse was first mooted in 1833, but the foundation stone was not laid until 1854, during the governorship of Lt.-Col. W.J. Butterworth, CB. The islet next to it is called Pulau Biola in Malay; which "the French have called the *Viol*, on account of its similitude to that instrument at a certain point of view" (*The Oriental Navigator or New*

plenty of fairway if he kept out far enough. Further, if the galleon grounded there, it is difficult to see why the tradition arose that she went ashore on or near Pulau Goa (present day Pulau Těmbakul). It seems much more likely that his fleet was following the new passage of Eredia, except that the commander was improving on it by keeping to seaward of the little cluster of islands round St John's Islands.[102]

Later Passages through the Old Strait

Though the *Globe* in her passage of 1613, and again the fleet accompanying the governor of the Philippines in 1616, sought courses south of Pulau Brani and Blakang Mati, it is clear that the *estreito velho* was already being used again. Yule quotes a passage from the *Viaggi di Carletti*, describing a voyage made in 1599, which must certainly have run through Keppel Harbour.[103] The narrowness of the channel of Santa Barbara is a matter of the fairway: on either side are wide reefs, not a steep-to rock as formerly stood at the western entrance to Keppel Harbour. Yule's quotation runs:

> In this voyage nothing occurred worth relating … except that after passing the straits of Sincapura … between the mainland and a variety of islands … with so narrow a channel that from the ship you could jump ashore or touch the branches of the trees on either side, our vessel stuck on a shoal.

The Chinese junks must also have been back on this route by this time, or only a little later (if indeed they ever really forsook it). The pilot's directory in the *Tung-hsi yang-k'ao* by Chang Hsi, dated 1618, has a section on the Keppel Harbour strait (again under the name of Lung-ya-men), which has been translated by Hsü Yün-ts'iao.[104] It starts by quoting from the account of this channel in the *Hsing-ch'a sheng-lan* (see above), and then continues:

> At present the ships still dare not sail in the night on account of the pirates as well as the *Liang-shan* Rocks in its mouth. Measuring the water, it is thirty *t'o* [fathoms] in the middle, twenty *t'o* in its south. Passing the Gate of *Tan-ma-hsi*, [the] ship sails to 262.5° and 292.5° by three watches towards *Chi-li-mea* [Karimun] Hill.

Directions for Sailing to and from the East Indies, China, New Holland, etc., 3rd ed., rev. John Stevens [London: Laurie & Whittle, 1826], p. 403); the name was actually of Portuguese origin, but the meaning as he says.

102 No doubt as the use of the new course was still in its infancy, he kept a little too far north when running west from off Kuala Johor, following the line of the old course, and then bore south to round Pulau Tembakul (Goa Island) and the St John's Islands. The governor with the fleet was Don Juan de Silva, Governor of the Philippines from 1609 to 1616. He was a sick man, and died on 19 Apr. 1616 while the fleet was at Melaka. The name *St John's* is a corruption of the Malay *Sa-Kijang*, as Crawfurd recognized. Eredia (fol. 45 recto) gives us *Pulo Siquijan*, which suggests that the Portuguese version may not have been current in 1600–05.

103 *Viaggi di Carletti* quoted in *Hobson-Jobson*, under *Singapore*.

104 See Hsü, "Notes on the Malay Peninsula", pp. 1–16, esp. p. 10. [E.N.: This article has been reproduced in this collection.]

Here, we may remark, as in the sailing directions given on the *Wu pei chih* charts, we have a clear association between the Dragons' Teeth Strait and the Karimun Islands, which effectively rules out any question of the former referring to a passageway near Lingga Island, at this period.

In 1637, John Weddell took his fleet of four vessels through the Keppel Harbour passage en route from Melaka to Macau.[105] The ships, he says, first "entred the streights of Pulo Symbilan or the nyne Islands and soe passed through Sincapura...." In running out of the latter, they experienced "much difficultie, for in the Channell we had but 4½ fathomes [8.2m] a shipps length from us, and on both sides but 17 and 18 foote hard rookie ground"; however, they "picked out the way and gott into deeper water and at last gott through these troublesome straights". It seems likely that their difficulties were augmented by the inexperience of their pilot, a Portuguese Eurasian whom they engaged at Melaka, and that he did not bear southeast soon enough at the exit from the strait. The reports read as if they came out by the northern channel and lay too close to the shoals off Tanjong Pagar.

We have a fuller account of this same passage from Peter Mundy, who had shipped as one of the two factors on the *Planter*, Captain Edward Hall, the fourth vessel in the fleet. In part his description runs as follows, the Selat Sembilan having been passed on the last day of May, and Keppel Harbour on 1 June:

> Passed through the old straightt.
>
> June Anno 1637. The First of this Month wee went through the old straightt which May bee aboutt a good league in length and not above ¼ Mile broade att the Comming in and going outt, butt within wider, with many little baies, Creeks, Ilands, etts., Where wee saw sundry companies of small boates covered over with Mattes, which is the Ordinary habitation of those thatt live among these Ilands, Where they have their wives, children and Household goods.
>
> Pretty Fishing.
>
> Here they broughtt us More Fish, Fresh and Dried, which I conceave is their Cheifest Mayntenaunce, Killing them with Fishgaes[106] in which they are very

---

[105] See R.C. Temple, ed., *The Travels of Peter Mundy in Europe and Asia, 1608–1667*, Hakluyt Society, 2nd ser., nos. 17, 35, 45, 55, 78, 5 vols. (Cambridge: Hakluyt Society, 1907–36), vol. 3 (1919), pp. 144–5 (passage of the Selat Sembilan) and pp. 146–8 (passage of Keppel Harbour). Temple attempts to fit Mundy's description into an account of a passage through the Johor Strait (Selat Tebrau), and his map, facing p.153, is valueless except as a pitfall for the dim-witted. Clearly the original narrative does not admit of this treatment, and subsequently Temple appreciated this point, after correspondence with Dr C.O. Blagden (see Temple, ed., *Mundy*, 2nd ser., no. 55, vol. 5 (1924), p. xiii, corrections of errors in vols. 45–6). Weddell's account of the voyage is in *EIC M.R.*, vol. 63 (India Office Library); not seen, the quotations here being from the notes by Temple in *Mundy*.

[106] Fishgaes = fishing spears, typically with three or more barbed heads, from the Spanish fisga, a harpoon. The word was variously spelt in the 17th century, but Mundy's rendering is unusual, and nearer to the original form than was customary. More general versions were *fishgig*, *fizgig*, *fisgig* or *visgee*. Dampier (J. Masefield, ed., *Dampier's Voyages, Consisting of a New Voyage Round the World*, 2 vols. [London: E. Grant Richards, 1906], vol. 1, p. 39), referring to the Indians of the east coast of Central America, says: "They are very ingenious at throwing the Lance, Fisgig, Harpoon, or any manner of Dart, being bred to it from their Infancy; for the Children imitating their Parents, never go aboard without a Lance in their Hands, which they

Dextrous, and a pretty sport it is to see them pursue the Fish with their little boates, who scudd before them as porpoises Doe before the stemme of a shippe in a gale of wynde untill they are strucke. They use allsoe netts, hookes and lynes.

There was likewise broughtt us From the shoare in those little hoates Plantanes, Sugarcanes[107] and pineapples,[108] which they sow and plant in certaine plottes, Butt all thatt wee could Discover by sightt, as well Ilands as Mayne, was quite overgrowne with trees and bushes.

Daunger escaped.

---

throw at any Object, till use hath made them masters of the Art". For an account of the Malay and Aboriginal Malay fishing spears, see T.W. Burdon, "Papers on Malayan Fishing Methods", *JMBRAS* 27, 2 (1954): 9–11, esp. fig. 3, D–F. The usual Malay word is *serampang*.

[107] *Sugarcanes*. It seems likely that sugarcanes were grown widely by the Aboriginal Malays in coastal areas from an early period. Groeneveldt, "Notes", p. 245, translating an early Chinese account of Melaka (*Ying-yai sheng-lan*, [1436], makes no mention of rice, but says that they had sago, sugarcane, plantains, nangka, wild *lichis*, etc. It seems, in fact, that in the southern part of the peninsula, rice was grown in appreciable quantities only in Pahang. According to the *Hsing-ch'a sheng-lan* of 1436 (Groeneveldt, "Notes", p. 236), on the Karimata Islands, "rice is not very abundant ... They plant bananas, and eat the fruit instead of rice". The same work in reference to the island of *Tong-si-tiok*, which was probably Singapore (ibid., pp. 258–9), says: "The ground is barren and not fit for agriculture; they always get their rice from the coast of Sumatra, and other countries". Alexander Hamilton, who if he did land on Singapore Island probably did so at the Singapore River, says that he saw "Sugar-cane five or six inches [13 to 15cm] round growing wild" (*A New Account of the East Indies*, 2 vols. [Edinburgh: John Mosman, 1727], vol. 2, p. 98). We must allow him to exaggerate a little, and six inches [15cm] in circumference gives a diameter of under two inches [5.1cm]; he may have come upon crops remaining from the settlement that the Portuguese destroyed in 1613, a hundred years earlier.

[108] *Pineapples*. The usual word at this period was *ananas*, from the Portuguese term *nanas*; the latter was itself derived from the name *nana*, employed by the aborigines of the Santa Cruz district of Brazil, through whom the Portuguese first came in contact with the fruit. From the various words used for the plant in the East Indies, it would seem that it was the Portuguese who introduced it to this area, where it was fairly widely distributed by the end of the 16th century. The Spaniards, who encountered the pineapple in the Caribbean region, considered that its tessellated fruit resembled a pine-cone, and called it *pinas*, a name which led to the English form *pine-apple*. It is interesting to find that the pineapple was well established in the region of the Singapore Strait as early as 1637, as its cultivation was widespread in this area in the early part of the last century. It was then being grown on many of the islands off Singapore, mostly by small groups of Bugis settlers; but the latter cannot have been resident here as early as the beginning of the 17th century, and it seems likely, in fact, that much of this later cultivation began after the establishment of the settlement of Singapore. In 1842, F.J. Bernard claimed that 20 years earlier he had cleared a large area of ground on Blakang Mati, which the temenggong had given him to start a pineapple plantation. According to Dr Robert Little, over 200 acres of Blakang Mati were devoted to pineapple cultivation in 1847, and the total area on the off-lying islands amounted to about 2,000 acres: at that time the fruit sold in Singapore at the rate of 300–400 for a Spanish dollar. About 1840, cultivation spread to the slopes of present-day Mount Faber. It was then held, in some quarters, that the effluvia from the rotting leaves was the cause of the virulent malaria which was prevalent on parts of Blakang Mati. When the signal station was transferred to Mount Faber in 1846, it was suggested that the temenggong be asked to prohibit the planting of pineapples on the hill, in the interests of

> This Day comming Forth of the old straightt, through Negligence of our Pilot (beeing a Portugall Mestizo taken in att Mallacca as a passenger), wee were in some Daunger when wee thoughtt ourselves Most secure, For hee Directed us on the starboard shoare when wee should [have] kept the larboard side, Falling among uneven ground and shallow water, having once butt 3½ Fathom [6.4m] and a coites cast farther[109] nott 10 Foote water. Butt God bee praised, wee gott clear off.

This is one of the best of the early accounts of the Aboriginal Malays actually living in the strait, and it gives a very similar picture to the one drawn by Crawfurd and Finlayson after their visit to New Harbour in January 1822.[110] A later note by John Nieuhoff, who was at Melaka in 1660, is less precise, but it mentions their presence in the neighbourhood of Singapore:[111]

> *Sinkapura* lies on the most southern point of all Asia, about half a degree to the north of the line, and twenty leagues from *Malaca*. This cape has imparted its name to the streights of *Sinkapura*. The country of *Sinkapura* had, before *Malaca* was built, its own kings, and was the chiefest place of trade on this coast, being much frequented by the Chinese merchants, and those of *Camboja*. The mountain near the straights of *Sinkapura*, bearing the same name, produces most excellent diamonds.
>
> About *Sinkapura* is a certain nation, which with their whole families live always at sea in their small vessels; they are called *Saletes*, live upon fishing, and are subject to the king *Jor* [king of Johor]. About two leagues beyond the streights of *Sinkapura* is the river *Johor*, at the entrance of which you see two mountains, or rather high islands shaped like sugar loaves; one is four times bigger than the

---

the men manning the station. The practice continued, however, and as late as 1892 there were still extensive areas under cultivation on its southwestern slopes. A photograph taken about 1905 shows a pineapple field covering the sides of the hill at Buona Vista.

[109] A quoit's cast, the distance to which a quoit is commonly thrown—that is, 19 yards [17.4m]—though it may legitimately vary from 15 to 20 yards [13.7 to 18.3m] (Carnac Temple).

[110] See also below. Compare with the account given by Dr Careri below.

[111] From "Mr. John Nieuhoff's Voyages and Travels to the East Indies", in *A Collection of Voyages and Travels*, publ. by H. Lintot and J. Osborn, 3rd ed., 6 vols. (London: Thomas Osborne, 1745). See J.J. Sheehan, "Seventeenth Century Visitors to the Malay Peninsula", *JMBRAS* 12, 2 (1934): 79. This is the only reference to the diamond-bearing Mount Sinkapura, and unfortunately Nieuhoff does not explain its exact position sufficiently clearly for it to be identified; possibly he means Bukit Serapong, on Pulau Blakang Mati. Actually, the only areas in the East Indies reliably known to produce diamonds are the southeast corner of Borneo, around Tanah Laut and the Martapura range, and the region of the Landak and Kapuas rivers in West Borneo. The taller of the two sugar-cane hills marking the entrance to Kuala Johor is Bukit Pengerang: at one time they were shown as *Barbucet* and *False Barbucet*. The hill "on the other side of the river" is Bukit Belungkor: it is in fact on the same side (the east side) of the estuary as Pengerang, but to the north of Pulau Tekong, and as you enter the channel between the island and the mainland it appears to lie on the right bank.

> other, lying NNE as you enter the river, and the other NE. On the other Side of the river you discover a high hill, tho' the southside of the river is a champain country.[112] There is ten fathom [18.2m] water at the mouth of this river.

William Dampier must have followed the same route as Peter Mundy outward bound from Melaka to Tonkin, as late as 1688, he says:[113]

> Our Captain being a Stranger to the Bay of Tonquin, as were all his Ship's Company, he hired a Dutch Pilot at Malacca; and having finished his Business there, we set sail, two Days after the Caesar. We were desirous to overtake these four Ships, and therefore crouded all the Sail we could make; having a strong westerly Wind, accompanied with many hard Gusts and Tornadoes: and the very next Day we got Sight of them; for they had not yet passed through a narrow Passage, called the Streights of Sincapore. We soon got up with them, and past through together; and sailing about three Leagues [16.7km] farther we anchored near an Island called Pulo Nuttee, belonging to the Kingdom of Jihore.
>
> Here Captain Weldon took in Wood and Water, and some of the Indian Inhabitants came aboard us in their Canoas, of whom we bought a few Coconuts, Plantains, and fresh Fish. We staid here not above four and twenty Hours; for the other Ships had filled most of their Water at other Islands near this, before we came up with them: for tho' Ships do usually take in Water at Malacca Town, yet they do as frequently discharge it again at some of these Islands, and take in better.
>
> We sailed the next Day, and kept near the Malacca Shore; and there passing by the Mouth of the River Jihore, we left many other Islands on our Starboard-side....

Dampier's "narrow Passage" was probably the Selat Sembilan, and his Pulo Nuttee, Pulau Blakang Mati. The earliest name for the island known to me is Wilde's, in a manuscript map dated about 1680: he calls it Burne Beard Island.[114] Several slightly later maps, however, give it names that seem to be variants on the Malay word

---

[112] A *champain country* = champaign, a broad, open country, from Campagna. The word was much employed by 17th-century travellers, though it is now rather out of fashion. For comparison see Alexander Hamilton, who wrote: "The middle cluster [of the Nicobars] is fine champain Ground" (*A New Account* [1727], vol. 2, p. 69); and William Dampier: "The Land for about 60 miles up in the Country [Tonquin, in present-day Vietnam] is still very low ... with some gentle risings here and there, that make it a fine pleasant Champian; and the further side of this also is more level than the Champian Country it self" (W. Dampier, *A New Voyage round the World* [London: For James Knapton, 1698], vol. 2, p. 19). Spelling (at this period) varies: *champain*, *champian*, *champion*, etc.

[113] Capt. William Dampier, *A New Voyage round the World*, 6th ed. of 1717. Quoted from the edition of Dampier's works prepared by John Masefield, 2 vols. (London: E. Grant Richards, 1906); see vol. 1, pp. 559–60. The voyage westbound occurs in ibid., vol. 2, pp. 39–40. "Jihore" is Dampier's rendering of "Johor". Moll's map (1688) illustrating Dampier's account puts Pulo Nuttee (see below) about where Pulau Bintan is, but this must, I think, be a mistake: in the extract given here Dampier clearly says that they kept near the Melaka shore and passed Kuala Johor after leaving the island. If Pulo Nuttee was not Pulau Blakang Mati, it must have been one of the islands in the St John's group, but this seems most unlikely.

[114] Wilde, MS map, ca. 1680: British Museum, MS Dept, Add. 15, 737 (10).

nyiur, a coconut: Hacke, in MS maps dated about 1690 and 1700,[115] labels the island Niry and P. Nirya: Eberard,[116] also about 1700, calls it *Isle Niry*. Later it appears as Toly, Thornton (1711),[117] and Jefferys (ca. 1770),[118] while the maps published by Lady Raffles and J.H. Moor call it P. Panjang, a term that was earlier applied to Singapore Island itself.[119] Variants of the present name appear first as Balakan Mati in the map by Captain James Franklin as amended by Lieutenant Jackson (and John Crawfurd) in 1825,[120] Blacan-mattee in Captain. Daniel Ross's survey of 1827, published in 1829, and Blaken Mattee in the latter's chart of 1830. Bonham in a letter of October 1842, refers to the island as "Pulo Panjang, usually called Blaken Mattie", though 20 years earlier Farquhar in official correspondence employed the name Blakan Mati alone.[121]

The last published description of a passage through the Old Strait in this period appears to be that in Dr Careri's account of his voyage from Melaka to Macau, beginning in July 1695.[122] It is of considerable interest, because he defines the three possible courses past Singapore Island very clearly: the Johor Strait, behind the island and used principally to reach "the metropolis of the same name"; the Strait of Singapore, the original passageway, which was apparently still the route most favoured by local craft; and the Governor's Strait, the present Main Strait, which the European vessels used "very much" because of its width, though much of it was so deep that it was not possible to anchor in it. As we have said, in spite of the apparent popularity of the Governor's Strait by this time, the pilot of his vessel chose to take her through the Old Strait.

> Monday the 11th [of July 1695] we pass'd by the island Pulcariman [Pulau Karimun], which, tho' large, is not inhabited any more than the rest. Then we came to an anchor at the mouth of the straight, before sun-set, both because the wind was contrary, and because we sounded all the way; for tho' the good pilots

---

[115] Hacke, MS maps, British Museum, Map Room: (a), undated, ca. 1690, 9. Tab. 37; (b), 1700, MSS. maps of the Indies by William Hacke, dedicated and presented to the Rt. Hon'ble John, Lord Sommers, etc.: K. Mar. VI. 1.

[116] Eberard, MS map, 1100: British Museum, MS Dept, Add. 15,738 (40).

[117] John Thornton, pub. 1111: British Museum, Map Room, 22.d.15.

[118] Thomas Jefferys, reprinted 1794: Raffles Museum collection [E.N.: Now in the National Archives of Singapore]. Jefferys died in 1771.

[119] (a) Anonymous (probably after Capt. Franklin, amended by Lt.-Col. W. Farquhar, 1822–23), published by Lady Raffles, "Memoir", opp. p. 377; (b) Compiled by J.B. Tassin, lithographer, dated 1836, publ. by J.H. Moor in *Notices of the Indian Archipelago* (Singapore: n.p., 1837), opp. p. 269.

[120] In Crawfurd, *Journal*, opp. p. 529.

[121] *EIC Rec*., V. 8: 331. Also ibid., L. 13: 68 and 108.

[122] Dr John Francis Gemelli Careri, *A Voyage Round the World*, in vol. 4 of *A Collection of Voyages and Travels*, ed. A. Churchill and J. Churchill, 3rd ed., 6 vols. (London: Henry Lintot and John Osborn at the Golden Ball, 1745); see Sheehan, "Seventeenth Century Visitors to the Malay Peninsula", *JMBRAS* 12, 2 (1934): 104–6. Dr Careri was a doctor of civil law from Naples. He began his travels on 13 June 1693 and arrived back in Naples on 3 Dec. 1699, having visited Turkey, Persia, Goa, Melaka, Borneo, Macau, China (where he remained for two years), the Philippines and Mexico.

of Macao sail that way twice a year, yet they never remember anything of it. On the left, going from Malacca, the mouth is four or five fathom [7.3 to 9.1m] deep, and six or seven [11 to 13m] on the right.

There are abundance of other islands between Sumatra and cape Ikor [Johor] which are not set down in the maps; tho' some of them are so large, that they are call'd kingdoms. Some of them belong to the kings of Jambi and Palumbon [Palembang], islands adjoining to Sumatra, on the coast opposite to Malacca, where the Dutch have a factory; and some to the king of Rioo [Riau],[123] on the right of the straight of Sincapura; all three kings Mahometanes as to their religion, and Malayes by descent.

This multitude of islands makes abundance of straights, all dangerous to pass; but particularly that of Sincapura, where we were, which yet is most frequented by the natives, to go to, and return speedily from Siam, Cochinchina, Tunchin [Tonkin], Manila, China, Japan and other kingdoms of Asia. The other call'd *del Governador*, or the Governor's, is so deep, that very often there is no anchoring in it; but being much wider than the other, the European ships, that is, French, English, Dutch and others, use it very much. The other straights are call'd Carvon [Sabon], Durion [Durian], Javon [Java, not identifiable] and Ikor [Johor]; besides many more, which take name from the islands that form them. That of Ikor is only passable betwixt the continent and the islands, where a long channel ends, which leads to the metropolis of the same name, consisting of cottages, and thence to the sea of *Contracosta*, or the opposite coast. The Dutch have a factory at that court to trade for pepper.

Tuesday the 12th we entred the mouth of the straight of Sincapura betimes, which is a quarter of a league over at first; but further in wider, tho' enclos'd by so many islands, that they are a meer labyrinth to ships; which those who have not seen it before, think they shall never get out of, seeing land on all sides. The second mouth is but half so wide as the first, but only a mile [1.6km] in length, and all the distance between the two mouths is eight miles [12.9km]. This narrow passage is rendered the more dangerous by the violent setting of the water backwards and forwards at ebb and flood. In other respects the eye is delighted with a beautiful green of so many islands adorn'd with tall and thick trees, which are never left naked like ours in Europe in winter.

The Malayes, call'd Salittes, live along this channel in portable and floating houses. They dwell on the water in boats cover'd with mats, with canes interwoven in the middle to lie on; nor are they disturb'd either at their brutal solitude, the ill air, or the dreadfulness of the neighbouring woods. They are ingenious at fishing, which they live, on, either angling, or striking the least fishes through with spears made of bamboo. Some of them came to our ship's side, with their women and children in their floating houses to get vessels, iron, knives, tobacco and other triffles, in exchange for fish; they having no knowledge of money. They are not satisfy'd if they had the value of a hundred pieces of eight in exchange, they are so mistrustful, false and wicked; but upon any slight occasion strike their spear

[123] In 1695 the Johor court was established at Kota Tinggi, on the Johor River. The sultan at the time was Mahmud, ascended 1685, murdered 1699, the last sultan to claim descent from the line of the former sultans of Melaka.

> in any man's body, or else a small knife call'd Crisi,[124] they wear by their side. They are subject to the king of Ikor, who therefore has a custom-house for fish in the midst of the channel. We came to an anchor near it by reason of the calm.
>
> Wednesday the 13th we got out of the straight, leaving behind us on the right the cottages cover'd with mats, set up on poles; and keeping along the coast of Ikor, where I said the other mouth of the channel of that name was, the wind came up contrary, which oblig'd us to cast anchor near that barbarous country.
>
> The kingdom of Ikor, as I said, abounds in pepper, a sort of white copper the Portuguese call'd *Calein*,[125] Indian canes, rice, areca, cocoa-nuts, and other things, which keep up its trade with other nations; particularly with the Dutch, who therefore use all their endeavours to hinder others from resorting thither, allowing no vessels to pass by Malaca without the governor's leave. The inhabitants of Ikor and the Salittes wear a garment to their waiste; and from thence down, both men and women cover themselves with a linen cloth. The women wear their hair dishevel'd without breading; but the men shave their heads and beards, only keep long whiskers. Instead of a turban, they tie a small linen rag, like a fillet, about their foreheads.

It is perhaps significant at this period that Dr Careri's passage was made eastward bound. The manuscript map by Wilde, referred to above, shows two tracks of a vessel past Singapore Island, with soundings marked at intervals.[126] One follows the present Main Strait, and the other the passage by way of the Selat Sembilan and Keppel Harbour, the old route. Presumably, they represent his outward and homeward courses on a single voyage, as anchors are drawn at irregular distances along both tracks; there is one about opposite Tanjong Rhu, one in the western part of Keppel Harbour, another off Pasir Panjang and a fourth just inside the eastern end of the Selat Sembilan. In addition, he gives a very pleasing marginal drawing, some six inches [15cm] long, depicting the western part of Keppel Harbour, with "Lott's Wife" shown and named at the north side of the entrance.[127] The picture is semi-diagrammatic, but nonetheless it must stand as the earliest known representation of a part of Singapore Island. It includes two small collections of houses, in among the trees on the shore, one on Tebing Tinggi, and the other on Pulau Hantu. Seemingly, then, there were settlements on the land at these two points by about 1680. Dr Careri, as we have seen, makes no mention of them, but his account indicates that the site in Telok Saga, on the north side of Pulau Brani, was already occupied by the end of the 17th century.

Wilde shows the mouth of the western entrance to the Johor Strait, and the Kuala Johor (which he labels "River Johore"), but he gives no indication of any communication between them, and treats Singapore Island as part of the mainland. The same pattern is followed in a rather cruder MS map by Kempthorne, dated

---

[124] *Crisi* = *kĕris*. In general, the Aboriginal Malays, or Salittes as Dr Careri called them, appear to have been fairly prosperous at this time. Not many other accounts accord two garments to the men.

[125] A "sort of white copper the Portuguese call'd *Calein*" must presumably be tin.

[126] Wilde, MS map, ca. 1680: British Museum, MS Dept, Add. 15,737 (map 10). See also Bellin 1755, who publishes the track of *l'Oiseau*, 1687.

[127] See also above.

1688–90,[128] which shows tracks along the two courses plotted by Wilde, but without soundings. However, he does label the western end of the Johor Strait, "The Wt Entring of the River Jantana", and must therefore have been aware of the connection. About the last map to show Singapore Island in this way appears to be one by Allard, dated 1710:[129] he marks the Keppel Harbour channel as Oude Straete; and the Main Strait as Nieuwe Straete, terms which were now coming to have different meanings.

Before we discuss the changes in the nomenclature of the straits, we may well consider another small point. Allard's map of 1710, noted above, is a printed map, and it does not show the tracks of a vessel. On the other hand, the maps by Wilde and Kempthorne are MS charts, and seemingly record round voyages to some point further east. Bellin's map of 1755, noted below, though printed, has a similar double track on it labelled "*Route du Vaisseau l'Oiseau en 1687*".[130] The account of Captain John Weddell's visit to Macau states definitely that, though the fleet went out eastbound by the old route in 1637, it returned the following year by the Main Strait. Similarly, in 1688 Dampier's captain brought him back by the latter passage, finishing by way of Brewer's Strait, though he suggests that this may have been partly due to force of circumstances. However, it seems probable that during the 17th century, English ship's captains not uncommonly took the old passage when sailing further east and then made the return voyage by the Main Strait. Two qualities are desirable in a course among islands and reefs. One is adequate depth of water, and room to sail in relation to the prevailing winds; the other is a satisfactory distribution of distinctive landmarks. There is no doubt that the old route was an easy one to follow, coming from the west, so long as there were a few trees on the white, sandy islet on Cyrene Shoal; but it was probably not quite so easy to run into Keppel Harbour from the east. From the space devoted to the subject in the later 18th-century directories, it seems likely that the most difficult point in sailing through the Main Strait was finding the way into it from the west.

If these suppositions are well founded, they would in part account for the continued use of the old passage through the 17th century, and for the undoubted fact that several of the recorded voyages from the time of Mundy onwards definitely show the vessel going out by one route and returning by the other. We must also, of course, take into account Dr Careri's contention that it was difficult to anchor in the Main Strait and, with no wind and the tide against a vessel, anchoring could be

---

[128] Kempthorne, MS map, 1688–90: British Museum, Map Room, Sloane. 3665, fol. 59 verso, 60 recto.

[129] Carel Allard, *Atlas Maior* (Amsterdam: Frederik de Wit, Pieter Mortier, 1710), vol. 3, map 471 (Sumatra).

[130] This vessel made two trips to Siam from France. In 1685 it carried six Jesuit monks who were going to China, as far as the Siamese capital. The following year *l'Oiseau* returned to France with the members of a Siamese embassy to the French court. Then in 1687 the vessel took the Siamese embassy home, and with them carried M. de la Loubère, French envoy extraordinary to the king of Siam. In 1688 she returned to France again. Bellin's map of 1755 shows the course followed on the second round voyage, though presumably it was the same as in 1685–86. M. de la Loubère wrote an account of his experiences, of which an English translation, *A New Historical Relation of the Kingdom of Siam*, was published in London in 1693.

very necessary. An account by the Reverend Dr Navarette,[131] who passed through the Old Strait westward bound from Manila to Melaka in 1669, certainly supports the idea that it was difficult to enter Keppel Harbour from the east without help:

> We made thence for the strait of Sincapuera; our pilot had never pass'd it; we came within musket-shot, and no sign of a passage appear'd: he was about to tack and steer away for the new strait call'd del Governador, which is wider, and at present most people go that way. Some aboard were satisfied the strait was there, as having passed it sometime; but honest Stephen Diaz was so perplex'd, he would believe nobody. At a point of land which conceal'd the passage, there was a great number of fishermen call'd Saletes, who always live upon the water, and in their boats carry their wife, children, cats, dogs, hens, etc, as I mention'd in the first book many liv'd in China. One of the boats made to us, the master of it came aboard and carried us thro' very safe ... Having discover'd the passage, which we admir'd to see how close nature had hid and conceal'd it, we sail'd easily along. I had heard it said at Canton, that when ships sail'd thro' there, the yard-arms hit against the trees on both sides, and that the current was so violent, it whirl'd a ship about with all her sails abroad. The first is mere fiction, the second is false; though perhaps when the south-west winds reign there may be something of it, but it is not likely, considering the position of the continent and islands about it. The passage is scarce a bow-shot in width, two ships cannot pass it board by board; it presently grows wider, and abundance of islands appear. Our obstinate pilot[132] would needs keep close under the shore; he lost the channel, and the ship struck upon the sand; being it sprung no leak, we were not much troubled. As soon as this happen'd, abundance of the Salsetes took their posts to observe us, to take their advantage in case the ship were cast away. Practice had made them very expert at it; the flood carried us off safe. On Saturday being the eve of the Purification, or Candlemas, we came to anchor in sight of Malacca...

As we have noted, round the end of the 17th century, we find a shift in the names generally applied to these straits. Linschoten says that one Portuguese commander was known to have used the Johor Strait "by chance". It seems likely that further vessels had penetrated the channel by the 1660s. A manuscript map dated 1667 attributed to Joannes Blaeu[133] shows Pulau Tekong and Pulau Ubin as distinct islands (though drawn relatively larger than they should be), and marks soundings at both ends or the Johor Strait (but not through the middle section), as well as along the Selat Sembilan and Keppel Harbour passage. An MS map by Thomas Bowrey,[134] dated about 1690, ignores the latter channel, but carries soundings over the whole

---

[131] Dr R.F.F. Dominick Fernandez Navarette, "An Account of the Empire of China", in *A Collection of Voyages and Travels*, vol. 1. See Sheehan, "Seventeenth Century Visitors to the Malay Peninsula", *JMBRAS* 12, 2 (1934): 90. Dr Navarette was Professor of Divinity at Manila.

[132] *Pilot*. That is, the ship's *pilot*, Stephen Diaz. At this period, the term pilot corresponded to the modern navigating officer.

[133] J. Blaeu (1596–1673), MS map, 1667: British Museum, MS Dept, Add. 9047. G. This map gives a name to Pulau Blakang Mati, apparently beginning with an "N", but it is not possible to read it clearly. See also above.

[134] T. Bowrey, MS map, ca. 1690: British Museum, MS Dept, Add. 5222 (10); Eberard, MS map, 1100: British Museum, MS Dept, Add. 15, 738 (40).

length of the passage behind the island, labelling it the Old Straits of Cincapura, and through the Main Strait, which he calls the Broad Straits. Eberard's MS map of about 1700 marks soundings in all three straits, but labels only two, the Johor Strait, Destroit de Sincapour, and the Main Strait, Destroit de Gebernapur. Manuscript maps, in so far as they are records of particular voyages, are more likely to reflect current practice than a printed map. A map published by W. and J. Mount and T. and T. Page in 1750,[135] shows tracks through the two straits south of the island, which they label Good Sernua Channel and The New Straits of Sincapour: the Johor Strait has no track through it, but is labelled the Old Straits of Sincapour. Bellin, in 1755,[136] five years later, gives the French equivalents of the same names (with a proper rendering of Governor), and again shows tracks through only the two southern straits, but they are marked as the route of a voyage made in 1687. Almost certainly, both these later maps really refer to conditions much nearer to 1700 than their dates alone indicate, and thus reflect a period when the Johor Strait was being used, to a small extent, by eastbound vessels making for the Johor River, while the original course which Linschoten described was still in limited use for passages to the South China Sea. In 1722 the itinerant Johor court finally vacated sites on the Johor River, and came to rest (rest of a sort) at Riau. There can have been no object in traversing the Johor Strait after this had happened, and it seems likely that from then onwards European vessels abandoned the shortlived northern route.[137] This would not, of course, retard

---

[135] W. and J. Mount, and T. and T. Page, *Atlas Maritimus Novus, or the New Sea Atlas, with 20 Charts* (London: Richard Mount and Thomas Page on Tower Hill, 1750), see map 7 ("A New and Correct Chart of the Straits of Malacca"), repr., 1755. The first edition of this work, with 22 charts, was published by R. Mount and T. Page in 1708; in spite of its title, much of the present map should probably be referred to that date, so far as the area now under discussion is concerned. Reissuing earlier maps with little or no amendment was a not uncommon practice in the 18th century. Thus the copy that we have of Thomas Jefferys' chart, "The Straits of Singapore, with Those of Durion, Sabon and Mandol", bears the cartographer's name with the title and "Published 12th May, 1794, by Laurie & Whittle, 53 Fleet Street, London" at the foot. But Jefferys died in 1771, and the original edition of this map must, in fact, have been prepared about 1766–70 (it shows the track of the East Indiaman *Bute* through the Straits of Durian in 1764–65). In the same way it seems likely that J.N. Bellin's map dated 1755 (see below) was in part based on a much earlier MS map. These two maps (Mount and Page, 1750 and 1755, and Bellin, 1755), do not, as we have said, indicate that the original strait was still in use at this period. We have drawn attention to them as showing that the passageway was still current on maps printed as late as the 1750s, just as Thornton's directions for sailing through it remained in print until the 1760s.

[136] Jean Nicholas Bellin, "Carte réduite des Détroits de Malaca, Sincapour, et du Gouverneur", Paris, 1755; said to have been drawn from the records and a manuscript map of "Sr. Dauge, Pilote du Service de la Compagnie des Indes", and, as we have noted, marked with the route of the ship *l'Oiseau*, in 1687. Like the previous map (n. 134), this very probably perpetuates the course favoured at a much earlier period. See also above: the route should be 1687–88.

[137] The Acehnese captured the Johor capital at Batu Sawar in 1613, and razed it to the ground. It was partly rebuilt in 1613–14, but in 1617 the sultan moved the court to Lingga. From then until the 1640s there can have been little European intercourse with the Johor River. In 1647 an Englishman named Wylde, in the *Supply*, tried to start up trade with Batu Sawar, and it seems that there was a limited commercial activity for the next 20-odd years. Then about 1669 Johor

the growing belief that the Johor Strait was the "Old Strait": it would, in fact, help to foster it.

Meanwhile the original passage (through the present Keppel Harbour) was apparently used much less frequently from about the turn of the century. Captain Alexander Hamilton, who visited Johor for the first time in 1695, and thereafter was round and about this part of the world at intervals until 1723, makes no direct mention of it, though from his employing the term "largest and easiest passage" to describe the Main Strait it might be taken that he was aware of the existence of a third route, particularly, if one has Dr Careri's note of the same period in mind. Hamilton's comments on the Singapore Straits are as follows:[138]

> *Johore Lami*, which is sometimes the Place of that King's Residence, and has the Benefit of a fine deep large River, which admits of two Entrances into it. The smallest is from the Westward, called by *Europeans* the Streights of *Sincapure*, but by the Natives *Sallita de Brew*. It runs along the Side of *Sincapure* Island for 5 or 6 Leagues together, and ends at the great River of *Johore* ... between the small *Carimon* and *Tanjong-bellong* on the Continent, is the Entrance of the Streights of *Sincapure* before mentioned, and also into the Streights of *Governadore*, the largest and easiest passage into the *China* Seas. There are many Islands lying thick hereabout, all under the Dominions of *Johore*.

At the same time the last two maps noted above show that notice of the Old Strait survived until well on in the 18th century, even if it was no longer used by European vessels. John Thornton, in his *Oriental Navigation* published in 1703, gives a tolerable description of the old passage, retaining for it the name Old Streights of Sincapore. In the interests of space we must confine ourselves to his account of the passage through Keppel Harbour from the west, beginning as he leaves the Selat Sembilan,

---

began a disastrous war with Jambi, which led to a second sack of Batu Sawar in 1673. For the next 15 years the Johor court was at Pahang and later Riau. Finally, from 1688 to 1722, the court was successively at Kota Tinggi, Panchor, Riau and back at Panchor (see Gibson-Hill, "Johor Lama and Other Ancient Sites on the Johore River", *JMBRAS* 28, 2 [1955]: 155–67, esp. the chart on p. 165). It seems likely that the period when the Johor Strait flourished as the "Old Strait of Sincapour" was restricted to this interval of about 30 to 35 years. Possibly it acquired its erroneous designation from the fact of its having been known as a way into the Johor River from the west before 1674, and so have come into use as the "old passage" when trade grew up again. It was probably explored by the Dutch, as it is a more natural approach to the river from Melaka, which they occupied in 1641. There was certainly English trade with Batu Sawar up to 1674, and according to Winstedt, "An English ship took the news [of its sack by the Pangeran of Jambi] to Bantam and said that an Englishman Mr Loch of Johor was captured with his ship and when he wished to complain to the sultan of Jambi was strangled by the Pati who said he had hanged himself"; but prior to 1683, when the East India Company was driven from Bantam, the majority of the English vessels probably reached Johor from the south, and at this period, for preference, they would have followed the course east of Bintan.

[138] Capt. Alexander Hamilton, *A New Account of the East Indies*, vol. 2, pp. 93, 123–4. Hamilton tells us definitely that he first visited the Johor River in 1695, and that he was there again in 1703. He finally returned to England in 1723: in the interval between 1703 and 1723 he seems to have visited much of the East Indies, Siam, Indo-China and Japan, but he mentions few dates and gives nothing in the way of an itinerary.

making for the "small Island with a white sandy Strand" which apparently still marked the eastern edge of the Cyrene Shoal:[139]

> in the way thither you will find 15, 14, 10, and 11 Fathom [18.2 to 27.4m], and as you draw near this Island, you will see a very fair and large Opening into the Sea, but you must not regard it, for it is full of Rocks and broken Ground, and no Passage through it. Thro' this Opening you will see the Island *Carimon*, and when the white Island bears West by South, the Island *Carimon* will be shut in with it, at which Time you have 15 Fathom [27.4m] Water; and then the *Old Streights* will shew its Opening quite through; steer over for the Mouth of the *Streights*, keeping the *Streights* quite open, your Soundings will be between 16 and 12 Fathom [22 to 29.2m] Water, and the Distance between the Mouth of the *Old Streights*, and the white Island is about 6 Miles [9.7m]: On the South-side of the *Streights* is a bluff Rock and smooth aloft, with Trees and Grass, and on the North-side is a scragged Rock, shewing like a ruined Wall; also several other Rocks close to the Shore, or not above half a Ship's length into the Sea; the Passage is between these two Rocks which is not above half a Cable's length [92.5m] in width; but there is very good Soundings, the least Depth being 12 Fathom [22m], and when you have entered the *Streights*, you will find it something wider, it being there a Cable's length [185.2m] or more in Width; as you enter into the *Streights*, you keep nearest the South Shore; but when you are within keep near the middle or nearest the North Shore, but not too near the first Point, for there is shoal rocky Ground. This is the narrowest part of the *Streights*, except the first. Entrance; from hence you may direct your Course through as you please, for there is no Rock or Shoal, but what lieth in the Bays, or within the Points, and in Sailing through you will have 10 and 9 Fathom [16.5 to 18.3m], the least Depth being seven and a half, but in many places it is coarse Ground; after you are out of the *Streights*, you must steer East and East by South, Depth 7, 8, and 9 Fathom [12.8 to 16.5m]; and being clear of the bluff Point, on the Larboard-side, you must luff up to the Southward, and in steering ESE, you will come in 7, 6, and 4 Fathom [7.3 to 12.8m] Water, in which Depth you may Anchor; it is coarse sandy Ground, which is on the Shoal that lieth on the South-side of the white sandy Bay; this Bay trendeth from the bluff brown Hill on the South-side of the *Streights*; and on the South-side of this Bay is a green Plat of Trees which grow in the Water; and from that Point, this shoal stretches East into the Sea, about a Mile, and from the North Point, which is a flat Point, with low green Trees, there is a Ledge of Rocks, which stretch nearest South, about half a Mile [805m] into the Sea, so that I would advise those that come this Way not to come in less than 7 Fathom Water…

[139] John Thornton, *Oriental Navigation* (London: J. How, 1703). There were subsequent editions in 1711, 1716, 1723, 1734, 1748, 1750 and 1761. The passage cited here was apparently retained, without appreciable amendment, throughout the life of the work: it was certainly repeated in the editions of 1711, 1734, 1750 and 1761 (M. Barnett, correspondence). The original edition of *Oriental Navigation* was by John Seller (1675), and comprised the third book of the *English Pilot* (not seen). Thornton gives no name to the island on the edge of Cyrene Shoal, though he marks it prominently on his map; it does not, in fact, seem to have had a name before Franklin's map of 1822. See above.

His description of Lot's Wife (Batu Berlayar) is apt, if we may judge by the watercolour painting of circa 1845–48,[140] though it scarcely redounds to the poor woman's credit.

Thornton's account of the passage through these straits was reprinted in the subsequent editions of his work, the last of which appeared in 1761. A few years earlier, however, William Herbert, giving "Directions for sailing from Malacca to Pullo Timoan", came down heavily in favour of the "*Governor's Straits*, commonly called the Straits of Sincapore", saying:[141]

> Beyond Tanjong-Bouro the coast of Malaya forms a bay, wherein some little rivers empty themselves, on the East side whereof is a little island, called the Island of Adders (or *Snake Island*), between which and the Westermost point of Pulau Panjang (*or Long Island, called also Sincapour, or Sincapore*), is the entrance of the Old Straits of Sincapour; and to the Southward of the said point you see also the entrance of the New Strait, so called. But most ships, at present, prefer Governor's Strait to either, as being both shorter and safer.

The latter is the only passage that he describes. From this time on we hear nothing more of the original strait ("the New Strait, so called"); and step by step it ceases to be even a clear channel on the maps, until, in fact in Horsburgh's chart of 1806 the area is such a muddle of rock, reef and islet, that no self-respecting navigator would have gone near the place, Before this we have Mannevillette, who in his *Neptune Oriental*, published in 1775, shows the Main Strait, well marked with soundings, but none on the other two channels.[142] The fifth edition of Herbert's directory, revised by Samuel Dunn and printed in 1780, mentions only the "Governor's Straits, commonly called the Straits of Sincapour", A sheet of views published for the benefit of ships' masters by Dalrymple in the same year,[143] gives a drawing of "the western entrance to the Strait of Sincapore", which, as far as he was concerned, was

---

[140] See above. The painting was probably the work of Miss Patience Thomson and executed about 1775–85, but based on a contemporay drawing by her father, J.T. Thomson, settlement surveyor from 1841 to 1855, who was responsible for the destruction of the stack in Aug. 1848, to widen the western entrance to Keppel Harbour. There is a picture of the point after the destruction of the stack and before any other development had taken place there, in John Cameron's *Our Tropical Possessions in Malayan India* (London: Smith, Elder & Co., 1865), opp. p. 33.

[141] William Herbert, *A New Directory for the East-Indies*, 2nd ed. (London: Printed for the Editor, 1759), pp. 17–59. First ed., the previous year, 1758 (not seen). "Tanjong-Bouro" = Tanjung Piai, See also above. "The Island of Adders" = Pulau Merambong: Eredia called it "Pulo Ular", and its name appears as a variant on this theme, mostly as "Isle de Cobra", until the middle of the 19th century. The first appearance of the present name known to me is on J.B. Tassin's map (in Moor [1837]), where it is called "P. Marambong". The Admiralty chart of 1840 gives "Cobra", plain and stark. The English edition of Linschoten (1598) interestingly calls it "old Sincapura", a name which does not appear to have been followed by any subsequent author, but which might repay a little investigation: Do any Portuguese accounts prior to 1600 use a variant of that name for it? Eredia, as we have noted, gives "Pulo Ular".

[142] J.B.N.D. d'Après de Mannevillette, *Le Neptune Oriental* (Paris: Brest, Demonville, Malassis, 1775), map 49. This map revives the name *Selat Tebrau*, in the form "Det. de Salete Baro", for the present Johor Strait: See also above.

[143] A. Dalrymple, publ. 17 Mar. 1780; copy, British Museum, Map Room, Maps 49. d. 2 (21).

14.7 New Harbour from the Proposed Site of the Dry Docks. Watercolour from the Charles Dyce Collection, National University of Singapore (NUS) Museums.

again the Main Strait. The drawings were from passages by the *Royal Charlotte*, East Indiaman (Joseph Cotton, 26 August 1748), the *Norfolk*, Man-of-War (M. Waghorn, 30 August 1762) and the *Earl of Ashburnham*, East Indiaman (R. Peirce, 19 August 1769). Dalrymple himself also used this passage on his voyage to and from Sulu in 1762–63,[144] and clearly by this time it had long been the official route for East Indiamen and HM vessels.

We have, in fact, no sure indications that the passage via the Selat Sembilan and Keppel Harbour was employed to any extent by European vessels after the close of the 17th century; though since mention of it survived on charts and in directories until about 1760, it can only have been in the last quarter of the 18th century "that its very existence was forgotten". Even this requires some qualification. There is no reason to doubt that local coasting vessels continued to employ it, and presumably the descendants of the Aboriginal Malays whom Tomé Pires, Mundy, Dr Navarette, Dampier and Dr Careri recorded remained there. In 1797 Captain Robert Scott passed through the strait in a Bugis *perahu*, but as he described Keppel Harbour as "too narrow for large ships", his notice of it can scarcely have done anything to bring to mind its earlier position as a passageway for European vessels. After its rediscovery in 1819, it is referred to by both Begbie and Newbold as a new channel, lately discovered.[145] On the other hand, as we note below (in relation to HMS *Rainbow*'s visit of 1826), obviously some recollection of its former significance remained, and at intervals the literate few must have stumbled on the old accounts, as one of the Logan brothers did in 1848, and J.T. Thomson again in 1852. Probably we should say no more than that, from the latter part of the 18th century, all effective knowledge of it died among European navigators.

In part, this was probably due to Horsburgh, who came near to acquiring pontifical ranking during the first half of the last century (though it is interesting to find that he was sufficiently fallible to cut the western end off Singapore Island, and set it up as an island on its own; and until 1828 at least, his general idea of the shapes of the smaller islands in this region were rather startling). In the first edition of his directory Horshurgh mentions only two straits hereabout, the Johor Strait and

---

[144] British Museum, MS Dept, James Rennell, "Journal of a Voyage to the Sooloo Islands and the North West Coast of Borneo, 1762–3".

[145] Capt. P.J. Begbie, Madras Artillery, *The Malayan Peninsula: Embracing Its History, Manners and Customs of the Inhabitants, Politics, Natural History etc. from its Earliest Records* (Madras: Vepery Mission Press, 1834): "A new passage, which has received the name of 'New Harbour', has been lately discovered to the westward of Singapore, through which vessels can pass, and thus avoid the circuitous route by St John's, when going to, or coming from, the Straits. The soundings are good, but the channel narrow, and not to be attempted but in daylight ... The inhabitants of New Harbour are generally employed in either fishing, or making *cadjangs*" (p. 354). Lt. T.J. Newbold, Madras Light Infantry, *Political and Statistical Account of the British Settlements in the Straits of Malacca*, 2 vols. (London: John Murray, 1839): "A narrow passage called New Harbour, has lately been discovered to the west of Singapore" (vol. 1, p. 267); on the previous page he erroneously refers to the Johor Strait as "formerly used by navigators sailing between India and China".

the "SINCAPOUR STRAIT (called Governor's Strait, or New Strait, by the French and Portuguese)"; of the former he says:[146]

> From Tanjong Boulus the coast trends to the N. Eastward, having near it the Isle Cobra, or Snake Island, on the West side of the entrance of Sincapour Old Strait, which is formed between it and Tooly Island to the S.E. This strait is from ½ a mile to 1½ miles [0.85 to 2.4km] broad, with soundings of 5 or 6, to 10 fathoms [9.1 to 18.2m]; it is bounded on the South side by the island of Tooly, the large island Sincapour, and their contiguous islands; and on the North side by the island Salat Boora, and the main. Betwixt the East point of Sincapour Island and Johore Hill, the eastern mouth of the Old Strait communicates with the large strait, now in general use; the former being more contracted, with strong tides, is now seldom chosen by any ship,

Copies of Franklin's map of Singapore must have come as quite a surprise to Horsburgh. Nonetheless, his statement on there being only two straits past Singapore Island, and the identity of the "Old Strait", apparently remained without overt correction until 1848; and even then the note fell on deaf ears.

The New Harbour

There is no doubt that Captain Daniel Ross, of HCSV *Margaret & Francis*, was ignorant of the existence of the Keppel Harbour waterway in February 1819, when he drew up the first rough survey of the Singapore roads.[147] Seemingly, also, neither Farquhar nor Raffles knew anything about it up to July of that year, when the latter left to return to Bencoolen. Then the following month Farquhar rediscovered it, though how much he was helped by information supplied by the local Malays or, as Wurtzburg suggests, the commander of the *Nearchus*, is not clear.[148] On the whole it is likely that his "discovery" amounted to no more than listening to what was told

---

[146] James Horsburgh, *The India Directory or Directions for Sailing to and from the East Indies, China, New Holland, Cape of Good Hope and the interjacent Ports*, 2 vols. (London: Printed for the Author, 1809–11) vol. 2 (1811), pp. 175–6. See also James Horsburgh, *Memoir of a Chart Elucidating the Navigation of the Straits of Malacca & Sincapour* (London: Printed for the Author, 1805), pp. 14–20 (new ed., 1812).

[147] Map published East India Company, London, 1 Jan. 1820. His memorandum to Raffles, accompanying it, appears in J.H. Moor's *Notices of the Indian Archipelago and Adjacent Countries* (Singapore: n.p., 1837), p. 275. There is also a contemporary MS copy in *EIC Rec*, L. 10: 19–21 (Raffles Museum Archives). [E.N.: Now deposited in the National Archives of Singapore.] In it he allows for an approach to the waterfront only from the east, or round "Peak Island" (Pulau Tembakul), that is, from the eastern part of the present Main Strait.

[148] *Prince of Wales Island Gazette*, vol. 5, no. 223, 21 Aug. 1819, says that according to accounts received from Singapore, Major Farquhar "was about to proceed in the schooner *Enterprize* to survey the straits and island". The information must have reached Penang via the brig *Ganges*, Chas Maybury which arrived there on 17 Aug. exited Singapore 11 Aug. (1819). If Farquhar did obtain information about the strait from the commander of the *Nearchus*, the latter himself must have learned of it after Raffles left Singapore for the second time in June 1819, as he was admittedly on friendly terms with Raffles, and would certainly have passed the information on to him personally.

to him, and then going out to verify it personally. Nonetheless, few enough people do that; and on 2 September 1819, he wrote to Raffles, much pleased with himself, and announced that he had found a "new harbour" to the west of the settlement. Two things are obvious from this letter: the passage was then looked on as a possible extension of the existing harbour area rather than as a strait; and even if its existence had been known to one or more of the ship's captains two months earlier, when Raffles was still in Singapore, there had been no discussion of it. Farquhar produces it, like Jack Horner's plum, as an indication of his zeal and enterprise, and he would scarcely have done so if he had thought that there was any chance that Raffles already knew about it.

Farquhar returned to the subject nearly a year later, in a letter to Raffles of 29 July 1820.[149] On this occasion he also sent a copy direct to Bengal: apparently he felt that Raffles had not shown sufficient interest in his first announcement. In 1820 he wrote:

> Reports having reached me that it has been asserted and credited in Calcutta that the Settlement of Singapore affords no adequate protection for shipping in times of war, I conceive it my duty in addition to what I noticed on this subject in my letter to your address under date the 2nd September last year to state that the harbour pointed out in that letter situated about three miles [4.8km] to the westward of the Town is capable of affording the most complete protection to ships of the largest size, the only entrances into which from the Eastward and Westward being sufficiently narrow to be defended in the most effectual manner from both shores, where from the nature of the ground being high and commanding the batteries would be quite secure against the fire of the enemy's ships.
>
> Inside the harbour there is good anchorage from 15 to 4 fathoms [7.3 to 27.4m], the latter depth being within pistol shot of a small elevated island situated about the centre of the harbour. The sea is at all times perfectly smooth here, being with the exception of the entrances above mentioned completely landlocked: in short nothing in my opinion is wanting to render this harbour a place of the greatest security in cases of danger from an enemy's shipping, and which will, I have no doubt, should this Settlement ever unfortunately fall into the hands of a foreign power be rendered a position of great strength and importance …
>
> A general survey of the Western or New Harbour as well as of the whole Settlement and environs is in great forwardness and would have been completed long ere this but from the circumstances of my time being completely occupied with the various other duties of the Residency and having had no assistant whatever in the Surveying Department.

To which, as a postscript, he adds another very good reason why the promised survey had proceeded slowly: "the surveying instruments written for to Calcutta and ordered by the Supreme Govt. to be furnished by the Surveyor-General" had never reached him. However, on 17 April the following year (1821), he was able to write:[150]

---

[149] *EIC Rec*., L. 4: 12–1.

[150] Farquhar to Raffles, 17 Apr. 1821 (EIC. Rec., L. 4: 346).

> Herewith I have the honour to transmit a general survey of the Town and environs of Singapore including the New Harbour … The soundings in the Harbour are the same as laid down in the chart by Captain D. Ross with the exception of those in the New Harbour which were taken under my own direction …

Nothing came of the suggestion in Farquhar's letter of July 1820, but the idea remained current for a number of years, and several officers returned to it later. Farquhar, we may note, was apparently the person responsible for the name "New Harbour", and if the latter had to be changed it should in all fairness have been changed to "Farquhar's Harbour".

The next account that we have of New Harbour, in point of origin, is from Dr Crawfurd, who visited Singapore for five weeks at the beginning of 1822, on his way to Siam and Cochinchina. Under the heading of 27 January, he says:[151]

> We went yesterday morning along the coast, to the westward, and visited the new harbour, or Selat Panikam, as it is called by the Malays. This harbour is formed by Singapore and the islets which lie off the western limit of the roadstead. The entrance is narrow and difficult; but when a ship is once moored within it, she is secure from every danger—from rocks, elements, and even from an enemy, for half a dozen guns would make it impregnable to any attack from the sea. The prospect we had on entering it was beautiful and unexpected. We found ourselves completely land-locked, in every direction, by the green and woody shores of the islands surrounding us; and the sea, though considerably ruffled without, was here as smooth as glass. This is a favourite retreat of the orang laut. On our arrival their proas were lying along the shore; but as the flood-tide made, they advanced into the middle of the channel, and began to fish. Their principal mode of taking fish is by spearing, and hence the native name of the Strait, which has this meaning. The larger fish are followed by the proas, and easily traced through the water, which is perfectly clear and transparent. They are speared with a long trident, and with such dexterity as to be seldom missed … The boats of the orang laut are mere canoes, covered by a light shed of palm-leaves. We saw their whole families on board, men, women, and children; and both in their fishing and management of the boats, the women appeared to take as active a share as the men.

At this period it seems that the strait was still inhabited only by Aboriginal Malays (the descendants of the "Indian Inhabitants" who sold Dampier's party a few fruits and fresh fish in 1688), under their own headmen. The great majority were living in boats at points along the south shore, in the Selat Sengkir and probably in Telok Chermin, near the western end of the strait, but it appears some at least had already built houses over the beach in Telok Saga (where Dr Careri had recorded houses "of poles" as early as 1695), and at Kampong Kopit, on Pulau Brani. Towards the end of 1822 arrangements begun to move the temenggong and his followers away from the upper part of the Singapore River. Early in March 1823, it was, agreed that he should be granted the use of a strip of ground along the beach between Tanjong

[151] Crawfurd, *Journal*, vol. 1, pp. 66–8. See also George Finlayson, *The Mission to Siam, and Hué, the Capital of Cochin-China in the Years 1821–22* (London: John Murray, 1826), pp. 72–4. Crawfurd's account of the fishing methods of the orang laut is very similar to that given by Peter Mundy, after his passage through Keppel Harbour in 1637. See also above.

Pagar and Telok Belanga: it was some 6,000 feet [1.8km] long, and extended inland for about 1,200 feet [366m]. At this period his compound on the north side of the Singapore River was said to contain 79 huts, with a total population of "607 souls".[152]

When Raffles and his party first landed on the island, in 1819, the temenggong's followers consisted mostly of orang laut from Siak, the great majority of whom were living in boats on the river. This community, we know, remained there until the 1840s at least.[153] A few may have adopted a terrestrial habitat before 1823, but certainly there cannot have heen many who came to live ashore. Nonetheless the population of the temenggong's compound apparently grew from about 25–30 persons to over 600 in four years, an increase that cannot be accounted for by this means, or by any natural process of reproduction. There must, in fact, have been a considerable addition to it from outside the settlement.

Early in 1820 a part-Bugis prince named Balarra or Bellara fled from Riau and sought sanctuary in Singapore. He was accompanied by his family and followers, making in all about 500 persons, including women and children. The Dutch authorities, who accused him of murder, piracy and treason, demanded his surrender, and an envoy was sent from Melaka to collect him. Farquhar, in a note of 20 February 1820, refused to give him up,[154] and at least the greater part of the group remained in Singapore. On his death, several years later, Balarra was buried in the temenggong's graveyard at Telok Belanga, not far from 'Abdu'r Rahman himself. There was already a small community of Bugis seamen and merchants in Singapore in 1820, settled near the sultan's compound at Kampong Gelam, but it looks very much as if the refugees from Riau were sheltered by the temenggong, and subsequently went with his party to New Harbour. This association of maritime Malays, displaced Bugis from Riau and orang laut, put in a place where they could not have grown rice effectively even if they had wished to do so, is worth noting. It goes a long way towards explaining the undoubted complicity of the Telok Belanga community in small-scale piracy in local waters during the period 1825–40.

About 1826 interest was revived in the possibilities of New Harbour as a passageway, though it never came into regular use again for this purpose alone. Early in the year the *William Parker*, a free trader, passed through on her way from Calcutta to Singapore. According to the editor of the *Singapore Chronicle*, writing some time later, she took this course "by mistake … and it was generally considered a very dangerous experiment", but it is probable that her commander had some idea of what he was doing, even if he subsequently looked back on his action with misgivings. In July that year HMS *Rainbow*, with 28 guns and under Captain

[152] The total includes women and children. Farquhar was authorised to give the temenggong $1,000, to compensate him for the expenses of moving his followers (Hull to Farquhar, 15 Mar. 1823, *EIC Rec*., L. 17: 190–1); later he obtained an additional sum from Crawfurd. For the grant of the land at New Harbour, see *EIC Rec*., L. 17: 181–2. For later reference to the conditions under which it was held, see S. 19: 120.

[153] See Gibson-Hill, "The Orang Laut of the Singapore River and the Sampan Panjang", *JMBRAS* 25, 1 (1952): 163–4. Bonham gave orders for them to move, but some families at least stayed on until the 1870s or later.

[154] Farquhar to Timmermann Thyssen, 20 Feb. 1820 (*EIC Rec*., L. 16: 262–4).

the Honourable Henry Rous, RN, investigated the passage. He had F.J. Bernard, Farquhar's son-in-law, on board as a passenger: at that time Bernard was a Lloyd's Agent. In reporting the event, the *Chronicle*[155] describes the *Rainbow* as "the first vessel that has ever come through intentionally", but on this occasion it is certain that her navigator was at least vaguely aware of the former use of the channel, as in the Captain's Log[156] the run is recorded under the heading "Thro' the Little Old Straits". The *Rainbow* came through very cautiously, towed by her boats: she entered the western end at 1 p.m. on 24 July, and was towed until 7 p.m., when Rous anchored for the night off Telok Belanga: towing was resumed again at 5:40 a.m. the next morning, and three hours later the *Rainbow* anchored in the roads off the mouth of the Singapore River.

The following year, 1827, Captain Daniel Ross, BM, surveyed the strait officially and prepared a chart (published in 1829), while G.D. Coleman was set to survey Blakang Mati. The same year (1827), Captain Edward Lake, Bengal Engineers, who had been sent to Singapore to report on the public works and fortifications, advocated the inclusion of the area in the defences of the settlement, and recommended the cutting of a canal from the Singapore River to Telok Belanga.[157] In part he based his proposals on recommendations given him by Lt. Phillip Jackson, Bengal Artillery,[158] who had been in the settlement since 1822, and it seems probable that the latter had himself received the germ of his ideas on the subject from Farquhar. Unfortunately, the only action taken on this portion of Lake's

---

[155] *Singapore Chronicle*, 3 Aug. 1826 (not seen). Reprinted in J.H. Moor, *Notices of the Indian Archipelago*, p. 274. There is also a reference to the passage, based on the notice in the *Singapore Chronicle*, in the *Asiatic Journal* 23 (1827): 278. Quotations used here are from Moor (1837).

[156] Captain's Log, PRO, Adm. 51/3381. Conditions are described as light, variable breezes, fine weather. HMS *Tees*, 26 guns, Capt. Thomas Coe, RN, circumnavigated the island in Dec. 1822, with Capt. William Flint, RN, Master Attendant, Singapore, on board as a passenger: she weighed from the roads at 10:30 a.m. on 2 Dec. for Kuala Johor, spent 4, 5 and 6 Dec. "working through [the] Old Straits", and anchored off the waterfront again at 1:20 p.m. on 7 Dec., but she did not return via New Harbour (Captain's Log, PRO, Adm. 51/3484). [E.N.: The records of the former PRO (Public Record Office) are now with the National Archives (TNA) in Kew.]

[157] Lake to Secretary to Govt. Singapore, 28 May 1827 (*EIC Rec*; A. 45: 36–7). Lake was stationed in Penang. His report on Singapore was not sent on to Bengal until 1829, and in 1830 Lake, his wife and children left Singapore for leave in England on the same ship as Presgrave's widow. The vessel cleared Sunda Head, but was never heard of again: presumably she sank somewhere in the Indian Ocean. Lake's death probably facilitated the pigeonholing of his report. By the end of 1829, Coleman had surveyed 1,038 acres [4.2km^2] on Pulau Blakang Mati and 215 acres [0.87km^2] on Pulau Brani.

[158] Lt. Jackson to Lake, 13 May 1827 (*EIC Rec.*, A. 45: 27–9). Lt. Phillip Jackson (1802–70) reached Singapore on 21 Jan. 1822, to take charge of the artillery unit stationed here: in October the same year, Raffles appointed him Assistant Settlement Engineer: the appointment was confirmed by Crawfurd on 7 June 1823, and he continued in this capacity (with change of title to Executive Officer on 18 Dec. 1824), and with the additional duty of surveyor of lands from Jan. 1823 until he left the settlement on sick leave on 1 July 1821. His departure was precipitated by the fact that he had been doing little or no survey work for some time: when Lake gave orders that he was to spend a definite proportion of each week on field surveys, he produced a certificate to the effect that it was not advisable for him to be out in the sun.

report was the construction of Fort Fullerton, on the site now occupied by Fullerton Building, and even this was the result of local panic at news of war having broken out between England and France in 1829. The proposal to fortify New Harbour was revived again in 1843 by Capt. James Best, Madras Engineers.[159] He wanted to place a chain of 12 batteries from Tanjong Berlayar to Kampong Gelam, with a redoubt at Tanjong Rhu: 7 of the batteries were to be sited to defend New Harbour, and the other 5 the water front from Telok Ayer to the Kalang basin. He also brought up the idea of moving part of the garrison from Sepoy Lines, and placing it on Blakang Mati (to which, following Captain Lake, he gives the alternative name of *Island of St George*). Nothing came of this proposal either, as it was still believed that the island was too unhealthy for habitation away from the fringe along New Harbour, and the only parts of his elaborate plan that were put into immediate effect were the construction of a sea wall around Fort Fullerton, in 1844–45, and the temporary rehabilitation of the battery on Scandal Point.[160]

By the late 1830s the European section of the town was becoming full, by contemporary standards, and some of the more enterprising merchants began to look further afield. Dr Oxley started the move towards the districts later known as Claymore and Tanglin, about 1837, when he acquired 173 acres of ground west of Tank Road (now Clemenceau Avenue) from the East India Company for Rs 2,342 and began the construction of Killiney Estate; but in the latter part of 1838 he was transferred to Melaka, and did not return to Singapore until October 1841. In the meantime William Cuppage had opened up Emerald Hill estate, beyond C.R. Prinsep's vast holding, and Charles Carnie had travelled further along Orchard Road, and built the first house on Carnie's Hill (now corrupted to Cairnhill). About the same time, W.W. Ker and James Guthrie moved out to join the Temenggong and Hodeen at New Harbour. Wemyss Ker erected a bungalow, later replaced by a "house of architectural appearance", on Bukit Chermin.[161] Guthrie, who whimsically named his house "St James", occupied Tanjong Aur, the spur to the east of Tebing Tinggi, close to the site of the present St James's Power Station. Several other merchants joined them in the late 1840s, but the New Harbour area proved less popular than

---

During 1826 he also held the acting appointment of Assistant to the Officer in Charge of the Residency. He did not return to Singapore: his service from 1827 was much broken by periods of ill-health, and on 6 Jan. 1836, he was allowed to retire on halfpay, at the rank of Captain.

[159] There are two maps showing the proposed positions of the batteries, etc., in the Raffles Museum collection; one is a MS map by Best, the other, annotations signed by Best on a printed map, J.T. Thomson, 1843.

[160] See "The Defences of Singapore", *Singapore Free Press Office* (1885): 22.

[161] Ker and Guthrie were the first European merchants to establish residences at New Harbour, though as early as 1822 the missionary C.H. Thomsen asked for the grant of an area of land which he had begun to clear there to establish a school to teach the arts of agriculture to young Malay boys, and at the beginning of 1823 F.J. Bernard claimed that the temenggong had given him (part of) Pulau Blakang Mati, and he was clearing it to plant pineapples. However, Bernard never took up residence at New Harbour, and the Rev'd Thomsen's school soon died a natural death. He lost several thousand dollars on the project in a few years, and then abandoned it. In 1835, prior to returning to Europe, he sold the land to a Chinese merchant known as "Hodeen" or "Hodin", who built a house on the ground and began the cultivation of nutmegs.

14.8 View of the towns and roads of Singapore from Government Hill. John Crawfurd, *Journal of an embassy from the Governor-General of India to the Courts of Siam and Cochin-China.* Singapore: Henry Colburn and Richard Bentley, 1828. NUS Libraries, Special Collections.

Tanglin, once the sites overlooking the strait had gone, as the men were separated from their offices by the Chinese section of the town and a length of very poor road.

Shortly after Wemyss Ker and James Guthrie moved to New Harbour, the temenggong began to develop his property there. About 1,843 samples of gutta percha were sent to England, and it was found to be a marketable commodity. Trade in it expanded rapidly, and proved very profitable for the temenggong, as the greater part of the supplies brought in by native boats found its way into his hands. In March 1848, it was suggested that he even sent men to "assist" the gatherers in taking it to his stores,[162] and there seems little doubt that his commercial methods were at times close to the piracy which he had renounced a few years earlier.[163] Still, Telok Belanga grew prosperous, and on 28 November 1848, the temenggong countered his critics, and rewarded his friends, with a spectacular public entertainment of fireworks: according to Abraham Logan,[164]

> The company were received in a rustic pavilion which had been erected at Pantei Chermin, on a rising ground overlooking the New Harbour, and it was decorated with a degree of taste which would have done no discredit to Edginton himself. The building was soon filled by such an assemblage of the "beauty and fashion" of the station, as we never remember to have witnessed before. The arrival of the Governor and Mrs. Butterworth, announced by the firing of a salute, was the signal for the commencement of the exhibition, and then firework succeeded firework in rapid succession, rockets, bluelights, flowerpots, wheels, ducks, and last, though not least, the Chinese drums with their minute population, who spend their brief existence in public in the uncomfortable position of suspension by the pigtails surrounded by an atmosphere of squibs and crackers that would choke even a Salamander.

---

[162] On 14 Mar. 1848, there was a meeting of the Chamber of Commerce at Singapore following which a letter was sent to the Resident Councillor, asking for action to be taken to maintain the freedom of the trade of the port. It was alleged that for some time past there had been increasing complaints of the temenggong's attempts to monopolize the trade in gutta perch. According to reports received he had boats stationed at strategic points manned by armed followers, and all native craft carrying gutta percha destined for Singapore were intercepted, and the occupants frightened or bullied into selling their cargo to his agents at a low price. The value of the trade was put at $150,000 to $200,000, and nine-tenths of it was said to pass through the temenggong's hands (*Singapore Free Press* [henceforth *SFP*], 16 Mar. 1848).

[163] On 1 Sept. 1846, the temenggong had been presented with a ceremonial sword by the governor, acting on behalf of the East India Company (not the Queen, as tradition has it), in recognition of his recent services in helping to discourage piracy in the waters round Singapore. The presentation took place on Government Hill (now Fort Canning) in the presence of representatives of all the different communities resident in Singapore (see *SFP*, 3 Sept. 1846). This is the scene that occupies the foreground of the picture of Singapore from Government Hill by J.T. Thomson, lithographed by Richardson & Co. and published in London in 1856. Incidentally, the background is the town as it was in Aug. 1846, not, as Buckley suggests, as it was in 1856.

[164] *SFP*, 30 Nov. 1848. Abraham Logan, brother of J.R. Logan (editor and publisher of the *Journal of the Indian Archipelago*), was editor of the *Singapore Free Press* from 1845 to 1865, in succession to Wm. Napier (correspondence, W.H.M. Read to C.B. Buckley), and proprietor from 1 Nov. 1848 onwards.

The performance drew the attention of the *Singapore Free Press* to the changes that had taken place at Telok Belanga, and two months later Logan published an interesting comment on the subject:[165]

> The great changes, and in most instances improvements, which have taken place of late years in Singapore, both as regards the architecture of the town, and the cultivation of the country, are nowhere so strikingly manifested as at Teluk Blangah, the residence of His Highness the Tumonggong. There, within a few years past, but especially in more recent times, the whole aspect of things has been changed, and everywhere improved. A few years ago, Teluk Belangah only presented the appearance of a very dirty Malay village, the royal residence being merely distinguished from its neighbours by being of brick, and if possible dingier and dirtier than the rest. Now everything has put on a new face. The money, which has flowed so copiously into the Teluk Blangah coffers, through the successful dealings of His Highness and his followers in the gutta trade, has been more judiciously applied than is generally the case when Malays become possessed of a little cash … His Highness has built for himself several extremely neat houses and *baleis* in the European style, which are gay with green and white paint, and many of his followers have done the same, their smart, green venetianed, tile-roofed houses, being an extreme contrast to the rude huts in which they formerly were content to live. The old palace, now the residence of the mother of the Tumonggong, has also been cleaned up and white-washed, and altogether has a very nice appearance … No less remarkable is the spirit of agricultural improvement which seems to have seized upon the Tumonggong and his followers. The hills overhanging the village, and which heretofore were covered with thick jungle giving shelter and cover to tigers, are now being rapidly divested of their coverings, and planted with fruit and spice trees.…

He finishes with a note of approval that they should have forsaken "the rude habitations and the idle and equivocal habits which formerly were the marks and distinguishing characteristics of the Teluk Blangah Malays".

On Not Building a Dry Dock

Meanwhile events had been adding up to produce a change in the local scene. In 1829 the PS *Enterprize* visited Singapore, and it was then suggested that a coaling depot should be established on the north side of Pulau Brani, in anticipation of further trips by steamers from India. Early in 1830 she was followed by the steam tug PS *Forbes*, towing the barque *Jamesina* with a cargo of 840 chests of opium and 52 tons of additional coal.[166] Under the terms of the charter the *Jamesina* had to reach

---

[165] *SFP*, 1 Feb. 1849. By this date Charles Spottiswoode and Gilbert Angus Bain had also built, or were building, houses on the north side of New Harbour. The firm of Spottiswoode & Connolly were acting as P&O Company's agents at this time, but in 1849 the latter opened their own offices in Battery Road. One of the "neat houses" built for the Temenggong is still standing though in a poor state of repair.

[166] The PS *Forbes*, 302 tons OM, was built at the New Howrah Dock Company's yard to the order of Mackintosh & Co. and launched on 21 Jan. 1826. She was constructed entirely of teak, had a copper boiler and was powered by two 60 hp engines made by Bolton & Watt, at the Soho Foundry, near Birmingham. Her total cost, ready for steaming, was Rs 310,000. She

Lintin within a month of leaving the *Hooghly* (in Bengal). With a moderate wind force they were able to make 4–5 knots [7.4–9.3km/h] against the monsoon, but the breeze freshened as they crossed the South China Sea, and their speed dropped to 2½ knots [4.6km/h]. Finally, with only four days' coal left, the *Forbes* was forced to cast off her tow, and the *Jamesina* reached Lintin under canvas, 38 days out from the Sandheads. The attempt to beat the monsoon failed in terms of the charter, but it provided useful data and showed that with careful planning the voyage might be undertaken with reasonable certainty of success in five weeks. There was, in fact, talk in Calcutta of a second tow that season, the PS *Irrawaddy* and the British barque *Isabella Robertson*, but the latter finally passed through Singapore unattended at the end of May (1830),[167] and the *Forbes*'s run remained unique.

Further attempts on the same lines would probably have been made in subsequent years, but at this period the performance of sailing vessels was being improved rapidly, and in the end they kept steamers out of the opium trade for another 20 years. The first successful passage against the monsoon by a small vessel was made by the Baltimore-built schooner *Dhaulle*, about 1827, but little notice appears to have been taken of her achievement. Then in 1829, the season before the *Forbes*'s effort, Captain Clifton made the run from Calcutta to Macau and back between 4 January and 1 April in the barque *Red Rover*, which had been specially built for him on the *Hooghly* by his father-in-law. She carried 800 chests of opium on the outward run, and the repetition of her performance during the next two seasons turned attention back to sailing vessels. In 1830 Clifton reached Canton on 7 February, 39 days out from Calcutta: in 1831 he was back in the *Hooghly* by 14 March, after a round trip of 76 days; in 1832 he reached Canton by 28 February. In the latter year he had three rivals on the same run, *Waterwich*, *Sylph* and *Lady*

---

was named in honour of Capt. W.N. Forbes of the Bengal Engineers, one of the pioneers in the development of steam vessels in India. In 1837 she was bought by the Calcutta Steam Tug Association, and thereafter she was used only on the *Hooghly*. Her commander in 1830 was Capt. Andrew Henderson, later one of the founders of the association. The log of her run to China towing the *Jamesina* is summarised by G.A. Prinsep, *An Account of Steam Vessels and of Proceedings Connected with Steam Navigation in British India* (Calcutta: From the Government Gazette Press, by G.H. Huttman, 1830), p. 18. See also *Singapore Chronicle*, 8 Apr. and 3 June 1830. And Gibson-Hill, "The Steamers Employed in Asian Waters, 1819–39", *JMBRAS* 27, 1 (1954): 145–7. According to the evidence given by Capt. Henderson to the Select Committee on Steam Communication with India, in 1831, the run to China towing the *Jamesina* was arranged in about a week. The sprightly *Jamesina* started her life as HM Brig *Curlew*, 18 guns, but in 1823 she was sold out of the navy and became the property of James Matheson. From 1827 Matheson was a partner in the firm of Magniac & Co., later known as Jardine, Matheson & Co.

[167] *Bengal Hurkaru*, 24 Mar. 1830. "It was yesterday determined by authority, we learn, to despatch the Steamer *Irrawaddy* to China. She is to tow the *Isabella Robertson* as far as Singapore in consideration of that vessel carrying 200 tons of coal for her." See also *Singapore Chronicle*, 20 May and 3 June 1830. But the project fell through. For a note on the PS *Irrawaddy*, 305 tons OM, see Gibson-Hill, "The Steamers Employed in Asian Waters, 1819–39", *JMBRAS* 27, 1 (1954): 142–3.

of the Lake; from then on no one thought of employing a steam tug to cross the South China Sea against the monsoon.[168]

No other steamer followed the PS *Forbes* to Singapore until the latter part of 1834, when the PS *Enterprize* turned up again, carrying the Bishop of Calcutta on a tour of his diocese. By this time the *Enterprize* was serving as a tug on the *Hooghly*, and her absence from Bengal was not popular.[169] Nonetheless, her visit revived the ideas of 1829, and drew attention to the absence of proper docking facilities at Singapore. For sailing vessels this was not so important, as they could be beached and hauled over on their beam ends, either for scouring or if urgent repairs were necessary; but the paddle boxes and paddlewheel shafts made it difficult to treat most steamers in this undignified manner. Accordingly, at the end of 1834, Dr W.M. Montgomerie applied for a lease of two areas of ground, one on Pulau Blakang Mati and the other on Pulau Brani, with permission to dam the strait between the two islands (the Selat Sengkir), to form a wet dock. His project was viewed with favour in Bengal, and the governor of the Straits Settlements was authorised to grant him the necessary leases for a period of 50 years.[170] This reply was passed on to Dr Montgomerie early in 1835, but thereafter he took no further action. Probably in the interval he had examined the Selat Sengkir more closely, and decided that the job would be too formidable. In addition, of course, the only other steamer to visit Singapore prior to 1837, when the PS *Diana* was stationed in the Straits on anti-piracy duties, was the PS *Jardine*, a vessel which can have done little to inspire local confidence in steam propulsion.[171]

---

[168] *Bengal Hurkaru*, 1821–32, passim; *Singapore Chronicle*, 1828–32, idem. On the history of the opium clippers in general, see Basil Lubbock, *The Opium Clippers* (Glasgow: Brown, Son & Ferguson, 1933). There is also useful data on vessels prior to 1840, in John Phipps, *A Collection of Papers Relative to Ship Building in India* (Calcutta: Scott and Co., 1840).

[169] This was the first PS *Enterprize*, 464 tons OM, built by Gordon & Co. at Deptford on the Thames and launched on 22 Feb. 1825. She left Falmouth on 16 Aug. of that year, and arrived off Calcutta on 8 Dec., 113 days and 11 hours later, of which she was at sea for just over 103 days. She was the first steamer to round the cape into the Indian Ocean, but nearly two-fifth of her voyage was made under sail, with her engines out of action. The first vessel to complete the run under steam was the PS *Atlanta*, 610 tons OM, in 1836: she was 68 days at sea between Falmouth and Bombay. The PS *Enterprize* was probably earning about Rs 8,000–10,000 a month as a tug on the *Hooghly* in 1834–35. She was finally broken up in 1838, and her engines used for a new vessel of the same name, built by the Kidderpore Docking Co., at a cost of Co. Rs 140,000. For a short biography of the PS *Enterprize*, see Gibson-Hill, "The Steamers Employed in Asian Waters, 1819–39", *JMBRAS* 27, 1 (1954): 134–9.

[170] Under-Secretary Bengal to Act. Governor, S.S., 6 Febuary 1835 (*EIC Rec.*, P. 21). A copy was sent to T. Church, Res. Councillor, Singapore, to inform Dr Montgomerie, 13 Apr. 1835. Butterworth to Under-Secretary, Bengal, 11 Mar. 1846 (*EIC Rec.*, R. 13: 78) also refers.

[171] For the PS *Jardine* debacle, see *Singapore Chronicle* and *SFP*, 1836, passim. Summary in Gibson-Hill, "The Steamers Employed in Asian Waters, 1819–39", *JMBRAS* 27, 1 (1954): 153–6. The PS *Jardine* was originally intended for service as a fast boat on the Canton River, but the Chinese authorities would not permit her to remain there. She was then sailed to Singapore, in an attempt to sell her to government or, failing government, to a group of merchants; but she was overengined and put up a very poor performance on her trial runs.

Towards the latter part of 1838, Dr Montgomerie's scheme was replaced by a less ambitious project originating with C.R. Prinsep of Calcutta, who asked for an outright grant, or a long-term lease, of the whole or a part of Pulau Brani, and part of Blakang Mati. It seems likely that initially he intended to carry out some form of works involving the use of the Selat Sengkir, but he later modified his request to part or all of Pulau Brani only, and announced his intention of erecting a patent slip in Telok Saga, on the north side of the island. Prinsep's application was referred to Dr Montgomerie, as the holder of an option on the land, and he replied saying that on mature consideration he had decided that only a grant of the property in perpetuity would provide a reasonable recompense for the outlay that would be involved in putting his plans into operation.[172] Accordingly, he waived any rights that he might have in favour of Prinsep; but as he had never previously suggested that the conditions on which the land had been offered to him should be revised in this way, it looks rather as if he had decided that his scheme was not practical and, at the same time, was trying to assist Prinsep to obtain the property that he required on the most favourable terms. Prinsep's application was warmly supported by Bonham, who recommended an outright sale, but at this time alienation in perpetuity was contrary to the policy of the Bengal government, and they only sanctioned the grant of a 50-year lease.[173] On 10 May 1839, Bonham wrote to the Resident Councillor Singapore:

> I have now the honour so far as I have the power to sanction a lease being issued to C.R. Prinsep of Calcutta for the Island of Ayer Brannie and 100 acres [$0.4km^2$] on Blakan Matti immediately opposite to that island ... As, however, no very protracted period will be required for putting the ground in a state proper for the reception of the Patent Slip and for the erection of the necessary buildings, I am of the opinion that the rent should commence from January 1843, and become payable in January 1844, and that the ground should be liable to resumption by government at the first mentioned period unless by that time it be absolutely in use, or such progress [have] been made towards the object for which it is leased as to render [it] clearly apparent that the parties intend fulfilling their part of the engagement.

The following year (1840), Prinsep made a formal application for a fifty-year lease of the island of Pulau Brani. His Singapore agents (Shaw, Whitehead & Co.) were told that no lease could be issued until the area had been surveyed, but that Prinsep had full authority to begin work on the property as soon as it was convenient for him to do so.[174] J.T. Thomson completed his survey of the island late in 1843, but Prinsep, like Dr Montgomerie before him, appears to have taken no further action once he had been told that he could make use of the land.

By this time there was every prospect of steamers reaching Singapore in increasing numbers. Eighteen steam vessels were sent to China at one stage or

---

[172] Dr W. Montgomerie to T. Church, Res. Councillor, Singapore, 16 Oct. 1838.

[173] Bonham to Shaw, Whitehead & Co., Singapore, as agents for C.R. Prinsep, 10 May 1839 (*EIC Rec.*, Z. 12: 71), following receipt of Under-Secretary Bengal to Governor, SS, 12 Dec. 1838 (*EIC Rec.*, S. 5: 124–1357 of 1838).

[174] Bonham to Shaw, Whitehead & Co., 3 Mar. 1840 (*EIC Rec.*, Z. 13: 66).

another of the Opium War of 1840–42, and some of them, employed as packet boats, made the trip to and from India more than once.[175] In itself, of course, this was no more than a temporary burst of activity, but it had forced the East India Company to augment their small fleet of steamers, and from the close of the war two were stationed permanently in the Straits. Moreover, by the end of 1843 active steps were at last being taken to intitute regular steam communication between India and Singapore. The matter was discussed in detail as early as 1825, when a small committee was formed in Singapore under the chairmanship of Captain William Flint, RN, the master attendant. It was broached again when the PS *Jardine* was sent down to Singapore from Lintin and hastily dropped after her abortive attempts to steam to Melaka. The Opium War showed clearly that steamers were already more reliable than they had been five to ten years earlier, and at the beginning of 1844 a company was formed locally to operate a monthly service between Calcutta and Singapore. Unfortunately their vessel, the PS *Fire Queen*, was constructed to the stockholders' specifications. She made her maiden run early in 1845, but proved so unreliable that after five dilatory trips she was withdrawn and sold for service as a tug on the *Hooghly*.[176]

In August 1845, while the *Fire Queen* was still trying to maintain a reasonable schedule, the P&O Company inaugurated a regular monthly service between Bombay and Hongkong, via Pont du Galle and Singapore: at the same time arrangements were made by the Netherlands Indies Government for a feeder service to operate between Batavia and Singapore.[177] The East India Company began by storing its coal in a shed near the point at the north side of the mouth of the river, close to the commissariat stores. Later, about 1847, someone had the bright idea of moving the store to Kampong Melaka further up the river: as a result, the coaling lighters had to run the full length of the pool to reach the roads. Private concerns had to go elsewhere from the start: the P&O Company vessels were supplied from stores on the beach at Telok Ayer; the Dutch company kept their coal at Kampong Melaka. Neither of these sites was really satisfactory, partly because the coal had to be handled in the roads; in 1847 300 tons were lost when a lighter was swamped by

[175] Gibson-Hill, "The Steamers Employed in Asian Waters, 1819–39", *JMBRAS* 27, 1 (1954): 158–61.

[176] PS *Fire Queen*, see *SFP*, 1844–46, passim. There are numerous references to her over this period, but they have never been summarised. Crane Brothers were the Singapore agents, but they may not have had much money invested in her. Sime & Co. and Ker, Rawson & Co., were the prime movers in the Straits.

[177] *SFP*, 7 Aug. 1845: "The Netherlands Government Steamer *Bromo* arrived here from Batavia on Tuesday afternoon, and will sail on her return trip to-day at noon. A regular monthly Steam communication is to be kept up by the Dutch Government between Batavia and Singapore. A Notification in the *Java Courant* states that the Dutch Government is to forward letters from Batavia to Holland, France or England on the payment at Batavia of two Guilders Copper for each letter or every Amsterdam ounce". For notes on earlier steamers in the Netherlands Indies, see Gibson-Hill, "The Steamers Employed in Asian Waters, 1819–39", *JMBRAS* 27, 1 (1954): 131–4 (PS *Van der Capellen*, launched at Surabaya 23 Nov. 1825, et al.), pp. 152–3 (PS *Willem de Eerste*, launched at Amsterdam 4 Aug. 1823, reached Onrust 7 Feb. 1836; lost near Ambon, 5/6 May 1837) and p. 158 (PS *Hekla* and PS *Etna*).

a choppy sea,[178] and the unloading and loading of coal was frequently held up for days at a time by unfavourable conditions. And, of course, the increase in steamer traffic again drew attention to the need for adequate docking facilities.

In January 1846, Jacob Clunis,[179] a former ship's captain who had set up as a blacksmith and shipwright at Telok Ayer in June 1841, published proposals for the erection of a dry dock on Pulau Brani, in place of the slip proposed (but still not built) by Prinsep.[180] He estimated that a dry dock (300 feet [91m] long, 68 feet [20.7m] wide, 15 feet [4.6m] deep, and 48 feet [14.6m] wide at the gate) could be built and equipped with a steam engine, buoys, gate, capstans, posts, chains and a counting house for less than $80,000: he put the annual recurrent costs at $10,000, and the receipts at $19,460, giving the investors "above 10½ per cent clear annual profit, no doubt increasing in after years"; and as a further inducement, he added:

> The above may not seem a very large amount of direct profit, but we think that on a little consideration many subsidiary advantages will present themselves. To the Ship-owners the facilities for repairing their vessels, with expedition and safety, are of the greatest importance. To the Merchants the large disbursements passing through their hands will give a handsome commission, besides the general advantage to the trade, of vessels resorting here. To the Tradesmen of every class, ship-chandlers, shipbuilders, carpenters, blacksmiths, brassfounders, &c., it will bring increase of business and profit. Should the scheme be carried into effect with spirit, [and] the necessary work be erected in a proper manner, there is no doubt that as its existence becomes known the Dry Dock at Singapore would be more and more resorted to, favourably situated as the place is from its central position with reference to China, Java, Australia, &c.

The European merchants in the town found the proposal extremely interesting, and at the request of the Chamber of Commerce the governor appointed a committee to examine the scheme in detail.[181] By a minute of 29 April (1846), the Bengal government agreed to alienate Pulau Brani or a part of Pulau Blakang Mati in perpetuity, at the discretion of the governor of the Straits Settlements, if work on

---

[178] In Keppel to Butterworth, 20 Sept. 1849 (*EIC Rec*., W. 14: 242).

[179] He usually spelt his name *Clunis*, as shown, but he was a cousin of John Clunies Ross (Ross from his mother), one of the founders of the settlement on the Cocos-Keeling Islands. He first appears east as a mate on the *Borneo*, 328 tons, commanded by the latter, in 1825–26. He subsequently held several commands in these waters, and then there is no notice of him for some years, until in June 1841, he settled in Singapore with his wife. He never seems to have made much money, and was still in business as a shipwright when he died here in a boarding house (probably no. 3) on Coleman Street in June 1866.

[180] *SFP*, 22 Jan. 1846. The lithograph sheet illustrating his proposals was inserted in a later issue of the paper (5 Feb. 1846).

[181] *EIC Rec*., U. 12: 118–20, refers. See also *SFP*, 4 June 1846. The committee consisted of Capt. Faber, Madras Engineers (Superintending Engineer, Straits Settlements), Samuel Congalton (commanding the HC steam vessel *Hooghly*), J.T. Thomson (Settlement Surveyor), Lt. H. Mann, Madras Engineers (Superintendent of Indian Convicts) and R.S. Ross (commanding the HCSV *Phlegethon*); the latter is omitted from the newspaper's list but included in the governor's minutes (EIC Rec. U. 12: 118–20).

14.9 Ships and staff in the dock of the Tanjong Park Dock Co. Ltd. Attributed to Lambert & Co, c.1890. Rijksmuseum, Amsterdam. RP-F-F01140-A.

the dock should start in the near future.[182] Subsequently, Captain Sir Edward Belcher, RN, who had put in at Singapore homeward bound in HMS *Samarang*, was asked for his views on the establishment of a coaling depot on Pulau Brani: he supported the idea enthusiastically:[183]

> With regard to New Harbour, and the proposed site for a coal depot on Pulo Brani (or Gage Island) I would most strenuously advise, under *any* circumstances, *peace* or *war*, adopting that position for coaling both the naval as well as packet service. I look beyond the mere *position* and facilities for coaling. I view it as a stride, not only to the opening, but also to the free navigation, of that channel, and, ultimately, to the *probable* formation of a new town and port for Singapore. In the event of distress, this position affords refuge; [and] secure facilities for grounding, or repairing defects, in many cases without lightening, either to naval or merchant shipping.

The Dry Dock Committee issued its report on 10 September 1846, fully in favour of the scheme in principle, but they gave a revised estimate of the probable cost of constructing the dock, raising it to $105,953.86, and finished by saying:[184]

---

[182] Minute by Resident Councillor, 15 June 1846 (*EIC Rec.*, U. 12: 116). The more favourable terms offered on this occasion were due to a change of policy on the part of the Bengal government in 1843, when it was then agreed that in the future islands in the Straits Settlements could be alienated in perpetuity, if there was no likelihood of their being wanted for defence purposes (letters 477 of 26 Apr. 1843, and 2922 of 30 Oct. 1841, refer).
[183] Capt. Sir Edward Belcher, *Narrative of the Voyage of R.M.S. Samarang, 1843–46*, 2 vols. (London: Reeve, Benham and Reeve, 1848), vol. 2, p. 186.
[184] Lt. H. Mann, on behalf of the Dry Dock Committee, to the Resident Councillor, Singapore, 10 Sept. 1846; published in the *SFP*, 24 Sept. 1846.

> To conclude, it is the opinion of the Committee that the only probable difficulty besetting the undertaking is want of patronage. No unusual or costly expedients are likely to be required for the execution of the work, and the Projector's Estimates have now well grounded pretensions to tolerable accuracy, and therefore it is the Committee's unanimous belief that every enquiry and investigation really necessary to warrant the formation of a joint stock Company have been made and that it rests with the Mercantile Community to adopt further measures for the development of the scheme.

Unfortunately, as the *Singapore Free Press*[185] had suggested earlier, it was not possible to raise the required capital locally. There was talk of trying to obtain a government loan, and of interesting outside investors: the discussions ran on into 1847, but in the end nothing came of them. In the meantime Clunis had squatted on the site on Pulau Brani, and ultimately used part of the land to erect a brickworks and a yard for repairing small boats.[186]

In May 1848, Captain the Honourable Henry Keppel, RN, reached Singapore in HMS *Mœander*, and took her into New Harbour for minor repairs. Under the date 30 May he notes:[187]

> In pulling about in my gig among the numerous prettily wooded islands on the westward entrance to the Singapore river, I was astonished to find deep water

---

[185] *SFP*, 24 Sept. 1846, "It is obvious, however, that a plan of such magnitude cannot be undertaken by parties in Singapore alone, where the limited number of mercantile establishments, and the nature of their transactions, renders it inconvenient to withdraw so much capital from trade and sink it in such an undertaking as that contemplated. We must look abroad therefore for assistance, and if it cannot be obtained from thence the scheme must be abandoned."

[186] Jacob Clunis was ejected from Telok Saga in the first half of 1854. The excuse given was that the island was required for defence purposes, but the only immediate use that government made of it was to establish its own coal stores on the east side of the little bay. Clunis had developed his undertakings there, in preference to elsewhere on the island, because of the advantages of the beach and the supply of labour from the kampong on the west side of the inlet. He retained part of his holdings, as in 1864 he wrote hopefully to the *Straits Times* (13 Feb. 1864), saying that in view of the discussion about extending the dock area, he would like to point out that he had a suitable stretch of ground facing the P&O wharf ready for development. This must have been the ground where Buyers & Robb subsequently built the Bon Accord dock (opened 2 Oct. 1866); see also Bogaars, "The Tanjong Pagar Dock Company", *Memoirs of the Raffles Museum*, no. 3 (1956): 259–60.

[187] Admiral of the Fleet, the Honourable Sir Henry Keppel, *A Sailor's Life under Four Sovereigns*, 3 vols. (London: Macmillan, 1899), vol. 2, p. 74. For the visit in 1849, see idem, p. 128 (20 Aug.): "Arrived at Singapore. Han with our cargo into New Harbour by the western entrance". The *Mœander* left to return to England via Australia and the Pacific on 24 Sept. (1849). With Keppel's instructions was a private letter from Rear-Admiral J.W. Dundas, Second Sea Lord:

I need not recommend Lead and Look Out to ye, but the Straits are difficult and so are the Society Islands.

Keep *Mœander* off the ground, and when there is a doubt, put her head round. God speed ye
Yours faithfully,
J.W.D. Dundas.

> close to the shore, with a safe passage through for ships larger than the *Mœander*, Now that steam is likely to come into use, this ready-made harbour as a depot for coal would be invaluable.
>
> I had the position surveyed, and sent it, with my report, to the Board of Admiralty; as it was, the forge was landed, boats repaired, and artificers employed under commodious sheds, all under the eyes of the officers on board.
>
> New Harbour has another advantage over Singapore Roads. In the latter a ship's bottom becomes more foul than in any known anchorage in these seas; perhaps from the near proximity to the bottom. This is not the case in New Harbour, through which there is always a tide running, while a current of air passing between the islands keeps it comparatively cool.

In part, Keppel's memory is at fault here: it was not until 1849 that he addressed the Board of Admiralty on the use of New Harbour,[188] and (he later alleged) received no acknowledgement. This in itself may not have been entirely due to inattention.

---

[188] In *A Sailor's Life* (cited above), under the heading of 24 Aug. 1849, it says:

> Having reported to the Admiralty the natural advantages of the Inner Harbour of Singapore as a coaling station over twelve months ago, and no notice having been taken of my letter, I now sent a similar statement, with survey, to the Secretary of the P. and O. Company.

But in a letter to Butterworth, written on 20 Sept. 1849, four days before the *Mœander* left for Australia, Keppel says:

> Being aware of the interest you take in everything connected with your Government, whether civil, military or naval, I beg leave to send you a rough copy of a survey we have made during our limited stay in New Harbour.
>
> There is no doubt from the central position of Singapore, that it ought to be the principal residence of the Naval Commander in Chief and of the advantages of New Harbour I have long been convinced. Its perfect security, the various points alongside which the largest steamers might take in coal, together with Pulo Brani in the centre on which to build storehouses, etc., and the incalculable advantages of a dry dock (already partially formed by nature) must render its possession most desirable by H.M. Government.
>
> New Harbour is the only place of refuge within reach of our Merchant Ships in case of war, and might easily be fortified.
>
> As a Harbour for the Mail Steamers it would be invaluable, and the saving of time and expense in coaling would soon repay the cost of the necessary buildings …
> Vessels coming down the Straits would, by entering New Harbour, avoid a circuit round the Rabbit and Coney Islands of twenty miles [32.2km] and the mails might be landed three hours earlier than they are at present …
>
> Under these impressions I have thought it right to bring the different advantages of New Harbour under the notice of the Commander in Chief, in case he should see fit to lay the same before the Lords of the Admiralty. (Keppel to Butterworth, 20 Sept. 1849, EIC Rec., W. 14: 242)

From which it is clear that the survey was not done until 1849, when he was in New Harbour for five weeks, and not engaged in repairs to the *Mœander*. And also that, in Sept. 1849, his principal concern was with New Harbour as a naval centre, and it was to the Commander in Chief that he wrote, not to the P&O Company. On the other hand, Butterworth may have passed some of Keppel's views on to the P&O agent, though they do not really go much further than those of Sir Edward Belcher, expressed in 1845, and published in 1848; also, of course, by the end of 1849, Butterworth should have had surveys of New Harbour from J.T. Thomson, available for transmission (or for Keppel).

As we have already noted, a chart of New Harbour had been published in London in 1829, and of the approaches in 1830; moreover the latter had subsequently been replaced by a new chart in 1840, and again in 1846 (Captain Samuel Congalton and J.T. Thomson). Captain Sir Edward Belcher had written in praise of the locality in 1846. Lake and Best had mentioned it as a refuge for shipping in time of war in their reports of 1827 and 1843. Applications to lease land to build a dock there had been approved in 1835, 1840 and 1846, though admittedly there was still no dock. Possibly even the Board of Admiralty had heard of New Harbour by this time. There is an intriguing, puckish look about the portraits of Keppel in youth and middle age. There is no doubt that he was a charming man: sometimes one almost feels that he must have been retained in HM Navy.

If Keppel did by any chance influence the course of events at New Harbour, his interference may not have been entirely helpful. Early in 1849 four of the local business firms (Hamilton, Gray & Co., Maclaine, Fraser & Co., A.L. Johnston & Co., and Shaw, Whitehead & Co.) again took up the matter of constructing a dry dock on Pulau Brani. This time they decided to work on a smaller scale, and Jacob Clunis drew up a set of revised plans for them. In a letter of 28 February, they made a formal request for the fee simple of Pulau Brani, accompanying it with the following statement of their proposal:[189]

> An estimate carefully made out has been procured from which it appears that a Dry Dock capable of docking vessels of 600 tons—or a steamer of large size by waiting for spring tides—can be constructed within from nine to twelve months at Pulo Brani for a sum of seven thousand dollars ($7,000), and warranted to last for 25 years. The dimensions of the dock to be,
> 140 feet [42.3m] long inside the gates,
> 80 feet [24.4m] broad at the top, and
> 60 feet [18.3m] broad at the bottom, and
> 50 feet [15.2m] to be the width of the gates.
> The pier heads to be of cut stone and the dock itself finished in a workmanlike manner (with suitable timber), as per plan and model. The above sum to include all necessary buildings.
>
> As it is not contemplated that the dock will require much outlay in the shape of repairs for a considerable time, and the expense of superintendence, clerks' salaries and wages for a couple of watchmen will only amount to a very moderate sum, this undertaking promises a profitable return upon the most moderate rate of employment for the dock, say,
>
> | | | |
> |---|---|---|
> | 20 vessels yearly at $100 each for entrance | … | $2,000 |
> | each vessel to be, in dock on all average three days, say 60 days at $20 per day | … | $1,200 |
> | | | --------- |
> | | | $3,200 |
> | | | --------- |
>
> The returns which may be expected from steamers are purposely omitted, that parties may form their own estimates according to circumstances, merely

[189] *EIC Rec.*, W. 14: 66 (letter 125 of 1849).

14.10 Blakan-Mati and the New Harbour in Singapore. Watercolour from the Charles Dyce Collection. Singapore: National University of Singapore (NUS) Museums. S1970-0052-041.

> remarking that Her Majesty's, the Honourable Company's and the Java and Australian Mail Packet Steamers would all probably avail [themselves] of the dock, and occasionally perhaps even P&O Company steamers.
>
> If the proposal be favourably received, and a capital of ten thousand dollars ($10,000) subscribed in twenty shares of $500 each or such other amount of capital or division of shares as may be ultimately decided on by the shareholders, the latter shall be immediately furnished with all the necessary plans, estimates &c., and they may then make the required arrangements.

A favourable reply was sent by Butterworth, dated 3 March (1849), the material portion of which runs:[190]

> The site selected for a Dry Dock is so peculiarly well situated for the purpose, and the result to the settlement of the construction of such a work would necessarily tend so materially to the advancement of the settlement, that I conceive it to be my imperative duty, as I am sure it will be my ernest desire, to forward the present movement to the utmost of my power, which however is limited by orders from the Hon'ble the Court of Directors and the Government of India.
>
> I am commanded in disposing of Pulo Ayer Brani to stipulate that such works as those in contemplation shall be commenced within a given period, and that on the abandonment of such the land shall revert to Government: also that Govemment shall have the right to occupy at any time such part of the said island as may be deemed necessary for any military purpose whatever, the claims of the present squatters on the land being respected and remuneration afforded them, should their removal be considered necessary.
>
> Under the above reservations the land will be granted on a lease of 999 years, at an Annual Quit Rent of 20 dollars on the completion of the work, prior to which an acknowledgement from Government will be given to the Company that such will be the case, should this communication be deemed insufficient for the purpose, which however must be considered to hold good only on the work being commenced within the next six months.

We are, therefore, now back in the same position as in March 1835, May 1839 and April 1846. On 3 March 1849, permission to take over Pulau Brani for the construction of a smaller dock was formally granted; and, of course, the result was the same as before. When on 20 August Keppel returned to Singapore, and ran with his cargo into New Harbour by the western entrance,[191] work had not begun on the proposed dock. This time the money had been subscribed rapidly enough. The trouble arose from the feeling that if a dock was to be built, it should be on the lines of the original proposal, so that it could also accommodate steamers. Unfortunately, the required increase in size and quality meant a tenfold increase in cost, and the shortage of capital locally was what had killed the project of 1846/47. It was here that Keppel came into the picture. Seemingly, he was asked if he could interest HM Navy in the plans for a large dry dock. On 18 September the four companies wrote to Butterworth:[192]

---

[190] *EIC Rec.*, V. 14: 193 (letter 82 of 1849).

[191] See also above.

[192] *EIC Rec.*, W. 14: 241.

> We are now making arrangements which we hope will result in placing on the island in question [Pulau Brani] a Dock suitable for the wants of HM Navy, and that of the Hon'ble East India Company, as also the increasing requirements of [other] steamers. As these arrangements will require to be completed in London, we beg to request that you will be pleased to extend the period stipulated [in your letter of 3 March] for entering upon the necessary operations for a further period of eighteen months from the third instant.

And on 20 September Keppel himself wrote to Butterworth, informing him that he had sent a report and survey to the commander-in-chief, China Station, in the hope that he would see fit to lay them before the Lords of the Admiralty.[193] As we have noted, there does not appear to have been any direct response to this approach, though ultimately the commander-in-chief did act in the matter.

The new company issued its prospectus towards the end of October 1849: according to the *Singapore Free Press* of 2 November:

> A glance at the map shows that this Port must ultimately become the central depot and naval station we have alluded to, and therefore it will be of the utmost importance to the Admiralty and the P&O Company to see suitable docks constructed here. This view of the case is taken by a prospectus now before us, issued a few days ago for the purpose of replacing the late Dock Company by one formed to carry out the original comprehensive scheme. This contemplates a capital of $100,000 in 1,000 shares of $100 each, and within twenty-four hours of its issue the original shareholders and others subscribed to a conditional share list for 140 shares, or $14,000, the list being still open. It will ultimately be circulated in China and elsewhere as well as in England, and we doubt not will be soon filled up. We observe that it contemplates an application to HM Government for its aid by guaranteeing a certain return upon its shares, according to the precedent established by the Hon'ble East India Company in the case of certain Indian Railways, the Dock Company offering to modify their plans, estimates and contracts so as to satisfy the Admiralty and the P&O Company.

Early in 1850 the committee of the new company approached the P&O Company, and in May of that year J.T. Thomson supplied their Singapore agent, Captain Shanks, with a report on Pulau Brani and the Dock Company's proposals.[194] Unfortunately the P&O Company was forced to watch its expenses fairly closely, and though willing to detail its requirements, it was not prepared to underwrite the new dock in any substantial manner. Sometime in the same year (1850), Jacob Clunis, sensing that sufficient capital for the construction of the larger dock would never be forthcoming, began work alone (and very slowly) on his small-scale dock of February 1849. An

---

193 See also above.

194 See above and also Bogaars, "The Tanjong Pagar Dock Company", pp. 256–8. In his report, Thomson assessed the likely cost of the new dock at $180,000, not $100,000 as claimed by the promoters of the company. This point probably carried some weight with the directors of the P&O Co., and may have been partly responsible for their final decision not to participate. Clunis' original estimate in 1846 of less than $80,000 was later increased by over $25,000. Possibly he was over-sanguine. He may have lacked experience: he never disclosed any details of earlier work.

Admiralty chart (No. 1341 of 1850) marks the site of the dock as a clear deep-water channel, but actually its excavation was still in progress four years later.

There were reasonable grounds for the P&O Company's reluctance to invest in the Pulau Brani Dry Dock scheme. It was in part itself dependent on the mail contracts. These were short-term contracts, and the directors could never be fully confident that they would be renewed. Moreover, from 1845 onwards the company had urgently required a coaling depot at Singapore; and while the local merchants were thinking in terms of a dock, the P&O Company began to explore the possibility of obtaining a suitable site for the construction of a deep-water pier and a coal store. Captain Sir Edward Belcher had considered the relative isolation of Pulau Brani an advantage, from a service point of view, on the grounds that it would be easier to maintain discipline there if a ship were held up for some time. For commercial interests, a freer access to the town for passengers and goods was more important than keeping their crews in purdah. Unfortunately, the middle section of the northern shore of New Harbour was taken up by the strip of ground to which Temenggong 'Abdu'r Rahman and his followers had moved in 1823, and by some misunderstanding this now extended further west than Raffles had originally intended. The Temenggong's[195] land ended a short distance beyond Tebing Tinggi,[196] and the only solid ground between this point and Tanjong Batu Berlayar was Bukit Chermin: for the rest, east and west of his demesne, the shore line was composed of swamps, mangrove at the edge, backed by *nipah* palms where the water became brackish.

The problem required a little thought. Meanwhile, in August 1848, J.T. Thomson, the Settlement Surveyor blew up Batu Berlayar (Lot's Wife),[197] to widen the western entrance to the channel. The following year (1849) the P&O Company asked formally for a new survey of the northern side of New Harbour. In November, Lieutenant-Colonel Butterworth, who was always anxious to comply with any legitimate requests from the commercial houses, arranged for Thomson to prepare the required maps before he proceeded to Melaka on official business early in 1850.[198] Before the end of the latter year the Company had made arrangements

---

[195] Daing Ibrahim, sometimes known as Daing Kechil, the second son of Temenggong 'Abdu'r Rahman. He succeeded to the leadership of the Telok Belanga Malays on his father's death in December 1825, and thereafter was usually referred to as the temenggong, though he was not actually installed in office until 19 Aug. 1841. The ceremony took place in the presence of the governor and the Dato' Bendahara of Pahang, and the title officially conferred on him was "Temenggong Seri Maha Raja" (*SFP*, 26 Aug. 1841). He died in 1862, and was succeeded by his eldest son, 'Abu-Bakar, who later assumed the titles of Maharajah (1868) and finally sultan (1885) of Johor, by gracious permission of Queen Victoria. Both 'Abdu'r Rahman and Ibrahim are buried in the family graveyard at the foot of Mount Faber.

[196] Even this did not prevent his selling the whole of Pantei Chermin to Capt. Cloughton and his partners in 1855: see also below.

[197] *SFP*, 17 Aug. 1848, records the demise of the lady, but without giving the reason for her sudden end. Possibly it was so that Keppel could sail in safely at night (compare his letter to Butterworth of 20 Sept. 1849). For her earlier role, see above.

[198] Butterworth to Church, 15 Nov. 1849 (*EIC Rec*, U. 19: 10–11), records authority for J.T. Thomson to survey in New Harbour, before proceeding to Melaka in Feb. 1850: "I beg that the survey of New Harbour may be made with sufficient minuteness to further the views of

with the temenggong for the outright purchase of Tebing Tinggi, the most prominent of the diminutive headlands on the north side of New Harbour. The governor gave formal approval to the transaction in 1851, and in 1852 the P&O Company opened up at New Harbour, with Jacob Clunis as their first official pilot.

The same year the Bengal Government, having received full information of the proceedings, wrote pointing out that while it was not proposed that the sale of Tebing Tinggi should be annulled, a stiff reprimand must be delivered to the temenggong;[199] as far as they were aware he was merely permitted to occupy his lands at New Harbour rent-free for so long as he and his family lived on Singapore Island, and he was not, therefore, in a position to dispose of any part of them in perpetuity; further, it was believed that Tebing Tinggi had been the residence of the temenggong's sister, and it was hoped that he had provided her with suitable alternative accommodation.

Thus, whatever may have been the fate of the temenggong's sister, by 1852 the P&O Company had dealt with their major problem. They now had a sheltered anchorage and a pier adapted for bunkering, together with space for a coal store and godowns adjacent to it. Butterworth considered that they could have excavated a dock on one side or other of Tebing Tinggi, but no attempt was made to do so. Meanwhile, the Pulau Brani Dock Company continued to look round hopefully for support, and for his part, Jacob Clunis pressed on slowly with his solitary labours, until the latter part of 1853, when the Lords of the Admiralty finally acted. By a letter and enclosures from the Honourable Court of Directors of the East India Company, dated 12 October, Butterworth was instructed "to take measures without delay, for securing from alienation any portion of the government land at Singapore, especially all sea frontages likely to be required for imperial and public purposes", and to report the measures that he had taken. Further and more specifically, at the request of the naval Commander-in-Chief, he had orders to requisition the islands of Pulau Brani and Blakang Mati, and place them at the disposal of HM Navy. Butterworth, as well pleased, believing that it meant that the navy was proposing to build the much-discussed dock, and that Singapore would become the naval headquarters for the Far East. But in the end, all that came of it was the eviction of Jacob Clunis from Telok Saga and later the construction there of a coal depot and loading pier for use by HM Navy. Subsequently, in 1861, after the naval authorities had come to appreciate that their requirements were indeed on this modest scale, the Messageries Imperiales was permitted to use the corner of the island to the west of Telok Saga for the same purpose.

---

the Mercantile Community to establish a Dry Dock in that locality and to enable the P&O Company to judge of the expediency of coaling their Steamers in that Harbour in preference to doing so off the Town of Singapore." Thomson must have started work immediately: his new chart (see pp. 46–7, above) is dated 1849, and it was published by the Admiralty on 1 Jan. 1851, less than 14 months after his receipt of Church's letter. Presumably also his draft of the chart reached the Admiralty within a few months of Keppel's despatch on New Harbour. It was certainly consulted by the hydrographic department in the production of the new edition of chart 1341, corrected up to 1850 (see also below).

[199] Secretary to Govt. Bengal to Resident Councillor, Singapore, 1852 (*EIC. Rec*, S. 19: 67 and 120).

The requisitioning of Pulau Brani ended the schemes for constructing a dry dock on the island, for a time at least. They had had a fairish run, after all: nearly 20 years, five projects, and not a sod cut other than by Jacob Clunis, who never held any legal title to any part of the island. It was quite an achievement, and even Clunis had not done too badly out of it. Apart from the fees for turning out several versions of the same essential theme, he had lived rent-free for nearly ten years. Unfortunately, however, when he was evicted he was promised compensation, and then in the end nothing was ever given to him. So the *Singapore Free Press*, eight years later (14 August 1862), lamenting the absence of a government dock in Singapore, stated:

> Government might long ago have had a dock of its own at Singapore for a very little outlay, if, when it took possession of the dock Mr Clunis spent so much time and money in constructing, it had enlarged and finished it. Instead however of this being done, the dock has been allowed to remain in an incomplete condition and it is of no use for any purpose. In this case the behaviour of government has been of a very dog in the manger character and marked by much shabiness. Mr Clunis was promised compensation, but up to the present moment he has not received one farthing.

No compensation was certainly regrettable, though as we have said, Clunis did not do too badly from the Pulau Brani dry dock schemes in other ways. Moreover, Abraham Logan seems to have forgotten two points in the eight years between 1854 and 1862: one is that apparently no one was willing to invest any money in Clunis's hole during the four years that he spent excavating it; and the other is that Butterworth resumed possession of the land on behalf of HM Navy, not on behalf of government.

Clunis's departure from Telok Saga, as we have seen, was ordered by the governor on the strength of the instructions that he had received from London. Buckley, of course, quotes as if correct a statement by Read that he was turned out by poor old Tom Church,[200] the resident councillor; whereas, in fact, the latter

[200] C.B. Buckley, *An Anecdotal History of Old Times in Singapore* (Singapore, 1902), vol. 2, p. 732. We have already drawn attention to Buckley's misleading comments on Keppel (see Gibson-Hill, "Singapore: Notes on the Old Strait", *JMBRAS* 27, 1 [1954]: 209n94), and to the unreliability of his book in general (ibid., pp. 235–43) which, while in no way reducing its attractions for those who do not mind if they are reading fact or fiction and do not wish to be enlightened, nonetheless renders it most dangerous as a work of reference. In the case of Keppel, as of Jacob Clunis, it seems likely that Buckley was misled by W.H.M. Read. Those interested will find the greater part of Buckley's astonishing comments on the subject in a note on Keppel's last book, signed "By One Who Knows about the Author", in the *Singapore Free Press* for 4 May 1899. On internal evidence, the author of the review must certainly have been read, as it requires a Singaporean who was here as early as 1848–9 and was on board the SS *Himalaya* in 1868 when she nearly ran aground on Pulau Brani, Read fulfils both qualifications. Moreover, in his own volume of "memories" and inventions, he claims to have known Keppel from 1843 onwards, and repeats the error of the reviewer in saying that Keppel advised the Admiralty to make use of the site in New Harbour, which the P&O Company afterwards used in place of them. This is quite wrong: the Admiralty did take over the site that Belcher and Keppel recommended, namely on Pulau Brani, and did build a coaling pier there. The P&O

14.11 Malay town on Pulau Brani at Singapore. Leiden: Royal Netherlands Institute for Southeast Asian and Caribbean Studies (KITLV).

merely passed on the governor's message in the course of his official duties; it is an interesting example of the manner in which Read distorted the stories that he relayed, and how Buckley accepted them without question.

On Building Dry Docks

Although the requisitioning of Pulau Brani put an end to the sequence of unimplemented projects, it did not shake the merchant community's firm conviction that what it really needed was a dry dock (though not, on past history, to put up the capital for its construction); it merely turned its attention for the time-being towards the north side of the waterway. Here, in 1846, eight years earlier, Joaquim d'Almeida, whose property overlooked the bay to the west of Tanjong Pagar (Telok Serian), had made enquiries about foreshore rights, and was apparently considering the construction of a dock or pier. In the end, however, he joined the committee of the company established in October, 1849, which was proposing to build a dry dock along the lines of the dock committee's revised version of Clunis's project of 1846.[201] Subsequently, on 2 April 1855, Captain William Cloughton (who had previously commanded one of the Apcar Line of opium schooners), William Paterson and William Wemyss Ker (owner of the Bukit Chermin property) purchased from the Temenggong of Johor the strip of land known as Pantei Chermin;[202] this lay south of the Pasir Panjang Road (as then named) and east of the effluent of the Sungei Chermin. It consisted largely of low-lying and partly marshy ground, but it included one small hillock. An interesting aspect of the sale is that it was situated well to the west of Tebing Tinggi, and thus began half a mile [805m] or so beyond the boundary of the area which Sir Stamford Raffles had assigned to Temenggong 'Abdu'r Rahman and his followers in 1823.[203]

Cloughton had already begun the excavation of a dock in this area. Initially work continued on the same site, but after a time it was considered unsuitable and abandoned. A fresh attempt was made a little further east, and here a dock 400 feet

---

Company built their wharf on the opposite side of the harbour, a spot that Keppel never mentions. The mistake gives us an interesting insight into Read's reliability. He was a partner in A.L. Johnston & Co. from 1 Jan. 1842, and senior partner from the time of A.L. Johnston's death in 1850 until his own retirement in 1887 (five years before the once prosperous firm went out of business); and A.L. Johnston & Company were one of the sponsors of the schemes for a dry dock on Pulau Brani from 1849 to 1854, until in fact Butterworth took over the site for the Admiralty. Moreover, Read was in Singapore in June/July 1861 when Admiral Jones inspected the site on Pulau Brani, and reported that the island was valuable as a coaling base but that he considered it unsuitable as a site for a naval dry dock.

[201] The committee sponsoring the revised scheme of 1849 (that is, the original project of 1845–46, as modified by Butterworth's Dry Dock Committee of the latter year) consisted of representatives of A.L. Johnston & Co., Hamilton, Gray & Co. and d'Almeida & Sons. See letter, Committee Pulo Brani Docking Company to Butterworth, 25 Nov. 1850 (*EIC Rec.*, W. 15: 283).

[202] Walter Makepeace in Makepeace et al., *One Hundred Years of Singapore*, 2 vols. (London: J. Murray, 1921), vol. 1, pp. 578–9 ("The Port of Singapore, Early Days"). W.W. Ker was Singapore partner in Ker, Rawson & Co. from the foundation of the firm in 1828.

[203] See also above.

[122m] long was completed in 1859.[204] The abandoned pit was known touchingly as Cloughton's Hole for many years. Work on it was resumed in the period 1899–1901, with improved equipment, but finally the site was abandoned, and use made of an area east of Cloughton's two docks.[205] At the end of December 1861, a seven-year partnership was concluded between Cloughton, Paterson, Wemyss Ker and six others for the purpose of operating the dry dock and slip. The new company took the name of the Patent Slip & Dock Company. The initial capital was Sp. $130,000, which was subscribed in equal shares of $100 each; 71 of the 130 shares were held by Paterson, Wemyss Ker and H.M. Simons between them, all of whom were partners in Paterson, Simons & Co. The latter firm thus held a controlling interest in the dockyard, and subsequently conducted the business side of the undertaking, while Cloughton continued as manager until his retirement in 1872. The patent slip was never used, so far as is known, and there is no mention of it (except in the title of the company) after 1863.[206]

Cloughton's dock was followed by the construction of two others. The various reclamations were still to come, and at this period Tanjong Pagar was a squat headland, rising in the centre to a low hillock. The property belonged to Gilbert Angus Bain, of Maclaine, Fraser & Co., and accordingly was known as Bain's Hill.[207] Bain retired to Scotland in 1854 leaving his affairs in the hands of a younger brother, Robert, who was at this time a partner in A.L. Johnston & Co. Robert Bain himself retired in 1857, and subsequently arranged for a series of trial borings on the west side of Tanjong Pagar. The following year he had a small lithograph map prepared, illustrating the position of the borings and providing other relevant data, as a preliminary to floating a company to construct a dock on the site. Unfortunately, at this point the resident councillor, Singapore, led him to believe that government was proposing to requisition the hill, with a view to placing a fort on it to protect the eastern entrance to New Harbour. There the matter rested for about six months,

---

[204] The dock was opened in Mar. 1859. See *SFP*, adv., 1 July 1863; and the *Straits Calendar and Directory* for 1861, 1862 and 1863.

[205] See Bogaars, "The Tanjong Pagar Dock Company", pp. 231–2. Seemingly the site was ill-chosen, and even if the excavation had succeeded, the approach was risky by lying too near Pulau Hantu.

[206] W.M. Cloughton, in a letter to the editor of the *Straits Times*, 17 Sept. 1863 (publ. 20 Sept.), recounting five "facts" why Singapore did not need another dock, says that up to that time he had never had any occasion to use his patent slip. Knowledge of this point had probably filtered through to the promoters of the Tanjong Pagar Dock Company a week or two earlier. Their original intention had been to build a slip, and later a dock, much as Robert Bain appears to have had in mind in 1858–59. But at their meeting on 14 Sept. (the prick that stimulated Capt. Cloughton to pen his mighty broadside) they decided to abandon the idea of a patent slip, and go straight ahead with a dock.

[207] Gilbert Angus Bain purchased the lot from government in Mar. 1847. Bain joined Maclaine, Fraser & Co. as a clerk at the firm's inception in 1827, became a partner in 1843, and retired in 1854, leaving his younger brother Robert Bain to act as "agent for the property of Tanjong Pagar". After Robert Bain's departure early in 1859, Maclaine, Fraser & Co. acted as agents, and ultimately sold the property to the embryo Tanjong Pagar Dock Co. for $24,000, after receiving an initial bid from them of $5,000.

during which time Bain took no further action over the formation of a company. Finally, in February 1859, when he was on the point of leaving the settlement, he was told that government had no immediate intention of taking over Tanjong Pagar. Bain had asked for compensation, on the grounds that he had been obstructed in his plans for developing the property by the statements that the hill was likely to be requisitioned. To which E.A. Blundell, who was then, governor, replied through his secretary that no written intimation of government action had ever been given to Bain, and that had he gone ahead with his plans and the hill then been requisitioned, his brother would have received suitable compensation.[208] At the same time, of course, it is doubtful if a company could have been floated successfully in such an atmosphere, but that was not Blundell's concern; he was a fully matured bureaucrat, aiming always at power without responsibility, the natural perquisite of the prostitute throughout history.

Apparently, nothing further was done about Tanjong Pagar for nearly four years. Probably the Bains, now in Scotland, and other interested parties in Singapore, were still held back by the possibility of the hill being required for defence purposes, as Pulau Brani had been, in 1854. It is not clear what plan, if any, was being followed by the military authorities at this point: several years earlier they had tried to modernise Fort Fullerton, with disastrous results; then in 1858 they had requisitioned Tan Tock Seng's hospital to provide quarters for the newly arrived European artillery unit, and less than two years later they had taken the men away and begun to convert the building into a commissariat store. But there is no doubt that in the scheme of defences drawn up by Lieutenant Best of the Madras Engineers in 1843, Bain's Hill is shown as the site of a coastal battery (No. 7).[209] Presumably, this point was known to the owners of the property.

Possibly Lieutenant-Colonel Cavenagh sought some clarification of the situation after his arrival in Singapore as governor of the Straits Settlements, in August 1859. Certainly towards the end of August 1862, James Guthrie purchased from government

---

[208] Verbal warning that Bain's property at Tanjong Pagar might be requisitioned by government under Act VI of 1857 was apparently first given to Robert Bain by H.S. Mackenzie, the resident councillor, Singapore, in July 1858. Seemingly, it was repeated on more than one occasion thereafter. Bain addressed the resident councillor on the matter officially in Jan. 1859, and getting no redress wrote to E.A. Blundell on 7 Feb. The latter replied through his Secretary on 9 Feb. 1859 (*EIC Rec.*, V. 26: 216), disclaiming any liability on the part of government, and informing Bain that in any case if he had any such claim to make, it would have to be made through the courts. There may have been further correspondence which has not been preserved. In his letter to Blundell, Bain says that he is about to leave Singapore, and will not therefore be able to float the proposed Joint Stock Company to develop the Tanjong Pagar property. But he was apparently still in Penang at the end of 1859, when he sent Col. Cavenagh, who had succeeded Blundell as governor, a formal letter to be forwarded to the under secretary to the Govt. of India on the subject. Unfortunately we have only a copy of his very brief covering letter, Bain to Cavenagh, 15 Dec. 1859 (*EIC Rec.*, W. 32: 675). Thereafter, the matter apparently ceases so far as the material preserved in the Government Archives, Singapore, is concerned.

[209] The original is in the Raffles Museum collection [E.N.: Now in the National Archives of Singapore]; see also the note on maps in Bogaars, "The Tanjong Pagar Dock Company", p. 269.

the foreshore adjoining his land near Tanjong Pagar,[210] and in February 1863, G.A. Bain similarly extended his holdings so that between them they owned the whole of the area in the neighbourhood of the point. Then on 1 September in the latter year, Guthrie called an informal meeting in his office to consider the possibility of floating a joint-stock company, for the purpose of constructing and operating a patent slip, and perhaps later a dry dock, in the vicinity of Tanjong Pagar. It was then estimated that the capital required would be in the region of $200,000, and that it should be possible to raise this by public subscription. A list was opened immediately, and on the strength of the response during the first ten days, subscribers were asked to attend a meeting on 14 September.[211] On this occasion those present appointed seven members who had each agreed to take up 20 or more shares as directors, approved the proposal to circulate the subscription list in England, India and China, and decided that the company should abandon the idea of making a patent slip, and that instead it should concentrate all its energies on the construction of a dry dock (later called *Victoria Dock*), to be built on land belonging to James Guthrie. At this stage it was provisionally agreed that the dock should be 550 feet [167.6m] long, 65 feet [19.8m] wide and 23 feet [7m] deep: later these figures were reduced to 450 feet [137m] and 20 feet [6.1m]. Finally it was resolved that a general meeting of the subscribers should be called at the begining of January 1864, to render these decisions effective and to make arrangements for registering the company.[212]

It is interesting to note that the idea of building the public wharf, which alone kept the company alive until conditions improved after 1869, was not broached at this meeting, or at the informal one that had preceded it on 1 September. The wharves were an addition suggested by George Lyon, a local shipwright, then in business on Tanjong Rhu, who was recruited at $200 a month as supervising engineer.[213] He had trouble later with his work on the dock, and in 1865 a second engineer, W.J. du Port, was brought out from Liverpool to take charge over him. Thereupon, Lyon resigned and returned to Tanjong Rhu before even the wharf was completed. Initially the wharf was intended only for use in bunkering and to allow vessels waiting to enter the dock to discharge and store their cargo. The first line of wharves, 750 feet

[210] G.A. Bain's original property, Bain's Hill, was conveyed to him on 26 Mar. 1847, on the completion of the survey; he may therefore have been in occupation before this date. His additional property, lot 1581, consisted of submerged land, amounting to 62½ acres [0.25km²]. The lease is dated 9 Feb. 1863; it is for 999 years, and no conditions were attached at the time when it was granted. Guthrie's additional land, a 500-foot [152.4m] frontage on the reef at Tanjong Pagar, was initially granted on condition that "the proposed works, to be carried out thereon, should be in an *advanced state* by the end of five years"; subsequently, on 15 Jan. 1864, he addressed the resident councillor asking that the clause should be removed, as there was no such clause attached to the grant to G.A. Bain, and that further, as the Tanjong Pagar Dock Company had selected his land as the site for their proposed dock, it was likely that substantial progress would have been made in utilising the land within five years (*EIC Rec.*, W. 49: 34).

[211] *SFP*, 13 Sept. 1863.

[212] *SFP*, 17 Sept. 1863.

[213] G.E. Bogaars, "The Effect of the Opening of the Suez Canal on the Trade and Development of Singpore", *JMBRAS* 28, 1 (1955): 126–7.

long [228.6m], was completed by du Port in 1866; two years later it was extended to 1,450 feet [442m] to provide accommodation for twelve vessels at a time.[214]

A further point of interest is that at the time of the general meeting at the beginning of January 1864, the future company still had no land, though it had decided on the approximate site of the proposed dock. It was clear that the land would have to be purchased, and there was at least this much simplicity about the matter: two people—G.A. Bain and James Guthrie—owned all that was likely to be required between them. The directors were authorised to go ahead and buy up their properties. They apparently began by offering Maclaine, Fraser & Co., who were acting as agents for G.A. Bain, $5,000 for the latter's holdings. Unfortunately, the Messageries Imperiales were also interested, and they promptly doubled the bid. In the end, by playing one against the other, Maclaine, Fraser & Co. finally sold Bain's Hill and adjacent properties to the Tanjong Pagar Dock Company for $24,000.[215] James Guthrie parted with his holdings more quietly, taking $25,000 for all except 22 acres; and for the latter, at a later date, shares to the value of $6,000.[216] It is not, perhaps, surprising that when the company was registered, in September 1864, the capital required was increased to $300,000.

Captain Cloughton strongly opposed the establishment of the Tanjong Pagar Dock Company on the grounds that there was not enough work for one dock, let alone two, and that it seemed likely that the growing use of iron hulls would reduce rather than increase the demand for docking facilities. The supporters of the new company, who apparently included John Cameron, the editor of the *Straits Times*, stoutly denied this, and a chorus was written for the *Christmas Epilogue* of the Corps Dramatique to prove their point.[217] Later, some faint hearts (or hard heads) seem to have had their misgivings, and in 1866 the directors tried to buy the Patent Slip & Dock Company, or failing that, to reach an agreement with them on prices. Neither effort was successful, and when the Victoria Dock was finally opened in October 1868 Captain Cloughton set out to break the new company by reducing his charges below cost.[218] The directors of the Tanjong Pagar Dock Company met this challenge by instructing their dock manager to quote the minimum possible figures above cost (which meant that the Victoria Dock received relatively little work, but that the company did not actually loose on the jobs that were undertaken):[219] at the same time they waived their own fees, and utilised the steadily increasing profits on the wharves to show a slight overall profit on the workings of the company as a whole.

---

[214] Ibid. See also Bogaars, "The Tanjong Pagar Dock Company", pp. 130ff.

[215] Walter Makepeace, "Rise and progress of the Tanjong Pagar Dock Co." (Singapore: Free Press, 1896). The Messageries Maritimes Imperiales opened up in Singapore in Mar. 1862, with offices in Flint Street (*Straits Calender & Directory* for 1862 and 1863). Their coal-sheds were built at the west end of Pulau Brani late in 1861; presumably permission for them to do so followed on from Admiral Jones's report that P. Brani was not suitable as a location for a naval dockyard.

[216] Bogaars, "The Tanjong Pagar Dock Company", p. 125.

[217] Anon., "The Tanjong Pagar Dock Company", *Straits Times*, 14 May 1864.

[218] Thomas Scott, chairman Tanjong Pagar Dock Company, reported in *Straits Times*, 20 Mar. 1869; and again, *Straits Times*, 23 Aug. 1869.

[219] *Straits Times*, 17 July 1869, reporting an Extraordinary General Meeting of the Tanjong Pagar Dock Company.

It is, of course, questionable how long they could have survived in this way. As it was, they were extricated from an increasingly difficult situation by the opening of the Suez Canal in 1869.[220] This lead to a great increase in the deep-water shipping entering the port of Singapore, and particularly in the use made of the Tanjong Pagar Company's wharves. On this latter score they were in effect operating a near monopoly, and as a result of the lead that it gave them, they were able to come to an agreement on docking charges with Cloughton's company in 1870. In that year, the Tanjong Pagar Dock Company paid its first dividend (amounting to 4 per cent), and in the following year the directors received their first fees of $2,000 each. From this time on, the total receipts continued to rise steadily, but it was several years more before there was a profit on the running of the dock.[221]

In spite of the arguments that Cloughton raised at the time when the Tanjong Pagar Dock Company was established, a firm of Telok Ayer shipwrights, J.C. Buyers & Daniel Robb, decided to build a small repairing dock on Pulau Brani. Work was begun at the end of 1865, and the dock was opened for use in August 1866. It was 300 feet [91.4m] long, 75 feet [22.9m] wide, and at spring tides capable of admitting a vessel with a draught of 18 feet [5.5m].[222] It was sited on the west side of the island, opening to the Selat Sengkir; thus it occupied roughly the position that Dr Montgomerie had planned to use some 30 years earlier (though in construction and function it was, of course, very different). Cloughton does not appear to have been unduly troubled by the opening of the Bon Accord Dock. He was a shrewd man, and he knew that he had the advantage of an extra hundred feet in length and of a much more direct access to the town. Also, seemingly, his views on how to deal with the competition from the Tanjong Pagar Dock Company changed: in 1869 he began to build another dock himself, so that by the latter part of 1870 there were four dry docks operating in Singapore. But the business proved too much for him. In 1872 his health broke down and he retired to England, where he died in March 1874.

When the price-cutting war began between Cloughton's Company and the Tanjong Pagar Dock Company, the Bon Accord Dock was, of course, the concern that suffered most severely. It was still a relatively new company, with little to show in the way of past profits and with no public wharves to provide a certain source of income. In addition, the directorates of the two larger companies consisted almost entirely of partners in important import-&-export firms and shipping agencies: as a result their respective docks could he sure of a certain amount of custom. Finally, therefore, when Cloughton and the Tanjong Pagar Company came to terms in 1870, they were in a position to take over a ten-year lease of the Bon Accord Dock, and run it jointly, so that between them they gathered in all the local docking fees. The agreement was not renewed in 1880, nor by this time were the owners of the Bon Accord in a position to start up again in competition with two better-equipped and well-established companies. As a result the directors of the Tanjong Pagar Company were able to buy up the independent dock at a relatively low figure. They had, of

---

[220] See Bogaars, "The Effect of the Opening of the Suez Canal", *JMBRAS* 28, 1 (1955): 99–143.

[221] Bogaars, "The Effect of the Opening of the Suez Canal", *JMBRAS* 28, 1 (1955): 128.

[222] See Bogaars, "The Tanjong Pagar Dock Company", p. 259, reproducing an account from the *SFP*, 1 Mar. 1866.

course, little intention of making much use of it, and after a few years it was put out of commission and the dock converted into a storage tank.

We started at the point where the present Keppel Harbour, populated only by a few groups of orang laut, first emerges as an essential section of the main sea route between the South China Sea and the Melaka Strait. We have seen how the Malays from Johor tried to block the passageway during one of their disputes with the Portuguese at Melaka, and how the shipping accordingly sought out an alternative route. The latter led to the use of the Singapore Main Strait, and thereafter, as vessels steadily increased in size, the old waterway was abandoned by all except local craft, and the still present orang laut. Finally, with the establishment of the modern settlement of Singapore, interest in the Old Strait was revived; but this time it was in the light of its potential value as a safe harbour in time of war, and ultimately as a site for the growing port's wharves and docks. By the latter part of 1870 there were four graving docks in operation in New Harbour, and (on the north side) private wharves belonging to the P&O Company, Jardine, Matheson & Company and the Borneo Company, and (on the south side) bunkering piers for the vessels of HM Navy and the Compagnie des Services Maritimes Messageries Imperiales; in addition, on the north side of the harbour there were the extensive public wharves of the Tanjong Pagar Dock Company, which provided godowns and bunkering facilities for the smaller independent companies. For the next 35 years, the history of the Old Strait is largely that of the Tanjong Pagar Dock Company, which follows in the succeeding pages of the present journal.

15

Peter Borschberg

A Portuguese-Dutch Naval Battle in the Johor River Estuary and the Liberation of Johor Lama in 1603*

General Background and Introduction

The maps and steel cuts of the three German publishers Theodore, Johann Theodore and Johann Israel de Bry have long been cherished among scholars of history and armchair travellers. In volume eight of their celebrated collection of voyages to the East and West Indies, one finds in appendix thirteen, under "Images or true and exact descriptions of all memorable things and events"[1] the sketch of a Dutch-Portuguese naval confrontation that took place in the Johor River (*Rio de Batusabar*) near Johor Lama (*Oud Ior*). De Bry and his sons also added a small commentary in German describing the various stages of the Luso-Dutch battle. The caption summarizes the more detailed account (liberally) rendered into Latin by M. Gotthard Arthus, a native of Danzig and co-rector of the Latin college in Frankfurt am Main. Arthus was also an associate of the de Bry publishing house.[2]

Like many other early accounts of Dutch voyages to the Indies, this story also found its way into the first "history" of the United Dutch East India Company (VOC)

---

* First published as a book chapter in *Early Singapore, 1300–1819. Evidence from Maps*, Texts and Artefacts, ed. John N. Miksic and Cheryl-Ann Low Mei Gek (Singapore: Singapore History Museum, 2004), pp. 106–17.

[1] *Icones seu gennuinae et expressae delineationes omnium memorabilium*, translation of the original Latin title by P.B. This is found in: *Ioannes Theodoricus et Ioannes Israel de Bry: Icones seu gennnuinae et expressae delineationes omnium memorabilium quae in hac octava Indiae Orientalis parte annotata sunt...* (Francofurti: In Officina typographica Wolfgangi Richteri, 1607). Source hereafter abbreviated as *IOPO*.

[2] *Allgemeine Deutsche Bibliographie*, vol. 1 (Leipzig: Duncker & Humblot, 1875), p. 613.

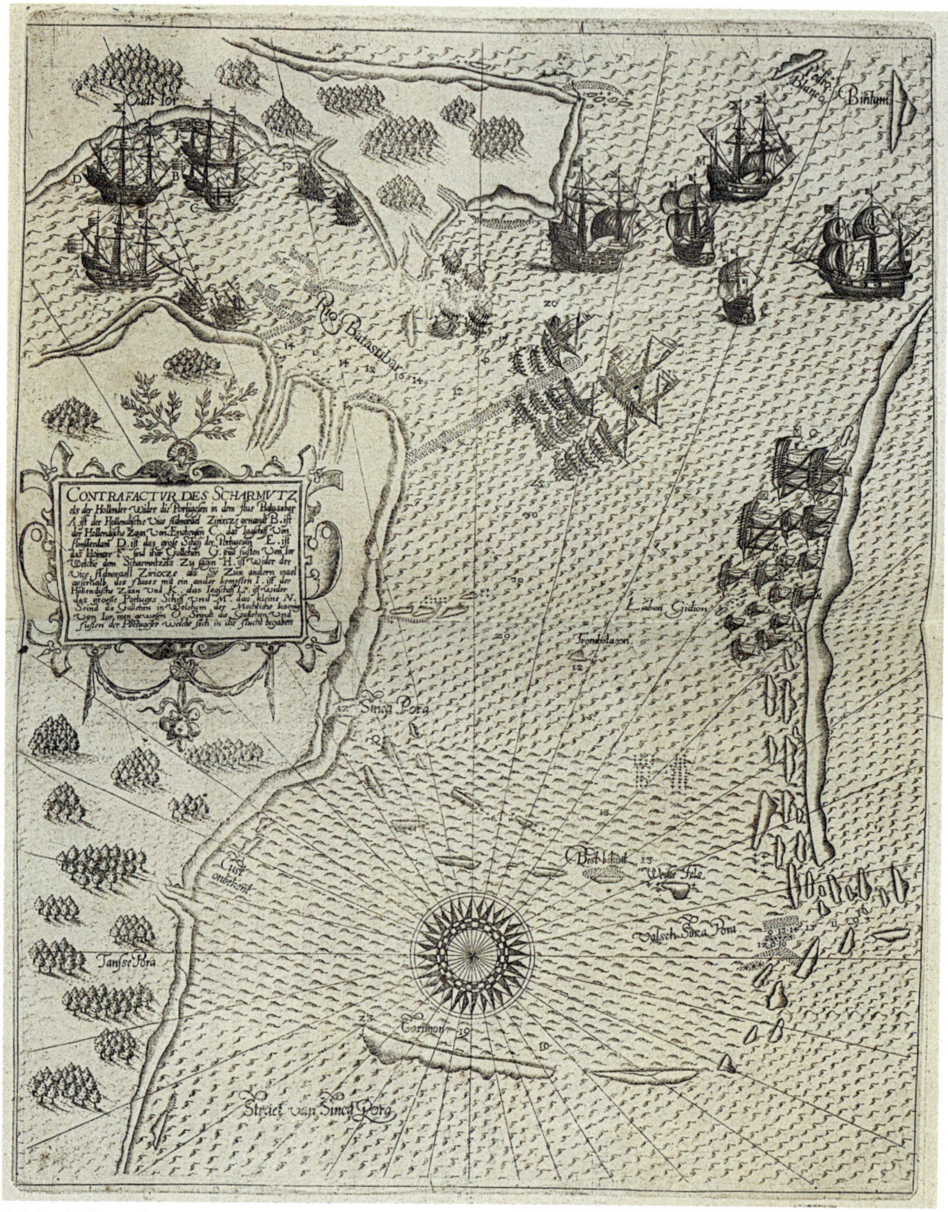

15.1 Schematic map depicting the various stages in the naval confrontation between Vice-Admiral Pietersz van Enkhuisen and Teixeira de Matos in the Johor River and the Straits of Singapore, October 1603. J.T. de Bry, *Icones seu Gennuinae et Expressae Delineationes Omnium Memorabilium* [Images or Authentic and Accurate Description of all Memorable Events], published in Frankfurt am Main, 1607. Leiden, Bibliotheca Thysiana, THYS 874, pl. 13.

that was published by Isaac Commelin.[3] Substantial sections of this monumental work were later translated into both French and English.[4] Commelin's compilation of early eyewitness accounts and historically relevant material contains several engravings that are similar or even identical to those printed by de Bry.

The map found in appendix thirteen reconstructs the sequence of armed engagements that took place from 6 to 11 October 1603, between three ships under the immediate command Dutch Vice-Admiral Jacob Pietersz van Enkhuisen,[5] and the Portuguese naval squadron under Captain Estêvão Teixeira de Matos.[6] This virtually unknown chapter in the history of the Straits of Singapore and the Johor River estuary during the early modern period of considerable significance for understanding both the origins, as well as the course of, Johor-Dutch relations in the first two decades of the 17th century.[7]

Teixeira de Matos' squadron had been dispatched to the Straits of Singapore to impose a blockade on the Johor River as well as to protect inbound vessels of the Portuguese China fleet. According to the testimony of one David van Lochum dated 10 October 1604, the Portuguese squadron consisted of vessels that had recently returned from battling the Dutch for supremacy in the Moluccas.[8] According to this testimony, Johor Lama had come under the direct control of the Portuguese assailants. It should be remembered that whilst the Portuguese had attacked and inflicted serious damage to the old royal residence of Johor in 1587, it still remained a viable settlement until 1604. Johann Verken, who visited Johor Lama in early 1609, observed that despite the complete destruction five years earlier, the city remained densely populated.[9]

---

[3] Translation P.B. Isaac Commelin, *Begin ende Voortgang Vande Vereenigde Nederlandsche Geoctroyeerde Oost-Indische Compagnie* [hereafter abbreviated as BV], facsimile reproduction of the original edition printed in Amsterdam, 1646, 4 vols. (Amsterdam: Facsimile Uitgaven Nederland, 1969).

[4] René Augustin Constantin de Renneville, *Recueil des voiages qui ont servi à l'établissement et aux progrès de la Compagnie des Indes Orientales, formée dans les Provinces-Unies des Païs-Bas* (Amsterdam: J.F. Bernard, 1725).

[5] Jacob Pietersz van Enkhuisen is erroneously attributed the name "Cornelis" by J.K.J. de Jonge, *Opkomst van het Nederlandsch gezag in Oost-Indië. Verzameling van onuitgegeven stukken uit het oud-coloniaal archief*, eerste reeks, vol. 3 (The Hague: Martinus Nijhoff, 1865), p. 17. Several authors have copied this error, including P.A. Tiele, N. Mac Leod and H. Terpstra. See also W. Ph. Coolhaas, "Een bron van het historische gedeelte van Hugo de Groots De Jure Praedae", *Bijdragen en Mededelingen van het Historisch Genootschap* 79 (1965): 505n4.

[6] The Portuguese naval officer is sometimes referred to as Teixeira de Made or Teixeira de Macedo. See for example M. Teixeira, *The Portuguese Missions in Malacca and Singapore*, vol. 1, Malacca (Lisbon: Agência Geral do Ultramar, 1961), p. 223n3; Charles Ralph Boxer and Frazão de Vasconcelos, *André Furtado de Mendonça, 1558–1610* (Macau: Fundação Oriente and Centro de Estudios Marítimo de Macau, 1989), appendix V, p. 127n1. *IOPO* refers on p. 85 to the Portuguese naval officer as *Estenao Teixeira de Made*.

[7] P.A. Tiele, "De Europeërs in den Maleischen Archipel", part 6, *BKI* 31 (1882): 217–8.

[8] Tiele "De Europeërs", p. 220; Coolhaas, "Een bron", p. 506.

[9] Johann Verken, "Molukkenreise 1607–1612", in *Reisebeschreibungen von Deutschen Beamten und Kriegsleuten im Dienst der Niederländisch West- und Ost-Indischen Kompanien, 1602–1797*, ed. S.P. L'Honoré Naber, vol. 2 (The Hague: Martinus Nijhoff, 1930), p. 58.

Only a few months earlier—on 25 February 1603, to be precise—the Johoreans attacked and seized, together with their new-found Dutch ally, the richly-laden Portuguese merchant vessel, *Santa Catarina*, off the East coast of Singapore.[10] The capture of the Portuguese trading ship by Captain Jacob van Heemskerk and the Johoreans dealt a serious blow to the merchants of Macau, who as a result of this loss became steeped in losses to the sum of one *conto de ouro*, or one million *cruzados*. At the time, this was a substantial sum that was equivalent to about 30,000 kilogrammes of coin grade silver. Around the year 1600 it could have bought at the trade fair in Canton between 20 and 25 million pieces of porcelain dishware![11]

The unusually rich cargo of the *Santa Catarina* was brought back to the Netherlands as a prize of war where at a public auction it raised the sum of three and a half million florins. At the time, this was equivalent to approximately half of the subscription capital of the Dutch East India Company (VOC) and more than double the capital base of its English counterpart, the Honourable East India Company, founded only two years earlier in 1600.[12]

The incident surrounding the seizure of the *Santa Catarina* certainly raised eyebrows in Europe and fired the imagination of traders over the riches to be "gained" in the East Indies. The capture of the *Santa Catarina* seriously alarmed the *Estado da Índia* over its vulnerability to such actions of hostile engagement and loss of merchant cargo. Not surprisingly, red-faced Portuguese officials from Melaka to Goa resolved that such an incident should not be able to repeat itself. They stepped up efforts to assert and defend, by force of arms, their claimed monopoly of trade with Europe.

It goes almost without saying that, with such profits and booty at stake, the Dutch would not be easily deterred from preying on Portuguese merchant shipping. The early years of the 17th century saw numerous Dutch fleets undertaking voyages to the Indonesian Archipelago, including notably the first VOC-organized expedition proper under the supreme command of Admiral Wijbrandt van Warwijk. On their arrival in the East Indies, Warwijk's fleet separated and proceeded to call at different destinations in India, China and Island Southeast Asia. While Warwijk set course for Patani and China, the three ships under Vice-Admiral Sebald de Weert headed for Ceylon and Aceh. After casting anchor off the coast of Baticaloa, De Weert travelled by elephant to the capital city Kandy where he was courteously received by its ruler,

---

[10] P. Borschberg, "The Seizure of the Sta. Catarina Revisited. The Portuguese Empire in Asia, VOC Politics and the Origins of the Dutch-Johor Alliance (1602–c.1616)", *JSEAS* 33 (2002): 31–65.

[11] Charles Ralph Boxer, *Fidalgos in the Far East, 1550–1770. Fact and Fancy in the History of Macao* (The Hague: Martinus Nijhoff, 1948), p. 50, places the losses at one *conto de ouro* which is the equivalent of one million Cruzados or 800,000 Cantonese *tael* of silver. The Italian merchant traveller Carletti who visited Canton around 1600 quotes a price of 22 *tael* for 650–700 pieces of porcelain dishware. See Francesco Carletti, *My voyage around the world*, tr. by Herbert Weinstock (New York: Pantheon Books, 1964), p. 149.

[12] C.R. Boxer, *Portuguese Merchants and Missionaries in Feudal Japan, 1543–1640* (London: Variorum Reprints, 1986), pp. 14–5; J.P. de Korte, *The Annual Accounting in the Dutch East India Company* (Amsterdam: NEHA, 2000), pp. 2–3.

the Maharaja Vimala Dharma Suriya I.[13] The monarch sought the assistance of the Dutch in expelling the Portuguese from their strongholds in Colombo, Cruz and Galle. De Weert promised to sail to Aceh and return with more ships.[14] He kept his word, and arrived in April 1603, from the North Sumatran city in the company of seven ships, three sloops and two Acehnese ambassadors. The Dutch managed to seize four Portuguese vessels off the coast of Ceylon, but the when the Maharaja of Kandy suspected that the Dutch were planning to capture and kill him, he had de Weert and 47 members of his crew murdered in cold blood on 1 June 1603.[15] Three days later, on 4 June, Jacob Pietersz[16] was elected by his peers to the position of vice-admiral to replace his assassinated predecessor.[17]

The new vice-admiral's ships set sail for Aceh. On 24 August 1603, Pietersz and the three vessels *Zierikzee*, *Hollandsche Tuin* and *Papagaaiken* set course for Patani in the hope of procuring a cargo of pepper there.[18] In the Melaka Straits, he intercepted several craft and exacted information about markets, cargo, trade routes and geography from their respective crews.[19]

Searching for the Straits of Singapore

In the final days of September 1603, Vice-Admiral Pietersz and his ships approached the Karimun Islands.[20] In these waters they encountered strong adverse currents and unpredictable winds. Although the Dutch ships reportedly carried two "Malay pilots" on board,[21] it does not appear that they were sufficiently familiar with the geo-morphology of the Straits of Singapore. The region presented itself to the Dutch crew and Malay pilots as a dangerous maze of islets, reefs and sandbanks that lay around shallow waters, or surfaced at low tide. The map of de Bry provides additional testimony to this by indicating the depth of water measured by the Dutch crew at several locations. The officers thus resolved, on 27 September, to man two skiffs[22] and charged these with finding a viable channel to the South China Sea. The search

---

[13] The incident is described at length in *IOPO*, pp. 51ff—The city of Kandy is located in the central highlands of present-day Sri Lanka.

[14] *IOPO*, pp. 53–4.

[15] *BV*, vol. 2, p. 23; *IOPO*, p. 65; Emanuel van Meteren, *Historiën der Nederlanden en haar Naburen oorlogen tot het Iaar 1612* (Amsterdam: Ian Iacobsz Schipper, 1652), fol. 495 verso; Coolhaas, "Een bron", p. 505; N. Mac Leod, *De Oost-Indische Compagnie als Zeemogendheid in Azië* (Rijswijk: Blankwaardt & Schoonhoven, 1927), vol. 1, pp. 13–4.

[16] Latinized as: Iacobus Petri Enchusanus.

[17] *IOPO*, p. 67; Mac Leod, *De Oost-Indische Compagnie*, vol. 1, p. 14.

[18] Heert Terpstra, *De factorij der Oostindische Compagnie te Patani* (The Hague: Martinus Nijhoff, 1938), p. 18; Mac Leod, *De Oost-Indische Compagnie*, vol. 1, p. 14.

[19] *IOPO*, pp. 78ff; *BV*, vol. 2, pp. 34–6.

[20] *BV*, vol. 2, p. 36.

[21] In the 16th and 17th century, the term "Malay" is applied generously to refer to several peoples in island and mainland Southeast Asia. Its meaning at this time is primarily cultural and not racial.

[22] The term *scapha* is used in the Latin text of 1607.

continued for several days through narrow passages and around small islands, but the Straits of Singapore remained elusive.[23]

On 30 September, seven mates went ashore to find fresh water and gather firewood. Unaware of any danger, the men were ambushed by angry locals, apparently mistaking the Dutch sailors for Portuguese soldiers. When their mates heard the commotion on land, they quickly dispatched a skiff to shore, finding one of the sailors dead and three mates seriously wounded. The native attackers meanwhile took flight in four *perahus* that had been left at the other side of the unnamed islet.[24]

As evening fell the following day, the crew spotted a number of *perahus* assembling nearby. Signalling to the native boatsmen that they should come closer, the Dutch hissed a white flag. Still, the local warriors or fishermen were too afraid and kept their cautious distance. Noting this, the Dutch launched a skiff, carrying on board one of the "Malay" pilots, a white flag and the important message that the ships were Dutch and not Portuguese. Sensing that this manoeuvre might be a trap, the native boatsmen used the approaching sunset to return to shore, but pledged to return at dawn.

The *perahus* regrouped the following morning as promised. As a matter of precaution, each party exchanged two members of the crew. On board the *Zierikzee*, the two native boatsmen explained that there was now great hostility between Johor and Portugal. Pietersz also learned on this occasion that two large ships (about the size of galleons), together with four galleys and between 20 and 25 bantins were holding guard in Johor River estuary.[25]

Sources reveal that the squadron of Teixeira de Matos was meant to fulfil a dual function. First, it imposed a blockade in punishment for Johorean co-operation with the Dutch, and specifically also for their active support lent to Heemskerk during the *Sta. Catarina* incident.[26] As long as the Portuguese vessels were holding guard in the Johor River, they disrupted direct trade between the sea and Johor's riverine towns, including the capital and royal residence at Batu Sawar, located about 36 kilometres upstream.[27]

Second, the Portuguese squadron was instructed to await the arrival of Portuguese carracks from Japan, China and Makassar and provide armed protection

---

[23] *BV*, vol. 2, pp. 36–7.

[24] *IOPO*, pp. 83–4; *BV*, vol. 2, p. 37.

[25] *BV*, vol. 2, p. 37.—Hugo Grotius, who is sometimes celebrated in modern times as the "father" of modern international law, briefly touches upon this incident in his *Law of Prize and Booty*. In this he claims that the Portuguese had "two galleons" and more than twenty five "foists and other long boats"; Hugo Grotius, *De Jure Praedae Commentarius*, edited by H.G. Hamaker (The Hague: Martinus Nijhoff, 1868), p. 331.—According to the testimony of David Lochum, the Portuguese fleet consisted of "two gallions or large ships, six galleys and 24 bantins or foists". See Coolhaas, "Een bron", p. 506.

[26] Concerning this cooperation, see also P. Borschberg, "Hugo Grotius, East India Trade and the King of Johor", *JSEAS* 30, 2 (1999): 225–48.

[27] *BV*, vol. 2, p. 38; A. Botelho de Sousa, *Subsídios para a historia militar-marítima da Índia* (Lisbon: Imprimeria da Armada, 1930), vol. 1, p. 554.

for their onward journey through the Singapore Straits to Melaka.[28] The Vice-Admiral also learnt at this juncture that, before returning to Europe, Heemskerk deployed members of his crew as resident agents, including Jacob Buijs who now headed the new VOC comptoir at Batu Sawar.[29]

Pietersz hesitated no longer. He asked the boatsmen to show his ships the passage through the Straits of Singapore, and even promised a reward for their effort. The Johoreans answered that they were not seeking reward or remuneration, but rather, they came to assist their Dutch friends on the instructions of their monarch, 'Ala'ud-din Ri'ayat Shah III. The Vice-Admiral issued orders to raise anchor, and with the two Malay boatsmen on board, he set course for the Straits of Singapore.[30] The local guides instructed the Dutch to "head back" because they were "not near the Straits".[31] It appears that the Dutch ships had proceeded too far south, and cast anchor near the Northern coast of present-day Bulan or Batam, which is marked on de Bry's map as *Valsch Sinca Pora* ("False" Strait of Singapore). Their further course cannot be reconstructed with certainty, but they did arrive at a location that clearly fits the description of the old Dragon Teeth Gate (also commonly known by its Chinese name, Lung-ya-men), located at Tanjong Berlayar, in the vicinity of present-day Labrador Park.

The "Old Strait" of Singapore is described (with some exaggeration, no doubt) as "a stone's throw" wide and "a cannon shot long".[32] Entering from the Northwest, the crew spotted on the left-hand side two columns or pillars. Nearby they sighted a "fine bay" as well as a town that is known by the name of "Singapura". Most unfortunately, the exact location of the latter cannot be ascertained on the basis of the early 17th century Dutch or Latin texts. In the afternoon a southwesterly breeze helped the ships steer clear of dangerous cliffs along the shores of Sentosa. Once the "Old" Strait had been cleared, the Vice-Admiral and his ships plied a North-Northeasterly course, skirting the Eastern shores of Singapore Island.[33]

Preparing for Battle

The following day, 4 October 1603, the three Dutch ships set course for "Patana". In the Latin text of Gotthard Arthus as well as in the Dutch-language equivalent

---

[28] *BV*, vol. 2, p. 38; Tiele, "De Europeërs", pp. 217–8; Botelho de Sousa, *Subsídios*, vol. 1, p. 553.

[29] Name latinized as *Buis[s]ius*; see *IOPO*, p. 85; MacLeod, *De Oost-Indische Compagnie*, vol. 1, p. 14; E. Netscher, *De Nederlanders in Djohor en Siak* (Batavia: Bruining & Wijt, 1870), p. 8.

[30] Tiele, "De Europeërs", p. 217.

[31] *BV*, vol. 2, p. 37.

[32] Ibid., pp. 37, 400; similar descriptions are found in other sources, see esp. C.A. Gibson-Hill, "Singapore: Note on the history of the Old Straits, 1580–1850", *JMBRAS* 27, 1 (1954): 163–214; and again in greater detail in: C.A. Gibson-Hill, "Singapore Old Strait & New Harbour, 1300–1870", *Memoirs of the Raffles Museum*, no. 3 (1956): 11–115. [E.N.: This text has been added to the present collection.]

[33] *BV*, vol. 2, pp. 37–8; Rouffaer, "Was Malaka emporium", pp. 388, 401. [E.N.: Portions of this text have been added in translation to this volume. See also the information regarding Pulau Patani in Rouffaer.]

reproduced by Commelin, this location described as the principal "port of Johor".[34] This is almost certainly the islet in the Johor River, known as Pulau Patani, that is located about five kilometres upstream from Johor Lama.[35] Several *perahus* are reported to have gathered around the Dutch ships. One of them ferried a Johorean official who is described as the "governor of Bintan".[36] A second *perahu* bore written messages from the Johor monarch, as well as the resident Dutch factor, Jacob Buijs.[37] These documents are said to have filled in the background events leading to the Portuguese blockade. Pietersz swiftly responded to these written messages with pledges to attack the Portuguese squadron—which was far superior in the number of vessels than his three ships—and to engage it against odds in battle. The vice-admiral also extended an invitation to King 'Ala'ud-din and Buijs join him aboard his flagship and participate personally in the planning for the attack.

The Dutch crew spotted a squadron of Portuguese craft that were evidently holding guard at the mouth of the Johor River. Under the cover of night, the Dutch dispatched a few skiffs and *perahus* for reconnaissance, but it is reported that the Portuguese immediately took flight when they suspected enemy craft approaching.

At dawn on 5 October 1603, a southerly breeze carried the Dutch ships further upstream. After passing two unidentified islands on their right-hand side,[38] numerous *perahus* suddenly appeared from all directions and gathered around them. These craft apparently belonged to small traders and peddlers who sought to break through the Portuguese blockade under the armed protection of the Dutch vessels. The full Portuguese squadron was now only about nine kilometres further upstream. The Dutch cast anchor and waited for the tide to turn. The currents of the rising tide would then assist Pietersz and his ships to glide up the river toward the enemy.

Evidently the Portuguese had spotted the Dutch as well. At about three o'clock in the afternoon, a few foists and other boats came to catch a better glimpse of the newcomers, but swiftly headed back after realizing that they were dealing with well-armed enemy vessels. That night the *Zierikzee* and *Hollandsche Tuin* hoisted anchor and quietly moved closer to the Portuguese vessels. The *Zierikzee* reportedly ran aground in this manoeuvre, but thanks to the swift response of its crew, the ship was soon afloat again, and ready for battle.

A Portuguese fugitive (*renegado*) named *Codsa de Delsab*,[39] who worked in the employ of the Johor monarch, arrived with a letter written in the Malay language and accompanied by a translation into Dutch prepared by Buijs. In his letter, King 'Ala'ud-din exhorted the vice-admiral to do all in his powers to deliver Johor from

---

[34] *IOPO*, p. 85: "... versus portum Ior, qui alias Portus de Patana vocatur... (toward the Port of Johor that is also called the Port of Patana)"; *BV*, vol. 2, p. 38.

[35] Rouffaer, "Was Malakka emporium", pp. 433, 438; N.B. Dennys, *Descriptive Dictionary of British Malaya* (London: London and China Telegraph Office, 1894), p. 273.

[36] *IOPO*, p. 85; "... Gubernator Insulæ Binthani ..."; *BV*, vol. 2, p. 38.

[37] D.F.A. Hervey, "François Valentyn's Account of Malacca", *JSBRAS* 16 (1885): 128; Teixeira, *The Portuguese Missions*, p. 223.

[38] *IOPO*, p. 86.

[39] Ibid., p. 86: *Codsa ab Delsab*. The term *renegado* encountered in Spanish and Portuguese texts from Southeast Asia of this period usually refers to a convert from Christianity to Islam.

the blockade and to drive the Portuguese out of the estuary. Accompanying the formal royal message and translation was also a private note from the resident factor Buijs. This told how King 'Ala'ud-din proclaimed before the people of Batu Sawar that the Dutch would come to their assistance and engage the Portuguese foe in battle. This news, Buijs explains, evoked much rejoicing among the people of the royal capital and raised hopes that the Portuguese blockade would soon be lifted.[40]

The Battle

At dawn the Dutch ships were now only two cannon shots' away from the Portuguese *squadron*. Slowly, they glided toward the eastern shores of the Johor River toward the enemy. The Dutch crew said their prayers and then engaged Teixeira de Matos with the first blast of the cannon. The Portuguese returned fire with their smaller artillery. The battle lasted for most hours of daylight. Just before dusk at five o'clock in the afternoon, the Portuguese flagship broke through the Dutch vessels.[41] It is believed that many *soldados* lost their lives in this tactical move, but with the benefit of hindsight, it saved the flagship and spared many of the remaining vessels of the Portuguese squadron from suffering more extensive damage. On the Dutch side, the vice-admiral counted on his ship three casualties and several men who had been wounded or crushed.

Throughout the hours of daylight one of the Johor monarch's half-brothers, Raja Bongsu,[42] Jacob Buijs and many *orang kaya* in their company held watch in *perahus* belonging to Johor's royal fleet. When the Portuguese flagship broke through the Dutch vessels, the Johoreans made their way across the river toward the victorious Dutch crew. Raja Bongsu presented Pietersz with a beautiful *keris* and thanked him for his contribution in lifting the crippling riverine blockade. The Johoreans also brought fruits and *arak* on board and celebrated with the Dutch sailors their victory over the Portuguese.[43] The following morning, 8 October 1603, the Dutch crew discovered that the Portuguese ships, at high tide and under the cover of darkness, made their way across the dangerous sand bank (upon which the *Zierikzee* had earlier run aground) and escaped downstream. As the tide had already reversed by the hours of dawn, it was not possible to raise anchor and chase after them.

Meanwhile, the king of Johor moved with the remaining part of his fleet, consisting of four to five "magnificent" galleys and about 40 *perahus* into the Johor River estuary.[44] He was determined to chase the remains of the Portuguese *squadron* from his waters. The map of de Bry places them near a finger-shaped shoal off the Eastern coast of Singapore that is now reclaimed land in the vicinity of Tanah Merah

---

[40] Ibid. and *BV*, vol. 2, p. 39.

[41] *IOPO*, p. 87; Tiele, "De Europeërs", p. 218; Boxer and Vasconcelos, *André Furtado de Mendonça*, appendix V, p. 127n1.

[42] Latinized as: *Rahu Bongso*, also referred to in many documents as Raja Sabrang or Raja di Ilir. Raja Bongsu already wielded considerable political power at the Johor court even before he succeeded his brother as king about 1613.

[43] *IOPO*, p. 87 : "... Araka et fructus offerentes ..."; *BV*, vol. 2, p. 40.

[44] *IOPO*, p. 87; Tiele, "De Europeërs", p. 218; MacLeod, *De Oost-Indische Compagnie*, vol. 1, p. 14.

and the Changi Naval Base. The king was aboard the largest of the galleys, and each of his two brothers, Raja Bongsu and the prince of Siak, aboard their own personal craft. During the morning hours they encountered strong adverse currents of the outgoing tide. By the afternoon, however, the tide began to reverse, and the proud Johorean fleet moved upstream. They spotted the enemy, anchored in the river estuary at a distance of about two Dutch sea-miles. Later they were also joined by the three Dutch ships. The king and the vice-admiral agreed to attack the following morning.

At dawn on 10 October 1603, Raja Bongsu, together with many *orang kaya* and the Dutch agent Jacob Buijs, transferred onto the *Zierikzee* from where they could better monitor the battle. A westerly breeze carried them toward the enemy, whose remaining vessels were quickly gathering in formation near the Eastern river bank. Pietersz resolved to attack the flagship. The crew again said their prayers and manoeuvred themselves near the Portuguese flagship. The exchange of fire began sometime between nine and ten o'clock in the morning and lasted for seven full hours. The Dutch crew fired at the sails of the enemy flagship in a tactical move to immobilize it. Pietersz and his Johorean guests observed how the Portuguese soldiers were abandoning ship, transferring personnel from the larger craft into their smaller galleys and *perahus*. The enemy ships under fire headed for the open sea, making their way toward Pedra Branca at the eastern entrance of the Straits. As evening fell, the remains of the Portuguese *squadron* regrouped and sought the protection of shallow waters off the northeastern coast of modern Batam, most probably around present-day Nongsa Point and Tering Bay.[45]

Raja Bongsu, who supervised the entire naval operation aboard the *Zierikzee*, transferred back to his personal galley at twilight. He left Buijs behind, issuing him with express instructions to keep a vigilant eye on all developments and to brief him the next morning.

At dawn of the following day, 11 October, the Dutch crew spotted whatever remained of the Portuguese *squadron* anchored off the coast of Batam, about six kilometres away. The Portuguese, too, were alert and had already spotted the Dutch ships which were now moving toward them. Dreading a third round of attacks, the Lusitanian mariners quickly hoisted sail and fled. Seeing this, Vice-Admiral Pietersz dispatched a skiff with a message for King 'Ala'ud-din, Raja Bongsu and the Johorean fleet that the enemy was now definitely taking flight.[46] The sea battle was won! With the Portuguese defeated and on the run, the King was now able to defeat the rest of the Portuguese forces and bring Johor Lama back under his control.[47]

Closer Ties

The vice-admiral moved his three ships into the safer waters of the Johor River where the crew could also rest for a few days from the exertions of combat. The

---

[45] *IOPO*, p. 88, rightly referred to in the Latin text by its commonly used Portuguese name *Pedra Branca*. This navigational landmark, however, is depicted on de Bry's map as *Pedro Blanco* (White Rock), a literal translation into Spanish of the Portuguese name *Pedra Branca*.

[46] *IOPO*, p. 88; *BV*, vol. 2, p. 41.

[47] Coolhaas, "Een bron", p. 506.

15.2 Artist's impression of Raja Bongsu's galley heading to greet Vice-admiral Pietersz van Enkhuisen in the Singapore Straits after his victory over the Portuguese in October 1603. J.T. de Bry, *Icones seu Gennuinae et Expressae Delineationes Omnium Memorabilium* [Images or Authentic and Accurate Description of all Memorable Events], published in Frankfurt am Main, 1607. Leiden, Bibliotheca Thysiana, THYS 874, pl. 7.

whole fleet of Johor, together with King 'Ala'ud-din, his two half-brothers brothers, and many *orang kaya* came toward the Dutch vessels. It was raining heavily that day. The vice-admiral and Buijs boarded the royal galley, where inside they found the king seated on a carpet and Raja Bongsu joined them soon after.

The king expressed his sincere gratitude to Pietersz for keeping good faith and also for lending armed assistance in such a time of need. Since he had little wealth to share, the king wondered aloud how he might be able to repay back his Dutch friends. Some days before—on 9 October to be precise—a man referred to as the "governor" of Kampar (who incidentally spoke Portuguese rather well) was asked to ascertain whether there would be sufficient pepper in stock, and whether this could be brought in from Kampar, Indragiri and other unspecified places, presumably all on Sumatra.[48] After preliminary investigations, King 'Ala'ud-din lamented that there was simply not sufficient pepper available.[49] He sought to console his Dutch friends with assurances that, should they return to Johor's waters in four or five months' time, or better even, if they would just simply stay put around Johor,[50] there would be abundant supplies at hand. Pietersz replied that the ships and crew were at sea for quite some time, and they would need to find cargo soon so that they could embark on their home voyage. The vice-admiral extended an invitation to the king to visit him aboard the *Zierikzee* for a farewell. This was accepted. Raja Bongsu then took his leave, and the Dutch party escorted him back to his galley.

Not long thereafter, the king, Raja Bongsu, the prince of Siak and several *orang kaya* arrived aboard the *Zierikzee* and entered the cabin of the vice-admiral.[51] Dressed in fine silk, the king seated himself with a pillow on a "table-shaped" *singgasana*. Next to him, on a "small bench", the prince of Siak took seat and Raja Bongsu made himself comfortable on a "Spanish chair".[52] The *orang kaya* seated themselves on mats.

King 'Ala'ud-din found many words of praise for his Dutch friends, and thanked Pietersz for delivering Johor from the Portuguese blockade. The vice-admiral presented the monarch with a silver-hilted Japanese sword and his brother, Raja Bongsu, received a musket.[53] The subsequent round of talks touched on various opportunities that had opened up in the aftermath of the Portuguese blockade. Now that the river was free from enemy craft, it was thought, pepper could be brought in from Sumatra and trade could flourish once more.

The Johorean guests bid their European hosts farewell. After bringing on fresh water and waiting for the wind to pick up, Vice-Admiral Pietersz issued orders, on 14 October, to raise anchor and set sail for Patani. He arrived there on 4 November 1603. The yacht *Papagaaiken* was dispatched to the Sundanese port of Bantam

---

[48] *BV*, vol. 2, p. 40.

[49] *IOPO*, p. 88.

[50] Ibid., p. 89; *BV*, vol. 2, p. 42; Tiele, "De Europeërs", part 6, p. 218.

[51] *IOPO*, p. 89. This visit is also mentioned by Grotius. See Grotius, *De Jure Praedae*, p. 331.

[52] Terms based on the Dutch text printed in Commelin. The Latin description reads as follows: *IOPO*, p. 89: "... Rex in mensam panno serico instratam, frater vero eius in scamnum (*bench, stool, footstool*) & Rahu Bongso in sellam ([*portable*] *chair*) iuxta eum consederunt."

[53] *IOPO*, p. 89; *BV*, vol. 2, p. 42; Teixeira, *The Portuguese Missions*, p. 223.

15.3 Portrait etching of the mature Hugo Grotius. Second Latin edition of his *Annales et Historiae de Rebus Belgicis* [Annals and Histories of the Low Countries], printed in Amsterdam in 1658. © Peter Borschberg, private collection.

where its crew delivered news to the Dutch factory of a successful engagement with the Portuguese enemy.[54] The words of the young lawyer and jurisconsult Hugo Grotius, who staunchly defended in writing Dutch aggression in the East Indies, are representative of an over-optimistic and greatly exaggerated view of the VOC's early accomplishments in the region: "… the whole [Portuguese] fleet was vanquished, Johor liberated, and a friendly king delivered from siege."[55]

The Aftermath

Jacob van Heemskerk's seizure of the *Sta. Catarina* off the eastern coast of Singapore and his primordial defence alliance with the king of Johor would herald an escalation of violence in the waters of the Straits of Singapore and the Johor River estuary.

The Portuguese, meanwhile, were seriously alarmed at the inherent vulnerability of their far-flung possessions in Asia. The Portuguese officials were already painfully aware that the Dutch competitors were not only seeking to wrest the spice producing islands of the Moluccas from their control, they were now engaging in acts that seriously disrupted vital trading routes linking Japan and China with the Malay Peninsula and India. The arrival of Vice-Admiral Pietersz surely gave cause for serious concern, as the Portuguese China fleet would now increasingly be exposed to the violent actions by what officials considered "Dutch thieves, liars and pirates". It can therefore hardly be surprising that the Portuguese *squadron*—or whatever parts of it might have remained seaworthy—reappeared just days after the Pietersz departed from Johor waters for Patani. Significantly also, the new Captain of Melaka, André Furtado de Mendoça, an officer seasoned in combat, assumed his office just shortly before hostilities erupted with Pietersz on 1 September, 1603. He used this change of political leadership to weaken the influence of Raja Bongsu (who was a staunch supporter of the Dutch cause at the Johor court) and strengthen the pro-Portuguese faction which was carried by the prince of Siak, as well as the *laksamanna*, *bendahara* and many *orang kaya*.[56] This diplomatic offensive (naturally backed by the force of arms) would yield dividends some years later. In 1610, Johor signed (under duress) a peace treaty with Portugal.[57]

On assuming office, Furtado de Mendoça was willing to hold out the olive branch to the Johor king, providing that he sever his good ties with the Dutch, expel the factors from Batu Sawar, and confiscate their property. On the advice of Raja Bongsu, however, the king replied on 8 February 1604, that he would rather lose

[54] *IOPO*, p. 89; *BV*, vol. 2, p. 42; Terpstra, *De factorij*, p. 18; MacLeod, *De Oost-Indische Compagnie*, vol. 1, p. 14.

[55] Grotius, *De Jure Praedae*, p. 331: "… tota classis victa, Jora liberata, rex amicissimus obsidio exemptus est." No doubt, his claim that the "whole [Portuguese] navy" was vanquished, is an exaggerated claim made in the heat of enthusiasm!

[56] Jonge, *De Opkomst*, vol. 3, p. 234: *Advies* of Admiral Matelieff de Jonge to Admiral Paul van Caerden, dated 4 January 1608; ibid., p. 241: letter of Admiral Matelieff de Jonge at Banten addressed to the first Admiral to arrive from the Netherlands, dated 28 January 1608.

[57] Jonge, *De Opkomst*, vol. 3, p. 305: letter of Jacques Obelaer to the VOC directors, dated 25 November 1610.

his entire kingdom than give in to such preposterous demands.[58] This surely ruffled Furtado's ego. It transpires from a number of studies that the early months of 1604 the Portuguese attacked targets along the Johor River. They failed to capture the capital Batu Sawar, but they did, once more, seize and occupy Johor Lama. It is said that the old capital was held by the Portuguese throughout this economically crippling blockade. Verken reports that in 1604, the old capital was destroyed and burnt to the ground.[59] Judging from what Winstedt and Gibson-Hill contended some decades ago,[60] it appears that the Portuguese did toy with the idea of reconstructing the old fortress to help them protect their shipping from attacks by the Johoreans and Dutch "pirates". The engineer and cartographer Manuel Godinho de Erédia, who also founded the fort at Muar,[61] spent some time examining the site at Johor Lama that very year.[62] But Portuguese influence in the region was always shrouded in uncertainty, and this, combined with the perennial dearth of funds, might very well explain why the plan to reconstruct the fort was never followed up by Furtado or his successors.[63]

Meanwhile co-operation of the Johoreans with the Dutch grew steadily. Admiral Wijbrand van Warwijk himself arrived at the mouth of the Johor River on 3 May 1604, much to the relief of the besieged monarch and Raja Bongsu.[64] On this occasion, Warwijk supplied the Johoreans with gunpowder, weapons, ammunition and armour so that he may better defend himself against the Portuguese enemy.[65]

Backed by their Johorean allies, the Dutch stepped up their attacks on Portuguese targets in the waters around the Peninsula and especially around the Straits of Singapore, the Johor River estuary, and the southeastern shores of the Malay Peninsula. In 1605, a Portuguese trading vessel arriving from Macau, the *Santo António*, was seized by the Dutch while making a distress call at the port of Patani.[66] The captured ship was dispatched by Admiral Warwijk in September 1605 to the Johor River with the aim of finding a cargo of pepper there.

The Portuguese suffered more losses to their merchant fleet. The Dutch soon captured a trading ship near Pedra Branca that was carrying a valuable cargo of

---

[58] Teixeira, *The Portuguese Missions*, pp. 224–5.

[59] Verken, "Molukkenreise 1607–1612", p. 58.

[60] R.O. Winstedt, *A History of Johore, 1365–1895*, MBRAS reprint no. 6 (Kuala Lumpur: MBRAS, 1992); C.A. Gibson-Hill, "Johore Lama and other ancient sites on the Johore River", *JMBRAS* 28, 2 (1955): 126–97.

[61] Boxer and Vasconcelos, *André Furtado de Mendonça*, p. 61.

[62] Rouffaer, "Was Malakka emporium", p. 402; Teixeira, *The Portuguese Missions*, p. 223.

[63] Gibson-Hill (1955), p. 157.

[64] Botelho de Sousa, *Subsídios*, vol. 1, p. 548.

[65] Hervey, "François Valentyn's Account", p. 131; Teixeira, *The Portuguese Missions*, p. 224.

[66] *BV*, vol. 2, pp. 82–3; Jonge, *De Opkomst*, vol. 3, p. 25; Terpstra, *De factorij*, pp. 24, 186, following Valentijn, claims that the *Santo António* was taken by Admiral Sebastiaanse; see also Boxer, *Fidalgos*, p. 51; Teixeira, *The Portuguese Missions*, p. 225. For an account of the Santo Antonio incident, see P. Borschberg, "The Seizure of the Santo Antonio at Patani. VOC Freebooting, the Estado da India and Peninsular Politics, 1602–1609", *JSS* 90, 1–2 (2002): 59–72.

textiles from Cochin-China.[67] They also seized nearby a junk bringing provisions for Melaka and a ship arriving from the island of Solor that was laden with sandalwood and sea turtle shell.[68]

The largest Dutch expedition to visit the region to that date arrived with fifteen ships in April 1606. Admiral Matelieff de Jonge concluded a treaty with the king of Johor.[69] This written agreement formalized the alliance between the Dutch and the Johoreans, ceded several rights and privileges to the VOC and foresaw a joint attack on Portuguese Melaka. In the event of victory, it was further agreed, the city of Melaka and some surrounding territory would be ceded to the Dutch. Despite heavy fighting, Matelieff's naval forces could not defeat the Portuguese. As history teaches, it would be another three and a half decades before the Dutch could wrest, once and for all, the legendary city of spice and trade from Portugal's control.

---

[67] António da Silva Rego, *Documentação Ultramarina Portuguesa*, vol. 1 (Lisbon Centro de Estudos Históricos Ultramarinos, 1962), p. 255; Hervey, "François Valentyn's Account", p. 130.

[68] Silva Rego, *Documentação*, vol. 1, p. 255; Hervey, "François Valentyn's Account", pp. 130–1.

[69] An English text version of this treaty is printed in Hervey, "François Valentyn's Account", pp. 136–7 and Winstedt, *A History of Johore*, pp. 31–3: the Dutch language original is printed as the *Accordt* of 17 May 1606, and its subsequent extension as the *Tweede Accordt* (second agreement), dated 23 September 1606, see Jonge, *De Opkomst*, vol. 3, pp. 214–8.

16

Victor Obdeijn

The Old Naval Trade Route through the Strait of Melaka in Connection with the Geomorphology of the Selat Islands*

Introduction

In my previous essays in this review I have connected the geographical knowledge of the ancients regarding South Sumatra with the geomorphology of the island. I think I have been able to produce some results in the matter.

Below I shall consider the geomorphology of the Selat Islands and try to show that it should be taken into account when studying the ancient history of the southeastern part of Asia and the naval trade route that led through the Strait of Melaka.

By the Selat Islands I mean the islands extending from the southeast point of the Malay Peninsula to the southeastern coast of Sumatra, which in the southeast part of the Strait of Melaka form a barrier, as it were, in which only a few passages give access to the South China Sea.

Those who were able to notice—as I have, frequently negotiating the straits between these islands on small government vessels—the strong tidal current between the islands, and were able to notice how much nautical knowledge and experience the *juragans* need in order not to run aground all the time, will automatically be confronted by the question whether these passages always existed, and whether some 20 centuries ago—around the beginning of the history of our Indian Archipelago—these islands were not connected with each other and with the peninsula, thus forming an extension of Melaka.

---

* First published as "De oude zeehandelsweg door de Straat van Malaka in verband met de geomorfologie der Selat-Eilanden", *TKNAG*, 2nd ser., 59 (1942): 742–70. The text reproduced below is a translation into English of the original Dutch text.

Every day the straits are still widened through scouring and the crumbling of the banks caused by that strong current; the northwest-southeast orientation of the islands is an indication of the scouring effect of the current over the centuries.

In his *Geologische verkenningen in den Riouw-Lingga Archipel* [Geological explorations in the Riau-Lingga Archipelago],[1] Mr Bothé notes that the current in the Strait of Batam, for instance, has a speed of five to six miles an hour. According to him, "*this current and the sea's impact on the coast have given rise to a speedy process of abrasion through which the straits of this archipelago have developed over the centuries*".[2]

Cornelis de Groot (*Herinneringen aan Blitong* [Memories of Belitung]) remarks: "Both chemically and mechanically, erosion restlessly continues through the action of atmospheric substances."[3]

In *De voor-historische verhouding van land en zee in den O.I. Archipel en de invloed daarvan op de verspreiding der diersoorten* [The prehistoric relation between land and sea in the East Indian Archipelago and its influence on the spread of animal species],[4] Mr L.J.C. van Es also considers the genesis of the straits in the Riau-Lingga Archipelago and between Bangka and Billiton [Belitung], judging as follows: "Now it cannot be denied that part of these channels was strongly influenced or *perhaps even produced solely by sea currents*, which are very powerful between the sometimes narrow straits and which have been able to contribute significantly to the deepening of the relief." Van Es specifically mentions the Singapore and Pengelap straits as straits whose great depth was probably caused by later erosion due to sea currents.

This is confirmed by the research of C.E. Jul. Mohr in *De grond van Java en Sumatra* [The soil of Java and Sumatra],[5] which led him to conclude that "at Bangka one finds a drowned or crumbled coast".

The judgement of Professor G.A.F. Molengraaff, is identical. *De zeeën van Nederlandsch Oost-Indië* [The seas of the Dutch East Indies],[6] in the chapter on geology, says: "The entire island world of the Riau Archipelago with its labyrinth of waterways characteristically shows the image of *a submerged land of hills, conquered in part by the sea.*"

The geographers and cartographers of the Middle Ages had already discovered the fact that the islands had once been connected to one another and to the peninsula. The maps from the 16th and 17th centuries show the islands from the Riau-Lingga Archipelago up to Bangka as an island group surrounded by a shallow sea or bank.

---

[1] [E.N.: A.C.D. Bothé, "Geologische verkenningen in den Riouw-Lingga archipel en de eilandengroep der Poelau Toejoeh (Anambas- en Naloena- eilanden)", *Jaarboek van het Mijnwezen in Nederlandsch-Indië* 54, 2 (1925): 101–52.]

[2] A.N.: the italics in this and subsequent quotations are mine.

[3] [E.N.: C. de Groot van Embden, *Herinneringen aan Blitong: historisch, lithologisch, mineralogisch, geologisch en mijnbouwkundig* (The Hague: H.L. Smits, 1887).]

[4] *Jaarboek van het Mijnwezen in Nederlandsch Oost-Indië* 45 (1916): 55–140.

[5] E.C.J. Mohr, *De Grond van Java en Sumatra* (Amsterdam: J.H. de Bussy, 1922).

[6] G.A.F. Molengraaff, "De Geologie der Zeeën van Nederlandsch Oost-Indië", in J.P. van der Stock, *De Zeeën van Nederlandsch Oost-Indië*, published on behalf of the *Koninklijk Aaardrijkskundig Genootschap* (Leiden: E.J. Brill, 1922), pp. 272–357.

We can see this in the maps by Pero Reinel (1517) and à Langren (1595), a map of Portuguese origin in *De eerste schipvaert der Nederlanders onder Cornelis de Houtman* [The first Dutch expedition under Cornelis de Houtman] which was copied from a map in Jan Huygen van Linschoten's *Itinerario* (1596), a map by Levinus Hulsius, Frankfurt (1605), and those by Izaak Tirion, Jodocus Hondius (1628), and Gerard Mercator (1631), among others. It appears from these maps that the Strait of Singapore was known already; the islands therefore were no longer connected to the peninsula.

On one of his maps, *Discripsao chorographico dos Estreitos de Sincapura e Sabam*,[7] in his *Declaraçam* (kept in the Koninklijke Bibliotheek [Royal Library] at Brussels), Manuel Godinho de Erédia (1604) indicates two straits: the Estreito Sabam along the east coast of Sumatra—Sabam is shown as an island off this coast[8]—and the Estreito Sincapura along the island of the same name, making a distinction between an Old (*Estreito Velho*) and a New Strait (*Estreito Novo*).

The Strait of Singapore was not yet easy to navigate then, for Giovanni Botero (*Relatione universale* [1595]) states that the channel was so narrow that the branches of the trees touched the ships' masts when they were passing through. This is recorded by Barros as well. Ferrand ("Malaka, le Malāyu et Malāyur"),[9] citing Barros' *Décadas*, reports "two channels we call straits, formed by the coast of Melaka and the island of Çamatra. One runs along the island called Sabam, the other along the Melakan coast called the coast of Cingapura. *In the middle of this space there are so many islands, shallows and hidden rocks that it is impossible to navigate there*; along the two coasts (that of Sumatra and the peninsula) only two straits remain through which the current flows in abundance".

The very fierce tidal currents are also mentioned by Barreto de Resende (*Livro de Estado do India Oriental* in the great Alfonso d'Albuquerque's *Comentários*),[10] who expressly states: "the currents of ebb and flow are very strong there (namely, in the Strait of Singapore) and extremely powerful", while Botero notes the small width: "so narrow that in certain parts the ships' yards touch the trees on the land".[11]

---

[7] [E.N.: The map in question appears in Eredia's *Declaraçam de Malaca* (Description of Melaka) as fol. 61. See: M. Godinho de Eredia, *Malaca l'Inde Méridionale e le Cathay: Manuscrit original autographe de Godinho de Eredia appartenant à la Bibliothèque Royale de Bruxelles*, trans. M.L. Janssen (Bruxelles: Librairie Européenne C. Muquardt, 1882).]

[8] On the old maps this Sabam, also spelt Saban and Sabi, occurs as a town on the east coast of Sumatra, situated approximately where in the earliest historic times Tebo should have been, taking into account the alluvion at this coast. Estreito Sabam is found as Sabaon on some of these maps, on those by Antonio Pigafetta and Abraham Ortelius. It would appear to be Ptolemy's Sabana Sea at the entrance to the Strait of Bangka, which reached further north because the islands were still connected.

[9] *JA*, 11 sér., vol. 12 (1918). [E.N.: Ferrand's long article was published in two parts, namely in *JA*, sér. 11, vol. 11 (1918): 391–484 and vol. 12 (1918): 51–154. Obdeijn evidently refers here to the second part.]

[10] [E.N.: Pedro Barreto de Resende's *Livro* has been added in Brás d'Albuquerque's *Commentaries of the Great Afonso Dalboquerque, Second Viceroy of India*, ed. and trans. W. de Gray Birch, 4 vols. (London: Hakluyt Society, 1875–84).]

[11] See Ferrand, "Malaka, le Malāyu et Malāyur" (1918).

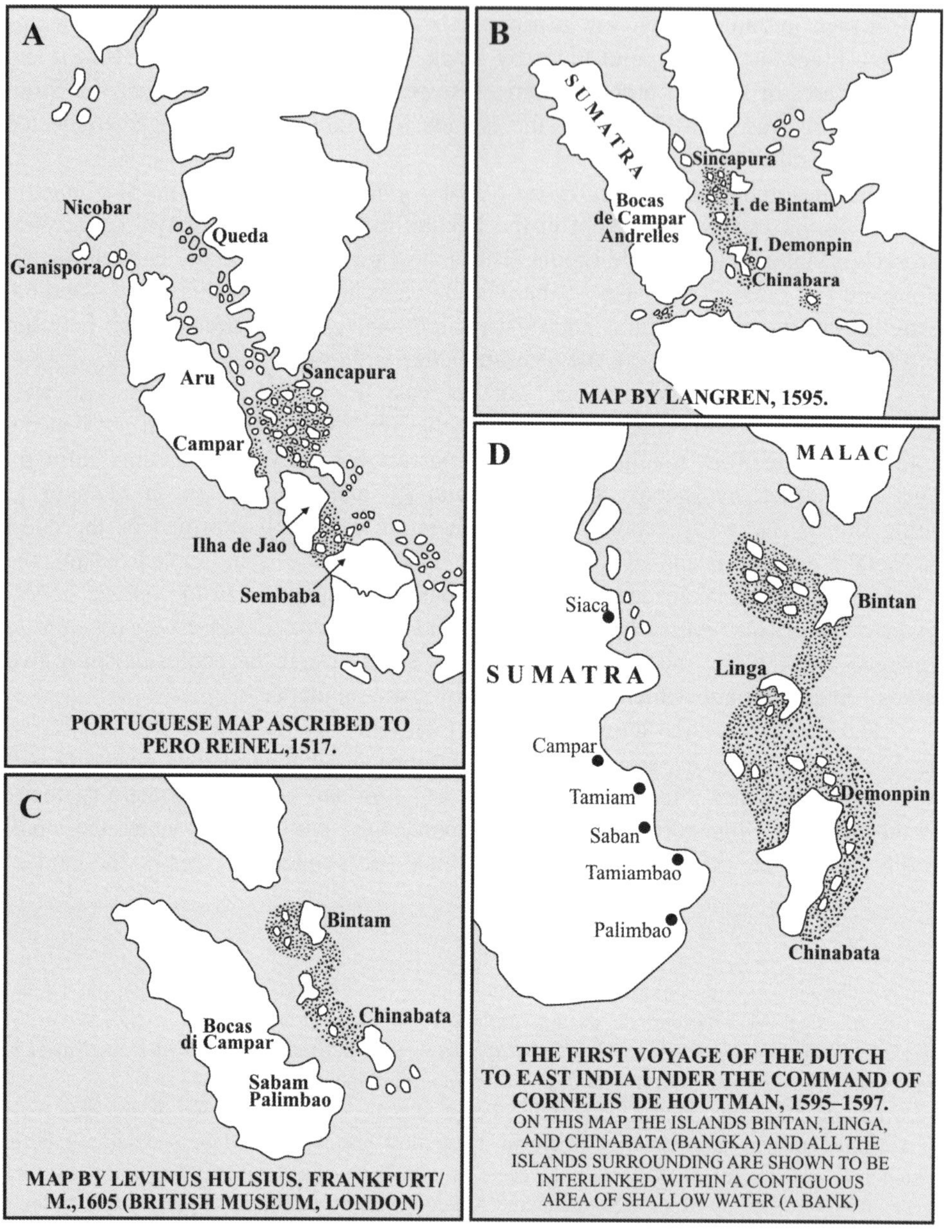

PORTUGUESE MAP ASCRIBED TO PERO REINEL,1517.

MAP BY LANGREN, 1595.

MAP BY LEVINUS HULSIUS. FRANKFURT/M.,1605 (BRITISH MUSEUM, LONDON)

THE FIRST VOYAGE OF THE DUTCH TO EAST INDIA UNDER THE COMMAND OF CORNELIS DE HOUTMAN, 1595–1597.
ON THIS MAP THE ISLANDS BINTAN, LINGA, AND CHINABATA (BANGKA) AND ALL THE ISLANDS SURROUNDING ARE SHOWN TO BE INTERLINKED WITHIN A CONTIGUOUS AREA OF SHALLOW WATER (A BANK)

16.1 A set of redrawn maps depicting (A) Portuguese map attributed to Pero Reinel, 1517. (B) Map by Van Langren, 1595. (C) Map by Levinus Hulsius, Frankfurt am Main, 1605. (D) The first Dutch voyage to the East Indies under the Command of Cornelius de Houtman, 1595–97. On this map are the islands Bintan, Lingga and Chinabata (Bangka) and all the surrounding islands are shown to be interlinked within a contiguous area of shallow water (a bank). All maps redrawn by Mrs Lee Li Kheng.

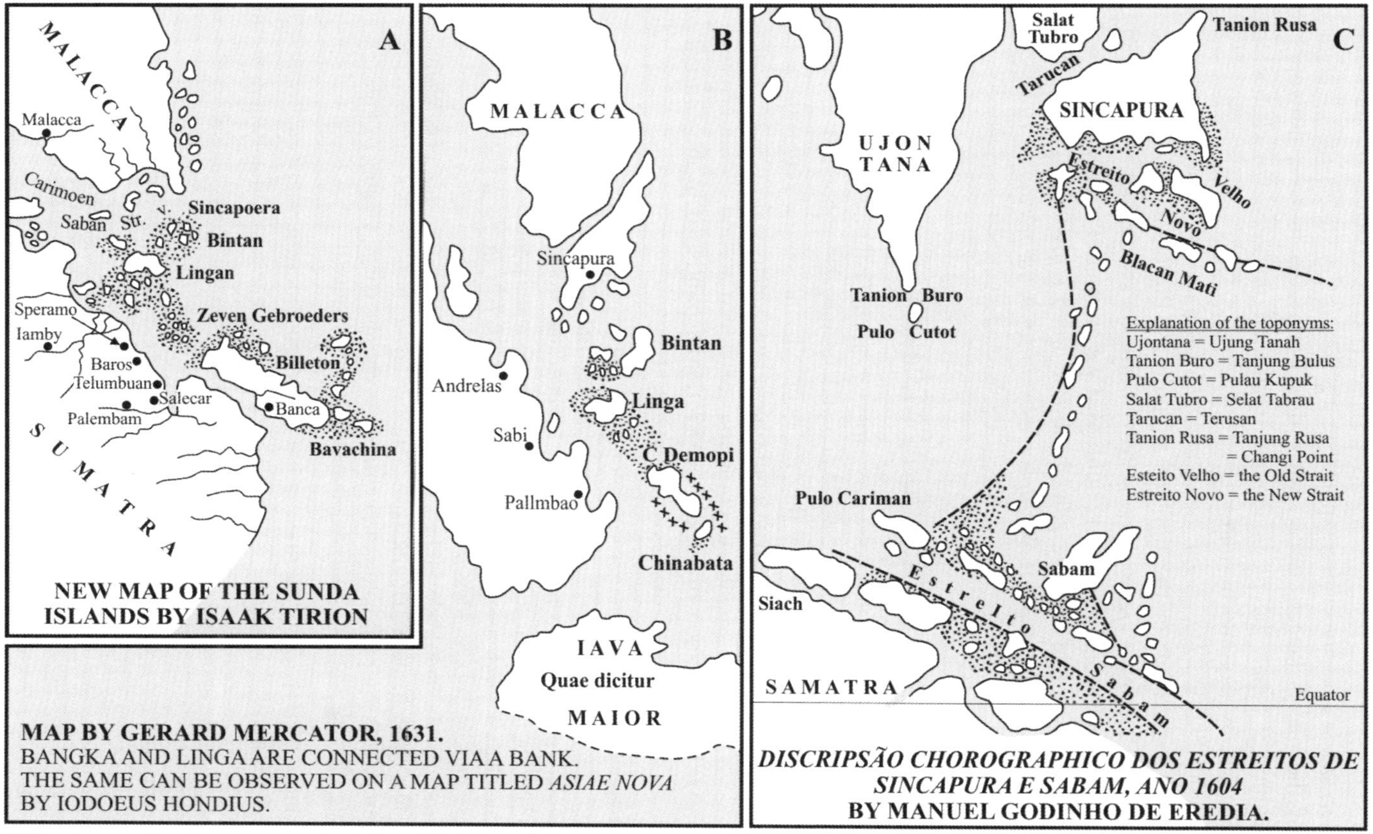

16.2 A set of redrawn maps depicting (A) Map of the Sunda Islands by Isaak Tirion. (B) Map by Gerard Mercator, *Insulae Indiae Orientalis*, 1631. Bangka and Lingga are connected via a bank. The same can be observed on a map titled *Asiae Nova* by Jodocus Hondius. *Discripsao Chorographico dos Estreitos de Sincapura e Sabam* [Chorographic Description of the Straits of Singapura and Sabam (present-day Straits of Kundur)], 1604 by C. Manuel Godinho de Erédia. All maps redrawn by Mrs Lee Li Kheng.

On a map by Antonio Pigafetta there is a note at the Strait of Singapore: "Magna hic pericula illis qui freta inter Malaccam et Singapura [*sic*, transl.] transeunt" [There are great dangers here for those who cross the sea between Melaka and Singapore].

The *Encyclopaedie van Nederlandsch-Indië* [Encyclopaedia of the Dutch Indies] under *Straat Singapore* [Singapore Strait] likewise mentions these dangers: "Because of the many dangers under water this strait used to be a difficult and perilous channel."[12] Since the placement of lights and markers, the channel has become navigable by day and by night.

In the work entitled *Das Land der Seide und Tibet im Lichte der Antike* [The land of the silk and Tibet in the light of antiquity],[13] Professor Albert Hermann, while discussing Ptolemy's *Geography*, states: "Cattigara's expulsion to Singapore, Changchou or Hangchou appears highly dubious if we compare Ptolemy's map to the Chinese tradition of which we have gained more detailed knowledge only recently. *According to it, no predecessor of Singapore existed until the period of Portuguese naval supremacy*".

The Spit of Land Extending from Melaka

Godinho de Eredia has a very noteworthy story about an isthmus which allegedly existed between Tanjung Tuan on the peninsula and Tanjung Balvala on the Sumatran opposite shore; an isthmus so narrow that the people living on the peninsula used it to cross to Sumatra. This isthmus then would have been destroyed by heavy storms, which caused the Strait of Melaka to come into existence around Ptolemy's time.

In J.V. Mills' translation of Eredia's *Declaraçam* published in the *Journal of the Malayan Branch of the Royal Asiatic Society*, it says:

> The present-day chart does not suggest an obvious land passage from Cape Rachado (Tanjong Tuan) to Pulau Rupat (Tanjong Balvala). On the contrary a more probable land connection appears to be indicated from Tanjong Bulus or again from the islands off Port Swettenham to the Sumatra coasts; in fact it has been said that in the Malaca straits *the sea bottom shelves up by Singapore to the south and by Port Swettenham to the north.*[14]
>
> From Cabo Rachado, "cloven headland", a promontory on the coast of Sungei Ujung, the Malay name is Tanjong Tuan. Tanjong Balvala possibly is a corruption of *berhala* (idol). No such name can be traced in the immediate vicinity of Pulau Rupat on the East coast of Sumatra opposite Cape Rachado.[15]

In fact the name of Balvala or Berhala is not found on the Sumatran coast opposite Tanjung Tuan; moreover, a narrow isthmus between this cape and Pulau Rupat would

---

[12] [E.N.: J. Paulus, ed., *Encyclopaedie van Nederlandsch-Indië*, 2nd ed., 8 vols. (The Hague and Leiden: Martinus Nijhoff and E.J. Brill, 1917–39).]

[13] [E.N.: A. Hermann, *Das Land der Seide und Tibet im Lichte der Antike. Quellen und Forschungen zur Geschichte der Geographie und Völkerkunde* (Leipzig: K.F. Köhlers Antiquarium, 1938).]

[14] J.V. Mills, "Eredia's Description of Malaca, Meridional India, and Cathay", *JMBRAS* 8, 1 (1930): 1–288.

[15] Pulau Rupat is an island situated on Sumatra's eastern coast, north of Bengkalis and therefore much farther to the north than the Selat Islands.

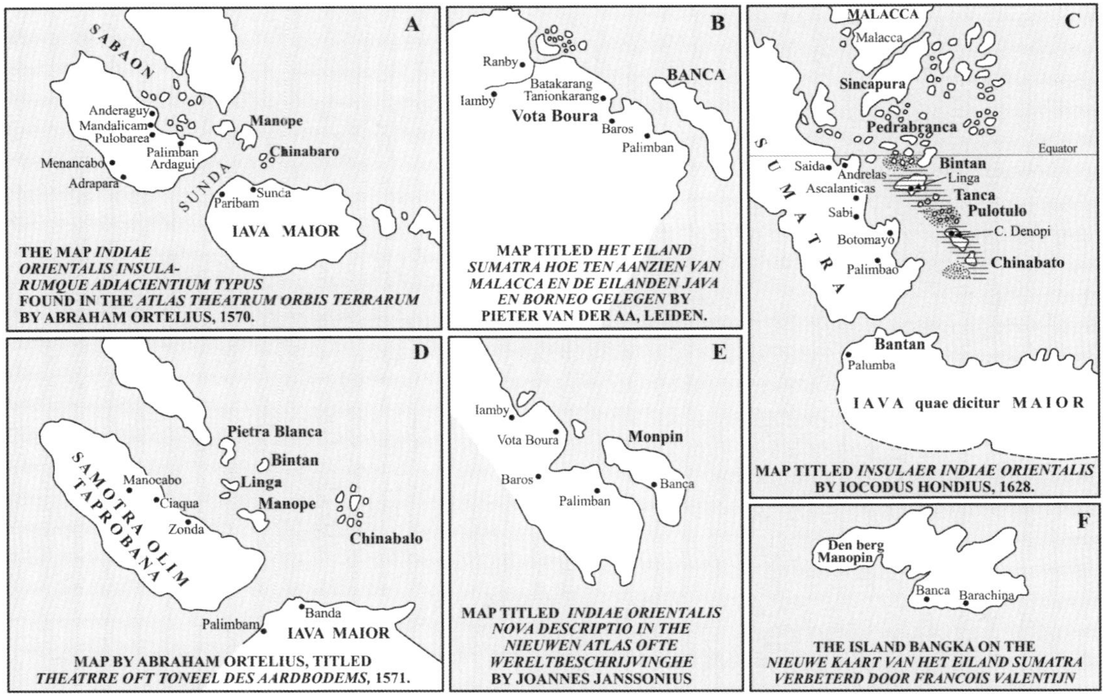

16.3 A set of redrawn maps depicting (A) The map *Indiae Orientalis Insularumque Adiacientium Typus* found in the *Atlas Theatrum Orbius Terrarum* by Abraham van Ortelius, 1570. (B) Map titled *Het Eiland Sumatra hoe ten Aanzien van Malacca en de Eilanden Java en Borneo Gelegen* [the island Sumatra with respect to Melaka and the location of the Java islands and Borneo] by Pieter van der Aa, Leiden. (C) The *Insulae Indiae Orientalis* by J. Hondius, 1628. (D) Map by Abraham Ortelius titled *Theatrre oft Toneel des Aardbodems* [Theatre or Stage of the World], 1571. (E) Map titled *Indiae Orientalis* in the *Nieuwen Atlas ofte Wereltbeschrijvinghe* [New Atlas, or Description of the World] by Joannes Janssonius. (F) The island Bangka on the updated map of the island Sumatra by François Valentijn. All maps redrawn by Mrs Lee Li Kheng.

be contrary to the geomorphological constitution of Sumatra's east coast, where the alluvial plains had not yet been formed in that period and the coastline had far receded, in other words, was much farther away from the peninsula than it is now. But one does encounter the name of Berhala as the name of an island opposite the coast of Jambi, an island already known to the earliest Arabic writers as Berthābīl, Berthāyīl or Brathāyīl,[16] belonging to the kingdom of the Mahārāja of Zābag, to which it was very close. Because of the "terrible noise"[17] on the island, perhaps caused by the collapse of its rocky coast,[18] it was thought to be the abode of the Antichrist.[19]

The existence of an isthmus before Ptolemy's time may well have been a fact, although such an isthmus could not have formed a connection with Sumatra, but from Tanjong Tuan on Melaka's west coast—or better still, Tanjong Bulus—to the Selat Islands, which were connected with each other by ridges as far as present-day Berhala. This Pulau Berhala was the southwest part (Balitung[20] being the southeast point) of a spit of land extending from the peninsula up to where the Strait of Bangka begins, consisting of the Riau-Lingga Archipelago, which had not yet broken up into islands. As the abrasion process continued, it became a group of islands in a shallow sea or surrounded by a bank, as still shown on geographers' maps in the 16th and 17th centuries.

---

[16] Found in Portuguese sources as Ilha Polvoreira = Pulu Varela (which the natives call Barala, Botero says), in Van Linschoten as Pulo Varella. On the *Wu pei pi-shu*, the Chinese map published by G. Phillips in "The Seaports of India and Ceylon, described by Chinese Voyagers of the Fifteenth Century", *JCBRAS* 21 (1886): 30–42, it occurs as *Tan-seu*. On Herman Moll's map (1710) it is seen as an island named Barella, drawn between Linga and Banca; on other old maps, by Janssonius, Ortelius, Van der Aa among others, as Vota Boura or Pulu Barea. They mistakenly locate this name on the east coast of Southern Sumatra, in Janssonius' case opposite an unnamed island; so the name probably belongs to that island. I would also suggest a connection between Pulau Berhala and a kingdom called P'o-huei-kia-lu in the *Hsin T'ang shu*: this could be a corruption of "Pulau Berhala". It is described as lying eight days' sailing east of Chö-p'o (Tebo), a position that would fit. According to the description, this P'o-huei-kia-lu was the royal residence; its remains, then, should now be on the bottom of the sea, something which is very well possible if one takes into account the crumbling of the island Berhala's coast.

[17] See G. Ferrand, *Relations de Voyages et textes géographiques arabes, persans et turcs relatifs à l'Extrême-Orient du VIIIe au XVIIIe siècles*, 2 vols. (Paris: Ernest Leroux, 1914).

[18] As indicated by the underwater ridges of which the surrounding smaller islands are the tops. See J.W.J. Wellan, "Het eiland Berhala bij Djambi" [The island Berhala near Jambi] *TKNAG*, 2nd ser., 42 (1925): 847, and the description there by Dr Aug. Tobler.

[19] As Kern informs us (*Verspreide geschriften*, vol. 9, p. 315), *berhala* in Malay—originating from *prākrit bharāla*—means "false god, idol". [E.N.: Reference to Hendrik Kern is to a collection of his minor works and essays published as: J.H.C. Kern, *Verspreide geschriften, onder zijn toezicht verzameld*, 17 vols. (The Hague: Martinus Nijhoff, 1913–28, 1936). Vol. 9 is entitled "Spraakkunst van het Oudjavaansch (slot) en diversen Oudjavaansch (eerste deel) (Linguistics of ancient Javanese, final part, and diverse papers on ancient Javanese, first part). The volume was published by Martinus Nijhoff in The Hague in 1920.]

[20] I use this spelling instead of "Billiton" [the common version in Dutch] on etymological grounds, I shall argue below.

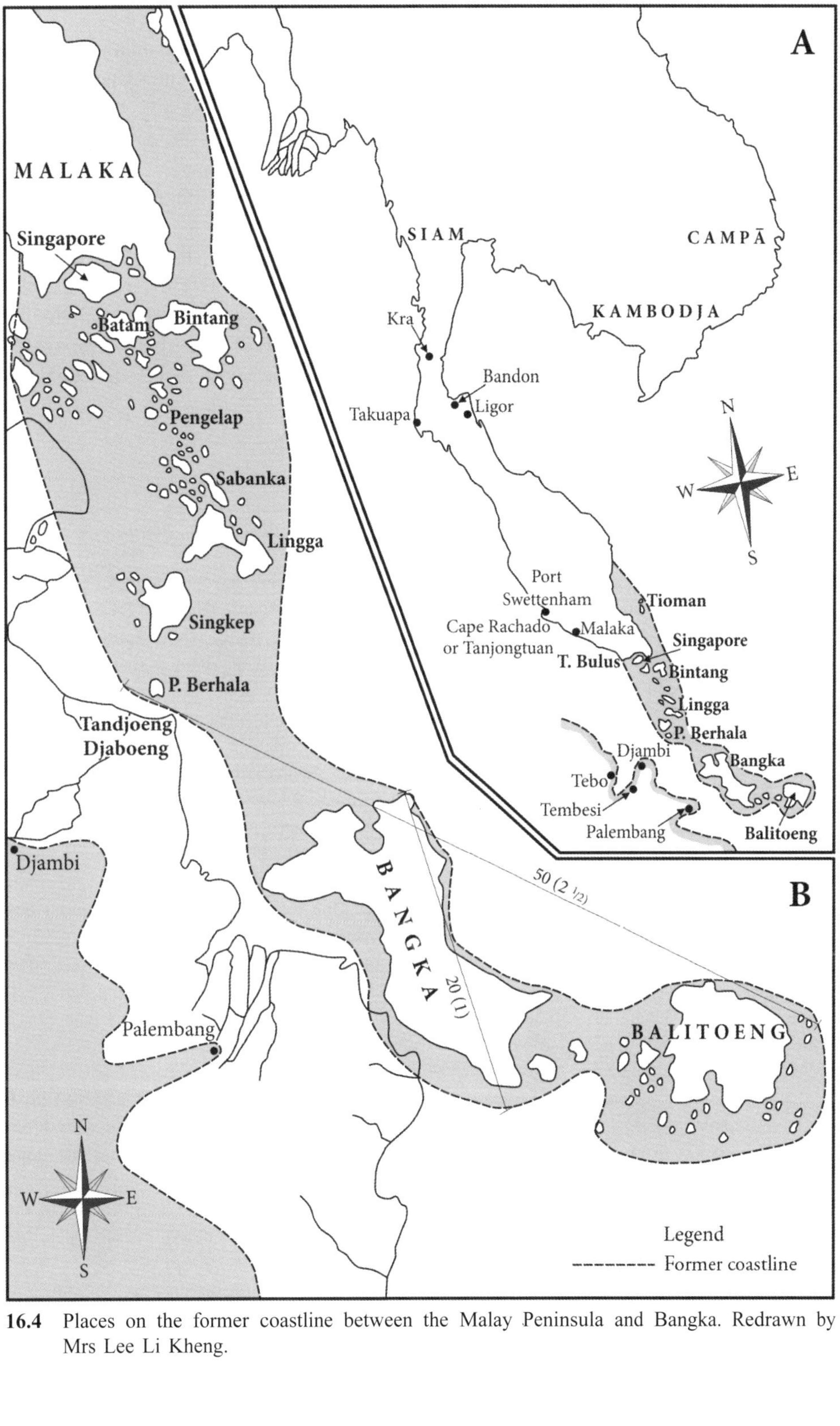

16.4 Places on the former coastline between the Malay Peninsula and Bangka. Redrawn by Mrs Lee Li Kheng.

This confirms "the shoal shelves up by Singapore to the south", which Mills notes and to which Frank Swettenham, in his *British Malaya*, likewise draws attention: "In the Harleian Mappemonde of 1536 a very distinct shoal or bank is marked exactly at the spot where Eredia places the narrow isthmus of sand between Cape Rachado and Sumatra. Pierre Descellier's Mappemonde of 1546 and 1550 give Sumatra and also indicate the shoal", that is, the bank or ridge representing the connection with the Selat Islands (p. 21).[21]

In the earliest historical times it was not the peninsula's southern point at Johor that was the Ujung Tanah as shown on Eredia's map and as Rouffaer also states in his "Was Malaka emporium vóór 1400 A.D.?" [Was Melaka an emporium before 1400 CE?];[22] it was situated at Pulau Berhala and at Balitung. This was the point where the mainland began, the *permulaän tanah* in Malay: it would seem to me that Ptolemy's "Perimula" and "Sinus Perimulicus" derive from this *permulaän*.[23] As they rounded Bangka and Balitung, seafarers saw the coast recede to the west,

---

[21] [E.N.: F. Swettenham, *British Malaya, an account of the origin and progress of British influence in Malaya* (London and New York: J. Lane, 1907).]

[22] *BKI* 77 (1921): 86ff. [E.N.: Portions of Rouffaer's long article have been included in this collection. It was published in two parts in 1921: *BKI* 77, 1 (1921): 1–171, and 77, 3–4 (1921): 359–604.] Rouffaer places ancient Langga or Lang-ga-su(-ka)—a polity which according to the Chinese chronicles existed as early as 500 CE, and which was then claimed to be 400 years old—later also called U-tang-ta-lim or Jiu-hut. This Ujung Tanah or Johor however was described by Minangkabau-Malay traditions as an island called Langkapura, situated between Palembang and Jambi; see W. Marsden, *History of Sumatra* (London: Longman, Hurst, Rees, Orme, and Brown, 1811). Rouffaer's conclusion goes: "I myself can say it without a shadow of a doubt: c. 100 CE Lanka was not Ceylon, but in fact Ujung Tanah, where one rounded the corner, so to speak, to the mysterious empire of China". If we assume with Rouffaer that Lanka is Ujung Tanah (Ferrand, Coedès and Huber are looking for it in Kedah, Groeneveldt in Western Java), the position of this Ujung Tanah corresponds even better with Pulau Berhala, the point of the extended chersonese, than with Johor. Around Bangka (the classical route between India and China) one "rounded the corner" to China. This Pulau Berhala lay between Palembang and Jambi as a protruding spit of land. For according to Van Linschoten, "the island of Pulo Varella [lies] straight opposite a hook on Sumatra called Tanjonbon" (that is, present-day Tanjung Jabung at the mouth of the Batanghari (Kuala Berhak). According to the Jambi tradition Berhala is the cradle of Jambi's royal line, and it was also at Tanjung Jabung that the Datuk of Berhala settled and built a city after marrying the daughter of Demang Lebar Daun from Palembang (Wellan, "Het eiland Berhala"). This does indicate that one should look for Lanka/Langga/Lang-ga-su (-ka) on Berhala, which was Ujung Tanah then. It is quite possible, even probable, that Johor became Ujung Tanah after the spit's disintegration into islands, because then it was the point behind which the mainland of Further India began. The Portuguese sources in any case locate their Ungentana here, while Eredia calls the coast of Melaka Vjontana as Ujung Tanah. In the Koṭ Monthīerabān from Siam, Ujung Tanah in 1360 was one of the southern vassal states, but its position is not indicated precisely.

[23] The hypothesis has often been brought forward that many names that the ancient historiographers use for places in the Far East had come to them through the Malays (who traded along the coasts of the archipelago, the peninsula and as far Siam and Cambodia). Consequently, Ptolemy's "Perimula" may have Malay origins as well.

forming a kind of bay; here was the Perimulicus Gulf, south of the Magnus Sinus, as the maps by Marinus of Tyre and Ptolemy indicate.

The Later Passages between the Selat Islands, Singapore and Melaka

The development of passages between the Selat Islands and the Strait of Singapore in particular (this probably was the first rupture) is connected with the rise of Singapore and Melaka—the former not before the mid-14th century, the latter around 1400.

"Tumasik" is the old name for Singapore in the *Sejarah Melayu*, an identification that is supported by Kern and Rouffaer. On the Chinese map *Wu-pei pi-shu*, probably deriving from that of Fei Hsin (1430), published by Philips, this Singapore/Tumasik is named Tan-ma-seih (Tan-ma-hsi).

The realm of Melaka was unknown before ca. 1400, unless one wishes to identify it with Malak by Yāḳūt (1179–1239) and Melk or Melke (Mellec) in John Mandeville (d. 1372).

In Ma Huan's *Ying-yai sheng-lan* (1432), the old name for Man-la-kia (Melaka) is given as Wu-hsü (the five small islands before the Melakan coast); on one of these islands, Pulau Besar, the market town Yiu-mên was known. The land was under the rule of Hsien-lo (Siam) and governed by a chief. In 1409 Cheng Ho delivered an imperial order from China that elevated the town from a city and the country to a kingdom; with that, it gained independence from Siam.[24]

"The probability that the foundation of Melaka which is usually laid in the middle of the 13th century must be put a century and a half later is supported by a certain amount of negative evidence", says C.O. Blagden.[25] In his "General Conclusion", this expert on the Malay Peninsula judges as follows:

(1) that the Malay colonisation of the peninsula was already in progress in the 13th century;
(2) that Singapore as a Malay settlement was founded in that century or possibly even earlier;
(3) that Singapore was still in existence throughout the first sixty or seventy years of the 14th century and must have been conquered and destroyed by the Javanese of Majapahit shortly after 1377; [and]
(4) that Melaka was not founded till some short time after 1377.[26]

Ferrand's judgement is the same. He states:

> The itineraries in the earliest Arabic geographical texts do not mention Melaka. Kilah or Kalah was an important stop, from which one proceeded either to Bālūs or to the island of Tiyūma [Tioman, the island before the peninsula's east coast, opposite Tanjung Penyabung]. *Nāgarakṛtāgama* does not mention Melaka.[27]

---

[24] See W.W. Rockhill, "Notes on the Relations and Trade of China with the Eastern Archipelago during the Fourteenth Century", *T'oung Pao* 15, 3 (1914): 419–47.

[25] Charles Otto Blagden, "Notes on Malay History", *JSBRAS* 53 (1909): 139–62.

[26] Ibid., p. 162.

[27] "Malakka, le Malāyu et Malāyur", *JA*, sér. 11, vol. 12 (1918): 51–154.

In his study in *BKI*, vol. 77, mentioned above, Rouffaer extensively argues that before 1400 Melaka was not known as a port of the great importance it was to acquire only later. The towns on the peninsula's south and southeast coasts, situated in a far corner of the Strait of Melaka and outside the great naval trade route, flourished and became trade centres, acquiring renown when the Strait of Singapore became easy to navigate and offered a shortcut on the long sea route between India and China.[28]

This circumstance, combined with the silting up of the South Sumatra Bay meant the downfall of the South-Sumatran Empire on the opposite side of the Strait of Melaka.

Their booming business fell and their position of power in the Strait declined, finally to be eclipsed completely by Melaka and Singapore, which gained a more favourable position when the Strait of Singapore became accessible to big ships.

Barros confirms this when he states that through this strait, goods were transported from the east (the countries on the China Sea) and from the west (those on the Indian Ocean); through the Strait of Sabam came the traffic to and from Java, Banda, the Moluccas and other islands south of the Equator.

For the other shifts in power and trade in the Indian Archipelago we may refer to B. Schrieke's *Prolegomena tot een sociologische studie over de volken van Sumatra* [Prolegomena to a sociological study of the peoples of Sumatra], from which we quote a passage to illustrate the rise of Melaka as a consequence of the changing world route:

> In the meantime Melaka had become the meeting point of the trade between East and West, as Palembang had been earlier, but because of the increased traffic along the new world route its importance was even greater. The Portuguese authors (Barros, Barbosa) never tire of painting this trade activity in glowing colours nor of sketching Melaka's favourable position as junction of the monsoon-determined trade routes.[29]

Melaka, formerly an insignificant fishing village, unknown to earlier writers, had now become a junction of trade routes at which all trade from East and West was aimed.

There must have been a very special factor at work to achieve this. That factor was the Strait of Singapore becoming navigable, so that Melaka gained a position on the world trade route. The second important factor was the fact that the two Malay kingdoms which had played such a prominent part in history had lost their political and commercial significance because of the progressing alluvion on the South Sumatran coast. Their position of power had been such that, according to the

[28] As a consequence Marco Polo, who mentions neither Singapore nor Tumasik, could not have sailed through the Strait of Singapore, but must have taken the classic route around Balitung; otherwise he would also have mentioned Singapore or Tumasik in his travelogue. If the Strait of Singapore already existed then, he certainly would have preferred this shortcut to the Strait of Melaka. The channel so shallow that ships had to take up their rudders consequently was not the Strait of Singapore, and Pentam was not Bintang. See the essay by V. Obdeijn, "De geografische kennis van Sumatra in de Middeleeuwen" [The geographical knowledge of Sumatra in the Middle Ages], *TKNAG* 59 (1942): 46–86.

[29] [E.N.: B.J.O. Schrieke, "Prolegomena tot eene sociologische studie over de volken van Sumatra. I. (A. Historische gedeelte)", *TBG* 15 (1925): 90–207.]

testimony of Chiu K'iu Fei and Chau Ju-kua, they dared use the most outrageous means to force ships to call in at their port: "If some foreign ship passing this place (San-fo-ts'i) should not enter here, an armed party would certainly come out and kill them to the last".[30] This San-fo-ts'i (Jambi) then was "the most important port-of-call on the sea-routes of the foreigners", "lying in the ocean and controlling the strait" (the Strait of Bangka, that is). That control often crossed the line, to such annoying obstructions that "vessels found it to their advantage to put into Ling-ya-mön (Lung-ya-men) and pay a toll to escape worse".[31]

Yet the route went past this vexing and trade-obstructing kingdom for another two centuries before a different route was chosen. The only probable reason for this is that the alternative route did not exist before then. But the Strait of Singapore was eagerly used as soon as it had become accessible to heavy vessels, which went hand in hand with Melaka's rise as a trade centre.

The other channel, the route around Pulau Berhala and Bangka that had been in use since ancient times, still existed as the Strait of Sabam. It lost its importance because the Strait of Singapore offered a shorter connection between East and West, and because the Malay South Sumatran kingdoms had lost much of their commercial significance as a consequence of the alluvion process at their coast.

The Kingdoms and Ports along the Strait of Sabam (the Strait of Bangka)

If in our study of the ancient history of the archipelago we take into account the geomorphological constitution of the Selat Islands, which were not separate islands at the time but a spit extending from the peninsula without passages from the Strait of Melaka to the China Sea and with the Strait of Sabam as the only classic naval route between India and China, then the regions, kingdoms and ports along this strait must be the places which were known to the early seafarers.

As Professor R.C. Majumdar remarks in his *Suvarṇadvīpa*: "The geographical position of Sumatra marks it out as pre-eminently the site of the earliest Hindu settlement in Indonesia. Being situated midway on the route between India and China important harbours and trading stations must have developed on its eastern coast

[30] See F. Hirth and W.W. Rockhill, trans. and annot., *Chau Ju-Kua: His Work on the Chinese and Arab Trade in the Twelfth and Thirteenth Centuries, Entitled* Chu-fan-chï (St Petersburg: Imperial Academy of Sciences, 1911).

[31] According to Hirth and Rockhill this was the Strait of Singapore, since it is said, "it was inhabited on both sides by a people called Tan-ma-shi" (Tumasik or Singapore). These people were also said to be active as pirates. Rouffaer in the *Encyclopaedie van Nederlandsch Indië* [Encyclopaedia of Netherlands India] under "Oudste ontdekkingstochten" [Earliest voyages of discovery], wants to identify Fei Hsin's Ling-ge-bun with the Strait of Lingga, known as the Strait of Durian during the Portuguese period and later, and dangerous because of the Celates or Selat pirates.

from an early period. The beginning of Hindu colonisation can be placed here two or three centuries before the Christian era".[32]

On the coast of Sumatra the most renowned and important kingdoms were those of Zaba, Thu-po, Tchu-po, Chö-p'o, Jāva, Zābag,[33] Tchan-pei, Che-li-fo-che (San-fo-ts'i), Srīvijaya, Sarboza and Ho-ling (Po-ling), Po-lin-pang, which I have already identified with Tebo, Jambi and Palembang in my articles of March, May and July 1941 in *Tijdschrift van het Koninklijk Nederlandsch Aardrijkskundig Genootschap* [Journal of the Royal Netherlands Geographical Society].[34] Farther south, the important kingdoms (although not situated directly at the sea route and perhaps visited by seafarers no more than incidentally as a consequence) at the mouths of the South Sumatran rivers discharging into the Java Sea—which also took care of the export of sought-after products like gold, pepper, sandalwood, ivory, and rhinoceros horn—were the Malay kingdoms of Tatang, Lematang,[35] Tulangbawang and Seputih. These are mentioned, albeit later than the aforementioned, as Ta-ta in I-tsing, Tan-tan in the *T'ai-p'ing huan-yu chi* and the *T'ang hui-yao*, To-mo-ch'ang in the *Old and New T'ang Annals*,[36] To-lang-p'o-huang (sometimes written as two separate words, embassies in 449–63 CE) in the *T'ai-p'ing huan-yu chi*, and Ch'ien or Ts'ien-chih-fu (which, taking into account the transposition of syllables or sounds

[32] [E.N.: Ramesh Chandra Majumdar, *Suvarṇadvīpa: Ancient Indian Colonies in the Far East*, 2 vols. (New Delhi: Cosmo Publications 1927).]

[33] Ptolemy's Sabana Sea on the east coast of Sumatra, found in Godinho de Erédia as the Estreito Sabam, is named after this Zaba. This also corresponds with Professor Hermann's argument in *Das Land der Seide*, p. 72, where on the basis of his research of Greek and Indian sources he concludes that Rabana or Sabana must be the same as Zabai in Ptolemy. This is likewise confirmed by G.E. Gerini (*Researches on Ptolemy's geography of Eastern Asia, Further India and Indo-Malay Archipelago* [London: Royal Geographical Society, 1909], p. 549), who identifies She-p'o with Ptolemy's Sabana, but places it on the western coast of the Malay Peninsula, where the small town of Sabah lies at the Berman River in Selangor. Ptolemy's Sabana is also thought to hide behind Yen-mo-na (Yavana or Yavanadvīpa), mentioned by the Chinese pilgrim Huen Thsang (Hsüen-tsang, 629–45 CE; see also Thomas Watters, *On Yuan Chwang's Travels in India, 629–645 A.D.*, 2 vols. [London: Royal Asiatic Society, 1904–05]); as a reminiscence of the famous Zaba in the old maps the names Sabi, Saban, Sabam, Sabaon and a Strait of Sabaon are found at the eastern coast of Sumatra.

[34] [E.N.: V. Obdeijn, "Zuid-Sumatra volgens de oudste berichten", parts 1–3, *TKNAG* 58 (1941): 190–216, 322–42, 476–503.]

[35] In the *Sejarah Melayu* the Muara Tatang is mentioned as the river of Palembang; according to L.C. Westenenk ("De Boekit Segoentang en de Goenoeng Mahameroe uit de Sedjarah Melajoe", *TBG* 63 [1924]: 212–26), it was called Sungei Melayu earlier. In his "Het land van Bittertong (Zuid-Sumatra)" (*Djawa* 1, 1 [1921]: 5–11), he furthermore says about the Upper Lematang: "The race of men that hewed these sculptures in a distant past had its main dwellings in the region of the Upper Lematang". As a consequence of the alluvion process on Sumatra's east coast, this river had its own discharge into the sea while its upper course lay closer to the sea.

[36] According to Pelliot the Chinese transliteration of K'ouen-louen or Kiun-t'oun (in Wang Ta-yüan) for Malay Kundur (Pulo Condor) shows that the Malay letter *l* in Chinese can be replaced by *t*. However, Ferrand disagrees with him in this matter.

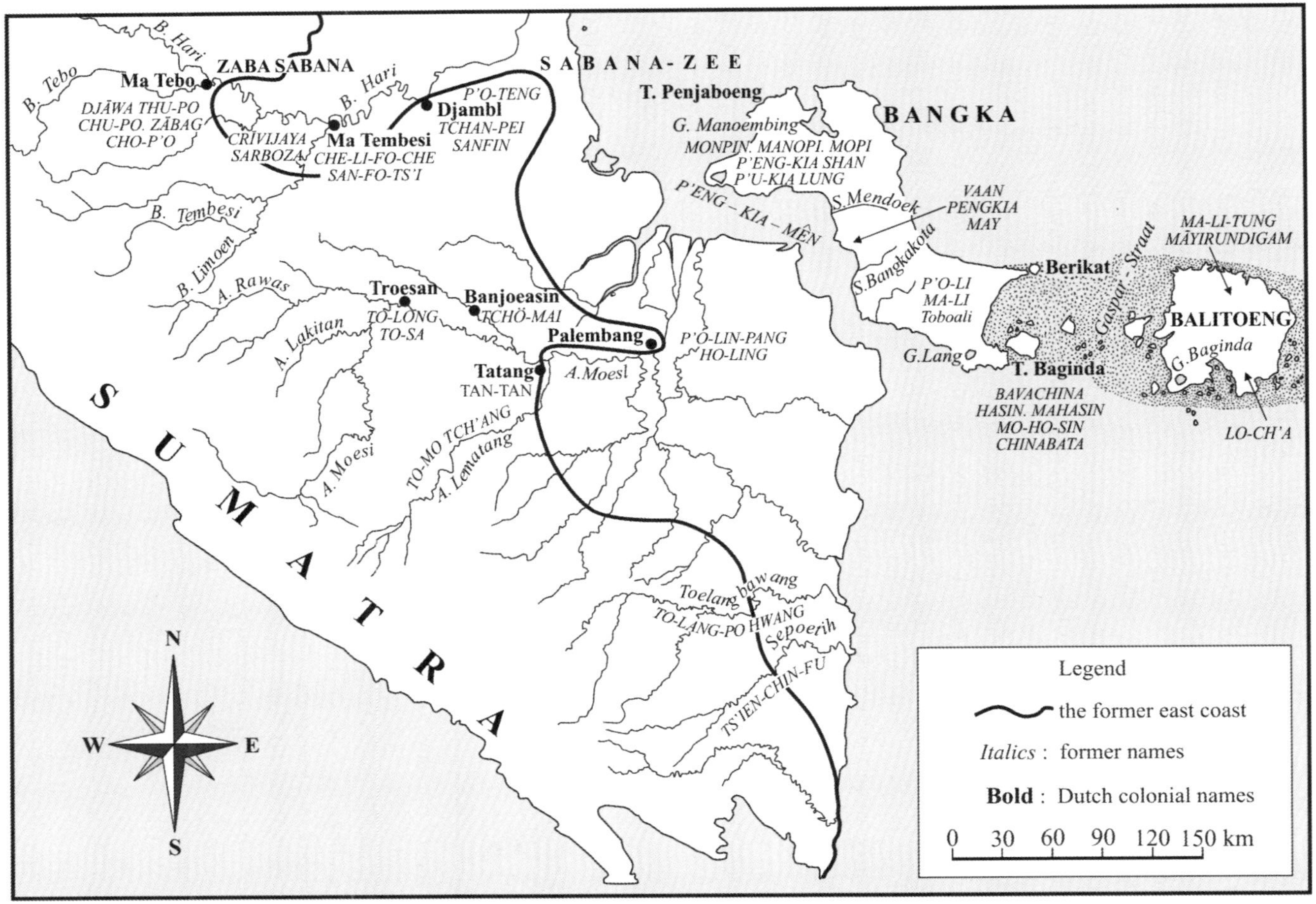

16.5 Map of places in Sumatra, Billiton and Bangka. Redrawn by Mrs Lee Li Kheng.

which sometimes occurs in Chinese transliteration of Indian and Indonesian words, could be Ts'ien-fu-chih)[37] in the Ts'e-fu yüan-kuei.[38]

Looking at the map of South Sumatra one notices that the geographical position of these places in relation to one another well matches this identification. After all, the *Old and New T'ang Annals* state that the position of Ho-ling (compare Gerini's *Researches* and Pelliot's *Deux itinéraires*) is east of P'o-teng or To-p'o-teng, west of P'o-li or Ma-li, south of Chen-la (Cambodia) and north of the sea and an island kingdom named To-mo-ch'ang (the Musi and Lematang delta islands). This To-mo-ch'ang again has To-long to the west, P'o-fong to the east and Ts'ien-chih-fu to the south. P'o-teng corresponds to the Malay *batang*, which means "stream, great river" and by which on South Sumatra specifically the Batanghari is meant.[39] That is why Marco Polo, Friar Odoric and Mandeville mention Pentan, Paten, Panthem [Batang(hari)], and why Ma Huan, Wang Ta-yüan and Fei Hsin call this river Tan-chiang (Tan River), Tan being short for Batang.[40]

Regarding the other names mentioned in the *T'ai-p'ing huan-yu chi* and the *T'ang hui-yao*, namely *To-long*, *Chö-mai* and *Po-leou*, Ferrand notes that these places must lie between Ho-ling and Sumatra, that is, the region on Sumatra's east coast currently taken up by Palembang and Jambi and surroundings.[41] To-long is placed at the western border of To-mo-ch'ang in the *Hsin T'ang shu* and according to Pelliot, it is transliterated as To-sa in the *T'ang hui-yao*. If we hold on to this transliteration, we can recognise Trusan on the Musi in it, where it is joined on the left side by its tributary the Rawas, and which indeed lies west (at the western border) of the Upper Lematang region (see the map of South Sumatra). This is precisely the place where the Musi meets the range of hills extending eastward up to Palembang and is thus forced to change its course in an eastern direction.[42] Another reason why it was an important place at the time is that the Rawas is the discharge from the Rawas and Limun region, rich in gold, toward Palembang. Trusan probably was a market place where the gold diggers came to sell the gold ore from upstream.[43]

---

[37] Compare Ferrand's identification of Ko-lo-fou-cha-lo = Ko-lo-cha-fou-lo (transposition of the third and fourth syllables) in the *Hsin T'ang shu* with Kalaçapura from the Kathāsaritsāgara ("Le K'ouen-Louen", *JA*, sér. 11, 14 [1919]).

[38] Regarding this Ts'ien-chih-fu, Pelliot says: "In the *New History of the T'ang*, halfway through the chapter on the countries of the southern seas, one finds the following passage: 'In the Hien-k'ing period (656–60), with the four kingdoms of P'o-ngan, Ts'ien-che-fu, Shö-pa-jo and Mo-la, he (the Chan-po) sent ambassadors to the court. Ts'ien-che-fu lies in the southwestern sea" (P. Pelliot "Deux itinéraires de Chine en Inde à la fin du VIIIe siècle", *BEFEO* 4 [1904]: 183–92).

[39] Compare with Rouffaer, "Was Malaka emporium vóór 1400 A.D.?", *BKI* 77 (1921): 12–3, 18.

[40] See V. Obdeijn, "De geografische kennis", *TKNAG* 59 (1942): 46–86.

[41] *JA*, sér. 11, vol. 14 (1919). [E.N.: This is a reference to Gabriel Ferrand's study "Le K'ouen-louen, et les anciennes navigations inter-oceaniques dans les mers du Sud", published in the *Journal Asiatique* (1919) in four parts and also as a separate book (Paris: Imprimerie Nationale, 1919).]

[42] See Obdeijn, "De geomorfologische gesteldheid van Zuid-Sumatra etc." [The geomorphological constitution of South Sumatra etc."], *TKNAG* 58 (1941): 190–216.

[43] R.D.M. Verbeek, in his "Topografische en geologische beschrijving van Zuid-Sumatra" [Topographical and geological description of South Sumatra], *Jaarboek van het Mijnwezen in Nederlandsch-Indië* 10, 1 (1881): 3–215, already notes that the gold from the Limun and Asai region was traded as "Korinchi" gold in Palembang, via the Rawas.

Chö-mai, according to Ferrand, is a toponym of Iliran and Bañuasin at Palemban, and thus likewise situated on the east coast of South Sumatra and the Strait of Bangka.

Po-leou has not been identified so far.

The Former Names of Bangka and Balitung

In the earliest historical times and long after, until ca. 1400, the naval trade route between India and China passed through the Strait of Bangka; at Bangka and Balitung the ships turned north to head for China. This means that the two islands, still connected with each other at that time,[44] and the Sumatran opposite shore were known to early seafarers already.

As a consequence Mr Takakusu (*A Record of the Buddhist Religion as Practised in India and the Malay Archipelago*)[45] must be wrong when on his map he notes in red at the location of Bangka: "This isle is never mentioned by special name in Chinese history".

In P'eng-kia shan ("Bangka mountain land") on the map *Wu-pei-pi-shu* (1430), P'eng-ka bun ("Bangka Strait") in Ma Huan's *Ying-yai sheng-lan* (1416), P'eng-kia men ("Bangka Strait" as well) in the *Tao-i chih-lüeh* by Wang Ta-yüan (1349), and P'u-kia lung ("Bangka Mountain") in Chau Ju-kua's *Chu fan chi* (1225)[46] it is obvious that P'eng-ka, P'eng-kia and the corrupted form P'u-kia are identical with Bangka.

---

[44] Regarding this connection, it is worthwhile to point out that the northwest and east extremities or points of Bangka, that is, those closest to Pulau Berhala and Balitung, are called Tanjung Penja(m)bung ("connected [to Berhala]") and Ujung Berikat ("tied [to Balitung]"). Bangka's southernmost point is Tanjung Baginda, opposite Gunung Baginda on Balitung. One of the Selat Islands (near Lingga) is called Sabangka, namely, "one with Bangka". These names point to a physical connection between the islands in a past not so distant that the tradition was lost.

[45] [E.N.: I-tsing, *A Record of the Buddhist Religion as Practiced in India and the Malay Archipelago*, trans. J. Takakusu (Oxford: Clarendon Press, 1896).]

[46] Chiu K'iu-fei and Chau Ju-kua (Hirth and Rockhill, *Chau Ju-kua*) say: "The kingdom of Chö-p'o which is also called P'u-kia lung", a name that was copied in the *Ming Annals*. Because this Chö-p'o was always assumed to be Java, P'u-kia lung is identified with Pekalongan on Java, which was completely unknown at that time. But Chö-p'o (Chau Ju-kua's "Great Chö-p'o"; he distinguishes between "Great Chö-p'o" and the "branches" or dependencies also called Chö-p'o) in fact was what the Chinese used to call Thu-po or Chu-po, Jāva of the Indies, the Arabs' Zābag. It was ruled by one of the richest and most powerful princes of the Far East (Ibn Rosteh), the Mahārāja, feared as far as Cambodia and Champā; he had the prince of Khmer beheaded for offending him and forced his successor to perform a shameful daily prostration to Zābag as *kibla* as a "token of respect" (Abū Zayd). According to Ferrand (*Le K'ouen-louen et les anciennes navigations*) *lung*, whose old pronunciation is **lun* = *non*, derives from Malay **gun-nun*, "mountain". So *P'u-kia lung*, like P'eng-kia shan, means Bangka Mountain. In fact the Gunung Manumbing on Bangka (455 metres high and north of Muntok, so on the part of the island facing the Strait of Melaka and well visible from it) is indicated on all the old maps of the archipelago as Manopin, Monpin, Mopi, Nopi, and even Popin. Valentijn names "Manopin Mountain" on his map of Bangka. To sailors coming from the Strait of Melaka the Manumbing was a beacon used for orientation when entering the Strait of Bangka.

Bangka was already known for its main product, tin (*vanga* or *vankam*) since antiquity. In the *Niddesa* the island of Vanga occurs among the first 14 islands (of the 34 mentioned there) which, lying outside the Indian subcontinent, were reached by merchants via the sea route (Professor Majumdar, *Suvarṇadvīpa*); Sylvain Lévi identifies Vankam as Bangka.[47] So this is not, as Rouffaer in *Oudheidkundige opmerkingen* [Archeological remarks] thinks, "Ship Island"—derived from *wangka* or *bangka*, as the old Indonesian sea ships used to be called that are better known nowadays under the nasal form *wangkang*—but "Tin Island".[48]

Another name for Bangka, one not recognised as such until now, is P'o-li, which was also called Ma-li according to the *New T'ang Annals* (618–906) and is identified with Bali on this ground and because it was said to be situated east of Ho-ling, which was always identified with Java.[49]

Although Kern does not identify P'o-li with exactitude, he is certain that it could not have been Bali.[50] Professor Majumdar also has reservations against the identification with Bali: "P'o-li etymologically corresponds to Bali but some

The identification of P'u-kia lung with Chö-p'o points to one of the phases of the battle for supremacy fought between Chö-p'o and Che-li-fo-che (San-fo-ts'i), the two mighty Malay kingdoms on the Strait of Melaka; they were mentioned in 992 by the embassy sent by the Mahārāja of Chö-p'o, according to the *Sung Chu*, and in 988 by the envoy of San-fo-ts'i. Both declared that their countries were engaged in continuous war with one another. To control the Strait of Bangka, Chö-p'o had to conquer Bangka's coast. In Chiu K'iu Fei's time Chö-p'o had succeeded in this, and Bangka had thus become Chö-p'o. As a consequence he rightly says that Chö-p'o lay to the east of San-fo-ts'i. The stone inscription of Kota Kapur states the contrary: then Chö-p'o (Jāva) had been beaten by its rival and San-fo-ts'i (Srīvijaya) controlled Bangka.

Regarding P'u-kia lung there is a story in the *Chu fan chi* (see Hirth and Rockhill, *Chau Ju-kua*) that "our Court has repeatedly forbidden all trade with this country, but the foreign traders for the purpose of deceiving the government changed its name and referred to it as Su-ki-tan". Rouffaer says the following about this: "So the clever South-Chinese adopted a different name for the forbidden land and kept sailing to it". But which was that other name? It cannot have occurred to them out of the blue. Opposite from P'u-kia lung (Chö-p'o) lay Ho-ling (Palembang), which belonged to Chö-p'o as well; here was the well-known hill Seguntang, that is, Su-ki-tan in Chinese pronunciation and transliteration. What would have been more natural for the clever South Chinese than adopting the name of Su-ki-tan for the forbidden island of Bangka and calmly continuing sailing to it?

With this note I have corrected the view I expressed in note 27 of my previous essay, "De geografische kennis omtrent Sumatra in de middeleeuwen", published in *TKNAG* 59 (1942): 46–86; I then thought that P'u-kia lung was identical with P'o-lu-kia-sze.

[47] [E.N.: Sylvain Lévi, "Ptolémée, le Niddesa et la Brhatkathā", in *Études Asiatiques publiées a l'occasion du vingt-cinquième anniversaire de l'École Française d'Extrême-Orient*, ed. G. van Oest, 2 vols. (Paris: Librairie Orientaliste Paul Geuthner, 1925), vol. 2, pp. 1–55 and 431–32.]

[48] Rouffaer, in *BKI* 74, 1 (1918): 138–66.

[49] And equally resists the identification of Ho-ling with Java on the grounds of geographical location. [E.N.: Lévi, "Ptolémée, le Niddesa et la Brhatkathā", pp. 1–55 and 431–2. Also, vol. 6 of Kern's *Verspreide geschriften* is entitled, "Indonesia in 't algemeen, inscripties van den indischen Archipel" (Indonesia in general, inscriptions of the Indian Archipelago), published by Martinus Nijhoff in The Hague in 1917.]

[50] In *Verspreide geschriften*, vol. 6, p. 217.

particulars about P'o-li are inapplicable to Bali. Thus there is a great deal of uncertainty about it. Schlegel and Groeneveldt have sought to identify it with the northern coast of Sumatra. Pelliot has identified it with Bali because a passage in the *History of the T'ang Dynasty* places P'o-li to the east of Ho-ling". But the position southeast of Canton (probably a rough approximation) and the indicated size (50 days east to west and 20 days north to south) do not fit Bali according to Majumdar, nor do they apply to North Sumatra.

Professor Krom likewise is skeptical about this identification with Bali: "a country equally shrouded in uncertainty which, lying on an island in the sea southeast of Canton, definitely belongs to the Archipelago and is called P'o-li; first located at Sumatra's north coast, later identified as Bali, although some of the reported details fit neither island".[51]

P'o-li counted 136 villages, the climate was warm, plant growth lush; rice was harvested twice a year. It was a civilised country; people used cotton for their clothes, while the king wore floral-patterned silk and a tiara made of gold and gems, his crown was made of gold and his sword inlaid with gold. His women servants fanned him with fans made of peacock feathers and white feathers. He rode on a wagon pulled by an elephant. The *Liang shu* (502–56) tell us that the king's family name was Kaundinya (the same as the name of the Brahman who founded Fu-nan (Cambodia) and that Çuddhodana's spouse was a woman from the country. According to Professor Krom and Professor Majumdar, it is evident from this story that the royal family of P'o-li came from India and practised Buddhism. In 518 an embassy brought the usual Buddhist letter; in 523 King Pin-ka through intervention of the envoy Chu-pa-ti[52] sent white parrots,[53] glass artefacts, cotton, shell bowls, perfume and medicine. The *Sui Annals* (589–618) report that the king's family name then was Ch'a-li-ya-ka, his own name Hu-lan-na-po, and that the officials were called

[51] N.J. Krom, *Hindoe-Javaansche geschiedenis* [Hindu-Javanese history] (The Hague: Martinus Nijhoff, 1926), p. 87.

[52] Is Pin-ka not the name spelled more correctly later as P'eng-ka or P'eng-kia, namely Bangka? That would mean that no King Pin-ka is meant here, but the king of Pin-ka, that is, Bangka. It would appear to me that Chu-pa-ti is (Da)tuk Patih.

[53] In 813 an embassy from Ho-ling went to China and offered the Chinese court Pinkia birds, among other things. Were these Pin'kia birds not parrots from Bangka = P'eng-kia, as is said here? In "Chinese Transcriptions of Tibetan Names", B. Laufer is looking for a link between this Pin-kia and the Sanskrit *kalavinka* "Indian cuckoo" (*T'oung Pao* 16 [1915]: 420–4). According to the *Encyclopaedie van Nederlandsch Indië* [Encyclopaedia of Netherlands India] parrots are common on Bangka. C. Parrot, writes that the Bangka birds are bigger than the corresponding species on Sumatra, Melaka and Java ("Beiträge zur Ornithologie Sumatras und der Insel Banka", *Abhandlungen der Bayerischen, Akademie der Wissenschaften*, Klasse 2, Band 24, Abteilung 1 [1907]: 186); J. Hendrik van Balen (*De dierenwereld van Insulinde in woord en beeld* [The animal world of the Dutch Indies in word and image], states (in vol. 2) that the long-tailed Alexander parakeet (*Palacorius longicauda*), which is also found on Bangka, is a highly intelligent bird, known for its gift to imitate speech and do tricks (2 vols. [Deventer and Jakarta: Van der Burgh, 1914]). [E.N.: The author seems to be confusing two species, currently known as *Psittacula alexandri* (red-breasted parakeet) and *Ps. longicauda* (long-tailed parakeet).]

tu-ka-ya-na, the lower officials *tu-ka-si-na*.[54] The sea produced corals. The embassies stopped appearing at the Chinese court after 630.

In these *Sui Annals* the size of P'o-li is enlarged. According to Pelliot ("Deux itinéraires") the *Annals* say: "Leaving Kiao-che (Chiao-chih, Tonkin) one goes south and passes through Che-t'ou (Siam) and Tan-tan; to cross P'o-li from east to west one needs four months, from north to south 45 days. The report in the *T'ang Histories* (embassies of 630) states that P'o-li measures several thousand *li* from north to south."

P'o-li's location (apart from its lying east of Ho-ling) is further indicated as being ten days south of Kalah (Kedah). The people of P'o-li had dark skin and ruddy frizzy hair, nails like talons and teeth like fangs. They wore cotton loincloths, their markets were held at night and were attended with veiled face. A soft kind of stone was found there called *kambala* (*napal*) from which one could cut figures that would harden through long exposure to air. The people were well versed in throwing the *çakra* (throwing wheel).

The *Sui Annals* also mention a kingdom Po-li, pronounced the same but different in transcription from P'o-li, which was situated at a bay south of the land of Chü-li or Kü-li. Gerini says of this: "This country seems to have no connection with P'o-li and must probably be sought at the east coast of Sumatra".[55]

In the *Hsin T'ang shu* one finds the interesting remark that P'o-li produced lenses or burning glasses that were called *p'o-li*, some as big as a hen's egg. Groeneveldt (*Notes on the Malay Archipelago and Malacca*)[56] calls them "fire pearls"; Professor Schlegel calls them "carbuncles".[57] According to the description they were round and white and radiated light up to several feet away. Lo-ch'a equally produced these carbuncles.[58] Between 650 and 755 such an egg-sized crystal from Lo-ch'a must have been sent to China as a tribute by Lin-yi (Champā).

Professsor Pelliot, in his publication "Le Fou-nan", notes that *p'o-li* also means "glass". The *T'ai-p'ing yu-lan* (977–83) tells us that "a junk from Fu-nan coming

---

[54] Were these not *(da)tuk rangkaya* or *(da)tuk karajaän* and *(da)tuk kalima*? The stone inscription of Kota Kapur on the Menduk River on Bangka provides evidence that there was an authentical Malay-Minangkabau government by *datuks* on the island. Then, Bangka had become a *kadatuan* of Srivijaya, and they were *datuks* of this kingdom. Here they were officials of the king of Bangka.

[55] This Kü-li or Kin-lin (Kin-chiu in I-tsing) was the gold island at the South Sumatra Bay (see the essay "*De goud- en specerij-eilanden*" [The gold and spice islands] published in May 1941). Although Bangka did not lie exactly at, but in any case opposite the South Sumatra Bay, the location of this Po-li makes me think that it is the same as P'o-li = Bangka. The people of Po-li are said to be "black-skinned with very white teeth", like those of P'o-li, although they are moreover said to go naked.

[56] [E.N.: W.P. Groenveldt, *Notes on the Malay Archipelago and Malacca. Compiled from Chinese Sources* (Batavia: W. Bruining, 1880).]

[57] "Geographical Notes", *T'oung Pao* 9 (1898): 177–200.

[58] This Lo-ch'a is said to lie east of P'o-li, its inhabitants populating a wide area and identical to those of P'o-li, with the same customs and values. Since it lies east of P'o-li, this Lo-ch'a can only be Balitung, which fits the similarity of the populations. If this Lo-ch'a is the same as Marco Polo's Locac, he did not stop at Singapore Island or Johor (commonly identified with Locac) but at Balitung.

from West India had a mirror for sale made of blue *p'o-li*, 5 *pouces*[59] in diametre and weighing 40 pounds."[60]

To conclude: regarding the island of P'o-li a good deal of information is available, both ethnological and geographical, that should enable us to identify it.

The geographical information shows that it was a big island in the Indian [Indonesian] Archipelago; according to the *T'ang Annals* it measured 50 days from east to west and 20 from north to south (travelling by foot). These measurements correspond quite well with the larger Bangka that existed at that time: connected to Balitung and Pulau Berhala. This larger Bangka does have an east-west versus north-south ratio of 50:20, or 2.5:1.

This big island lay southeast of Canton, east of Palembang and ten days south of Kedah. Coming from Tonkin one reached it over Siam and Tatang (the mouth of the Musi River, see above). Apparently one first set course to the Sumatra shore before putting in at P'o-li (because of wind and current?). Taking into consideration that in those days of sailing, being dependent on wind and current, season and lucky navigation, the travel time of ten days was not completely dependable (according to I-tsing, it took 15 days to get from Kedah to Malayu), the position of P'o-li corresponds with that of Bangka with a reasonable degree of exactness.

Taking the etymological approach one arrives at the same result.

In the *Wu-pei-pi-shu*, to the west of Kia-li-ma-ta (= Karimata in the South China Sea), there is an island Ma-li-tung, west of which the island of P'eng-kia = Bangka has been sketched in. This can only be Balitung, which is called Ma-yi-tung in Fei Hsin's *Hsing-ch'a sheng-lan*. The last character in Chinese, *tung*, means east: Ma-li-tung therefore is the island east of Ma-li. Since according to the *Hsin T'ang shu* P'o-li was also named Ma-li, the P'o-li to the east of which Ma-li-tung lay can only be Bangka. This corresponds perfectly with the *Wu pei pi-shu*: P'eng-kia to the west of Ma-li-tung.

In his *Herinneringen aan Blitong* [Memories of Belitung] Cornelis de Groot reports that according to native traditions the name of Blitong derived from Bali-potong, "the piece cut off from Bali".[61] His conclusion that the island of Bali, which the natives held in high regard, had been cut to pieces, Blitong being one of them, must be considered very far-fetched.

It would be more logical to consider this Bali as Ba-li again, which again, P'o-li, and to think that Balitung was separated from this P'o-li by the centuries of scouring and abrasion (which gave rise to the Straits of Gaspar between Bangka and Balitung). Opposite Balitung on the other side of the Straits of Gaspar, on the southeast spit where Cape Baginda still points to a former connection with the Gunung Baginda on Balitung, lies the district of Toboali. As (To)boali it could have been the origin of the names Ma-li (Ba-li) and P'o-li. Then Bali-potong would not

---

[59] Old French measure, about 2.7 centimetres.

[60] P. Pelliot, "Le Fou-nan", *BEFEO* 3 (1903): 248–303.

[61] According to another tradition—to be found in F.S.A. de Clercq's "Bijdragen tot de geschiedenis van het eiland Bangka" [Contributions to the history of the island Bangka] *BKI* 6, 1 [1895]: 113–63—Bangka originally was a strip of land that had become separated from Johor. Here we see once more the former connection between the Selat Islands and their being joined to the peninsula as a spit of land.

indicate a separation from the distant Bali (which is impossible), but a tearing apart from Toboali = Bangka.[62]

The identification of Bangka with the Arabs' island of Māyiṭ corresponds with this. After all, Ibn Khordādzbeh (844–48) says that there is little distance between Jāba (on the east coast of South Sumatra) and Māyiṭ. On the journey to China, coming from Māyiṭ one stops at Tiyūma (the island Tioman at the east coast of the peninsula), which is on the left side (that is, to the west, which fits well); from there it is five days to Khmer (Cambodia). Idrīsī (1154) has a similar report (Ferrand, *Relations des voyages*): "Quite close to the island of Jāba lies that of Māyiṭ. It is subject to the king of Jāba [this is also said in the *Chu fan chi*, see note above]. To the left of the island of Māyiṭ, at a day's distance, lies that of Tiyūma".[63] Ibn al-Wardī (1340) still mentions Māyiṭ, but the name disappears in Arabic literature after that; the island's importance declined, because the Strait of Singapore became navigable and provided a shorter route than that round Bangka and Balitung. The Turkish admiral Sīdī 'Ali Čelebī (1554) does not speak of the island Māyiṭ, but of Fulo Bang when he means Bangka.

In the great Tanjore inscription of 1030 describing the Chola prince Rājendracoladeva Ị's military campaign to the peninsula and the archipelago, a "Māyirunḍingam" is mentioned in which we can see the Chinese Ma-yi-tung for Balitung (switch of dentals *r* and *t*). The description "surrounded by the deep sea like a moat around a castle" fits Balitung very well.

Rouffaer ("Was Malaka emporium vóór 1400 A.D.?", *BKI* 77) locates this Māyirunḍingam on the southeast extremity of the mainland, near Cape Romania. But in ca. 1000 the mainland's southeast extremity did not lay at Cape Romania but on the island of Balitung, because the Strait of Singapore did not exist yet and the Selat Islands had not crumbled up. The order in the Tanjore inscription, in which Māyirunḍingam comes after Malayur on South Sumatra's east coast, also points to Rājendracoladeva's fleet being in the vicinity of Balitung.

Checking if there is any further mention of Bangka and Balitung in the Chinese sources, we find that Chau Ju-kua in his enumeration of the 15 dependencies of Chö-p'o has Ma-tung or Ma-yi-tung or Balitung under number 2, and Ma-li as P'o-li or Bangka under number 9.

The occurrence of Ma-yi-tung in Fei Hsin's *Hsing-ch'a sheng-lan* has been mentioned above. In Wang Ta-yüan's *Tao-i chih-lüeh* we find a P'eng-kia-lo, which could be a misspelling of P'eng-kia long or Bangka. The Ma-lin we encounter in the *Ming shu* could stand for Ma-li—especially since the next place name is La-sa ("some port near Ma-lin", Rockhill says), which could represent Lo-ch'a: Bangka and Balitung.

In order to see whether the ethnological details fit Bangka and Balitung, let us first look into the information on the carbuncles or fire pearls.

In his article "Çrīvijaya, Yava en Katāha",[64] J.L. Moens, writes: "P'o-li in fact had a different name, but was called this because it produced rock crystal (*sphaṭika*,

[62] Which is geologically quite probable; see above.

[63] This is possible if the journey started from the north coast of Bangka.

[64] [E.N.: J.L. Moens, "Çrīvijaya, Yava en Katāha", *TBG* 77, 3 (1937): 317–487.]

Chinese *p'o-li*)." In the *New T'ang Annals* (618–906), after the remark that P'o-li is also called Ma-li, the note is included that "in this country" rock-crystal lenses or burning glasses occur which are traded elsewhere by the people of Lo-ch'a. Groeneveldt's *Notes*, state that in P'o-li a kind of "fire pearls" is found, some as big as a hen's egg, white and emitting light as far as several feet away. If one catches the sun's rays in it, any tinder held under it will catch fire. The so-called sun-stone is a many-speckled felspar, but the crystals from P'o-li are a different kind of mineral—a pure quartz. The name "fire pearl" is a literal translation of Chinese *huo-chu* and Sanskrit *agnimani*. The latter mineral has the ability to produce the stone sūryahanta, that is "beloved by the sun so called because it produces fire under the influence of the solar rays".[65] The Sanskrit name for rock crystal is *sphaṭika*, whose Chinese equivalent according to Pelliot is *p'o-li*. This makes it likely that the Chinese called the land that produced this *sphaṭika* P'o-li after this natural product. Bangka is known to have produced these crystals (or to have produced them as well). Radermacher's *Sumatra* (1824):[66] "Gemstones are not found on Bangka, but there is a kind of crystal that is dug up at the tin mines; the richer the mine in tin, the more of these crystals are found as well. This crystal ware was part of the goods brought to China as tribute; compared with the embassy from King Kalavinka in 523 mentioned in the *Liang Annals*".[67]

Above I brought forward the suggestion that the names of Ma-li (Bali) and P'o-li could derive from (To)boali. Mr Moens suggests another possibility: that the names originated from the natural product *p'o-li*. In any case, both views give reason to conclude that the old P'o-li was the same as Bangka.

Another valuable piece of information is found in the *Chiu T'ang shu*: on the island P'o-li the plant *ku-pei* (*ki-pei*, Sanskrit *karpāsa* or *kapas*, cotton) grew.[68] It is known that on the infertile Bangka soil, cotton is one of the few plants that are grown. This detail, combined with the information mentioned above that the inhabitants of P'o-li used cotton for their clothes, even the primitive dark-coloured people wore cotton loincloths, and cotton was sent to the Chinese court as tribute, points to Bangka.

The mention of the elephant used by the king for his royal wagon could also point to Bangka, if one connects it to the find of an elephant's tusk in the ore layer of mine number 8; a tusk that seems to have come from the *Elephas sumatranus*

---

[65] [E.N.: W.P. Groeneveldt, *Notes on the Malay Archipelago and Malacca, compiled from Chinese sources* (Batavia: W. Bruining, 1877), p. 206.]

[66] [E.N.: J.C.M. Radermacher, "Beschrijving van het eiland Sumatra", *Verhandelingen van het Bataviaasch Genootschap* 10 (1824): 1–89. The work had been originally published in vol. 3 in 1781.]

[67] Radermacher, *Sumatra*, p. 142. Reference should also be made to Berthold Laufer, "Optical Lenses", in *T'oung Pao* 16 (1915): 169–228. He shows that at the beginning of the 7th century China received rock-crystal "burning lenses" from the Indies—which must have copied their use from the Greeks—via Lo-ch'a and Champa. Laufer's remark—"It is curious that a tribe of such a low degree of culture as the Lo-ch'a possessed burning lenses and was instrumental in conveying this Indian article to Champa and China"—might find an explanation in the fact that the Lo-ch'a were pirates and could take the lenses from Indian/Indonesian ships. Later on, they may have ground the lenses themselves out of rock crystal from neighbouring P'o-li (Bangka).

[68] See Pelliot, "Le Fou-nan", *BEFEO* 3 (1903): 248–303.

(Temminck) which still survives on Sumatra (R.D.M. Verbeek in *Topografische en geologische beschrijving van Zuid-Sumatra* [Topographical and geological description of South Sumatra]).

According to the *Sui Annals* the sea around P'o-li produced corals. This is a known fact about the sea surrounding Bangka and Balitung. In *De zeeën van Nederlandsch Oost-Indië* [The Seas of the Dutch East Indies], chapter on geology, Professor G.A.F. Molengraaff correctly notes: "It is only in a few places, such as Bangka and Balitung according to Verbeek, that corals have been found up to 2 metres above sea level. This indicates that in the most recent period the land has risen a little in relation to the sea, perhaps in connection with small fluctuations, probably climate fluctuations."

Regarding the black population with the frizzy hair: Bangka and Balitung always were notorious for piracy. The VOC representatives and later the residents of Palembang often complained about Balitung "and its inhabitants, a heap of rabble and all kinds of thugs who now form a perfect corps of thieves and pirates. They went privateering on the coasts of Java, Cirebon and other neighbouring islands, sold the men they caught as slaves, and came to sell the spoils they had taken at sea there" (Cornelis de Groot, *Herinneringen aan Blitong*).

The Portuguese knew them as Ceilates or Cellates [Celates]: the Strait robbers. The Chinese also mention these pirates. According to Pelliot ("Deux itinéraires"), Chau Ju-kua speaks of Ma-wu or Ma-lo-nu, known as Malātu in the *Kitāb 'Ajāib al-Hind*—Van der Lith and Devic suggest reading Malāyu there, a correction with which Pelliot agrees. In the southeastern sea lies the kingdom of Chao-hwa [Java], whose inhabitants were pirates. The people they took prisoner were sold in Chö-p'o (it should be noted that a distinction is made here between Chao-hwa and Chö-p'o, so that the latter is not Java). The barbarian pirates are called Ma-wu or Ma-lo-nu. If we accept the equation with Malāyu, the meaning of Chau Ju-kua's story becomes clear: these were Malay pirates haunting the coasts of Java and taking Javanese prisoners to Chö-p'o [Bangka] to be sold there as slaves. The Portuguese were to tell the same story later of the Celates, and the Dutch of the pirates of Balitung, who were also known in the Javanese inscriptions as the Malay *wong asin*.

The Arabs refer to the Fanjab or Pangan, who, seated in their perahus, attacked the ships with poisoned arrows; they likewise had frizzy hair and strange faces. They were the Orang Laut or Orang Sekah who are still found on the Selat Islands and along the Inderagiri coast, for instance. Gerini, in his *Researches* (p. 503n1), identifies these Fanjab, mentioned by Ma'sūdī and Idrīsī, with the Orang Sekah of Balitung, who differ so greatly from the Malays and in fact have an appearance of the Negrito type: "Everyone is struck by the fact that the Sekahs are not Malays. Against this speaks not only the fact that their language is entirely different but also the occurence of their hairy, frizzle-haired men and women, true Papuan types" (A.B. Meyers in *Negritos*).[69] The reddish colour of their hair is caused, I think, by contact with seawater and constant exposure to salty sea air.

---

[69] [E.N.: Adolf B. Meyers, *The Distribution of Negritos In the Philippines end Elsewhere* (Dresden: Stengel & Co., 1899).]

This anthropological information is another argument for identifying P'o-li with Bangka.

A large island like Bangka (and it used to be larger than it is now) would have been known under different names, depending on the direction from which a traveller came. Gerini already notices this, after reporting that from 630 onward the Chinese annals no longer mention P'o-li but speak of *Dva-pa-tan* instead, which like P'o-li is said to lie east of Ho-ling (Palembang): "It is no objection to this identification that the island is also known by a different name P'o-li, for the Chinese are in the habit of calling the same island or different parts of it by different names."

Coedès puts it even more generally: "People have in fact always had a tendency to call a foreign land by the name of the population of the province, the river or the mountain they encountered first as they entered the country."

On the island Bangka, the mountain Manumbing therefore gave the name of *Manopin*, *Monpin*, *Nopi* or even *Popin* to north Bangka, because it served as a beacon for seafarers coming from the Strait of Melaka and entering the Strait of Bangka. Consequently, on all the old maps of the archipelago north Bangka is found under one of these names, sometimes as a separate island, not attached to the rest of Bangka. This mountain should also be regarded as the origin of the Chinese P'eng-kia shan or P'u-kia lung (Bangka Mountain).

Bangka's middle region occurs as *Banca* on those maps. The river Banca Kota is sketched in there as well, and this region (best known for the stone inscription of Kota Kapur dating from 608 Çaka, 686) may have given the *Niddesa* occasion to name the entire island Vanga, since the port from which tin (*vankam*) was exported was situated here. The mouth of the Bangka Kota probably gave access to that port, which lay on the great trade route between India and China here and had a well-sheltered roadstead.

Bangka's southeast part is indicated on the old maps, for instance those by Abraham Ortelius (1570 and 1571), Joan Martines (1576), à Langren (1595), Van Linschoten (1596), Cornelis de Houtman (1595–97), Levinus Hulsius (1605), Jodocus Hondius (1628), Gerard Mercator (1631), Izaak Tirion, and Willem Jansz. Blaeu (1650), Jean Baptiste Nolin (1687), Joachim Ottens (1700) as Chinobata(m), Chinabara, Chinabalo, or Bara- or Bavachina (the latter in Izaak Tirion, Joachim Ottens, Pierre Mortier, Hubert Jaillot, Pater Coronelli and François Valentijn). H.M. Lange (*Het eiland Bangka en zijne aangelegenheden*[70] [The island of Bangka and its matters]) reports that Bangka was also called China Batta.[71]

This *Bava-china* or *Maha-china* as the name for South Bangka could be the Cīna in the *Milindapanha*, which is mentioned with Takkola and Suvannabhūmi as a place where ship owners sent their ships over the high seas to get rich cargo.

I also think that it was the origin of Mo-ho-sin in I-tsing and the *T'ai-p'ing huan-yu chi*, in which Mo-ho-sin is part of an enumeration of kingdoms on or near

---

[70] [E.N.: H.M. Lange, *Het eiland Bangka en zijne aangelegenheden* (Hertogenbosch: Bij Gebroeders Muller, 1850).]

[71] In several old maps the island of Bangka has been split into two separate islands: a northern island named Manopin, Mopin, Mopi, Nopi and the like, and a southern one called Chinabalo or Chinabara, etc. (Ortelius, Mercator, à Langren and Hondius, among others).

South Sumatra: Tan-tan (Tatang, the mouth of the Musi), Ho-ling (Palembang), Mo-ho-sin (south Bangka), To-long (To-sa/Trusan), Chö-mai (Banyuasin), P'o-leou (?), To-lang P'o-hwang (Tulangbawang), Mo-lo-che (Malayu). Amid these countries on and near the Strait of Bangka, a country on Bangka's southeast coast fits in well and is indeed indispensable in a list of these countries.

On the map in part three of Stanislas Julien's *Hiouen Thsang, voyages des pèlerins bouddhistes* [Hsien-tsang, Journeys of the Buddhist pilgrims][72] Mo-ho-sin is an island opposite Mo-lo-yu (which is on an island apparently meant as South Sumatra, for Che-li-fo-che and Po-lu-sse are also located on it). The island opposite the South Sumatran coast is no other than Bangka.

Kern, in *Een Chineesch reiziger op Sumatra* [A Chinese traveller on Sumatra], makes the following remark on I-tsing's Mo-ho-sin: "To the east of Po-lu-sse lies Çribhoya [Srivijaya]; then follows Mo-ho-sin, it is said. This can be nothing but the Syrian missionaries' Masin, the Indians' Mahācīna. This name, which in fact means Great China, is often the equivalent of China, but distinguished from Katai by the Arab writers. How the Chinese monk came to apply the Sanskrit name of his own country to a region near Sumatra is an unsolvable riddle to us."[73]

So Kern looked for this Mo-ho-sin in the vicinity of Sumatra; this fits Bavachina = south Bangka quite well.

Mr Takakusu, (*A Record*) does the same, for at the island of Balitung he notes in red: "This may be Mahâsin from its position", that is, precisely where the old maps located Bavachina.

The Arab writer Yāḳūt (1179–1229) mentions a country named *Čīn* with a city called Čīnīyya off the coast of Jāwa. From this Jāwa aloe, camphor, perfume oil, cloves, medicinal Chinese herbs and Chinese vases were exported. The mention of camphor points to South Sumatra, the Chinese herbs and vases to trade with China. Lying off the coast of South Sumatra, this country Čīn could also be taken for Bavachina or Chinabata = South Bangka.

Rouffaer, in "Was Malaka emporium vóór 1400 A.D.?" (*BKI* 77), goes into great detail about Tumasik, which he places in Johor or on the island of Singapore, and which he identifies with Hasin and Mahasin. His question—"Is it possible that Singapore existed before 900, and if so, under which name?"—is answered as follows by himself: "Under that of Hasin = Salt City or Sea City, and even under that of Mahasin = Great Hasin, I-tsing's Mo-ho-sin, at that time a very powerful city on the south point of the Malay peninsula."[74]

As explained above, the geomorphological constitution of the Selat Islands contradicts this view. It is well possible that on the location of present-day Singapore and Johor, on the eastern shore of the Malay Peninsula, there once was a Malay kingdom and a port, but this part of the peninsula did not then form the south point of the Further Indian [Southeast Asia] mainland, because at that time (before 900)

---

[72] [E.N.: Hiouen-Thsang, *Histoire de la vie de Hiouen-Thsang et de ses voyages dans l'Inde depuis l'an 629 jusqu'en 645*, trans. S. Julien (Paris: Imprimerie Impériale, 1853).]

[73] In *Verspreide geschriften*, vol. 6.

[74] To Rouffaer, the foundation of Tumasik "renamed Singapore" is certain, based on stories two and three of the *Sejarah Melayu*.

16.6 Photograph portrait of the Dutch orientalist and linguist Hendrik Kern. Leiden: Royal Netherlands Institute for Southeast Asian and Caribbean Studies (KITLV).

the Strait of Singapore did not exist yet—that was only the case after ca. 1350. That south point was on Bangka or Balitung; this is where one should look for the Salt or Sea City Hasin, not in Johor or on the island of Singapore.

But it is possible, even quite probable, that Tasik-Tumasik lay here. On Stanislas Julien's map Ta-che-po occurs as a big island not far from South Sumatra. This Ta-che-po may have been an abbreviation of Ta-che-pu-lo (the Tasik Island), predecessor of Tumasik-Singapore. There is all the more ground for this because according to Pelliot ("Deux itinéraires")[75] "a late Chinese text claims that Melaka had equally been called Ta-chö-p'o". This corresponds to Chau Ju-kua's Ta-shi, of which he says (see Hirth and Rockhill, *Chu fan chi*): "Sailing five days (from Shö-p'o or P'u-kia lung or Bangka) one comes to a country of the Ta-shi." In those days of sailing, a duration of five days may be correct for the distance between the south coast of Bangka and Tasik-Tumasik-Singapore.

Ta-che is also found in the story of Queen Si-Mo of Ho-ling in the *Hsin T'ang shu*, according to which in the Shang-yüan Age (674–75) the people of Ho-ling (Palembang) had elevated a woman by the name of Si-Mo to royal dignity, and she was a very strict but just ruler. If her subjects saw something lying on the road that did not belong to them, they dared not pick it up. The prince of Ta-che [Ta-shi] heard this and had a bag of gold put on the road. No one dared touch the bag. Only the crown prince touched the bag with his foot as he passed by. The queen had his toes cut off for it instead of his head, but only after repeated intervention by the ministers.

The Arabs were usually called *Ta-che*, *Tâzi* or *Tajik*; but here, considering the distance and the unlikelihood of an Arab prince giving a thought to an internal matter of Ho-ling, one should rather think of a kingdom in the vicinity of Ho-ling, and identification with Tasik-Tumasik-Singapore is more plausible.

This was not Hasin, however. This Hasin-Mahasin or Mo-ho-sin, later Bavachina on the old European maps and in the traditions, lay on Southeast Bangka, already infamous in Airlangga's time for its pirates, who from here extended their raids to Java's north coast, plundered towns on that coast, robbed ships, and sold Javanese merchants and sailors as slaves (see above).[76]

The inscription in copper, now lost, dating from 956 Çaka, 1034 and copied onto stone in the Majapahit era speaks of Hasin as a country hostile toward Java,

---

[75] However, he identifies this Ta-chö-p'o with Great Java.

[76] Since we are dealing with Java here in any case, we should ask if this Bavachina or Chinabata is not in fact meant with "China" in the *Carita Parahyangan*. It is stated that the Pati Sarikaladarma was defeated by Sanjaya there (R.N. Poerbatjararaka, "De Tjarita Parahijangan", *TBG* 19 [1920]: 403–16); that does not point to China, the "Heavenly Empire", but to a little South-Sumatran state, just like Malayu and Barus in this *Carita*. The Keling mentioned above could be Pasemah, since Westenenk in "De Hindoe Javanen in Midden- en Zuid-Sumatra" (*Handelingen van het eerste congres voor Taal-, Land- en Volkenkunde te Solo, 25–26 December 1919* [Weltevreden: Albrecht & Co., 1921]) [Communications (of the) first Congress of Linguistics and Ethnology at Solo]) locates a Benuwa Keling on the upper course of the Musi. So the *Carita Parahyangan* describes a military expedition overseas (*sabrang*) by Rahyang Sanjaya which however did not go beyond South Sumatra (apart from Bali and Bima; see N.J. Krom in *Hindoe Javaansche Geschiedenis*).

almost certainly Malay, and defeated by the Javanese king Airlangga.[77] We need hardly inquire after the reason: it is rather obvious that once Java had recovered from the *pralaya* that had it in its grip, Airlangga made an end to the piracy it had to endure from the infamous Hasin on the south coast of Bangka and on Balitung.

The Malay *wong asin*[78] from the Bantam *pijagem* who are mentioned by Rouffaer should likewise certainly be identified with the notorious pirates from Mahasin-Bavachina on Southeast Bangka.

That was not the end of Hasin, however: its piracy was not so easily exterminated, especially since it was favoured by Palembang. Prince Kṛtanagara had to become involved as well, as Rouffaer states: "The Pamalayu sent by prince Kṛtanagara of Tumapel in 1275 also destroyed the old Mahasin, Java's former enemy. A first wave of exiled sea Malays (still named *wong asin* later) fled to safety in the northwest."[79] These, then, were the pirates still prowling the Strait of Singapore in later years, who were called the "Tan-ma-hsi (Tumasik) barbarians" by Wang Ta-yüan and Cellates or Celates by the Portuguese. There was, however, no sign of a thriving and "supremely powerful" kingdom on Singapore Island at that time, for Marco Polo does not report on it in his travelogue—something he certainly would have done had he sailed by it, and he definitely would have sailed by it if the Strait of Singapore had existed then as a shortcut between the China Sea and the Strait of Melaka.

Nāgarakṛtāgama and Pararaton are silent regarding Hasin or Mahasin, but they do mention Tumasik, which appears as Tan-ma-seih on Philips's map. The Portuguese are ignorant of this Tumasik or Mahasin; they only know Cinquapura, Cingapura or Sincapura at the strait of the same name.

Balitung, however, kept up its bad repute as a pirate's nest, as appears from reports of Dutch residents of Palembang to the government at Batavia. Piracy existed up to 1850, even close to the coast of Tegal on Java, as Cornelis de Groot tells us.

If we may conclude from the above that before ca. 1350 no other sea route between India and China was known but the Strait of Bangka, around Bangka and Balitung, then there is all the more reason to assume that in order to shorten this long journey seafarers must have used a route across the peninsula's isthmus. The latest research done by H.G. Quaritch Wales, field director of the Greater India Research Committee, has made it clear that this route connected Takupa—Ptolemy's ancient Takkola—on the west coast with the Bay of Bandon on the east coast of the peninsula.

---

[77] Rouffaer, "Was Malaka emporium vóór 1400 A.D.?", p. 73.

[78] Rouffaer translates *wong asin* as "salty people" or "sea people", but shouldn't it be "wong Hasin", "people of Hasin"?

[79] Rouffaer, "Was Malaka emporium vóór 1400 A.D.?", p. 106.

17

Purnadi Purbatjaraka

Shahbandars in the Archipelago*

Stimulated by the publications of Moreland and Blagden who have both discussed the institution of the *shahbandar*,[1] this paper presents the results of some further research on this subject. It gives special attention to some specific points, such as the origin of the institution in the Malay Archipelago and the functions of the shahbandar from the viewpoint of international relations, that is, his dealings with foreigners and foreign powers.

It is well known that the archipelago formerly was divided into numerous independent or semi-independent states or principalities. At the beginning of the 20th century, no less than 350 of those states existed side by side with the Netherlands Indies "Minor" (1800–ca. 1900), and before that with the VOC (Dutch East India Company ca. 1680–1800).[2] Both the VOC and the Netherland Indies Minor, as well as the aforementioned states and principalities, were international legal personalities, each with their own subjects.[3]

The following are some preliminary findings resulting from this study:

1. The approximate beginning of the institution in the archipelago can be traced.
2. Shahbandars were known in almost all parts of the archipelago.

---

* First published in the *JSEAH* 2, 2 (1961): 1–9. [E.N.: Purnadi's mix of spellings for place names have been retained].

[1] See W.H. Moreland, "The Sharbanda in the Eastern Seas", *JRAS* (1920): 517–33; and C.O. Blagden, "Shahbanda and Bendahara", *JRAS* 53, 2 (1921): 246–8.

[2] The full colonial period (ca. 1900–K.War II) = Netherlands Indies "Major".

[3] J.H. Zeeman, *De Kustvaart in Nederlandsch-Indië* (Amsterdam: J.H. de Bussy, 1824), p. 37; *Publication of the International Bureau of the Permanent Court of Arbitration* (The Hague: Martinus Nijhoff, 1928), p. 44; as well as G.H.J. van der Molen, *Subjecten van Volkenrecht* (The Hague: Martinus Nijhoff, 1949), p. 11.

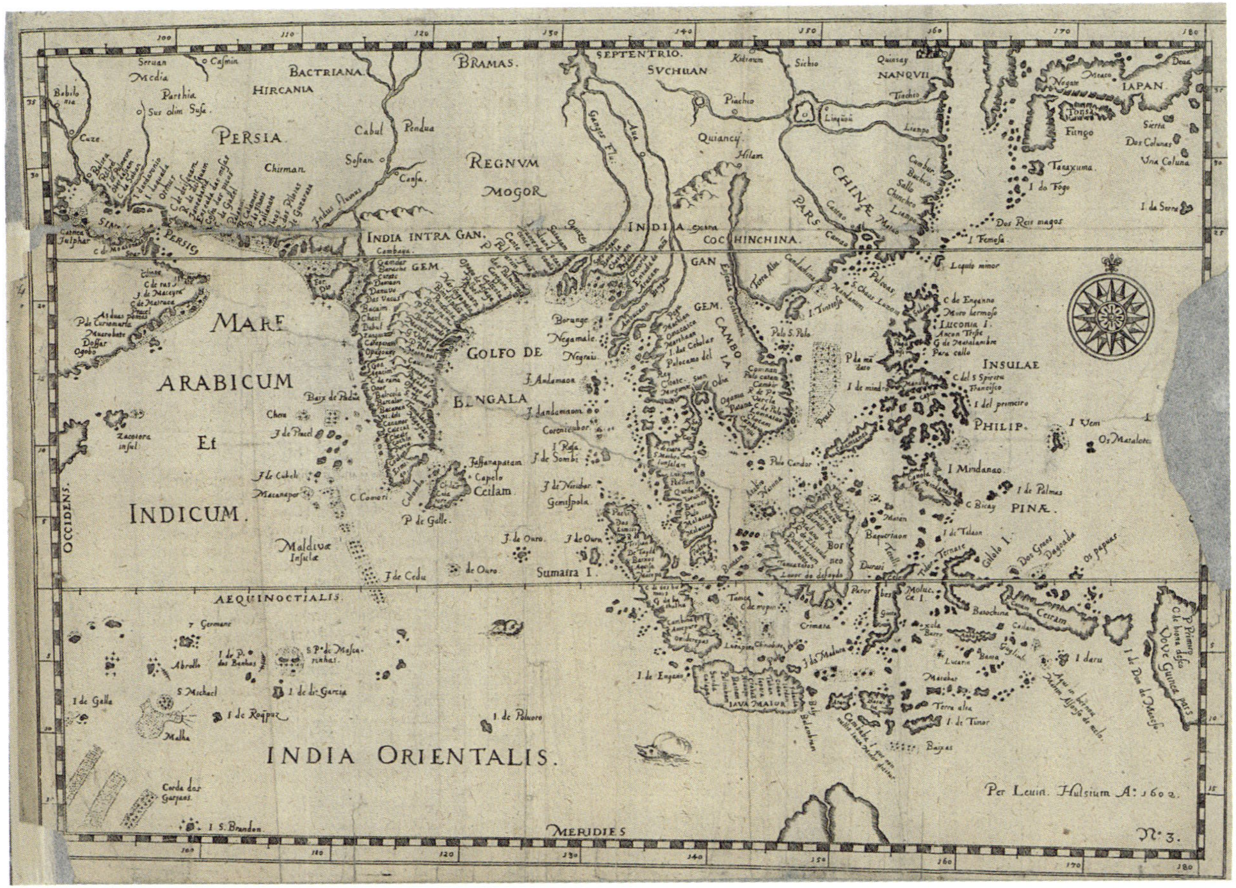

17.1 Map of Asia by Theodore de Bry. Isaac Genius and Levinus Hulsius, *Neundte Schiffart* [Ninth Voyage to the East Indies], Frankfurt M., 1612. Koninklijke Bibliotheek, The Hague, 2112C4.

3. There existed a great variety of local terms side by side with the original name.
4. He fulfilled an important role in international relations.
5. A foreigner could hold the post of shahbandar.

I

There need not be any doubt about the Persian origin of the word *shahbandar*. Its English translation, "king of the haven"[4] or the German version "Hafenkönig"[5] is, in our opinion, not entirely correct, for although the word *shah* means "king or lord", *Bandar* does not exactly mean a harbour. Emporium or trade centre on the coast or a major riverbank would be more correct.[6]

In Indonesia, the Persian word shahbandar was probably introduced by (pre-Islamic) Persian traders who visited and settled the archipelago since the 3rd century CE.[7] Sumatra's northeast coast, on the trade routes between China and other Asian countries, was the area where they first settled.

A well-known state in Southeast Asian history where they may have ruled is Pasei. It is not entirely impossible that the name Pasei signifies the place where Persians or Parsis lived.

In step with the commercial success and increasing prosperity of those Persian settlers, their headmen or leaders became "Havenkoninkjes" (kinglets of the port) in the trade centres of that particular part of Sumatra.[8]

It is therefore not impossible that from that time shahbandars were known in the archipelago.

II

Because shahbandars were known to act as authorities in trade centres on the north coast of Sumatra, it seemed later on not unusual that one of the authorities in other emporia throughout the archipelago was also called *shahbandar*. This assumption is based on the historical fact that shahbandars were found to be authorities in most of the trade centres.

It is regretable that the existing records do not allow us to list the chronological sequence in which shahbandars make their appearance in other areas outside Pasei up to the beginning of this century. Hence only the names of the principalities, states or places where shahbandars have functioned can be given.

---

[4] H. Yule, and A.C. Burnell, *Hobson-Jobson, A Glossary of Colloquial Anglo-Indian Words and Phrases, and of kindred Terms, Etymological, Historical, Geographical and Discursive*, 2nd ed., ed. W. Crooke (London: J. Murray, 1903); see under "Shabunder".

[5] J. Verken, *Molukkenreise 1607–1612*; ed. S.P. l'Honoré Naber (The Hague: Martinus Nijhoff, 1930), p. 76.

[6] H.C. Klinkert, *Nieuw Maleisch-Nederlands Woordenboek* (Leiden: E.J. Brill, 1916); see under "Bandar".

[7] J.L. Moens, "De Noord-Sumatraanse rijken der Parfums en Specerijen, in voor-Moslimse tijd", *TBG* 85 (1955): 325–64.

[8] Ibid., p. 358.

17.2 Batavia fish market. Johan Nieuhof, *Voyages and Travels, into Brazil, and the East-Indies*. London: Printed for Awnsham and John Churchill at the Black Swan in Pater Noster Row, 1703. NUS Libraries, Special Collections.

In this listing we will start with the principalities, states and places on the island of Sumatra as the areas that first became familiar with the institution of the shahbandar. We will then move, without regard for historical sequence, towards the eastern part of the archipelago.

On the island of Sumatra, shahbandars were found in: Aceh, Pasei, Samudera, Pedir, Lhosumawe, Tapa'tuan, Langkat, Serdang, Pelalawan, Melaju, Indragiri, Reteh, Lingga, Jambi, Palembang, Lampung, Kalianda, Kota-Agung, Pedada, Indrapura, Pariaman, and Tiku.

In Borneo (Kalimantan) they were found in: Kotawaringin, Banjermasin, Negari/Kajutangi, Tatas, Pasir, Kutai, Sambaliung, Gunungtabur, and Samarinda.

On the island of Java we found them in: Banten, Kalapa/Jakatra/Batavia, Krawang, Tjiasem, Pamanukan, Tanjongpura, Waringinpitu, Tjidjuhung, Indramaju, Cirebon, Mataram, Tegal, Pemalang, Kendal Kaliwungu, Semarang, Demak, Japara, Pati, Juwana, Rembang, Lasem, Wedung, Kaligawe, Majapahit, Tuban, Sidaju, Gresik, Jortan, Surabaja, Pasuruan, Probolinggo, and Blambangan (in Madura: Arosbaja, Bangkalan, Sumenep).

In Nusatenggara (Lesser Sunda Islands) one could find them in: Bali, Tedjakula, Buleleng, Lombok/Selaparang/Sasak, Ampenan, Sanggar, Dompo, and Bima Ende.

On the island of Celebes (Sulawesi) they were found in: Makassar, Gowa, Bone, Kalingsusu, Supa, Mondano, Balantak, Palu, and Tolitoli.

In the eastern part of the archipelago: Ternate, Tidore, Batjan, Ambon, Banda, Labetaka/Lautaka, Neira, Lontor, Ortatan, Ratu, Kombir, Pulau Run, and Pulau Ai.[9]

This list, which mentions no less than one hundred places, covers all parts of the archipelago, starting from the northern tip of Sumatra and ending in the Banda Archipelago. It may be said here in passing, that the latter group of islands is of great historical significance, especially with regard to the history of international relations, within as well as without the archipelago.

In particular, it should be noted that the institution of the shahbandar was also used by the VOC and later by the Netherlands Indian state. This is evidenced by the fact that the shahbandar was also found in the city of Batavia.

III

As has already been mentioned, the word *shahbandar* is Persian in origin, but like so many other foreign words it underwent some changes because of its adaptation by the various indigenous languages in the archipelago.

I. It is sometimes used in compound with other names or words, such as, in Banten: Kijahi Sabandar; in Indragiri: Datokh Sjahbandar; in Ende; Radja Sabandar; while outside the Indonesian Archipelago; as in Perak: Datu Shabandar; in Melaka: Tuan Shabandar.

II. In other areas the word *shah* was discarded or instead some local word was used to replace it, such as in Aceh: Panglima Bandar; in Deli: Datuk

[9] [E.N.: This listing includes place names in current and Dutch orthography as well as place names of port and riverine settlements with islands, inland residencies and historic kingdoms. An editorial attempt at sorting out some of these place names is appended to this essay.]

Bandar; in Palawan: Datuk Bandar; in Reteh: Bandar; in Indragiri: Bandar; on the west coast of Sumatra: Radja Panglima Bandar; in Lampung: Bandar; in Banjermasin: Djuru Bandar, Mantri Bandar; in Gunung Tabur: Pangeran Bandar, Datu Bandar; in Dajak: Bandar; in Central Java: Tuwan Bandar; on the island of Madura: Tuwan Bandar; and in Bali and Lombok: Bandar.

Taking a closer look one will notice that those indigenous words; used together with the word Bandar, it had more or less the same meaning as the word *shah*. Apparently difficulties in its pronunciation resulted in these changes.

III. In some other areas the word *shahbandar* was transformed by the local language, such as in: Aceh: Sabonda and Tja(h)bonda; Minangkabau: Sihibanda(r); Toradja: Sabandara; Makassar and Bone: Sabânârâ; Bali and Lombok: Subandar: Bima Sabanda(r).[10]

From these examples one can see that the acceptance of the word *shahbandar* by the various regional languages in the archipelago. For this reason that, apart from the original Persian word, attention must also be paid to those indigenous names denoting the functions of the shahbandar.

IV

From the history of international relations in the archipelago, one learns that the shahbandar played an important role, perhaps the most important role.

His functions not only covered matters connected with foreigners; in interstate relations, he was also an important factor.

In commentaries on the "Adat Atjeh", Drewes and Voorhoeve mentioned the shahbandar as the "beneficiary of the *adat nan diluar*".[11]

The term *adat* is meant as a synonym of the word *hukum* (law),[12] and as a consequence, *adat nan diluar*—as distinguished from *adat lafaf* (internal court law)—can be interpreted as the law—concerning foreigners or foreign powers; in short, international law.

Ancient Balinese codes for the island of Lombok regulate the relations between the shahbandar and the "wong dagang sunantara" (nusantara), thus showing that his activities also covered relations with trading foreigners, because the word *wong dagang* or *orang dagang*, which means foreigners![13]

---

[10] See above.

[11] G.W.J. Drewes and P. Voorhoeve, "Adat Atjeh", *VKI* 24 (1958): 28.

[12] *Adat* = native common-law; *Hukum* = Islamic-law. See T.A. Juynboll, *Handleiding tot de kennis van de Mohammedaansche wet*, 4th ed. (Leiden: E.J. Brill, 1903), p. 44n3.

[13] F.A. Liefrink, *De landsverordeningen der Balische vorsten van Lombok*, II (The Hague: Martinus Nijhoff, 1915), pp. 12, 274–5; see also J. Hageman, "Aanteekeningen ontrent een gedeelte der Oostkust van Borneo", *TBG* 1 (1853): 78, and N. Adriani, "Mededeelingen omtrent de Toradjas van Midden-Celebes; lezing gehouden door Dr N. Adriani den 3.en September, 1900", *TBG* 44 (1901): 222.

In the field of interstate relations, records show us that the functions of the shahbandar covered all forms of international public activities, such as: (1) legislation, (2) judicature, (3) police, and (4) administration.

I. The shahbandar's role in the field of international legislation can be concluded from various treaties between the VOC or the Netherlands Indian state, and numerous principalities in the archipelago.

Those treaties also showed that the shahbandar could and did act as a sole, principal or a fellow representative of one of the contracting parties. This was for instance the case in treaties concluded between the VOC and, respectively, Jacatra (1614), Banjermasin (1635), Bacan (1667), Makassar (1710), and Indragiri (1758); also between the Netherlands Indies and, respectively, Kutai (1825), Endeh (1869) and Gunung Tabur (1893).[14]

II. Some of the activities of the shahbandar in the international judicial field, such as his dealings with disputes between foreigners and subjects of his principality, were expressly regulated by treaty, while others were regulated by customary law or decrees issued by a prince.

This judical function was carried out by way of mixed tribunals or single judges. Shahbandars of Jacatra (1611), Bantam (1684) and Palembang (1691) had their functions regulated by treaty. Those of Jacatra and Palembang were allowed to act as sole judges, while those of Bantam sat together in tribunals with officials of the VOC.[15]

In Aceh, Kota Waringin and South Celebes functions of the shahbandar were regulated by various codes or princely decrees, the one of South Celebes allowing him to sit in mixed tribunals.[16]

In an international arbitration concerning a dispute between Jambi and Palembang (1682), a VOC shahbandar acted as one of the arbitrators.[17]

III. Police activities of the shahbandar covered both repressive as well as preventive measures, some of them were also regulated by treaty. Preventive police action against individuals were regulated by treaties concluded between the VOC and princes of Sumatra's West Coast (Priaman) [Pariaman] in 1671, e.g. control of crews of in and outgoing foreign ships.

Treaties between the VOC and Jambi (1683, 1709, 1721), and Palembang (1722, 1763) were more or less concerned with the same matter.[18]

---

[14] *CD*, vol. 1, pp. 117–9, 271; vol. 2, pp. 359–63; vol. 4, pp. 372–6; vol. 6, pp. 158–61. Treaties after 1900 are deposited in the Arsip Nasional in Jakarta.

[15] *CD*, vol. 1, p. 91; vol. 3, pp. 349, 554.

[16] Drewes and Voorhoeve, "Adat Atjeh", p. 26; A.A. Cense, "De Kroniek van Bandjarmasin", Dissertation, University of Leiden, 1928, p. 402; L.T.J. Caron, "Het handels-en zeerecht in adatrechtsregelen van de rechtskring Zuid-Celebes", Dissertation, University of Utrecht, 1937, p. 39.

[17] L.W. Alders, "Internationale rechtspraak tussen Indonesische rijken en de VOC tot 1700", PhD dissertation, Catholieke Universiteit, Nijmegen, 1955, p. 101.

[18] *CD*, vol. 2, p. 450; vol. 3, p. 326; vol. 4, pp. 337, 533, 540; vol. 6, p. 225.

Treaties regulating repressive power of the shahbandar were those concluded between the VOC and Banjermasin (1733), stipulating his participation in confiscatory measures against apprehended smugglers.

The same goes for treaties between Palembang and the VOC (1763).[19] An example of repressive police action was the extradition of a prisoner by the shahbandar of Tjiasem (in the territory of Cirebon) to an envoy of the VOC government in Batavia in 1664.[20]

Investigation of prisoners and taking back escaped slaves caught abroad were also examples of this repressive power.

The above-mentioned actions were taken by the shahbandar of Batavia, while the shahbandar of Cirebon was the captor of the escaped slaves.[21]

Intervention by a VOC shahbandar in Johor-Acehnese relation—by which he threatened to take drastic measures if good relations were not restored—may serve as an example of interstate police action.[22]

IV. Shahbandars also carried out international administrative functions, and one might say that it was in this field that their main activities lay.

It covers everything which is not already included in the three other functions mentioned earlier.

A distinction is made here between activities concerning foreigners and those concerning states, both of which could be respectively unilateral or multilateral.

Unilateral activities towards foreigners were, for instance, the issuing of permits, allowing them to enter a certain territory or to import goods. Apart from that, rendering assistance to ships in distress might also be included in this function, as laid down in the decrees of Balinese princes for Lombok mentioned earlier.[23]

Multi-lateral activities were those where the shahbandar contracted treaties of commerce with foreigners.

Shahbandar Mistaha of Ternate fulfilled a unilateral administrative function when he cosigned a treaty between Banggai and the VOC (1773) as a witness. The same was done by Codjarabo (from Kodja or Gujarat) a shahbandar from Bima in a treaty between Sanggar and Dempo.[24]

Examples of multilateral interstate activities by the shahbandar were the international negotiations and sometimes also the rendering of good offices or mediation, events of frequent occurrence but often none too successful. Negotiations between the Shahbandar Paravicini from Batavia and the Sultan of Banjermasin

[19] *CD*, vol. 5, p. 167; vol. 6, p. 325.

[20] *DRB*, entry for 14 July 1664, p. 282.

[21] F. de Haan, *De Preanger-Regentschappen onder het Nederlandsch Bestuur tot 1811* 4 vols. (Batavia: Kolff, and The Hague: Martinus Nijhoff, 1910–12), vol. 4, p. 143; *DRB*, entry for 17 Nov. 1659, p. 230.

[22] Alders, *Internationale Rechtspraak*, p.42.

[23] *CD*, vol. 3, pp. 464–5; Liefrinck, *De landsverordeningen*, p. 290.

[24] *CD*, vol. 6, p. 343; vol. 2, p. 501.

which to the utter astonishment: of Paravicini himself were very successful, may serve as an example.[25]

V

Thus we have clearly seen that the shahbandar had an important role to fulfill both in relation to foreigners as well as to foreign powers.

One can even say that almost all of his activities were in the field of international relations.

Moreland, who made a special study, came to a fourfold classification of the shahbandar. According to him, a shahbandar could have the function of a minister, a president, a consul or a harbourmaster.

One could agree with the use of the terms *consul* and *harbourmaster*, but as regards the first two terms, it would be better if the words "native high official" and "chief native authority" were used instead.

In accordance with the shahbandar's activities in the international sphere, it was not impossible—except for the second category mentioned above—that the post was held by a foreigner.[26]

With regards to the third category (consul), described by Moreland as "appointed or elected head of the body of merchants of any nation resident in a foreign seaport or town, to settle disputes among them and be their channel of communication with the local government", chances were very small that he was not a foreigner to the locality. But his assertion that shahbandars with consular capacity were only found in Melaka,[27] and by inference therefore not in the Indonesian Archipelago, is open to many doubts—especially in view of the fact that, in one of the Indonesian principalities, there were at the same moment several shahbandars in charge of foreigners. Such was the state of affairs in Palembang, where the Malays, Javanese and Chinese each had their own shahbandar.[28] In our opinion, the same can be concluded from the words used in a treaty between the VOC and Palembang (1678, art. 3): "de volkeren van den sabandaar" [The people of/subject to the shahbandar].[29]

Is it then not possible that in Palembang or other areas in Sumatra, situated opposite Melaka, there were also shahbandars with consular capacities?

In any case, it is beyond doubt that, in the archipelago, the post of shahbandar could be held by foreigners. Here follows a list of the places, areas or principalities in which foreigners have acted as shahbandars. As before, it starts from the western part of the archipelago:

In Aceh an Indian shahbandar, in Chillebaer a Chinese; in Bantam an Indian, a Chinese and a Gujarati; in Batavia a Japanese; in Cirebon a Dutchman; in Mataram a Chinese; in Tuban a Portuguese; in Majapahit a Kodja (Gujarati); in Arosbaja and

---

[25] N.C. Noorlander, "Bandjarmasin en de Compagnie in de 2e helft der 18e eeuw", PhD dissertation, University of Leiden, 1935, p. 27.

[26] W.H. Moreland, "The Shahbandar in the Eastern Seas", *JRAS* 52 (1920): 532.

[27] Ibid.

[28] *VKI* 3 (1787): 62, 71–2.

[29] *CD*, vol. 3, pp. 138ff.

17.3 Batavian Malays. Johan Nieuhof, *Voyages and Travels, into Brazil, and the East-Indies: Containing, an exact description of the Dutch Brazil, and divers parts of the East-Indies*. London: Printed for Awnsham and John Churchill at the Black Swan in Pater Noster Row, 1703. NUS Libraries, Special Collections.

Bambangan a Chinese; in Banjermasin a Gujarati and a Chinese; in Kutai an Arab; in Makassar a Dutchman; in Kendari Bay a Buginese; in Mendano also a Buginese; in Tejakula a Chinese; in Ampenan an Englishman; and finally, in Ternate a Dutchman.

In this article the author has attempted to sketch in brief and preliminarily outline the history of the institution of the shahbandar in the Indonesian archipelago until approximately the beginning of the 20th century. This study was undertaken not only as a modest contribution to Indonesian institutional history, but also because, in the opinion of the author, the results of an inquiry into the history of common institutions and common cultural phenomena in Indonesia also serve the wider purpose of the rewriting of Indonesia's history, however limited in scope and however particular in form these results might be. In order to attain this goal, it will be necessary for us to be guided not only by our Indonesia-centric vision but also our approach to Indonesia's history as an integrated structure, has to be inspired by the concept expressed in the motto in Indonesia's coat of arms: "Unity in Diversity" (Bhinneka Tunggal Ika), and more precisely, by our awareness of the *Unity* in that *Diversity*.

Editorial Appendix

The present list represents the editors' own identification of the place names, with reference to the authoritative *Atlas van Tropisch Nederland*.[30] We have included those that we can find in its geographical and historical context. Others we have tried to use a phonetic equivalence in order to deduce the possible places.

For our confirmed list, we begin with Sumatra (east and west coast, south, Riaus) and Borneo/Kalimantan (south to north) before we proceed to Java (north coast, west to east), followed by Nusatenggara (Bali, Lombok, Sumbawa), Elebes/ Sulawesi-Maluku and Ternate-Tidore.

On the island of Sumatra, shahbandars were found in:

East coast: Aceh, Pasai, Samudera, Pedir, Langkat, Belawan, Serdang, Melayu-Jambi, Indragiri, and Palembang.

West coast: Lhok Sumawe, Tapa Tuak, Tiku, Pariaman, and Indrapura.

South Sumatra and Riaus: Lampung, Kalianda (provincial capital today), Kota Agung, Reteh, and Lingga.

In Borneo (Kalimantan), south to north: Kota Waringin, Banjermasin, Pasir, Kutai, Negari, Samarinda, Sambaliung (on the Krangan River, today a district), and Gunung Tabur.

On the island of Java (north coast, west to east): Banten, Jakarta (Kelapa or Batavia), Krawang [river], Ciasem, Indramayu, Cirebon, Tegal, Pemalang, Kendal, Semarang, Tanjongpura, Rembang, Waringinpitu, Demak, Japara, Juana, Wedung, Tuban, Gresik, Surabaya, Sidoarjo, Probolinggo, Pasuran, Bangkalan (island of Madura), and Sumenep (Madura).

---

[30] *Atlas van Tropisch Nederland* (Batavia: Reproductiebedrijf van den Tropischen Dienst in Nederlandsch-Indië, 1938).

In Nusatenggara, in Bali: Tejakula (north coast), Buleleng (north coast district); in Lombok: Selaparang (east coast), Ampenan (west coast); in Sumbawa: Sanggar, Dompo (both north coast), and Bima (north coast).
On Sulawesi or Maluku: Makassar, Bone, Gowa, Paul (north coast), Tolitoli (north Sulawesi), Balantak (district, not port, north Sulawesi), and Mondano (south Sulawesi).
In Ternate or Tidore: Tidore, Bacan, Ambon Bandar (now capital of province), Neira Banda and Lontor.

Those not included in the list are as follows:

Sumatra: Pedada [possibly Pedada Bay in the Sunda Straits but there is also a Tanjungpedada in the Riaus].
Borneo: Kajutangi [plausibly Kayu Tangi], Tatas [unlikely to be Pulau Tatas].
Java: Pamanukan, Tjidjujung, Mataram [A powerful central Javanese Sultanate that controlled much of the north coast; it is difficult to attribute a shahbandar to it], Pati, Lasem, Kaligawe, Majapahit [there is no evidence that they had a shahbandar in their inland capital at Trowulan], Jortan [possibly Yortan], Arosbaja [Arosbaya].
Lombok: Sasak [an ethnic group; a categorical error to attribute a shahbandar to them].
Sulawesi: Kalingsusu [possibly Kulisusu] and Supa [probably Suppa, South Sulawesi, exact location is uncertain].
Ternate: Lebetakka/Lautaka, Ratu, Pulau Run, Palau Ai, Kombir (Combi) and Ortatan (Orantatta). [These are villages or islands in Ternate again; it would be difficult to attribute a shahbandar to them].

18

Kwa Chong Guan

Singapore in 1819: The Beginnings of a New *Kerajaan*[*]

Much of the credit for the founding of modern Singapore has been given to Thomas Stamford Raffles. He is eulogised by Sir Frank Swettenham as the man to whom "we owe the possession of Singapore, the Gate of the Further East, a naval base of the highest importance, a great commercial centre, and the most prosperous of the British Crown Colonies".[1] The role of Temenggong 'Abdu'r-Rahman in welcoming Raffles to Singapore and Tengku Husain in granting "full permission to the Honourable English East India Company to establish a factory or factories at Singapore"[2] is noted but not considered significant in most textbook accounts of Singapore's

---

* First published as a chapter in *Malays/Muslims in Singapore: Selected Readings in History 1819–1965*, ed. Khoo Kay Kim et al. (Subang Jaya, Selangor: Pelanduk Publications, and Singapore: Association of Muslim Professionals [AMP], 2006), pp. 1–36.

[1] *British Malaya: An Account of the Origin and Progress of British Influence in Malaya* (London: John Lane the Bodley Head, 1906), pp. 72–3. Swettenham was one of those who not only made history as Governor-General of the Straits Settlements and High Commissioner for the Federated Malay States, but lived long enough after retirement to write and rewrite it, even though, as Sir Richard Winstedt commented, "his education had not been such as to qualify him for research" in his notice on Swettenham in *Dictionary of National Biography 1941–50*, ed. L.G. Wickham Legg and E.T. Williams (Oxford: Oxford University Press, 1959), p. 856. Swettenham revised his *British Malaya* twice, in 1929 and 1948 and in between, saw the book reprinted several times. The text, for better or worse, set the framework for much of Malayan historiography in the pre- and post-World War II eras. C.M. Turnbull, in her textbook *A History of Singapore 1819–1988* (Singapore: Oxford University Press, 1989), p. 31, continues this assessment of Raffles when she wrote that "Singapore was fortunate in her three early pioneer administrators: Raffles, a man of extraordinary vision, but for whom Singapore would never have existed".

[2] Article 3 of Johor treaty of 6 Feb. 1819.

18.1 Cropped map of Asia used during the 1824 Anglo-Dutch negotiations. The pencil line cutting across the Singapore and Melaka Straits was drawn by A.R. Falck in his proposal to C.J. Canning to divide the Straits into Dutch and British spheres of influence. This division was confirmed by the Anglo-Dutch Treaty of 17 March 1824. National Archives of the Netherlands. 4.AANW-1455.

past. C.M. Turnbull's textbook A *History of Singapore 1819–1988* contains one paragraph reference to Raffles recognising Tengku Husain as the elder claimant to the throne of Johor who had been bypassed in 1812.[3] A more recent *A History of Singapore* edited by Ernest C.T. Chew and Edwin Lee makes no reference to Temenggong 'Abdu'r-Rahman's and Tengku Husain's role or place in the founding of modern Singapore. The textbook locates the British decision to establish a presence at the southern end of the Straits of Melaka within the framework of 18th century Anglo-French global rivalry.[4]

The story of why and how Raffles founded an East India Company settlement on Singapore is well documented. Raffles in part ensured that in his correspondence and reports on the subject. But the story of why Temenggong 'Abdu'r-Rahman and Tengku Husain chose to sign with Raffles on 6 February 1819 the agreement permitting the Honourable Company to establish a factory on the island is not so well documented and known. Neither the temenggong nor Tengku Husain left any records of their rational for joining the British in establishing a new entrepot on Singapore.[5] We are left to infer their rationale from contemporary European accounts of the doings of the Johor *istana* at Lingga and Bintan. Major Peter J. Begbie,[6] who served with the Madras Artillery in the Naning Campaign in 1831, utilised his time in Malaya to research into its past and present circumstances. He has left us a graphic and dramatic account of how Tengku 'Abdu'r-Rahman, the younger and religiously inclined son of Sultan Muhmad Shah who had no political ambitions was forced to ascend the throne when his father unexpectedly died in 1810 after sending his elder brother Tengku Husain off to Pahang to get married. The new sultan was apparently prepared to abdicate in favour of his elder brother who their late father had nominated to succeed him. Nevertheless, *istana* factions pressured him to remain and leave his elder brother to move out from Lingga, where the late Sultan Muhmad Shah had moved the *istana* to from Pulau Penyengat, off Bintan Island. It was to

[3] Turnbull, *A History of Singapore*, p. 9.

[4] In the essay by Wong Lin Ken, "The Strategic Significance of Singapore in Modern History", in *A History of Singapore*, ed. Ernest C.T. Chew and Edwin Lee (Singapore: Oxford University Press, 1991), pp. 17–35.

[5] The problems of attempting to reconstruct a Malay view of history without any Malay records of what the sultans thought was highlighted by John Bastin in his inaugural lecture at the University of Malaya in Kuala Lumpur in 1959 on "The Western Element in Modern Southeast Asian History", reprinted in his *Essays on Indonesian and Malayan History* (Singapore: Eastern Universities Press, 1961), pp. 10ff and "Problems of Personality in the Reinterpretation of Modern Malayan History", in *Malayan and Indonesian Studies, Essays Presented to Sir Richard Winstedt on his Eighty-Fifth Birthday*, ed. J. Bastin and R. Roolvink (Oxford: Clarendon Press, 1964), pp. 141–53.

[6] Major P.J. Begbie, *The Malayan Peninsula: Embracing its History, Manners and Customs of the Inhabitants, Politics, Natural History, etc. from its Earliest Records*, repr. ed. (Kuala Lumpur: Oxford University Press, 1967), pp. 72–7. Begbie's account is quoted *in extenso* by Richard Winstedt in his "A History of Johore (1365–1895)", *JMBRAS* 10, 3 (1932): 75–6. According to the *Tuhfat al-Nafis*, Mahmud, shortly before he unexpectedly died, reversed his earlier choice of Tengku Husain as his successor and appointed Tengku 'Abdu'r-Rahman, p. 264, of Virginia Matheson's romanised text of the *Tuhfat al-Nafis* (Kuala Lumpur: Penerbit Fajar Bakti, 1982).

the *istana* of his stepmother at Pulau Penyengat that Tengku Husain moved to plot and politick for the next nine years, until Stamford Raffles arrived in January 1819. Tengku Husain is therefore perceived to have welcomed Raffles, hoping that he could, with British support, reclaim the succession and become sultan of Johor.[7]

Granted that without Raffles,[8] the fortunes of Tengku Husain and Temenggong 'Abdu'r-Rahman would probably not have changed and they would have continued eking out their living on Pulau Penyengat or Singapore. But their decision to enter into treaties with Raffles provided the British with a modicum of a locus standi in an area the Dutch considered to be within their sphere of control. "Mynheer", Raffles wrote to Charles Assey in England, "will probably enter into a paper war on the subject but we may, I think, combat their arguments without any difficulty. They had established themselves at Rhio, and by virtue of a Treaty, which they had forced the Raja of that place to sign, they assume a right of excluding us from all the islands and declaring the people their vassals. The legitimate successor to the empire of Johor is with us, and on the ruins of the ancient capital, has signed a Treaty with us which places Singapore and the neighbouring islands under protection".[9] The intentions of Tengku Husain and Temenggong 'Abdu'r-Rahman in deciding to enter into treaties with Raffles therefore deserves better recognition. For without their decision to ally with the British, Raffles may well have not located in Singapore the East India Company factory he was authorised to establish. This essay attempts to reconstruct a context for Tengku Husain's actions in signing the 6 February 1819 treaty and, more significantly, the 2 August 1824 treaty ceding Singapore in perpetuity to the British.

Raffles, Farquhar and the Choice of Singapore for an East India Company Factory

William Farquhar could not be unaware of these differences and tensions within the Johor *istana* after he left Pulau Penyengat in August 1818 and negotiating with the Bugis Yamtuan Muda a commercial treaty awarding the British most-favoured nation privileges. It would appear that the Yamtuan Muda might have tacitly welcomed a British presence in the area to counter a growing Dutch presence that he was apparently finding constraining. He agreed to Farquhar's 15 October 1818 request

---

7 "The Temenggong and the newly elevated Sultan Husain", Christopher Wake surmised, "had good reason to be pleased with themselves in January 1819. The British alliance transformed the balance of power within the Johor empire", in his "Raffles and the Rajas; The Founding of Singapore in Malayan and British Colonial History", *JMBRAS* 48, 1 (1975): 61. Carl A. Trocki, *Prince of Pirates: The Temenggongs and the Development of Johor and Singapore 1784–1885* (Singapore: Singapore University Press, 1979), p. 45, writes: "the coming of Raffles and William Farquhar in 1819 was a godsend for the Temenggong. It gave him a change to enter into a privileged relationship with another important European power".

8 As Swettenham argued counterfactually, "if there had been no Raffles in 1819, there would have been no British Singapore today". F.A. Swettenham, *British Malaya: An Account of the Origin and Progress of British Influence in Malaya* (London: Allen & Unwin, 1955), p. 71.

9 Quoted in C.E. Wurtzburg, *Raffles of the Eastern Isles* (London: Hodder Stoughton, 1954), p. 506.

to explore the suitability of the Karimun for a British post.[10] Strangely, it was not Singapore that Farquhar asked for, since he was supposed to have been secretly negotiating with Tengku Husain for it, and was later to claim that he was the one who advised Raffles to consider it for the location of the East India Company factory that he had received Calcutta's approval to establish. Geographically, Farquhar was right to look first to the Karimun for a strategic location to check Dutch influence in the area. The Karimun controlled not only the approach to the Main Straits past Singapore, but also to the Durian Straits which led south to Bangka and on to the Sunda Straits and the Java Sea. Lying directly north of the Kampar River mouth, the Karimun also controlled access to the Kampar and the Minangkabau highlands the river leads to. So it was to Karimun that Farquhar led Raffles to explore in January 1819.

But sailing around the Karimun for three days failed to locate a suitable location for the proposed East India Company factory. The records are equivocal on how Singapore then came to be selected. It is not clear that Raffles, as Lady Sophia Raffles and later biographers claim, had thought of Singapore as early as 1817 and went to the Karimun "out of courtesy"[11] to Farquhar who later registered a claim to be the one to suggest that "they stopped on the 19th [sic] January at Singapore, then the residence of a native prince called the Tumung'gong of Johor".[12] Farquhar, in the Malay social memory, was the mastermind for bringing the British to Singapore. He had been meeting the Malay chieftains, among who was Tengku Husain. He corresponded with the Tengku and according to Abdullah bin Kadir,[13] may have been promised Singapore in return for which he paid Tengku Husain "a great deal of money". Raffles' meeting Temenggong 'Abdu'r-Rahman on 28 January 1819 was therefore not serendipity, but foresight of Farquhar.

The decision to search further for a suitable location was made after dinner on 27 January on board Raffles' ship the *Indiana*. Raffles may have had in mind a site in the estuary of the Johor River where he was aware the Johor *istana* was earlier located. But it was Raffles' hydrographer, Captain Daniel Ross, according to his assistant Captain J.G.F. Crawford, who pointed out to Raffles after dinner on 27 January "a spot [on the navigation chart] he considered more eligible than Karimun] in point of harbour, cleared of jungle and advantageous for trade to the north east of St John's Island which he had observed, on our passage to China, when it was agreed we should in the morning get under weigh and examine this port before deciding on

[10] Farquhar's letter to the Yamtuan Muda is cited by E. Netscher, *De Nederlanders in Djohor en Siak, 1602 tot 1865; Historische beschrijving*, Verhandelingen Bataviaasch Genootschap 35 (Batavia: Bruining & Wijt, 1870), p. 266.

[11] Lady Sophia Raffles, *Memoir of the Life and Public Services of Sir Thomas Stamford Raffles*, repr. ed. (Singapore: Oxford University Press, 1991), p. 370; Wurtzburg, *Raffles of the Eastern Isles*, p. 454, also concludes that Raffles had Singapore in his mind for a long time.

[12] Farquhar's claim is contained in his memorial to the Court of Directors of the Hon. Company, quoted in D.C. Boulger, *The Life of Sir Stamford Raffles*, repr. ed. (Singapore: Graham Brash), pp. 353–5.

[13] A.H. Hill, trans., *The Hikayat Abdullah; The Autobiography of Abdullah bin Abdul Kadir (1797–1854)*, repr. ed. (Singapore: Oxford University Press, 1969), p. 140.

any other".[14] It was to St John's Island that they sailed on 28 January where they anchored for the night before landing on Singapore the following day for what has become a historic meeting with Temenggong 'Abdu'r-Rahman.[15]

Tengku Husain: "Lord of the Straits"

Tengku Husain must have been pleased with the news that the orang laut Batin Sapi and his sons brought to him at the end of January 1819. The news they brought from the temenggong on Singapore was that the British were in Singapore and prepared to recognise him as sultan of Johor in return for the right to establish a *loji* or factory on the island. Within the social memory[16] of the temenggong and Tengku Husain, a British presence was to be welcomed for reasons not too different from those which led Tengku Husain's forebears to link up with the Dutch to besiege the Portuguese in Melaka, or call in the Bugis to help oust the usurper Raja Kecik or the Illunun to get rid of the Dutch. Tengku Husain probably perceived the British as a counter to Dutch support for the Bugis and his diffident brother 'Abdu'r-Rahman, and hoped that with British backing he could establish a new *negeri* on Singapore.

In crossing the straits, or *menyeberang*, a term that connotes more than physically crossing a body of water, Tengku Husain was following the footsteps of his father and forefathers. Sultan Mahmud had no compunction abandoning his *istana* in Bintan to move to Lingga, where he established a new *istana* at Daik when he found the Dutch Resident imposed on him by the 1784 treaty he was forced to sign too demanding. In relocating to Diak, Sultan Mahmud was also accentuating the scission in the political power of the kingdom created in 1722 when the Malay heir to the throne, Raja Sulaiman, recruited Bugis warriors to help him drive out the Minangkabau usurper Raja Kecik. As reward for their success, the sultan's office of

---

[14] Quoted by Wurtzburg, *Raffles of the Eastern Isles*, p. 483.

[15] Dr John Crawfurd, who first visited Singapore in February 1822 and then became its second resident, and should therefore have personal memories of the background to the founding of Singapore, recorded in his 1856 *A Descriptive Dictionary of the Indian Islands & Adjacent Countries*, repr. ed. (Kuala Lumpur: Oxford University Press, 1971), p. 407, that "in the first instance the island of Singapore did not occur, either to (Raffles) or anyone else ... The first place thought of was Rhio, but it was found to be already in the occupation of the Netherland government. The next was the Carimon Islands, out, however, of the convenient tract of navigation, and here, Sir Stamford and his expedition tarried three days, but found the place unsuitable. The river of Johor was then thought of, but on the way to it, the expedition touched at Singapore to make enquiries, and then for the first time, the advantages and superiority of its locality presented themselves".

[16] The French sociologist Maurice Halbwachs has shown how our personal memories can only function within a social memory of the society we are members of and how these memories—personal and collective—shapes our identity of who we are as a community and our behaviour and actions in his *The Collective Memory*, trans. F.J. Ditter, Jr. and V.Y. Ditter (New York: Harper & Row, 1980) and *Les cadres sociaux de la mémoire*, trans. L.A. Coser, *On Collective Memory* (Chicago: Chicago University Press, 1992). The continuity and centrality of social memories in the Riaus today is investigated by Vivienne Wee, "Melayu: Hierarchies of Being in Riau", unpublished PhD dissertation, Australian National University, 1985.

Yang Dipertuan, "he who is made lord" was split between the Bugis who became the *Yang Dipertuan muda*, the "junior lord" or "Underking" in the contemporary European records, and the Malay *Yang Dipertuan besar*, the "senior lord". Over the decades after 1722 the Bugis lineage rose to dominate the *istana*, becoming the defacto ruler of the realm.[17]

This scission of power that Tengku Husain was perpetuating was not peculiar to Johor. Perak in 1746 and between 1773 and 1788 was also divided between a ruler living upstream (*hulu*) and a ruler living downstream (*hilir*) the Perak River. For much of the period from the late 16th to the early 19th centuries Barus on the north-west coast of Sumatra was also ruled by two families living "upstream" and downstream" of the Batu Garigis River.[18] The Minangkabau heartland was split in a succession dispute in 1674 when the sultan died and the realm divided between his nephew and his adopted son. The underlying theme of the history of the northeast Sumatra kingdoms of Pasai and Semudra is their rivalry between their rulers who were descendants of two brothers.

Such divisions in Malay royalty, leading to the creation of two royal families in one kingdom was however antithetic to the classical Malay world view of itself as a *kerajaan*, the condition of having a *raja*.[19] The classical Malay texts are clear that a society without a *raja* as its focal point, and against which Malays define who they are, is a society in "utter confusion" (*sangatlah huru-haranya*). Similarly, having more than one *raja* also creates confusion and disarray. The Perak text the *Misa Melayu* describes the events of 1746 leading to "*negeri sebuah, Raja dua*" [one realm, two rulers] as *huru-hara*. The Bugis *Tuhfat al-Nafis* equates Raja Kecik's seizure of the Johor throne to creating two kings in one kingdom like "a *perahu* with two captains". It remains then for the texts like the *Hikayat Raja-Raja Pasai* to rationalise these divisions of royalty through arguments of which royal family has a more impeccable lineage, commands more wealth and whose *istana* is a better exemplar and therefore a better claim to be the *kerajaan*.

This fundamental issue of the indivisibility of the *raja* and the unity of the *kerajaan* must have weighed heavily on Tengku Husain and Temenggong 'Abdu'r-Rahman. It is expressed in a series of letters the new Sultan Husain and Temenggong 'Abdu'r-Rahman despatched to Sultan 'Abdu'r-Rahman at Lingga, to the Yamtuan Muda Raja Ja'far at Bintan and to Engku Sayid. The contents of these letters

---

[17] The *Tuhfat al-Nafis* narrative of these events by Raja Ali Haji, the Bugis champion of Malay language and culture, has become part of the standard interpretation of Johor-Riau history. But the *Tuhfat* is an essentially Bugis version of these events which reduces the Malay role in their history. Virginia Matheson in her "Strategies of Survival: the Malay Royal Line of Lingga-Riau", *JSEAS* 17, 1 (1986): 5–38 summarises a 1930 Malay draft *Keringkasan Sedjarah Melayu* attempt to counter-balance the *Tuhfat* version of their history and reassert their identity.

[18] Jane Drakard, *A Malay Frontier; Unity and Duality in a Sumatran Kingdom* (Ithaca, NY: Cornell University South East Asia Program, 1990) on the hilir/hulu duality in Barus. More generally, J. Kathirithamby-Wells, "Hulu-hilir unity and conflict: Malay statecraft in East Sumatra before the mid-nineteenth century", *Archipel* 45 (1993): 77–96.

[19] Anthony Milner argues for the centrality of the *raja* as the idiom through which Malays experienced the world in his *Kerajaan: Malay Political Culture on the Eve of Colonial Rule*, Association of Asian Studies, monograph 40 (Tucson, AZ: University of Arizona Press, 1982).

are about how Tengku Husain hurriedly left Bintan to check a report from the temenggong that a flotilla of British ships had appeared in Singapore waters. According to the temenggong, he could not resist the British landing and erecting quarters for themselves. Tengku Husain, when he arrived in Singapore, was detained by Stamford Raffles who then installed him as a Raja with the title Sultan Husain Shah and gave him a seal acknowledging his new title. The underlying tone of these letters is that both the temenggong and Tengku Husain could not resist the British and therefore had no choice but to comply with Raffles' intentions. The new sultan informs that he was not even allowed to return to Bintan to fetch his family to Singapore and asked the Yamtuan Muda permission for them to depart Bintan.[20]

From his brother and the Yamtuan Besar, the new Sultan Husain begged forgiveness for his actions and assured he intended no harm. To Sultan 'Abdu'r-Rahman he writes that "although your brother may comply with the British, never fear, nor entertain the least suspicion that he intends to do anything that will cause future ill-will or animosity". From the Yamtuan Muda, Tengku Husain "asks pardon and forgiveness, hoping that it will be granted. Your son is his father's son in this world and the world to come; he will never do anything against his father nor abandon him". The thrust of these letters appears to be to assure that Tengku Husain's installation as sultan by Raffles and his accepting it (under duress) is not a challenge to his brother and the Yamtuan Muda. In their translated form[21] these letters clearly addresses Sultan 'Abdu'r-Rahman as *Yang Dipertuan besar* and Raja Ja'far as *Yang Dipertuan muda*. More significant, Tengku Husain does not use his new title, but refers to himself as the *Yang Dipertuan* of Singapore" in his letters. Tengku Husain is therefore not challenging his brother for the title of *Yang Dipertuan besar* and

---

[20] These letters became ammunition for the Dutch to challenge Raffles' arguments for his settlement on Singapore in ensuring "paper war" between the Dutch and English. The letters were cited by the Dutch governor-general Van der Capellen in his 25 March 1819 letter to his English counterpart reproduced by P.H. van der Kemp in his "De Singapoorsche papieroorlog", *BKI* 49 (1898): 496.

[21] T. Braddell provided a translation of three of these letters (Temenggong to the Yamtuan Muda; Husain to Sultan 'Abdu'r-Rahman and to the Yamtuan Muda) in his "Notices of Singapore" in J.R. Logan's *Journal of the Indian Archipelago and Eastern Asia* 9 (1855): 444–6. These "Notices" reproduced official reports and documents Braddell had collected with the intent of writing a history of the early years of the Straits Settlement, which he unfortunately never did. They are reproduced by C.B. Buckley in *An Anecdotal History of Old Times in Singapore 1819–1867*, repr. of 1902 ed. (Singapore: Oxford University Press 1984), pp. 50–1. Netscher collated seven letters in his *De Nederlanders in Djohor en Siak*, pp. 269–73. More recently, Hj. Buyong Adil reproduced three of these letters in his *Sejarah Johor* (Kuala Lumpur: Dewan Bahasa dan Pustaka, 1980), pp. 191–3. Unfortunately in these translations the formal salutations and Arabic exordium that preceded the main texts of the letters have been omitted. In the world of Malay letters these "compliments" often critically determined the relative status of sender and recipient of the letter. See Anabelle Teh Gallop and B. Arps, *Golden Letters; Writing Traditions of Indonesia/Surat Emas: Budaya tulis di Indonesia* (London: British Library and Jakarta: Yayasan Lontar, 1991), pp. 51–8, and transcription of the letters displayed in this exhibition catalogue on pp. 127–40. Also see R.J. Wilkinson, "Notes on Malay Letter Writing", in R.O. Winstedt, *Malay Grammar* (Oxford: Clarendon Press, 1939), pp. 183–205, and A.T. Gallop, *The Legacy of the Malay Letter: Warisan warkah Melayu* (London: British Library, 1994).

continues to acknowledge Raja Ja'far as the *Yang Dipertuan muda*. Tengku Husain is only claiming to be the *Yang Dipertuan* of Singapore.

Tengku Husain and the temenggong appear to have convinced the *istanas* at Lingga and Penyengat of their good intentions. The legendary Raja Ali Haji ibn Ahmad recorded these events of January 1819 some five decades later in his *Tuhfat al-Nafis* without rancour:[22] "Engku Temenggong ... then sent Raja Ambung to Riau to fetch Tengku Lung [Husain], and when Raja Ambung met Tengku Lung he informed him of all the secret plans of Mr Raffles, Colonel Farquhar, and the Temenggong. Tengku Lung was amenable and when night fell he set sail with Raja Ambung for Singapore. When he arrived, the temenggong and Mr Farquhar took him aboard the warship to meet Mr Raffles, who honoured Tengku Lung in the way kings are honoured, by firing cannon, beating drums, and so forth. Afterwards he was taken below and given a chair sitting beside Mr Raffles and Mr Farquhar. Mr Raffles told him everything, using courteous words, advising him, and paying him delicate compliments. And Tengku Lung agreed to whatever Mr Raffles proposed, and so the affair was settled, and the discussions and agreements were put into effect". Significantly, Raja Ali Haji did not perceive Tengku Lung's actions as causing "confusion" [*huru-hara*] by creating two *rajas* in one kingdom. For in the view of Raja Ali Haji, Tengku Husain was installed not as sultan of Johor, but as "Sultan Husain Syah, son of the late Sultan Mahmud Syah in the state of Singapore and all its subject territories".[23] Hereafter Raja Ali Haji refers to Tengku Husain in the *Tuhfat* as the "Yang Dipertuan selat", the "Lord of the Straits", never as Sultan Husain. The indivisibility of the *raja* and the unity of the *kerajaan* were preserved. Sultan 'Abdu'r-Rahman was still *Yang Dipertuan besar* at Lingga and Raja Ja'far the *Yang Dipertuan muda* at Penyengat while Tengku Husain was the *Yang Dipertuan selat* at Singapore.

That the *istana* on Pulau Penyengat continued to be the seat of the *kerajaan*, the focal centre of the kingdom, appeared to have been accepted by Tengku Husain and Temenggong 'Abdu'r-Rahman and his descendants. In 1868, Abu Bakar, the grandson of Temenggong 'Abdu'r-Rahman thought it appropriate to petition the Riau *istana* for a royal title even before approaching the British to formally recognise him as "Maharaja of Johor". Sir Richard Winstedt summarises a Malay manuscript account of this petition to the Riau *istana*:[24]

> On 18 April 1869, Abu Bakar sent his cousin Engku Haji Muhammad and his Dato' Bentara (Ja'far bin Haji Muhammad) to Riau to that genealogist and prolific historian Raja Haji 'Ali to needle the way to the Yamtuan Muda and enquire if the Temenggongs could now assume 'sovereign power'—which in fact they had assumed already, but at Riau it was a euphemism for a 'royal title.' The envoys

[22] Quoted from Virginia Matheson and Barbara Watson Andaya, trans., *The Precious Gift* (Tuhfat al-Nafis) (Kuala Lumpur: Oxford University Press, 1982), pp. 227–8.

[23] The Malay text reads: "Tuan Gebernur Jenderal Benggal mengangkat Tengku Long bergelar Sultan Husin Syah bin al-Marhum Sultan Mahmud Syah di dalam negeri Singapura rantau takluk jajahannya", in Virginia Matheson, ed., *Tuhfat al-Nafis* (Kuala Lumpur: Penerbit Fajar Bakti, 1982), p. 278.

[24] Winstedt, "History of Johore", pp. 108–9.

> met that student of Islamic mysticism, the Yamtuan Muda, in his half-finished stone palace, partook of cakes and coffee, talked of the wonders of London and the powers of the white man ... They scanned Raja Haji's genealogies and talked of the time of the first Bendahara sultan, son of Tun Habib. The critical historian put some shrewd questions to the visitors. Was Johor ever the property of Sultan Husain, seeing that his brother was sultan of Lingga? Why had Sultan Husain delayed appointing a successor to Temenggong 'Abdu'r-Rahman? Who installed Sultan 'Ali [on the death of his father Sultan Husain] and did the English inform all Malay rulers as was the custom? ... On the last day the oracle spoke, 'Tell the Temenggong to study all my genealogies. I and the Yamtuan Muda would like him to become Raja. It can be done, if he will let the Yamtuan Muda go to Singapore and install him. The Bendahara too, can be made Raja, but it would be difficult. If the Temenggong's people want it, that will be one good reason. Try and persuade Sultan 'Ali also to agree. But we must call the Temenggong by some name other than sultan or Yamtuan, and I must come to Teluk Blanga to arrange things.' On 7 May Raja Haji 'Ali and his son arrived; they were taken to see the noonday gun fired from the Fort [Canning]; they saw gas for the first time; after twelve days they left for Riau with the present of a twin-screw steamer from the Temenggong. On 30 Jun Abu Bakar wrote to the Governor, Sir Harry Ord, thanking Her Majesty's Government for acceding to his wish to be styled Maharaja.

The 1824 Anglo-Dutch Treaty may have politically divided the Johor *kerajaan* but it would appear from this event, not its cultural and social unity.

18.2 Rade de Sincapour [Harbour of Singapore]. Jules-Sébastien-César Dumont d'Urville, *Voyage pittoresque autour du monde; resumé general des voyages de découvertes, de Magellan, Tasman, Dampier* [*et autres*]. Paris: L. Tenré, 1834–35. © Peter Borschberg, private collection.

Kerajaan Singapura versus Honourable Company Factory[25]

The 6 February 1819 treaty, Dr John Crawfurd was to subsequently point out, "amounted to little more than a permission for the formation of a British factory and establishment, along two miles of the northern shore, and inland to the extent of the point-blank range of a cannon shot. There was in reality no territorial cession giving a legal right of legislation. The only law which could have existed was the Malay code. The native chief was considered to be the proprietor of the land, even within the bounds of the British factory, and he was to be entitled, in perpetuity, to one-half of such duties of customs as might hereafter be levied at the port".[26] The newly elevated Sultan Husain and Temenggong 'Abdu'r-Rahman appeared to have little doubt that Singapore in 1819 was a new *negeri* they ruled. William Farquhar, as the first Resident, attempted to administer the new settlement within the framework of this 6 February 1819 treaty.[27] However, this was not the view of Stamford Raffles. For him Singapore was *his* "new colony [that] thrives most rapidly". In a letter to Colonel Addenbrooke, Raffles claimed Singapore as his "child … which in every way it can be viewed, bids fair to be one of the most important … which we possess".[28] A series of differences between the Malays and the British was inevitable given these different perceptions of Singapore.

One issue was the "presents" (*hantar-hantaran*) the sultan and temenggong from the captains of vessels calling at Singapore, as was the custom at other Southeast Asian ports. It was a practice contrary to British principles, but both Raffles and Farquhar had to initially condone lest they antagonise Sultan Husain and the temenggong. The compromise was that the *nakodas* of native vessels will continue to call on the sultan and temenggong with "presents" but this was optional for the captains of British and other European vessels. They need only pay their respects to the sultan and the temenggong when they reported to the Master Attendant. Another was the administration of justice which was resolved by creating a "Council" of three (resident, sultan and temenggong, or their representatives) meeting weekly in the courthouse to hear complaints and cases. Slavery and debt-bondage, one of the traditional institutions of a *kerajaan*, was yet another issue between the sultan, the temenggong and Raffles and Crawfurd.[29]

---

[25] The East India Company found that in contrast to its operations in Europe, its "factors" or agents in Asia needed secure, protected premises against vagaries of local conditions from which to operate. These fortified settlements near or enclaves within Asian cities were "factories" which eventually linked up to form a system through which the Company ran its Asian operations.

[26] Crawfurd's remarks on the 1819 treaty are contained in his *Journal of an Embassy from the Governor General of India to the Courts of Siam and Cochin China*, repr. 1828 ed. (Kuala Lumpur: Oxford University Press, 1967), p. 566. Crawfurd stopped in Singapore in 1822 on this mission to Siam. Crawfurd's remarks have been reproduced by Buckley, *Anecdotal History*, p. 40.

[27] Wake, "Raffles and the Rajas", p. 63, described it as a "condominium of Company officials and Malay rajas".

[28] In a letter to the Duchess of Somerset on his third visit to Singapore in June 1819 in Lady Raffles, *Memoir*, p. 383; letter to Addenbrooke on ibid., p. 379.

[29] Wake, "Raffles and the Rajas", pp. 62–3.

For Sultan Husain and Temenggong 'Abdu'r-Rahman, Singapore was their *negeri* from which they were fully entitled to a share of its wealth because their presence created and defined the settlement. As a *negeri*, Singapore was not defined by the boundaries demarcated by the British in their treaties and memorandums with Sultan Husain, but by his very presence. The *Sejarah Melayu* and other classical texts argue that the *raja* was society; that he personified it and gave it form and purpose. Without a *raja* society dissolves into chaos. It was a view that Tengku Husain almost certainly subscribed to and may have believed his presence was sufficient to create a new *negeri* on Singapore in February 1819. The sultan was the link between the world of the gods and the world of men. At his coronation the sultan was, and still is, crowned as a representative of Indra, King of the Gods, in the world of mortals. He is also the "shadow of Allah" on earth. Spiritual salubrity flowed from his actions at the apex of society. From him all wealth emanated and to him all wealth flowed. That wealth was however not actively and overtly sought, as a merchant seeks wealth. To seek wealth is to demonstrate a lack of status and prowess as sultan. Sultan Husain's reply to Raffles' proposal that he supplements the Honourable Company's allowances to him through trade sums up this view of the sultan: "It is not the custom of rulers to engage in trade for they would lose their dignity before other rulers."[30]

In the Malay *negeri* wealth from taxes and tribute was not to be accumulated as capital and power, but to be expended or *belanja* on building and maintaining networks of allies and retinues. For political influence and control in the geographically fragmented island world of the Malay *negeri* was and is, difficult to institutionalise. Ecological constraints on population size and density created small, highly mobile self-sufficient communities that were difficult to control except through a network of kingship ties and alliances. Political power therefore flowed from patronage of a network of kin-related alliances and the prowess to lead and move these networks of alliances and retinues.

Sultan Husain's expectations of establishing a new *negeri* with British support were however to be rapidly shattered. The British were not to be like the Dutch, who did not dominate the Riaus although they had been in the area for 35 years.[31] Sultan Husain and Temenggong 'Abdu'r-Rahman should have recognised the growth of the Country Trade or private trade in the latter half of the 18th century and realised their need for a base after they lost Bintan as a base for their private trading operations.[32] It was these country traders who pressured the East India Company to reverse its policy of refusing to establish and maintain new factories in the Straits

---

[30] Abdullah bin Kadir reports the sultan's reply to Raffles' proposal that he goes into trading, *Hikayat Abdullah*, trans. A.H. Hill, repr. ed. (Kuala Lumpur: Oxford University Press 1969), p. 163. Milner, *Kerajaan*, pp. 20ff, demonstrates the importance of wealth in Malay society and argues that it was more an attribute than resource of the sultan.

[31] Dianne Lewis, *Jan Companie in the Straits of Malacca, 1641–1795* (Athens, OH: Ohio University Press, 1995); R.C. Vos, *Gentle Janus, Merchant Prince: The VOC and the Tightrope of Diplomacy in the Malay World, 1740–1800* (Leiden: KITLV Press, 1993).

[32] Dianne Lewis, "The Growth of the Country Trade to the Straits of Malacca, 1760–1777", *JMBRAS* 43, 2 (1970): 114–29.

of Melaka.[33] These country traders and the East India Company combined to build up a much larger and more dominant presence than Sultan Husain and Temenggong 'Abdu'r-Rahman anticipated. Both were no match for a British empire that emerged after the depression and setbacks of the 1770s and was at the height of its power.[34] Stamford Raffles and John Crawfurd epitomised this resurgent British empire in their imperious dealings with Sultan Husain and Temenggong 'Abdu'r-Rahman and other Malay and Javanese rulers and reagents.

The "sweet words" that Raffles spoke to Tengku Husain on 6 February 1819 was not born out in his deeds. He consistently referred to Singapore as "his" colony that he was shaping. The provisions of the 6 February treat were temporary expedients while Britain resolved its relations with the continent. On his three visits Raffles attempted to put the government of Singapore on what he considered a "proper" footing.[35] On his June 1819 visit, Raffles negotiated a new arrangement on the administration of Singapore. On his last visit before his final departure for England, Raffles negotiated a second memorandum on the administration of Singapore which formalised his efforts to curtail and reduce the power and influence of the sultan and temenggong granted by the 6 February 1819 treaty.

1824: Demise of a *Kerajaan*

Dr John Crawfurd, whom Stamford Raffles appointed Resident, taking over from William Farquhar, continued a number of Raffles' plans for Singapore while discontinuing others. Among the plans he continued was the reduction of the sultan's and temenggong's influence in government. He questioned the sums paid to them under the June 1823 agreement on the government of Singapore, claiming that the agreement had never been ratified by Calcutta, and payments made under that agreement were therefore unauthorised. Crawfurd attempted to recover the sums "unlawfully" paid by stopping all payments to the sultan and temenggong from 1 June 1824. Crawfurd then proposed that they cede Singapore to the British in return for the cancellation of their "debts", resumption of payments under the terms of the February 1819 treaty and a lump sum payment of Sp. $20,000. Negotiations over this British offer for Singapore's future were apparently difficult, with the sultan threatening at one point to leave the settlement. Lack of funds is perceived to be the factor that finally forced Sultan Husain and Temenggong 'Abdu'r-Rahman to give in to Crawfurd and signed away Singapore on 2 August 1824.

---

[33] Dianne Lewis, "British Policy in the Straits of Malacca to 1819 and the Collapse of the Traditional Malay State Structure", in *Empires, Imperialism and Southeast Asia: Essays in Honour of Nicholas Tarling*, ed. B. Barrington (Clayton: Monash Asia Institute, 1997), pp. 17–33.
[34] *The Founding of the Second British Empire, 1763–1793* (London: Longman, 1952–64) as Victor Harlow termed it, may not have been that liberal reformist as many historians make it out to be; but more a reflection of the neo-absolutism of 18th century Europe and Britain. C.A. Bayly, *Imperial Meridian; The British Empire and the World, 1780–1830* (London: Longman, 1989).
[35] These reforms to put the administration of Singapore on a "proper footing" was driven as much by Raffles' disregard for the Malay chieftains as his dislike for Farquhar. See Wake's review of Raffles moves against the Malay chieftains and Farquhar in "Raffles and the Rajas", pp. 64–8.

On that morning Sultan Husain and Temenggong 'Abdu'r-Rahman drove up Government Hill, as Fort Canning was then known, to call on Dr John Crawfurd at his official residence. The ensuring scene is described by Abdullah bin Abdul Kadir, who appears to have heard enough about the meeting to offer the following reconstruction of what transpired.[36] "On arrival they were greeted by Mr Crawfurd and invited into his house where they sat down. After they had been seated for a few moments, Mr Crawfurd said 'Is it true that Your Highness is ready to accede to the wishes of the Governor-General?' The sultan said 'It is true.' Then Mr Crawfurd asked the temenggong who also gave his assent. After that Mr Crawfurd took two pieces of parchment out his writing-box saying 'This is a copy of the agreement for Your Highness and this one for the temenggong. May Your Highness be pleased to listen while I explain its provisions to you in Malay. This document is to certify that I, Sultan Husain Shah ibn Al-Marhum Sultan Mahmud Shah, ruler of the Kingdoms of Johor and Pahang, whose sovereignty extends over the settlement of Singapore, do sincerely declare in this Treaty of my own free will I have ceded this Settlement of Singapore and all authority over it to the East India Company.'"

As with the 6 February 1819 treaty which we have a detail account of British intentions in signing the treaty, but not a Malay version of why they signed that treaty, so too with the 2 August 1824 treaty. Dr John Crawfurd's rational for the treaty he persuaded or pressured the sultan and the temenggong into signing are fairly clear. In a memorandum to George Swinton, Secretary to Government at Fort William in Bengal, Crawfurd demeaned the character and capabilities of Sultan Husain and his temenggong, depreciated their contributions to the administration of the port and recommended they be paid off. Crawfurd though the sultan and the temenggong got more from port duties and tributes or gifts and profits on monopolies and revenue farms than they contributed to the development and well being of the settlement and argued this should be rectified.[37] But the sultan and the temenggong have not left similar records of their rational for signing away Singapore for 33,200 Spanish dollars (Sp. $) and a monthly stipend of Sp. $1,300 for life for the sultan; and Sp. $26,800 to the temenggong with a monthly stipend of Sp. $700. The sums of money were unattractive and they bargained with Crawfurd for three months for more. Was it finally their increasingly urgent need for money which lead them to consider Singapore insignificant enough to sign away?

The answer to the preceding issue may well lie in attempting to understand how Tengku Husain interpreted the title of sultan of Johor accorded to him by the British and his own claim to be the *Yang Dipertuan selat*. Did he conceive of himself as ruler of a clearly demarcated territory, or "lord" of a defined stretch of sea? In the worldview of the *kerajaan*, it is the sultan or *raja* who is more significant than the territory of the *negeri*. A *negeri* without a sultan or *raja* is by not by definition a *negeri*. The *Sejarah Melayu* account of Sultan Muhmud's dilemma after losing Melaka to the Portuguese and moving to Bintan where he attempted to re-establish himself and was again besieged by the Portuguese, establishes this priority in the

[36] *Hikayat Abdullah*, 1969 reprint of A.H. Hill's translation, pp. 218–21.

[37] The text of Crawfurd's 3 Aug. 1824 memorandum to Calcutta is reproduced by Buckley in his *Anecdotal History*, pp. 170–3.

relationship of a sultan to the territory of his *negeri*. The Sri Nara Diraja urged him [the sultan] to leave Bentan now that the city had fallen. But he replied, "it is the custom of Rajas that when their country falls to the foe, they die". And the Sri Nara Diraja said, "Your Highness is mistaken. Every country has a Raja, and if Your Highness is granted length of days, we can find ten countries for you."[38]

The Portuguese in 1511 therefore captured only the empty shell of a entrepôt, for in the mindset of the *Sejarah Melayu*, the structure of Malay power was the network of allegiances binding the sultan and the aristocracy and their subjects which Sultan Muhmud carried with him on his flight through the jungles of Pahang to the court of his cousin in Pahang and then to Bintan. Sultan Muhmud was however not "granted the length of days" to establish a new *negeri*. It fell to his son, Sultan 'Ala'u'd-din to bring this network of allegiances with him up the Sungei Johor to its junction with the Sungei Serting, where he established a new *negeri* which would reclaim the glory of Melaka. From his new *negeri* 'Ala'u'd-din and his successors ventured forth into the Straits of Melaka to alternately challenge the Portuguese and the Achenese for control of Melaka Straits shipping and trade. When attacked by the Portuguese or Achenese the Johor sultans withdrew with their people into the jungle to re-emerge further upstream or downstream to they built a new *istana*.[39]

Sultan Husain and Temenggong 'Abdu'r-Rahman were probably aware that their forebears never fought to the last warrior to defend their *istanas* along the Johor River. In the under populated Malay world of the Melaka Straits, people were more important than land. Attracting and holding the loyalties of people was more critical than controlling land, which in the Malay perception, was just occupied and used, but not owned or inherited. W.H. Maxwell's explanation of Malay land tenure is that "land is abundant, but the population sparse; there is no restriction upon the selection and appropriation of forest land, and a propriety right is created by the clearing of the land *followed by continuous occupation*. Forest land and land which, though once cleared, has been abandoned and bears no trace of appropriation (such as fruit trees still existing) are said technically to be *tanah mati* or 'dead land'. He who, by clearing or cultivation, or by building a house, causes that to live which was dead (*meng-hidop-kan bumi*) acquires a propriety right in the land, which now becomes *tanah hidop* ('live land')."[40]

If this was Sultan Husain's and the temenggong's memory of the value of land, then the island of Singapore which Raffles made much of its strategic location, was of no great significance. After all, Sultan Husain's great-grandfather, the Bendahara

---

[38] *Sejarah Melayu* is quoted from C.C. Brown's translation of Raffles MS 18 in *JMBRAS* 25, 2–3 (1952): 189; Malay text transcribed by R.O. Winstedt and revised by Abdul Rahman Hj. Ismail, repr. ed. 17 (Kuala Lumpur: MBRAS, 1998), p. 294.

[39] 'Ala'u'd-din's venture is described in detail in the "long" version of the *Sejarah Melayu* (which concludes with mention of the 1673 Jambi attack on Johor), ed. W. Shellabear, *Sejarah Melayu* (Kuala Lumpur: Oxford University Press, 1967). The archaeological evidence for the peregrination of the Johor sultans along the Johor River is reviewed by C.A. Gibson-Hill, "Johore Lama and other ancient sites on the Johore River", *JMBRAS* 28, 2 (1955): 127–97.

[40] Maxwell, "The Laws and Customs of the Malays with Reference to the Tenure of Land", *JSBRAS* 13 (1884): 77–9.

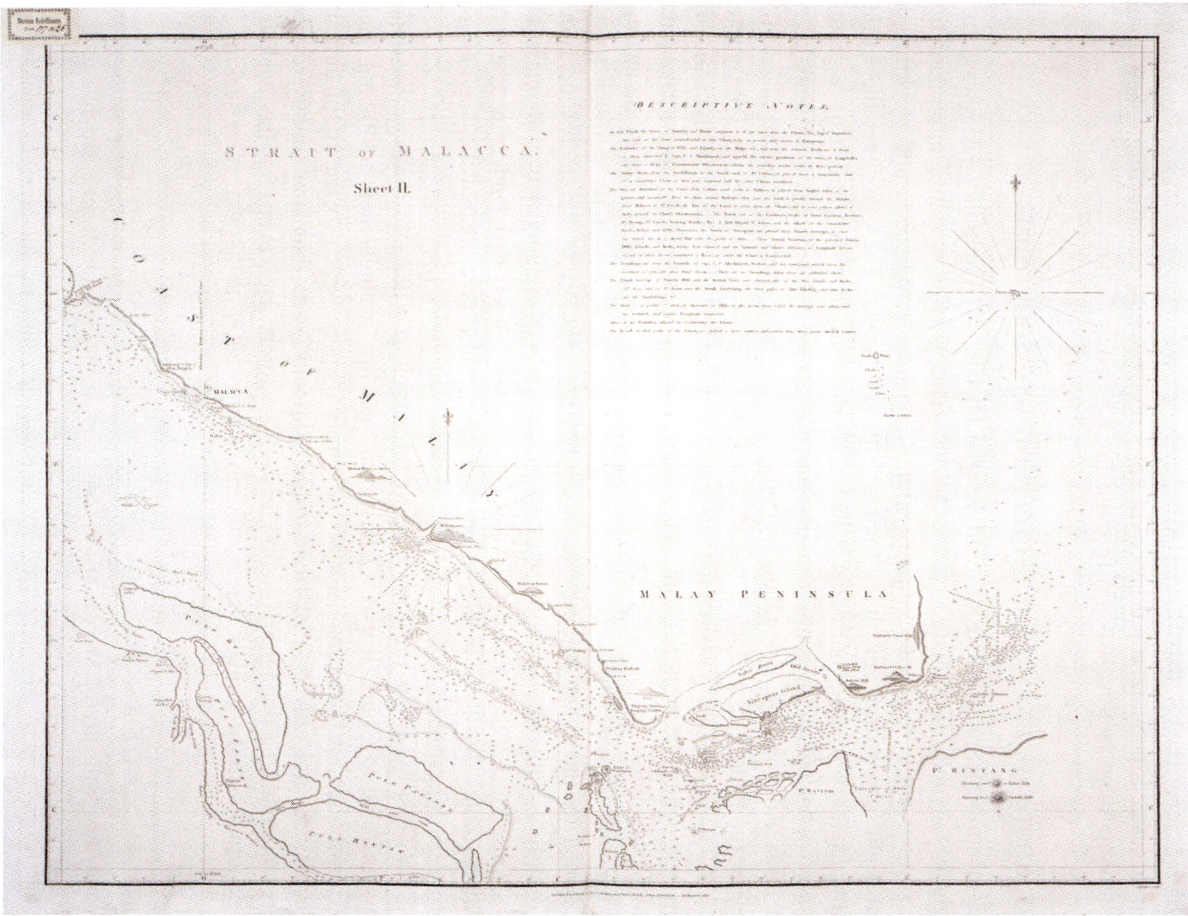

18.3 Strait of Malacca, Sheet II. James Horsburgh, 1823. Leiden University Library, H1823 177-26.

Sultan 'Abdu'l-Jalil, to whom the Johor sultans traced their ancestry, rated Singapore insignificant enough to be offered as a present to an English trader with whom he was fairly well acquainted with. Captain Alexander Hamilton recorded the offer in his travelogue: "In Anno 1703 I called at Johor on my Way to China, and he [the sultan] treated me very kindly, and made me a present of the island of Singapore, but I told him it could be of no Use to a private person tho' a proper Place for a company to settle a Colony on." Sultan Husain probably realised too late the implications of his signing away Singapore when he could not stop Crawfurd constructing a new road (following Victoria Street today) through his Kampong Gelam.

Singapore in 1819: The Transition to Modernity

The meeting of Stamford Raffles and Tengku Husain on 1 February 1819 was, this essay has argued, the meeting of two worlds. One was the world of an expanding British mercantile empire seeking to maximise its wealth and power and blocking its continental rivals from enhancing their wealth and power. The other was the world of the Malay *kerajaan* continuing a historical dynamic that was began by a group of *datus* who in the 7th century made their home base around Bukit Seguntang on the Musi River where Palembang is today, the premier entrepot in the Straits of Melaka for some five centuries. Paramesvara, as we know him from the Portuguese records, fled the Bukit Seguntang complex and carried that historic dynamic to Temasek, which he renamed Singapura, and then to Melaka.[41] From Melaka this historic dynamic of a "circle" or "*mandala*" of Malay rajas and sultans vying among themselves[42] to make their *negeri* the premier entrepot in the Straits of Melaka was continued by the Johor sultans from their bases on the Johor River. The decision of Stamford Raffles and Tengku Husain to meet was a convergence of a series of events emerging out of the British and Malay past that created modern Singapore. Neither Raffles nor Tengku Husain on their own could have created the beginnings of modern Singapore.

Singapore was, for the British, the culmination of a search for a base for their ships en route to China. It was a search that had first brought them to Pinang. But once in the region the rational for settling in Singapore widen to the establishment of a base for not only official Honourable Company trade, but also equally, if not more important, growing private trade in the region. However, for the Malays, Singapura was only another *negeri*, another settlement with its own ruler seeking a

---

[41] O.W. Wolters, *The Fall of Srivijaya in Malay History* (London: Lund Humphries, 1970), explores this continuity of Malaya history contained in the *Sejarah Melayu* narrative of the transmission of sovereignty from Srivijaya to Melaka.

[42] Wolters has termed this pattern of intra-regional relations in Southeast Asia in which geographically adjacent rulers and *rajas* interacted to form a "circle" in which one *raja* would emerge *primus inter pares* a "mandala" in his benchmark *History, Culture, and Region in Southeast Asian Perspectives*, rev. ed. (Ithaca and Singapore: Cornell University South East Asia Program and Institute of Southeast Asian Studies, 1999), pp. 27–40, 126–54. This framework of geographically adjacent *rajas* vying to dominate each other to become the centre of their world and symbolically, their *mandala*-like universe was borrowed by Southeast Asian *rajas* from classical Indian statecraft.

18.4 View of Singapore from Sandy Point (Tanjong Rhu). Watercolour from the Charles Dyce Collection. Singapore: National University of Singapore (NUS) Museums. S1970-0052-036.

niche in the evolving "circle" of sultans in the Malay world of the Riaus and South Sumatra. A sultan's position in this circle of kings was to a large extent dependent upon his ability to display wealth, which was an indicator of his prowess. Sultan Husain realised too late that he had lost his prowess after he signed the 1824 treaty with John Crawfurd. In contrast, the descendants of the temenggong were in 1869 able to claim membership of this circle of kings on the basis of having displayed sufficient new wealth.

Singapore's rapid development after 1819 appeared to have surprised not only Stamford Raffles, but almost certainly, also Sultan Husain. The British Country Traders and, more important, the Asian traders who migrated to Singapore, principally from Bintan,[43] enable the new settlement to take off and assume a life of its own that became a challenge for both the East India Company Resident and the sultan and his temenggong to control and administer. In hindsight could Sultan Husain and his temenggong successfully controlled and administered Singapore to make their new *kerajaan* the new centre of the *mandala* of Malay *rajas* in the Malay world of the Straits of Melaka? From the perspective of the 20th century that has just ended, the answer is a resounding "no". Sultan Husain and his temenggong were anachronisms attempting to make a "last stand" for Asian autonomy[44] against Western colonialism and imperialism. But from the perspective of the new 21st century this perception of Sultan Husain and Temenggong 'Abdu'r-Rahman may change. In choosing to depart Bintan, this essay has suggested, Tengku Husain was attempting to redirect the past he came out from into a new future. But that new future was not what he envisaged. He simply could not envisage the new global forces impacting on his world. The legacy he and Temenggong 'Abdu'r-Rahman may have left to their descendants and people was the unwitting break with their past in Bintan[45] and Lingga and the opportunity to come to terms with the modern world.[46] The origins of the ongoing Malay effort to come to terms with modernity may have been made in Singapore between 1819 and 1824.

---

[43] Anthony Reid and Radin Fernando, "Shipping on Melaka and Singapore as an Index of Growth, 1760–1840", *South Asia* 19 (1996): 59–84, documents this growth of not only the country trade, but more important, Asian trade, which migrated to Singapore and enabled it to take off.

[44] See the essays edited by Anthony Reid, *The Last Stand of Asian Autonomies; Responses to Modernity in the Diverse States of Southeast Asia and Korea, 1750–1900* (Houndmills: Macmillan Press, 1997) on the attempts by Asian societies to grapple with the pressures of modernity.

[45] This Riau heritage continues to challenge the definition and development of Malay culture today. See for example, the papers in Zahrah Ibrahim, ed., *Tradisi Johor-Riau; Kertas kerja hari sastera 1983* (Kuala Lumpur: Dewan Bahasa dan Pustaka, 1987).

[46] Anthony Milner argues that Abdullah bin Kadir's autobiography was a critique of the ancien regime of the *kerajaan* and marks the transition to a new discourse of politics in Malay society: *The Invention of Politics in Colonial Malaya; Contesting Nationalism and Expansion of the Public Space* (Cambridge: Cambridge University Press, 1994).

Index

In the absence of a consolidated bibliography, a comprehensive index has been prepared where authors and their works can be easily referenced. The index has taken into consideration as far as possible variant transliterations from Malay, Javanese, Chinese and Arabic and are rendered using only a basic set of diacritical characters. Readers should note the following collective entries: Bt (Bukit), G. (Gunung), I. (Isa,Ile), K. (Kuala), Kg (Kampung), Mt (Mount), P. (Pulau), S. (Sungei), Tg (Tanjong or Tanjung), and separately also for hikayat, kota, orang, Raja, Seri or Sri (title, honorific), ship names, straits, tanah, telok, Tengku (title), Tun (title) and university. Key works of history and literature as well as the names of newspapers have been italicized.